PRENTICE HALL
PORTFOLIO EDITIONS

Prentice Hall is pleased to introduce *Making a Nation: The United States and Its People, Portfolio Edition.* Prentice Hall Portfolio Editions feature a collection of concise textbooks on a variety of subjects. Written in classic narrative form, these books allow for the flexibility to incorporate the use of other material such as primary source documents, readings, and technology resources. As you use *Making a Nation, Portfolio Edition,* complete your portfolio by selecting one of many Prentice Hall resources to enhance your course:

Included with *Making A Nation, Portfolio Edition*

U.S. History Documents CD-ROM. *Provided at no additional charge with this textbook,* the U.S. History Documents CD-ROM enables one to access over 300 primary source documents relevant to the study of American history.

The Study Portfolio

Includes *Practice Tests* and *Evaluating Online Resources for History 2003 with Research Navigator.* Free when bundled with the text.

The Penguin Portfolio

Adopters of *Making a Nation, Portfolio Edition* can receive significant discounts when orders for the text are bundled with Penguin titles in American history. As a special offer from Prentice Hall, Thomas Paine's, *Common Sense* and Upton Sinclair's, *The Jungle* are available for free when bundled with *Making a Nation, Portfolio Edition.*

The Technology Portfolio

Includes the *Mapping American History* CD-ROM and the *Exploring America: Interactive Learning Activities from the Sixteenth Century to the Present* CD-ROM. Free when bundled with the text.

Create your own portfolio. Customize any of these portfolio options to suit your specific needs and interests. For additional details, please see the Preface or contact your local Prentice Hall representative.

MAKING A NATION

The United States and Its People
Volume Two

Jeanne Boydston
University of Wisconsin

Nick Cullather
Indiana University

Jan Ellen Lewis
Rutgers University, Newark

Michael McGerr
Indiana University

James Oakes
The Graduate Center, The City University of New York

PEARSON
Prentice
Hall

Upper Saddle River, New Jersey 07458

Library of Congress Cataloging-in-Publication Data

Making a nation: the United States and its people / Jeanne Boydston . . . [et al.]. — Brief ed.
  p. cm.
  "Combined volume."
  Includes bibliographical references and index.
  ISBN 0-13-111454-9
  1. United States—History. 2. United States—Economic conditions. I. Boydston, Jeanne.
E178.1.M22 2003
973—dc21

                                                                        2002035905

Editorial Director: Charlyce Jones-Owen
Senior Acquisitions Editor: Charles Cavaliere
AVP, Director of Production and Manufacturing:
  Barbara Kittle
Editor in Chief of Development: Rochelle Diogenes
Development Editor: Elaine Silverstein
Production Editor: Jan H. Schwartz
Prepress and Manufacturing Manager: Nick Sklitsis
Prepress and Manufacturing Buyer: Sherry Lewis

Media Editor: Deborah O'Connell
Marketing Managers: Claire Rehwinkel,
  Heather Shelstad
Creative Design Director: Leslie Osher
Interior and Cover Design: Nancy Wells
Line Art Supervisor: Guy Ruggiero
Editorial Assistant: Adrienne Paul
Cartographer: CartaGraphics
Cover Photos: Bettmann/CORBIS

This book was set in 10/11 New Baskerville by TSI Graphics, Inc. and was
printed and bound by R.R. Donnelly, Inc. The cover was printed by Phoenix
Color Corporation.

 © 2004 by Pearson Education
Upper Saddle River, New Jersey 07458

Printed in the United States of America
10 9 8 7 6 5 4 3 2 1

ISBN 0-13-111453-0

PEARSON EDUCATION LTD.
PEARSON EDUCATION AUSTRALIA PTY. Limited
PEARSON EDUCATION SINGAPORE, Pte. Ltd.
PEARSON EDUCATION NORTH ASIA Ltd.
PEARSON EDUCATION CANADA, Ltd.
PEARSON EDUCATION DE MEXICO, S.A. de C.V.
PEARSON EDUCATION—Japan
PEARSON EDUCATION MALAYSIA, Pte. Ltd.

BRIEF CONTENTS

16. Reconstructing a Nation, 1865–1877   369

17. The Triumph of Industrial Capitalism, 1850–1890   401

18. Cultural Struggles of Industrial America, 1850–1895   425

19. The Politics of Industrial Society, 1870–1892   450

20. Industry and Empire, 1890–1900   473

21. A United Body of Action, 1900–1916   496

22. A Global Power, 1914–1919   520

23. The 1920s   544

24. A Great Depression and a New Deal, 1929–1939   568

25. The Second World War, 1941–1945   591

26. The Cold War, 1945–1952   615

27. The Consumer Society, 1950–1960   639

28. The Rise and Fall of the New Liberalism, 1960–1968   664

29. Living with Less, 1968–1980   692

30. The Triumph of a New Conservatism, 1980–1988   718

31. A New America? 1989–   743

CONTENTS

Preface   x
About the Authors   xvi

16. Reconstructing a Nation, 1865–1877   369

John Dennett Visits a Freedmen's Bureau Court   369

Wartime Reconstruction   372

Presidential Reconstruction, 1865–1867   375

Congressional Reconstruction   380

The Retreat From Republican Radicalism   386

Reconstruction in the North   390

The End of Reconstruction   392
Conclusion   397
Chronology   398
Further Readings   400

17. The Triumph of Industrial Capitalism, 1850–1890   401

Rosa Cassettari   401

The Political Economy of Global Capitalism   403

The Rise of Big Business   407

A New Social Order   412

Clearing the West for Capitalism   416

The Economic Transformation of the West   419
Chronology   422
Conclusion   423
Further Readings   423

18. Cultural Struggles of Industrial America: 1850–1895   425

Anthony Comstock's Crusade Against Vice   425

The Varieties of Urban Culture   427

The Elusive Boundaries of Male and Female   432

Immigration as a Cultural Problem   434

The Creation of High Culture   438

Artistic Realism Embraces Urban and Industrial America   443
Conclusion   447
Further Readings   447
Chronology   448

19. The Politics of Industrial America, 1870–1892   450

The "Crusade" Against Alcohol   450

Two Political Styles   452

Economic Issues Dominate National Politics   456

Government Activism and Its Limits   459

Middle-Class Radicalism   464

Discontent Among Workers   467

Chronology   470

Conclusion   472

Further Readings   472

20. Industry and Empire, 1890–1900   473

Dealmaking in the White House   473

The Crisis of the 1890s   475

A Modern Political Economy   479

The Retreat From Politics   481

American Diplomacy Enters the Modern World   486

Conclusion   493

Chronology   494

Further Readings   495

21. A United Body of Action, 1900–1916   496

Alice Hamilton   496

Toward a New Politics   497

The Progressives   502

Progressives in State and Local Politics   507

The Presidency Becomes "The Administration"   509

Rival Visions of the Industrial Future   515

Conclusion   517

Chronology   518

Further Readings   518

22. A Global Power, 1914–1919   520

Walter Lippmann   520

The Challenges of Revolution and Neutrality   521

The Drift to War   525

Mobilizing the Nation and the Economy   528

Over There   535

The Black Cloud in the East   539

Chronology   542

Conclusion   543

Further Readings   543

23. The 1920s   544

"The Queen of Swimmers"   544

A Dynamic Economy   545

A Modern Culture   549

The Limits of the Modern Culture   555

A "New Era" in Politics and Government   561

Conclusion   565

Chronology   566

Further Readings   566

24. A Great Depression and a New Deal, 1929–1939   568

Sidney Hillman and the Search for Security   568

The Great Depression   569

The First New Deal   575

The Second New Deal   581

Crisis of the New Deal   587
Chronology   589
Conclusion   590
Further Readings   590

25. The Second World War, 1941–1945   591

A. Philip Randolph   591

Island in a Totalitarian Sea   592

Turning the Tide   598

Organizing for Production   604

Between Idealism and Fear   607

Closing with the Enemy   609
Conclusion   612
Chronology   613
Further Readings   614

26. The Cold War, 1945–1952   615

The Fall of Esther and Stephen Brunauer   615

The Origins of the Cold War   617

Fighting the Cold War Abroad   621

The Reconversion of American Society   626

The Frustrations of Liberalism   631

Fighting the Cold War at Home   634
Chronology   637
Conclusion   638
Further Readings   638

27. The Consumer Society, 1950–1960   639

E.J. Korvettes   639

Living the Good Life   640

A Homogeneous Society?   646

The Eisenhower Era at Home and Abroad   651

Challenges to the Consumer Society   657
Conclusion   661
Chronology   662
Further Readings   662

28. The Rise and Fall of the New Liberalism, 1960–1968   664

"We Would Never Be Beaten": Vietnam, 1968   664

The Liberal Opportunity   665

Implementing the Liberal Agenda   670

Winning Civil Rights   673

Fighting the Cold War   677

The American War in Vietnam   679

The Great Society Comes Apart   683
Conclusion   689
Chronology   690
Further Readings   690

29. Living with Less, 1968–1980   692

"Panic at the Pump," 1973–1974   692

A New Crisis: Economic Decline   693

Confronting Decline: Nixon's
Strategy 695

Refusing to Settle for Less:
Struggles for Rights 700

Backlash: From Radical Action to
Conservative Reaction 707

Political Crisis: Three Troubled
Presidencies 709
Conclusion 715
Further Readings 715
Chronology 716

30. The Triumph of a New Conservatism, 1980–1988 718

The Trumps' American Dream 718

A New Conservative
Majority 720

The Reagan Revolution at
Home 724

The Reagan Revolution
Abroad 727

The Battle Over Conservative
Social Values 732

The Limits of the New
Conservatism 736
Chronology 741
Conclusion 742
Further Readings 742

31. A New America? 1989– 743

Felix Andreev and "The Blessing of America" 743

A New Economy 744

Political Deadlock 748

Struggles Over Diversity and
Rights 752

From the Cold War to the War on
Terrorism 760
Chronology 766
Conclusion 768
Further Readings 768

Appendix A-1
Bibliography B-1
Credits C-1
Index I-1

PREFACE

Every human life is shaped by a variety of different relationships. Cultural relations, diplomatic relations, race, gender, and class relations, all contribute to how an individual interacts with the larger global community. This was the theme of the full-length version of *Making a Nation*. For this concise edition, the authors have worked hard to retain the theme while reducing some of the illustrious material. This allows us to retain our emphasis on the relationships that have historically shaped and defined the identities of the American people. So, for example, to disentangle the identity of a Mexican American woman working in a factory in Los Angeles in the year 2000 is to confront the multiple and overlapping "identities" that define a single American life. There are many ways to explore these and similar relationships. *Making a Nation* views them through the lens of *political economy*.

In March of 1776, a few months before American colonists declared their independence from Great Britain, Adam Smith published his masterpiece, *The Wealth of Nations*. Smith had delayed publication of his work for a year so that he could perfect a lengthy chapter on Anglo-American relations. Thus *The Wealth of Nations*, one of the most important documents in a new branch of knowledge known as political economy, was written with a close eye to events in the British colonies of North America, the colonies that were soon to become the United States.

What did Smith and his many American followers mean by political economy? They meant, firstly, that the economy itself is much broader than the gross national product, the unemployment rate, or the twists and turns of the stock market. They understood that economies are tightly bound to politics, that they are therefore the products of history rather than nature or accident. And just as men and women make history, so too do they make economies—in the way they work and organize their families as much as in their fiscal policies and tax structures.

Political economy is a way of thinking that is deeply embedded in American history. To this day we casually assume that different government policies create different "incentives" shaping everything from the way capital gains are invested to how parents raise their children, from how unmarried mothers on welfare can escape from poverty, to how automobile manufacturers design cars for fuel efficiency and pollution control. Political economy is the art and science that traces these connections between government, the economy, and the relationships that shape the daily lives of ordinary men and women. But that connection points in different directions. Politics and the economy do not simply shape, but are in turn shaped by, the lives and cultural values of ordinary men and women.

Put differently, political economy establishes a context that allows students to see the links between the particular and the general, between large and seemingly abstract forces such as "globalization" and the struggles of working parents who find they need two incomes to provide for their children. *Making a Nation* shows that such relationships were as important in the seventeenth and eighteenth centuries as they are today.

In a sense, globalization has been a theme in American history from its earliest beginnings. As the opening chapters demonstrate, Europe, Africa and the Americas were linked to each other in an Atlantic world across which everything was exchanged, deadly diseases along with diplomatic formalities, political structures and cultural assumptions, African slaves and Europeans servants, colonists and commodities.

In subsequent chapters *Making a Nation* traces the development of the newly formed United States by once again stressing the link between the lives of ordinary men and women to the grand political struggles of the day. Should the federal government create a centralized bank? Should it promote economic development by sponsoring the construction of railroads, turnpikes and canals? At one level, such questions exposed competing ideas about what American capitalism should look like and what the implications of those ideas were for American democracy. But a closer look suggests that those same political quarrels were propelled by the concerns that farmers, workers, and businessmen were expressing about the pace and direction of economic change.

Similarly, the great sectional struggle over slavery and freedom is told as the story of dramatic political maneuvers and courageous military exploits, as well as the story of women who created the modern profession of nursing by caring for civil war soldiers and of runaway slaves who helped push the United States government into a policy of emancipation. The insights of political economy likewise frame the way *Making a Nation* presents the transition from slave to free labor in the South after the Civil War. In the twentieth century, as America became a global power, the demands of the new political economy of urban and industrial America inform our examination of both U.S. diplomacy and domestic affairs. It was no accident, for example, that the civil rights leader A. Philip Randolph took advantage of the crisis of the Second World War to threaten Franklin Roosevelt's administration with a march on Washington. For Randolph, the demand for racial equality was inseparable from the struggle for a more equitable distribution of the rewards of a capitalist economy.

The United States victory in World War II, coupled with the extraordinary burst of prosperity in the war's aftermath, gave rise to fantasies of omnipotence that were tested and shattered by the American experience in Vietnam. Presidents, generals, and ordinary soldiers alike shared in the illusion of invulnerability. America's was the greatest democracy and the most powerful economy on earth. Thus did Americans in Southeast Asia in the late twentieth century find themselves in much the same place that Christopher Columbus had found himself centuries before: halfway around the world, face to face with a people whose culture he did not fully understand. And even today, the unparalleled military might and economic power of the Unites States have not proved enough to make ordinary Americans feel secure from recession at home and deadly attack from abroad. History cannot provide lessons on how to navigate this paradox, but a fuller understanding of the present begins with a better understanding of the past. We trust that this concise edition of *Making a Nation* will help make that possible.

TOPICS AND COVERAGE

Because *Making a Nation* was written from the very beginning with an organizing theme in mind, we have been able to incorporate many topics relatively smoothly within the larger narrative. For example, this textbook includes some of the most extensive coverage of Indian and western history available, but because our coverage is integrated into the larger narrative, there is no need to provide a separate chapter on either topic. At the same time, the theme of political economy allows us to cover subjects that are often missed in standard texts. For example, *Making a Nation* includes more than the usual coverage of environmental history, as well as more complete coverage of the social and cultural history of the late twentieth century than is available elsewhere. And in every case the politics of globalization and environmentalism, of capitalist development and democratic reform, of family values and social inequality are never far from view. *Making a Nation* also provides full coverage of the most recent American history, from the end of the Cold War to the rise of a new information economy and on to the terrorist attacks against the World Trade Center and the Pentagon in September 2001. Here, again, the organizing theme of political economy provides a strong but supple interpretive framework that helps students understand developments that are making a nation in a new century.

Student Learning Aids

To assist students in their appreciation of this history, we have added several distinctive features and pedagogical aids.

Chapter-Opening Vignettes
The vignettes that open each chapter are intended to give specificity as well as humanity to the themes that follow. From the witchcraft trials in Salem to the Trumps' American dream, students are drawn into each chapter with compelling stories that illustrate the organizing factor of political economy.

Chronologies
Found at the end of each chapter, chronologies organize key events into sequential order for quick review.

Further Readings
An annotated list of helpful books related to the key topics of each chapter is located at the end of each chapter.

U.S. History Documents CD-ROM
Bound in every new copy of *Making a Nation, Portfolio Edition*, and organized according to the main periods in American history, the U.S. History Documents CD-ROM contains over 300 primary-sources in an easily-navigable PDF file. Each document is accompanied by essay questions that allow students to read important sources in U.S. history via the CD-ROM and respond online.

Appendix
In addition to providing several key documents in United States history, the Appendix presents demographic data reflecting the 2000 census. An extensive Bibliography offers an expanded compilation of literature, arranged by chapter.

Supplementary Materials

Making a Nation comes with an extensive package of supplementary print and multimedia materials for both instructors and students.

Instructor's Resource Manual and Test-Item File
The Instructor's Resource Manual contains chapter outlines, detailed chapter overviews, discussion questions, lecture strategies, essay topics, and tips on incorporating Penguin titles in American history into lectures. The Test-Item File includes over 1000 multiple-choice, true-false, essay, and map questions, organized by chapter.

Practice Tests (Volumes I and II)
Free when packaged with the text, Practice Tests provide students with chapter outlines, map questions, sample exam questions, analytical reading exercises, collaborative exercises, and essay questions.

American Stories: Biographies in United States History
This two-volume collection of sixty-two biographies in U.S. history is free when packaged with *Making a Nation*. Introductions, prereading questions, and suggested readings enrich this attractive and useful supplement.

Transparencies
 This collection of over 150 full-color transparencies provides maps, charts, and graphs for classroom presentations.

Retrieving the American Past 2003 Edition (RTAP)
RTAP enables instructors to tailor a custom reader whose content, organization, and price exactly match their course syllabi. Edited by historians and educators at the Ohio State University, this online database offers instructors the freedom and flexibility to choose selections of primary and secondary source readings—or both—from 81 (8 new) chapters. Contact your local Prentice Hall

representative for details about RTAP. Discounts apply when copies of RTAP are bundled with *Making a Nation*.

Prentice Hall and Penguin Bundle Program

Prentice Hall and Penguin are pleased to provide adopters of *Making a Nation* with an opportunity to receive significant discounts when orders for *Making a Nation* are bundled together with Penguin titles in American history. Please contact your local Prentice Hall representative for details.

Reading Critically about History

This brief guide provides students with helpful strategies for reading a history textbook and is available free when packaged with *Making a Nation*.

Understanding and Answering Essay Questions

This helpful guide provides analytical tools for understanding different types of essay questions and for preparing well-crafted essay answers. It is available free when packaged with *Making a Nation*.

MULTIMEDIA SUPPLEMENTS

Companion Web site™

The Companion Web site™ for *Making a Nation* is available at www.prenhall.com/boydston and offers students one of the most comprehensive Internet resources available. Organized around the primary subtopics of each chapter, the Companion Web site™ provides detailed summaries, multiple-choice, true-false, essay, identification, map labeling, and document-based questions. Unique Web Connections, directly tied to the content of the text, combine primary sources, interactive maps, audio clips, and numerous visuals to explore key topics in depth. The Faculty Module contains a wealth of material for instructors, including an online instructor's manual and maps, charts, and graphs that can be imported into electronic presentations.

Exploring America CD-ROM

The new Exploring America CD-ROM features thirty-one activities that drill down to explore the impact of key episodes and developments in United States history. Each activity combines primary sources, illustrations, graphics, audio clips, and interactive maps to provide opportunities to further explore the key themes of *Making a Nation*. Available free when packaged with *Making a Nation*.

Research Navigator™

Prentice Hall's new Research Navigator™ helps students make the most of their research time. From finding the right articles and journals, to citing sources; drafting and writing effective papers, and completing research assignments, Research Navigator™ simplifies and streamlines the entire process. Complete with extensive help on the research process and three exclusive databases full of relevant and reliable source material including EBSCO's ContentSelect Academic Journal Database, *The New York Times* Search by Subject Archive, and "Best of the Web" Link Library, Research Navigator™ is the one-stop research solution for students. Research Navigator™ is free when packaged with any Prentice Hall textbook. An Access Code for Research Navigator™ is provided in every copy of Prentice Hall's Evaluating Online Resources guide. Contact your local representative for more details or take a tour on the web at http://www.researchnavigator.com.

Maps and Graphics CD-ROM

Available in Windows and Mac formats for classroom presentations, this CD-ROM includes the maps, charts, tables, and graphs from *Making a Nation*.

Course Management Systems

As the leader in course-management solutions for teachers and students of history, Prentice Hall provides a variety of online tools. Contact your local Prentice Hall representative for a demonstration, or visit www.prenhall.com/demo.

ACKNOWLEDGEMENTS

We would like to express our thanks to the reviewers whose thoughtful comments and insights were of great value in finalizing *Making a Nation*:

Tyler Anbinder, George Washington University
Debra Barth, San Jose City College
James M. Bergquist, Villanova University
Robert Brandfon, College of the Holy Cross
Stephanie Camp, University of Washington
Mark T. Carleton, Louisiana State University
Jean Choate, Northern Michigan University
Martin B. Cohen, George Mason University
Samuel Crompton, Holyoke Community College
George Daniels, University of South Alabama
James B. Dressler, Cumberland University
Elizabeth Dunn, Baylor University
Mark Fernandez, Loyola University of New Orleans
Willard B. Gatewood, University of Arkansas
James Gilbert, University of Maryland at College Park
Richard L. Hume, Washington State University
Frederic Jaher, University of Illinois at Urbana-Champaign
Glen Jeansonne, University of Wisconsin-Milwaukee
Constance Jones, Tidewater Community College
Laylon Wayne Jordan, University of Charleston
Peter Kirstein, St. Xavier University
John D. Krugler, Marquette University
Mark V. Kwasny, Ohio State University-Newark
Gene D. Lewis, University of Cincinnati
Glenn Linden, Southern Methodist University
Robert McCarthy, Providence College
Andrew McMichael, Vanderbilt University
Dennis N. Mihelich, Creighton University

Patricia Hagler Minter, Western Kentucky University
Joseph Mitchell, Howard Community College
Reid Mitchell, University of Maryland Baltimore County
Carl Moneyhon, University of Arkansas at Little Rock
James M. Morris, Christopher Newport University
Earl Mulderink III, Southern Utah University
Alexandra Nickliss, City College of San Francisco
Chris S. O'Brien, University of Kansas
Peter Onuf, University of Virginia
Annelise Orleck, Dartmouth College
Richard H. Peterson, San Diego State University
Leo R. Ribuffo, George Washington University
Kenneth Scherzer, Middle Tennessee State University
Sheila Skemp, University of Mississippi
Kevin Smith, Ball State University
Michael Topp, University of Texas at El Paso
Gregory J. W. Urwin, University of Central Arkansas
Paul K. Van der Slice, Montgomery College
Jessica Weiss, California State University of Hayward
James A. Wilson, Southwest Texas State University
John Wiseman, Frostburg State University
Andrew Workman, Mills College

We also wish to thank the reviewers whose feedback on the concise edition was invaluable:
J. Christopher Arndt, James Madison University
Edward Baptist, University of Miami
Laura Graves, South Plains College
Raymond M. Hyer, James Madison University
Timothy Koerner, Oakland Community College

The authors would like first to acknowledge their co-authors: Without the patience, tenacity, and intellectual support we received from each other, we could scarcely have continued to the end. And we are grateful of course to our families, friends, and colleagues who encouraged us during the planning and writing of *Making a Nation*.

The authors would like to thank the editors, staff, and freelance support at Prentice Hall, especially our acquisitions editor, Charles Cavaliere; editorial director and vice president, Charlyce Jones-Owen; development editor, Elaine Silverstein; editor-in-chief of development, Rochelle Diogenes; production editor, Jan Schwartz; marketing managers, Claire Bitting and Heather Shelstad; and designer, Nancy Wells. We have benefited at each stage from their patience, their experience, and their commitment to this project. Thanks also to Maria Piper who formatted the line art; Nick Sklitsis, manufacturing manager; Sherry Lewis, manufacturing buyer; and Jan Stephan, managing editor; and many other people behind the scenes at Prentice Hall, for helping make the book happen.

ABOUT THE AUTHORS

Jeanne Boydston is Professor of History at the University of Wisconsin-Madison. She is the author of *Home and Work: Housework, Wages, and the Ideology of Labor in the Early American Republic,* coauthor of *The Limits of Sisterhood: The Beecher Sisters on Women's Rights and Woman's Sphere,* co-editor of *The Root of Bitterness: Documents of the Social History of American Women* (second edition), as well as author of articles on the labor history of women in the early republic. Professor Boydston teaches in the areas of early republic and antebellum United States history and United States women's history to 1870. Her BA and MA are from the University of Tennessee, and her PhD is from Yale University.

Nick Cullather is Associate Professor at Indiana University, where he teaches courses on the history of United States foreign relations. He is on the editorial boards of *Diplomatic History* and the *Encyclopedia of American Foreign Policy,* and is the author of *Illusions of Influence* (1994), a study of the political economy of United States-Philippines relations, and *Secret History* (1999), which describes a CIA covert operation against the government of Guatemala in 1954. He received his AB from Indiana University and his MA and PhD from the University of Virginia.

Jan Ellen Lewis is Professor of History and Director of the Graduate Program at Rutgers University, Newark. She also teaches in the history PhD program at Rutgers, New Brunswick and was a Visiting Professor at Princeton University. A specialist in colonial and early national history, she is the author of *The Pursuit of Happiness: Family and Values in Jefferson's Virginia* (1983), and co-editor of *An Emotional History of the United States* (1998) and *Sally Hemings and Thomas Jeffer-*son: *History, Memory, and Civic Culture* (1999). She is currently completing an examination of the way the Founding generation grappled with the challenge presented to an egalitarian society by women and slaves and a second volume of the Penguin *History of the United States.* She received her AB from Bryn Mawr College, and MAs and PhD from the University of Michigan.

Michael McGerr is Associate Professor of History and Associate Dean for Graduate Education in the College of Arts and Sciences at Indiana University-Bloomington. He is the author of *The Decline of Popular Politics: The American North, 1865–1928* (1986). With the aid of a fellowship from the National Endowment for the Humanities, he is currently writing a book on the rise and fall of Progressive America. Professor McGerr teaches a wide range of courses on modern American history, including the Vietnam War, race and gender in American business, John D. Rockefeller, Bill Gates, and the politics of American popular music. He received his BA, MA, and PhD degrees from Yale University.

James Oakes is Graduate School Humanities Professor and Professor of History at the Graduate Center of the City University of New York, and has taught at Purdue, Princeton, and Northwestern. He is author of *The Ruling Race: A History of American Slaveholders* (1982) and *Slavery and Freedom: An Interpretation of the Old South* (1990). In addition to a year-long research grant from the National Endowment for the Humanities, he was a fellow at the Center for Advanced Study in the Behavioral Sciences in 1989–90. His areas of specialization are slavery, the Civil War and Reconstruction, and the history of American political thought. He received his PhD from The University of California at Berkeley.

CHAPTER

16

Reconstructing a Nation

1865–1877

John Dennett Visits a Freedmen's Bureau Court
Wartime Reconstruction • Presidential Reconstruction, 1865–1867
Congressional Reconstruction • The Retreat from Republican
Radicalism • Reconstruction in the North
The End of Reconstruction
Conclusion

JOHN DENNETT VISITS A FREEDMEN'S BUREAU COURT

ohn Richard Dennett arrived in Liberty, Virginia, on August 17, 1865, on a tour of the South during which he sent back weekly reports for publication in *The Nation*. The editors wanted accurate accounts of conditions in the recently defeated Confederate states and Dennett was the kind of man they could trust. He graduated from Harvard, was a firm believer in the sanctity of the Union, and belonged to the class of elite Yankees who thought of themselves as the "best men" the country had to offer.

At Liberty, Dennett was accompanied by a Freedmen's Bureau agent. The Freedmen's Bureau was a branch of the U.S. Army established by Congress to assist the freed people. Dennett and the agent went to the courthouse because one of the Freedmen's Bureau's functions was to adjudicate disputes between the freed people and southern whites.

The first case to arrive was that of an old white farmer who complained that two blacks who worked on his farm were "roamin' about and refusin' to work." He wanted the agent to help find the men and bring them back. Both men had wives and children living on his farm and eating his corn, the old man complained. "Have you been paying any wages?" the Freedmen's Bureau agent asked. "Well, they get what the other niggers get," the farmer answered. "I a'n't payin' great wages this year." There was not much the agent could do. He had no horses and few men, but one of his soldiers volunteered to go back to the farm and tell the blacks that "they ought to be at home supporting their wives and children."

A well-to-do planter came in to see if he could fire the blacks who had been working on his plantation since the beginning of the year. The planter complained that his workers were unmanageable now that he could no longer punish them. The sergeant warned the planter that he could not beat his workers as if they were still slaves. In that case, the planter responded, "Will the Government take them off our hands?" The Freedmen's Bureau agent suspected that the planter was looking for an excuse to discharge his laborers at the end of the growing season, after they had finished the work but before they had been paid. "If they've worked on your crops all the year so far," the agent told the planter, "I guess they've got a claim on you to keep them a while longer."

Next came a "good-looking mulatto man" representing a number of African Americans. They were worried by rumors that they would be forced to sign five-year contracts with their employers. "No, it a'n't true," the agent said. They also wanted to know if they could rent or buy land so that they could work for themselves. "Yes, rent or buy," the agent said. But the former slaves had no horses, mules, or ploughs to work the land. So they wanted to know "if the Government would help us out after we get the land." But the agent had no help to offer. "The Government hasn't any ploughs or mules to give you," he said. In the end the blacks settled for a piece of paper from the Freedmen's Bureau authorizing them to rent or buy their own farms.

The last case involved a field hand who came to the agent to complain that his master was beating him with a stick. The agent told the field hand to go back to work. "Don't be sassy, don't be lazy when you've got work to do; and I guess he won't trouble you." The field hand left "very reluctantly," but came back a minute later and asked for a letter to his master "enjoining him to keep the peace, as he feared the man would shoot him, he having on two or three occasions threatened to do so."

Most of the cases Dennett witnessed centered around labor relations. The southern economy had been devastated by the war, and successful rebuilding depended on the creation of a political economy based on free labor. There was, however, little agreement about what kind of free labor system should replace slavery. The cases John Dennett saw showed how difficult the labor problem was. The freed people preferred to work their own land, but they lacked the resources to rent or buy farms. Black workers and white owners who negotiated wage contracts had trouble figuring out the limits of each other's rights and responsibilities. The former masters wanted to retain as much of their old authority as possible, while the former slaves wanted as much autonomy as possible.

The Freedmen's Bureau was placed in the middle of these conflicts. Most agents tried to ensure that the freed people were paid for their labor and that they were not brutalized as they had been as slaves. Southern whites resented this intrusion, and their resentment filtered up to sympathetic politicians in Washington, DC. As a result, the Freedmen's Bureau became a lightning rod for the political conflicts of the Reconstruction period.

Reconstruction raised challenging questions for Americans: What conditions should the federal government impose on the southern states before they could be readmitted to the Union? Should these conditions be set by the president or by Congress? How far should the federal government go to protect the economic well-being and civil rights of the freed people? Politicians in Washington disagreed violently on these questions. At one extreme was Andrew Johnson who, as president, believed in small government and a speedy readmission of the southern states and looked on the Freedmen's Bureau with suspicion. At the other extreme were radical Republicans, who believed that the federal government should redistribute confiscated land to the former slaves, guarantee their civil rights, and give African-American men the vote. They viewed the Freedmen's Bureau as too small and weak to do the necessary job. Between the radicals and the president's supporters were moderate Republicans who at first tried to work with the president but later shifted toward the radical position.

Regardless of where they fell on the political spectrum, policymakers in the nation's capital responded to what went on in the South. Events in the South were shaped in turn by the policies emanating from Washington. What John Dennett saw in Liberty, Virginia, was a good example of this. The Freedmen's Bureau agent listened to the urgent requests of former masters and slaves, his responses shaped by the policies established in Washington. But those policies were, in turn, shaped by reports on conditions in the South sent back by Freedmen's Bureau agents like him and by journalists like John Dennett. From this interaction the political economy of the "New South" slowly emerged.

WARTIME RECONSTRUCTION

Long before the Civil War was over, Republicans in Congress and the White House had considered the reconstruction of the southern states. What system of free labor would replace slavery? Under what political conditions should the southern states be read-mitted to the Union? What civil and political rights should the freed people receive? As Congress and the Lincoln administration responded piecemeal to developments in regions of the South under Union control, a variety of approaches to Reconstruc-tion emerged. Some approaches, notably those developed in Louisiana, established precedents that shaped Reconstruction for many years.

Experiments with Free Labor in the Lower Mississippi Valley

Southern Louisiana came under Union control early in the war. The sugar and cot-ton plantations around New Orleans therefore provided the first major experi-ments in the transition from slave to free labor. The Union commander of the area, General Nathaniel Banks, hoped to stem the flow of black refugees to Union lines. Unsympathetic to the former slaves, Banks issued harsh labor regulations designed to put the freed people back to work quickly. The Banks Plan required freed peo-ple to sign year-long contracts to work on their former plantations, often for their former owners. Workers would be paid either five percent of the proceeds of the crop or three dollars per month. The former masters would provide food and shel-ter. African-American workers were forbidden to leave the plantations without per-mission. So stringent were these regulations that to many critics Banks had simply replaced one form of slavery with another. Nevertheless, the Banks Plan was im-plemented throughout the lower Mississippi Valley, especially after the fall of Vicksburg in 1863.

The Banks Plan touched off a political controversy. Established planters had the most to gain from the plan, which allowed them to preserve much of the prewar labor system. Louisiana Unionists, who had remained loyal to the government in Washington, formed a Free State Association to press for more substantial changes. Lincoln publicly supported the Free State movement and issued a Proclamation of Amnesty and Reconstruction to undermine the Confederacy by cultivating the sup-port of southern Unionists. The Proclamation contained the outline of the so-called Ten-Percent Plan, which turned out to be not much of a plan at all.

Lincoln's Ten-Percent Plan versus the Wade–Davis Bill

The Ten-Percent Plan promised full pardons and the restoration of civil rights to all those who swore loyalty to the Union, excluding only a few high-ranking Con-federate military and political leaders. When the number of loyal whites in a for-mer Confederate state reached ten percent of the 1860 voting population, they could organize a new state constitution and government. The only stipulation was that they recognize the abolition of slavery. Abiding by these conditions, Free State whites met in Louisiana in 1864 and produced a new state constitution. It provided for free public education, a minimum wage, a nine-hour day on public works proj-ects, and a graduated income tax. However, although it abolished slavery, it also de-nied blacks the right to vote.

By the spring of 1864 such denials were no longer acceptable to radical Republicans, a small but vocal wing of the Republican Party. They were active in many parts of the South immediately after the war, and they developed strong ties to leading radicals in Congress, such as Thaddeus Stevens of Pennsylvania and Charles Sumner of Massachusetts. Despite their differences, most radicals favored distributing land to the former slaves and federal guarantees of the civil rights of former slaves, including the right to vote. Radicals were prepared to use the full force of the federal government to enforce Congressional policy in the South. Although the radicals never formed a majority in Congress, they gradually won over the moderates to many of their positions. As a result, when Congress took control of Reconstruction after the elections in 1866, the process became known as radical Reconstruction.

The radicals were particularly strong in New Orleans, thanks to the city's large and articulate community of free blacks. In the spring of 1864 they sent a delegation to Washington to meet with President Lincoln and press the case for voting rights. The next day Lincoln wrote to the acting governor of Louisiana suggesting a limited suffrage for the most intelligent blacks and for those who had served in the Union Army. The delegates to Louisiana's constitutional convention ignored Lincoln's suggestion. Shortly thereafter free blacks in New Orleans and former slaves together demanded civil and political rights and the abolition of the Banks labor regulations. Radicals complained that Lincoln's Ten-Percent Plan was too kind to former Confederates and that the Banks Plan was too harsh on former slaves.

Moved largely by events in Louisiana, congressional radicals rejected the Ten-Percent Plan. In July 1864 Congressmen Benjamin F. Wade and Henry Winter Davis proposed a different Reconstruction plan. Under the Wade–Davis Bill, Reconstruction could not begin until a majority of a state's white men swore an oath of allegiance to the Union. In addition, the Wade–Davis Bill guaranteed full legal and civil rights to African Americans, but not the right to vote. Lincoln pocket vetoed the bill because he was still interested in cultivating southern Unionists. By the spring of 1865, however, Lincoln had shifted toward the radical position. In his last speech Lincoln publicly supported voting rights for some freedmen.

The Louisiana experience made several things clear. The radical Republicans were determined to press for more civil and political rights for blacks than moderates initially supported; however, the moderates showed a willingness to move in a radical direction. Equally important, any Reconstruction policy would have to consider the wishes of southern blacks.

The Freed People's Dream of Owning Land

Freedom meant many things to the former slaves. It meant they could move about their neighborhoods without passes, that they did not have to step aside to let whites pass them on the street, and that their marriages would be secured by the law. Following emancipation, southern blacks withdrew from white churches and established their own congregations, and during Reconstruction the church emerged as a central institution in the southern black community. Freedom also meant literacy. Even before the war ended northern teachers poured into the South to set up schools. The American Missionary Association organized hundreds of such northern teachers. When the fighting stopped, the U.S. Army helped recruit and organize thousands more northern women teachers. The graduates of the missionary schools sometimes became teachers themselves. As a result, hundreds of thousands of southern blacks became literate within a few years.

But even more than churches and schools, the freed people wanted land. Without land, the former slaves saw no choice but to work for their old masters on

Charlotte Forten, born to a prominent African-American family in Philadelphia, was one of many northern women who went to the South to become a teacher of the freed slaves. Forten helped found the Penn School on St. Helena's Island in South Carolina.

their farms and plantations. As the war ended many African Americans had reason to believe that the government would assist them in their quest for independent land ownership.

Marching through the Carolinas in early 1865, Union General William Tecumseh Sherman discovered how important land was to the freed people on the Sea Islands. "The way we can best take care of ourselves is to have land," they declared, "and turn it out and till it by our own labor." Persuaded by their arguments, Sherman issued Special Field Order No. 15 granting captured land to the freed people. By June 1865, 400,000 acres had been distributed to 40,000 former slaves.

Congress seemed to be moving in a similar direction. In March 1865, the Republicans established the Bureau of Refugees, Freedmen and Abandoned Lands, commonly known as the Freedmen's Bureau, which quickly became involved in the politics of land redistribution. The Freedmen's Bureau controlled the disposition of 850,000 acres of confiscated and abandoned Confederate lands. In July 1865, General Oliver Otis Howard, the head of the Bureau, issued Circular 13, directing his agents to rent the land to the freed people in 40-acre plots that they could eventually purchase. Many Bureau agents believed that to re-educate them in the values of thrift and hard work, the freed people should be encouraged to save money and buy land for themselves. From the Bureau's perspective, redistributing land was like giving it away to people who had not paid for it.

From the perspective of the former slaves, however, black workers had more than earned a right to the land. "The labor of these people had for two hundred years cleared away the forests and produced crops that brought millions of dollars annually," H. C. Bruce explained. "It does seem to me that a Christian Nation

Before the Civil War it was illegal in most southern states to teach a slave how to read. With emancipation, the freed people clamored for schools and teachers, such as the one pictured here. Within a few years, hundreds of thousands of former slaves became literate.

would, at least, have given them one year's support, 40 acres of land and a mule each." Even Abraham Lincoln seemed to agree. But in April 1865 Lincoln was dead and Andrew Johnson became president of the United States.

PRESIDENTIAL RECONSTRUCTION, 1865–1867

When Andrew Johnson took office in April 1865, it was still unclear whether Congress or the president would control Reconstruction policy, and whether that policy would be lenient or harsh. Like so many Democrats, Johnson's sympathy for the common man did not extend to African Americans. Determined to reconstruct the South in his own way and blind to the interests of the freed people, Johnson grew increasingly bitter and resentful of the Republicans who controlled Congress. As a result, presidential Reconstruction was a monumental failure.

The Political Economy of Contract Labor

In the mid-nineteenth century, Congress was normally out of session from March until December. Having assumed the presidency in April 1865, Johnson hoped to take advantage of the recess to complete the Reconstruction process and present the finished product to lawmakers in December. At the end of May the president offered amnesty and the restoration of property to white southerners who swore an oath of loyalty to the Union, excluding only high-ranking Confederate military and political leaders and very rich planters. He named provisional governors to the seceded states and instructed them to organize constitutional conventions. To earn readmission to the Union, the seceded states were required to nullify their secession ordinances, repudiate their Confederate war debts, and ratify the Thirteenth Amendment abolishing slavery, terms far more lenient than those Lincoln and the

Congressional Republicans had contemplated. They did nothing to protect the civil rights of the former slaves.

Johnson's leniency encouraged defiance among white southerners. Secessionists had been barred from participating in the states' constitutional conventions, but they participated openly in the first elections held late in the year because Johnson issued thousands of pardons. Leading Confederates thus assumed public office in the southern states. Restored to power, white southerners demanded the restoration of all properties confiscated or abandoned during the war. In September 1865 Johnson ordered the Freedmen's Bureau to return all confiscated and abandoned lands to their former owners.

In late 1865 thousands of black families were ordered to give up their land. On Edisto Island off South Carolina, for example, the freed people had carved farms out of the former plantations. But in January 1866 General Rufus Saxton restored the farms to their previous owners and encouraged the freed people to sign wage contracts with their old masters. The blacks unanimously rejected his offer, whereupon the general ordered them to evacuate their farms within two weeks. By the end of 1865 former slaves were being forcibly evicted from the 40-acre plots they had been given by the Union Army or the Freedmen's Bureau.

The Johnsonian state governments enacted a series of "Black Codes" severely restricting the civil rights of freed people. Vagrancy statutes, for example, allowed local police to arrest and fine virtually any black man. If he could not pay the fine, the "vagrant" was put to work on a farm, often the one owned and operated by his former master. Even more disturbing to the former slaves were apprenticeship clauses that allowed white officials to remove children from their parents' homes and put them to work as "apprentices" on nearby farms.

Presidential Reconstruction left the freed people with no choice but to sign labor contracts with white landlords. The contracts restricted the personal as well as the working lives of the freed people. In one case, a South Carolina planter

Slaves in parts of coastal South Carolina were freed early in the Civil War. Here the freed people in Edisto Island in 1862 are shown planting sweet potatoes rather than cotton. In other parts of the South, the former slaves returned to the cultivation of cash crops.

contractually obliged his black workers to "go by his direction the same as in slavery time." Contracts required blacks to work for wages as low as one-tenth of the crop, and cotton prices were steadily falling. It is no wonder that contract labor struck the freed people as little different from slavery.

Resistance to Presidential Reconstruction

In September 1865 blacks in Virginia issued a public appeal for assistance. They declared that they lacked the means to make and enforce legal contracts, because the Black Codes denied African Americans the right to testify in court in any case involving a white person. In many areas planters blocked the development of a free labor market by agreeing among themselves to hire only their former slaves and by fixing wages at a low level. Finally, there were numerous incidents in which black workers who had faithfully obeyed the terms of their contracts were "met by a contemptuous refusal of the stipulated compensation."

Across the South whites reported a growing number of freed people who would not abide by the humiliating conditions of the contract labor system. Some blacks refused to perform specific tasks while others were accused of being "disrespectful" to their employers or to whites in general. Most important, thousands of freedmen declined to renew their contracts for another year.

As black defiance spread, reports of a violent white backlash flooded into Washington. A former slave named Henry Adams claimed that "over two thousand colored people" were murdered around Shreveport, Louisiana, in 1865. Near Pine

In this satirical cartoon, Andrew Johnson and Congress square off against one another. The political struggle over who should control Reconstruction policy led to Congress's impeachment and trial of the president.

Bluff, Arkansas, in 1866 a visitor arrived at a black community the morning after whites had burned it to the ground. Blacks were assaulted for not speaking to whites with the proper tone of submission, for disputing the terms of labor contracts, or for failing to work up to the standards white employers expected. Through relentless intimidation, whites prevented blacks from buying their own land or attending political meetings to press for civil rights.

Northerners read these reports as evidence that "rebel" sentiment was reviving in the South. When Congress came back into session in December 1865, moderate Republicans were already suspicious of presidential Reconstruction. Radicals argued that the contract system made a mockery of their party's commitment to free labor and insisted that the only way to protect the interests of the freed people was to grant them the right to vote.

Congress Clashes with the President

Increasingly distressed by events in the South, Republican moderates in Congress moved toward the Radical position of active government in the South and voting rights for black men. President Johnson, meanwhile, became obsessed with fears of "negro rule" in the South. When he insisted on the swift readmission of southern states that were clearly controlled by unrepentant Confederates, Congress refused. Instead, the Republicans formed a Joint Committee on Reconstruction to propose the terms for readmission. Established in December 1865, the Joint Committee reflected Congress's determination to follow its own course on Reconstruction.

In February 1866 Congress voted to extend the life of the Freedmen's Bureau and empowered the Bureau to set up its own courts, which would supersede local jurisdictions. The Bureau's record during its first year had been mixed. It provided immediate relief to thousands of individual freed people, and it assisted in the creation of schools. But in the crucial area of labor relations, the Bureau too often sided with the landowners and against the interests of the freed people.

Nevertheless the understaffed and overworked Bureau agents often acted under difficult circumstances to protect the freed people from racist violence, unfair employers, and biased law enforcement officials. For this reason, thousands of freedmen and freedwomen looked to the Bureau as their only hope for justice. For the same reason, however, thousands of southern whites resented the Bureau, and they let Andrew Johnson know it.

To the amazement of moderate Republicans, Johnson vetoed the Freedmen's Bureau Bill, complaining that the legislation would increase the power of the central government at the expense of the states. He invoked the Jacksonian political economy of the free market, insisting that the "laws that regulate supply and demand" were the best way to resolve the labor problem. Republicans fell just short of the two-thirds vote they needed to override the veto. Johnson reacted to his narrow victory with a speech attacking the Republicans in Congress and questioning the legitimacy of the Joint Committee on Reconstruction.

Origins of the Fourteenth Amendment

In March 1866 Congress passed a landmark Civil Rights Act. It overturned the Dred Scott decision by granting United States citizenship to Americans regardless of race. This marked the first time that the federal government intervened in the states to guarantee due process and basic civil rights. But President Johnson vetoed the Civil Rights Act of 1866. In addition to the usual Jacksonian rhetoric

Led by President Andrew Johnson, attacks on the Freedmen's Bureau became more and more openly racist in late 1865 and 1866. This Democratic Party broadside was circulated during the 1866 election.

about limited government, Johnson made an overtly racist argument to justify his veto. He doubted that blacks "possess the requisite qualifications to entitle them to all the privileges and immunities of citizens of the United States."

Johnson's actions and rhetoric forced the moderate Republicans to confront the president. The Republican Congress overrode Johnson's veto of the Civil Rights Act and passed another Freedmen's Bureau Bill. Once again Johnson vetoed it, but this time Congress overrode his veto.

To ensure the civil rights of the freed people, the Joint Committee on Reconstruction proposed a Fourteenth Amendment to the Constitution. The most powerful and controversial of all the Constitution's amendments, it guaranteed citizenship to all males born in the United States, regardless of color (see Table 16–1). Although the amendment did not guarantee blacks the right to vote, it based representation in Congress on a state's voting population. This punished southern states by reducing their representation if they did not allow blacks to vote.

By mid-1866, Congress had refused to recognize the state governments established under Johnson's plan, and it had authorized the Freedmen's Bureau to create a military justice system to override the local courts. Congress thereby guaranteed the former slaves basic rights of due process. Finally, it made ratification of the Fourteenth Amendment by the former Confederate states a requirement for their readmission to the Union. Congress and the president were now at war, and Andrew Johnson went on a rampage.

Race Riots and the Election of 1866

A few weeks after Congress passed the Civil Rights Act, white mobs in Memphis rioted for three days. They burned hundreds of homes, destroyed churches, and attacked black schools. Five women were raped and 46 blacks died. Three months later, white mobs in New Orleans rioted as well. They focused their fury on a convention of radical leaders who were demanding constitutional changes that would give black men in Louisiana the right to vote. Disciplined squads of white police and firemen marched to the convention site and proceeded to slaughter the delegates. Thirty-four blacks and three whites were killed.

TABLE 16–1

Reconstruction Amendments, 1865–1870			
Amendment	Main Provisions	Congressional Passage (2/3 majority in each house required)	Ratification Process (3/4 of all states including ex-Confederate states required)
13	Slavery prohibited in United States	January 1865	December 1865 (twenty-seven states, including eight southern states)
14	1. National citizenship	June 1866	Rejected by twelve southern and border states, February 1867
	2. State representation in Congress reduced proportionally to number of voters disfranchised		Radicals make readmission of southern states hinge on ratification
	3. Former Confederates denied right to hold office		Ratified July 1868
	4. Confederate debt repudiated		
15	Denial of franchise because of race, color, or past servitude explicitly prohibited	February 1869	Ratification required for readmission of Virginia, Texas, Mississippi, Georgia Ratified March 1870

The Memphis and New Orleans massacres quickly became political issues in the North, thanks in large part to Andrew Johnson's reaction to them. In late August the president undertook an unprecedented campaign tour designed to stir up voters' hostility to Congress, but his trip backfired. The president blasted Congressional Republicans, blaming them for the riots. At one point he suggested that Radical Congressman Thaddeus Stevens should be hanged. Republicans charged in turn that Johnson's own policies had revived the rebellious sentiments in the South that led to the massacres.

The elections of 1866 became a referendum on presidential Reconstruction. The results were "overwhelmingly against the President," the *New York Times* noted, "clearly, unmistakably, decisively in favor of Congress and its policy." The Republicans gained a veto-proof hold on Congress, and Republican moderates moved further to the radical position. Congressional Reconstruction was about to begin.

CONGRESSIONAL RECONSTRUCTION

Johnson's outrageous behavior during the 1866 campaign, capped by a Republican sweep of the elections, ended presidential Reconstruction. Congressional Reconstruction would be far different. It was an extraordinary series of events, second only to emancipation in its impact on the history of the United States.

Origins of the African-American Vote

The Congress that convened in December 1866 was far more radical than the previous one. Nothing demonstrated this as clearly as the emerging consensus among moderate Republicans that southern blacks should be allowed to vote. Radical Republicans and black leaders had been calling for such a policy for two years, but moderate Republicans initially resisted the idea. At most, moderates like Abraham Lincoln contemplated granting the vote to veterans and to educated blacks who had been free before the war. Not until early 1867 did moderates conclude that the way to avoid a lengthy military occupation of the South was to put political power into the hands of all male freedmen.

Andrew Johnson finally pushed the moderate Republicans over the line. Ignoring the results of the 1866 elections, Johnson urged the southern states to reject the Fourteenth Amendment. Frustrated moderates thereupon joined with radicals and repudiated presidential Reconstruction. On March 2, 1867, Congress assumed control of the process by passing the First Reconstruction Act. It reduced the southern states to the status of territories and divided the South into five military districts directly controlled by the army (see Map 16–1). Before the southern states could be readmitted to the Union they had to draw up new "republican" constitutions, ratify the Fourteenth Amendment, and allow African-American men

Map 16–1   Reconstruction and Redemption
By 1870 Congress readmitted every southern state to the Union. In most cases the Republican Party retained control of the "reconstructed" state governments for only a few years.

to vote. The Second Reconstruction Act, passed a few weeks later, established the procedures to enforce African-American suffrage by placing the military in charge of voter registration. Johnson vetoed both acts, and in both cases Congress immediately overrode the president. This was Congressional Reconstruction at its most radical, and for this reason it is often referred to as radical Reconstruction.

Radical Reconstruction in the South

Beginning in 1867, the constitutions of the southern states were rewritten, thousands of African Americans began to vote, and hundreds of them assumed public office. Within six months 735,000 blacks and 635,000 whites had registered to vote across the South. African Americans formed electoral majorities in South Carolina, Florida, Mississippi, Alabama, and Louisiana. In the fall these new voters elected delegates to conventions that drew up progressive state constitutions that guaranteed universal manhood suffrage, mandated public education systems, and established progressive tax structures.

The Republican governments elected under Congressional authority were based on an unstable political coalition. Northern whites occupied a prominent place in the southern Republican Party. Stereotyped as greedy carpetbaggers, they included Union veterans who stayed in the South when the war ended, idealistic reformers, well-meaning capitalists, and opportunistic Americans on the make. More important to the Republican coalition were southern whites, or scalawags. Some of them lived in upcountry regions where resistance to secession and the Confederacy had been strongest. Others had been Whigs before the war and hoped to regain some of their former influence. But new black voters were

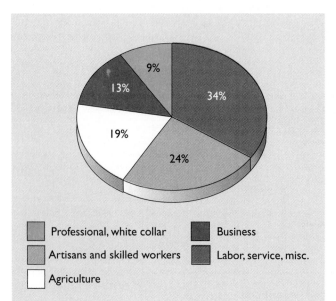

Figure 16–1 Occupations of African-American Officeholders During Reconstruction
Source: Eric Foner, Freedom's Lawmakers: A Directory of Black Officeholders during Reconstruction, 2d. ed. (Baton Rouge, LA), p. xxi

the Republican Party's core constituency in the South. Like the carpetbaggers and scalawags, black voters were a varied lot. Elite black artisans and professionals did not always share the interests of poor black farmers and farm laborers. Nevertheless, most African Americans were drawn together by a shared interest in securing civil rights.

In the long run the class and race divisions within the southern Republican coalition weakened the party, but in the late 1860s and early 1870s the southern Republicans launched an impressive experiment in interracial democracy in the South. Racist legend paints these years as a dark period of "negro rule" and military domination, but military rule rarely lasted more than a year or two, and in only one state, South Carolina, did blacks ever control a majority of seats in the legislature. Blacks who held office came largely from the ranks of the prewar free African-American elite. Teachers, ministers, and small businessmen were far more common among black elected officials than were field hands and farmers. Nevertheless, these Reconstruction legislatures were more representative of their constituents than most legislatures in nineteenth-century America (see Figure 16–1).

Achievements and Failures of Radical Government

Once in office, southern Republicans had to cultivate a white constituency and at the same time serve the interests of their black constituents. To strengthen this biracial coalition, white Republican leaders emphasized active government support for economic development. Republican legislatures granted tax abatements for corporations and spent vast sums to encourage the construction of railroads. They preached a "gospel of prosperity" that promised to bring the benefits of economic development to ordinary white southerners.

In the long run, the gospel of prosperity did not hold the Republican coalition together. Outside investors were unwilling to risk their capital on a region marked by political instability. By the early 1870s, black politicians questioned the diversion of scarce revenues to railroads and tax breaks for corporations. Instead, they demanded public services, especially universal education. But more government services meant higher property taxes at a time of severe economic hardship. Small white farmers had been devastated by the Civil War. Unaccustomed to paying high taxes and strong believers in limited government, they grew increasingly receptive to Democratic appeals for restoration of "white man's government." Thus southern Republicans failed to develop a program that could unite the diverse interests of their party's constituents.

Despite powerful opposition at home and lukewarm support from Washington, DC, radical governments in the South boasted several important achievements. They funded the construction of hospitals, insane asylums, prisons, and roads. They introduced homestead exemptions that protected the property of poor farmers. One of their top priorities was the establishment of universal public education. Republican legislatures established public school systems that were a major improvement over their antebellum counterparts. The literacy rate among southern blacks rose steadily.

Nevertheless, public schools for African Americans remained inadequately funded and sharply segregated. In Savannah, Georgia, for example, the school board allocated less than five percent of its 1873 budget to black schools, although white children were in the minority in the district. In South Carolina, fewer than one in three school-age children were being educated in 1872.

RADICAL MEMBERS
OF THE So. CA. LEGISLATURE.

One of the greatest achievements of Congressional Reconstruction was the election of a significant number of African Americans to public office. Only in South Carolina, however, did African Americans ever form a legislative majority.

The Political Economy of Sharecropping

Congressional Reconstruction made it easier for the former slaves to negotiate the terms of their labor contracts. Republican state legislatures abolished the Black Codes and passed "lien" laws, statutes giving black workers more control over the crops they grew. Workers with grievances had a better chance of securing justice, as southern Republicans became sheriffs, justices of the peace, and county clerks, and as southern courts allowed blacks to serve as witnesses and sit on juries.

The strongest card in the hands of the freed people was a shortage of agricultural workers throughout the South. After emancipation thousands of blacks sought better opportunities in towns and cities or in the North. And even though most blacks remained as farmers, they reduced their working hours in several ways: Black women withdrew from field work in significant numbers, and children attended school. The resulting labor shortage forced white landlords to renegotiate their labor arrangements with the freed people.

The contract labor system that had developed during the war and under presidential Reconstruction was replaced with a variety of arrangements in different regions. On the sugar plantations of southern Louisiana, the freed people became wage laborers. In low-country South Carolina, former slaves became independent farmers. But in tobacco and cotton regions, where the vast majority of freed people lived, a new system of labor called *sharecropping* developed. Under the sharecropping system, an agricultural worker and his family typically agreed to work for one year on a particular plot of land, the landowner providing the tools, seed, and work animals. At the end of the year the sharecropper and the landlord split the crop, perhaps one-third going to the sharecropper and two-thirds to the owner.

Sharecropping shaped the political economy of the postwar South by transforming the way cash crops were produced and marketed. Most dramatically, it required landowners to break up their plantations into family-sized plots, where sharecroppers worked in family units with no direct supervision. Each sharecropping family established its own relationship with local merchants to sell crops and buy supplies. Merchants became crucial to the southern credit system because during the Civil War, Congress had established nationwide banking standards that most southern banks could not meet. Therefore storekeepers were usually the only people who could extend credit to sharecroppers. They provided sharecroppers with food, fertilizer, animal feed, and other provisions over the course of the year, until the crop was harvested.

These developments had important consequences for small white farmers. As the number of merchants grew, they fanned out into upcountry areas inhabited mostly by ordinary whites. Reconstruction legislatures meanwhile sponsored the construction of railroads in those districts. The combination of merchants offering credit and railroads offering transportation made it easier for small farmers to produce cash crops. Thus Reconstruction accelerated the process by which the southern yeomen abandoned self-sufficient farming in favor of cash crops.

Sharecropping spread quickly among black farmers in the cotton South. By 1880, 80 percent of cotton farms had fewer than 50 acres, the majority of which were operated by sharecroppers (see Map 16–2). Sharecropping had several advantages for landlords. It reduced their risk when cotton prices were low and encouraged workers to increase production without costly supervision. Further, if sharecroppers changed jobs before the crop was harvested, they lost a whole year's pay. But the system also had advantages for the workers. For freed people who had no hope of owning their own farms, sharecropping at least rewarded those who worked hard. The bigger the crop, the more they earned. It gave the former slaves more independence than contract labor.

Sharecropping also allowed the freed people to work in families rather than in gangs. Freedom alone had rearranged the powers of men, women, and children within the families of former slaves. Parents gained newfound control over the lives of their children. They could send sons and daughters to school; they could put them to work. Successful parents could give their children an important head start in life. Similarly, African-American husbands gained new powers.

The laws of marriage in the mid-nineteenth century defined the husband as the head of the household. Once married, women often found that their property belonged to their husbands. The sharecropping system assumed that the husband was the head of the household and that he made the economic decisions for the

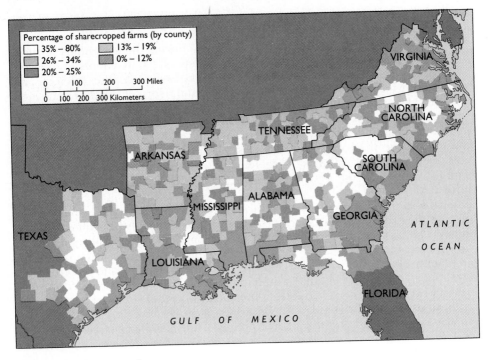

Map 16–2 Sharecropping
By 1880 the sharecropping system had spread across the South. It was most common in the inland areas where cotton and tobacco plantations were most common before the Civil War.

entire family. Men signed most labor contracts, and most landlords assumed that the husband would take his family to work with him.

Sharecropping thereby shaped the political economy of the postwar South: It influenced the balance of power between men and women; it established the balance of power between landowners and sharecroppers; and it tied the southern economy to agriculture, in particular to cotton production, seriously impeding the region's overall economic development. Yet even as this new way of life was taking shape, the Republican Party was retreating from its commitment to the freed people.

THE RETREAT FROM REPUBLICAN RADICALISM

By the late 1860s the Republican coalition was splintering in ways that weakened the party's continued commitment to radical Reconstruction. By 1868 the Republicans were presenting themselves to voters as the party of moderation. The success of this appeal brought in its wake the last major achievements of Reconstruction.

The Impeachment and Trial of Andrew Johnson

Throughout 1866 and much of 1867, President Johnson waged a relentless campaign against Congress and the radicals. Inevitably, this conflict led to a struggle over control of the military in the South. The First Reconstruction Act placed the entire South under direct military power. The Freedmen's Bureau itself was a branch of the

Court proceedings were held in the Senate chambers during the impeachment trial of President Andrew Johnson. It was an extraordinary thing to put a president on trial.

U.S. Army. Judicial authority was vested in the provost marshals. The military also oversaw voter registration. But the president was the commander in chief of the military, and exercising his authority over the military, Andrew Johnson removed dozens of Freedmen's Bureau officials who enforced the Civil Rights Act of 1866. He replaced Republican provost marshals with men who were hostile to Congress and contemptuous of the former slaves. In short, Johnson went out of his way to undermine the law.

Radicals called for Johnson's impeachment, but moderates and conservatives resisted. Instead, Congress hoped to restrain the president by refining the Reconstruction Acts and by using the Tenure of Office Act of March 2, 1867. This act prohibited the president from removing officials whose appointments required Congressional approval. One purpose of the law was to prevent Johnson from firing Secretary of War Edwin M. Stanton, who was sympathetic to the Republicans. A related statute required that all presidential orders to the military pass through General Ulysses S. Grant. Republicans hoped that this would prevent the president from removing military officials who enforced the Reconstruction Acts.

Congress's actions only provoked the president. In his veto messages and public pronouncements Johnson indulged in blatant racist pandering. He played on fears of "amalgamation," "miscegenation," and racial "degeneration." He expressed fear for the safety of white womanhood. In the off-year elections of 1867, northern Democrats played the race card relentlessly and successfully. Democratic victories erased many of the huge Republican gains of 1866 and inspired the president to defy Congressional restraints. As a deliberate provocation, Johnson asked Secretary of War Stanton to resign on August 5, 1867. Stanton refused, and the president appointed General Grant as interim Secretary of War. Still Stanton would not budge, so in February 1868 Johnson fired him. For this the House of

Representatives voted to impeach the president and put him on trial in the Senate. Yet for all the Congressional animosity that Johnson had aroused by his obnoxious behavior, the Senators trying him took their job seriously. Many were concerned that the Tenure of Office Act, which Johnson was accused of violating, was in fact unconstitutional. Others wondered whether his technical breach of the law was serious enough to warrant his removal from office. These and other doubts, along with Johnson's promise of good behavior in the future, led the Senate to acquit the president by a single vote.

Republicans Become the Party of Moderation

While Andrew Johnson was on trial in the Senate, voters in Michigan went to the polls and overwhelmingly rejected a new state constitution that granted blacks the right to vote. Coming on the heels of Democratic victories in 1867, Republicans read the Michigan results as a rejection of radical Reconstruction.

During the 1868 elections Republicans repudiated the radicals' demand for nationwide black suffrage, arguing that the black vote was a uniquely southern solution to a uniquely southern problem. The northern states should be free to decide for themselves whether to grant African-American men the vote. Congress

The Ku Klux Klan was one of a number of racist vigilante groups trying to restore the Democratic Party to power in the postwar South.

readmitted six southern states to the Union, thereby demonstrating that Republican policies had successfully restored law and order to the South. By nominating General Ulysses Grant as their presidential candidate, the Republicans confirmed their retreat from radicalism. "Let Us Have Peace" was Grant's campaign slogan.

In sharp contrast, the Democrats nominated Horatio Seymour, who ran a vicious campaign of race baiting. The Democratic platform denounced the Reconstruction Acts and promised to restore white rule to the South. Seymour suggested that a Democratic president might nullify the governments organized under Congressional Reconstruction. Where the Republicans promised order and stability, the Democrats seemed to promise continued disruption. Northern fears were confirmed by the violence that swept the South during the election, incited by Southern Democrats to keep black voters from the polls.

The Ku Klux Klan, which systematically intimidated potential black voters, was one of several secretive organizations dedicated to the violent overthrow of radical Reconstruction and the restoration of white supremacy. They included the Knights of the White Camelia, Red Shirts, and Night Riders. Some tried to force blacks to go back to work for white landlords. Some attacked African Americans who refused to abide by traditional codes of racial etiquette. But in the main, such organizations worked to restore the political power of the Democratic Party in the South. They intimidated white Republicans, burned homes of black families, and lynched African Americans who showed signs of political activism. It is fair to say that in 1868 the Ku Klux Klan served as the paramilitary arm of the southern Democratic Party.

As a means of restoring white supremacy, the Klan's strategy of violence backfired. A wave of disgust swept across the North, and the Republicans regained control of the White House, along with 25 of the 33 state legislatures. The victorious Republicans quickly seized the opportunity to preserve the achievements of the Reconstruction.

The Grant Administration and Moderate Republicanism

The Republicans reinforced their moderate image by attempting to restore law and order in the South. Congressional hearings produced vivid evidence of the Klan's violent efforts to suppress the black vote. Congress responded with a series of Enforcement Acts, designed to "enforce" the recently enacted Fifteenth Amendment (see the following section). After some initial hesitation, the Grant administration used the new laws to initiate anti-Klan prosecutions that effectively diminished political violence throughout the South. As a result the 1872 presidential elections were relatively free of disruption.

In this period the Republicans shifted to an aggressive foreign policy. Before the Civil War, Republicans associated expansionism with the slave power and the Democratic Party. But with the triumph of nationalism, the Republicans equated American overseas expansion with the spread of liberty. They went on the offensive: In 1867 Secretary of State William Seward successfully negotiated the purchase of Alaska from Russia. The administration was equally adroit in its negotiations with Great Britain over the settlement of the so-called *Alabama* claims. In 1872 the English accepted responsibility for having helped equip the Confederate Navy during the Civil War and agreed to pay over $15 million for damage to American shipping by the *Alabama* and other southern warships built in England.

But Grant's aggressive foreign policy did not go uncontested. In 1869 the president set his sights on Santo Domingo (now the Dominican Republic), but the administration bungled the deal. Grant's private secretary negotiated a treaty without informing the cabinet. Grant tried to bulldoze the treaty through Congress, but succeeded only in alienating members of his own party. The Senate rejected the annexation of Santo Domingo, and the Republicans were weakened by the debacle.

RECONSTRUCTION IN THE NORTH

Although Reconstruction was aimed primarily at the South, the North was affected as well. The struggle over the black vote spilled beyond the borders of the defeated Confederacy. Although not as dramatic as developments in the South, the transformation of the North was still an important chapter in the history of Reconstruction.

The Fifteenth Amendment and Nationwide African-American Suffrage

Before the Civil War African Americans in the North were segregated in theaters, restaurants, cemeteries, hotels, streetcars, ferries, and schools. Most states denied them the vote. The Civil War galvanized the northern black community to launch an assault on racial discrimination, with some success. In 1863 California removed the ban on black testimony in criminal courts. Two years later Illinois did the same. During the war, many northern cities abolished streetcar segregation. But when they considered black voting, northern whites retained their traditional racial prejudices. In 1865 voters in three northern states (Connecticut, Wisconsin, and Minnesota) rejected constitutional amendments to enfranchise African-American men. In 1867, even as the Republican Congress was imposing the black vote on the South, black suffrage was defeated by voters in Ohio, Minnesota, and Kansas.

The shocking electoral violence of 1868 persuaded many northerners that, given the chance, southern whites would quickly strip blacks of the right to vote. In Iowa and Minnesota, voters finally approved black suffrage. Emboldened by their victory in the 1868 elections, the following year Republicans passed the Fifteenth Amendment to the Constitution. It prohibited the use of "race, color, or previous condition of servitude" to disqualify voters anywhere in the United States. By outlawing voter discrimination on the basis of race, the Fifteenth Amendment protected the most radical achievement of Congressional Reconstruction.

The Fifteenth Amendment brought Reconstruction directly into the North by overturning the state laws that discriminated against black voters. In addition, Congress required ratification of the amendment in those southern states still to be readmitted to the Union. Virginia, Mississippi, and Texas did so and were restored to the Union in early 1870. On March 30, 1870, the Fifteenth Amendment became part of the Constitution. For the first time, racial criteria for voting were banned everywhere in the United States, North as well as South.

Women and Suffrage

The issue of black voting divided northern radicals, especially feminists and abolitionists, who had long been allies in the struggle for emancipation. Signs of trouble appeared as early as May 1863 when a dispute broke out at the convention of the Woman's

Elizabeth Cady Stanton, a leading advocate of women's rights, was angered when Congress gave African-American men the vote without also giving it to women.

National Loyal League in New York City. One of the convention's resolutions declared that "there never can be a true peace in this Republic until the civil and political rights of all citizens of African descent and all women are practically established." For some of the delegates, this went too far. The Loyal League had been organized to assist in defeating the slave South. Some delegates argued that it was inappropriate to inject the issue of women's rights into the struggle to restore the Union.

By the end of the war, radicals were pressing for black suffrage in addition to emancipation. This precipitated an increasingly rancorous debate among reformers. Abolitionists argued that while they supported women's suffrage, the critical issue was the protection of the freed people of the South. This, abolitionist Wendell Phillips argued, was "the Negro's Hour." Phillips's position sparked a sense of betrayal among women's rights activists. For 20 years they had pressed their claims for the right to vote. They were loyal allies of the Republican Party, and now the Republicans abandoned them. It would be better, Elizabeth Cady Stanton argued, to press for "a vote based on intelligence and education for black and white, man and woman." Voting rights based on "intelligence and education" would have excluded virtually all the freed slaves as well as the working-class Irish, Germans, and Chinese. Thus, Stanton's remarks revealed a strain of elitism that further alienated abolitionists.

Not all feminists agreed with Stanton, and as racist violence erupted in the South, abolitionists argued that black suffrage was more urgent than women's suffrage. The black vote "is with us a matter of life and death," Frederick Douglass argued. "I have always championed women's right to vote; but it will be seen that the present claim for the negro is one of the most urgent necessity."

Stanton was unmoved by such arguments. For her the Fifteenth Amendment barring racial qualifications for voting was the last straw. Supporters of women's suffrage opposed the Fifteenth Amendment on the ground that it subjected elite, educated women to the rule of base and illiterate males, especially immigrants and blacks. Abolitionists were shocked by such opinions. They favored universal suffrage, not the "educated" suffrage that Stanton was calling for. The breach among reformers weakened the coalition of radicals pushing to maintain a vigorous Reconstruction policy in the South.

The Rise and Fall of the National Labor Union

Inspired by the radicalism of the Civil War and Reconstruction, industrial workers across the North organized dozens of craft unions, Eight-Hour Leagues, and working men's associations. The general goal of these associations was to protect northern workers who were overworked and underpaid. They called strikes, initiated consumer boycotts, and formed consumer cooperatives. In 1867 and 1868 workers in New York and Massachusetts launched campaigns to enact laws restricting the workday to eight hours. Shortly thereafter workers began electing their own candidates to state legislatures.

The National Labor Union (NLU) was the first significant postwar effort to organize all "working people" into a national union. William Sylvis, an iron molder, founded the NLU and became its president in 1868. Like most worker organizations of the time, the NLU subscribed to a "producers ideology." It sought to unify all those who produced wealth through their own labor and skill. The NLU targeted bankers, financiers, and stockbrokers as the enemies of the producing classes.

Under Sylvis's direction the NLU advocated a wide range of political reforms, not just bread-and-butter issues. Nevertheless, the NLU was thwarted by the limits of producer ideology. Sylvis believed that through successful organization American workers could take the "first step toward competence and independence." Thus Sylvis's NLU clung to the Jeffersonian vision of a society of independent petty producers. By the 1860s this vision was an outdated relic of an earlier age, because wage labor rather than economic independence had become the rule for the majority of American workers. Sylvis showed little interest in organizing women, blacks, rural workers, or unskilled wage laborers. After a miserable showing in the elections of 1872, the NLU fell apart. By then Reconstruction in the South was also ending.

THE END OF RECONSTRUCTION

National events had as much to do with the end of Reconstruction as did events in the South. A nationwide outbreak of political corruption in the late 1860s and 1870s provoked a sharp reaction. Influential northern Liberals, previously known for their support for Reconstruction, abandoned the Republican Party in disgust in 1872. The end of Reconstruction finally came after electoral violence corrupted the 1876 elections. Republican politicians in Washington, DC, responded with a sordid political bargain that came to symbolize the end of an era.

Corruption as a National Problem

Postwar Americans witnessed an extraordinary display of public dishonesty. Democrats were as prone to thievery as Republicans. Northern swindlers looted the public treasuries from Boston to San Francisco. In the South, both black and white legislators took bribes. Corruption, it seemed, was endemic to postwar American politics.

If corruption was everywhere in the late 1860s and 1870s, it was largely because there were more opportunities for it than ever before. The Civil War and Reconstruction had swollen government budgets. Never before was government so active in collecting taxes and disbursing vast sums for the public good. Under the circumstances, many government officials accepted bribes for votes, embezzled public funds, or used insider knowledge to defraud taxpayers.

The federal government set the tone. In the most notorious case, the directors of the Union Pacific Railroad set up a dummy corporation called the Credit Mobilier, awarded it phony contracts, and protected it from inquiry by bribing influential congressmen. The Grant administration was eventually smeared with scandal as well. Although personally honest, the president surrounded himself with rich nobodies and army buddies rather than respected statesmen. Grant's own private secretary was exposed as a member of the "Whiskey Ring," a cabal of distillers and revenue agents who cheated the government out of millions of tax dollars every year.

State and city governments in the North were no less corrupt. Wealthy businessmen curried favor with politicians whose votes would determine where a railroad would be built, which land would be allocated for rights of way, and how many government bonds had to be floated to pay for such projects. State officials regularly accepted gifts, received salaries, and sat on the boards of corporations directly affected by their votes. Municipalities awarded lucrative contracts for the construction of schools, parks, libraries, water and sewer systems, and mass-transportation networks, creating temptations for corruption. The Tweed Ring alone bilked New York City out of tens of millions of dollars. By these standards the corruption of the southern Reconstruction legislatures was relatively small.

William Marcy Tweed, the boss of New York's notoriously corrupt, "Tweed Ring" was parodied by the great cartoonist, William Nast. Nast's portrayal of the bloated public official became an enduring symbol of governmental corruption.

But corruption in the South was real enough, and it had particular significance for Reconstruction. Southern Republicans of modest means depended heavily on the money they earned as public officials. These same men found themselves responsible for the collection of unusually high taxes and for economic development projects. As elsewhere in industrializing America, the lure of corruption proved overwhelming. The Republican governor of Louisiana grew rich while in office by "exacting tribute" from railroads seeking state favors. Corruption on a vast scale implied petty corruption as well. Individual legislators sold their votes for as little as $200.

In many cases opponents of Reconstruction used attacks on corruption to mask their contempt for Republican policies. Their strategy helped galvanize opposition, destroying Republican hopes of attracting white voters. Finally, corruption in the South helped provoke a backlash against active government nationwide, weakening northern support for Reconstruction. The intellectual substance of this backlash was provided by influential liberal Republicans, many of whom had once been ardent supporters of radical Reconstruction.

Liberal Republicans Revolt

The label "liberal Republicans" embraced a loosely knit group of intellectuals, politicians, publishers, and businessmen from the northern elite who were discouraged by the failure of radical Reconstruction to bring peace to the southern states and disgusted by the corruption of postwar politics. Although small in number, liberals exercised important influence in northern politics.

At the heart of liberal philosophy was a deep suspicion of democracy. Liberals argued that any government beholden to the interests of the ignorant masses was doomed to corruption. They believed that public servants should be chosen on the basis of intelligence, as measured by civil-service examinations, rather than by patronage appointments that sustained corrupt party machines. Indeed, to liberals, party politics was the enemy of good government.

Liberals therefore grew increasingly alienated from the Republican Party and from President Grant. Above all they resented the fact that the Republican Party had changed as its idealistic commitment to free labor waned and its radical vanguard disappeared. To the rising generation of Republican leaders, getting and holding office had become an end in itself.

As Republicans lost their identity as moral crusaders, liberal reformers proposed a new vision of their own. In 1872 they supported Horace Greeley as the Democratic presidential candidate. The liberal plank in the Democratic platform proclaimed the party's commitment to universal equality before the law, the integrity of the Union, and support for the Thirteenth, Fourteenth, and Fifteenth Amendments. At the same time, liberals demanded "the immediate and absolute removal of all disabilities" imposed on the South as well as a "universal amnesty" for ex-Confederates. Finally, the liberals declared their belief that "local self-government" would "guard the rights of all citizens more securely than any centralized power." In effect, the liberals were demanding the end of federal efforts to protect the former slaves.

In the long run, the liberal view would prevail, but in 1872 it did not go over well with the voters. The liberals' biggest liability was their presidential candidate. Horace Greeley's erratic reputation and Republican background were too much, and Democrats refused to vote for him. Grant was easily re-elected, but he and his fellow Republicans saw the returns as evidence that Reconstruction was becoming a political liability.

The 1874 elections confirmed the lesson. Democrats made sweeping gains all across the North, and an ideological stalemate developed. For a generation, neither party would clearly dominate American politics. The Republicans would take no more risks in support of Reconstruction.

During his second term, therefore, Grant did little to protect black voters from violence in the South. Not even the Civil Rights Act of 1875 undid the impression of waning Republican zeal. Ostensibly designed to prohibit racial discrimination in public places, the Civil Rights Act lacked enforcement provisions. The bill's most important clause, prohibiting segregated schools, was eliminated from the final version. Southern states ignored even this watered-down statute, and in 1883 the Supreme Court declared it unconstitutional. Thus the last significant piece of Reconstruction legislation was an ironic testament to the Republican Party's declining commitment to equal rights.

A Depression and a Deal "Redeem" the South

Angered by corruption and high taxes, white Republicans across the South succumbed to the Democratic Party's appeal for restoration of white supremacy. As the number of white Republicans fell, the number of black Republicans holding office in the South increased, even as the Grant administration backed away from civil rights. But the persistence of black officeholders only reinforced the Democrats' determination to "redeem" their states from Republican rule. Democrats had taken control of Virginia in 1869. North Carolina was redeemed in 1870, Georgia in 1871, and Texas in 1873. Then depression struck.

The severe depression that followed the financial panic of 1873 drew the attention away from the problems of Reconstruction.

In September 1873 America's premier financial institution, Jay Cooke, went bankrupt after overextending itself on investments in the Northern Pacific Railroad. Within weeks hundreds of banks and thousands of businesses went bankrupt as well. The country sank into a depression that lasted five years. Unemployment rose to 14 percent as corporations slashed wages. To protect their incomes, railroad workers tried to organize a nationwide union and attempted to strike several times. Their employers, however, repeatedly thwarted such efforts, and the strikes failed.

As the nation turned its attention to labor unrest and economic depression, the Republican Party's commitment to Reconstruction all but disappeared. Democrats regained control of the governments of Alabama and Arkansas in 1874. In the few southern states where black Republicans clung to political power, white "redeemers" used violence to overthrow the last remnants of Reconstruction.

Mississippi established the model in 1875. Confident that authorities in Washington, DC, would no longer interfere in the South, Democrats launched an all-out campaign to regain control of the state government. The Democratic campaign was double edged. Crude appeals to white supremacy further reduced the dwindling number of scalawags. To defeat black Republicans, White Leagues organized a campaign of violence and intimidation to keep blacks away from the polls. Republicans were beaten, forced to flee the state, and in several cases murdered. Washington turned a deaf ear to African-American pleas for protection. In the end

By the mid-1870s the Republican Party lost its zeal to sustain Reconstruction. In many parts of the South, violent repression left African Americans feeling abandoned by the Republican Party to which they had been so loyal.

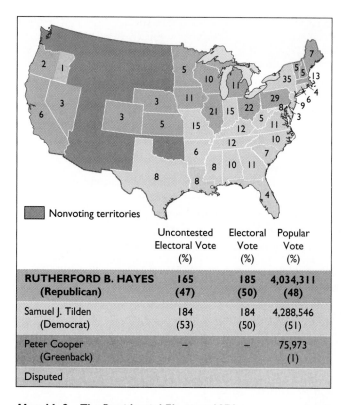

	Uncontested Electoral Vote (%)	Electoral Vote (%)	Popular Vote (%)
RUTHERFORD B. HAYES (Republican)	165 (47)	185 (50)	4,034,311 (48)
Samuel J. Tilden (Democrat)	184 (53)	184 (50)	4,288,546 (51)
Peter Cooper (Greenback)	–	–	75,973 (1)
Disputed			

Nonvoting territories

Map 16–3   The Presidential Election, 1876
In 1876 the Democratic presidential candidate, Samuel Tilden, won the popular vote but was denied the presidency because the Republicans who controlled Congress chose to interpret voting irregularities in Louisiana, South Carolina, Oregon, and Florida in a way that gave their candidate, Rutherford B. Hayes, all of the disputed electoral votes.

enough blacks were kept from the polls and enough scalawags voted their racial prejudices to put the Democrats in power. Mississippi was redeemed.

The tactics used in Mississippi were repeated elsewhere the following year, with dramatic consequences for the presidential election of 1876. Amidst a serious economic depression, and with an electorate tired of Reconstruction, the Democrats stood a good chance of winning the presidency. In fact, the Democratic candidate, Samuel J. Tilden, won 250,000 more votes than the Republican, Rutherford B. Hayes (see Map 16–3). But electoral fraud in South Carolina, Louisiana, Florida, and Oregon threw the results into doubt.

If all of the electoral votes from those states had gone to Hayes, he would win, but if even a single electoral vote went to Tilden, he would have won, the first Democrat to win the presidency in 20 years. The outcome was determined by an electoral commission with a Republican majority, and the commission awarded every disputed electoral vote to the Republican candidate. When Hayes was inaugurated on March 4, 1877, the legitimacy of his presidency was already in doubt. But what he did shortly after taking office made it appear as though he had won thanks to a sordid "compromise" with the Democrats to end Reconstruction in the South. There is no solid evidence that such a deal was ever

CHRONOLOGY

1863	Lincoln's Proclamation of Amnesty and Reconstruction
1864	Wade–Davis Bill
1865	General Sherman's Special Field Order No. 15 Freedmen's Bureau established Lincoln's second inaugural Lincoln assassinated; Andrew Johnson becomes president General Howard's Circular 13 President Johnson orders the Freedmen's Bureau to return confiscated lands to former owners Joint Committee on Reconstruction established by Congress
1866	Congress renews Freedmen's Bureau; Johnson vetoes renewal bill Civil Rights Act vetoed by Johnson Congress overrides presidential veto of Civil Rights Act Congress passes Fourteenth Amendment Congress passes another Freedmen's Bureau Bill over Johnson's veto Johnson begins "swing around the circle" Republicans sweep midterm elections
1867	First and Second Reconstruction Acts Tenure of Office Act
1868	Johnson fires Secretary of War Stanton House of Representatives impeaches Johnson Senate trial of Johnson begins Acquittal of Johnson Fourteenth Amendment ratified Ulysses S. Grant wins presidential election
1869	Congress passes Fifteenth Amendment
1870	Fifteenth Amendment ratified
1872	"Liberal Republicans" leave their party Grant re-elected
1873	Financial "panic" sets off depression
1875	"Mississippi Plan" succeeds Civil Rights Act of 1875 enacted
1876	Disputed presidential election
1877	Electoral commission awards presidency to Rutherford B. Hayes

actually made. Nevertheless, Hayes ordered the federal troops guarding the Republican statehouses in South Carolina and Louisiana to leave. This order marked the formal end of military occupation of the South and the symbolic end of Reconstruction. By late 1877, every southern state had been redeemed by the Democrats.

The following year the Supreme Court began to issue rulings that further undermined the achievements of Reconstruction. In *Hall v. DeCuir* (1878) the Supreme Court invalidated a Louisiana law that prohibited racial segregation on public transportation. In 1882, the justices declared unconstitutional a federal law that protected southern African Americans against racially motivated murders and assaults. More important, in the Civil Rights Cases of 1883, the Supreme Court declared that the Fourteenth Amendment did not pertain to discriminatory practices by private persons. The Supreme Court thus put the finishing touches on the national retreat from Reconstruction.

CONCLUSION

Inspired by an idealized vision of a political economy based on free labor, Republicans expected emancipation to bring about a dramatic transformation of the South. Freed from the shackles of the slave power, the entire region would soon become a shining example of democracy and prosperity. If the results were less than Republicans expected, the achievements of Reconstruction were nonetheless impressive. Across the South, African-American men and women carved out a space in which their families could live more freely than before. Black men by the tens of thousands elected to office some of the most democratic state legislatures of the nineteenth century. Thousands more black workers repudiated an objectionable contract labor system in favor of an innovative compromise known as sharecropping. Furthermore, Reconstruction added three important amendments to the Constitution that transformed civil rights and electoral laws throughout the nation.

Nevertheless, the Republicans washed their hands of Reconstruction with unseemly haste. The Republicans left the former slaves unprotected in a hostile world. Sharecropping offered them a degree of personal autonomy but little hope of real economic independence. Democratic redeemers excluded blacks from the substance of power. Tired of Reconstruction, Americans turned their attention to the new and difficult problems of urban and industrial America.

FURTHER READINGS

Michael Les Benedict, *The Impeachment and Trial of Andrew Johnson* (1973). Especially strong on the constitutional issues and highly critical of Andrew Johnson.

Dan T. Carter, *When the War Was Over: The Failure of Self-Reconstruction in the West* (1985). Reveals the weaknesses of presidential Reconstruction.

W. E. B. DuBois, *Black Reconstruction in America, 1860–1880* (1935). This classic is one of the greatest American history books ever written.

Eric Foner, *Reconstruction: America's Unfinished Revolution, 1863–1877.* (1988). The best one-volume treatment of the period.

John Hope Franklin, *Reconstruction: After the Civil War* (1961). The first modern treatment of African-American politics in the South.

Jacqueline Jones, *Labor of Love, Labor of Sorrow: Black Women, Work, and the Family from Slavery to the Present* (1985). This text includes a pioneering treatment of women's experience of Reconstruction.

Leon Litwack, *Been in the Storm So Long* (1979). This is a detailed and poignant treatment of the former slaves' first experience of freedom.

Roger Ransom and Richard Sutch, *One Kind of Freedom* (1977). The authors provide a clear picture of the breakup of the plantation system and the emergence of sharecropping.

Kenneth M. Stampp, *The Era of Reconstruction* (1965). Stampp gives a lucid overview of events in Washington, DC.

Mark W. Summers, *The Era of Good Stealings* (1993). *Good Stealings* is a lively treatment of the corruption issue.

 Please refer to the document CD-ROM for primary sources related to this chapter.

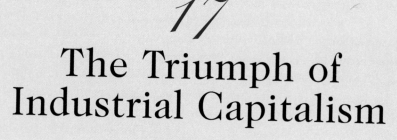

17
The Triumph of Industrial Capitalism
1850–1890

Rosa Cassettari • The Political Economy of Global Capitalism
The Rise of Big Business • A New Social Order • Clearing the West
for Capitalism • The Economic Transformation of the West
Conclusion

ROSA CASSETTARI

In 1884 Rosa Cassettari left the Italian village of Cugiono, near Milan, to marry a man named Santino, a miner in Union, Missouri. Rosa was reluctant to go, especially because she had to leave behind her infant son. "It is wonderful to go to America even if you don't want to go to Santino," Rosa's friends told her at the train station in Milan. "You will get smart in America. And in America you will not be so poor." Along with millions of others, Rosa entered a stream of migrants coming from the far corners of Europe. At Le Havre, France, she embarked on a ship for America. "All us poor people had to go down through a hole to the bottom of the ship," she remembered. But she was going to "America! The country where everyone would find work! Where wages were so high that no one had to go hungry! Where all men were free and equal and where even the poor could own land!"

Rosa's first taste of America did not live up to such dreams. In New York she was cheated and forced to make the long trip to Missouri with nothing to eat. When she arrived at the town of Union she found a shabby collection of tents and shacks. Life in the mining camp lived up to her fears rather than her hopes. With no doctors or midwives available, Rosa gave birth to a premature child alone on the floor of her cabin. Santino was an abusive husband and a cruel father. Rosa had to supplement his earnings by cooking for 12 additional miners.

Yet Rosa was impressed by many things about America. Poor people did not behave humbly in the presence of the rich, for example, and even in the difficult circumstances of the mining camp Rosa became accustomed to wearing decent clothing and eating meat every day, things she could never do back in Europe.

When Rosa discovered that her husband planned to spend all their savings to open a house of prostitution, she separated from Santino. With the help of her immigrant friends from Missouri, Rosa moved to Chicago with her two children. She took a job at a place called Hull House where the social workers were so impressed by her life story that they wrote it down and published it *as Rosa Cassettari's Autobiography.*

Rosa was one of millions of men and women who were moving around the world in the late nineteenth century. They moved from the countryside to the city or from town to town. They moved from less developed regions to places where industrialization was well underway. The nerve center for all of the movement was a powerful core of industrial capitalist societies, and at the center of the core was the United States. Migrants were on a worldwide trek, but more of them came to the United States than any other nation.

Perpetual human migration, global in its extent, had become a hallmark of the political economy of industrial capitalism. Common laborers moved from place to place because jobs were unsteady. Railroads hired construction workers who moved as the track was laid and had to find other work when the line was finished. African-American sharecroppers in the South moved at year's end. Over time they moved into cotton-growing districts, into towns and cities, or out of the South. White tenant farmers moved into mill towns. Native Americans were pushed off their lands throughout the trans-Mississippi West, making room for a flood of white settlers. And all across America the children of farmers abandoned the rural life: They went to mill villages and to huge cities like New York, Chicago, and Philadelphia.

They went looking for work, and for most migrants that meant working in a bureaucracy under professional managers who controlled the work process. It meant working with new and complicated machines. It meant working with polluted air, dirty rivers, or spoiled land. Most of all, industrial capitalism meant wage labor. Working people had been freed from the things that tied them to the land in other places and earlier times, such as feudal dues, slavery, and even independent farming. But wage labor released men and women to move about from community to community, from country to country, and finally from continent to continent. To watch Rosa Cassettari as she traveled from Cugiono to Missouri and Chicago is to witness one small part of a global process set in motion by the triumph of wage labor.

THE POLITICAL ECONOMY OF GLOBAL CAPITALISM

The economic history of the late nineteenth century was sandwiched between two great financial panics in 1873 and 1893. Both were followed by prolonged periods of high unemployment and led directly to tremendous labor unrest. The years between the two panics were marked by a general decline in prices that placed a terrible burden on producers. Farmers found that their crops were worth less at harvest time than they had been during planting season. Manufacturers increased production to maintain profits, but the more they produced, the lower prices for their products fell. In search of an inexpensive work force that could produce more for less, industrialists turned to an international labor market. Amidst financial panics and nationwide strikes, depressions and deflation, Americans experienced a dramatic economic transformation. When it was over, the United States had become the leading capitalist nation on earth.

The "Great Depression" of the Late Nineteenth Century

On July 16, 1877, workers for the Baltimore and Ohio Railroad struck at Martinsburg, West Virginia. Within days the strike spread to the Pennsylvania Railroad, the New York Central, the Great Western, and the Texas Pacific. Governors issued orders for the strikers to disperse and asked for federal assistance. Federal troops were sent to major cities, but confrontations between workers and armed forces only fanned the flames of insurrection. "Other workingmen followed the example of the railroad employees," explained Henry Demarest Lloyd, a prominent social critic. "At Zanesville, Ohio, fifty manufactories stopped work. Baltimore ceased to export petroleum. The rolling mills, foundries, and refineries of Cleveland were closed. . . . Merchants could not sell, manufacturers could not work, banks could not lend. The country went to the verge of a panic." A strike in one key industry now threatened the entire nation.

The railroad strike of 1877 was fueled by an economic depression that began with the Panic of 1873 (see Chapter 16, "Reconstructing A Nation") and spread throughout the developed world. The number of immigrants who had arrived in New York—200,000 every year between 1865 and 1873—fell to less than 65,000 in 1877. Although employment recovered in the 1880s, prices and wages continued to fall. Then in 1893 another panic struck. Once again several major railroads went bankrupt and more than 500 banks and 15,000 businesses shut down. From 1873 to 1896 a "Great Depression" blighted much of the globe.

The world was shrinking, and most Americans knew it. In 1866 a telegraph cable was laid across the Atlantic Ocean. From that moment, Americans could read about events in Europe in the next morning's newspaper. Railroads slashed the distances that separated Eastern from Western Europe and the East Coast from the West Coast of the United States. Steamships brought distant ports into regular contact. Midwestern farmers sold their wheat in Russia. Chinese workers laid the tracks of the Union-Pacific Railroad. Eastern Europeans worked the steel mills of Pittsburgh. The political economy of capitalism was tying the world's nations together.

The clearest sign of this linkage was the emergence of an international labor market. As economic change swept through the less developed parts of the world, men and women were freed from their traditional ties to the land and hurled into a global stream of wage laborers. Irish women went to work as domestic servants. African Americans took jobs as railroad porters. Wage laborers built and maintained the transportation network, the steel mills, and the petroleum refineries; slaughtered beef in Chicago; sewed ready-made clothing in factories; and staffed department store sales counters.

The Political Economy of Immigration

Nineteenth-century migrants tended to leave areas already in the grip of social and economic change. Rosa Cassettari, for example, had worked in a silk-weaving factory in Italy. At first, the largest numbers emigrated from the most developed nations, such as Great Britain and Germany. Later in the century, as industrial or agricultural revolution spread, growing numbers of immigrants came from Scandinavia, Russia, Italy, and Hungary (see Map 17–1). As capitalism developed in

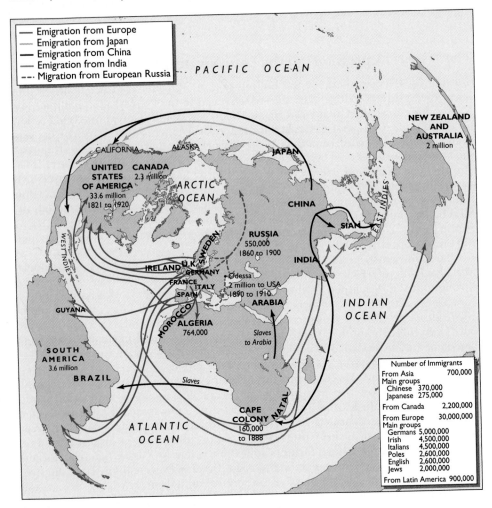

Map 17–1   Patterns of Global Migration, 1840–1900
Emigration was a global process by the late nineteenth century, but more immigrants went to the United States than to every other nation combined.
Source: London Times Atlas.

these areas, small farmers were forced to produce for a highly competitive international market. The resulting upheaval sent millions of rural folk into the worldwide migratory stream.

Improvements in transportation and communication were a sign that capitalism was spreading; they also made migration easier. In 1856, more than 95 percent of immigrants came to America aboard sailing vessels. By the end of the century, more than 95 percent came in steamships. The Atlantic crossing took one to three months on a sailing ship, but only 10 days on a steamship. Beginning in the 1880s fierce competition among steamship lines dramatically lowered the cost of a trans-Atlantic ticket, making two-way movement easier. Many immigrants went back and forth across the Atlantic, particularly workers in seasonal trades like construction.

But the great migrations of the late nineteenth century were also related to political upheaval. In China, for example, the Taiping Rebellion of 1848 was accompanied by an economic disaster rivaling the Irish potato famine of the same decade. This combination of economic and political disruption sent some 300,000 Chinese to the Pacific Coast of North America between 1850 and 1882. They labored in mines and panned for gold, and large numbers of Chinese workers helped build the transcontinental railroad. Desperate for employment and willing to work for low wages, the Chinese soon confronted racist hostility from American and European workers. Union organizers in San Francisco argued that the Chinese threatened the "labor interests" of white workers. In 1882 Congress responded by passing the Chinese Exclusion Act, banning further immigration from China.

A similar combination of economic and political forces lay beneath European immigration. The revival of employment in the 1880s brought with it a revival of movement. After 1890 immigration from Northern and Western Europe fell off sharply, as capitalist development made labor scarce in those areas. But by then agrarian crisis and political disruption had set off a wave of emigration from Eastern and Southern Europe. In Austria-Hungary, for example, the revolution of 1848 brought with it economic and political changes that resulted, by the 1880s, in a profound agrarian crisis. In southern Italy, citrus fruits from Florida and California arrived on the market, and protective tariffs thwarted the sale of Italian wines abroad. Desperate farmers from southern Italy started coming to the United States.

Jewish immigration was propelled by a different combination of politics and economics. The assassination of Czar Alexander II in 1881 was followed by a surge of Russian nationalism. Anti-Jewish riots (called pogroms) erupted in 1881–1882, 1891, and 1905–1906, during which countless Jews were massacred. Anti-Semitic laws forced Russian Jews to live within the so-called Pale of Settlement along Russia's western and southern borders, and the May Laws of 1882 severely restricted Russian Jews' religious and economic life. In the 1880s, Russian Jews began moving to America in significant numbers.

Most immigrants came to America looking for work. Some came with education and skills; some were illiterate. Most came with little more than their ability to work, and they usually found their jobs through families, friends, and fellow immigrants. Letters from America told of high wages and steady employment. Communities of immigrant workers provided the information and the connections that newcomers needed. Large Scandinavian communities settled the upper Midwest; the Chinese were concentrated on the West Coast. Some immigrants settled directly on farms, but the overwhelming number lived in cities.

America Moves to the City

Between 1850 and 1900 the map of the United States was redrawn thanks to the appearance of dozens of new cities (see Figure 17–1). Of the 150 largest cities in the United States in the late twentieth century, 85 were founded in the second half of the nineteenth century. In 1850 the largest city in the United States was New York, with a population of just over half a million. By 1900 New York, Philadelphia, and Chicago each had more than a million residents.

The industrial city was different from its predecessors. By the middle of the nineteenth century the modern "downtown" was born, a place where people shopped and worked but did not necessarily live. Residential neighborhoods separated city dwellers from the downtown districts and separated the classes from one another. Streetcars and commuter railroads brought middle-class clerks and professionals from their homes to their jobs and back, but the fares were beyond the means of the working class. The rich built their mansions uptown, but workers had no choice but to remain within walking distance of their jobs.

As cities became more crowded they became unsanitary and unsafe. Yellow fever and cholera epidemics, were among the scourges of urban life in the nineteenth century. Fires periodically wiped out entire neighborhoods. In October 1871 much of Chicago went up in flames. Along with fires and epidemics, urban life was marred by poverty and crime. Beginning in New York in the 1880s, immigrants lived in a new kind of apartment building—the "dumb bell" tenement, five- or six-story walkups housing huge concentrations of people. Immigrant slums appeared in most major cities of America, as well as mill towns and mining camps. In 1890 Jacob Riis published *How the Other Half Lives*, his famous exposé of life in the immigrant slums of New York. He described a dark three-room apartment inhabited by six people. The two bedrooms were tiny, the beds nothing more than boxes filled with "foul straw." Such conditions were a common feature of urban poverty in the late nineteenth century.

Yet during these same years urban reformers set about to make city life less dangerous and more comfortable. Professional fire departments were formed in most big cities by the 1860s. Professional police departments appeared around the

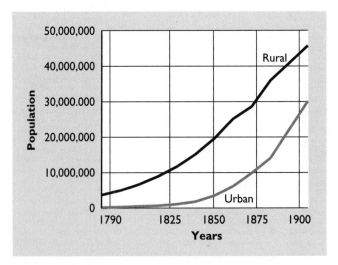

Figure 17–1   Proportion of Population Living in Cities, 1790–1900

A growing proportion of Americans lived in cities, but not until the twentieth century did city dwellers outnumber rural Americans.

same time, greatly reducing urban violence. In 1866 New York City set up the first board of health.

In the second half of the nineteenth century American cities undertook the colossal task of making urban life decent and safe. To a large degree they succeeded: Cities provided clean drinking water, efficient transportation, and great museums, public libraries, and parks. And so the city, which the Jeffersonian tradition had long associated with corruption and decay, was increasingly defended as an oasis of diversity and excitement.

Annie Aitken, who moved from Scotland to Pittsburgh, Pennsylvania, in 1840, would have agreed. Aitken was prospering in the United States while her sister Margaret's family back in Scotland was sinking fast. Margaret's husband, Will, had been a traditional handloom weaver whose livelihood was destroyed by the rise of textile mills. With Aitken's encouragement, in 1848 Will and Margaret Carnegie and their two sons, Tom and Andrew, left Scotland and moved to Pittsburgh. Annie Aitken let her sister's family live rent-free in a small house she owned. Her nephew, Andrew, took a job in a textile mill for $1.20 a week. Fifty years later, Andrew Carnegie sold his steel mills to J. Pierpont Morgan for $480 million.

THE RISE OF BIG BUSINESS

Before the Civil War the only enterprises in the United States that could be called "big businesses" were the railroads. Indeed, railroads became the model for a new kind of business—big business—that emerged during the 1880s. Big businesses had massive bureaucracies that were managed by professionals rather than owners and were financed through a national banking system centered on Wall Street. They marketed their goods and services across the nation and around the world and generated wealth in staggering concentrations, giving rise to a class of men whose names—Carnegie, Rockefeller, Morgan, and Vanderbilt—became synonymous with American capitalism.

The Rise of Andrew Carnegie

Andrew Carnegie was an immigrant, whereas most businessmen were native born. His childhood in Scotland was marked by poverty, whereas most of America's leading men of business were raised in relative prosperity. Certainly few working families in the late nineteenth century could hope to match Carnegie's spectacular climb from rags to riches. Nevertheless, Andrew Carnegie was the perfect reflection of the rise of big business. In the course of his career, Carnegie mastered the telegraph, railroad, petroleum, iron, and steel industries and introduced modern management techniques and strict accounting procedures to American manufacturing. Other great industrialists and financiers made their mark in the last half of the nineteenth century—Henry Clay Frick, Collis P. Huntington, George M. Pullman, John D. Rockefeller, and Cornelius Vanderbilt—but none of their lives took on the mythic proportions of the Scottish lad who came to America at the age of 12 and ended up the richest man in the world.

"I have made millions since," Carnegie once wrote, "but none of these gave me so much happiness as my first week's earnings." Young Andrew might have been happy to earn a wage, but he was not content with his job in a mill. He enrolled in a night course to study accounting, and a year later got a job as a messenger boy in a telegraph office. So astute and hard working was Andrew that by

1851 he was promoted to telegraph operator. In his dealings with the other operators, Carnegie soon displayed the leadership ability that served him throughout his career. He recruited talented, hard-working men and organized them with stunning efficiency.

The most successful businessmen in Pittsburgh, such as Tom Scott, a superintendent for the Pennsylvania Railroad, noticed Carnegie's talents. In 1853, Scott offered Carnegie a job as his secretary and personal telegrapher. Carnegie stayed with the Pennsylvania Railroad for 12 years during a time when railroad construction soared. Railroads stood at the center of the booming industrial economy. They would become the steel industry's biggest customer. Petroleum refiners shipped their kerosene by rail. Mining corporations needed railroads to ship their coal and iron. Ranchers shipped their cattle by rail to the slaughterhouses of Chicago, and meat packers distributed butchered carcasses in refrigerated railroad cars. Thus his position at the Pennsylvania Railroad gave Carnegie an unrivaled familiarity with the workings of big business.

By the mid-1850s, the largest factory in the country, the Pepperell Mills in Biddeford, Maine, employed 800 workers, while the Pennsylvania Railroad had more than 4,000 employees. If the men who maintained the track fell down on the job, if an engineer arrived late, or if a fireman came to work drunk, trains were wrecked, lives were lost, and business failed. The railroads thus borrowed the disciplinary methods and bureaucratic structure of the military to ensure that the trains ran safely and on time.

The man who introduced this organizational discipline to the Pennsylvania Railroad was Tom Scott, the man who hired Andrew Carnegie. J. Edgar Thomson, the Pennsylvania's president, was a pioneer of a different sort. He established an elaborate bookkeeping system that provided detailed knowledge of every aspect of the Pennsylvania's operations. Scott used the statistics Thomson collected to reward managers who improved the company's profits and eliminate those who failed.

Carnegie succeeded. After Scott was promoted to vice president in 1859, Carnegie took Scott's place as superintendent of the western division, where he helped make the Pennsylvania Railroad into a model of industrial efficiency. By 1865 the Pennsylvania had 30,000 employees and had expanded its line east into New York City and west to Chicago. It was the largest private company in the world.

Carnegie's experience at the Pennsylvania Railroad gave him a keen understanding of the modern financial system. Railroads dwarfed all previous business enterprises in the amount of investment capital they required and in the complexity of their financial arrangements. Railroads were the first corporations to issue stocks through sophisticated trading mechanisms that attracted investors from around the world. To organize the market in such vast numbers of securities the modern investment house was developed. J. Pierpont Morgan grew rich selling railroad stocks. The House of Morgan prospered greatly from its association with Andrew Carnegie, for there was no shrewder investor in all of America.

Carnegie Becomes a Financier

Carnegie began making money from money in 1856. On Tom Scott's advice Carnegie borrowed $600 and invested it in Adams Express Company stock, which soon began paying handsome dividends. Carnegie had become a successful capitalist, and for the next 15 years he made a series of financial moves that earned him several more fortunes.

Carnegie invested in the Woodruff Sleeping Car Company in the late 1850s and, a decade later, used his shares and influence to help win George Pullman near-monopoly control of the industry—and make millions in the bargain. Carnegie brokered a similar deal that created the Western Union monopoly of the telegraph industry. He invested in an oil company in western Pennsylvania and demonstrated that strict management would produce steady profits. He made shady deals on the international financial markets; he made millions selling worthless bonds to naïve German investors. More substantially, he created the Keystone Bridge Company, which built the first steel arch bridge over the Mississippi River and provided the infrastructure for the Brooklyn Bridge over New York's East River. With Keystone, Carnegie perfected a model of managerial organization that was the envy of the industrial world.

By 1872 Carnegie was tired of financial speculation and ready for something new. He was 37 years old and had proven himself a master of the railroad industry, a brilliant manager, and a shrewd financial manipulator. Now Carnegie wanted to create an industry of his own. "My preference was always for manufacturing," he explained. "I wished to make something tangible." He would make iron and steel.

Carnegie Dominates the Steel Industry

In 1865 Carnegie acquired a controlling interest in the Union Iron Company. Carnegie's first goal was to speed the flow of materials to his Keystone Bridge Company. This was an important innovation. Iron manufacturing in America had always been decentralized, with each stage of production handled by a different manufacturer. But Carnegie forced Union Iron and Keystone Bridge to coordinate their operations, thereby eliminating middlemen and making production more efficient.

Andrew Carnegie won the bid to provide much of the steel for the construction of the Union-Pacific railroad. Here Chinese workers are pictured laying the tracks at Promontory Point, Utah, in 1869.

Carnegie also forced Union Iron to adopt the managerial techniques and accounting practices he had learned at the Pennsylvania Railroad. By keeping a strict account of all costs, Carnegie could locate the most wasteful points in the production process and reward the most efficient workers. Because he knew exactly what his costs were, Carnegie figured out that his iron mill would be more profitable if he invested in expensive new equipment. He ran his furnaces at full blast, wearing them out after only a few years and replacing them with still more modern machines. Carnegie's great achievement was his introduction of modern management techniques to American industry, but it was in steel rather than iron that Carnegie would prove the worth of those techniques.

As with so many industries, the development of steel was driven by the development of railroads. Traditional iron rails deteriorated rapidly, and as trains grew larger and heavier, iron withered under the load. J. Edgar Thomson, head of the Pennsylvania Railroad, began experimenting with steel rails in 1862. Steel was also a better material for locomotives, boilers, and railroad cars themselves. In the 1860s two developments cleared the path for the transition from iron to steel. First, Henry Bessemer's patented process for turning iron into steel became available to American manufacturers. Second, iron ore began flowing freely onto the American market from deposits in northern Michigan.

Andrew Carnegie was uniquely situated to take advantage of these developments. His experience with Union Iron taught him how to run a mill efficiently, and he had access to investment capital. In 1872 Carnegie built a steel mill, the Thompson Works. Despite a worldwide depression, the steel mill was profitable from the start.

Big Business Consolidates

In the late nineteenth century the names of a handful of wealthy capitalists became closely associated with different industries: Gustavus Swift in meat packing, John D. Rockefeller in oil refining, Collis P. Huntington in railroads, J. P. Morgan in financing, and Andrew Carnegie in steel (see Map 17–2). These powerful individuals, sometimes called "robber barons," represented a passing phase in the history of American enterprise. Most big businesses were so big that no single individual or family could own them. They were run by professionally trained managers, and the highest profits went to companies with the most efficient bureaucracies. Because the businesses were so big and their equipment was so expensive, they had to be kept in operation continuously. An average factory could respond to an economic slowdown by closing its doors for a while, but big businesses could not afford to do that.

Beginning in the 1880s big businesses developed strategies designed to shield them from the effects of ruinous competition. The most common strategy was vertical integration, the attempt to control as many aspects of a business as possible, from the production of raw materials to the sale of the finished product. Carnegie integrated the steel industry from the point of production forward to the distribution of steel but also backward to the extraction of iron ore. He bought iron mines to produce his own ore and railroads to ship the ore to his mills and the finished product to market. His Keystone Bridge Company then purchased the steel.

In 1882 John D. Rockefeller devised a new solution to the problem of ruinous competition by forming the Standard Oil Trust. Rockefeller had founded Standard Oil in 1867 in Cleveland, Ohio. Like Carnegie, Rockefeller surrounded himself with the best managers and financiers to build and run the most efficient modern refineries, but he was more willing than Carnegie to use ruthless tactics to wipe out

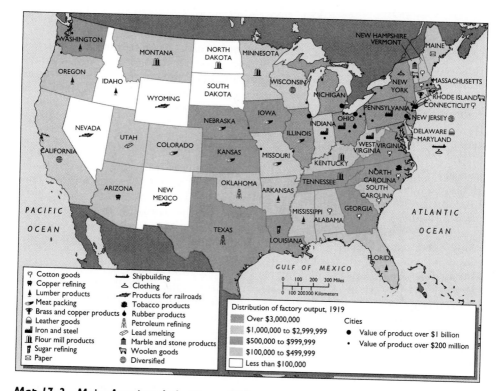

Map 17–2 Major American Industries c. 1890
An industrial map of late nineteenth century America shows regions increasingly defined not by their crops but by their major industries.

his competitors. Rockefeller extracted preferential shipping rates from the railroads, giving him a critical advantage in the savagely competitive oil business. In 1872 Rockefeller began imposing on the national oil refining industry the same control that he had already achieved in Ohio. As president of the National Refiner's Association he formed cartels with the major operators in other states. But the cartels were too weak to eliminate independent refiners.

Rockefeller therefore set out to control the entire oil industry by merging all of the major companies together under Standard Oil. By 1879 the Standard Oil monopoly was largely in place, but not until 1882 was it formalized as a "trust," an elaborate legal device by which different producers came together under the umbrella of a single company that could police competition internally. In 1889 the New Jersey legislature passed a law that allowed corporations based in that state to form "holding companies" that controlled companies in other states. Thus the trust gave way to the holding company, with Standard Oil of New Jersey as its most prominent example. Within a decade many of the largest industries in America were dominated by massive holding companies.

Rockefeller's Standard Oil monopoly was a notorious example of how big business had changed the American economy. Rockefeller himself came to represent a powerful new class of extraordinarily wealthy businessmen. Their names—Carnegie, Rockefeller, Morgan, Harriman, and others—soon became associated with the upper class of the new social order of industrial America.

A New Social Order

Classes were not supposed to exist in the United States the way they existed in Europe, as many Americans continued to believe in the late nineteenth century. Yet the reality of class divisions was so obvious that it had become part of public discussion. It was hard not to notice the conspicuous gap between the astonishing wealth of Andrew Carnegie and the daily struggles of Rosa Cassettari.

Lifestyles of the Very Rich

Between 1850 and 1890 the proportion of the nation's wealth owned by the 4,000 richest families nearly tripled. At the top of the social pyramid rested some 200 families worth more than $20 million each. Concentrated in the Northeast, especially in New York, these families were known throughout the world for their astonishing wealth. Spread more evenly across America were the several thousand millionaires whose investments in cattle ranching, agricultural equipment, mining, commerce, and real estate made them wealthy capitalists.

As a group America's millionaires had a lot in common. Most traced their ancestry to Great Britain. Most were Protestant, usually Episcopalians, Presbyterians, or Congregationalists. By the standards of their day they were unusually well educated. Except in the South, America's upper class voted Republican.

The upper classes lived in spectacular houses in neighborhoods that became famous for their wealth: Fifth Avenue in Manhattan, Nob Hill in San Francisco, Rittenhouse Square in Philadelphia, and Boston's Back Bay. Wealthy suburbs (Brooklyn Heights, Philadelphia's Main Line, and Brookline, Massachusetts) acquired similar reputations as privileged retreats. The richest families also built rural estates that rivaled the country homes of England and the chateaus of France. In the late nineteenth century the richest families built a string of spectacular summer homes along the Newport, Rhode Island, shoreline.

The leading figures in New York's high society competed with one another to stage the most lavish balls and dinner parties. The competition reached a climax on March 26, 1883, when Mrs. William Vanderbilt staged a stupendous costume ball that challenged Mrs. William Astor's long-standing position as the queen of New York's upper class. The ball was a great success. All of New York society turned out at the magnificent Vanderbilt mansion where the hostess made a grand entrance dressed as a Venetian princess.

It was left to the new middle class to preserve the traditional virtues of thrift and self-denial.

The Consolidation of the New Middle Class

In 1889 *The Century Dictionary* introduced the phrase "middle class" in the United States. The new term reflected a novel awareness that American society had become permanently divided in a way that earlier generations had stoutly denied.

Professionals were the backbone of the new middle class that emerged in the nineteenth century. All professions defined what it meant to be a member of their tribe, organized themselves into professional associations, and set educational standards for admission. By these means professionals could command high salaries and enjoy both prestige and a comfortable standard of living. Between 1870 and 1890 some 200 societies were formed to establish the educational requirements and maintain the credentials of their members. Even the management of corporations became a professional occupation, as business schools appeared to train professionals in the science of accounting and the art of management. Some professionals succeeded in having their standards written into law. In most states, by 1900 doctors and lawyers could practice legally only when licensed under the auspices of professional associations.

Behind the new professional managers marched an expanding white-collar army of cashiers, clerks, and government employees. They were overwhelmingly men, and they earned annual incomes far beyond those of independent craftsmen and factory workers. They also enjoyed much better opportunities for upward mobility. A beginning clerk might make only $100 a year, but within five years his salary could be closer to $1,000. At a time when the average annual income of a skilled factory worker in Philadelphia was less than $600, over 80 percent of the male clerks in the Treasury Department earned over $1,200 a year.

As it developed, the middle class withdrew from the messy uncertainties of the central city. Improved roads and mass-transit systems allowed middle-class families to escape the urban extremes of great wealth and miserable poverty. Middle-class residents idealized the physical advantages of trees, lawns, and gardens, as well as the comfortable domestic life that suburbs afforded.

Only the most successful craftsmen matched the incomes and suburban lifestyles of white-collar clerks. Butchers might earn more than $1,600 annually, for example, but shoemakers averaged little more than $500. A shoemaker who owned his own tools and ran a small shop maintained the kind of independence that was long cherished among middle-class Americans, yet his income scarcely distinguished him from skilled factory workers. The manual crafts were therefore a bridge between the remnants of the independent middle class and the growing industrial working class made up of men and women like Rosa Cassettari.

The Industrial Working Class Comes of Age

"When I first went to learn the trade," John Morrison told a Congressional committee in 1883, "a machinist considered himself more than the average workingman; in fact he did not like to be called a workingman. He liked to be called a mechanic." Morrison put his finger on one of the great changes in the political economy of nineteenth-century America. Before the Civil War, urban workingmen were skilled laborers who were referred to as artisans and mechanics. "Today," Morrison explained, the mechanic "is simply a laborer." Big businesses replaced mechanics with semiskilled or unskilled factory laborers. For traditional mechanics, this felt like downward mobility.

But most factory operatives and common laborers were migrants (or children of migrants) from small towns and farms. Few, therefore, experienced factory work as a degradation of their traditional skills, as John Morrison did. But most migrants did experience industrial labor as a harsh existence. Factory operatives worked long hours in difficult conditions performing repetitive tasks with little job security.

The clothing industry is a good example of the lives of urban workers. The introduction of the sewing machine in the 1850s gave rise to sweatshops where work was subdivided into simple, repetitive tasks. One group produced collars for men's shirts, another produced cuffs, and another stitched the parts together.

Jobs were defined to ensure that workers could be easily replaced. Factory operatives learned this lesson quickly. They were young; often they were women or children who moved into and out of different factory jobs with astonishing frequency. But even among men, factory work was at best unsteady. The business cycle swung hard and often, leaving few factory operatives with secure, long-term employment.

At the bottom of the hierarchy of wage earners were the common laborers, whose trademark was physical exertion. Their numbers grew throughout the century until by 1900 common laborers accounted for a third of the industrial work force. Hundreds of thousands of common laborers worked for railroads and steel companies. Before Andrew Carnegie and his competitors revolutionized their industry, for example, no more than 20 percent of iron and steel workers were common laborers. By the 1890s 40 percent of steel workers were common laborers.

Common laborers were difficult to organize into effective unions. A large proportion were immigrants and African Americans, and ethnic differences and language barriers often frustrated the development of workers' alliances. Even the kind of work common laborers performed inhibited the growth of effective unions. It was rarely steady work. Men who laid railroad tracks or dug canals and subway tunnels generally moved on when they finished. Common labor was often seasonal; as a result unskilled workers changed jobs frequently. Common laborers were unusually mobile and easily replaceable, and they increasingly came from parts of the world where the idea of organized labor was unknown. Even when they did organize, common laborers faced the biggest, most powerful, most effectively organized corporations in the country.

A great deal of the wage work done by women fell into the category of common labor. In 1900 women accounted for nearly one of every five gainfully employed Americans. They stood behind the counters of department stores and young Irish women worked as domestics in northern middle-class homes. In the South, African-American women worked as domestics. A smaller proportion of women held white-collar jobs, as teachers, nurses, or low-paid clerical workers and sales clerks.

The same hierarchy that favored men in the white-collar and professional labor force existed in the factories and sweatshops. In the clothing industry, for example, units dominated by male workers were higher up the chain of command than those dominated by women. Indeed, as the textile industry became a big business, the proportion of women working in textile mills steadily declined. The reverse trend appeared among white-collar workers. As department stores expanded in the 1870s and 1880s, they hired low-paid women, often Irish immigrants, with none of the prospects for promotion still available to men. White-collar work was not a signal of middle-class status for women as it was for most men in the late nineteenth century.

The story was somewhat different for married women and their children. As few as one in 50 working-class wives and mothers took jobs outside the home. Women supplemented the family income by taking in boarders or doing laundry. Most often, however, working-class families survived by sending their children to work. Even in the families of the highest paid industrial workers, 50 percent of the children worked. Among the poorest working-class families, three out of four children worked. Child labor was a clear sign of class distinction. The rich sent their daughters to finishing schools and their sons to elite boarding schools, middle-class parents sent their children to public schools, and working-class families sent their children to work. This was especially true in the South, where sharecropping was becoming a form of wage labor.

Sharecropping Becomes Wage Labor

As the southern economy recovered from the devastation of the Civil War many observers predicted a bright future for the region. Optimists saw a wealth of untapped natural and human resources, a South freed from the constraints of an inefficient slave labor system ripe for investment, brimming with opportunities, and ready to go.

In an age when Americans were building railroads at an exuberant clip, southerners built them faster. By 1890 nine out of ten southerners lived in a county with a railroad. By then impressive steel mills were coming to life in Birmingham, Alabama. The Piedmont plateau (running along the eastern foothills of the Appalachian Mountains from Virginia to Georgia) was dotted with textile mills bigger and more efficient than those in New England. Southerners were migrating from the countryside to the towns, expanding the production of cotton into new areas, bringing the rich soil of the Mississippi Delta under cultivation. For ordinary southerners, however, especially African Americans, there was no great prosperity in the New South.

After the war most blacks returned to work on land they did not own (see Chapter 16). In place of the master–slave relationship emerged a new labor relationship between landlords and sharecroppers. Between the landlords and croppers, supplying the credit that kept the system alive, arose a powerful class of merchants. At the beginning it was unclear how much power the landlords, the merchants, and the sharecroppers each had. The most important question was who owned the cotton crop at the end of the year: the sharecropper who produced it, the landlord who owned the farm, or the merchant who loaned the supplies needed until the crop came in. The answer would be decided in the state legislatures and courts where the credit laws were written and interpreted.

The resolution was legally complete by the middle of the 1880s. First the courts defined a sharecropper as a wage laborer. The landlord owned the crop and paid his workers a wage in the form of a share of what was produced. Landlords also won a stronger claim on the crop than the merchant creditors. The struggle among landlords, sharecroppers, and merchants was therefore settled in favor of the landlord.

Under the circumstances, merchants were reluctant to loan money to sharecroppers. Many left the plantation districts and moved to the upcountry where they established commercial relations with white yeomen farmers. Trapped in a cycle of debt, white farmers in the 1880s began losing their land and falling into tenancy. Meanwhile in the "black belt" (where most African Americans lived and most of the cotton was produced), successful landlords became merchants while successful merchants purchased land and hired sharecroppers of their own. By the mid-1880s, black sharecroppers worked as wage laborers for the landlord-merchant class across much of the South.

Sharecropping differed in two critical ways from the wage work of industrial America. First, sharecropping was family labor, depending on a husband and father who signed the contract and delivered the labor of his wife and children to the landlord. Second, because sharecropping contracts were year long, the labor market was restricted to a few weeks at the end of each year. If croppers left before the end of the year, they risked losing everything.

The political economy of sharecropping impoverished the South by binding the region to a single crop—cotton—that steadily depleted the soil even as prices fell. Yet for most southern blacks there were few alternatives. Over time a small percentage of black farmers purchased their own land, but their farms were generally tiny and the soil poor. The skilled black artisans who had worked on plantations before the Civil War moved to southern cities where they took unskilled, low-paying jobs. Industrialization was not much help for African Americans. Northern factories were segregated, as were the steel mills of Birmingham, Alabama, and the Piedmont textile mills. Black women worked as domestic servants to supplement their husbands' meager incomes. Wage labor transformed the lives of southern blacks, but it did not bring prosperity.

Hoping to escape the poverty and discrimination of southern life, a number of former slaves moved west. One group, the Exodusters, began moving to the Kansas prairie during the mid-1870s. By 1880 more than 6,000 blacks had joined them, searching for cheap land on which to build independent farms. The Exodusters became locked in the same battles with cattlemen that troubled white farmers, and blacks who settled in cowtowns like Dodge City and Topeka found the same pattern of discrimination they had known in the South. Nevertheless, some of the Exodusters did manage to buy land and build farms. In this respect, the black exodus was similar to the movement of Americans headed west for relief from the constraints of urban and industrial America.

CLEARING THE WEST FOR CAPITALISM

The Homestead Act, passed by Congress during the Civil War, was designed to ensure that the West would be settled by hard-working, independent small farmers. And millions of farmers actually did settle in the West during the second half of the nineteenth century. Their movement has become the stuff of legend.

But these hardy individuals did not settle an empty prairie. Waiting for them in the West were native peoples, some helpful and many hostile. And far from escaping the hierarchy of industrial capitalism, the settlers brought it with them. By the time the director of the U.S. Census declared the frontier "closed" in 1890, the political economy of the American West was composed of railroad tycoons and immigrant workers, commercial farmers and impoverished Native Americans.

The Overland Trail

"Left home this morning," Jane Gould wrote in her diary on April 27, 1862. Along with her husband, Albert, and their two sons, Jane loaded a covered wagon in Mitchell, Iowa, and joined a group of migrants on the Overland Trail to California (see Map 17–3). It would be a long and difficult journey. Albert got sick shortly after they left, and Jane had to nurse him, drive the wagon, and care for the children. The farther they traveled the more distressed Jane became. The Overland Trail was littered with the remnants of wagon trains that had gone before, including discarded furniture, dried bones, and lonely graves. In early October the Goulds reached their new home in the San Joaquin Valley. Five months later, Jane's husband died.

A popular image pictures the West as a haven for rugged men who struck out on their own, but most migrants went in family groups, and the families were mostly middle class. Few poor people could afford the expense of the journey and still hope to buy land and set up a farm in the West.

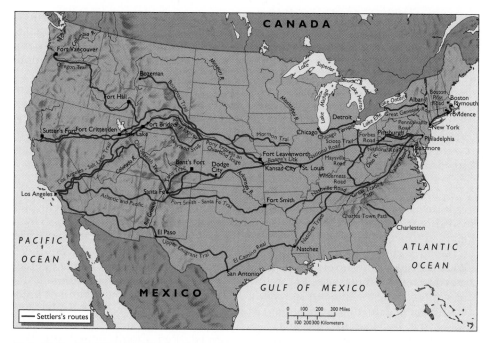

Map 17–3   The Overland Trail
There was no transcontinental railroad until the late 1860s. Before then, and even thereafter, most settlers moved west on a series of well-developed overland trails.

The journey across the Overland Trail became safer over the years. In the late 1840s the U.S. government began building forts along the overland routes. Besides protecting migrants from Indians, the forts became resting points for wagon trains. By the 1850s Mormon settlers in Utah had built Salt Lake City into a major stopping point. Migrants came to rely on the facilities there to ease the journey. Also during the 1850s the government began to pursue a long-term solution to the growing problem of Native American–white relations in the West.

The Origins of Indian Reservations

In 1851 more than 10,000 Native Americans from across the Great Plains converged on Fort Laramie in Wyoming Territory. All the major Indian peoples were represented: Sioux, Cheyenne, Arapaho, Crow, and many others. They came to meet with government officials who hoped to develop a long-term solution to the growing problem of Indian–white relations. Since the discovery of gold a few years earlier, white migrants had been crossing through Indian territory on their way to California, most of them already prejudiced against the Indians. U.S. officials wanted to prevent hostility between whites and Indians from breaking out into violence and to restrain the conflicts among Indians themselves. They proposed the creation of a separate territory for each Indian tribe, with government subsidies to entice the Indians to stay within their territories. This was the beginning of the reservation system, and for the rest of the century the U.S. government struggled to force the Indians to accept it.

From the start the reservation system was corrupt and difficult to enforce. Agents for the Bureau of Indian Affairs cheated Indians and the government alike, sometimes reaping huge profits. But primarily, the reservations failed because not all Indians agreed to restrict themselves to their designated territories, leading to armed confrontations and reprisals.

By the late 1860s the tensions between Indians and whites were at a fever pitch, as Senator James R. Doolittle of Wisconsin discovered on a fact-finding mission through the West. In Denver he asked an audience of whites whether they preferred outright extermination of the Indians to a policy of restricting Indians to reservations. The crowd roared its approval for extermination. Army officers agreed. The government "must act with vindictive earnestness against the Sioux," General William Tecumseh Sherman declared.

Senator Doolittle and his colleagues resisted the calls for extermination, opting instead for a more comprehensive reservation policy. The government pursued this approach by means of two important treaties that divided the Great Plains into two huge Indian territories. The Medicine Lodge Treaty, signed in Kansas in October 1867, organized thousands of Indians across the Southern Plains. In return for government supplies, most of the Southern Plains peoples agreed to restrict themselves to the reservation. The Northern Plains Indians did not sign onto the reservation so readily. A treaty was drafted, but a band of holdouts demanded further government concessions. Inspired by their leader Red Cloud, the Indians insisted that U.S. forces abandon their forts along the Bozeman Trail. When the government agreed, Red Cloud signed the Fort Laramie Treaty in November 1868.

Red Cloud respected the treaties for the rest of his life, but they nevertheless failed. Most white settlers still preferred extermination to reservations, and not all the Plains Indians approved of the treaties. Nor did the U.S. Army abide by the reservation policy. Within weeks of Red Cloud's signature on the Fort Laramie Treaty, for example, the Seventh Cavalry led by Colonel George Armstrong Custer massacred Cheyenne at Washita, Oklahoma, on November 27, 1868. As long as the U.S. Army sustained the settlers' hunger for extermination, Indian "policy" was made on the battlefield rather than in government offices.

By 1870 it was clear that western Indians would not voluntarily retire to reservations and that the military could not force them into surrender. If any further evidence of the Indian resistance was needed, it came in South Dakota, where, after discovery of gold in the Black Hills, thousands of whites poured onto Indian territory. When the Lakota Sioux rejected demands that they cede their lands to the miners, the government sent in the Army led by General Custer. Custer was an arrogant man, and he made two critical mistakes. First he divided his army in two, and then he failed to keep them in communication with each other. Custer and hundreds of his men were slaughtered at Little Bighorn, Montana, in 1876 by 2,000 Indian warriors led by Sitting Bull and Crazy Horse.

The Destruction of Indian Subsistence

Custer's Last Stand did not signal any change of fortunes for the Plains Indians. By the 1870s whites had learned that they could undermine Native American society most effectively by depriving Indians of their sources of subsistence, especially the bison. "Kill every buffalo you can," a U.S. Army colonel urged one hunter, "Every buffalo dead is an Indian gone." Federal authorities did not actually sponsor the mass killing of the bison; they merely turned a blind eye. Railroads joined the process, sponsoring mass kills from slow-moving trains as they crossed the prairies. Some 13 million bison in 1850 were reduced, by 1880, to only a few hundred.

With their subsistence destroyed, Chief Sitting Bull and his starving men finally gave up in 1881. The Sioux war ended in 1890 with a shocking massacre of 200 Native American men, women, and children at Wounded Knee, South Dakota.

In the Northwest in 1877 the Nez Percé, fleeing from Union troops, set out on a dramatic trek across the mountains into Yellowstone in an attempt to reach Canada. The Nez Percé eluded government troops and nearly made it over the Canadian border. However, hunger and the elements did what the Union Army had failed to do. Chief Joseph and his exhausted people agreed to go to their reservations.

Reformers who advocated reservations over extermination always believed that the Indians should be absorbed into the political economy of capitalism. By "confining the Indians to reservations," explained William P. Dole, Lincoln's Commissioner of Indian Affairs, "they are gradually taught and become accustomed to the idea of individual property." Most white settlers considered Native Americans an inferior race worthy of destruction. By contrast, Dole believed that "Indians are capable of attaining a high degree of civilization." But reformers like Dole equated civilization with the cultivation of "individual property." Accordingly, reformers set out to destroy Native American society. They introduced government schools on Indian reservations to teach children the virtues of private property, individual achievement, and social mobility.

The reformers' influence peaked in 1887 when Congress passed the Dawes Severalty Act, the most important piece of Indian legislation of the century. Under the terms of the Dawes Act, land within the reservations was broken up into separate plots and distributed among individual families. The goal was to force Indians to live like stereotypical white farmers. But the lands allotted were generally so poor, and the plots so small, that their owners sold them as soon as they were allowed. By the early twentieth century there were virtually no reservations left, except for a few parcels in the desert Southwest. With the Indians subdued, the path was cleared for the capitalist transformation of the West.

THE ECONOMIC TRANSFORMATION OF THE WEST

A few hundred civilians died in Indian attacks during the late nineteenth century. More than 5,000 died building the railroads. Lawless violence and wild speculation were very much a part of the western experience, as were struggling families, temperance reformers, and hard-working immigrants. By 1900 the West provided Americans with the meat and bread for their dinner tables, the wood that built their homes, and the gold and silver that backed up their currency. The West was being drawn into the political economy of global capitalism.

Cattlemen: From Drovers to Ranchers

The cowboy is the great mythic figure of the American West: a rugged individual, a silent loner who scorned society for the independence of the trail. Like many myths, this one has elements of truth. Cowboys were usually unattached men. They worked hard, but when their work was over they played just as hard, spending their earnings on a shave, a new suit of clothes, and a few good nights in town. Driving cattle was hard work, often dangerous, and even more often boring. Civil War veterans, emancipated slaves, displaced Indians, and Mexican *vaqueros* all became cowboys at various times. Cowboys were poorly paid, their work was unsteady, and their chances of reaching real independence were slim.

Longhorn cattle were as much a part of western legend as the cowboys who drove them. With the destruction of the bison and the westward spread of the railroads, it became possible to drive huge herds of Texas longhorns north onto the Great Plains. With relatively little capital, cattle herders could make substantial profits. Cowboys drove gigantic herds, sometimes numbering half a million, to a town with a railroad connection from which the cattle could be shipped, such as Abilene, Wichita, or Dodge City, Kansas. Cattlemen sold half of their stock to eastern markets and the other half in the West, to Californians, or to the government, which purchased beef to feed soldiers and Indians on reservations.

But the Texas longhorn had several drawbacks that eventually led to its replacement. Most seriously, it carried a tick that devastated many of the grazing animals that came into contact with it. In addition, the longhorn took a long time to fatten up and never produced good beef. Wealthy investors began to experiment with hybrid cattle that did not carry the deadly tick, fattened up quickly, and produced higher quality meat. By the early 1880s investors were pouring capital into mammoth cattle-herding companies. At the same time it was becoming clear that the Great Plains were seriously overstocked. The grazing lands were depleted, leaving the cattle weak from malnutrition. In the late 1880s several severe winters devastated the sickly herds.

Open-range herding became so environmentally destructive that it was no longer economically feasible. In addition, long drives became increasingly difficult as farmers settled the plains and fenced in their lands. By the 1890s huge cattle companies were giving way to smaller ranches that raised hybrid cattle. The western railroad network was by then so extensive that it was no longer necessary to drive herds hundreds of miles to reach a railhead. Cowboys became ranch hands who worked for regular wages, like miners and factory workers.

In the mid-1880s, more than 7 million head of cattle roamed the Great Plains, but their numbers declined rapidly, and in their place came sheep. Sheep fed on the growths that cattle would not eat. In fact, the sheep ate so many grasses that they proved even more ecologically destructive than cattle. Nevertheless, by 1900 sheep herding had largely replaced the cattle industry in Wyoming and Montana and was spreading to Nevada. Sheep herding had one other crucial advantage: It did not interfere with small farmers as much as cattle driving did.

Commercial Farmers Subdue the Plains

Between 1860 and 1900, the number of farms in America nearly tripled, thanks largely to the economic development of the West. On the Great Plains and in the desert Southwest, farmers took up former Indian lands. From San Francisco to Los Angeles, white settlers poached on the estates of Spanish-speaking landlords, stripping them of their natural resources and undermining their profitability. Over time Hispanic ranchers gave way to Euro-American farmers. The Hispanic population of Los Angeles fell from 82 percent in 1850 to 19 percent in 1880. A similar pattern displaced the Mexican-American landowners in New Mexico and Texas.

This ethnic shift signaled profound changes in the ecology and political economy of the West, driven by the exploding global demand for western products. Cattle ranchers were feeding eastern cities. Lumber from the Pacific

Northwest found its way to Asia and South America. By 1890 western farmers produced half of the wheat grown in the United States, and they shipped it across the globe.

But farming in the arid West was different from farming in the East. To begin with, the 160-acre homesteads envisioned by eastern lawmakers were unrealistic: Farms of that size were too small for the economic and ecological conditions of western agriculture. From the beginning, western farmers were businessmen. To produce wheat and corn for the international market they needed steel plows, costly mechanical equipment, and extensive irrigation. To make these capital investments, western farmers mortgaged their lands. For mechanized, commercial agriculture to succeed on mortgaged land, western farms had to be much bigger than 160 acres.

Most western agricultural settlement took place not on government-sponsored homesteads but through the private land market. By some estimates land speculators bought up nearly 350 million acres of western lands from state or federal governments or Indian reservations. Railroads were granted another 200 million acres by the federal government. The more farmers who settled in the West, the more agricultural produce they could regularly ship back East. Therefore, railroads set up immigration bureaus and advertised for settlers, offering cheap transportation, credit, and agricultural assistance, filling up the Great Plains with settlers from the East Coast and from Ireland, Germany, and Scandinavia. In 1890 the director of the Bureau of the Census reported that the frontier had at last been filled.

Changes in the Land

The trans-Mississippi West was no Garden of Eden waiting for lucky farmers to move in and reap the land's abundant riches. The climate, particularly in the Great Plains and the desert Southwest, was too dry for most kinds of farming. The sod on the plains was so thick and hard that traditional plows ripped like paper; only steel would do the job. With little wood or stone to build houses, farmers lived first in dugouts or sodhouses. Fierce winter blizzards gave way to blistering summers, each rocked by harsh winds. Yet settlers seemed determined to overcome, and to overwhelm, nature itself. To build fences where wood was scarce, manufacturers invented barbed wire. Windmills dotted the prairie to pump water from hundreds of feet below ground. Powerful agricultural machinery tore through the earth, and new strains of wheat from Europe and China were cultivated to withstand the brutal climate.

The western environment was transformed. Wolves, elk, and bear were exterminated as farmers brought in pigs, cattle, and sheep. Tulare Lake, covering hundreds of square miles of California's central valley, was sucked dry by 1900. Hydraulic mining sent tons of earth and rock cascading down the rivers flowing out of the Sierra Nevada, raising water levels to the point where entire cities became vulnerable to flooding. The skies above Butte, Montana, turned grey from the pollutants released by the copper smelting plants. Sheep herding destroyed the vegetation on the eastern slopes of the Rocky Mountains and the Sierra Nevada.

By the turn of the century, the bison had all but disappeared, and the Indians had been confined to reservations. Industrial mining corporations, profitable cattle ranches, and mechanized farms now dominated the West. The frontier was gone, and in its place were commercial farmers whose lives were shaped by European weather, eastern mortgage companies, commodity brokers, and railroad conglomerates. Cowboys sold their labor to cattle companies owned by investors in

CHRONOLOGY

1848	Taiping Rebellion spurs Chinese emigration to U.S. Revolution in Austria-Hungary Andrew Carnegie emigrates to U.S.
1851	Fort Laramie Treaty establishes Indian reservations
1856	St. Paul's boarding school opens
1857	Henry Bessemer develops process for making steel
1862	Pacific Railroad Act Homestead Act Rebellion of Dakota Sioux in Minnesota
1864	Sand Creek Massacre
1865	First trans-Atlantic telegraph cable begins operation
1866	Battle of One Hundred Slain
1867	Medicine Lodge Treaty
1868	Second Fort Laramie Treaty Washita Massacre
1871	October: Great Chicago fire
1872	Edgar Thompson Steel Works open near Pittsburgh
1873	Financial panic, followed by depression
1876	Custer's Last Stand at Little Bighorn
1877	"Great Strike" of railroad workers begins
1878	American Bar Association founded
1881	Czar Alexander II of Russia assassinated
1882	Chinese Exclusion Act John D. Rockefeller forms Standard Oil "Trust" Edison Electric Company lights up New York buildings
1887	Dawes Severalty Act
1890	Jacob Riis publishes *How the Other Half Lives* Massacre at Wounded Knee, South Dakota Director of U.S. Census declares frontier "closed"
1893	Financial panic, followed by depression

Boston and Glasgow. Mining and lumber corporations employed tens of thousands of wage laborers.

Big cities sprang up almost overnight. San Francisco had 5,000 inhabitants in 1850, but by the time the Gold Rush was over, in 1870, there were 150,000 people living there. Denver was incorporated in 1861 but its population hovered at just below 5,000 until the railroad came in 1870. Twenty years later Denver had more than 100,000 inhabitants.

CONCLUSION

Rosa Cassettari and Andrew Carnegie never met, but together their lives suggest the spectrum of possibilities in industrializing America. Both were immigrants who, caught up in the political economy of industrial capitalism, made their way to the United States. Yet the same grand forces touched the two immigrants in different ways. Cassettari moved to a mining camp west of the Mississippi River before making her way to Chicago—the city that opened the west to the dynamism of industrial capitalism. Carnegie migrated, almost overnight, from the preindustrial world of Scotland to the heart of the industrial revolution in America—Pittsburgh, with its railroads, oil refineries, and steel mills. Cassettari struggled all her life and achieved a modest level of comfort for herself and her children. She did as well as most immigrants could hope for, and in that sense her biography reflects the realities of working-class life in industrial America. Cassettari's experience with failure—the harsh life of the mining camp and a bad marriage—impelled her to move on in search of something better. It was success, however, that made Carnegie itch for something different. By 1890, having made his millions, he remade himself by becoming a patron of culture. He moved to New York and traveled the world, befriending the leading intellectuals of his day. He built libraries and endowed universities. He had helped create an industrial nation. Now he set out to re-create American culture.

FURTHER READINGS

Alfred D. Chandler, *The Visible Hand: The Managerial Revolution in American Business* (1977). The standard account of the rise of corporate bureaucracy.

William Cronon, *Nature's Metropolis: Chicago and the Great West* (1991). Meticulously charts the way Chicago's influence stretched across much of the West.

Eric Hobsbawm, *The Age of Empire: 1875–1914* (1987). Establishes the global context for the industrial transformation of the United States.

Maldwyn Jones, *American Immigration*, 2nd ed. (1992). Unusually sensitive to the political and economic background to global migration.

Harold Livesay, *Andrew Carnegie and the Rise of Big Business* (1975). Does an unusually fine job of placing Carnegie in historical context.

David Montgomery, *The Fall of the House of Labor: The Workplace, the State and American Labor Activism, 1865–1925* (1987). Shows how the rise of big business changed the daily labor of the American working class.

Gregory Nobles, *American Frontiers: Cultural Encounters and Continental Conquest* (1997). A brief survey reflecting the latest scholarship in western history.

Henry Nash Smith, *Virgin Land: The American West as Symbol and Myth* (1950). The premier example of the much-maligned "myth and symbol" approach to American studies, this is a classic account of the "image" of the West in the nineteenth century.

C. Vann Woodward, *Origins of the New South, 1877–1913* (1951) is one of the great works of American historical literature.

Richard White, *'It's Your Misfortune and None of My Own': A History of the American West* (1991) is a comprehensive survey by a leading historian of the West.

Please refer to the document CD-ROM for primary sources related to this chapter.

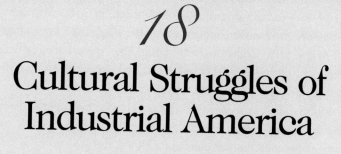

CHAPTER

18

Cultural Struggles of Industrial America

1850–1895

Anthony Comstock's Crusade Against Vice • The Varieties of Urban Culture • The Elusive Boundaries of Male and Female Immigration as a Cultural Problem • The Creation of High Culture • Artistic Realism Embraces Urban and Industrial America • Conclusion

ANTHONY COMSTOCK'S CRUSADE AGAINST VICE

Anthony Comstock devoted most of his adult life to putting the owners of brothels, gambling dens, abortion clinics, and dance halls out of business. "You must hunt these men as you hunt rats," Comstock declared, "without mercy." There was little in his background to foreshadow such zeal. While still a young man, Comstock had moved from rural Connecticut to New York City, where he worked as a clerk in a dry goods store. White-collar careers of this sort were a familiar path for native-born Protestant men in the middle of the nineteenth century. Fame came to him in 1873 when the United States Congress enacted a statute that bore his name. The Comstock Law banned the production, distribution, and public display of obscenity. Thereafter, Comstock spent much of his life chasing down and prosecuting pornographers, prostitutes, and strippers.

Comstock and like-minded citizens were disturbed by the municipal corruption that kept police departments from enforcing obscenity laws. To overcome this obstacle, reformers established private organizations with quasi-official authority. Among the most influential was Anthony Comstock's New York Society for the Suppression of Vice, commonly known as the SSV. Founded in 1873, the SSV was dedicated to "the enforcement of laws for the suppression of the trade in, and circulation of, obscene literature and illustrations, advertisements, and articles of indecent or immoral use."

As head of the SSV, Comstock was appointed a special agent of the U.S. Post Office. Along with other SSV leaders Comstock disregarded the rights of due process by entrapping his victims. But they always defended their actions by claiming that the established legal procedures of the police and the judiciary were ineffective in preventing the sale of smut.

Comstock maintained that his chief concern was the protection of children. In his most famous book, *Traps for the Young* (1883), he warned that obscenity was enticing American youngsters into deviant ways by artificially nourishing youthful appetites and passions until they exerted "a well-nigh irresistible mastery over their victim." The evils that trapped America's children were thought to be concentrated in the cities that, in the late nineteenth century, attracted millions of young people. Urban life was relatively anonymous and it was also driven by vast amounts of cash. In the last third of the nineteenth century the income of nonfarm employees in America rose steadily, while prices declined. Except for the very poorest workers, urban Americans had more money to spend and more time to spend it than ever before. And if industrial workers enjoyed more leisure time, white-collar employees enjoyed even more. The big city offered Americans new entertainments that frequently provoked the ire of those determined to defend traditional standards of respectability.

For Comstock urban culture was a cesspool of vice and corruption. For modern historians, a great deal of urban culture resided in its immigrant neighborhoods, with their distinctive family structures and religious practices. But at the time, many Americans looked at immigrant slums as utterly devoid of culture. To them, culture referred only to the great works of Western art, literature, and music. High culture, in this sense, was seen as an alternative to the sordid realities of urban and industrial America. Ironically, the best artists and writers of the late nineteenth century were "realists." While Anthony Comstock tried to suppress the vices of the city, realists embraced them, translating them into compelling fiction and dramatic canvases.

In the second half of the nineteenth century, cultural clashes were as much a part of the political economy of industrial capitalism as were class conflict and political upheaval. Rural America reacted defensively to the culture of the city. Native-born Protestants struggled against the cultures of immigrants. Defenders of high culture fought against the rise of popular culture. Amateur sportsmen sniffed at the emergence of spectator sports. Victorian moralists were shocked by the apparent collapse of traditional gender distinctions. Yet these struggles reflected the efforts of Americans to absorb the dramatic social transformations that accompanied the rise of industrial capitalism.

The Varieties of Urban Culture

In 1850 nonfarm workers comprised just over 35 percent of all workers; by 1890 the figure was almost 60 percent. Americans moved to the city in vast numbers during these years, and they both loved and hated the cities in which they lived. Their mixed feelings showed up in the varieties of entertainment they embraced during the second half of the nineteenth century. In unprecedented numbers Americans went to theaters, music halls, concert saloons, baseball stadiums, and sports arenas. City life, long associated with poverty and crime, now came to mean fun and excitement as well.

Minstrel Shows as Cultural Nostalgia

In the late nineteenth century the western frontier became one of the most popular themes in American show business. As rugged pioneers gave way to wage earners, commercial farmers, and industrialists, the mythology of the West grew. The most spectacular example of this was Buffalo Bill Cody's hugely successful Wild West Show, which toured the country parading live Indians before delighted urban spectators. Audiences watched displays of horsemanship and highly stylized reenactments of the Plains wars. America's fascination with a romanticized frontier was one example of a popular nostalgia for ways of life that were thought to have been simpler than the life of the city. Nowhere was this nostalgia more obvious than in the minstrel shows.

Minstrel shows were the most significant form of public entertainment for most of the nineteenth century. During the 1830s and 1840s minstrel shows were dominated by white performers in blackface. Although the minstrels stereotyped plantation slaves as happy and carefree, the earliest performances were not as viciously racist as they became later. In the mid-1850s, however, the tone of blackface minstrel shows changed. As the slavery controversy forced white northerners to take sides on a divisive issue, popular troupes like New York's Christy Minstrels took the side of the slaveholders. During the Civil War and Reconstruction, minstrel shows attacked white reformers in the North who supported emancipation and black rights. They portrayed blacks with gross racial stereotypes and subjected abolitionists to ridicule. Minstrel troupes staged corrupted versions of *Uncle Tom's Cabin*, stripped the novel of its abolitionist theme, and reduced the plot to a simplistic story of beleaguered southern whites. Yet throughout the period, minstrel shows continued to poke fun at the aristocratic pretensions of cultural elites. Indeed, minstrel shows commonly combined racism with populism, lampooning elites by playing them in blackface wearing fancy clothes and putting on airs.

In the 1870s minstrel shows grew larger and more elaborate. J. H. Haverly led the way: He hired the most players, dressed them in the gaudiest costumes, placed them in the most spectacular sets, and had them perform the widest variety of numbers. He toned down the emphasis on blackface singers and plantation themes and added scantily clad women and off-color routines. Haverly expanded his audiences with extensive advertising. By 1881 he had theaters in New York, Brooklyn, Chicago, and San Francisco; three national minstrel troupes; and four touring comedy theaters. Of Haverly's three companies, two were white and one was black. There were other black companies as well. As national minstrel shows abandoned their commitment to authentic representations of southern life, blacks often took to the stage and kept the plantation theme alive, operating within the racial stereotypes established by prewar whites in blackface. The most famous black minstrel of the nineteenth century, Billy Kersands, drew huge audiences with his portrayals of ignorant and comical characters. Yet as the plantation theme became the preserve of black players, some of the early criticism of slavery crept back into the productions. When black minstrels romanticized the Old South, their nostalgia was reserved for slaves. Meanwhile, the largest and most successful minstrel shows retained their exclusively white casts and their heavy-handed racism.

As productions grew more ornate and expensive, show business entrepreneurs put smaller local troupes out of business or swallowed them up into national companies. From more than 60 troupes in the late 1860s, the number of minstrel troupes fell to just 13 by the early 1880s. Differences from one company to the next diminished as minstrel shows became uniform and somewhat bland. Yet, more popular than ever, they expanded their audiences into the far West and the deep South. By 1890 a handful of huge entertainment moguls controlled the minstrel shows.

Minstrel shows never lost their nostalgic appeal to rural America. However, by the late nineteenth century they looked more and more like vaudeville, an art form that was born and bred in the big city.

The Origins of Vaudeville

Unlike the minstrels, vaudeville shows did not rely on nostalgia. Rather, vaudeville and its cheaper cousins (concert saloons and dollar theaters) flourished in American cities after elites succeeded in distinguishing serious theater from variety shows. As the cost of a ticket to a Shakespeare production rose beyond the means of most working people, urban audiences turned to inexpensive houses that offered music, singing, sketches, and variety acts. At first the audiences in such theaters were rowdy and exclusively male. Yet these concert saloons and variety theaters attracted patrons from up and down the social scale. In 1883 a Chicago guidebook claimed that the city's variety theaters were patronized not only by "the lower class of society, but [by] journalists, professional men, bankers, railroad officials, politicians, and men of rank in society." Even so, there were no blacks.

Increasingly, however, there were women. Beginning in the 1880s, a handful of show business entrepreneurs tried to develop variety theaters that appealed to audiences with both men and women. The respectability of a mixed audience was one of the distinguishing signs of vaudeville. Vaudeville producers booked a variety of acts to appeal to a broad audience. They also developed continuous performances, which allowed patrons to come to a vaudeville show any time of the day or evening.

Continuous performances kept the prices down, thereby increasing the size of the potential audience. Locating downtown in the heart of the city had the same effect. Theater owners also regulated smoking and, over time, banned alcohol consumption, thus promoting the image of family entertainment. Finally, they booked great opera singers or distinguished musicians for brief appearances, in a conscious effort to enhance vaudeville's reputation for respectability.

Growing audiences made it possible for vaudeville producers to construct huge and ornate theatrical "palaces" that housed ever more elaborate productions. The high cost of such theaters kept the number of competitors down. As a result, a handful of companies came to dominate the vaudeville theater industry, much as minstrel companies had become concentrated in the hands of a few owners. By the turn of the century, vaudeville was one of the most popular forms of public entertainment in American cities. But minstrel shows and vaudeville theaters were not the only places Americans went during their leisure time.

Sports Become Professional

As growing numbers of Americans went to the theater to be entertained, still more went to the baseball park or sports arena. For a significant segment of the urban population, sports was becoming something to watch rather than something to do.

As the number of spectators increased, baseball and prizefighting became professionalized. Prizefighting had long been a disreputable amusement of shady bars and lower class streets, but during the 1880s, it became an organized sport attracting a huge national audience. Richard Kyle Fox, owner of the *National Police Gazette,* used his popular magazine and his considerable financial resources to transform boxing. Because Fox put up the prize money, he had the power to reform the sport. He made it both more profitable and more respectable and introduced standardized rules.

As the sport grew in popularity, entrepreneurs sponsored fights at indoor rings where they could control unruly audiences with police and security guards. Thereafter, as prizefighter John L. Sullivan explained in 1892, "the price of admission is put purposely high so as to exclude the rowdy element, and a gentleman can see the contest, feeling sure that he will not be robbed . . . or in any way be interfered with." Although prizefighting never completely lost its aura of disrepute, by the 1890s it was one of the most popular spectator sports in America, second only to baseball.

Like prizefighting, baseball was professionalized in the last half of the nineteenth century. By the 1860s baseball had become tremendously popular among city dwellers, particularly immigrants and their children. They formed leagues in urban neighborhoods all across the country. But not until 1869, when the Cincinnati Red Stockings went on tour and charged admission, did baseball become a professional spectator sport. Soon thereafter standardized rules appeared for the first time.

Within a decade the owners of eight baseball clubs had formed a National League that had all the earmarks of a corporate cartel. It restrained the power of players, restricted the number of teams to one per city, prohibited Sunday games, banned the sale of alcohol at ballparks, hired umpires, and set schedules and admission prices. Chafing under these restrictions, many players jumped to a new American Association that formed in 1882. The owners regrouped, however, and within a year the two leagues merged and quickly reinstated the restrictions on players. In reaction the players formed a league of their own but were unable to match the wealth and power of the owners. By the mid-1890s the National League controlled professional baseball.

Baseball idealized the principle of success based purely on merit. Objective statistics identified the best players without respect to their personal background. A model of ordered competition, the baseball meritocracy provided a useful lesson in the way capitalist society was supposed to work. Professional players became working-class heroes, many of them having risen from factories and slums. But professional baseball reflected the realities as well as the ideals of American capitalism. The owners' cartel prevented professional athletes from taking advantage of the market. In addition, baseball's meritocracy had no place for the merits of black players, who were excluded from the professional sport. Even the seating arrangements in ballparks reflected America's social divisions. Working-class fans sat in the bleachers, the middle class occupied the stands, and elites took the box seats.

The popularity of sports was reflected in the growing numbers of participants as well as spectators. As daily work became more sedentary, especially for white-collar workers, Americans spent more time in physical recreation. During the late nineteenth century, "the sporting life" became an American pastime. The popularity of bicycling exploded, for example, particularly after the invention of the modern "safety bike" in 1888. Within a decade there were 10 million bicycles in the United States. Men joined the YMCA or organized local baseball teams. At Harvard, Yale, and Princeton young men took up football, basketball, and rowing. At Smith, Vassar, and Berkeley young women played baseball, basketball, and tennis. In urban neighborhoods ethnic groups organized Irish, Italian, and German baseball teams. Women began riding bicycles, swimming, and playing golf and croquet.

But appearances were deceptive. The sports craze mirrored the inequalities and anxieties of industrial America. Men who believed that independence was a sign of masculinity became concerned that wage labor would make them soft and "feminine." A vocal segment of the American elite turned to athletic activities as an antidote to the supposedly feminizing tendencies of industrial capitalism. Theodore Roosevelt, the product of an old and wealthy New York family, who became president of the United States, believed that "commercial civilization" placed too little stress on "the more virile virtues." There was, Roosevelt argued, "no better way of counteracting this tendency than by encouraging bodily exercise and especially the sports which develop such qualities as courage, resolution and endurance."

As baseball and prizefighting became both popular and professional, elites reacted by glorifying the amateur ideal, embracing vigorous athletic activity for its own sake rather than for monetary reward. In the late nineteenth century wealthy Americans pursued the sporting life at elite colleges, exclusive race tracks, and private athletic clubs, country clubs, and yacht clubs. By the turn of the century, the most exclusive colleges in the Northeast had formed football's Ivy League, a designation that became synonymous with elite private universities.

The rigors of sport taught elite men how to face the rigors of business competition, weeded out the weak, and prepared society's leaders for the contest of daily life. Thus the elite's attraction to rugged sports reinforced a self-serving view of American society: In the political economy of competitive capitalism the best nations, like the best men, would rise to the top.

The most significant attempt to spread such values more widely was the founding of the Young Men's Christian Association (YMCA) in 1851. By 1894 there were 261 YMCAs across the nation. A strong reform impulse sustained the YMCA movement. Its founders hoped that organized recreational activity would distract workers from labor radicalism and that classes and games would assimilate immigrants to the laws, customs, and language of the United States. In many ways the YMCA was an extension of Anthony Comstock's movement to suppress vice: It hoped to provide wholesome amusements to young men who might otherwise succumb to the temptations of city life.

World's Fairs: The Celebration of the City

To celebrate the accomplishments of urban and industrial society, the city of London hosted a spectacular world's fair at the Crystal Palace in 1851. Over the next 50 years the cities of the Western world became showcases for the technological and cultural achievements of industrial capitalism. By 1900 there had been expositions in Paris, Vienna, Brussels, Antwerp, Florence, Amsterdam, Dublin, and even Sydney, Australia. Most celebrated the achievements of the host countries and the civic pride of their sponsoring cities, as well as the triumph of technology and the progress of humanity. American fairs were no exception. A dozen major American cities sponsored world expositions in the late nineteenth and early twentieth centuries.

The first major world's fair in the United States took place in Philadelphia in 1876, timed to commemorate the centennial of American independence. In keeping with the theme of global interaction, the fair's sponsors asked the nations of the world to build pavilions of their own. The pavilions were arranged to reflect not the harmony of nations, but the differences among the world's "races." Americans were only beginning to develop such ideas in 1876, but the broad outlines of the racial categories were already evident. France and its colonies, "representing the Latin races," were grouped together, as were England and its colonies, "representing the Anglo-Saxon races," and "the Teutonic races," represented by Germany, Austria, and Hungary. Within 20 years, these racial categories would harden into an elaborate hierarchy that embraced all the peoples of the world.

The World Columbian Exposition in Chicago was the largest of the world's fairs that became popular in the late nineteenth century. Among other things, they were celebrations of the technology and city life that were becoming the characteristics of modern, industrial civilization.

Nowhere was this hierarchy more visible than at the greatest fair of the century, the World's Columbian Exposition in Chicago in 1893. Built on Lake Michigan several miles south of downtown, the Chicago fair had twice as many foreign buildings as its Philadelphia predecessor, covered 686 acres, and attracted 25 million visitors. The exposition was divided between the White City and the Midway Plaisance. The White City showcased American industrial might with immense steam engines and the latest consumer goods. But the Midway Plaisance featured carnivals, the first ferris wheel, games, and sideshows. It also featured an ethnographic exhibit providing a popular rendition of principles of scientific racism. The exhibit portrayed the "races" of the world in a hierarchy from the most civilized (Europeans) to the least civilized (Asians and Africans).

Where earlier forms of popular entertainment had romanticized preindustrial society and the rural life, the world's fairs celebrated the new political economy of cities and industry. The White City, the heart of the World's Columbian Exposition in Chicago, was an idealized vision of urban life. Rural simplicity had given way to the majestic city as the model for civilization.

The Elusive Boundaries of Male and Female

Anthony Comstock saw the city as a place where traditional morality broke down, particularly standards of sexual propriety. In fact, the political economy of industrial capitalism and the triumph of wage labor compelled men and women to rethink traditional conceptions of masculinity and femininity. As they did so, spectacular new cities and newfound leisure time offered Americans unprecedented opportunities to test the conventional boundaries of sexual identity.

The Victorian Construction of Male and Female

Until the mid-1700s most European doctors believed that there was only one sex: Females were simply inferior, insufficiently developed males. Sometime after 1750, however, scientists and intellectuals began to argue that males and females were fundamentally different, that they were "opposite" sexes. For the first time it was possible to argue that women were naturally less interested in sex than men or that men were "active" while women were "passive." Nature itself seemed to justify the infamous double standard that condoned sexual activity by men but punished women for the same thing.

In the nineteenth century Victorians drew even more extreme differences between men and women. Victorian boys were reared on moralistic stories of heroes who overcame their fears. In this way boys were prepared for the competitive worlds of business and politics, worlds from which women were largely excluded. To be a "man" in industrial America was to work in the rough-and-tumble world of the capitalist market. Men proved themselves by their success at making a living and therefore at taking care of a wife and children.

Victorian men defined themselves as rational creatures whose reason was threatened by their overwhelming sexual drives. Physical exertion was an important device for controlling a man's powerful sexual urges. Because in Victorian America masturbation was an unacceptable outlet for these drives, men were urged to channel their sexual energies into strenuous activities such as sports and, conveniently enough, wage labor. Masculinity was defined as the ability to leave the confines of the home and compete successfully in the capitalist labor market.

Where masculinity became a more rigid concept, femininity became less certain. Women's schools established their own sports programs. Thousands of women took up bicycling, tennis, and other physical activities. Yet at the same time the stereotype persisted that women were too frail to engage in the hurly-burly of business and enterprise. Lacking the competitive instinct of the male, the female was destined to become a wife and mother within the protective confines of the home. Just as men congregated in social clubs and sports teams, a "female world of love and ritual" developed. Middle-class women often displayed among themselves a passionate affection that was often expressed in nearly erotic terms. But genuinely passionate female sexuality was deeply disturbing to the Victorians. Evidence of sexual passion among women was increasingly diagnosed, mostly by male doctors, as a symptom of a new disorder called "neurasthenia."

Over time the differences between men and women were defined in increasingly medical terms. Victorian doctors redefined homosexuality as a medical abnormality, a perversion, and urged the passage of laws outlawing homosexual relations. The new science of gynecology powerfully reinforced popular assumptions about the differences between men and women. Distinguished male physicians argued that the energy women expended in reproduction left them unable to withstand the rigors of higher education. In extreme cases physicians would excise a woman's clitoris to thwart masturbation or remove her ovaries to cure neurasthenia.

On the assumption that motherhood was a female's natural destiny, doctors pressed to restrict women's access to contraception and to prohibit abortion. Before the Civil War abortion in the first three months of pregnancy was tolerated, although not necessarily approved. This began to change as the medical profession seized control over the regulation of female reproduction. The American Medical Association (AMA, founded in 1847) campaigned to restrict the activities not only of quacks and incompetents but also of female midwives and abortionists. Doctors, most of whom were males, accepted prevailing assumptions about the maternal destiny of women. Hence doctors opposed attempts by women to interfere with pregnancy. The AMA supported passage of the Comstock Law, which outlawed the sale of contraception. Doctors also pushed successfully to criminalize abortion.

Victorians Who Questioned Traditional Sexual Boundaries

In a new political economy based on wage labor, large numbers of Americans, especially young men, now found themselves with cash and leisure time. The anonymity of huge cities gave them the opportunity to defy established standards of sexual behavior. Freed from the constraints of parents and the scrutiny of small-town life, wage earners frequented prostitutes in unprecedented numbers, attended shows that featured sexually provocative entertainers, read erotic novels, and purchased pornographic prints. Many Americans began to explore unconventional sexual practices.

The major venues of popular entertainment increasingly displayed a looser, more relaxed attitude toward sex. Can-can girls, off-color jokes, and comedy skits focusing on the war of the sexes all contradicted Victorian propriety. Even the styles of clothing that consumers purchased in mass quantities were a rejection of the stifling conventions of the Victorian middle class. Trousers got looser, starched collars disappeared, and women's dresses were simplified and rendered considerably more comfortable. The sensuous human body became an object of fascination in much of the popular culture. Minstrels, musical variety shows, and the vaudeville theater all glorified female sexuality. For the first time male sports heroes were openly admired for their physiques. Much of the literature of the day was infused with the theme of homosexual relations. Walt Whitman's poems celebrated sexual attraction among men, and some scholars see elements of homoeroticism in Huckleberry Finn's relationship with Jim in Mark Twain's famous novel. A more obvious case is Horatio Alger. In the late nineteenth century he wrote a series of books about young boys who lived on the streets of New York and made their way out of poverty. Alger's heroes thus embody the American dream of upward mobility. Alger began his own career as a Unitarian minister in Brewster, Massachusetts, but he was expelled from his pulpit for "the revolting crime of unnatural familiarity with boys." Alger left New England in disgrace and moved to New York, where he developed a keen interest in the problems of young boys who roamed loose on the city streets.

Alger's charity work became the basis of his fiction. In most of his novels, the young heroes shared the same physical attributes. They were dirty but handsome. In most cases it was the boy's good looks that attracted the attention of the wealthy male patron. Alger's novels depicted the relationships between men and boys in terms reminiscent of a seduction. Once rescued from rags and gainfully employed, Alger's hero typically set up house with a roommate. These households were fastidiously neat, and their inhabitants were thrifty and sober. The only difference from an ideal middle-class household was that both inhabitants were male. In one case, two male roommates, having both been saved and made respectable, actually "adopted" a little boy, a street urchin named "Mark the Matchboy."

Few readers saw Horatio Alger's novels as experiments in unconventional sexuality, but their homoeroticism was consistent with the increased sexual frankness of urban life in the late nineteenth century. It was not surprising that reformers like Anthony Comstock looked at the city and saw an explosion of vice. Others, however, were struck less by urban sexuality than by the profusion of immigrants who were transforming the culture of the city.

IMMIGRATION AS A CULTURAL PROBLEM

When novelist Henry James returned to the United States in 1907 after a quarter of a century in Europe, he was stunned and disgusted by the pervasive presence of immigrants in New York City. On the streetcars he confronted "a row of faces, up and down, testifying, without exception, to alienism unmistakable, alienism undisguised and unashamed." James was one of the many native-born Americans who assumed that their culture was Protestant, democratic, and English-speaking. They were deeply disturbed, therefore, by the arrival of vast numbers of immigrants who were none of those things and by the way ethnic subcultures seemed to flourish in United States cities. Yet among immigrants and their children, an ethnic identity was often a sign of assimilation into a broader American culture.

Josiah Strong Attacks Immigration

"Every race which has deeply impressed itself on the human family has been the representative of some great idea," Josiah Strong wrote in *Our Country*. Greek civilization was famed for its beauty, he explained, the Romans for their law, and the Hebrews for their purity. The Anglo-Saxon race had two great ideas to its credit, Strong argued. The first was the love of liberty, and the second was "pure spiritual Christianity." Published in 1885, Strong's bestselling book was revised and reprinted in 1891 and serialized in newspapers across America. Strong spoke to the concerns of vast numbers of native-born Americans who saw themselves as the defenders of Anglo-Saxon culture. Strong was optimistic that as representatives of "the largest liberty, the purest Christianity, the highest civilization," the powerful Anglo-Saxon race would "spread itself over the earth."

But there was a problem. To Strong and his readers, the Anglo-Saxon in America was threatened by the arrival of vast numbers of immigrants. The typical immigrant, he warned, was not a freedom-loving Anglo-Saxon Protestant but a "European peasant." Narrow-minded men and women "whose moral and religious training has been meager or false," immigrants brought crime to America's cities and undermined the nation's politics. Immigrants voted in blocks, and their influence was enhanced by the fact that they were concentrated in big cities. "[T]here is no more serious menace to our civilization," Strong warned, "than our rabble-ruled cities."

At the core of the problem was the fact that immigrants could not be assimilated into the American way of life. "Our safety demands the assimilation of these strange populations," Strong wrote. But they were coming in such huge numbers that assimilation was becoming impossible (see Map 18–1). Worst of all, the Catholic Church held millions of immigrants in its grip, filling their heads with superstition rather than "pure Christianity." It did not help that immigrants had large numbers of children. Through its elaborate network of parochial schools, the Catholic Church was training new generations to love tyranny rather than liberty.

Strong and his readers need not have worried. The millions of immigrants who came to the United States adapted quickly to American society. Indeed, Strong misread much of his own evidence. By cultivating the German vote or the Irish vote,

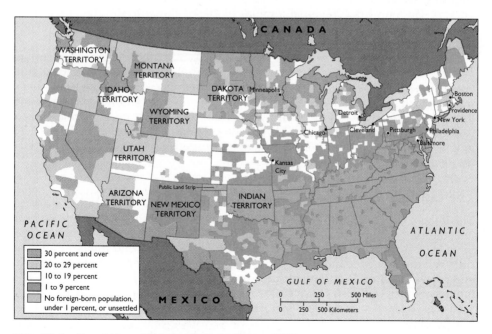

Map 18–1 Population of Foreign Birth by Region, 1880

Source: Clifford L. Lord and Elizabeth H. Lord, Lord & Lord Historical Atlas of the United States (New York: Holt, 1953).

for example, politicians went far toward assimilating immigrants into American political culture. Nor were immigrants as slavishly subservient to the Catholic Church as Strong thought. In the end, the Church played an ambiguous role in the cultural history of American immigrants.

From Immigrants to Ethnic Americans

Critics like Strong scarcely noticed the regional and class differences that immigrants brought with them. In the middle of the nineteenth century, most immigrants came with loyalties to their regions and villages, but not to their nationality. In New York City German-speaking immigrants thought of themselves primarily as Bavarian or Prussian rather than as German. Irish immigrants identified with their home counties more than their native country. Immigrant churches across America were torn by such regional conflicts.

After immigrants arrived in the United States, however, regional differences began to decline. One reason was the growth of secular fraternal organizations. Fraternal organizations often began as mutual aid societies designed to help newcomers find jobs and housing. In 1893 mineworkers formed the Pennsylvania Slovak Catholic Union to help cover burial expenses for those killed in the mines. Most often, however, middle-class immigrants took the lead in forming fraternal organizations; in other cases local priests played prominent roles. Regardless of their leadership, about half of all immigrants eventually joined ethnic fraternal societies.

As they grew, fraternal organizations became national in their scope, as immigrants constructed a new "ethnic" identity that united all members under a single national rubric. In some cases immigrant businessmen led the drive toward the development of a unified ethnic identity. Marco Fontana, who ran the Del Monte company in California, encouraged the growth of an "Italian" identity among his workers. He found that regional loyalties hindered the efficient operation of his enterprises. Eventually, immigrants began to think of themselves as members of ethnic groups that shared the same national ancestry.

It was not merely coincidental that immigrants developed "national" identities in the United States. Nationalism was spreading throughout the Western world during the nineteenth century. While immigrants in America were coming to see themselves as Irish or Italian, the same thing was happening back home in Ireland and Italy. In the United States the Civil War had unleashed a wave of nationalistic fervor, and a series of liberal revolutions did the same thing in Europe. As the decades passed immigrants brought to America an increasingly powerful sense of their ethnic identities.

The Catholic Church and Its Limits in Immigrant Culture

The Roman Catholic Church played a complicated role in the development of ethnic cultures among immigrants. In some cases churches were established to preserve Old World traditions. In 1841, for example, the Reverend Johann Raffeiner collected the money to build Holy Trinity, a German-speaking Catholic church. In other ways the church smoothed the transition into American life by serving as a mutual aid society. Polish churches in Chicago and German parishes in Milwaukee used their women's groups and youth clubs as mutual aid societies for their local immigrants.

The church sometimes unintentionally sped the development of ethnic identities. The Irish became more devout in America as they came to rely on the church to assist them in resisting an overwhelmingly Protestant culture. Germans also grav-itated toward the church and in the process overcame their regional differences. But the more they came to equate their German identity with Catholicism, the more they resented Irish domination of the church hierarchy. Thus German Catholics worked to establish their own churches and parish schools or to have ser-mons preached in German. By contrast, the Italians were largely alienated from the official church, the hierarchy of which was largely Irish. By the late nineteenth cen-tury North American bishops were trying to standardize Catholicism in America. They published uniform catechisms, established powerful bureaucratic structures, and tried to suppress the folk rituals of Italian Catholicism. Thus Italians were iron-ically united in their suspicion of the church.

The church's power was reinforced by the struggle for control over the educa-tion of immigrant children. Throughout the nineteenth century public schools were heavily Protestant. Josiah Strong and other native-born reformers tried to use public education to "Americanize" immigrant children. They taught the Protestant Bible. They shifted the focus in the classroom away from the classics and toward "practical" education and language training, with the goal of turning immigrants into reliable workers and patriotic citizens. But immigrants fiercely resisted such efforts, and the bulwark of their resistance was the church.

During the second half of the nineteenth century both the Catholic and Lutheran Churches established parochial school systems to protect immigrant chil-dren from the biases of public education. So comprehensive was the Catholic Church's effort that by 1883 all but two parishes in the city of Chicago had their own parochial schools.

Ironically, parochial education contributed to assimilation among immigrants. Catholic or Lutheran schools in Irish or German parishes reinforced the growth of distinctively American ethnic identities and bound ethnicity to an increasingly stan-dardized and Americanized Catholicism or Lutheranism.

The Political Economy of Immigrant Culture

Despite assimilation, the ethnic identities that immigrants developed in America remained distinctive. Irish Americans, for example, fused together songs from var-ious parts of Ireland and added piano accompaniment. Similarly, Polish immi-grant bands expanded beyond the traditional violin of their homelands by adding accordions, clarinets, and trumpets. But the results were still distinctively Polish-American or Irish-American music. Hundreds of immigrant theaters sprang up of-fering productions that adjusted traditional plot lines to the New World. Jewish plays told of humble peddlers who outwitted their prosperous patrons. Italian folk tales emphasized the importance of the family. In these ways distinctive ethnic identities, adapted to urban and industrial America, developed.

One of the most distinctive features of immigrant culture was family size. At a time when middle-class families had only two or three children, immigrant families remained large. There were sound economic reasons for this. There were no child-labor laws restricting the employment of minors and few compulsory-education laws requiring children to attend school. Working-class families relied heavily on the incomes of their children, particularly teenagers. Children in the immigrant working class were expected to contribute to the economic well-being of their families.

At the turn of the century, Italian mothers in Buffalo, New York, had an aver-age of 11 children. Among Polish wives the average was closer to eight. In

Pennsylvania's coal-mining district, working-class immigrant women had 45 percent more children than native-born women. But the death rate among immigrant children was also high. In 1900, one out of three Polish and Italian mothers had seen one of their children die before his or her first birthday.

As ethnicity developed in the late nineteenth century, class divisions were increasingly difficult to isolate from cultural distinctions. The middle class, for example, was overwhelmingly native born, white, Anglo-Saxon, and Protestant. The working class was, by contrast, African American, foreign born, Catholic, or Jewish. By 1900, 75 percent of the manufacturing workers in the United States were immigrants or the children of immigrants. In large cities, five out of six new manufacturing jobs were filled by immigrants and their children. In the South, wage laborers were overwhelmingly black sharecroppers. It was in this context that educated elites constructed a definition of high culture that would distinguish the middle classes from the allegedly uncultivated and uncultured working classes.

THE CREATION OF HIGH CULTURE

During the second half of the nineteenth century many leading intellectuals sought to isolate and define a tradition, *high culture*, that stretched through Western history from ancient Greece and Rome to the present. By the 1890s high culture embodied principles of social, cultural, and political hierarchy that were firmly installed in museums, libraries, and universities across the United States. A high culture had been created.

High Culture Becomes Sacred

The leading advocate of high culture was an Englishman, Matthew Arnold. In *Culture and Anarchy*, published in 1869, Arnold promoted the study of "the best which has been thought and said in the world" as an antidote to the "anarchy" of capitalist society. Similar views about high culture spread on both sides of the Atlantic. "Certain things are not disputable," *Harper's Magazine* declared in 1867; authors such as Homer, Shakespeare, and Dante "are towering facts like the Alps or the Himalayas. . . . It is not conceivable that the judgment of mankind upon those names will ever be reversed." American elites looking for firm moral guidelines were turning to a canon of great cultural achievements the way earlier generations had looked to holy scripture, and secular culture therefore assumed sacred qualities.

Lurking beneath the sacred view of culture was the fear that the modern world had undermined traditional values, especially religious values. "Organizations are splitting asunder, institutions are falling into decay, customs are becoming uncustomary," one observer complained in 1865. Particularly troubling was the apparent decline in religious fervor. Middle-class men and women often confessed to a loss of their own faith.

The middle class never lost its faith entirely. On the contrary, Victorians retained their overwhelmingly Protestant orientation and their deep suspicion of Roman Catholicism. What they lost was a strong theology and missionary zeal. Victorians moved restlessly from one denomination to another, but few found the spiritual satisfaction or moral guidance they sought. As religious fervor waned, the Victorian middle class looked for comfort in more secular pursuits.

Jacob Riis, who included this photo in his classic study of immigrant slums, How the Other Half Lives, *believed that immigrant neighborhoods were plagued by the absence of culture.*

Thomas Wentworth Higginson typified this shift. Nurtured in the reform movements of antebellum New England, Higginson had been an abolitionist and supporter of women's rights and during the Civil War commanded a regiment of African-American troops. Fully engaged in the politics of his day, Higginson was equally at home in the literary culture of his native New England, turning to culture for relief from the sordid realities of capitalist political economy.

In 1871, two years after Matthew Arnold published *Culture and Anarchy*, Higginson made a strikingly similar case. Culture, he explained, "pursues" art and science for their intrinsic worth. It "places the fine arts above the useful arts." It sacrifices "material comforts" for the sake of a "nobler" life. At its best, Higginson believed, culture "supplies that counterpoise to mere wealth which Europe vainly seeks to secure by aristocracies of birth." Like Matthew Arnold, Higginson saw culture as a defense against materialism.

Despite his contempt for the European aristocracy, Higginson could write just as condescendingly about ordinary people. He thus shared the Victorian conviction that culture was an attribute of the middle classes. At the top of the social order stood an increasingly dissolute and unrestrained capitalist class. At the bottom, poor working men and women lived lives utterly devoid of gentility and refinement. To many progressive intellectuals, therefore, saving America from barbarism required an infusion of culture into the lives of ordinary city folk.

Yet these very classes, the greedy capitalists at the top and the ignorant masses below, seemed to grow in influence as cities grew in size. To counteract this threat, American elites worked to transform American cities into centers of high art and cultural distinction.

The Creation of a Cultural Establishment

In the early nineteenth century Shakespeare was the most popular playwright in America. Traveling through the country in the 1830s, Alexis de Tocqueville encountered Shakespeare even in "the recesses of the forests of the New World. There is hardly a pioneer's hut that does not contain a few odd volumes of Shakespeare." In established theaters, Shakespearean plays were performed more than any others, and the repertoire was not limited to a few classics. American audiences were familiar with a substantial body of Shakespeare's work.

A Shakespearean play was usually performed as the centerpiece of an entire evening's entertainment that included music, dancing, acrobats, magicians, and comedians. The show generally ended with a short humorous skit, or farce. Audiences attending these shows came from all walks of life, and they often made a noisy crowd.

Americans preferred highly melodramatic renditions of Shakespeare. It was best if the moral ambiguities were smoothed out, the lessons made sharp and clear. Ideally the ending was always satisfying. Good always triumphed over evil. Instead of committing suicide, Romeo and Juliet lived happily ever after. By 1850 Americans were so familiar with Shakespeare that politicians could safely make allusions to his plays without fear of losing an audience.

All of this changed in the second half of the nineteenth century. Shakespeare was redefined as high culture, anwd performances of his plays were separated from popular entertainment. This shift was evident as early as the 1850s, when a San Francisco theater announced that its production of *A Midsummer Night's Dream* would be performed by itself, with "NO FARCE." The entertainments that had once accompanied Shakespearean performances became the basis of the vaudeville theater, and theater audiences became segregated by class. The respectable classes retreated from the boisterous houses into quieter theaters, where the prices rose beyond the means of ordinary working people.

The same thing happened to opera and to orchestral music. Opera changed from an eclectic and highly popular art form to an elite entertainment. Opera became associated with high fashion and elite culture, and the opening of the opera season became synonymous with the opening of the "social season" among the very rich.

In the first half of the nineteenth century, local bands sprang up in thousands of communities across America (3,000 of them by 1860) with a repertoire that included popular and classical pieces. Beginning in the 1840s, classical music became the preserve of elite symphony orchestras in large cities.

To sound their best, orchestras like the New York Philharmonic and the Chicago Symphony needed expensive new halls. Opera companies needed endowments. Serious theater needed generous patrons. Thus great infusions of private wealth were necessary to support lavish arts programs. In the late nineteenth century, the rich formed an alliance with leading performers and intellectuals to create a cultural establishment that endures to this day. Opera houses and symphony halls were built with and sustained by the patronage of the wealthy. They were the architectural embodiment of high culture.

Great cities required great museums as well. Americans built a stunning array of secular temples devoted to the world's great art. Major museums were founded in New York, Boston, Philadelphia, and Chicago in the 1870s. Spectacular new public libraries appeared at the same time. By 1900 many Americans had come to associate culture with impressive institutions lodged in major cities. By this reasoning, for example, the cultural life of Chicago was embodied not in the immigrant neighborhoods or the popular theaters, but in the Art Institute, Symphony Hall, and the Chicago Public Library.

Orchestra Hall in Chicago was one of many stately auditoriums built to house America's major symphony orchestras in the second half of the nineteenth century.

The Emergence of the Modern University

At the same time that American elites were endowing museums and libraries they stepped up their commitment to the establishment of distinguished private universities. Cornell, Johns Hopkins, Vanderbilt, Stanford, and the University of Chicago all appeared between the late 1860s and the 1890s. Wealthy businessmen had good reason to endow great universities. The political economy of industrial capitalism rested on technological developments, which in turn depended on up-to-date scientific learning. Research universities played a central role in such developments and provided the training for the new business and engineering elite. And finally, corporate philanthropists agreed with many Americans that a great Western nation required great universities.

The new colleges reflected a new conception of how universities should be organized. Daniel Coit Gilman, the first president of the Johns Hopkins University in Baltimore, created specialized departments of history, English, and the various sciences that were responsible for recommending appointments and promotions and for developing courses. He encouraged the publication of academic journals and established the first university press in 1878. Gilman had created the modern university with a faculty of specialists dedicated to research and the training of other scholars. His innovations spread quickly and led to the undergraduate major, the system of numbered courses, unit requirements, electives, and PhD programs with research seminars and dissertations based on original research.

In this new setting, the study of modern literature entered the college curriculum for the first time. Some professors, influenced by German scholarship, emphasized sentence structures, word roots, and forms of publication. This approach appealed to those who sought to make the study of literature into a science. But beneath the surface was a set of assumptions about the intrinsic superiority of Western European languages. A leading Oxford scholar, Friedrich Max Muller, saw "an unbroken chain between us and Cicero and Aristotle." Muller and his American followers created a canon of great works that they believed defined culture of the "West." They also defined the study of literature as the preserve of specialists.

Leading scholars in the new "social sciences" of sociology, anthropology, and political science also divided the world into great and inferior nations. Best of all were the so-called Teutonic nations of western Europe and North America. Anthropologists, sociologists, and professional economists also claimed that the human hierarchies they constructed were grounded in the objective methods of pure science. Science was becoming the model for the production of all human knowledge.

Social Darwinism and the Growth of Scientific Racism

In 1859 Charles Darwin published his masterpiece of evolutionary theory, *On the Origin of Species*. Several scientists had already suggested that life had evolved over a long period of time, but Darwin offered the first persuasive theory of how this might have taken place. He argued that a process of "natural selection" favored those biological changes that were most suited to the surrounding environment. In Darwinian theory, natural selection was the single most important explanation for the vast array of life forms on earth. American scientists were remarkably receptive to Darwinism. Asa Gray at Harvard and Joseph LeConte at the University of California spread the evolutionary word in their influential textbooks on botany and geology. By 1900 virtually all the science textbooks used in American high schools embraced evolution.

Darwin's remarkable influence did not stop with the natural sciences. Social scientists applied the theory of natural selection to social evolution. This combination of social theory with evolutionary science was known as social Darwinism. Social Darwinists argued that human inequality was the outcome of a struggle for survival in which the fittest rose to the top of the social ladder. This theory made the rich seem more fit than the poor; it made blacks seem less fit than whites. To social Darwinists, inequality was the natural order of things. In this way Darwinism was put to use in defense of the political economy of industrial capitalism.

From the moment he published *On the Origin of Species* in 1859 Darwin's theory of natural selection was used to support a theory of African racial inferiority. Racists had argued that emancipation would force blacks to compete with their white superiors and that this competition would end in the disappearance of the African race. When the 1890 census seemed to show that blacks were withering under the strain of competition with whites, racial theorists unleashed a volley of influential studies.

In 1892 biologist Joseph LeConte weighed in with an article on "The Race Problem in the South." In conditions of free competition with whites, LeConte argued, blacks faced either "extinction" or permanent subordination. Only the protection of whites could shield blacks from their natural fate.

Far more influential than the LeConte article was Frederick L. Hoffman's full-length treatise, *Race Traits and Tendencies of the American Negro*, published in 1896. Hoffman's book quickly established itself as one of the most important studies of race relations written in the nineteenth century. Hoffman himself was a statistician, and the tables and figures scattered throughout his book gave it the authoritative air of the new social sciences. Yet from beginning to end the book was an ideological rant. Ever since they had left the protective cover of slavery, Hoffman argued, blacks had shown clear signs of moral degeneration and were doomed to poverty and social inferiority.

Social scientists like Hoffman prided themselves on their commitment to the truth as it was revealed in facts and statistics. Like advocates of high culture, sociologists and anthropologists claimed to have isolated the definitive truths of human society. But not all "realists" sought solace in the past or justified the inequalities of the present. The best American artists of the late nineteenth century openly embraced the realities of urban and industrial America.

ARTISTIC REALISM EMBRACES URBAN AND INDUSTRIAL AMERICA

"This is the age of cities," writer Hamlin Garland declared. "We are now predominantly urban and the problem of our artistic life is practically one of city life." In the second half of the nineteenth century, artists and writers embraced the world that Anthony Comstock wanted to suppress and that Matthew Arnold wanted to escape. They called themselves realists and saw themselves as part of the first major artistic movement that was grounded in urban and industrial America. As writer Fanny Bates put it, the people of the cities "live more in realities than imagination."

The Triumph of Literary Realism

In April 1861 the *Atlantic Monthly* published a powerful story called "Life in the Iron Mills" by a writer named Rebecca Harding. Her story created a sensation. Rarely had the dreary lives of ordinary workers been presented in such relentless detail. In the decades to come, the best writers in America joined in the crusade to make fiction realistic. "The public demands realism," Willa Cather explained, "and they will have it." The leading spokesperson for realistic fiction was William Dean Howells, the author of one of the best realist novels, *The Rise of Silas Lapham*, and editor of the *Atlantic Monthly*, one of a handful of influential magazines that championed literary realism.

Realists tried to bridge the gap between "high" and "popular" culture by making great literature out of the details of everyday life. To "enjoy the every-day life," Sarah Orne Jewett explained in *Deephaven*, one must "find pleasure in thought and observation of simple things, and have an instinctive, delicious interest in what to other eyes is unflavored dullness." By writing about failed businessmen or runaway slaves, writers like Howells and Mark Twain hoped to reveal both courage and cowardice in the lives of ordinary men and women. This was the great achievement of Twain's *Huckleberry Finn*.

The characters in realistic novels were flawed men and women who struggled with the moral dilemmas they encountered in their daily lives. In Howells's greatest novel, Silas Lapham had to decide whether to mislead the men who wanted to buy his failing paint company. Huck Finn had to decide whether to turn in a runaway slave. Yet neither Lapham nor Finn was "heroic" in the way that earlier heroes were. Lapham was an ill-educated social climber who drank and talked too much. Huck Finn was a barely literate seeker of adventure who played hooky, spoke improper English, and spun absurd fantasies. In the end both Silas Lapham and Huck Finn made the right moral decisions, but neither found his decision easy to make, and Lapham suffered for having done so.

The realist movement was greeted with shock by the defenders of the genteel tradition of American letters. In March 1885 the public library committee of Concord, Massachusetts, banned *Huckleberry Finn* from its shelves, denouncing it as "the veriest trash." Members of the committee characterized Twain's masterpiece as "rough, coarse and inelegant, dealing with a series of experiences not elevating, the whole book being more suited to the slums than to intelligent, respectable people."

Realists dismissed such criticism as evidence of the "feminine" taste that prevailed in American letters and saw realism as a "masculine" alternative to sentimental writing that appealed to women novel readers. In their commitment to the unvarnished truth, realists thought of themselves as "virile and strong." But female realists such as Kate Chopin also rejected the assumption, common to sentimental fiction, that women's lives should be bounded exclusively by the needs of their husbands and children. Louisa May Alcott wanted her female characters to be "strong-minded, strong-hearted, strong-souled, and strong-bodied." Realistic writers thus challenged the sentimental depiction of women as nervous, frail, and destined only for the domestic life.

Other authors, most notably Walt Whitman, pushed the radical possibilities of realism even further. Like most realists, Whitman aspired to "manly" writing. Through his poems he hoped "to exalt the present and the real, to teach the average man the glory of his daily walk and trade." He was the poet of the city who filled his verse with vivid details of urban life. For Whitman that meant he would embrace the "goodness" as well as the "wickedness" of modern America. Just as vaudeville flirted more and more openly with sexual titillation, Whitman wrote more and more openly about eroticism. Thus Whitman, like so many realists, fused the themes of popular culture with the forms of "high" art.

Painting Reality

In 1878 New York artist John Ferguson Weir declared that "art, in common with literature, is now seeking to get nearer the reality, to 'see the thing as it really is.'" Like the best writers of the post-Civil War era, the finest painters rejected romanticism in favor of realism. Winslow Homer and Thomas Eakins shifted the emphasis of American painting from sentiment to realism, from unspoiled nature to the facts of social life in urban and industrial America. Realists did not always paint the city, but even when they depicted rural life, or in Winslow Homer's case the life of the seafarer, realists generally avoided romanticism.

Homer was, in the words of one critic, a "flaming realist—a burning devotee of the actual." He left several important bodies of work, all realistic in different ways. A series of Civil War studies, notably *Prisoners From the Front* (1866), presented ordinary soldiers with ragged uniforms and worn, tired expressions. This was a sharp departure from a tradition of painting military men in heroic poses. As an illustrator for *Harper's Weekly*, the first successful mass-circulation magazine in America, Homer also drew realistic scenes of factories, railroad workers, and other aspects of industrial life.

Two of Homer's most enduring contributions were his sensitive depictions of African Americans and his remarkable portrayals of seafaring men struggling against nature. At a time when intellectuals were perfecting theories of black racial inferiority and minstrel shows presented blacks in the grossest stereotypes, Winslow Homer represented blacks as varied men and women who worked hard and struggled with dignity against the difficulties of everyday life. In the process, Homer produced some of his finest paintings.

Thomas Eakins was an even more thoroughgoing realist, determined to drain his paintings of all romantic sentiment. He wielded his paintbrush with the precision of a scientist in a laboratory. Indeed, in his effort to represent the human body with perfect accuracy, Eakins attended medical school. After studying for several years in Europe, Eakins returned to his native Philadelphia in 1870 and was soon shocking viewers with warts-and-all portraits of his own sisters. Eakins, one critic sniffed, "cares little for what the world of taste considers beautiful."

Eakins established his reputation with a series of lifelike paintings of rowers. Even at the beginning of his career, Eakins could render scenes with startlingly three-dimensional effects. In 1875, he shocked the art world once again with *The Gross Clinic*, a large canvas depicting the gruesome details of a surgical procedure. The selection committee for the 1876 Philadelphia Centennial Exposition rejected *The Gross Clinic* on the grounds that "the sense of actuality about it was . . . oppressive."

Eakins was fascinated by the human form. He photographed dozens of naked men and women and used some of them as the basis for full-scale paintings. *The Swimming Hole* (ca. 1884) was based on a photograph Eakins had taken. By 1886 the directors of the Academy had had enough. Eakins was fired after he pulled the loincloth from a male model posing before a group of female students.

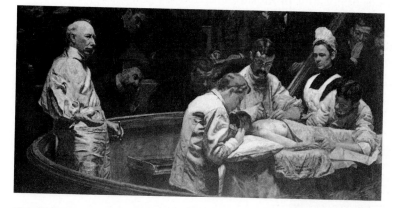

Thomas Eakins was a pioneer in the artistic use of photography. By using photography as the basis for painting, and by using scenes of ordinary life as the basis of high art, Eakins demonstrated his commitment to artistic realism in paintings such as The Agnew Clinic.

Critics complained that Eakins was obsessed with nudity, but for Eakins himself the exact details of the human body were merely the entryway into a deeper exploration of the characters and personalities of his subjects. In the late 1880s and 1890s Eakins produced a number of portraits that were stunning both for their physiological accuracy and their psychological penetration. Like Winslow Homer's portrayals of blacks, Eakins's women were thoughtful and dignified. *Miss Amelia C. van Buren* (1891) conveys its subject's intelligence and complexity with no sacrifice of accuracy. Eakins thereby did for painting what Henry James did for literature. Both demonstrated that distinguished works of art could be impressively realistic and at the same time deeply insightful.

Is Photography Art?

As city life became the subject matter of painters and writers, a major technological development—photography—created a new medium of artistic expression. In the fall of 1862 Mathew Brady mounted an exhibit of Civil War photographs in his New York gallery. This was the first time a large viewing public was able to see realistic pictures of the most gruesome facts of war. The camera had been invented scarcely a generation earlier, in 1839, by a Frenchman named Louis Daguerre. By the early 1860s photographic technology had improved dramatically, and Mathew Brady knew how to take advantage of it. His 1862 exhibition had electrifying effects.

By the 1880s journalists used photographs to heighten the reality, the sense of "truth," conveyed by their stories. The effect of Jacob Riis's *How the Other Half Lives*, published in 1890, was enhanced by the fact that he included a series of dramatic photographs documenting the misery of the urban poor. Photography had become part of the body of factual evidence.

The camera's eye inevitably fascinated realistic writers and artists. In the second half of the nineteenth century photography set the standard for accurate representation to which many artists aspired. Thomas Eakins, for example, used the camera to freeze images that he intended to paint on canvas. He photographed horses in motion to guide him as he painted. Eakins soon became a skilled photographer, producing hundreds of portraits of his subjects. He took numerous photos of the naked human form, and not always as a basis for later paintings. Eakins was thus one of the first artists to recognize the artistic element of photography itself. His work thereby raised questions that remain unanswered: Is a painting based on a photograph a work of art? Is photography art?

Civil War photography, pioneered by Mathew Brady's New York studio, was part of a larger artistic movement toward realism. The photos were not simply graphic; the best of them were works of art.

Some writers applauded the camera's capacity to capture the "truth." Writers as varied as Walt Whitman and Harriet Beecher Stowe used photographic metaphors to describe the effects they hoped to achieve with their words. But others were not persuaded that the photograph could ever be a genuine work of art. The camera captures only "the external facts," *The Galaxy* magazine declared, it "does not tell the whole truth."

Anthony Comstock worried a great deal about the difference between art and photography. Millions of copies of great and not-very-great works of art flooded the market in the late nineteenth century. Photographs of naked men and women suddenly became a new form of readily accessible pornography. "Is a photograph of an obscene figure or picture a work of art?" Comstock asked. "My answer is emphatically, No." Artists who paint nude portraits use lines, shadings, and colors in ways that "seem to clothe the figures"; their artistry diverts the viewers' attention from the nudity. Photographers have no such artistic devices at their disposal, Comstock explained. "A photograph of a nude woman in a lewd posture, with a lascivious look on her face," was to Comstock no work of art, for it lacked "the skill and talent of the artist."

CONCLUSION

When Comstock questioned whether photography could be art he was participating in a larger debate about what counted as culture in the new political economy of industrial capitalism. Did it include the popular culture of the city, or was American culture restricted to the nation's great libraries, universities, museums, and opera houses? And what was culture supposed to do for people? Americans argued over whether culture should maintain traditional values or boldly face up to the realities of the new political economy.

These cultural struggles easily spilled over into politics. Urban reformers proposed public policies to elevate the cultural level of slum dwellers. Elites convinced politicians to subsidize the construction of huge public libraries. Nevertheless, American politics in the late nineteenth century had not yet become cultural politics. The issues that brought Americans into the streets and into the voting booths remained, for the most part, economic issues. Just as American culture was transformed by the rise of cities and industry, the problems of the capitalist political economy became the focus of American politics in the late nineteenth century.

FURTHER READINGS

John D'Emilio and Estelle Freedman, *Intimate Matters: A History of Sexuality in America* (1988). This text is an innovative overview with important chapters on the late nineteenth century.

Elliot J. Gorn and Warren Goldstein, *A Brief History of American Sports* (1993). True to its title, this provides a brief but intelligent introduction to the subject.

John Higham, *Strangers in the Land: Patterns of American Nativism, 1860–1925* (1955). Higham has prepared a classic study of the response of native-born Americans to immigrants.

CHRONOLOGY

1851	YMCA is founded First world's fair is held at Crystal Palace in London
1859	Charles Darwin publishes *On the Origin of Species*
1861	Rebecca Harding publishes "Life in the Iron Mills"
1862	Mathew Brady exhibits Civil War photos at his New York studio
1866	New York Athletic Club opens Horatio Alger expelled from his pulpit in Brewster, Massachusetts Winslow Homer paints *Prisoners From the Front* and *Near Andersonville*
1869	Cincinnati Red Stockings charge admission to watch baseball games Matthew Arnold publishes *Culture and Anarchy*
1870	Metropolitan Museum of Art and Boston Museum of Fine Arts are founded
1870s	National League is formed; baseball becomes professional
1871	Walt Whitman publishes *Democratic Vistas* Thomas Eakins paints *Max Schmitt in a Single Scull*
1873	New York Society for the Suppression of Vice (SSV) founded Congress enacts the Comstock Law
1875	First Harvard-Yale football game is played Thomas Eakins paints *The Gross Clinic*
1876	World's Fair held in Philadelphia Philadelphia Museum of Art founded

Lawrence Levine, *Highbrow/Lowbrow: The Emergence of Cultural Hierarchy in America* (1988). Levine, a leading cultural historian, has effected a masterful study.

Roy Rosenzweig, *Eight Hours for What We Will: Workers and Leisure in an Industrial City, 1870–1920* (1983). Rosenzweig demonstrates the importance of leisure time to industrial workers.

David Shi, *Facing Facts: Realism in American Thought and Culture, 1850–1920* (1995). Refer to this for a broad introduction to the topic.

	Daniel Coit Gilman becomes first president of Johns Hopkins University
1878	Johns Hopkins establishes the first university press
1879	Art Institute of Chicago founded
1880s	Richard Kyle Fox professionalizes boxing
1883	Anthony Comstock publishes *Traps for the Young*
1884	Mark Twain publishes *The Adventures of Huckleberry Finn* Winslow Homer paints *The Life Line* Thomas Eakins paints *The Swimming Hole*
1885	William Dean Howells publishes *The Rise of Silas Lapham* Josiah Strong publishes *Our Country*
1888	Modern "safety" bike invented
1890	Jacob Riis publishes *How the Other Half Lives*
1891	Thomas Eakins paints *Miss Amelia C. van Buren*
1893	World's Columbian Exposition held in Chicago
1894	Vaudeville producer B. F. Keith opens the New Theatre in Boston
1896	Frederick L. Hoffman publishes *Race Traits and Tendencies of the American Negro*
1899	Winslow Homer paints *The Gulf Stream*

Robert Toll, *Blacking Up: The Minstrel Show in Nineteenth-Century America* (1974). *Blacking Up* is very good at tracing changes over time.

Alan Trachtenberg, *The Incorporation of America: Culture and Society in the Gilded Age* (1982). Trachtenberg gives a brief, spirited overview of the topic.

 Please refer to the document CD-ROM for primary sources related to this chapter.

19
The Politics of Industrial America
1870–1892

The "Crusade" Against Alcohol • Two Political Styles • Economic Issues Dominate National Politics • Government Activism and Its Limits • Middle-Class Radicalism • Discontent Among Workers Conclusion

THE "CRUSADE" AGAINST ALCOHOL

A few days before Christmas in 1873, Dr. Diocletian Lewis arrived in Hillsboro, Ohio, to speak on the evils of alcohol. He had given the speech many times before, but on this occasion the women who came proved unusually responsive. Lewis told them how, when he was a boy, his mother saved his father from drink by persuading a local saloonkeeper to stop selling liquor. The next morning a group of Hillsboro women met for prayer and then marched through the town urging local merchants to stop selling liquor. Inspired by their success, the women kept up the pressure through the winter of 1873–1874.

The Crusade, as it came to be called, quickly spread to more than 900 towns and cities in 31 states and territories. The women closed down thousands of liquor stores and saloons and secured written pledges from hundreds of druggists and hotel-keepers not to sell alcohol. With the dramatic success of the Crusade of 1873–1874, temperance was reborn as a movement dominated by women. The Woman's Christian Temperance Union (WCTU), organized in late 1874, would eventually bring tens of thousands of women directly into the political arena.

The WCTU dwarfed all other women's political organizations in the late nineteenth century. By the early 1890s, for example, the National American Woman Suffrage Association had 13,000 members; the less-radical General Federation of Women's Clubs had 20,000. The WCTU had 150,000 adult members and 50,000 in its young women's auxiliary.

Much of this success could be attributed to the WCTU's powerful and charismatic president, Frances Willard. The child of well-educated parents, she attended college in Milwaukee and completed further studies in Rome, Berlin, and Paris. While in Europe, she settled on the question that would guide her life: "What can be done to make the world a wider place for women?" In her early 30s, Willard attended the founding convention of the WCTU and was appointed corresponding secretary. At first "conservatives" who wanted to restrict its activity to the suppression of liquor dominated the organization. But Willard had grander visions, and so, apparently, did the WCTU's members. In 1879 they elected Willard their national president, a position she held until her death in 1898.

The temperance movement broadened its interests and grew steadily more radical and more popular. It embraced women's suffrage, workers' rights, and finally "Christian socialism." Nevertheless, the WCTU's appeal and its radicalism were restricted by its predominantly prosperous membership. The middle-class Protestant bias of the WCTU was consistent with its disdain for most forms of party politics.

To be sure, the WCTU convened huge rallies, but Willard contrasted them to party conventions. WCTU gatherings were depicted as clean, well-disciplined affairs with oratory that was substantive rather than bombastic. Unlike the major parties, the WCTU combined education with interest-group pressure. Willard and her associates gave speeches, wrote articles, published books and newspaper columns on the evils of drink, organized petition campaigns, and lobbied officeholders. The crusade against alcohol grew into a broad-ranging political campaign to alleviate the problems of a new industrial society. In this sense the WCTU was typical of American politics in the late nineteenth century.

The political economy of industrial capitalism had thrown into doubt long-standing beliefs about the limited role of government in the regulation of the economy. The spectacular growth of big business worried voters, so politicians responded with the first tentative steps toward government regulation of commerce. But a growing number of Americans, though, stepped outside the two-party system to propose more radical solutions to social problems. Dissatisfied with party politics itself, many activists turned to wholesale political reforms. The WCTU tried all of these approaches, imitating the tactics of party politics while positioning itself outside the political mainstream. The effect of these competing styles was a dramatic increase in the number of politically active Americans, most of them demanding that their government actively confront the problems of industrial society.

TWO POLITICAL STYLES

There were two distinct political styles in late nineteenth-century America. One was partisan, the other was voluntary. Partisan politics included all the eligible voters who counted themselves as Democrats or Republicans, attended party parades and electioneering spectacles, and cast their ballots in record numbers. This was largely a world of men. The second political style, voluntarism, embraced a vast network of organizations, including women's assemblies, reform clubs, labor unions, and farmers' groups.

The Triumph of Party Politics

In the late nineteenth century American men voted along very strict party lines. Political parties printed and distributed their own ballots, and loyal Republicans and Democrats simply dropped a party ballot in the appropriate box. Party allegiances and discipline were strict, and campaigns were carefully organized. At no other time in American history did voters ally themselves so tightly to the two major parties.

And never again would so large a proportion of American men participate in presidential elections. From the 1840s through the 1860s an average of 69 percent of those eligible voted in presidential elections. During the final quarter of the century, the average rose to 77 percent. The figures were less impressive in the South, although they followed the same general pattern. Between 1876 and 1892, nearly two out of three southern men cast ballots in presidential elections. In the North 82 percent of men went to the polls every four years between 1876 and 1892. In the presidential elections of 1896 and 1900, northern voter turnout peaked at 84 percent.

Newspapers played a critical role in maintaining this level of political participation. Most editors were strong party advocates. Papers survived with the help of official advertisements and contracts to print ballots and campaign documents. Strong-willed editors such as Horace Greeley of the *New York Tribune* and William Cullen Bryant of the *New York Evening Post* became influential party leaders. Papers editorialized relentlessly in favor of their candidates and their party and slanted stories to show their party in the most favorable light. Some papers printed logos boasting of their partisan affiliation. "Republican in everything, independent in nothing," the *Chicago Inter Ocean* declared. Newspapers thus presented to their readers a starkly partisan world in which the difference between parties was the same as the difference between good and evil.

Spectacular political campaigns reinforced the partisan attachments promoted by newspapers. The parties organized political clubs to drum up enthusiasm for elections. Military marching companies organized the party foot soldiers as well. The clubs and marching groups in turn organized an endless series of competing party parades. Marchers rang bells, set off cannons, raised banners, and unfurled flags. Millions of American men, perhaps a fifth of all registered voters, participated in these huge spectacles.

Conspicuously absent from these events were the candidates themselves, particularly in presidential contests. Throughout the nineteenth century it was considered unseemly for presidential candidates to stump for votes. Those who did campaign—for example, Stephen Douglas in 1860, Horace Greeley in 1872, or James G. Blaine in 1884—were notoriously prone to losing the election. As the *Philadelphia Inquirer* explained in 1884, "It is better that the country should make its choice between the two candidates from what they know of their public records rather than from what they may learn of their personal appearance."

Masculine Partisanship and Feminine Voluntarism

Party politics was a largely masculine activity in the late nineteenth century. Both major parties functioned like fraternal organizations, and voting was increasingly referred to as a "manly" or a "manhood" right. Denying a man his right to vote was like denying his masculinity.

If the electoral sphere of campaigns and voting was a man's world, the private sphere of home and family was widely understood as a woman's world. In practice, women always participated in the background of popular politics. They sewed the banners, decorated the meeting halls, prepared the food for rallies and picnics, and joined the parades dressed as symbolic representations of the Goddess of Liberty or some similarly feminine icon. Nevertheless, politically active women opted for a different style of politics.

The stereotypes of the public man and the private woman rested on the assumption that women were destined to remain at home as protectors of the family's virtue. By the middle of the century, increasing numbers of women used that female stereotype to develop their own form of political activism. Female virtue justified women's support for moral reform movements such as abolitionism and temperance. Thus many women entered the public sphere to protect the private sphere. By defining "the family" in broad terms, women expanded the horizons of political activity beyond the confines of the two-party system. Thus a stereotype that initially restricted feminine political activity became a justification for women's increasing participation in public crusades.

Women pursued politics as representatives of voluntary associations that were dedicated to specific reforms, such as Sabbatarian laws that would prohibit working and drinking alcohol on the Sabbath or the struggles against slavery, prostitution, and poverty. Because it grew out of voluntary associations rather than political parties, this style of political activity is known as voluntarism.

Most of those who joined voluntary associations came from the educated middle class, and voluntary associations inevitably reflected the class biases of their members. By upholding the home as the special preserve of feminine authority, for example, reformers ignored the fact that working-class families depended heavily on the labor of children.

Sometimes women's associations copied the style of partisan politics. The WCTU staged mass marches and rallies. But because many politically active women were critical of the emotional style of mass politics, voluntary associations concentrated less on rousing voters than on educating them and lobbying elected officials.

Although men also joined voluntary associations, they were dismissed by mainstream politicians as "namby-pamby, goody-goody gentlemen." In the late nineteenth century, voluntarism was associated with feminine politics and party politics was associated with masculinity.

The Critics of Popular Politics

The combination of partisanship and voluntarism made American politics more "popular" than ever before. Women and men, blacks and whites, immigrants and the native born, working class and middle class all found places in the popular politics of the late nineteenth century. But not all Americans appreciated popular politics. After the Civil War a small but influential group of conservatives reacted with disgust to the American rage for politics. Contemptuous of partisanship, they advocated a new style of nonpartisan politics and questioned the

A satirical cartoon from 1869 belittled the campaign for women's suffrage. Entitled "Women on Top," the image reflected the common assumption that electoral politics was a strictly masculine activity.

principle of universal suffrage. Because they laid the groundwork for a new style of politics that would prevail in the twentieth century, the critics were ahead of their time.

"Universal suffrage can only mean in plain English the government of ignorance and vice," Charles Francis Adams complained in 1869. Adams spoke for a traditional American elite that saw popular politics as a degradation of public life. To such men, economic independence was the precondition for political virtue, among voters and public officials alike. The fact that the American working class was made up largely of blacks, Asians, and Catholic immigrants only made matters worse.

But blatantly antidemocratic rhetoric was a losing proposition in the late nineteenth century. Elites who hoped to maintain political influence learned to avoid direct assaults on the principle of universal suffrage. Instead they became advocates of good government, government run by professionals rather than party bosses and staffed by civil servants rather than party favorites. They became, in short, advocates of *nonpartisan* politics.

Nonpartisan politics was a reaction against the upheavals of the political economy of industrial capitalism. Many elites were haunted by what they saw as the twin evils of radicalism and immigration. In the wake of the nationwide strikes of 1877, *The Nation* magazine, a reliable barometer of elite opinion, asked whether an "alien" proletariat had transformed universal suffrage from a democratic blessing into a nightmare for the "well-to-do and intelligent" classes. In 1881, supporters of good government organized the National Civil Service Reform League to prevent political parties from filling government positions with their supporters. Victory came two years later with the establishment of a Civil Service Commission that would assign federal jobs on the basis of merit rather than patronage.

But civil service reform would not stop the phenomenal growth of a working-class electorate made up largely of recent immigrants. Political opposition to immigration, known as nativism, had enjoyed some success in the 1850s, and in 1882 nativists had secured a Congressional ban on the further immigration of Chinese. Anti-Catholicism spread across the country, especially in the Midwest in the late 1880s. Immigrants were Catholic and working class, so Yankee Protestants often saw working-class radicalism as a double threat. One nativist pointed to the "two lines" of foreign influence that were threatening the American republic. One line led to the radical politics of "agrarianism" and "anarchy." The second line tended toward Catholic "superstition." Both led "by different roads to one ultimate end, despotism!"

By the mid-1890s, as the number of immigrants from Eastern and Southern Europe increased, nativist rhetoric grew more racist. It was no longer merely radicals and Catholics who were swarming into the United States, but darker skinned peoples from Italy, Russia, and Eastern Europe. Social scientists wrote treatises on the inherent intellectual inferiority of such peoples, giving the imprimatur of science to the most vicious stereotypes. Italians were said to be genetically predisposed to organized violence, Jews to thievery and manipulation. Anti-immigrant parties and nativist societies appeared across America.

Throughout most of the nineteenth century, however, the critics of popular politics remained a vocal minority. Most Americans entered the political arena with deep concerns over the problems of a society that was rapidly becoming more urban and industrial. The political economy of industrial capitalism generated the issues that dominated American public life in the late nineteenth century.

As the number of immigrants to America swelled, so did opposition to them. This 1891 cartoon blames immigration for causing a host of social and political evils.

ECONOMIC ISSUES DOMINATE NATIONAL POLITICS

By the late nineteenth century Americans were accustomed to the idea that government should oversee the distribution of the nation's natural resources. After the Civil War federal officials distributed public lands to homesteaders and railroads and granted rights to mining, ranching, and timber companies. By the late nineteenth century, the rise of big business led growing numbers of Americans to believe that the government should regulate the currency and also protect American commerce and workers from ruinous foreign competition. To undertake these new responsibilities fairly and professionally, government employees had to be freed from the hold of political parties. These issues, all of them touching on the government's role in the regulation of the economy, dominated party politics in the late nineteenth century.

Weak Presidents Oversee a Stronger Federal Government

Starting in the mid-1870s, the Democrats and Republicans had nearly equal electoral strength, and from 1876 through 1896, not a single president enjoyed a full term during which his own party controlled both houses of Congress, nor did any president during these years take office with an overwhelming electoral mandate. After Grant's re-election in 1872, no president was re-elected to two consecutive terms until 1900.

In some cases, a president took office already tainted by the process that put him there, as was certainly true of Rutherford B. Hayes's election in 1876. Hayes's fellow Republicans were annoyed by his efforts to conciliate the southern Democrats who were conducting Congressional investigations of his election and frustrated by the president's contradictory position on civil service reform. Hayes forbade his party from raising money by assessing Republican officeholders, and he wrestled with the mighty Roscoe Conkling, Republican boss of New York City, for control of the New York Customs House—the most lucrative source of patronage in America. But although Hayes spoke for civil service reform, he acted the role of the party patron by lavishly rewarding his own supporters. Civil service reformers soon turned away from Hayes.

In 1877 Hayes took one important step toward strengthening the presidency. When railroad workers went on strike, Hayes dispatched federal troops to suppress them. This was an important precedent. Later presidents would often exercise their authority to intervene directly in disputes between workers and employers. But except for calling out the troops, Hayes's policy was to do nothing whatsoever to relieve the distress caused by the depression of the 1870s. Millions of Americans were suffering from the sharp fall in wages and prices, yet Hayes vetoed a bill that would have modestly inflated the currency. By 1880 the president was so unpopular that his fellow Republicans happily took him up on his offer not to run for re-election.

The results of the 1880 election were typical of the era. Republican James A. Garfield won the presidency by a tiny margin. He received 48.5 percent of the votes, and Democrat Winfield Hancock received 48.1 percent. As usual, the Republicans did best in New England, the upper Midwest, and the West. The Democrats swept the South but also took New Jersey, Nevada, and California. As a general rule, the Republicans appealed to southern blacks and to a northern middle class that was native born and overwhelmingly Protestant. The Democrats could count on strong support from working-class immigrants and southern whites.

As usual, economic issues dominated the 1880 campaign. But this did not mean that the Democrats and Republicans differed on economic policy. Both parties were addicted to the patronage system, so neither pressed for civil service reform. In theory the Democrats favored lower tariffs than the Republicans. In practice, neither party advocated free trade, and both parties had strong "protectionist" blocks (those who supported high tariffs to protect American business) as well as significant numbers who favored lower tariff rates. Neither party wanted to reverse the prevailing deflationary policies. Finally, while Republicans made periodic gestures in support of southern blacks, they had abandoned the freed people of the South. Thus Garfield's victory for the Republicans in 1880 did not foreshadow any major shifts in government policy.

On July 2, 1881, the president was shot by a lunatic who claimed to be a disappointed office-seeker. Garfield died two months later, and Chester A. Arthur, the product of a powerful patronage machine, became president. The assassination that put him in office made it dangerous for the president to resist the swell of popular support for civil service reform. The Republicans in control of Congress did resist, however, and Democrats swept into office on a tide of resentment against Republican corruption and patronage. The following year Congress passed, and President Arthur signed, the landmark Pendleton Civil Service Act.

The Pendleton Act prohibited patronage officeholders from contributing to the party machine that gave them their jobs. More important, the law authorized the president to establish a Civil Service Commission to administer competitive examinations for federal jobs. Before the century ended, the majority of federal jobs were removed from the reach of the patronage machines. The Pendleton Act was a major turning point in the creation of a stable and professional government bureaucracy.

Although Arthur signed the Pendleton Act, he squandered his chance of gaining popular credit as a reformer by distributing lavish patronage to his supporters in a shameless bid for re-election in 1884. He likewise threw away an opportunity to lead the way on tariff reform. With the return of prosperity in the late 1870s and early 1880s, government coffers bulged with surplus revenues from import taxes. Cries for lower tariffs grew louder, but the president succumbed to the political manipulations of the high-tariff forces in Congress. The so-called Mongrel Tariff he signed in 1883 did nothing. Arthur was no more successful in his attempts to strengthen the Navy or carry out an aggressive foreign policy. To make matters worse, the economy began to slow down again. Arthur approached the 1884 elections a tainted president. His fellow Republicans would not even renominate him.

The Democrats nominated Grover Cleveland. In his brief career as mayor of Buffalo and governor of New York, Cleveland had developed a reputation as an honest man and a moderate. Cleveland, the first Democrat elected to the presidency in nearly 30 years, made reconciliation between the North and the South a theme of his administration.

Cleveland's conviction that the federal government should defer to southern whites derived in part from his commitment to local government. Accordingly, Cleveland was not an activist president. During his first two years in office he initiated no new programs, but neither did he thwart Congressional moves to strengthen the authority of the central government. Cleveland approved legislation that raised the Agriculture Department to the status of a cabinet office and signed the Dawes Severalty Act of 1887, which placed the federal government in direct control over most Native Americans (see Chapter 17, "The Triumph of Industrial Capitalism"). In the same year, Cleveland signed the Interstate Commerce Act, the first federal legislation designed to regulate big business. It empowered a five-member Interstate Commerce Commission to curb monopolistic and discriminatory practices by railroads.

Cleveland earned few points for merely signing laws passed by Congress, so when his fellow Democrats lost control of the House of Representatives in 1886, he decided to take the lead on some important issue. The issue he chose was the tariff. In December 1887, shortly before his re-election campaign was to begin, Cleveland devoted his annual message to Congress almost entirely to sharp reductions in the tariff. He insisted that he was not an advocate of free trade; he simply thought that the tariff was too high.

But having staked so much on tariff reduction, the president merely watched passively as Congress produced a doomed bill that was biased in favor of southern interests. When his own party included only a weak endorsement of tariff reform in the 1888 platform, Cleveland did nothing. Throughout his campaign for re-election, he spoke not one word on the subject. Cleveland went before the voters with no tariff reform, and little else, to show for his four years in office.

Running a skillful campaign on an overtly protectionist platform, the Republicans won back the White House in 1888. A Republican president, Benjamin Harrison, at last presided over a Republican majority in Congress. Making good on their campaign promises, Republicans enacted high tariff rates. The Harrison–McKinley Tariff of 1890 also gave the president the authority to raise or lower tariffs with nations that opened their markets to American businesses. Thus the legislation gave the president important new authority in the conduct of foreign affairs. Also in 1890 the Republicans passed the Sherman Anti-Trust Act, declaring it illegal for "combinations" to enter into arrangements that would restrain competition. By failing to define precisely what constituted a "restraint of trade," the Sherman Act left it to the probusiness courts to decide. Still, the Sherman Anti-Trust Act was yet another indication of the federal government's increasing involvement in the regulation of the economy.

The Republicans received little credit for their efforts, and part of the problem was the president himself. Nicknamed "the human iceberg," Harrison was too stiff and pompous to rally the people. But the larger problem was the rising discontent among voters. In 1890 they put the Democrats back in control of the House of Representatives, and in 1892 they re-elected Grover Cleveland president. Once again, however, a president took office without a popular majority. Cleveland was the last of a string of relatively weak presidents (see Table 19–1).

TABLE 19–1

Electoral Margins in the Gilded Age

Year	Popular Vote	% of Popular Vote	Electoral Vote
1876	4,036,572	48.0	185
	4,284,020	51.0	184
1880	4,453,295	48.5	214
	4,414,082	48.1	155
	308,578	3.4	—
1884	4,879,507	48.5	219
	4,850,293	48.2	182
1888	5,477,129	47.9	233
	5,537,857	48.6	168

But the weakness of the executive did not indicate an inactive central government. In addition to the Pendleton Act, the Interstate Commerce Act, and the Sherman Anti-Trust Act, the government tried to inflate the currency by modestly increasing the amount of silver in circulation. By maintaining high tariffs politicians effectively protected the wage rates of workers and the economic security of businesses. Nevertheless, the weakness of the federal government left growing numbers of Americans with the impression that the political system could not solve the problems associated with the political economy of industrial capitalism.

GOVERNMENT ACTIVISM AND ITS LIMITS

There are two standard themes in the political history of the late nineteenth century. The first theme stresses that government in this era was replete with corruption and bribery. The second theme emphasizes that the late nineteenth century was the great age of limited government and unregulated markets. After the retreat from Reconstruction, the government stepped back and allowed the new industrial economy to grow at its own rapid pace. There is a kernel of truth in each of these themes. Corruption was a real problem in late-nineteenth-century politics, and the government's regulatory powers were trivial compared to what would come later. Nevertheless, government in the late nineteenth century did become more centralized and somewhat more involved in the regulation of the economy. The conflicting impulses toward limited and active government can be seen most clearly in one of the most disruptive issues of late-nineteenth-century American politics, the regulation of the currency.

Greenbacks and Greenbackers

People have always disagreed over how much money governments should produce and how they should produce it. During the eighteenth century, American colonists complained that there was not enough money in circulation to sustain their economic needs. In the first half of the nineteenth century Americans fought over how much power the government should give to banks to regulate the amount of money in circulation. After the Civil War, capitalist development sparked another political debate over the role of government in the organization of the economy.

During the Civil War, the U.S. government printed $450 million worth of *greenbacks* to support the Union effort. Greenbacks were paper bills that were backed by the government's word, but not by the traditional reserves of gold or silver. When the war ended most Americans agreed that the greenbacks should be withdrawn from circulation. But after the depression of the 1870s a growing number of Americans demanded that the government keep the greenbacks in circulation. Those who wanted to return to the gold standard by making greenbacks convertible for "specie"—gold or silver—were called *resumptionists*, that is, they wanted the government to resume specie payments. Those who wanted the government to keep greenbacks in circulation to help inflate the currency were called greenbackers.

The supporters of the gold standard associated sound money with sound religion. In 1878, for example, the *Christian Advocate* compared greenbackers to atheists. And in fact, greenbackers were often radical critics of the new political economy. They formed a Greenback-Labor Party, which garnered more than 1 million votes in the 1878 Congressional elections and elected 14 members of

This cartoon belittles those who advocated a more inflationary policy by using silver as well as gold as the basis of the money supply. The implication of the image is that "bimetallism"—the use of both gold and silver—would create economic instability.

Congress. But the sound money forces won out, and in 1879 the $300 million in greenbacks that were still in circulation were made convertible into gold.

Supporters of inflation next took up the issue of "free silver." To counteract the deflationary trend, they argued, the government should add to the amount of money in circulation by allowing the unlimited coinage of silver. In 1878 the inflationists and sound money forces in Congress passed the Bland–Allison Act authorizing the Treasury to purchase silver and mint it in amounts tied to the amount of gold being minted. With the return of prosperity in the 1880s the currency question died down, to be revived with the arrival of another severe depression in the 1890s.

Foreign Policy and Commercial Expansion

Capitalist development reshaped American foreign policy just as it dominated domestic politics. In the 1860s William Henry Seward shifted the emphasis of American foreign policy from the acquisition of territory to the expansion of American commerce. As the Secretary of State for Abraham Lincoln and Andrew Johnson, Seward argued for foreign and domestic policies that promoted industrial expansion. Prewar southern expansionism had dampened Seward's enthusiasm for the acquisition of more land: He came to believe that "political supremacy follows commercial supremacy," and so he shifted his attention to the opening of American markets in Latin America, Canada, and the Pacific region, including Asia.

In the late 1860s, as Congressional Republicans struggled with President Johnson over Reconstruction, many of Seward's plans got caught in the crossfire. His biggest success came on April 9, 1867, when the Senate ratified the treaty purchasing Alaska for $7.2 million (see Map 19–1). A few months later, however, the Senate blocked a treaty with Denmark for the purchase of the Virgin Islands. Seward likewise failed to win approval for a naval base in Santo Domingo and a treaty with Colombia giving the U.S. exclusive rights to build a canal across the isthmus of Panama. Nevertheless, Seward established the principle that commercial interests would drive American foreign policy.

Those commercial interests were increasingly global. Between 1860 and 1897 American exports tripled, surpassing $1 billion per year. After 300 years of trade deficits, in 1874 America's exports began to surpass its imports. Nearly 85 percent of those exports were agricultural commodities, but the growth of industrial exports was even more spectacular. Iron and steel exports jumped by 230 percent between 1888 and 1898. John D. Rockefeller's Standard Oil corporation shipped three-quarters of its kerosene overseas between the 1860s and the 1880s. In the 1880s, U.S. multinational corporations became a fixture of international commerce.

This expansion of overseas commercial interests did not mean that the U.S. had abandoned its territorial ambitions. President Grant and Senator Charles Sumner revived long-standing American hopes of annexing Canada, but the Canadians seemed intent on cementing their ties to Great Britain. Nevertheless, until the twentieth century many Americans cherished the dream of absorbing Canada into the United States.

European powers similarly thwarted U.S. territorial ambitions in Latin America, but so did racist concerns about bringing large numbers of nonwhites into the United States. A rebellion in Cuba in 1868 heightened American interest in annexing the island. But Secretary of State Hamilton Fish had long resisted the idea of

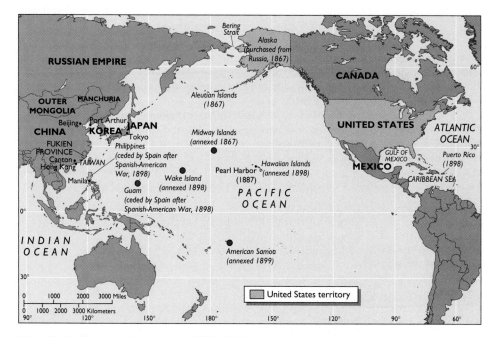

Map 19–1   American Expansion, 1857–1898
By the 1860s, Secretary of State William Henry Seward established the principle that American foreign policy would be driven by commercial interests.

absorbing half a million Cubans of "every shade and mixture of color." Similar inhibitions led the Senate to reject President Grant's 1869 treaty with Santo Domingo.

Despite the territorial restraints imposed by European power and racial ideology, aggressive secretaries of state reaffirmed Seward's commitment to commercial expansion. In 1886, for example, James G. Blaine worried openly that rapidly industrializing European nations were diverting Latin American commerce away from the United States. Concern for access to foreign markets pushed successive administrations to assert America's exclusive right to build a canal across Central America. The canal, President Harrison argued in 1891, "is the most important subject now connected with the commercial growth and progress of the United States." Hoping to thwart European commercial expansion by forging ties of friendship with Latin America, the United States convened the first Pan-American Conference in 1889.

Mexico provided the most vivid demonstration of U.S. commercial expansion. Although Americans had been buying up property in Mexico since before the Civil War, political instability limited Mexico's attractiveness as an investment. In 1876, however, Porfirio Díaz seized power in Mexico and began a reign of 35 years that proved a boon to American commercial interests. American investors quickly swarmed into Mexico, building railroads, selling life insurance, and digging oil wells. By 1910 Americans owned 43 percent of all the property in Mexico, more than Mexicans themselves owned.

United States attention also turned toward Asia and the South Pacific. In the 1880s the United States nearly went to war with England and Germany over disputed claims to Samoa. An 1876 reciprocity treaty gave Hawaiian sugar favored treatment on the American market, prompting a huge influx of Hawaiian sugar into the U.S. market (along with a backlash against the treaty by sugar producers on the mainland). By 1886, however, two-thirds of Hawaiian sugar was produced on American-owned plantations. Consequently, President Cleveland supported the treaty's renewal by referring to "our close and manifest interest in the commerce of the Pacific Ocean." By the 1890s American power in Hawaii had grown so great that it provoked among native Hawaiians a backlash that culminated in Queen Liliuokalani's ascension to the throne in January 1891. Two years later Hawaiians favorable to the United States dethroned the queen and President Harrison sent a treaty of annexation to the Senate.

The United States treaded somewhat more cautiously in East Asia, where European powers had long-established ties. The United States negotiated treaties with Japan and Korea that substantially increased American access to Asian markets.

From 1865 to 1890 the Senate repeatedly rejected treaties negotiated by presidential emissaries, but a succession of powerful secretaries of state compensated for a succession of weak presidents. By the late 1880s America's extensive global interests began to shape the nation's military policy. In 1890 Congress approved the construction of the first modern warships and the Supreme Court extended the president's control over "our international relations." The growing links between commercial and diplomatic interests were reviving the powers of the American presidency.

Growth of the Central Government

Despite its archaic rules and outdated structure, the central government grew steadily after 1860. Even after the inevitable retrenchment that followed the Civil War, the government continued to grow as new bureaucracies were created: Congress consolidated the United States Geological Survey in 1879, established the

Interstate Commerce Commission in 1887, and created the Department of Justice in 1870 and the Department of Agriculture in 1889.

The number of civilian federal employees rose from 53,000 in 1871 to 256,000 in 1901. The growth of the civil service provides the clearest evidence of the emergence of a permanent government bureaucracy. In 1883, when Congress passed the first civil service law, 13,780 federal jobs were "classified," meaning that applicants had to pass an exam to qualify. Fifteen years later, 89,306 federal positions were classified, amounting to nearly half of the jobs in the national government. This expansion of the number of civil service jobs substantially weakened the power of the Democratic and Republican Parties. As the proportion of "classified" federal jobs swelled, the patronage well dried up.

By the turn of the century the rudiments of a permanent federal bureaucracy were in place. The Interstate Commerce Commission lacked the power to enforce its own rulings, so it was forced to rely on the courts, which were dominated by supporters of big business. The Sherman Anti-Trust Act was even weaker. Few monopolies were broken up, much less threatened, by it. Finally, only about 15 percent of the wage labor force was actually protected by the high tariffs. By 1900 the federal government had developed in important ways, yet it remained small and weak by later standards. Indeed, it was not the federal, but rather the state and municipal governments that responded most aggressively to the problems of the new political economy.

States Regulate; Municipalities Reform

Even as Americans called on their government to do more and more, politicians proclaimed their opposition to the taxes and bureaucracies that active government required. The result was a jarring contradiction. At the state level, politicians enacted policies of retrenchment. In contrast to the federal government, for example, late-nineteenth-century state legislatures passed fewer laws, lowered their taxes, and balanced their budgets.

State politicians also established new regulatory bodies to govern the exploding municipalities of urban and industrial America. During the late nineteenth century state officials often transferred municipal power from elected officials and party politicians to experts and specialists on unelected boards. Mayors, city council members, and aldermen lost much of their authority over budgets, schools, police, and parks. For example, reformers handed control of the police to commissions staffed by middle-class citizens rather than by working-class immigrants. Parks commissions, sanitation commissions, public health commissions, and transportation commissions were generally staffed by middle-class professionals who were appointed to their posts and who prided themselves on their "nonpartisan" approach to government. The quality and professionalism of police and fire services increased dramatically over the course of the nineteenth century.

At least as important for the proper functioning of city government was the willingness of municipalities to raise taxes. As states retrenched, cities increased their property taxes to pay for streets, sewers, reservoirs, and public transportation. In the late nineteenth century city governments produced some of the great urban achievements of American history. Huge public parks, such as Central Park in New York and Golden Gate Park in San Francisco, sprang up across the country. At the same time cities sponsored spectacular feats of engineering and architecture. New Yorkers built the Brooklyn Bridge; Chicagoans literally reversed the flow of the Chicago River. Municipal governments went a long way toward enhancing the civility and decency of urban life in America.

San Francisco's Golden Gate Park, designed by Frederick Law Olmsted, was one of the most impressive of the great municipal parks built in cities across America in the late nineteenth century.

Yet Americans grew dissatisfied with their governments. Some were disgusted by corruption and inefficiency; others were offended by the hoopla of popular politics. To a significant number, government policies seemed inadequate to the demands of a new political economy. The powers of government grew slowly, but they were dwarfed by the private power of huge new corporations. Frustrated by piecemeal reforms, middle-class Americans turned to radical campaigns for social and economic transformation.

MIDDLE-CLASS RADICALISM

In the late nineteenth century a number of middle-class radicals argued that the political economy of industrial capitalism had undermined individual liberty and equality. Yet while their attacks on capitalism were severe, their assumptions were surprisingly traditional. They were usually frightened, not motivated, by socialism. They often worried that if substantial reforms were not undertaken, a discontented working class would overthrow the reign of private property. Their radical critiques of industrial society exposed deep wells of discontent among Americans.

Henry George and the Limits of Producers' Ideology

Henry George was born in Philadelphia in 1839, the son of middle-class parents. Although his formal education was limited, George traveled extensively and read widely. Like many middle-class Americans of his generation, he was shocked by the fact that as the United States grew richer the number of poor people grew as well. He studied the problem for many years and in 1879 published his conclusions in a bestselling book called *Progress and Poverty.*

George's explanation rested on what historians have called producers' ideology. It started from the assumption that only human labor could create legitimate wealth. Anything of value, such as food, clothing, or steel rails, came from the world's producing classes. By contrast, stockbrokers, bankers, and speculators made money from money rather than from the goods they produced. Producers' ideology therefore deemed their wealth illegitimate. Starting from these premises, Henry George divided the world into two classes: producers and predators.

The harmony of capital and labor was a central theme of producers' ideology. Henry George dreamed of a world in which working people owned their own farms and shops, making them both capitalists and laborers. His critique of industrial capitalism thus harkened back to Thomas Jefferson's vision of a society of small farmers and independent shopkeepers. America used to be that way, George believed, but as society "progressed," the land was monopolized by a wealthy few. Producers were forced to go to work for wealthy landholders. Employers then invested in technology that increased the productivity of their workers, but they kept the added wealth for themselves. Technology thus multiplied the wealth of the predators at the expense of the producers.

George's solution for the inequities of industrial society was a so-called Single Tax on rents. Because all wealth derived from labor applied to land, he reasoned, rents amounted to an unnatural transfer of wealth from the producers to the landlords. To thwart that transfer, George suggested taxing rents and improvements on land at prohibitive levels. This would discourage the accumulation of land by the landowning class. All other taxes would be abolished, including the tariffs that protected big business.

George presented his Single Tax as an alternative to the dangerous socialist doctrines that he thought were spreading among the working class. George attacked as "faulty" the socialist idea that there was an inherent conflict between labor and capital. He opposed government regulation of the economy, and he was a fiscal conservative, suspicious of proposals to counteract deflation by putting more money in circulation. Despite his apparent radicalism, George's popularity testified to the strength of middle-class concerns about the political power of the working class.

John F. Weir's 1877 painting, Forging the Shaft: A Welding Heat, graphically depicts the forms of industrial wage labor that Henry George feared. His response was to propose the restoration of a Jeffersonian economy of small, independent producers.

Edward Bellamy and the Nationalist Clubs

In 1888 Edward Bellamy, a 38-year-old Massachusetts editor, published a bestseller with a critique of capitalism even more powerful than Henry George's. Bellamy's *Looking Backward* was a utopian novel set in the future. The plot revolves around Julian West, who goes to sleep in Boston in 1887 and wakes up in the year 2000. His host, Doctor Leete, introduces West to the miraculous changes that have taken place. Technological marvels have raised everyone's standard of living. Boston has become a clean and orderly city. The great problems of industrial civilization have been solved. This was possible, Doctor Leete explains, because Americans had overcome the "excessive individualism" of the late nineteenth century, which "was inconsistent with much public spirit."

What about "the labor question?" Julian West asks. It had been "threatening to devour society" in 1887 when West fell asleep. Bellamy's critique of capitalism is contained in Doctor Leete's answer to West's question. In the early years of the American republic, the doctor explains, workers and employers lived in harmony. Upward mobility was common. This changed when "great aggregations of capital" arose. Like Henry George's, Bellamy's criticism of capitalism was grounded in traditional Jeffersonian ideals. For both authors the triumph of wage labor led to concentrations of wealth that undermined the harmony of capital and labor.

But where *Progress and Poverty* proposed the restoration of the simple virtues of Jeffersonian society, *Looking Backward* imagined a high-tech future in which consumer goods were provided in abundance. Henry George reasserted the values of hard work and self-restraint, whereas Edward Bellamy embraced the modern cult of leisure. For Henry George technology led to misery and inequality, but for Edward Bellamy machines would free mankind from the burdens and inequities of the modern world.

In spite of these differences, Bellamy and George were both motivated by a profound fear of militant workers. *Looking Backward* catered to a middle class craving for order amidst the chaos of industrial society. Superficially, Bellamy's futuristic Boston appeared to be a socialist utopia. Decisions about what to produce were made collectively, and society as a whole owned the means of production. Yet Bellamy was contemptuous of socialism and called his vision "nationalism." Under nationalism, the restoration of social peace was so complete that there was little or no need for government. This vision inspired thousands of middle-class Americans to form "Bellamy Clubs" or "Nationalist Clubs," particularly in New England.

The Woman's Christian Temperance Union

"Edward Bellamy's wonderful book" likewise inspired Frances Willard, president of the WCTU. She called nationalism "the fulfillment of man's highest earthly dream." Fifteen years earlier such support would have been impossible. The temperance movement that had revived in the early 1870s had initially restricted itself exclusively to the suppression of alcohol.

Even under Frances Willard's direction the WCTU never lost sight of its central goal. All across America, new laws established prohibitive license fees for the sale of liquor. Others banned the sale of liquor on Sunday. States passed "local option" laws giving communities the power to regulate the sale of liquor. But to temperance purists such victories presented a problem. Liquor licenses implied the government's endorsement of alcohol; local option meant that towns were free to permit the consumption of liquor. Thus the ultimate goal of the WCTU became prohibition of the manufacture and sale of alcohol throughout the United States.

Under Willard's direction, temperance became the springboard to a wide range of political and social reforms. The WCTU endorsed women's suffrage and formed an alliance with the country's largest labor union. She supported laws restricting the workday to eight hours and prohibiting child labor. Even the WCTU's attitude toward alcohol changed. By the 1890s Willard viewed drunkenness as a public health problem rather than a personal sin, a problem of political economy rather than individual failure. Accordingly, temperance advocates supported reforms designed to relieve poverty, improve public health, raise literacy, alleviate the conditions of workers, reform prisons, suppress public immorality, and preserve peace. In the end, Willard attributed the evils of liquor to the inequities of corporate capitalism.

Three factors explain the WCTU's success. The first was Frances Willard's paradoxically conservative approach to radical reform. Her justification for female political activism always came back to women's distinctive calling as protectors of the home. The second reason for the WCTU's success was its decentralized structure. Willard left the local chapters of the Union free to adjust their activities to suit their particular needs. In the southern unions there was little talk of women's suffrage. Willard called this the "Do Everything" policy. Finally, the WCTU appealed to middle-class women who felt isolated by a culture that restricted them to the home. Women found in the WCTU a source of camaraderie as well as political activism.

For all its success, however, temperance remained a middle-class reform movement. The organization rested on a constituency that was concentrated in cities, especially in the North.

The WCTU did not attract many immigrants, for example. The official policy of toleration was undermined by the prejudices of middle-class members. For many temperance advocates immigrants were the Union's targets rather than its constituents, and the strong Protestant identity of the WCTU limited its appeal among working-class Catholics. One of its first major campaigns in the 1870s was aimed at replacing altar wine with grape juice in Christian services, a switch that Catholics and Lutherans were unwilling to make. As radical as it was, the WCTU would never reflect the interests of black sharecroppers, white tenant farmers, or immigrant workers. Nevertheless, like the Single-Taxers and the Bellamy Clubs, WCTU reformers reflected a growing sense that the American political system was unable to solve the problems of an industrial political economy.

DISCONTENT AMONG WORKERS

Radicalized workers shared the conviction that mainstream politics could not confront the problems of industrial capitalism. Workers turned to violence, and employers demanded that government use its police powers to put down strikes. Labor radicals began to question one of the premises of producers' ideology: that American democracy was secured by a unique harmony between capital and labor. But if the harmony of capital and labor had been destroyed, advocates of the producers' ideology continued to search for a political solution to the labor problem.

The Knights of Labor and the Haymarket Disaster

Between 1860 and 1890 wages overall grew by 50 percent, but the bulk of the growth was confined to elite skilled and semiskilled workers in a handful of industries, such as printing and metalworking. The vast majority of workers suffered directly from the deflation and economic instability of the late nineteenth century. By 1880, 40 percent of industrial workers lived at or below the poverty line, and the average worker was unemployed for 15 to 20 percent of the year. To relieve their plight, American workers sought political solutions to economic problems.

The most important labor organization to emerge from the crisis of the 1870s was the Noble and Holy Order of the Knights of Labor. Founded in 1869, the Knights of Labor was inspired by the producers' ideology and admitted everyone from self-employed farmers to unskilled factory workers. It appealed to a nostalgic vision of a world dominated by ordinary working people. Nevertheless the Knights of Labor advocated a host of progressive reforms, including the eight-hour day, equal pay for men and women, the abolition of child and prison labor, inflation of the currency to counteract the deflationary spiral, and a national income tax.

By the late 1870s leaders realized that the union needed a strong national organization to hold various locals together. A new constitution, drawn up in 1878, required all members to pay dues and allowed the national organization to support local boycotts and thereby boost its credibility among workers. Thereafter the Knights grew rapidly, from 19,000 members in 1881 to 111,000 in 1885. True to the producers' tradition, leader Terence Powderly favored the consumer boycott over the strike. His approach proved most successful during the sharp recession of 1884, when trade union strikes were being broken. By 1886 membership in the Knights skyrocketed to more than 700,000.

But the more the Knights of Labor grew, the more the strains among its members showed. The interests of shopkeepers and small factory owners were very different from those of wage laborers. The critical issue dividing self-employed producers from wage-earning producers was the use of the strike as a weapon of organized labor. Self-employed producers preferred the consumer boycott, and so did the leadership of the Knights of Labor. By contrast, wage laborers saw the strike as their most powerful weapon.

With the return of prosperity, trade unions called for a nationwide strike for the eight-hour day. On May 1, 1886, workers across the country walked off their jobs in one of the largest and most successful labor walkouts in American history. In Chicago 80,000 workers went out on strike. The Chicago job action was largely peaceful until May 4, when at an Anarchist rally at Haymarket Square near downtown, someone from the crowd tossed a bomb into a line of police. One policeman was killed instantly, and seven more died within days. The number of civilian casualties was never determined. Although the bomb thrower was never identified, eight anarchists were tried for inciting violence, and four were put to death.

Anarchists—who questioned the legitimacy of all government power—had been active in Chicago for several years. Although they had little influence on the labor movement, their fiery rhetoric advocating the use of violence made them conspicuous. At the Haymarket rally on the evening of May 4 anarchist speakers used the same violent rhetoric. Samuel Fielden, for example, urged his listeners to "throttle" and "kill" the legal system or else, he warned, "it will kill you." This remark provoked Captain James Bonfield to rush 170 policemen to the dwindling rally, and into this crowd of policemen someone threw a bomb.

Haymarket was a turning point in American labor politics. With the support of its president, Terence Powderly, the Knights of Labor had tried to prevent its locals from supporting the May Day walkouts. Powderly had put himself into a bind. Members resented his failure to support the strikes, while outside the union a wave of revulsion against labor agitation swept the country. The Knights of Labor never recovered from the Haymarket disaster. Thereafter worker agitation split dramatically into two competing wings. Small farmers formed their own organizations, and wage laborers organized separately into industrial trade unions.

Agrarian Revolt

The late nineteenth century was a desperate time for American farmers, especially in the West and South. To compete they had to buy expensive agricultural equipment, often from manufacturers who benefited from tariff protections. Then they had to ship their goods to market on railroads that charged higher rates to small farmers than to big industrialists. When their goods reached a market, they faced steadily declining prices..

As the economy became global, southern cotton had to compete against cotton from India and the Near East. Western wheat competed with Russian and Eastern European wheat. To keep up, farmers increasingly went into debt, and in a deflationary spiral the money they borrowed to plant their crops was worth more when it came time to pay it back, while their crops were worth less. Farmers mortgaged their homes and land. The proportion of owner-occupied farms declined while the number of tenants rose.

Farmers were traditionally opposed to active government, but they began to press for government action, beginning with inflation of the currency. Inflation lowered the value of the money farmers borrowed while it raised the value of the crops they produced. Farmers also sought railroad regulations to end rate discrimination. They sought to reform a tariff system that protected manufacturers but left them exposed to the insecurities of an international market. Eventually, militant farmers began to press for antitrust legislation to break up concentrations of wealth in the steel, oil, and railroad industries.

But farmers were notoriously hard to organize. They were scattered over large sections of the country, they were committed to an ideology of economic independence, and they were traditionally hostile to government intervention. If American farmers were to pursue their political agenda effectively, they needed to overcome these and many other obstacles.

One of the first attempts to organize farmers was the Patrons of Husbandry, generally called the Grange. The Grange began to attract large numbers of farmers during the depression of the 1870s and claimed 1.5 million members by 1874. Consistent with producers' ideology, the Grange organized cooperatives designed to eliminate the role of merchants and creditors. By storing grain collectively, farmers held their products back from the market in the hope of gaining control over commodity prices. But inexperience made the Grange cooperatives difficult to organize and sustain. After 1875 their membership dwindled.

The National Farmers' Alliance and Industrial Union, known simply as the Farmers' Alliance, was much more effective than the Grange. Founded in Texas in 1877, the Farmers' Alliance spread rapidly across the South. Its potency was demonstrated at a huge meeting at Ocala, Florida, in 1890. The Ocala Platform supported a host of reforms, many of which had been staples of radical politics for a generation: currency inflation through the free coinage of silver, lower tariffs, and a constitutional amendment providing for direct election of senators. The Ocala Platform also demanded that the government establish a system of "subtreasuries," or public warehouses in which farmers could store their crops until they could get the best prices. Finally, the Alliance called for strict government regulation, and if necessary direct government ownership, of the nation's railroad and telegraph industries.

The Farmers' Alliance steered clear of politics and instead judged political candidates by the degree to which they supported the reforms advocated in the Ocala Platform. But very little such support was forthcoming from either of the major parties. Farmers' Alliance members therefore formed their own third parties, with

CHRONOLOGY

1867	U.S. purchases Alaska from Russia Patrons of Husbandry (the Grange) founded
1869	Noble and Holy Order of the Knights of Labor founded Suez Canal opened
1870	Department of Justice created
1872	Grant re-elected
1873	"Crusade" against alcohol begins in Hillsboro, Ohio
1874	WCTU is formed
1876	Rutherford B. Hayes elected president Porfirio Díaz seizes power in Mexico
1877	Farmers' Alliance founded
1878	Bland-Allison Act
1879	Frances Willard becomes president of the WCTU Henry George publishes *Progress and Poverty*
1880	James Garfield elected president
1881	Garfield assassinated; Chester Arthur becomes president WCTU endorses women's suffrage
1883	Pendleton Civil Service Act "Mongrel Tariff"

some success on the Great Plains in the election of 1890. Out of these initial forays into politics came the most significant third party of the late nineteenth century, the People's Party, otherwise known as the Populists.

The Rise of the Populists

On February 22, 1892, a huge coalition of reform organizations met in St. Louis, including Single Tax advocates inspired by Henry George, greenbackers who wanted an inflationary currency policy, representatives of the Knights of Labor, and members of the Farmers' Alliance. Together they founded the People's Party and called for a presidential nominating convention to meet in Omaha, Nebraska, on July 4. There they nominated General James B. Weaver of Iowa for president and drew up the famous Omaha Platform.

Inspired by the producers' ideology, the People's Party called for the unity of all working people and for harmony of interests between small property holders and wage earners. The Populist platform was a vigorous restatement of the

1884	Grover Cleveland elected president
1886	Nationwide strike for eight-hour day Riot at Haymarket Square in Chicago
1887	Interstate Commerce Act Four Haymarket anarchists executed Dawes Severalty Act
1888	Benjamin Harrison elected president Edward Bellamy publishes *Looking Backward*
1889	U.S. convenes first Pan-American Conference Department of Agriculture created
1890	Harrison–McKinley Tariff Sherman Anti-Trust Act Ocala Platform
1891	Queen Liliuokalani assumes the Hawaiian throne
1892	Omaha Platform of the People's Party Grover Cleveland re-elected
1893	Queen Liliuokalani overthrown
1898	Frances Willard dies

proposals laid out two years earlier by the Farmers' Alliance. Like the Ocala Platform, the Omaha Platform demanded an inflationary currency policy and subtreasuries. The Populists called for a graduated income tax, direct government ownership of the railroad and telegraph industries, and the redistribution of lands owned by the railroads.

In the 1892 elections the Populist presidential candidate won about 1 million votes and elected several senators, representatives, governors, and state legislators. But there was no support among wage earners outside the South and West. The producers' ideology, for all its talk of the unity of working people, was frankly incompatible with the interests of industrial workers, who had little reason to oppose protective tariffs that shielded the industrial economy. Inflation would only undermine the value of their wages and raise the price of commodities, and income taxes would shift the tax burden from landowners and importers to wage laborers. Conversely, farmers had every reason to oppose the eight-hour day and laws restricting child labor. In short, Populism was grounded in a rural society of independent farmers and craftsmen, a world that was rapidly disappearing.

CONCLUSION

After the Civil War the problems of industrial capitalism placed increasing strain on the political system. The two major parties were so closely matched in electoral strength that neither could risk bold new programs to meet the needs of a new political economy. So restless workers, desperate farmers, and an anxious middle class turned in increasing numbers to voluntary organizations, labor unions, and farmers' alliances.

The politics of industrial society reached a dramatic turning point in the 1890s. During that decade American voters went to the polls in record numbers. Organized farmers made their most radical demands; labor agitation reached a violent climax. And as night follows day, a conservative reaction set in. Movements to restrict the number of voters emerged, particularly in the South. Opponents of immigration made significant strides. The Supreme Court declared constitutional one of history's greatest social experiments, systematic racial segregation. In short, radicalism and reaction reached their peak in the 1890s. During the closing decade of the nineteenth century, a recognizably modern America was born.

FURTHER READINGS

Paul Avrich, *The Haymarket Tragedy* (1984). This is an exhaustive account by the leading historian of American anarchism.

Ruth Bordin, *Woman and Temperance: The Quest for Power and Liberty, 1873–1900* (1981). *Women and Temperance* is the best single volume available on the subject.

Leon Fink, *Workingmen's Democracy: The Knights of Labor and American Politics* (1983). This case study, with broad implications, shows the connections between political mobilization and labor organization.

Lawrence Goodwyn, *Democratic Promise: The Populist Moment in America* (1976). Goodwyn traces the roots of populism to the Farmers' Alliance.

Walter LaFeber, *The New Empire: An Interpretation of American Expansion, 1860–1898* (1963). LaFeber ties American foreign policy to commercial expansion.

Michael McGerr, *The Decline of Popular Politics: The American North, 1865–1928* (1986). This text is particularly strong on the culture of popular politics in the late nineteenth century.

John L. Thomas, *Alternative America: Henry George, Edward Bellamy, Henry Demarest Lloyd, and the Adversary Tradition* (1983). Thomas's work is a sensitive examination of middle-class radicalism and its limits.

Please refer to the document CD-ROM for primary sources related to this chapter.

20

Industry and Empire

1890–1900

Dealmaking in the White House • The Crisis of the 1890s
A Modern Political Economy • The Retreat From Politics
American Diplomacy Enters the Modern World • Conclusion

DEALMAKING IN THE WHITE HOUSE

On an icy February morning, J. Pierpont Morgan walked the short distance from his hotel to the White House. He pulled his scarf up around a scowling face known to millions of newspaper readers. He had not wanted to come to Washington. The commander in chief of the nation's bankers was going to meet the president to keep the United States from going bankrupt.

The events leading up to this urgent meeting stretched back five years, to 1890, when business failures in Argentina toppled London's venerable Baring Brothers investment house and triggered a collapse in European stock prices. As depression spread, European investors sold off their American holdings, and in early 1893 the panic reached the United States. Fourteen thousand businesses soon folded, along with more than 600 banks.

Wall Street went into a tailspin. In New York 55,000 men, women, and girls in the clothing industry were thrown out of work. Banks refused to cash checks, and coins vanished from circulation. The governor of Nebraska instructed the police to deal leniently with the thousands of homeless people on the roads. Breadlines formed.

The anger of workers and farmers, which had been simmering for decades, was about to boil over. President Grover Cleveland called Congress into special session and pledged to keep the dollar on the gold standard, but it was not enough. A wave of strikes swept the country. Unemployed workers battled police on the Capitol grounds. By January 1895, as panicky investors cashed government bonds, the Treasury's gold reserve was half gone. Reluctantly, President Cleveland opened negotiations with Morgan.

Admired and reviled, Morgan was the preeminent financial manipulator of the late nineteenth century. Like his contemporaries, steelmaker Andrew Carnegie and oil magnate John D. Rockefeller, Morgan's skill lay in organization. He restructured railroads, rooting out waste and competition and driving down wages. Cleveland was about to place the Treasury in this man's hands.

The president opened the meeting by suggesting that a new bond issue might stabilize the Treasury. No, Morgan replied flatly, the run on gold would continue until European investors regained confidence. If the president agreed, Morgan would arrange a private loan and personally guarantee the solvency of the U.S. Treasury. After a stunned silence, the two men shook hands. News of the deal instantly calmed the bond markets. The crisis was over.

Culminating two decades of economic turbulence, the Panic of 1893 and the depression that followed permanently transformed the American political economy. Businessmen like Morgan created enormous corporate combinations and placed them under the control of professional managers. They used technology and "scientific management" to control the workplace and push laborers to work faster and harder. Workers resisted, and the 1890s witnessed brutal clashes between capital and labor.

The 1890s were also a turning point in American politics. After the 1896 election, many Americans withdrew from the electoral process. African-American leaders and union organizers urged their followers to turn away from politics in favor of "bread and butter" economic issues. Patriotism, once synonymous with partisanship, now became identified with the United States' global military and economic ambitions. As Americans became more conscious of their military power, they watched the horizon, fearing that well-being at home could hinge on far-away events.

Americans began to feel that their economy's links to the world—and the changes manufacturing and rapid communications brought to politics and daily life—had transformed society fundamentally. Morgan's rescue required simultaneous transactions on two continents. The speed of industry, trade, and information, and the ability of machines and technology to span distance and time created a sense that the environment and the future could be controlled.

Between 1890 and 1900 Americans made their country recognizably modern. Financiers and giant corporations assumed control of a vast portion of the American economy. The significance of voting declined, and a decade that opened with a global economic catastrophe ended with a dramatic display of the global reach of U.S. power.

THE CRISIS OF THE 1890S

Financial convulsions, strikes, and the powerlessness of government against wealth rudely reminded Americans of how much their country had changed since the Civil War. When Illinois sent Abraham Lincoln to Congress, Chicago's population was less than 5,000; in 1890 it exceeded 1 million. Gone was the America of myth and memory, where class tensions were slight and upward (or at least westward) mobility seemed easy. Many Americans, one British diplomat noted, predicted the imminent collapse of civilization: "They all begin with the Roman Empire and point out resemblances." Others, however, felt that the United States was passing into a new phase of history that would lead to still greater trials and achievements.

Hard Times

Chicago in 1893 captured the hopes and fears of the new age. To celebrate the 400th anniversary of Columbus's discovery of America, the city staged the World's Columbian Exposition, transforming a lakefront bog into a gleaming vision of the past and the future, but just outside the exposition's gates lay the city of the present. In December 1893 Chicago had 75,000 unemployed, and the head of a local relief committee declared that "famine is in our midst." In the nation's second largest metropolis, thousands lived in shacks or shared rooms in high-rise tenements in which each floor had only a single bathroom. Jobs were hard to find, and when groups of men gathered at the exposition's gates to beg for work, the police drove them away.

As the depression deepened, the Cleveland administration ordered troops to guard Treasury branches in New York and Chicago. Jobless people began banding together, forming "industrial armies," many with decidedly revolutionary aims. Hundreds heeded the call of Jacob Coxey, a prosperous Ohio landowner and Populist. Coxey appealed in 1894 to the unemployed to march on Washington and demand free silver and a public road-building program that would hire a half-million workers. When Coxey set out with 100 followers, reporters predicted the ragged band would disintegrate as soon as the food ran out, but well-wishers turned out by the thousands to greet the Coxeyites and offer supplies for the trip.

Industrial armies set out from Boston, St. Louis, Chicago, Portland, Seattle, and Los Angeles. When Coxey arrived in Washington on May 1 with 500 marchers, Cleveland put the U.S. Army on alert. The march ended ignominiously. In front of the Capitol, police wrestled Coxey into a paddy wagon, and his disillusioned army dispersed. Still, after the march no one could deny that something was seriously wrong. Ray Stannard Baker, a reporter for the *Chicago Record*, acknowledged that "the public would not be cheering the army and feeding it voluntarily without a recognition, however vague, that the conditions in the country warranted some such explosion."

The Overseas Frontier

At noon on September 16, 1893, thousands of settlers amassed along the borders of the Cherokee Strip, a 6-million-acre tract in northwestern Oklahoma. In the next six hours, the last great land rush came to an end. The line of settlement that had been marked on census maps throughout the nineteenth century had ceased to exist.

Frederick Jackson Turner, a historian at the University of Wisconsin, explained the implications of this event. Steady westward movement had placed Americans in "touch with the simplicity of primitive life," he explained, and allowed the nation to renew the process of social development continuously. The frontier furnished "the forces dominating the American character," and without its rejuvenating influence, democracy itself might be in danger. Turner's thesis resonated with Americans' fears that modernity had robbed their country of its unique strengths. For the previous ten years, Populists and financiers had worried that the end of free lands would signal trials for free institutions. "There is no unexplored part of the world left suitable for men to inhabit," Populist writer William "Coin" Harvey claimed, "and now justice stands at bay."

That assertion turned out to be premature. More homesteaders claimed more western lands after 1890 than before, and well into the twentieth century new "resource frontiers"—oil fields, timber ranges, Alaskan ore strikes—were explored. Irrigation technology and markets for new crops created a bonanza for dry-land farmers. Nonetheless, the economic and social upheavals of the 1890s seemed to confirm Turner's contention that new frontiers would have to be found overseas.

While farmers had always needed to sell a large portion of their output abroad, until the 1890s manufactured goods had sold almost exclusively through domestic distribution networks. As the total volume of manufactured goods increased, the composition of exports changed. Oil, steel, textiles, typewriters, and sewing machines made up a larger portion of overseas trade. American consumers still bought nine-tenths of the output of domestic factories, but by 1898 the extra tenth was worth more than $1 billion (see Figure 20–1).

As American firms entered foreign markets they discovered that other nations and empires guarded their markets with restrictive tariffs just as the United States did, to promote domestic manufacturing. Government and business leaders acknowledged that to gain a larger share of world trade, the United States might have to use political or military leverage to pry open foreign markets. Their social Darwinist view of the world—as a jungle in which only the fittest nations would survive—justified engaging in global competition for trade and economic survival.

Recognizing that naval power could extend economic influence, and wanting to find a use for surplus steel, Congress authorized the construction of three large battleships in 1890. In 1894, Congress sent a commission to Nicaragua to study the feasibility of a canal across Central America. In 1895 industrialists organized the National Association of Manufacturers to urge the government to help open for-

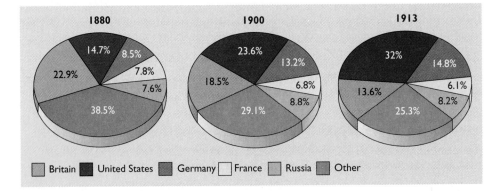

Figure 20–1   Relative Shares of World Manufacturing
The United States was a significant industrial power by 1880, but by the turn of the century it moved into a position of dominance.

eign markets. The administration created a Bureau of Foreign Commerce and urged U.S. consuls abroad to seize opportunities to extend sales of American industrial products.

Congress also knew that tariff rates could influence the expansion of trade. Before 1890 taxes on imports had been set high to raise revenue and to help domestic manufacturers by making foreign goods unaffordable. The Harrison–McKinley Tariff of 1890 did something different. It allowed the president to use the tariff to punish countries that closed their markets to U.S. goods or reward them for lifting customs barriers. This "bargaining tariff" put the full weight of the U.S. economy behind the drive to open markets around the world.

The United States began to reorganize itself to compete in a global marketplace. The struggle required the executive branch to enlarge the military and take on additional authority. It also meant that domestic industries had to produce higher quality goods at less cost to match those being turned out in Germany or Japan. Employers and workers had to gear up for the global contest for profits.

The Drive for Efficiency

In mines, factories, and mills production depended on the knowledge of skilled workers. Laborers used their knowledge to rationalize their work, to set work routines, and to bargain with managers who wanted to change the pace or conditions of work. As profits stagnated and competition intensified, managers tried to prevent labor from sharing control over production. In the struggle for control in the workplace, employers relied on three allies: technology, scientific management, and federal power. Workers resisted, organizing themselves and enlisting the support of their communities.

Advances in management techniques enabled employers to break routines favored by laborers and to dictate new methods. Frederick Winslow Taylor, the first "efficiency expert," reduced each occupation to a series of simple, precise movements that could be easily taught and endlessly repeated. To manage time and motion scientifically, Taylor explained, employers should collect "all of the traditional knowledge which in the past has been possessed by workingmen" and reduce "this knowledge to rules, laws, and formulae."

Taylor's stopwatch studies determined the optimal load of a hand shovel (21.5 pounds), how much pig iron a man could load into a boxcar in a day (75 tons), and the amount the man ought to be paid (3.75 cents per ton). Even office work could be separated into simple, unvaried tasks. Taylorism created a new layer of college-educated "middle managers" who supervised production in offices and factories.

Although Taylorism accelerated production, it boosted absenteeism and job turnover. Telephone operators had a 100 percent yearly turnover rate. Another new technique, "personnel management," promised to solve this problem with tests to select suitable employees, team sports to ward off boredom, and social workers to regulate the activities of workers at home.

As the nineteenth century ended, management was establishing a monopoly on expertise and using it to set the rhythms of work and play, but workers did not easily relinquish control. In the 1890s, the labor struggle entered a new phase. New unions confronted corporations in bloody struggles that forced the federal government to decide whether communities or property had more rights. Skilled workers asserted leadership over the labor movement, and they rallied to the cause of retaining control of the conditions of work.

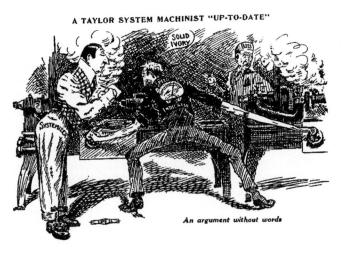

A TAYLOR SYSTEM MACHINIST "UP-TO-DATE"

An argument without words

Corporations used stop-watches and social workers to stretch each machine and worker to full capacity. The method was called Taylorism.

Progress and Force

To accelerate production, employers aimed to seize full control over the workplace. They had private detective agencies at their disposal, the courts on their side, and federal troops ready to act. In Pennsylvania and Chicago this antagonism led to bloody confrontations.

In 1892 Andrew Carnegie's mill at Homestead, Pennsylvania, the most modern steel works in the world, turned out armor plating for American warships and steel rails for shipment abroad. In June Carnegie's partner, Henry Clay Frick, broke off talks with the plant's American Federation of Labor affiliated union and announced that the plant would close on July 2 and reopen a week later with a nonunion work force. The union contended that Frick's actions constituted an assault on the community, and the town agreed. On the morning of July 6, as 300 armed detectives tried to land from barges, they were raked by gunfire. Townspeople forced the detectives to surrender.

The victory was short-lived. A week later the governor of Pennsylvania sent in the state militia, and under martial law strikebreakers reignited the furnaces. Homestead became one of labor's most celebrated battles, but it broke the union and showed that corporations, backed by government, would defend their prerogatives at any cost.

The Pullman strike, centered in Chicago, paralyzed the nation's railroads for two weeks in the summer of 1894. It pitted the American Railway Union (ARU) against 24 railroads and the powerful Pullman Company over the company's decision to cut pay by 30 percent. The calm at the center of the strike was Eugene V. Debs, charismatic president of the ARU, who urged strikers to obey the law, avoid violence, and respect strikebreakers. When Cleveland sent in the Army over the governor's protests, enraged crowds blocked tracks and burned railroad cars. Police arrested hundreds of strikers. Debs went to jail for six months and came out a Socialist. Pullman and Homestead showed that the law was now on the side of the proprietors.

Newspapers, magazines, and novels portrayed Pullman and Homestead as two more battles in an unending war against the savage opponents of progress. Frederic Remington, famous for his reporting on wars against the Navajo and Apache Indians, covered the Pullman strike for *Harper's Weekly*. In his account, rough-hewn cavalrymen, having defeated the Sioux, now came to rescue civilization from the unions.

The business elite's influence over cultural expression (see Chapter 18, "Cultural Struggles of Industrial America") allowed it to define the terms of this contest, to label its enemies as enemies of progress. Workers did not object to efficiency or modernization, but they wanted a share of its benefits and some control over the process of change. With state and corporate power stacked against them, these goals appeared beyond reach.

Just as the massacre at Wounded Knee in 1890 had ended the armed resistance of Native Americans, the violence at Homestead and Chicago signified that the struggle of industrial workers had entered a new phase.

Corporate Consolidation

In a wave of mergers between 1897 and 1904, investment bankers consolidated leading industries under the control of a few corporate giants, and J. P. Morgan led the movement. His goal was to take industry away from the industrialists and give it to the bankers. Bankers, he felt, had better information about the true worth of an industry, and they could make better decisions about its future. Financiers could create the larger and leaner firms needed to take on foreign competitors.

Morgan's greatest triumph was the merger of eight huge steel companies, their ore ranges, rolling mills, railroads, and shipping lines into the colossal U.S. Steel. Announced in March 1901, the merger created the world's largest corporation. Its capital amounted to 7 percent of the total wealth of the United States (by comparison, Microsoft's total assets in 1998 amounted to less than one-third of 1 percent of the gross national product). U.S. Steel's investors (Morgan especially) earned profits "greatly in excess of reasonable compensation," according to one government report.

Bankers outnumbered steelmakers on U.S. Steel's board, and they controlled the company. *McClure's* magazine reported that the new company was "planning the first really systematic effort ever made by Americans to capture the foreign steel trade." Morgan's son wrote to his stepmother that "Father is in the same category with Queen Victoria." He did not say what category U.S. Steel's employees and customers fell into.

A MODERN POLITICAL ECONOMY

Grover Cleveland's bargain with Morgan revived the industrial economy, but farm prices, wages, and the president's popularity remained flat. The escalating cycle of economic and political crises, farmer and labor insurgencies, middle-class radicalism, and upper class conservatism fractured political parties. Democrats, Republicans, and Populists all called for stronger government action, but each party split over what action to take. In 1896 the "currency question" dominated a watershed election that transformed the two major parties and destroyed the third.

Currency and the Tariff

The soundness of the dollar, which Morgan and Cleveland worked so hard to preserve, was a mixed blessing for Americans. Based on gold, the dollar helped sell American goods in foreign markets, especially in Europe, where currencies were also based on gold. The United States traded on a much smaller scale with countries—

like Mexico or China—that used silver. "Without exception," Cleveland's Secretary of Commerce explained, "prices are fixed in the markets of countries having a gold standard." Gold, however, was valuable because it was scarce, and many Americans suffered from that scarcity. The low prices and high interest rates Populists complained of were a result of the gold standard.

Increasing the money supply would reduce interest rates and make credit more available. There were two ways to put more money in circulation: The government could print paper greenbacks, or it could coin silver (see Chapter 19, "The Politics of Industrial America"). "Free silver" advocates generally favored coining a ratio of 16 ounces of silver for each ounce of gold. Populists initially wanted greenbacks but later found silver an agreeable compromise. Western mining interests pushed silver as well. To Americans in the 1890s, the crucial political issues—jobs, foreign trade, the survival of small farms, and the prosperity of big corporations—boiled down to one question: Would the dollar be backed by gold or silver? The election of 1896 was "the battle of the standards."

The Cross of Gold

A dark mood hung over Chicago as delegates arrived at the Democratic Convention in July 1896. They had come to bury Cleveland and the party's commitment to the gold standard along with him. The draft platform denounced Cleveland for imposing "government by injunction" during the Pullman strike. When the platform came before the full convention, delegates had to decide whether the party would stand for silver or gold and who would replace Cleveland as the candidate for president.

Both questions were decided when a former congressman from Nebraska, William Jennings Bryan, mounted the stage. Handsome and only 36 years old, he was an electrifying speaker. "You come and tell us that the great cities are in favor of the gold standard," he said. "Destroy our farms, and the grass will grow in the streets of every city in the country!" Bryan delivered his lines in the rhythmic cadence of a camp preacher. "We will answer their demand for a gold standard by saying to them"—he paused stretching out his arms in an attitude of crucifixion—"You shall not press down upon the brow of labor this crown of thorns. You shall not crucify mankind upon a cross of gold!" The hall exploded with cheers. Bryan won the nomination handily.

Two weeks later the Populists, meeting in St. Louis, also nominated Bryan. The Ocala and Omaha platforms, which imagined comprehensive changes in the money system and American institutions, had been reduced to a single panacea: silver. Republicans overwhelmingly adopted a progold plank drafted with the approval of J. P. Morgan and nominated William McKinley, the governor of Ohio, a supporter of industry. The parties could hardly have offered two more different candidates or two more different visions of the future.

The Battle of the Standards

In one of the most exciting contests since the Civil War, the candidates employed new techniques in radically different ways. McKinley ran like an incumbent: He never left his home. Instead, delegations came to him. Some 750,000 people from 30 states trampled McKinley's grass and listened to speeches affirming the candidate's commitment to high tariffs and sound money. The speeches were set in type and distributed as newspaper columns, fliers, and pamphlets throughout the country. The campaign used public relations techniques to educate the electorate on the virtues of the gold standard. Posters reduced the campaign's themes to pithy slogans like "Prosperity or Poverty," or "Vote for Free Silver and be Prosperous Like Guatemala."

The genius behind the campaign was a Cleveland coal-and-oil millionaire named Marcus Hanna who bankrolled his publicity blitz with between $3 million and $7 million raised from industrialists. He assessed a share of the campaign's expenses from corporations and banks based on calculations of the profitability and net worth of each. The combination of big money and advertising revolutionized presidential politics.

With only $300,000 to spend, Bryan ran like a challenger even though his party occupied the White House. He logged 29,000 miles by rail and buggy and made more than 500 speeches in 29 states. Oratorical ability had won Bryan the nomination, but audiences were unaccustomed to hearing a candidate speak for himself, and many considered it undignified. "The Boy Orator has one speech," wrote an unsympathetic Republican, John Hay. "He simply reiterates the unquestioned truths that . . . gold is vile, that silver is lovely and holy."

Industrialists genuinely feared the prospect of a Bryan presidency. Factory owners threatened to close shop if Bryan won. Just before election day, crop failures abroad doubled the price of wheat in the Midwest. In the final tally, Bryan won the South and West decisively, but McKinley won the populous states of the industrial Northeast, as well as several farm states in the upper Midwest, capturing the electoral college by a majority of 271 to 176.

The election of 1896 changed the style of campaigns and shifted the political positions of both major parties. By pushing currency policies, Bryan's Democrats abandoned their traditional commitment to minimal government. The Republicans recognized that the electorate would judge the president on his ability to bring prosperity to the country. As president, McKinley asserted his leadership over economic policy, calling Congress into special session to pass the Dingley Tariff Act, which levied the highest taxes on imports in American history.

In the election of 1896 fundamental economic questions—Who is the economy supposed to serve? What is the nature of money?—were at stake in a closely matched campaign. No wonder voter turnout hit an all-time high, and Americans long remembered that raucous campaign when the nation's economic future was up for grabs.

THE RETREAT FROM POLITICS

The economy improved steadily after 1895 but this latest business panic and its aftermath left lasting marks on corporate and political culture. Industrial workers made a tactical retreat in the face of a new political and legal climate. In the South, depression, urbanization, and the modernizing influence of railroads accelerated the spread of legalized racial segregation and disfranchisement. What was happening in the South was part of nationwide decline of participatory politics. With the slackening of agrarian unrest and the exhaustion of resistance to corporate capitalism, politics lost some of its value. Voter participation declined, and Americans felt less of a personal stake in election campaigns. Disaffected groups—such as labor and African Americans—had to devise new ways to build community and express resistance.

The Lure of the Cities

In the South as in the North people left the countryside and moved to towns and cities. By 1900 one out of six southerners lived in town. With the lone exception of Birmingham, Alabama, southern cities were not devoted to manufacturing but to commerce and services. Doctors' offices, haberdasheries, dry goods stores, and groceries could be found near warehouses where cotton was stored, ginned, and pressed and near the railway station where it was shipped to textile mills.

The growth of villages and towns in the South was the product of rural decay. Crop liens, which gave bankers ownership of a crop before it was planted, and debt drove people from the countryside. The young and the ambitious left first, while older and poorer residents stayed behind.

While white newcomers settled on the outskirts of towns, African Americans moved into industrial districts along the railroad tracks. Cities became more segregated as they grew, and by 1890 most blocks in the larger cities were either all black or all white. Still, towns offered things that were missing in the country, such as schools. A Little Rock, Arkansas, resident noted that newly arrived African-American parents were "very anxious to send their children to school." Jobs were often available, too, although more frequently for women than for men. Men looked for seasonal labor at farms or lumber camps some distance from town. This meant families faced a tough choice between poverty and separation.

Despite setbacks, the newcomers gained a place for themselves in urban life. By 1890 every southern city had an African-American business district with churches, insurance companies, lawyers, doctors, undertakers, and usually a weekly newspaper. Benevolent and reform organizations, sewing circles, and book clubs enriched community life. There were limits to how high educated African Americans could ascend. Professionals like lawyers, doctors, and nurses had to work within their community. Jobs on the bottom rung of the corporate ladder—clerk, salesman, telephone operator, stenographer, railroad conductor—were reserved for whites.

Inventing Jim Crow

In June 1892 Homer Plessy boarded the East Louisiana Railway in New Orleans for a trip to Covington, Louisiana. Having purchased a first-class ticket, he attempted to board the whites-only car and was arrested under a Louisiana law that required African Americans and whites to ride in "equal but separate accommodations." Before Judge John H. Ferguson could try the case, Plessy's lawyer appealed on the grounds that the separate car law violated the Constitution's Fourteenth Amendment.

When *Plessy* v. *Ferguson* came before the Supreme Court in April 1896, lawyers for the state of Louisiana argued that the law was necessary to avoid the "danger of friction from too intimate contact" between the races. In separate cars, all citizens enjoyed equal privileges. Plessy's lawyer, Albion Tourgée, replied that the question was not "the equality of the privileges enjoyed, but the right of the state to label one citizen as white and another as colored." In doing so, the government gave unearned advantages to some citizens and not to others. The issue for Tourgée was not racial conflict or even prejudice, but whether the government should be allowed to divide people arbitrarily. The court upheld the "separate but equal" doctrine. The Plessy decision provided legal justification for the system of official inequality that expanded in the twentieth century. Informal segregation had existed since the Civil War. People associated with members of their own race when they could, and when they could not—at work, in business, or when traveling—unwritten local customs usually governed their interaction. By the 1890s those informal customs were being codified in law. Railroads, as symbols of progress, were a chief point of contention.

The political and economic tensions created by the depression helped turn racist customs into a rigid caste division. Competition for jobs fed racial antagonisms, as did the migration into cities and towns of a new generation of African Americans, born since the war, who showed less deference to whites. New notions of "scientific" racism led intellectuals and churchmen to regard racial hostility as natural. Angry voters in many southern states deposed the coalitions of landowners and New South industrialists that had governed since Reconstruction and replaced them with Populist "demagogues."

Between 1887 and 1891 nine states in the South passed railroad segregation laws. Trains began pulling separate cars for African Americans, called "Jim Crow" cars after the name of a character in a minstrel show. Soon Jim Crow laws were extended to waiting rooms, drinking fountains, and other places where African Americans and whites might meet.

Segregation was also enforced by terror. The threat of lynching poisoned all relations between the races, and African Americans learned that they could be tortured and killed for committing a crime, talking back, or simply looking the wrong way at a white woman. Lynchings occurred most frequently in areas thinly populated by whites, but killings and mob violence also occurred in the largest cities. Between 1882 and 1903, nearly 2,000 African-American southerners were killed by mobs. Victims were routinely tortured, flayed, castrated, gouged, and burned alive, and members of the mob often took home grisly souvenirs like a piece of bone or a severed thumb.

Many African-American southerners fought segregation with boycotts, lawsuits, and disobedience. Ida Wells-Barnett, a Nashville journalist, organized an international antilynching campaign (see Chapter 21, "A United Body of Action"). Segregation was constantly negotiated and challenged, but after 1896 it was backed by the U.S. Supreme Court.

The Atlanta Compromise

When Atlanta invited African-American educator Booker T. Washington, to address the Cotton States Exposition in 1895, northern newspapers concluded that a new era of racial progress had begun. The speech made Washington the most recognized African American in the United States. Starting with 40 students and an abandoned shack, Washington had built Tuskegee Institute into a nationally known institution, the preeminent technical school for African Americans. Washington was a guest in the stately homes of Newport and at Andrew Carnegie's castle in Scotland. When Atlanta staged an exposition to showcase the region's industrial and social progress, the organizers asked Washington to speak.

Washington's address stressed racial accommodation. It had been a mistake, he argued, to try to attain equality by asserting civil and political rights. "The wisest among my race understand that agitation of questions of social equality is the extremest folly," he said, "and that progress in the enjoyment of all the privileges that will come to us must be the result of severe and constant struggle rather than artificial forcing." He urged white businessmen to employ African-American southerners "who have, without strikes and labor wars, tilled your fields, cleared your forests, builded your railroads and cities." Raising his hand above his head, stretching out

Lynchings were public spectacles. When 17-year-old Jesse Washington was killed in Waco, Texas in 1916, a crowd of several thousand, including the mayor, police chief, and students from Waco High, attended the event on the lawn of city hall. Afterwards, the murderers posed for a photograph and sold their victim's teeth for $5 apiece.

his fingers and then closing them into a fist, he summarized his approach to race relations: "In all things that are purely social, we can be as separate as the fingers, yet one as the hand in all things essential to mutual progress." The largely white audience erupted into applause.

Washington's "Atlanta Compromise" stressed the mutual obligations of African Americans and whites. African Americans would give up the vote and stop insisting on social equality if white leaders would keep violence in check and allow African Americans to succeed in agriculture and business. White industrialists welcomed this arrangement, and African-American leaders felt that for the moment it might be the best that could be achieved.

Disfranchisement and the Decline of Popular Politics

After the feverish campaign of 1896, elections began to lose some of their appeal. Attendance fell off at the polls. Some 79 percent of voters cast ballots in the battle of the standards; eight years later the figure was down to 65 percent. More visibly, the public events surrounding campaigns drew thinner crowds. Organizers fretted about apathy, which seemed to have become a national epidemic.

In the South, the disappearance of voters was easy to explain. As Jim Crow laws multiplied, southern states disfranchised African Americans (and one out of four whites) by requiring voters to demonstrate literacy, property ownership, or knowledge of the Constitution before they could register. Louisiana added the notorious grandfather clause, which denied the vote to men whose grandfathers were prohibited from voting (see Table 20–1).

Whites saw disfranchisement and segregation as modern, managed race relations. Demonizing African Americans enforced solidarity among white voters, who might otherwise have voted on local or class interests.

No new legal restrictions hampered voting in the North and West, but participation fell there, too. This withdrawal from politics reflected the decline of political pageantry as an element of cultural and social life, but it also reflected the disappearance of intense partisanship. For American men, the cliffhanger contests of the late nineteenth century provided a sense of identity that matched and strengthened ethnic, religious, and neighborhood identities.

A developing economy with new patterns of recreation, class relations, and community participation undermined the habits of partisanship, but so did the new style of campaigns. The emphasis on advertising, education, and fundraising reduced the personal stakes for voters. Educated middle- and upper-class voters liked the new style, feeling that raucous campaigns were no way to decide important issues. They sought to influence policy more directly, through interest groups rather than parties. Unintentionally, they discarded traditions that unified communities and made voters feel connected to their country and its leaders.

TABLE 20–1

The Spread of Disfranchisement		
	State	**Strategies**
1889	Florida	Poll tax
	Tennessee	Poll tax
1890	Mississippi	Poll tax, literacy test, understanding clause
1891	Arkansas	Poll tax
1893, 1901	Alabama	Poll tax, literacy test, grandfather clause
1894, 1895	South Carolina	Poll tax, literacy test, understanding clause
1894, 1902	Virginia	Poll tax, literacy test, understanding clause
1897, 1898	Louisiana	Poll tax, literacy test, grandfather clause
1899, 1900	North Carolina	Poll tax, literacy test, grandfather clause
1902	Texas	Poll tax
1908	Georgia	Poll tax, literacy test, understanding clause, grandfather clause

Organized Labor Retreats From Politics

Workers also withdrew from politics as organized labor turned away from political means and goals and redefined objectives in economic terms. As traditional crafts came under attack, skilled workers created new organizations that addressed immediate issues: wages, hours, and the conditions of work. The American Federation of Labor (AFL), founded in 1886, built a base around skilled trades, and grew from 150,000 members to more than 2 million by 1904. The AFL focused on immediate goals that would improve the working lives of its members. Its founder, Samuel Gompers, was born in London's East End and apprenticed as a cigar maker at the age of ten. Three years later his family moved to New York, where Gompers joined the International Cigar Makers Union.

Although affiliated with the Knights of Labor, the cigar makers were more interested in getting higher wages than in remaking the economy. They concentrated on shortening work hours and increasing pay. High dues and centralized control allowed the union to offer insurance and death benefits to members while maintaining a strike fund. Gompers applied the same practices to the AFL. His "pure and simple unionism" made modest demands, but it still encountered fierce resistance from corporations, which were backed by the courts.

In the 1895 case of *In re Debs*, the Supreme Court allowed the use of injunctions to criminalize strikes. The court then disarmed one of the few weapons left in labor's arsenal, the boycott. In the 1908 case of *Loewe* v. *Lawlor*, popularly known as the Danbury Hatters case, the court ruled that advertising a consumer boycott was illegal under the Sherman Anti-Trust Act.

Gompers believed that *industrial unions*, associations that drew members from all occupations within an industry, lacked the discipline and shared values needed to face down corporations and government, and that unions organized around a single trade or craft would break less easily. However, because the AFL was organized by skill, it often ignored unskilled workers, such as women or recent immigrants. Because employers used unskilled newcomers to break strikes or to run machinery that replaced expert hands, Gompers excluded a large part of the labor force. Organizers recruited Irish and German workers through their fraternal lodges and saloons while ignoring Italian, African-American, Jewish, and Slavic workers. The union attacked female workers for stealing jobs that rightfully belonged to men.

Even leaders who rejected Gompers's philosophy and strategy built unions that represented the immediate interests of their members. Under the leadership of Eugene V. Debs, railroad workers merged the old railroad brotherhoods into the ARU in 1893. The United Mine Workers (UMW), founded in 1890, unionized the bituminous (soft coal) mines of Pennsylvania, Ohio, Indiana, and Michigan. The ARU and the UMW were industrial unions that tried to organize all of the workers in an industry. These new unions faced determined opposition from business and its allies in government.

AMERICAN DIPLOMACY ENTERS THE MODERN WORLD

The Republican victory in 1896 encouraged proponents of foreign trade. Before the turn of the century, the new president announced, the United States would control the markets of the globe. Many in McKinley's party wanted both war and colonies. Called "jingoes," they included Assistant Secretary of the Navy Theodore Roosevelt; John Hay, the ambassador to London; and Senators Albert Beveridge and Henry

Cabot Lodge. Britain, France, and Germany were seizing territory around the world, and jingoes believed the United States needed to do the same. McKinley, at first reluctantly but later enthusiastically, pushed for the creation of an American empire that stretched to the far shores of the Pacific.

Sea Power and the Imperial Urge

Few men better exemplified the jingoes' combination of religiosity and martial spirit than Alfred Thayer Mahan. A naval officer and strategist, Mahan connected naval expansion and empire to the problem of overproduction in the United States. A great industrial country needed trade, trade required a merchant fleet, and merchant shipping needed naval protection and overseas bases. Colonies could provide markets for goods and congregations for Christian missionaries, and naval forces could protect sea lanes and project United States power abroad.

World leadership, Mahan argued, belonged to the nation that controlled the sea. He urged the United States to build a canal across Central America, allowing manufacturers on the Atlantic coast to "compete with Europe . . . for the markets of eastern Asia." He felt that naval bases should be established along routes connecting the United States with markets in Latin America and the Far East. Congress and the Navy Department began implementing these recommendations even before McKinley took office.

If subduing continents with cross, Constitution, and gatling gun appealed to anyone, it was Theodore Roosevelt. Imperialism seemed to him the essential characteristic of modernizing countries. Roosevelt was acutely conscious of how modern forces—globalized trade, instant communications, the reach of modern navies, and imperialism—had altered domestic and international politics. He sought to position the United States at the center of these modernizing currents, a place that would have to be earned, he felt, both on foreign battlefields and at home, where the material and technological gains of the nineteenth century had not yet been translated into the social and moral advancement that marked a true civilization. Sharing the social Darwinist belief (see Chapter 18) that nations and races were locked in a savage struggle for survival, Mahan and Roosevelt expected the United States to prevail and benefit from the approaching conflict.

The Scramble for Empire

For jingoes, China was the ultimate prize in the global contest for trade and mastery. It had more people than any other country, hence more customers and more souls to be brought to Christ: The number of American missionaries in China doubled in the 1890s. Even though no more than 1 or 2 percent of U.S. exports went to Chinese ports, manufacturers believed that China could absorb the output of America's overproductive factories. In 1890 Standard Oil began selling kerosene in Shanghai. Fifteen years later, China was the largest overseas market for American oil.

In 1894 Japan declared war on China, and within months it occupied Korea, Manchuria, and China's coastal cities. When the fighting was over, Western powers seized slices of Chinese territory. In November 1897, German troops captured the port of Qingdao on the Shandong Peninsula. An industrial area on the northeast coast, Shandong was the center of American missionary activity, investment, and trade. To Americans, the invasion of Shandong presaged the beginning of an

Thanks to the work of missionaries in China, Mark Twain observed, "the people who sit in darkness ... have become suspicious of the blessings of civilization."

imperial grab for territory and influence. The McKinley administration watched the events unfolding in China carefully, but in the winter of 1897–1898 the Departments of State and War had more pressing concerns closer to home.

War With Spain

While other European powers were expanding their empires, Spain was barely hanging on. Since the 1860s its two largest colonies, Cuba and the Philippines, had been torn by revolution. Between 1868 and 1878 Cuban nationalists fought a prolonged war of independence. Spain ended the war by promising reforms but U.S. tariffs ruined the island's chief export industry, sugar, and plunged the colony into debt. When rebellion resumed in 1895, the rebels practiced a "scorched earth" policy, dynamiting trains and burning plantations to force Spain to withdraw or the United States to intervene.

Spain retaliated with a brutal campaign of pacification. General Valeriano Weyler herded civilians into reconcentration camps enclosed by barbed wire. Nearly 100,000 died, many of them women and children. William Randolph Hearst's *New York Journal* and other newspapers provided readers with lurid details that fixed the public's attention on Cuba.

Cleveland had tried to minimize U.S. involvement in Cuba, but McKinley moved quickly toward confrontation. In July 1897 he demanded that Spain withdraw from Cuba. The government in Madrid retreated, and McKinley breathed a sigh of relief. Despite his bluster, he realized that he could pay for a war only by coining silver. However, events in Havana were soon outracing policy. Riots erupt-ed, and American expatriates demanded protection. The president asked the Navy to send a warship to Havana, and Theodore Roosevelt selected the *Maine*, one of the new battleships that had been built at Mahan's urging (see Map 20–1).

The arrival of the *Maine* reduced tensions for a while, but on February 15 an explosion ripped through the ship. Almost the entire crew of 266 perished. Navy investigators later concluded that the explosion had been internal, probably in the new oil-fired boilers, but the newspapers had already blamed Spanish treachery.

McKinley hesitated, mindful of the budget and the unfolding events in China, but Roosevelt ordered Commodore George Dewey's Asiatic Squadron to Hong Kong to prepare for an attack on Spain's colony in the Philippines. Congress appro-priated $50 million for arms.

In March the economic picture took a turn for the better, and McKinley sent Spain an ultimatum demanding independence for Cuba. On April 11 he asked Congress for authorization to use force, and Congress passed a declaration of war. Expansionists such as Roosevelt, Mahan, and Adams would not have had their way if war had been less popular. Corporate interests favored it, immigrants and south-erners saw it as a way to assert their patriotism, and newspapers found it made good copy. "We are all jingoes now," declared the *New York Sun*.

The war opened with a cliffhanger that even Hearst could not have invented. On May 1 news arrived that Dewey's Asiatic Squadron was battling the Spanish fleet in Manila Bay in the Philippines. The war had begun half a world away on the far edge of the Pacific Ocean. The telegraph cable connecting Manila to the outside world was cut, and for six anxious days the American public awaited word from the Far East.

It arrived in the early morning of May 7, interrupting a poker game in the news-room at the *New York Herald*. The paper's Hong Kong correspondent reported that Dewey had destroyed Spain's entire fleet of 12 warships. The country went wild with relief and triumph. McKinley consulted a map to see where the Philippines were, and Roosevelt quit his job and ordered Brooks Brothers to make him a uniform.

The war in Cuba unfolded less spectacularly. The Navy bottled up Spain's Atlantic fleet in the Bay of Santiago de Cuba. A bit of drama was provided by the voyage of the U.S.S. *Oregon*, which left its West Coast base and traveled around the southern tip of South America in 68 days to join the Atlantic fleet too late for the fighting. Its journey dramatized the need for a canal connecting the Atlantic and the Pacific.

In the years before the war, Congress had poured money into the Navy but not the Army, and it took some time before soldiers could be trained and equipped. Recruits were herded into camps in Florida without tents, proper clothing, or latrines. Soldiers in woolen uniforms died of dysentery and malaria, a scandal that forced the government to elevate the status of the surgeon general and to regard disease prevention as important to national defense.

The Army landed on the Cuban coast and marched inland to engage Spanish defenders. Roosevelt came ashore with the First Volunteer Cavalry, known as the Rough Riders. He recruited, trained, and publicized the regiment, and afterwards he wrote its history, all with an eye to symbolism. The regiment traveled with its own film crew and a correspondent from the *New York Herald*.

Spanish forces stubbornly resisted around the city of Santiago. At San Juan Hill, 500 defenders forced a regiment of the New York National Guard to retreat. The all-African-American 9th and 10th Cavalry took their place along with the Rough Riders, with Roosevelt cautiously waiting until artillery could be brought up from the rear. The capture of Santiago effectively ended Spanish resistance. When fighting

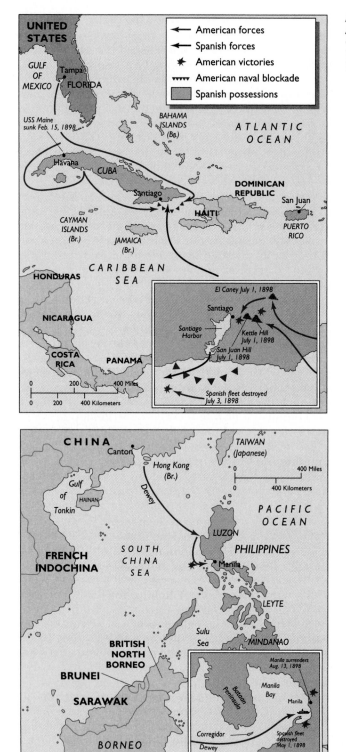

Map 20–1   The Spanish–American War in the Caribbean. The Spanish–American War in the Pacific

ended, U.S. troops occupied Cuba, Guam, Puerto Rico, and the city of Manila. The war had lasted only four months.

As American and Spanish diplomats concluded a peace treaty, McKinley had to decide which occupied territories to keep as colonies. Congress, not wanting to inherit the island's $400 million debt, had already resolved not to annex Cuba. McKinley decided that Guam and Puerto Rico would make ideal naval bases.

The president also seized the opportunity to annex the island nation of Hawaii. In 1893 American sugar planters, led by Sanford Dole, overthrew the islands' last queen, Liliuokalani, and petitioned for annexation (see Chapter 19). They had a powerful ally in the U.S. Navy: Mahan had identified the deep-water port at Pearl Harbor, on Oahu, as a vital base. McKinley now decided to take up Dole's annexation offer.

The Philippines presented more of a problem. Its 7,000 islands were far from the United States and had a population of several million. What the United States needed was a naval base and a fuel station close to the China coast, but holding just one island would be impossible: Shortly after Dewey's victory, British and German warships anchored in Manila Bay, intending to divide up whatever territory the United States did not claim. McKinley felt that he could not let go.

However, the United States did not actually control the Philippines, and in Manila it was increasingly clear that it would take a war to do so. Rebels led by Emilio Aguinaldo had seized most of the country outside of the capital. Rather than surrender to the Filipinos, the Spanish surrendered to the Americans on August 13, 1898. At Malolos, 25 miles north of Manila, Aguinaldo proclaimed himself president of the independent Philippines and issued a constitution modeled on that of the United States. When the U.S. Army finally arrived, American troops filled Spanish trenches opposite the Philippine lines. At the end of 1898, the two armies still faced each other across a no-man's land.

Spanish negotiators recognized Cuban independence and surrendered most of the Spanish empire to the United States for free, but they gave up the Philippines only after the United States agreed to pay $20 million. The treaty was signed December 10, 1898.

The Anti-Imperialists

Many prominent Americans opposed both the annexation of new colonies and the approaching war with the Philippines. The movement included ex-presidents Grover Cleveland and Benjamin Harrison, William Jennings Bryan, labor and business leaders including Samuel Gompers, Eugene Debs, and Andrew Carnegie, and writers such as Mark Twain and Ambrose Bierce. The anti-imperialists advanced an array of moral, economic, and strategic arguments. Filipinos and Hawaiians, they said, had sought American help in good faith and were capable of governing themselves. The islands could not be defended. Imperialism distracted attention from domestic problems and took tax money that could be spent at home. White supremacists asked whether Filipinos would become citizens or be allowed to vote and emigrate to the mainland.

The most moving objections came from those who believed imperialism betrayed America's fundamental principles. "Could there be a more damning indictment of the whole bloated ideal termed 'modern civilization' than this amounts to?" William James asked. To Mark Twain imperialism was the modern form of greed. Opponents of annexation organized an Anti-Imperialist League and lobbied for the rejection of the Paris Treaty.

Congress whittled away at anti-imperialist objections, banning Philippine immigration, placing the colonies outside the tariff walls, and promising eventual self-government. Jingoes had military victory and public acclaim on their side. Anti-imperialists could not offer a vision comparable to naval supremacy, the evangelization of the world, or the fabled China market. On February 6, 1899, the Senate ratified the Paris Treaty and annexed the Philippines. A day earlier, on the other side of the world, the Philippine–American War began.

The Philippine–American War

McKinley believed he had annexed islands full of near savages "unfit for self-rule," but the Philippines by 1899 had an old civilization with a long tradition of resistance to colonialism. When Magellan discovered the islands in 1521, he found a literate population linked by trade to India, Japan, and China. By 1898 much of the upper class, the *illustrados*, had been educated in Europe. Aguinaldo convened a national assembly comprised of doctors, lawyers, professors, and writers.

Dewey had given Aguinaldo his word that America desired no colonies. Aguinaldo continued to have faith in that word long after the occupation of Manila made it clear that the United States intended to stay. On February 4 an argument between American and Filipino sentries ended in gunfire.

By midsummer the Filipino armies fell back into the mountains and abandoned conventional warfare for guerilla tactics. Some 4,000 Americans were killed and another 3,000 wounded out of a total force of 70,000. Frustrated by guerilla conflict, American soldiers executed and tortured prisoners, looted villages, and raped Filipino women. An American general on the island of Samar ordered his soldiers to kill everyone over the age of ten.

Newspaper accounts of torture and massacres fueled opposition to the war, but just as the anti-imperialist movement gained steam, U.S. forces scored some victories. Recognizing that they were fighting a political war, U.S. officers took pains to win over dissidents and ethnic minorities. In early 1901 this strategy paid off when Brigadier General Frederick Funston, leading a band of Filipino fighters working for the U.S., entered Aguinaldo's camp and kidnapped the president.

After three weeks in a Manila prison, Aguinaldo surrendered. "Enough of blood, enough of tears and desolation," he pleaded. Resistance continued for another year. The U.S. Army increased the pressure by imposing the same reconcentration policies the United States had condemned in Cuba, and produced the same result. On July 4, 1902, President Theodore Roosevelt declared the war over.

The Open Door

As Americans celebrated their victories, European powers continued to divide China into quasi-colonial "concessions." An alarmed imperial court in Beijing began a crash program of modernization, but reactionaries within the government overthrew the emperor and installed the conservative "dowager empress" Ci Xi. In the countryside, Western missionaries and traders came under attack from local residents led by street-corner martial artists known as Boxers. Americans feared that the approaching disintegration of China would mean the exclusion of U.S. trade.

To keep China's markets open, Secretary of State John Hay drafted an official letter known as the Open Door Note. Sent to each of the imperial powers, it acknowledged the partitioning of China into spheres, and urged that each of the powers keep its areas open to the trade of other countries.

The Open Door was mostly bluff. The United States had no authority to ask for such a pledge and no military power to enforce one. The foreign ministers of Germany, Japan, Russia, Britain, and France replied cautiously, agreeing to issue a declaration when the others had done so, but Hay adroitly played one power off another. Once Britain and Japan, the two strongest powers in China had agreed, France reluctantly acquiesced, as did Russia and Germany. Hay proclaimed the Open Door as a diplomatic watershed on the order of the Monroe Doctrine. The United States had secured access to China without war or partition, but the limits of Hay's success soon became apparent.

In early 1900, the antiforeign Boxer movement swept through Shandong province, attacking missions and foreign businesses, destroying railroads, and massacring Chinese Christians. Empress Ci Xi recruited 30,000 Boxers into her army and declared war on all foreign countries. The Western powers rushed troops to China, but before they arrived, Chinese armies laid siege to Western embassies in Beijing. An international force of British, Russian, Japanese, and French troops gathered at Tianjin to capture the Chinese capital.

Without consulting Congress, McKinley ordered American troops from Manila to Tianjin. John Hay issued a second Open Door Note, asking the allied countries to pledge to protect China's independence. Again, the imperial powers reluctantly agreed. On August 15, 1900, U.S. cavalry units under General Adna Chaffee reached Beijing along with Russian, French, British-Indian, German, and Japanese troops. After freeing the captive diplomats, the armies looted the city. The United States was unable to maintain the Open Door in China, because Russia and Japan established separate military zones in northeast China in defiance of the Beijing government and American protests. However, the principle of the Open Door, of encouraging free trade and open markets, guided American foreign policy throughout the twentieth century. It rested on the assumption that, in an equal contest, American firms would prevail, spreading manufactured goods around the world, and American influence with them. Just one year after the Spanish–American War, Hay's notes rejected imperial expansion in favor of trade expansion. This bold new strategy placed the United States on a collision course with the great empires of the world.

CONCLUSION

In the turbulent 1890s the social and economic divisions among Americans widened. The hope that a solution to these divisions could be found outside the United States was short-lived. Imperialism promised new markets and an end to the wrenching cycle of depression and labor strife. The United States conquered an overseas empire and challenged other empires to open their ports to free trade, but the goal of prosperity and peace at home proved elusive.

In many ways social Darwinism became a self-fulfilling prophecy, as competition rather than compromise prevailed. Workers and businessmen, farmers and bankers, middle-class radicals and conservatives, whites and African Americans saw each other as enemies. Racial segregation showed that middle ground, where whites and African Americans could meet on equal terms, had disappeared. Workers, farmers, African Americans, radicals, and reformers had to decide what was politically possible and devise new bargaining strategies.

Economic recovery and victory in global conflict closed the decade on an optimistic note. Prosperity, power, and technology seemed to have rewritten the rules of human affairs to America's advantage. Henry Adams, standing in the American

CHRONOLOGY

1890	Global depression begins United Mine Workers founded Battle of Wounded Knee ends Indian wars Harrison–McKinley Tariff passed Standard Oil markets kerosene in China
1892	Homestead strike
1893	Financial crisis leads to business failures and mass unemployment World's Columbian Exposition in Chicago Cherokee Strip land rush American sugar planters overthrow Queen Liliuokalani of Hawaii
1894	Coxey's Army marches on Washington Pullman strike U.S. commission charts canal route across Nicaragua
1895	Morgan agrees to Treasury bailout Booker T. Washington gives "Atlanta Compromise" address Revolution begins in Cuba Japan annexes Korea and Taiwan
1896	*Plessy* v. *Ferguson* declares "separate but equal" facilities constitutional William McKinley elected president
1897	Germany captures Qingdao, on China's Shandong Peninsula
1898	Maine explodes in Havana's harbor U.S. declares war on Spain Dewey defeats Spanish fleet at Manila Bay In the Treaty of Paris, Spain grants Cuba independence, cedes Guam, Puerto Rico, and the Philippines to the United States Aguinaldo proclaims Philippine independence
1899	Senate votes to annex Puerto Rico, Hawaii, and the Philippines Philippine–American War begins Hay issues first Open Door Note
1900	Hay issues second Open Door Note U.S. Army joins British, French, Russian, German, and Japanese forces in capture of Beijing Great Exposition of Paris showcases American technology William McKinley re-elected
1901	Aguinaldo captured McKinley assassinated; Theodore Roosevelt becomes president
1902	Roosevelt declares Philippine–American war over

exhibit at the Paris Exposition of 1900 contemplated a 40-foot dynamo—a "huge wheel, revolving within arm's-length at some vertiginous speed, and barely murmuring"—and felt as if he had crossed a "historical chasm." The machine's immense force, scarcely understood or controlled and emanating from "a dirty engine-house carefully kept out of sight," seemed a metaphor for the power of the modern age.

FURTHER READINGS

Edward L. Ayers, *The Promise of the New South: Life After Reconstruction* (1992). A study of daily life, work, and politics in the turn-of-the-century South.

H. W. Brands, *The Reckless Decade: America in the 1890s* (1995). A lively look at some of the decade's noteworthy events and characters.

Ron Chernow, *The House of Morgan: An American Banking Dynasty and the Rise of Modern Finance* (1990). The life and business of J. P. Morgan and his heirs, the lions of Wall Street for more than a century.

James B. Gilbert, *Perfect Cities: Chicago's Utopias of 1893* (1991). The fears and dreams that led Chicago's elite to create the World's Columbian Exposition.

Robert Kanigel, *The One Best Way: Frederick Winslow Taylor and the Enigma of Efficiency* (1997). The most famous efficiency expert and how his system changed the world.

Stanley Karnow, *In Our Image: America's Empire in the Philippines* (1989). America's colonial venture in the Philippines from 1898 to 1986.

David L. Lewis, *W. E. B. Du Bois: Biography of a Race, 1868–1919* (1993). The story of the man who "pleaded with a headstrong, careless people to despise not Justice," and the era that produced him.

Ivan Musicant, *Empire by Default: The Spanish American War and the Dawn of the American Century* (1998). A misnamed but thorough account of the war and its meaning.

Nick Salvatore, *Eugene V. Debs: Citizen and Socialist* (1982). From the railroad yards to federal prison, the story of one of America's great labor leaders.

Please refer to the document CD-ROM for primary sources related to this chapter.

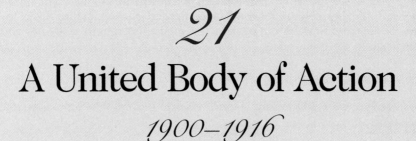

CHAPTER

21

A United Body of Action

1900–1916

Alice Hamilton • Toward a New Politics • The Progressives
Progressives in State and Local Politics • The Presidency Becomes
"The Administration" • Rival Visions of the Industrial Future
Conclusion

ALICE HAMILTON

On an October morning in 1902, three friends, Maude Gernon of the Chicago Board of Charities, Gertrude Howe, director of the kindergarten at Hull House, and Dr. Alice Hamilton, a professor of pathology at Northwestern University, stood over two open sewer drains catching flies. Hamilton had organized the hunting expedition to prove a point. Chicago was in the grip of a typhoid epidemic. The disease had ravaged the city's 19th Ward, a working-class neighborhood. To find out why, Hamilton "prowled about the streets and the ramshackle wooden tenement houses," which often had illegal outdoor privies because landlords refused to install plumbing. It was then that she noticed the flies. Army doctors in the Spanish–American War had found a link between flies, poor sanitation, and the spread of typhoid. Hamilton incubated her test tubes for several days, examined the contents under a microscope, and confirmed that Chicago's flies carried the typhoid bacillus.

When her findings appeared in the *Journal of the American Medical Association*, they touched off a furor. Hull House attacked the Board of Health for failing to enforce sanitary codes, and an inquiry discovered that landlords bribed sanitation inspectors to overlook the outdoor privies. Further investigations found that tap water was pumped straight from Lake Michigan and that broken pumping equipment channeled raw sewage into the water mains. Chicago's city government was directly responsible for an epidemic that killed hundreds of people.

Hamilton chose to become a doctor because "I could go anywhere I pleased . . . and be quite sure that I could be of use anywhere." She attended the Fort Wayne College of Medicine and in 1892 entered the University of Michigan, later doing advanced work in bacteriology and pathology at Leipzig and Munich. Despite her training, she was not able to find work anywhere she pleased, but in Chicago she found a university position and a supportive environment in Hull House, a "settlement house" founded by women who wanted to live among the poor and avoid patronizing forms of charity. Hamilton lived there for 22 years while conducting research on tuberculosis among Jewish garment workers in the neighborhoods nearby. Hamilton pushed for state laws on occupational disease, and in 1911 Illinois became the first state to pass legislation giving workers compensation for job-related disability. By the 1930s, all major industrial states had similar laws.

Alice Hamilton was among the thousands of "progressives" who reshaped government and business by intervening in politics in new ways. Responding to the challenges of immigration, industrialization, and urbanization, Americans agitated for change on a broad variety of issues. Women, who did not have the vote, took the lead and created a new style of political activism.

Some reformers feared the uncontrolled wealth and power of corporations, while others feared losing wealth and power to the uncontrolled political passions of the poor. Although they disagreed on many of their goals and methods, progressives saw politics and economics, according to W. E. B. Du Bois, as "but two aspects of a united body of action and effort." They were pessimistic about the ability of people, particularly nonwhite people, to improve themselves. Science and evangelical Protestantism, as progressives understood them, justified the supervision of human affairs by qualified experts and the state.

Although reformers accepted capitalism and industry as fixtures of a modern political economy, they were outraged by the disease, waste, and corruption the factory system left behind. They sought a middle ground between revolutionary socialism and uncontrolled corporate capitalism. Progressivism, as it came to be called, was the first and perhaps the only reform movement experienced by all Americans.

TOWARD A NEW POLITICS

The political and economic crises of the 1890s contributed to the strength of progressivism. Politics became less participatory, and millions of Americans lost the strong loyalties they once had to traditional parties. Egged on by a national press, progressives organized at the local, state, and national levels to solve the problems of the new industrial world. Progressives recognized that large-scale industrial capitalism was here to stay and worked to make an erratic and brutal system more predictable, efficient, and humane. In pushing for reform, however, they were willing to use state power to tell people what was good for them and then make them do it. The movement rewrote the Democratic and Republican platforms and gave politics a new purpose.

The Insecurity of Modern Life

Most people who lived in cities at the turn of the century had grown up in the country or in smaller towns. They remembered living in communities where people knew each other, where many of the foods they ate and clothes they wore were made locally. In contrast, life in a modern metropolis, connected by rail, telephone, and telegraph to other cities and the world beyond meant depending on strangers. Meat and bread came not from a familiar butcher or baker, but from distant packinghouses and producers. Tap water, gas for heating and lighting, and transportation were all supplied by large, anonymous corporations. City dwellers felt more sophisticated than their parents but also less secure.

City living carried risks. In Chicago marketplaces journalist Upton Sinclair found milk preserved with formaldehyde, peas colored green with copper salts, and smoked sausage doctored with toxic chemicals. Druggists sold fraudulent cures for imaginary diseases. Cures available over the counter included wood alcohol, cocaine, heroin, and other dangerous substances.

Simply finding a place to live could involve hazards. Tenement blocks housing hundreds of people often had no fire escapes or plumbing. Unscrupulous bankers and real estate brokers could hoodwink families out of their savings. Consumers were at the mercy of unrestrained monopolies and hucksters.

Tragedy reminded New Yorkers of these dangers on March 25, 1911, when fire engulfed the Triangle Shirtwaist Company. On the top three floors of a ten-story building, 500 Jewish and Italian women manufactured blouses. When fire broke out, they raced for the exits, which had been locked to discourage employees from taking breaks. Desperate to escape the flames, many women jumped from ledges in groups, holding hands. Others dove into empty elevator shafts. In all, 146 died. Such episodes demonstrated to many Americans that although the political economy was enormously productive, it was also deadly.

Government not only failed to address these problems, it contributed to them. Regulation by legislature or elected city officials often supplied a pretext for kickbacks and bribery. City and state machines were riddled with graft. In 1904 and 1905, journalists and investigators uncovered corruption in state after state. Trials in San Francisco disclosed that Boss Abraham Ruef ruled the city with a slush fund donated by public utilities. The Minneapolis police, with the connivance of the mayor's office, protected brothels and gambling dens in return for bribes. By creating a demand for campaign contributions and jobs for loyal party officials, elections became invitations to graft. Politics, journalist Lincoln Steffens complained, merely amplified the power of big corporations.

Around many urban centers a ring of "street car suburbs" grew in the latter years of the nineteenth century, filled with Victorian homes belonging to business managers, accountants, engineers, lawyers, doctors, and highly skilled workers. These citizens became conscious of themselves as a class, with common interests and common ideas on how cities should run. Modern corporations had to have clear lines of authority, an emphasis on efficiency, and reliable sources

Employers had locked the emergency exits when fire broke out at the Triangle Shirtwaist Factory. The death toll provoked state and federal investigations and a public clamor for regulation.

of information. Yet these virtues were frustratingly absent from civic life. Government needed to become more responsive, accountable, and vigilant against dangers to the public.

The Decline of Partisan Politics

In the early twentieth century many Americans, particularly the middle and upper classes, began seeking new ways to compel government to deal with the problems of industrial, urban society. They demanded civil service reform, the regulation of monopolies, and an end to the rule of party machines. They voted not as members of a party but as independents.

As the new activism increased, popular party politics declined. Participation in national and state elections dropped off sharply (see Figure 21–1). Literacy tests accounted for much of the decline in the South, but in all regions the old spectacular style of electioneering gave way to campaigns that were more educational and less participatory. "Listless" was how one observer described the 1904 turnout. Worse from the parties' point of view, more voters split their tickets. The ethnic and sectional loyalties that led people to vote a straight party ballot in the late nineteenth century were weakening.

Increasingly, Americans participated in politics through voluntary associations. Pressure groups took over important functions that formerly belonged to the parties: educating and socializing voters and even making policy. Some voluntary organizations were concerned with public morals, others with urban corruption, restraining monopolies, or caring for the poor. A few functioned almost as parties did, even running candidates for local office, but most worked outside the system to gather support for a particular cause or proposal. Built on the idea that reform was a continuous process, they strove for permanence. Some, like the National Association for the Advancement of Colored People (NAACP), the Salvation Army, and the Sierra Club, remain prominent today.

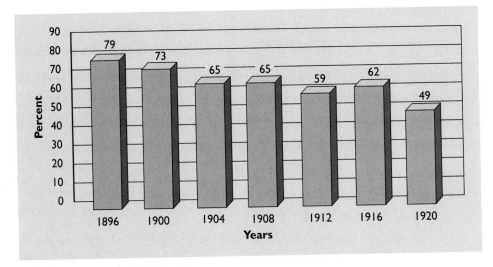

Figure 21–1   Voter Participation, 1896–1920
After the intense partisanship and high-stakes elections of the 1890s, campaigns became more "educational" and voters lost interest.
Source: Michael E. McGerr, The Decline of Popular Politics (New York: Oxford University Press, 1986), pp. 185–186.

Social Housekeeping

The growing clamor for social change aroused latent political strength in unexpected places. Women's social clubs had been nonpolitical before the turn of the century. Club women, generally white and upper or middle class, enjoyed sufficient freedom from housework to attend meetings dedicated to art, speaking, reading, and conversation. They met "without some work of benevolence or reform in view," but were nonetheless highly organized, with local, state, and national chapters. The urgency of social problems led many clubs to launch campaigns on behalf of free kindergartens, civil service reform, and public health.

Club women explained that activism was a natural outgrowth of their domestic responsibilities as wives and mothers. One could hardly keep a safe, comfortable home in the midst of a dangerous and corrupt community. Club membership grew alongside activism. The 50,000 members of the General Federation of Women's Clubs in 1898 expanded by 1914 to well over a million, and the organization became a powerful lobby. In some communities the women's club was the only organized voice for civic improvement.

By the turn of the century, the first generation of graduates from the new women's colleges had reached adulthood—and some, like Alice Hamilton, had attained advanced professional degrees—at a time when few men had a college education. These "new women," as historians have called them, had different ambitions and values from women of their mothers' generation. About half of the female college graduates did not marry. Because the career paths their male classmates followed were closed to them, educated women served in voluntary organizations. Reform politics allowed them to use their talents for a larger purpose.

Educated women found careers by finding problems that needed solving. Florence Kelley, trained as a lawyer, became Illinois' first state factory inspector and later directed the National Consumers' League. Margaret Sanger, a New York public health nurse, distributed literature on birth control and sex education when it was illegal to do so. Female activists "discovered" problems, publicized them, lobbied for new laws, and then staffed the bureaus and agencies created to administer solutions.

Middle-class women remained concerned with the welfare of women and children and with issues related to their homes and neighborhoods. By uniting with others around the country, however, they changed the political culture. Activities that had once been considered charity or volunteer work became political. Through national networks, activists learned that the problems of their neighborhoods arose elsewhere and could not be solved at the local level. Ultimately, to maintain decent and safe homes, women needed the help of the state.

The logic of social housekeeping called for enlarging state powers and increasing women's influence over the state. The experiences of women's clubs and associations taught political activists the importance of cooperation, organization, and expertise. When women's clubs built a playground and donated it to the city or urged lawmakers to address an issue, they increased their own stake in the political system. They gave themselves new reasons to demand full citizenship.

The women's suffrage movement quietly built momentum in the early years of the century. Women had gained the vote in four states—Colorado, Wyoming, Utah, and Idaho—early on, but between 1896 and 1910 no other states adopted a women's suffrage amendment.

Competing suffrage organizations joined forces under the National American Women's Suffrage Association (NAWSA), which developed a strategy based on professional lobbying and publicity. Suffragists appealed to club women and middle-class reformers by linking suffrage to moderate social causes, such as temperance and education. This strategy paid off: After 1910, five states adopted suffrage amendments in rapid succession, but the opposition rallied and defeated referendums in three eastern states.

Frustrated with the glacial pace of progress, Alice Paul's National Woman's Party adopted more radical tactics, picketing the White House and staging hunger strikes. Despite setbacks, women led the transformation of politics through voluntary organizations and interest groups and were on the threshold of even greater gains.

Evolution or Revolution?

No group was more buoyantly optimistic about the prospects for revolutionary change than the Socialists. The Socialist Party of America (SPA) met in Indianapolis in the summer of 1901 and declared its confidence in the inevitability of capitalism's downfall. By 1912, Eugene V. Debs, the party's candidate for president, garnered almost 1 million votes, some 6 percent of the total. Socialists elected two members of Congress, 56 mayors, and 33 state legislators.

Even more impressive was their influence within the labor movement. A third of the delegates to the AFL's 1912 convention had party cards. Jewish workers in New York and Germans in Milwaukee formed powerful urban voting blocs. "Gas and water" Socialists, who demanded public ownership of utilities, captured municipal offices in smaller cities across the country. In the plains states, socialism drew strength from primitive Baptist and Holiness churches and held revival-style tent meetings.

Debs's party dreamed of a peaceful evolution to an economy that rewarded cooperation and valued human labor. Although tinged with religion, Socialists' analysis of modern problems was economic. They maintained that the profit motive distorted human behavior, forcing people to compete instead of joining together to promote the common good. Driven by the need for profits, corporations could not be trusted to look after the welfare of their customers or workers. Socialists demanded the collective ownership of industries, starting with railroads and city utilities. They were sure socialism was coming "like a prairie fire," a socialist newspaperman told his readers, "You can see it in the papers. You can taste it in the price of beef."

When the Industrial Workers of the World (IWW), known as the Wobblies, talked about revolution they meant a war, not an election. Founded in 1905, the IWW unionized some of the most rugged individuals in the West: miners, loggers, and even rodeo cowboys. Wobblies organized unskilled workers, challenging both the AFL's elite unionism and the Socialists' gradualism. Membership remained small, fewer than 100,000, but the union frightened people with its calls for sabotage and a general strike. At IWW strikes in Lawrence, Massachusetts, and Paterson, New Jersey, strikers clashed with police and paraded with red flags. To sensationalist newspapermen and anxious middle-class readers, these activities were signs of approaching class warfare.

Socialism's greatest influence might have been the push it gave conservatives to support moderate reform. Theodore Roosevelt worried that unless something was done the United States might split into two parties, one representing workers, the other capital.

The failure of the two parties to deal with urgent social problems created a chance to redefine politics and citizenship. Precisely because they had been outside the system, women—particularly middle-class, educated, Protestant women—gained a moral authority that enabled them to transform humanitarian concerns and voluntary activities into a new kind of politics. The specter of revolution aided their efforts. As the new century began, Americans were scrapping their old political rules and getting ready to fashion new institutions to deal with the challenges of modern society.

THE PROGRESSIVES

As the old politics declined, a new politics of associations and activists took its place. Historians have found it difficult to define the progressives. Progressives addressed a wide variety of social problems with many different tactics, but for people of the time the connectedness was apparent. A rally to end child labor, for instance, might draw out young lawyers, teachers, labor unionists, woman suffragists, professors, and politicians. A series of overlapping movements, campaigns, and crusades defined the era from 1890 to 1920.

Progressivism was not a unified movement with a platform or set of goals. It was more like a political style, a way of approaching problems. Progressives had no illusions that wage labor or industrialism could be eliminated or that it was possible to re-create a rural commonwealth, but they shared an optimistic conviction that modern institutions could be made humane, responsive, and moral.

In choosing solutions, progressives relied on scientific expertise. Rival points of view could be reconciled more easily by impartial authority. Like the salaried managers many of them were, progressives valued efficiency and organization. No problem could be solved in a single stroke. Instead, remedies could be enforced only by repeated actions by institutions dedicated to reform. Instead of organizing a reform party, progressives formed interest groups to lobby government and raise public awareness.

Convinced that science and God were on their side, progressives often imposed their views on others. Such measures as identifying "born criminals" who could be put on probation for life without ever having committed a crime would be described as "progressive." To southern progressives "scientific" principles of race justified segregation and paternalism. Reforms could be unpopular—as the drive to ban alcoholic beverages was—but this posed a strategic rather than a philosophical problem. Progressives demanded more democracy when it led to "good government," but if, in their view, the majority was wrong progressives readily handed power to unelected managers.

Progressives shared the conviction that social problems required urgent action. "There are two kinds of people," Alice Hamilton learned from her mother, "the ones who say 'Someone ought to do something about it but why should it be I?' and the ones who say, 'Somebody must do something about it, then why not I?'" Hamilton and other progressives were the second kind.

Social Workers and Muckrakers

Among the first to hear the call to service were the young women and men who volunteered to live among the urban poor in "settlement houses." Stanton Coit established the first on New York's lower east side in 1886, but the most famous was Hull House, which opened in Chicago three years later. Its founders, Jane Addams and Ellen Starr, bought a run-down mansion, formerly a country estate, that now stood among sweatshops, factories, and overcrowded tenements. Poverty, back-breaking labor, and disease blighted life for residents of the 19th Ward. The women of Hull House attacked these problems by opening a kindergarten and a clinic, taking sweatshop bosses to court, investigating corrupt landlords, criticizing the ward's powerful alderman, and building the first public playground in Chicago.

Addams drew together a remarkable group of women with similar backgrounds. Florence Kelley pushed some of the nation's first occupational safety laws through the Illinois legislature. Julia Lathrop headed the state's Children's Bureau. All three women were raised in affluent Quaker homes, and their parents were all abolitionists. Like Alice Hamilton, all three attended college and afterward traveled or studied in Europe.

As the fame of Hull House spread, women (and some men) organized settlement houses in other cities. By 1910 there were more than 400. Reformers often began by using social science techniques to survey the surrounding neighborhoods, gathering information on the inhabitants' national origins, income, housing conditions, and occupations. One of the most ambitious research projects was the Pittsburgh Survey, a six-volume study of conditions in the steel city published between 1909 and 1914. By relying on survey data, progressives acknowledged that the causes of poverty were social, not personal. Because economic conditions, not laziness or immorality, caused poverty, progressives did not offer charity; they were social workers.

This outlook motivated settlement workers to attack urban problems across a broad front. Social workers labored to improve the urban environment by making food safe, repairing housing, and sponsoring festivals and pageants. Working conditions, especially for women and children, drew special attention, but the "young enthusiasts" attacked with equal indignation working-class vices—gambling dens, saloons, and brothels.

Settlements touched many lives. Harry Hopkins, Eleanor Roosevelt, and Frances Perkins, who would each attain political prominence in the 1930s, acquired a taste for activism in settlement houses. Others participated vicariously by reading popular books written by settlement workers. Newspaper accounts and memoirs awakened readers to the suffering of the urban poor and carried the hopeful message that action and intelligence could change things for the better.

The loudest voice of progressivism came from a new type of journalism introduced on the pages of *McClure's* magazine in 1902. *McClure's* published Lincoln Steffens's investigation of graft in St. Louis, "The Shame of the Cities," and Ida Tarbell's "History of the Standard Oil Company," two sensational exposés that disclosed crimes of the nation's political and economic elite. As cities grew and periodicals competed for a mass readership, newspapers and magazines enticed readers with promotional stunts, crusades, celebrity correspondents, and "sob sister" features. The new ten-cent magazines, like *Everybody's, Cosmopolitan,* and *McClure's,* had national audiences and budgets big enough to pay for in-depth investigations. The result was a type of reporting Theodore Roosevelt disdainfully called "muckraking." An article exposing some new corporate or public villainy could easily sell half a million copies.

Upton Sinclair described the grisly business of canning beef. Ray Stannard Baker investigated railroads and segregation. Samuel Hopkins Adams cataloged the damage done by narcotics in popular medicines. Tarbell's articles in *McClure's* exposed John D. Rockefeller's methods: camouflaged companies, espionage, sweetheart deals, and predatory pricing. The series shattered the notion that industrial giants competed in a free market. Amid a national outcry, the Justice Department sued Standard Oil in 1906 for conspiracy to restrain trade.

The ten-cent magazines reached subscribers across the country and projected local problems onto a national canvas. Newspapers had covered municipal corruption before, but Steffens's series revealed that bribery, influence peddling, and protection rackets operated in nearly every major city. Magazines also carried news of progressive victories, allowing solutions adopted in one city to spread to others. Muckraking translated the outrage of millions of readers into "public opinion," a force that could shake politicians and powerful corporations.

Dictatorship of the Experts

For doctors, lawyers, engineers, and members of other licensed occupations, progressive reforms offered a chance to apply their special skills to urgent problems. Experts like Alice Hamilton led crusades and adorned the boards of reform leagues. Much of the reformers' optimism came from their faith in the powers of science and expertise to solve modern problems. Rapid advances seemed to justify this faith. In just a generation, antiseptic techniques and a new understanding of disease transformed medicine from a collection of folk beliefs into a science. Advances in engineering, architecture, chemistry, and agriculture confirmed science's ability to shape the future.

Crime, education, labor relations, and other problems came under attack from social engineers using scientific or pseudoscientific methods. Social workers copied doctors, diagnosing each case with clinical impartiality and relying on tests and individual histories. Dietitians descended on school cafeterias, banishing pierogies and souvlaki and replacing them with bland but nutritionally balanced meals.

Trust in science sometimes led to extremes. One was the practice of eugenics, an attempt to rid society of crime, insanity, and other defects through selective breeding. In 1907 Indiana passed a law authorizing the forced sterilization of "criminals, idiots, rapists, and imbeciles." Seven other states followed suit.

Behind progressives' emphasis on expertise lay a thinly veiled distrust of democracy. Education reform was one example. Professional educators took control of the schools, certified teachers, and classified students based on "scientific" intelligence tests. Reformers wanted to consolidate schools and extend education beyond the eighth grade. The new "high schools" had courses that prepared students to become experts themselves. To reformers, education was far too important to be left to amateurs, like teachers, parents, or voters.

Progressivism created new social sciences, such as sociology, changed the agendas of others, and made universities into centers of advocacy. The study of government became political science, and "scientific" historians searched the past for answers to modern problems. John R. Commons, Richard Ely, and Thorstein Veblen used economics to study modern institutions. Legal scholars like Louis Brandeis and Roscoe Pound called for revising the law to reflect social realities.

This stress on expertise made progressive-era reforms different from earlier ones. Instead of trying to gain success at a single stroke—by passing a law or trouncing a corrupt politician—progressives believed reform had to be a process. When they could, progressives set up permanent organizations and procedures that would keep the pressure on and make progress a habit.

Progressives on the Color Line

In her international crusade against lynching, Ida B. Wells-Barnett pioneered some of the progressive tactics of research, exposure, and organization. She documented mob violence against African Americans and mobilized opinion in the United States and Britain. As her Afro-American Council took on national and then international scope, she joined forces with white suffragists, social workers, and journalists, but her cause fell outside of the progressive mainstream. Theodore Roosevelt's Progressive Party refused to seat African-American delegates to its convention or even to hear a resolution that called for equal rights.

Wells-Barnett referred to lynch mobs and their supporters as "barbarians," inverting the progressives' code word for peoples eligible for patronizing. Reformers debated how much progress Native Americans, African Americans and other non-Anglo-Saxons were capable of, but they were inclined to be pessimistic. Following educated opinion, public policy incorporated assumptions about the diminished capabilities of various races. Trade schools, not universities, were deemed appropriate for educating Filipinos and Hawaiians. Progressives took Indian children from their families and placed them in boarding schools. The "scientific" racism of the day classified nonwhites as subjects to control rather than citizens.

Wells-Barnett was not alone in finding doors through this stone wall of racial ideology. William Edward Burghardt Du Bois documented the costs of racism in *The Philadelphia Negro* (1898). Sponsored by settlement workers, the survey spoke the progressives' language, insisting that discrimination was not just morally wrong but inefficient, because it took away steady work and encouraged alcoholism and crime. Du Bois soon transformed the politics of race in America as profoundly as Addams had transformed the politics of the cities.

Raised in Massachusetts in a large family that had been free citizens for three generations, Du Bois learned Latin and Greek in public schools. At 17, he received a scholarship to Fisk University in Tennessee, where he "came in contact for the first time with a sort of violence that I had never realized in New England." He also had his first encounter with African-American religion and gospel music, which stirred him deeply. Du Bois later studied at Harvard and the University of Berlin.

Du Bois and Booker T. Washington (see Chapter 20, "Industry and Empire") espoused opposing visions of African Americans' place in the political economy of the United States. Both emphasized the importance of advancement through thrift and hard work. Du Bois, however, rejected Washington's willingness to accept legal inequality. Gradually, Du Bois believed that the Atlanta Compromise led to disfranchisement and segregation and disliked the way Washington's influence with the national press and his standing with white philanthropists silenced other voices.

In *The Souls of Black Folk* (1903), Du Bois argued that the strategy of accommodation contained a "triple paradox": Washington had urged African Americans to seek industrial training, build self-respect, and become successful in business, but to stop striving for higher education, civil rights, or political power. How could a people train themselves without higher education or gain self-respect without having any of the rights of citizens? Economic, political, and educational progress had to move together. African Americans could not stop demanding the right to vote, civic equality, or education at all levels.

In July 1905, Du Bois and 28 prominent African-American leaders met on the Canadian side of Niagara Falls (hotels on the United States side would not accept African-American lodgers) to declare that "the voice of protest of ten million Americans must never cease to assail the ears of their fellows, so long as America is unjust." The Niagara Movement was one of several organizations formed to lobby against racial violence, segregation, and disfranchisement. In 1909, Ida Wells-Barnett,

Editor of The Crisis (circulation 103,000), William Edward Burghardt Du Bois was the voice of African-American progressives. "We expect revolutionary changes to come mainly through reason, human sympathy, and the education of children," he wrote.

Lillian Wald, Jane Addams, and other reformers formed the NAACP and named Du Bois as editor of its newspaper, *The Crisis.* The NAACP attacked segregation and disfranchisement in print and the courts. In 1915 it won a Supreme Court decision outlawing the grandfather clause, which denied the vote to descendants of slaves.

In the towns and modern cities of the South, whites struggled to maintain their system of social and legal supremacy, while African Americans fought to fulfill the promise of freedom. By challenging the laws and customs that supported injustice, Du Bois anticipated the struggle against segregation and disfranchisement that would take the next 60 years to complete. "The problem of the Twentieth Century," he predicted, "is the problem of the color line."

PROGRESSIVES IN STATE AND LOCAL POLITICS

Progressives were of two minds about the public. Walter Lippmann, a journalist and reformer, wrote fondly of "the voiceless multitudes," but contemptuously of the "great dull mass of people who just don't care." As reformers engaged in politics, their tactics betrayed this split vision. To bring the cities and states under control, they made changes that enlarged the influence of the small-town and urban-middle-class reform constituency while reducing that of immigrants and the working class.

Redesigning the City

The political insiders who ran American cities proved remarkably adaptable to the changing political environment. To immigrants and factory workers, the local boss was one of the few people looking out for the interests of the average person. He rushed to fire scenes to offer help to victims. He distributed turkeys at Christmas. When a family member was jailed or out of work, he was ready to help. Jane Addams acknowledged that as a benefactor to the city's disinherited, Hull House had nothing on Johnny Powers, boss of Chicago's 19th Ward, "a stalking survival of village kindness."

Yet Powers and other aldermen also sheltered the brothels, saloons, gambling dens, and petty "boodlers" who, in Addams's view, exploited honest workers. Big corporations could do what they liked, so long as they padded the right wallets. As city budgets and tax burdens grew, voters turned to reform candidates. Decrying the faults and ignoring the merits of machine politics, progressives set out to replace the fatherly generosity of the ward boss with efficient, scientific administration.

After the depression of 1893, scores of city improvement leagues and good government associations sprang up. The structure of many cities resembled the federal government in miniature. A mayor, elected by the whole city, presided over a council comprised of representatives from each neighborhood, or ward. This system diluted the influence of the "better classes," reformers argued, and allowed the chiefs of a few powerful wards to rule the city. In 1899 Louisville's Conference for Good City Government proposed a new model, the "strong mayor" system. It abolished wards, gave more power to the mayor, and required that the council be chosen in citywide elections. Two years later, Galveston, Texas, experimented with an even bolder plan, placing power in the hands of a nonpartisan commission of five officials, each of whom managed a city department. Des Moines, Iowa, copied and improved on Galveston's design, and by 1911 some 160 cities had commission governments.

The city commission plan imitated features of the modern corporation. The commission was comparable to a board of directors. The honesty and skills that made for business success, reformers argued, could improve a city, too. This philosophy led Detroit voters to elect Ford Motor Company's chief efficiency expert, James Couzens, as mayor. Other cities, led by Dayton, Ohio, placed government in the hands of an unelected "city manager."

Middle- and upper-class professionals led this revolution in city government, and they gained the most from it. The new city officials could explain where tax money was spent, and they responded to criticisms from leading citizens and newspapers, but there were no turkeys at Christmas. Reform administrations targeted urban "vice," which included prostitution and drugs, but also working-class recreations like drinking and gambling. Businesslike efficiency did not lower taxes: Budgets continued to grow along with the public's demand for services.

Reform Mayors and City Services

A new breed of reform mayors gained heroic reputations by cleaning up and humanizing their cities. Samuel "Golden Rule" Jones won election three times as the independent mayor of Toledo. He enacted the eight-hour day for city employees, pushed for public ownership of city utilities, built kindergartens and public playgrounds, and staged free concerts in the parks. "Everyone was against him," one of his aides remembered, "except the workers." Reform mayors worried less about inefficiency and saloons and more about thieving public utility magnates. Vice raids and blue laws, they agreed, paled next to the larceny of public contracts, tax breaks, and exclusive franchises for favored businesses. Milwaukee, Schenectady, and other cities bought or regulated the private monopolies that supplied street lighting, garbage removal, water, and streetcars.

Architects, engineers, and planners also endeavored to improve urban life through the reform of public space. Voluntary art and planning commissions formed a City Beautiful movement that sought to soften the urban landscape with vistas, open spaces, and greenery. New York enacted zoning laws in 1916, and planning became a permanent feature of city administration.

Progressivism and the States

Reform at the state level displayed a regional character. In the East it mimicked the tactics and agenda of urban reform. New York's progressive governor, Charles Evans Hughes, passed laws prohibiting gambling and creating a state commission to regulate public utilities. In southern states, progressivism often meant refining the techniques of segregation and disfranchisement. White leaders justified segregation and disfranchisement using the same terms that justified urban reform in the North: The "better classes" had an obligation to prevent the disorder and corruption that came from too much democracy.

States in the West and Midwest produced the boldest experiments in governmental reform. In Oregon the drive was led by William S. U'Ren, an itinerant farmer who went into politics after reading Henry George's *Progress and Poverty* (see Chapter 19, "The Politics of Industrial America"). Under U'Ren's guidance, Oregon adopted the secret ballot and voter registration to protect the polls from manipulation and passed three Populist measures: the initiative, recall, and referendum. The initiative allowed voters to place legislation on the ballot by petition; the referendum let the legislature put proposals before the voters for approval; and

"Annual Parade of the Cable Trolley Cripple Club," from The Verdict, *March 20, 1899. Injuries attributed to private firms that ran city transportation, water, and sewage monopolies led to demands for public supervision or control of essential services.*

the recall gave voters the chance to remove officials from office. Other states soon adopted all or part of the "Oregon system."

The best known of the progressive governors was Robert M. "Fighting Bob" La Follette. La Follette claimed that as a young congressman the offer of a bribe had awakened in him a resolve to break the power of "corrupt influence." More probably, La Follette responded to his constituents' demands for state action against corporate interests.

Elected governor in 1900, La Follette pushed through a comprehensive program of social legislation. Powerful railway and public utility commissions placed some of the state's largest corporations under public control. A tax commission designed a "scientific" distribution of the tax burden, including a state income tax. Other commissions regulated hours and working conditions and protected the environment. Wisconsin also implemented the direct primary, which allowed party nominees to be chosen directly by the voters. Defying laissez-faire prescriptions, the state's economy prospered under regulation.

By shaking up city halls and statehouses, progressives made government more responsive, but they knew that social problems did not respect city and state boundaries. National corporations and nationwide problems had to be attacked at the federal level, and that meant capturing the White House.

THE PRESIDENCY BECOMES "THE ADMINISTRATION"

If Theodore Roosevelt stood at the center of the two great movements of his age, imperialism and progressivism, it was because he prepared himself for the part. The Roosevelt family was one of the oldest and wealthiest in New York, but Theodore embarked instead on a series of pursuits that were unusual for a man of his class. After graduating from Harvard in 1880, he married, started law school, wrote a history of the War of 1812, bought a cattle ranch in the Dakota Territory, and most surprisingly, ran for the state legislature.

Roosevelt's political bid stunned his family and friends, who believed that government was no place for gentlemen. Roosevelt felt avoiding the "rough and tumble" only conceded high offices to those less fit to lead. Roosevelt's flair for publicity got him noticed, and in 1886 the Republican Party nominated him for mayor of New York. He finished a poor third, lagging behind the Tammany nominee and the United Labor Party candidate. Losing to a Socialist gave him a conviction, shared by many progressives, that reform was necessary to keep voters from turning to more radical, or even violent, alternatives.

A turn as head of New York's board of police commissioners from 1895 to 1897 deepened Roosevelt's commitment to reform. While supervising 38,000 policemen, Roosevelt made friends with two muckraking journalists, Lincoln Steffens and Jacob Riis, with whom he stalked the dark streets looking for officers on the take. Roosevelt's crackdown on saloons and corruption in the police department earned him a reputation as a man who would not be intimidated, even by his own party's bosses, and when McKinley captured the presidency he named Roosevelt Assistant Secretary of the Navy. The Spanish–American War catapulted him to national fame (see Chapter 20), and in quick succession he became governor of New York, vice president, and then president of the United States.

The Executive Branch Against the Trusts

Roosevelt approached politics the way Jane Addams approached poverty, studying it, living in its midst, and carefully choosing his battles. His fear that economic desperation could lead to political violence was borne out in September 1901 when President William McKinley was assassinated by Leon Czolgosz, who came from the slums of Cleveland. Czolgosz claimed to have done it on behalf of the poor.

Roosevelt entered the White House at the age of 42. With characteristic vigor, he moved to increase the power of the presidency and bring order and efficiency to governmental administration. The first president to call himself a progressive, Roosevelt set out to remake the executive as the preeminent branch of government, the initiator of legislation, molder of public opinion, and guardian of the national interest at home and abroad. Instead of asking Congress for legislation, he drafted bills and lobbied for them personally. He believed federal administrators should intervene in the economy to protect citizens or to save business from its own shortsightedness. McKinley had already decided that action against the trusts was necessary, but his plans were not as bold as his successor's.

Challenging the megacorporations would be no easy task. Roosevelt took office less than a decade after J. P. Morgan saved the federal Treasury. In an 1895 decision, the Supreme Court gutted the Sherman Anti-Trust Act, one of the few laws that allowed federal action against monopolies. The underfunded Interstate Commerce Commission (ICC) possessed only theoretical powers. In 1903 Roosevelt established a Department of Commerce and Labor with a Bureau of Corporations to penetrate the shroud of secrecy surrounding mergers and corporate activities and to put business information before the public.

The Justice Department revitalized the Sherman Act with vigorous prosecutions. Selecting cases for maximum publicity, Attorney General Philander Knox filed suit against J. P. Morgan's holding company, Northern Securities. Morgan expected that the matter could be settled in the usual way, and his attorney asked how they might "fix it up." "We don't want to fix it up," Knox replied. "We want to stop it." When the court handed Roosevelt a victory in 1904, Americans cheered.

With this case, Roosevelt gained an undeserved reputation as a "trust buster." Although he opposed serious abuses, he distinguished between good and bad trusts and believed government should restrain the bad and encourage the good. His thinking mirrored that of progressives who imagined a professionalized central government staffed by nonpartisan experts who would monitor the activities of big corporations to ensure efficiency and head off destructive actions.

Progressives had different ideas of what the ideal corporation should look like. Brandeis and Woodrow Wilson envisioned a political economy of small, highly competitive firms kept in line by regular applications of the Sherman Act. To Roosevelt, large combinations were necessary, even desirable, fixtures of modern life. It was government's obligation not to break them up but to force them to serve the public interest.

To this end, Roosevelt revitalized the ICC. He secured passage of the Hepburn Act (1906), which allowed the commission to set freight rates, and banned special deals between carriers and favored clients. The Elkins Act (1910) gave the ICC authority over telephone, telegraph, and cable communications and allowed the commission to act without waiting for an injured party to file a complaint. The Pure Food and Drug Act (1906) made it a crime to ship or sell contaminated or fraudulently labeled food and drugs. Under Roosevelt, the federal government gained authority and tools to counterbalance the power of business, and the number of federal employees almost doubled between 1900 and 1916.

The Square Deal

Roosevelt's exasperation with big business reached a peak during the anthracite strike of 1902. The UMW represented 150,000 miners in the coal fields of eastern Pennsylvania. The miners, mostly Polish, Hungarian, and Italian immigrants, earned less than $6 a week in a dirty, hazardous line of work. More than 400 died underground yearly. Seventy percent of the mines were owned by six railroads, which in turn fell under the control of Morgan, Rockefeller, and other financiers. The owners refused to deal with the UMW, declaring it a band of outlaws. When the miners struck in May 1902, they had the public's sympathy; newspapers urged the president to take the mines away from the owners.

The "gross blindness of the operators" infuriated Roosevelt. A coal shortage might kill hundreds in the cities and lead to class warfare. Rumors spread of a general strike in support of the miners. Roosevelt exhausted the options his office allowed, publicly and privately urging the two sides to settle. In early October, as schools in New England closed for lack of heat, he invited UMW officials and the

Nearly one of every five American children worked full time in 1900. This Pennsylvania coal mine started its workers at age eight.

operators to Washington for arbitration. John Mitchell, head of the mineworkers, eagerly accepted, but the owners refused to deal with "criminals" and "anarchists."

Roosevelt drew up plans for the Army to place the mines under government control. The Secretary of War warned Morgan of the impending move, and the owners agreed to submit the dispute to a federal commission. The commission produced a compromise: Miners received a 10 percent pay increase and a nine-hour workday, but owners did not have to recognize the union.

Roosevelt's direct action set precedents that made the federal government a third force in labor disputes. For the first time a strike was settled by federal arbitration and a union struck against a strategic industry without being denounced as revolutionary. The government would no longer automatically side with the corporations. Instead, Roosevelt acknowledged the legitimacy of labor, farm, and consumer groups who would work to make a corporate economy more congenial to wage earners and families.

Conserving Water, Land, and Forests

Roosevelt enraged Congress by stretching the definitions of presidential power, nowhere more so than in the area of conservation. When Congress sent him a bill to halt the creation of new national forests in the West, Roosevelt created or enlarged 32 national forests, then signed the bill. To stop private companies from damming rivers, he set aside 2,500 of the best hydropower sites as "ranger stations." The energy behind his program came from Gifford Pinchot, the chief forester of the United States, who saw conservation as a new frontier. Unsettled, undeveloped lands were growing scarce, and Pinchot convinced the president that hope for the future lay in using the available resources more efficiently. Preserving nature for its own sake had no place in his plans. Forests, deserts, and ore ranges were to be used, but wisely, scientifically, and in the national interest.

One of the first victories for the new policy of resource management was the Newlands Reclamation Act (1902), which gave the Agriculture Department authority to build reservoirs and irrigation systems in the West. To prevent waste, Roosevelt put tighter controls on prospecting, grazing, and logging. Big lumber and mining companies had few complaints about rationalized resource administration, but small-scale prospectors and ranchers were shut out of federal lands. Naturalists, like John Muir, also resisted, pointing out that nature was to be appreciated, not used.

By 1909, conservation had become a national issue. Hikers, sightseers, and tourism entrepreneurs drawn to the new parks and forest reserves were forming a powerful antidevelopment constituency. By quadrupling the acreage in federal reserves, professionalizing the forest service, and using his "bully pulpit" to build support for conservation, Roosevelt helped create the modern environmental movement.

Roosevelt and Big Stick Diplomacy

The expansion of U.S. overseas investment and new threats to American security placed greater demands on foreign and military policy. American investors wanted assurances that Washington would protect their overseas factories and railroads. The diplomatic and military budgets grew to meet these demands, and the United States staffed permanent embassies in many Latin American capitals, staffed with trained, professionalized Foreign Service officers. Conducting foreign relations was no longer a matter of weathering "incidents" but of making policy.

Roosevelt's view of world affairs flowed from his understanding of both history and the future. Global trade and communications, he believed, separated civilized nations from savage and barbarian peoples. His foreign policy aimed to keep the United States at the center of global trends such as commerce, imperialism, and military (particularly naval) modernization. The United States had a moral duty, he felt, to interfere with "barbarian" governments in Asia, Latin America, or Africa that blocked progress.

Building an interoceanic canal topped Roosevelt's list of foreign policy priorities. A canal would be a hub of world trade and naval power in the Atlantic and Pacific. He pressed Britain to drop its claim to joint control over a canal, urged Congress to choose the Colombian province of Panama as the site, and bought out a failed French canal venture. He manipulated the Colombian government to agree to the canal, and when that failed, encouraged Panama to secede from Colombia. Congress launched an investigation of his behavior, but while that went on, so did the building of the canal.

Engineers, led by George W. Goethals, removed a mountain to let water into the isthmus and built another to shore up an artificial lake (see Map 21–1). Colonel William C. Gorgas defeated malaria and yellow fever, reducing the death rate in Panama to below that of an average American city. The canal, a 50-mile cut built at a cost of $352 million and more than 5,600 lives, opened in 1914.

Once construction was underway, Roosevelt protected the canal from other imperial powers. Poverty and unrest in the Caribbean states created opportunities for European navies to establish bases on Panama's doorstep. Neighboring nations owed millions to European investors, and imperial practice allowed creditor nations to seize the ports and customs houses of debtors. In 1904 a civil war caused the Dominican Republic to renege on its loans.

As four European nations laid plans for a debt-collecting expedition, Roosevelt went before Congress in December 1904 and announced a policy later known as the Roosevelt Corollary. It stipulated that when chronic "wrongdoing or impotence" in a Latin American country required "intervention by some civilized nation" the United States would do the intervening. Its language captured the president's worldview. White "civilized" nations acted; nonwhite "impotent" nations were acted on.

By enforcing order and administrative efficiency in the Caribbean, Roosevelt extended progressivism beyond the borders of the United States; the movement gained footholds in the Far East, too. Governor General William H. Taft took municipal reform to Manila. In 1906 the U.S. federal courts created a court outside the United States, in Shanghai, China, to control prostitution in the American community.

Roosevelt extended American stewardship to conflicts in Asia and Africa. He won the Nobel Peace Prize for mediating the end of the Russo–Japanese War in 1905, and he proposed a compromise settlement to the British–French–German dispute over Morocco. In each case, the solution involved extending open door trade.

Taft and Dollar Diplomacy

Enormously popular at the end of his second term, Roosevelt chose his friend, William H. Taft, to succeed him. Taft easily defeated William Jennings Bryan in the 1908 election, and as president he began consolidating Roosevelt's programs with the help of a more progressive Congress. He sent to the states constitutional amendments for the

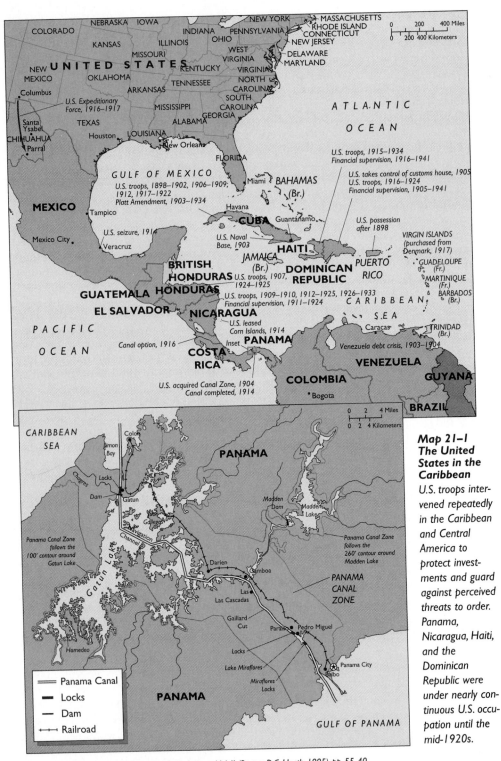

Map 21–1 The United States in the Caribbean

U.S. troops intervened repeatedly in the Caribbean and Central America to protect investments and guard against perceived threats to order. Panama, Nicaragua, Haiti, and the Dominican Republic were under nearly continuous U.S. occupation until the mid-1920s.

Source: Thomas Patterson, American Foreign Relations, Vol. II (Boston: D.C. Heath, 1995), pp. 55, 40.

direct election of senators and the income tax. His administration increased antitrust enforcement and levied the first tax on corporations.

In the Caribbean, Taft put the Roosevelt Corollary into action. The United States bought up the debts of Honduras and Nicaragua to prevent another incident like the one in the Dominican Republic. Taft persuaded four New York banks to refinance Haiti's debt to prevent German intervention. For Caribbean nations, American financial protection meant allowing the Americans to impose high import taxes, and a revolt usually followed. Marines went into Honduras and Nicaragua in 1912.

Dollar diplomacy also aimed to harness corporate investment power to foreign policy. Shortly after his inauguration, Taft mobilized a consortium of financiers to invest in China's planned Chinchow-Aigun railway. With one railroad Taft felt he could drive a wedge between the imperial powers—Britain, Russia, and Japan—and compel them to resume open door trade. Instead, they joined forces and signed a protocol opposing U.S. interference in China. Roosevelt criticized the China venture, but Taft believed that he was only taking his mentor's vision of modern diplomacy seriously. Military force was outmoded, he felt, and soon economic power would be the only kind that mattered.

Taft disappointed both conservatives and progressives in his party. He urged Congress to reduce the tariff, but when protectionists in the Senate put up a fight he retreated and signed the Payne–Aldrich Tariff in 1909, lowering rates for some goods but raising rates on steel, cotton, silk, and other important imports. Taft's flip-flop disgusted La Follette and other midwestern progressives.

Taft's Secretary of the Interior, Richard Ballinger, siding with ranchers and miners who opposed resource management, opened a million acres of public land to private development. When Pinchot publicly accused Ballinger of catering to corporate interests, the party's divisions over conservation came into the open.

Taft maintained but did not extend Roosevelt's reforms. To the former Rough Rider, that was not enough. Enlarging the president's powers did no good unless the president was willing to use them. Roosevelt began to believe his country needed him back.

RIVAL VISIONS OF THE INDUSTRIAL FUTURE

After Roosevelt returned from a safari in Africa in 1910, Pinchot, La Follette, Croly, and others trooped to his home at Sagamore Hill to complain about Taft. Roosevelt re-entered politics because his views had evolved, and because politics was what he knew best. Just 54 years old, his energy was undiminished. He took more radical positions on corporations, public welfare, and labor than he had during his presidency. The election of 1912 defined the future of industrial America.

The New Nationalism

At a sunbaked railroad stop in Osawatomie, Kansas, in August 1910, Roosevelt declared that "the essence of any struggle for liberty . . . is to destroy privilege, and give the life of every individual the highest possible value." He laid out a political program he called the New Nationalism. It included the elimination of corporate campaign contributions, regulation of industrial combinations, an expert commission to set tariffs, a graduated income tax, banking reorganization, and a national workers' compensation program. The message drew cheers from some, but to the *New York Times*, the speech crossed "the ultimate boundary line of radicalism."

From the beginning, Roosevelt had the newspapers while Taft had the delegates. The nomination fight tested the new system of direct primaries. Taft's control of the party machinery gave him an advantage in states that chose delegates by convention, but in a number of key states Roosevelt could take his campaign to the voters. When the convention met in Chicago in June 1912, Taft's slim but decisive majority allowed him to control the platform and win over undecided delegates. Grumbling that he had been robbed, Roosevelt walked out.

Roosevelt returned to Chicago in August to accept the nomination of the newly formed Progressive Party. The party platform endorsed the New Nationalism, along with popular election of senators, popular review of judicial decisions (which would allow the voters to second-guess the courts), and women's suffrage. Women served as delegates, and Jane Addams gave the speech seconding Roosevelt's nomination. The gathering had an evangelical spirit. "We stand at Armageddon," Roosevelt declared, "and we battle for the Lord."

The 1912 Election

Meanwhile in Baltimore the Democratic convention nominated a former college professor and governor of New Jersey. Woodrow Wilson entered politics by an unusual route, the university. Obtaining a doctorate in government from Johns Hopkins University in 1886, he published his first book, *Congressional Government,* at age 28. It advocated reforming the federal structure by enlarging the power of the executive branch. As a professor and later president of Princeton University, he became a well-known lecturer and commentator for national political magazines. In 1910 he won election as governor of New Jersey and enacted a sweeping program of progressive reforms. For Democrats, Wilson offered a new image and the ability to unite the South and the East under a progressive program.

With Roosevelt in the race, Wilson had to stake his own claim to the progressive constituency. To compete with the New Nationalism, Wilson devised a program called the New Freedom that challenged Roosevelt's fundamental approaches to the economy and politics. Simply regulating the trusts, Wilson argued, would not make the economy friendly to consumers, workers, or small entrepreneurs. He wanted antitrust laws that would allow a lean but powerful government to return competition and economic mobility to the marketplace. While Roosevelt appealed to a collective, national interest, Wilson stressed the needs of individual consumers and investors. In contrast to the New Nationalism's evangelical style, Wilson appealed to reason and self-interest.

On election day, the split in the Republican Party gave Wilson a plurality. He won 42 percent of the popular vote, compared to 27 for Roosevelt, 23 for Taft, and 6 for Debs, the Socialist candidate. Although his margin was thin, Wilson could interpret the large combined vote for the progressive candidates as a mandate for change.

The New Freedom

Within a year and a half of his inauguration, Wilson produced one of the most coherent and far-reaching legislative programs ever devised by a president. The New Freedom advocated lower tariffs, increased competition, and vigorous antitrust enforcement. Three monumental bills passed through Congress in rapid succession.

The first bill was the Underwood–Simmons Tariff, which made the first deep cuts in tariff rates since before the Civil War. The bill overturned the protectionist tariff and it helped farmers and consumers by lowering prices and increasing competition, but Wilson argued that its real beneficiaries would be manufacturers. Lower tariffs would help persuade other countries to reduce taxes on imports from the United States, he reasoned. The Singer, Ford, and Camel brand names began appearing in bazaars, souks, and godowns from Caracas to Mandalay. The Underwood–Simmons Tariff (1913) also permanently shifted the revenue base of the federal government from tariffs to income taxes.

Wilson's next target was the banking system. The Federal Reserve Act of 1913 set up a national board to supervise the banking system and created 12 regional reserve banks. Banks were now watched to ensure that their reserves matched their deposits. The system's real advantage was the flexibility it gave the currency. The Federal Reserve Board could put more dollars into circulation when demand was high and retire them when it subsided. Regional banks could adjust the money supply to meet the needs of different parts of the country. The system broke Wall Street's stranglehold on credit and opened new opportunities for entrepreneurship and competition.

Finally, Wilson attacked the trusts. He established the Federal Trade Commission (FTC) to enforce free and fair competition. It had the right to sub-poena corporate records and issue cease-and-desist orders. The Clayton Antitrust Act (1914) prohibited price fixing, outlawed interlocking directorates, and made it illegal for a company to own stock in its competitor. In 1916 Wilson produced another crop of reform legislation, including the first national workers' compensa-tion and child-labor laws, the eight-hour day for railroad workers, and the Warehouse Act, which extended credit to cash-strapped farmers.

These programs furthered Wilson's goal of "releasing the energies" of con-sumers and entrepreneurs, but they also helped business. Businessmen headed many of the regulatory boards, and the FTC and Federal Reserve Board brought predictability to unruly markets. The New Freedom linked liberal reform to indi-vidual initiative and the free play of markets.

Conclusion

By 1900 America's political economy had outgrown the social relationships and laws that served the earlier rural republic. Squeezed between the indifference of corpo-rate elites and the large, transient immigrant communities that controlled urban politics, middle-class reformers experimented with the structure of decision making at the municipal and state levels and vested the state with responsibility for the qual-ity of life of its citizens. Progressives challenged but never upset the system. Above all, they wanted managed, orderly change. Science and the pressure of informed opinion, they believed, could overcome resistance without open conflict.

The progressive presidents continued this movement on the national stage. Roosevelt and Wilson helped position the federal government as a broker among business, consumer, and labor interests. In less than two decades, the federal gov-ernment overcame its reputation for corruption and impotence and adapted to a new role at the center of economic and social life. The concept of a "national inter-est" that superseded individual and property rights was now firmly ingrained. The president's leadership now extended beyond the administration to Congress and public opinion. These achievements created a modern central government just at the time when military, diplomatic, and economic victories made the United States a global power. The consensus favoring a strong central government and the strength of American influence abroad would both be tested by events unfolding in Europe.

CHRONOLOGY

1889	Hull House founded
1890	General Federation of Women's Clubs founded
1893	Illinois passes eight-hour day for women
1895	National Association of Manufacturers organized
1900	Robert La Follette elected governor of Wisconsin
1901	Socialist Party of America founded Galveston introduces commission government McKinley assassinated; Theodore Roosevelt inaugurated president
1902	Newlands Reclamation Act funds construction of dams and irrigation systems Alice Hamilton investigates Chicago's typhoid epidemic *McClure's* publishes first episodes of Ida Tarbell's "History of the Standard Oil Company" and Lincoln Steffens's "The Shame of the Cities" Roosevelt settles anthracite strike
1903	Roosevelt establishes Department of Commerce and Labor Panama declares independence from Colombia W. E. B. Du Bois publishes *The Souls of Black Folk*
1904	Justice Department sues Standard Oil under the Sherman Anti-Trust Act U.S. Supreme Court orders Northern Securities Company dissolved as an illegal combination Roosevelt elected president The Roosevelt Corollary announced
1905	U.S. takes over Dominican customs Industrial Workers of the World founded Roosevelt mediates end to Russo–Japanese War

FURTHER READINGS

Jane Addams, *Twenty Years at Hull House* (1910). In her autobiography, Addams urges respect for the traditions of immigrants and action against the causes of crime and poverty.

John Milton Cooper, Jr., *The Warrior and the Priest: Theodore Roosevelt and Woodrow Wilson in American Politics* (1983). A dual biography of the progressive presidents compares their backgrounds, philosophies, and political styles.

J. Anthony Lukas, *Big Trouble: A Murder in a Small Western Town Sets off a Struggle for the Soul of America* (1997). The anxiety and tension of the progressive-era West comes to the surface in the trial of three labor leaders for the murder of a former governor of Idaho.

1906	Hepburn Act passed, allowing the Interstate Commerce Commission to set freight rates Pure Food and Drug Act requires accurate labeling
1907	Indiana passes forcible sterilization law
1908	William H. Taft elected president Supreme Court upholds maximum-hours laws for women in *Muller* v. *Oregon*
1909	Payne–Aldrich Tariff goes into effect NAACP founded
1910	Taft fires chief forester Gifford Pinchot Elkins Act authorizes Interstate Commerce Commission to regulate electronic communications Roosevelt announces the New Nationalism
1911	Triangle Shirtwaist Company fire
1912	U.S. troops occupy Nicaragua Woodrow Wilson elected president
1913	Federal Reserve Act reorganizes banking system Underwood–Simmons Tariff
1914	Panama Canal completed Clayton Act strengthens antitrust enforcement
1916	New York City enacts zoning laws Federal workers' compensation, child labor, and eight-hour-day laws passed

Kevin Starr, *Inventing the Dream: California Through the Progressive Era* (1985). The century's first decade in a state that was defining a distinct local identity through planning, art, and reform.

David Thelen, *Robert M. La Follette and the Insurgent Spirit* (1976). The life and philosophy of the progressive governor and senator from Wisconsin.

Robert H. Wiebe, *The Search for Order, 1877–1920* (1967). This classic study of progressivism traces the movement's origins to the middle class's yearning for a lost Eden of small towns and personal relationships.

Please refer to the document CD-ROM for primary sources related to this chapter.

CHAPTER

22

A Global Power

1914–1919

**Walter Lippmann • The Challenges of Revolution and Neutrality
The Drift to War • Mobilizing the Nation and the Economy
Over There • The Black Cloud in the East • Conclusion**

WALTER LIPPMANN

"War in Europe is impending," Walter Lippmann wrote in his diary on July 29, 1914. Vacationing in Belgium, the 24-year-old journalist witnessed the aftershocks of a crisis in the Balkans. Four weeks earlier, the heir to the throne of Austria-Hungary, Archduke Ferdinand, had been shot as he drove through the Serbian city of Sarajevo, plunging Europe into war. As stock markets tumbled and refugees crowded train stations, Lippmann found himself caught up in a conflict between the world's most powerful states: Austria and Germany on one side, and Russia, France, and Britain on the other.

In the twilight of August 4, Britain's foreign minister, Sir Edward Grey, asked Parliament for a war resolution. Two hours later, in Berlin, the Reichstag declared war on France. "We sit and stare at each other and make idiotically cheerful remarks," Lippmann wrote, "and in the meantime, . . . nothing can stop the awful disintegration now."

Lippmann had come of age in the progressive era. As a student at Harvard, he came to believe that reason and science would allow his generation to "treat life not as something given but as something to be shaped." He worshiped Theodore Roosevelt, and after graduation he set out to become a political journalist. "It was a happy time, those last few years before the First World War," he remembered many years later; " . . . it was easy for a young man to believe in the inevitability of progress, in the perfectibility of man and of society, and in the sublimation of evil."

The European war crushed those hopes. Just days after Lippmann left Belgium, German armies sliced through the neutral nation in a maneuver that aimed to encircle the French Army, but reserve troops from Paris struck the German flank and stopped the advance at the Marne River in northeastern France. By November, the western front had stabilized into the bloody stalemate that would prevail for four years, absorbing between 5,000 and 50,000 lives a day.

The carnage horrified Americans. German soldiers used terror against Belgian civilians, killing more than 5,000 hostages. Two weeks after the invasion began, German troops burned the picturesque medieval city of Louvain in retaliation for a Belgian attack.

"We Americans have been witnessing supreme drama, clenching our fists, talking, yet unable to fasten any reaction to realities," Lippmann told his readers. For three years, Americans watched as a civilization they had admired sank into barbarism. They recoiled from the war's violence and the motives behind it, and they debated what, if anything, they could do to stop it.

When the United States entered the fight in 1917, it mobilized its economy and society. The war both interrupted and culminated the progressive movement. In the name of efficiency, government stepped in to manage the economy as never before. The war transformed many of the most controversial items on the progressive social agenda—women's suffrage, prohibition of alcohol, restrictions on prostitution—into matters of national urgency. On the battlefield, American forces brought swift triumph, but victory failed to impose a stable peace. The experience of war brought home the dangers of a modern, interdependent world, but it also revealed the United States' power to shape the global future.

THE CHALLENGES OF REVOLUTION AND NEUTRALITY

The Great War disturbed the American president's sense that order could be imposed on foreign relations. Like other progressives, Wilson saw similar evils assailing the United States from within and without. Wilson opposed revolutionary radicalism, and he tried to fashion "organic" institutions and processes to mediate disputes and foster orderly change. However, Wilson believed order had to be forced on those who resisted. Opponents of reform "who will not be convinced," he wrote, deserved to be "crushed."

Imposing order, the president believed, was both a political duty and an economic opportunity for the United States. Imperialism and revolution endangered the free trade that was necessary for world peace and the economic health of the United States. It was the government's duty to ensure the safety of foreign travel, investments, and markets to secure American prosperity and its benefits for the world.

This combination of idealism and self-interest, humanitarianism and force, produced a foreign policy that seemed contradictory. Wilson renounced "dollar diplomacy" but used Taft's tactics when the open door was threatened in China. He atoned for the imperialism of prior administrations but intervened repeatedly in Central America. He believed the United States had a mission to promote democracy, yet he considered many peoples unready to govern themselves.

These contradictions are explained by Wilson's view of history. As he saw it, the modernizing forces of commerce and communications were creating a global society with new rules of international conduct. With Europe aflame, the United States remained the sole voice of reason, the hope for the future, and therefore had to remain out of the war. He was also preoccupied with matters closer at hand. In April 1914 American troops had invaded Mexico in an attempt to overthrow its revolutionary government.

The Mexican Revolution

In May 1911, Francisco Madero's rebels overthrew Mexican dictator of Porfirio Díaz, ending more than three decades of enforced order and rapid industrialization. Díaz and a clique of intellectuals and planners known as *científicos* had spanned the country with railroads, built up Mexican industry, and turned Mexico into one of the world's leading exporters of petroleum. Foreign investment poured in, and by 1911 Americans owned 40 percent of the property in the country (see Chapter 19,"The Politics of Industrial America"). Mexicans grew to resent the privileged colonies of foreign businessmen and the heavy taxes needed to keep industrialization going. When Madero's revolt broke out, the army folded, Díaz fled to Spain, and power changed hands in a nearly bloodless coup.

The fall of Díaz gave the United States little cause for concern: Madero left foreign investments undisturbed and held an election to confirm his presidency, but in February 1913, just two weeks before Wilson's inauguration, General Victoriano Huerta seized power and had Madero shot. Outraged Mexican states raised armies and revolted against Huerta's regime, beginning a long and bloody civil war. In the mountains south of Mexico City, Emiliano Zapata led a guerrilla resistance; along Mexico's northern border, Venustiano Carranza organized a constitutionalist army and bought weapons in Texas and New Mexico.

Wilson denounced Huerta, warning that he would "teach the South American republics to elect good men." He gave arms to Carranza's soldiers and sent 7,000 U.S. Marines to occupy Mexico's largest port city, Veracruz, in April 1914. The invasion radicalized the revolution, unifying all sides against the United States. When Carranza deposed Huerta a few months later, he promised to nationalize oilfields owned by Americans.

Still determined to "put Mexico on a moral basis," Wilson pressured Carranza to resign while providing arms to his enemy, Francisco "Pancho" Villa. Joining forces with Zapata, Villa briefly seized the capital at the end of 1914, but Carranza counterattacked, reducing Villa's army to outlaw bands. Reluctantly, Wilson recognized the Carranza government and cut off supplies to Villa; stung by Wilson's betrayal, Villa attacked the U.S. Thirteenth Cavalry outpost at Columbus, New Mexico.

Wilson responded with a "punitive expedition" of 10,000 troops under General John J. Pershing who pursued Villa 400 miles into Mexico and clashed with Carranza's army. Like the Veracruz adventure, Pershing's invasion unified Mexicans against the United States. Facing a choice between declaring war on Mexico and

In April 1914, Wilson ordered the capture of Mexico's largest port, Veracruz. The Mexican population resisted, and American warships shelled the city before Veracruz was taken in bitter street fighting.

giving up the hunt for Pancho Villa, Wilson ordered Pershing home with nothing to show for his efforts. Villa was still at large, Carranza was seeking German arms, the civil war still raged, and American lives and property were still in danger.

Bringing Order to the Caribbean

In principle, Wilson opposed imperialism and gunboat diplomacy, but his desire to impose order on neighboring countries led him to use force. He sent Marines into more countries in Latin America than any other president. United States troops quashed a revolution in Haiti in 1915 and landed in the Dominican Republic the following year, where they stayed until 1924. Wilson kept in place the Marines that Taft had sent to occupy Honduras, Panama, and Nicaragua, and briefly sent troops into Cuba. From each of these countries Wilson obtained the right to intervene if necessary to restore order. These agreements reassured American business that the United States would maintain what Wilson called "orderly processes" in foreign markets.

Congress had less enthusiasm for treaties that promised to embroil American soldiers in one crisis after another. Senator Robert La Follette explained that corporations were in the business of exploitation, whether in Wisconsin or Mexico. La Follette and Senator George W. Norris argued that in some countries revolutions might be necessary to protect the rights of the many against the power of the few.

Opponents of Wilson's policies in Mexico and the Caribbean also urged the United States to stay out of the Great War in Europe. In April 1916, progressive writers and social workers met at New York's Henry Street Settlement House to organize the American Union Against Militarism and protest against intervention in Mexico. Jane Addams and Carrie Chapman Catt founded the Woman's Peace Party, whose 25,000 members supported a mediated settlement to the European conflict. Peace advocates supported Wilson's policy of neutrality but saw signs that the United States was being drawn into war.

A One-Sided Neutrality

As German armies crossed Belgium in August 1914, Woodrow Wilson declared a policy of strict neutrality. The war took him by surprise, and like Addams he found it "incredible" that civilized nations could display such savagery. His first worry was that America's immigrant communities, filled with people newly arrived from the warring countries, would split into "camps of hostile opinion, hot against each other."

With 32 million Americans either born abroad or having at least one parent from overseas, and more than 10 million with family ties to Germany and Austria-Hungary, Wilson's concern was understandable. The Allies (Britain, France, Italy, and Russia) and the Central Powers (Germany, Austria-Hungary, and Turkey) did their best to sway opinion. Britain cut the telegraph cable between Germany and the United States to ensure that news had to pass through censors in London. In 1915 a New York City subway policeman found a German secret plan to fund peace groups in the United States. Both the president and the press worried that propaganda could push the electorate to demand American intervention.

Wilson did his best to appear completely neutral. He told Americans that this was a war "whose causes cannot touch us," but privately he believed that a German victory would be a catastrophe. With Europe and possibly Asia controlled by a single power, the United States would be vulnerable and alone.

Modern warfare and commerce made true neutrality difficult, and Wilson's bias soon became clear. The belligerent powers desperately needed United States exports: food, textiles, steel, chemicals, and fuel. The economy rose on a tide of war orders, mainly from the Allies. American trade with the Allies grew to more than $3 billion by 1916, while trade with the Central Powers sank from $170 million to less than $1 million. U.S. loans to the Allies grew to $2.5 billion by 1917, but the Central Powers received only $127 million in credit. The American economy was already in the war on the side of the Allies.

Wilson's reaction to the British and German naval blockades helped the Allies capture American trade. The British fleet closed European ports and laid mines across the North Sea, preventing American ships from reaching Germany. London's actions violated the "freedom of the seas," but the Wilson administration never strenuously protested or used force to break the blockade. Wilson reacted differently to Germany's violations. On February 4, 1915, Berlin announced a policy of "unrestricted submarine warfare" against ships entering a "war zone" around the British Isles. A German *Unterseeboot* or U-boat, a small, fragile submarine with a crew of only 32 men, could not stop, board, and escort ships into port, as required by law, without giving up the stealth and surprise that were its only weapons, but while Wilson was willing to excuse the British blockade, he insisted that German U-boats observe the letter of international law.

The *Lusitania's* Last Voyage

Germany posted advertisements in American newspapers warning passengers not to travel on ships bound for the war zone; Americans were horrified by the targeting of ships carrying civilian men, women, and children. Wilson declared that Germany would be held to "strict accountability" for American lives or property destroyed by U-boats.

On the afternoon of May 7, 1915, submarine U-20 sighted the luxury liner *Lusitania* off the coast of Ireland. A torpedo struck the starboard side behind the bridge, and the massive ship broke apart and sank. Of almost 2,000 passengers aboard, 1,198 drowned, including 94 children. Of these, 124 were Americans. Newspaper headlines accused Germany of savagery. A German in Berlin remarked that although the Americans she knew "had always professed to be neutral . . . a sudden change now took place. . . . Their rage and horror at the idea that Americans had been killed knew no bounds."

Wilson demanded that Germany pay reparations and stop attacking ships without warning. He hinted that unless these demands were met, the United States would break relations. Accusing Wilson of pushing the country into war, Secretary of State William Jennings Bryan resigned.

Public opinion was also divided. Newspapers called for war, but as Lippmann wrote to a friend in England, "the feeling against war in this country is a great deal deeper than you would imagine by reading editorials." When Germany promised not to attack passenger liners without warning, this guarantee, known as the Sussex Pledge, restored calm. However, official and public opinion had turned against Germany. American involvement no longer seemed impossible.

THE DRIFT TO WAR

The *Lusitania* disaster opened an unbridgeable gap among progressives on the issue of the war. Peace advocates like Addams, Bryan, and La Follette urged a stricter neutrality to prevent another tragedy that might require retaliation. Others believed war, or preparations for war, were justified. The *Lusitania* incident "united Englishmen and Americans in a common grief and a common indignation" and might "unite them in a common war," Lippmann predicted. Thousands of preparedness supporters marched down New York's Fifth Avenue under an electric sign declaring "Absolute and Unqualified Loyalty to our Country."

The preparedness leagues, headed by businessmen and conservative political figures, called attention to the pathetic state of the armed forces. When Pancho Villa attacked the 13th Cavalry at Columbus, New Mexico, every one of the Americans' machine guns jammed. Pershing's punitive expedition suffered from chronic shortages of trucks, planes, and supplies. The preparedness campaign adopted patriotic rituals once reserved for elections. Wilson himself led the parade in Washington in 1916, wearing a red tie, white trousers, and a blue blazer.

The Election of 1916

In campaigning for re-election, Wilson had to reconcile the public's overwhelming desire for peace with his own feeling that the United States could not remain uninvolved. Nonetheless he campaigned under the slogan "He kept us out of war." It was a sure vote-getter.

The preparedness issue reunited Theodore Roosevelt with the Republicans. Bringing the Progressive Party with him, he endorsed Supreme Court Justice Charles Evans Hughes, the Republican candidate. The party organizations took a back seat to modern advertising campaigns waged by poster and press release. Democrats charged Hughes with sympathy to Germany, while Republicans accused Wilson of "leniency with the British Empire." Woman suffragists campaigned against Wilson. They picketed the White House with signs asking "Mr. President? How long must women wait for liberty?"

Although the country remained strongly Republican, Hughes proved an inept campaigner. He won pivotal states in the North and East but lost in the South and West. Wilson won narrowly; a shift of a few thousand votes in California would have cost him the election. Republicans gained seats in the House and the Senate. Still, re-election freed Wilson to pursue a more vigorous foreign policy. As Lippmann realized, "What we're electing is a war president—not the man who kept us out of war."

The Last Attempts at Peace

After the election, Wilson launched a new peace initiative. Looking for an opening for compromise, he asked each of the belligerent powers to state its war aims. The results were disappointing. Each side insisted on punishing the other and enlarging its own territories. Going before Congress in January 1917, the president called for a "peace without victory," based on self-determination of all nations and the creation of an international organization to enforce peace.

Germany toyed with accepting Wilson's proposals and decided to wait. Having subdued the Balkans and pushed deep into Russia by February 1917, it could begin shifting armies from the Eastern front to France. It seemed that the summer of 1917 might bring a German victory. To accelerate that outcome, Germany resumed unrestricted submarine warfare. U-boats torpedoed British passenger liners and American merchant ships. In late February, British intelligence officers showed the U.S. ambassador in London an intercepted telegram from the German foreign minister, Arthur Zimmermann, to his ambassador in Mexico City. It instructed the ambassador that if the United States joined the war on the Allied side he should invite Carranza to ally with Germany. Together, Germany and Mexico would fight to regain "lost territories" in Arizona, California, and New Mexico. The Zimmermann Telegram confirmed Americans' darkest fears about the implications of a German victory, and it provoked alarm in the West, where antiwar feeling had been strongest.

Americans disagreed then, as historians do today, on why the United States went to war. Economic and strategic issues were at stake, as was national honor and the ability to shape the peace. Critics pointed to the influence of munitions makers and banks that stood to gain from war. Publicly and in private, Wilson stressed two considerations that led to his decision: First, attacks on American ships had forced him to retaliate. Second, joining the war was necessary for the United States to influence the peace settlement. Unless it took part in the conflict, Wilson told Jane Addams, the United States would have to shout "through a crack in the door."

Wilson's War Aims

On the evening of April 2, 1917, Wilson asked Congress for a declaration of war. The conflict, he told his audience, was in its last stages and American armies could bring it to a quick, merciful end. Neutrality had provided no safety for American travelers or American trade. The only hope for avoiding future wars that might pose even graver dangers was to place the United States in a position to dictate the peace. This would be a war to end all wars, to make the world safe for democracy.

In urging Congress to vote for war, the president explicitly rejected the war aims of the Allies. "We have no quarrel with the German people," he said. "We have no feeling towards them but one of sympathy and friendship." His argument was with the Kaiser and all other emperors and autocrats who stood in the way of his plan to rebuild the world on "American principles."

Allied diplomacy contradicted Wilson's sense of what a progressive foreign policy should be. He wanted to prevent the kind of peace that would lead to more imperialism, absolutism, and war, and he believed the conclusion of the war would allow only a momentary chance to establish institutions that could enforce a durable peace.

A national preparedness movement campaigned for compulsory military training and modernization of the U.S. Army, which ranked 17th in the world. Campaigners used parades, such as this one in Mobile, Alabama, to overcome public doubts. Some residents of Mobile could remember greeting the U.S. Army on different terms.

Wilson's trusted advisor, Edward House, assembled a secret committee, known as the Inquiry, to draft a peace proposal, based on "American principles," that would be both generous enough to show "sympathy and friendship" to the German people and harsh enough to punish their leaders. Made up of economists, historians, geographers, and legal experts, it met in New York, with Lippmann as secretary. The Inquiry produced a set of 14 recommendations that redrew the boundaries of Europe, created a league of nations, and based peace on the principles of freedom of the seas, open door trade, and ethnic self-determination.

The Fight in Congress

After Wilson's war message to Congress, Robert La Follette told his colleagues that if this was a war for democracy, it should be declared democratically. He asked for a national referendum on the war. The country had voted only five months earlier for the peace candidate for president, and there were strong reasons to suspect a declaration would fail a national vote.

Prowar representatives blocked the referendum and brought the declaration to a vote on April 6, when it passed by a margin of 82 to 6 in the Senate and 373 to 50 in the House. As debate turned to questions of how to pay for the war and who would fight in it, the divisions resurfaced. Wilson wanted universal conscription, the first draft since the Civil War. The 1917 draft law created a selective service system comprised of 4,000 local boards manned by volunteers. Men between the ages of 18 and 45 were required to register. The draft would be a "melting pot," said one representative, that would "break down distinctions of race and class and mold us into a new nation."

Congressman Claude Kitchin argued that if young men were to be drafted, profits should be drafted too. He proposed to pay for the war with increased taxes on incomes, corporations, and war profits. Business interests wanted to finance the war instead with sales taxes and bonds, passing the cost on to consumers and future generations. Senator Porter J. McCumber (R–ND) worried that if the rich were taxed heavily it would "dampen their ardor and destroy their war spirit."

In the end, antiwar progressives had too few votes to stop conscription, but they managed to make an exemption for conscientious objectors and to reduce some of the taxes on sugar, bread, and coffee used to pay for the war. Voices of opposition were soon silenced by patriotic calls for unity at all costs.

Mobilizing the Nation and the Economy

News of the war declaration, carried in banner headlines on Easter Sunday, 1917, set the nation astir with activity. William Percy, a college student from Mississippi, rushed home to Greenville and found women "knitting and beginning to take one lump of sugar instead of two, men within draft age were discussing which branch of the service they had best to enter, men above draft age were heading innumerable patriotic committees and making speeches." Businesses converted to war production. Hull House started a bond drive, eventually raising $50,000 from its neighbors in the 19th Ward.

Wilson recognized that he was asking the nation to undertake an unprecedented effort. Raising an army of more than 3 million men, supplying it, and transporting it across submarine-infested waters to France were Herculean feats. Americans would spare from their dinner plates and send to Europe 1.8 million tons of meat, 8.8 million tons of cereals, and 1.5 million tons of sugar. Factories that produced sewing machines, automobiles, and textiles would retool to make howitzers, tanks, and explosives.

Wilson and others feared that the strain of war could widen political divisions and destroy the achievements progressives had made in the previous 15 years, but some felt that sharing sacrifices would consolidate the progressives' gains. Lippmann hoped the war would open Americans to new ideas. "We are living and shall live all our lives now," he predicted, "in a revolutionary world."

Enforcing Patriotism

The summons to a war to end all wars allowed many progressive pacifists to put aside their opposition and join in the task at hand. Still, some resistance remained. The Socialist Party, whose presidential candidate polled more than half a million votes in 1916, maintained its opposition. Midwestern farmers continued to grumble about the draft and taxes on consumption, but expressing dissent openly soon came to be seen as dangerous.

Since 1914, mysterious explosions had disrupted American munitions factories and ports. On July 30, 1916, across the river from New York City, the largest arms storage facility in the country, known as Black Tom, exploded. Thousands of pounds of shells and guns bound for Russia were destroyed. Four days after Wilson declared war, saboteurs blew up a munitions factory outside of Philadelphia and killed 112 workers, mostly women and girls. Federal agents rounded up large numbers of aliens, but the fear of internal enemies persisted.

Congress gave the president sweeping powers to suppress dissent. The Espionage Act (1917) and the Sedition Act (1918) effectively outlawed opposition to the war and used the postal service and the Justice Department to catch offenders. The Justice Department raided the Chicago offices of the Industrial Workers of the World and imprisoned 96 of the union's leaders on charges of sedition. Eugene V. Debs, leader of the Socialist Party, received ten years for telling a Cincinnati audience that "You need to know that you are fit for something better than slavery and cannon fodder."

The Justice Department organized a volunteer auxiliary, the American Protective League (APL), with a quarter of a million members who opened mail, wiretapped phones, and conducted searches. In September 1918, the APL conducted a "slacker raid" in downtown Manhattan, arresting suspected draft dodgers in offices, subways, and shops. The dragnet pulled in more than 50,000 people. States also passed laws criminalizing opposition to the war and deputizing volunteer enforcers.

Towns, schools, and clubs with German-sounding names changed them. East Germantown, Indiana, became Pershing. Hamburgers became "liberty sandwiches." Americans who had once proudly displayed their ethnicity now took pains to disguise it.

Mennonites, Jehovah's Witnesses, and other pacifist faiths faced their own ordeals. Some sects had come to America to avoid conscription in Germany or Russia. Many could not comply even with the conscientious objector statute, which required submission to military control. Fifteen hundred Mennonites and Hutterites fled to Canada to avoid being placed in camps, while others obeyed their consciences by going to prison.

Advertising the War

Josephus Daniels, the Secretary of the Navy, enlisted the new art of mass advertising to overcome the public's indifference and mold the American people into a "white-hot mass." He turned to former muckraker George Creel, who had helped to mastermind Wilson's publicity campaign in 1916. Creel's propaganda bureau, the Committee on Public Information (CPI), made films, staged pageants, dispatched public speakers, and churned out display ads, billboards, posters, leaflets, and press releases. The CPI sold the war by telling Americans they were fighting to save their own homes. In a famous poster, a fleet of German bombers pass over a shattered, headless Statue of Liberty while New York burns in the background.

Propaganda images represented Germany as menacing and bestial. Following Wilson's example, propaganda distinguished between Germany and the German people, especially Germans who had emigrated to the United States. The CPI distributed leaflets in German offering "Friendly Words to the Foreign Born." Billboards encouraged the foreign born to think of themselves as Americans.

Creel cast women as symbols of progress and patriotism, depicting them as mothers, nurses, and patriotic consumers. The National Woman's Party seized on this theme and began highly publicized pickets outside the White House. Wilson endorsed the suffrage amendment in January 1918 in words that might have been lifted from a CPI poster: "We have made partners of the women in this war. Shall we admit them only to a partnership of suffering and sacrifice and toil and not to a partnership of privilege and right?" Advertising mobilized Americans for war while advancing progressive agendas like assimilation of immigrants, women's suffrage, and reconciliation between labor and management.

Regimenting the Economy

The first prolonged conflict between industrial nations, World War I introduced the public to the term "total war." It was a struggle to protect not just territory or state interests but fundamental values and ways of life. It subordinated all human efforts,

THE NAVY NEEDS YOU! DON'T READ AMERICAN HISTORY— MAKE IT!

U·S·NAVY RECRUITING STATION
34 EAST 23rd ST., NEW YORK
THE MAYOR'S COMMITTEE ON NATIONAL DEFENSE

The new business of commercial advertising came to the aid of the war effort, producing memorable images and slogans for mass-circulation magazines.

ideas, and institutions to the needs of the nation. When the War Department laid plans to place a million-man American Expeditionary Force in Europe by the spring of 1918, it became clear that the economy would have to be reorganized, planned, and centralized. The government began issuing contracts, enlisting men, and building camps on a gigantic scale.

To build ships to carry an army across the Atlantic, the United States commissioned the construction of a vast shipyard on Hog Island, outside Philadelphia. It was to have 250 buildings and 80 miles of railroad track, employ 34,000 workers, and have facilities to build 50 ships simultaneously. Wilson asked steelmaker Charles M. Schwab to build the facility, and Schwab signed contracts for the delivery of machinery, cement, steel, and timber. Manufacturers loaded goods on trains headed for Hog Island. The result was the Great Pile Up, the biggest traffic jam in railroad history. Within weeks railroad cars could get no closer than Pittsburgh or Buffalo. Schwab begged the railroads to cooperate, to no avail. The voluntary system for mobilizing the nation's resources had failed, and on January 1, 1918, Wilson nationalized the railroads.

The Hog Island fiasco demonstrated the need for national supervision of the economy. Wilson created a War Industries Board (WIB) to set prices, regulate manufacturing, and control transportation. Wilson found the overseer he needed in Bernard Baruch, a Wall Street financier, who believed in central control of the economy by "socially responsible" businessmen. He drafted corporate executives to fill the top positions and paid them a salary of a dollar a year.

The dollar-a-year men regimented the economy and put business at the service of government, but they also guaranteed profits and looked after manufacturers' long-term interests. One of their innovations was the "cost-plus" contract, which assured contractors the recovery of costs plus a percentage for profit. Under these arrangements, the Black and Decker Company used its factories to make gun sights, and Evinrude stopped making outboard motors and turned out grenades instead. The contract allowed companies to build up revenues to reconvert or to launch new product lines after the war.

Not all businesses submitted willingly to "war socialism." The Ford Motor Company, unwilling to scrap its network of dealerships, refused to completely stop making cars. When other automakers followed suit, the board threatened to cut off the industry's supply of coal and steel. After months of negotiations, the auto manufacturers agreed to cut production by three-fourths. The delay hurt. When American troops went into battle, they had only two tanks.

The war economy was a culmination of two movements: Wall Street's drive for corporate consolidation and the progressives' push for federal regulation. Businessmen recognized that the WIB could rationalize the economy. These "New Capitalists" wanted to end cutthroat competition and bring central organization and "scientific management" to the economy, and they saw the war as their chance. They established the National Foreign Trade Council and other trade associations to represent them in government. They worked to control price fluctuations, share technology, make business predictable, and make workers identify with the company through stock sharing and bonus plans.

The WIB prevented economic chaos, held down inflation, standardized products, and forced manufacturers to pay attention to quality. It changed fashion, removing metal stays from corsets and saving enough metal to build two battleships. Above all, it demonstrated how a corporate economy could work for the national interest.

The Great Migration

The war economy gave Americans new choices and opportunities. As factories geared up for war production, corporate managers, facing a shortage of labor, found a ready supply in the South. In small towns and rural junctions, labor recruiters offered free rides to the North and well-paid employment on arrival. Large manufacturers came to rely on the labor of former sharecroppers. In some northern cities, African-American migrants arrived at the rate of 1000 a week. The massive movement of African Americans from the rural South to the urban North and West that began during World War I came to be called the Great Migration.

Almost half a million people came north during the war years, emptying out some counties in the South and creating panic among the whites left behind. Mississippi lost 75,000 African-American workers, leaving farms without tenants and delivery wagons without drivers. Southern states passed laws banning recruiters and free passes on the railroads. In some places, migrants were discouraged by violence, and the number of lynchings increased, provoking still more migration.

Memories of discrimination and brutality made the decision to move an easy one for many African Americans, but encouragement also came from the *Chicago Defender*, an African-American newspaper available in any county that had a railroad. The paper estimated the war would create 1.5 million jobs for African Americans in northern cities. Classified ads promised jobs in factories. For the price of a $20 ticket, a sharecropper could be at a factory in St. Louis or Cleveland in six hours.

African-American workers moved into low-paying jobs as janitors, domestics, and common laborers in stockyards, steel mills, and factories. The work was back-breaking and often dangerous, and the migrants faced hostility from employers and unionized white workers. Prices were substantially higher in the cities. Still, African-American workers could earn wages 70 percent higher than in the South. Almost no one went back.

The new arrivals found apartments and boarding houses in ghetto neighborhoods and adapted to the rhythms of city life. "South State Street was in its glory then, a teeming Negro street with crowded theaters, restaurants, and cabarets," Langston Hughes wrote of Chicago in 1918. "Midnight was like day. The street was full of workers and gamblers, prostitutes and pimps, church folks and sinners."

With new construction stopped by the war, housing was in short supply, and African-American renters found their options limited to overcrowded districts wedged between industrial zones and unfriendly white neighborhoods. Ghetto neighborhoods were both expensive and decrepit. On Chicago's South Side, rents were 15 to 20 percent higher than in white neighborhoods, and the death rate was comparable to that of Bombay, India.

White property owners and real estate agents worked hard to create the ghettos and define their boundaries. In Chicago's South Side, the Hyde Park-Kenwood Property Owners Association organized to "Make Hyde Park White." When discrimination failed to deter "undesirables" from owning homes, the neighbors used dynamite. From 1917 to 1919 there were 26 bombings of African-American residences in Chicago. On July 2, 1917, in East St. Louis, Illinois, rumors that Republicans were "colonizing" the county with African Americans led a mob of white workers to attack a black neighborhood, killing 47 people and leaving 6,000 homeless.

Three years later, in Washington, DC, when a mob invaded the ghetto, residents fought back and retaliated against white neighborhoods. "This new spirit is but a reflex of the great war," an African-American newspaper explained. The "New Negro," urban, defiant, demanding rather than asking for rights, became the subject of admiring and apprehensive reports. Editorials in African-American newspapers urged readers to recognize their own beauty and prowess: "The black man is a power of great potentiality upon whom consciousness of his own strength is about to dawn."

Reforms Become "War Measures"

"Why not make America safe for democracy?" asked the signs carried by marchers protesting racism in New York. The NAACP, in response to the East St. Louis riots, urged Congress to outlaw lynching as a "war measure." African Americans were not alone in using the war emergency to justify immediate reform. Carrie Chapman Catt told Wilson that he could enact women's suffrage "as a 'war measure' and enable our women to throw, more fully and wholeheartedly, their entire energy into work for their country." On a variety of issues, reformers used the war to advance the progressive agenda.

Catt's National American Woman Suffrage Association (NAWSA) worked to identify women with the war effort. NAWSA members sold liberty bonds and knitted socks for the Red Cross, making clear to the president and Congress that they expected to be rewarded with suffrage. Alice Paul's National Woman's Party (NWP) contrasted the nobility of the administration's war aims with its treatment of American women. Pickets at the White House carried signs insisting, in Wilson's own words, on "the right of those who submit to authority to have a voice in their own governments." When Wilson announced his support for suffrage in 1918, he cited women's war service as the reason. The Nineteenth Amendment was finally ratified in 1920, "so soon after the war," according to Jane Addams, "that it must be accounted as the direct result of war psychology."

As it had for African Americans, the wartime shortage of labor increased opportunities for women. Women replaced men as bank tellers, streetcar operators, mail carriers, and laborers in factories. Women in low-skilled and low-paid occupations found room for upward movement. Cashiers became sales clerks, file clerks became stenographers, and line workers became supervisors. Most of these opportunities vanished when the war ended, but in rapidly expanding sectors like finance, communications, and office work women made permanent gains. By 1920, more than 25 percent of working women labored in offices or as telephone operators, and 13 percent were in the professions. The new opportunities made work a source of

Members of the National Woman's Party picket outside the White House in 1917. Founded by Alice Paul, the NWP campaigned for suffrage through civil disobedience.

prestige and enjoyment for women. War propaganda enhanced the glamour, portraying working women as "our second line of defense."

The general appreciation for women's sacrifices afforded a chance to revisit the issue of special protection for female workers. Sociologist Mary Van Kleeck and Mary Anderson of the Women's Trade Union League persuaded the Army Ordnance Department to recommend uniform standards for women's work, including an eight-hour day, prohibitions on working at night or in dangerous conditions, and provisions for rest periods, lunchrooms, and bathrooms. For military contractors the standards were mandatory, but a number of other firms voluntarily followed them, and several states enacted them into law.

The shortage of labor and high turnover in industrial jobs, combined with strikes in critical industries and an increase in the number of labor disputes, threatened to slow the war effort. Union leaders recognized that the war affected labor relations. Samuel Gompers believed it would lead to a "general reorganization" of the economy that could either help or hurt labor. Workers were prepared to make "any sacrifice which may be necessary to make our triumph sure," he told mineworkers, "but we are not going to make sacrifices that shall fill the coffers of the rich." Conservative unions like the AFL supported the war and backed the administration's repression of more radical unions.

In return, Wilson went further than any previous president had in recognizing the interests of labor. He authorized a National War Labor Board to intervene in critical industries. The board set an unofficial minimum wage based on the cost of living. For the first time the federal government recognized workers' rights to organize, bargain collectively, and join unions. Wilson ordered a wage hike for railroad workers after nationalization.

Beer, wine, and spirits were early casualties of war. The Anti-Saloon League and the Woman's Christian Temperance Union had assembled a powerful antiliquor coalition by 1916. Congress would have passed prohibition without war, but in the rush to mobilize, temperance became a patriotic crusade. Temperance groups touted the liquor ban as the cure for slums, insanity, poverty, high taxes, and inefficiency.

Military regulations prohibited the sale of liquor in the vicinity of Army camps and outlawed selling or giving alcohol to men in uniform. Food conservation laws made it illegal to use grain to make liquor. Finally, on December 22, 1917, Congress passed the Eighteenth Amendment, banning the "manufacture, sale, or transportation of intoxicating liquors." The amendment was ratified in 1919, and Congress passed a "bone dry" enforcement act, sponsored by Congressman Andrew J. Volstead, that defined liquor as any beverage containing half a percent of alcohol or more. Wilson opposed the Volstead Act, favoring restrictions on hard liquor only, but Congress overrode his veto. At midnight on January 28, 1920, the Anti-Saloon League celebrated the dawn of "an era of clear thinking and clean living." Bootleggers, smugglers, and organized crime continued to slake American thirsts, but liquor prices rose and consumption declined.

The war also lent patriotic zeal to antivice crusaders. During the progressive era, vice commissions attacked gambling dens, brothels, and dime-a-dance parlors, while muckrakers exposed the police-protection rackets that allowed them to thrive. Within days of the declaration of war, reformers identified prostitutes as domestic enemies who sabotaged the health of American troops. Gonorrhea reportedly afflicted a quarter of the Allied forces in France, and proper middle-class Americans worried what might become of soldiers sent to such a moral wilderness.

The administration mobilized against venereal disease. The president formed an Interdepartmental Board of Social Hygiene, which implemented severe restrictions known as the "American Plan." Military police could arrest any woman found within five miles of a military cantonment in the United States and force her to submit to medical tests. If infected, she could be sentenced to a "detention home" until cured. Authorities confined 15,520 afflicted women during the war and closed vice districts in port cities. Cities and states followed the Army's lead and mounted their own attacks on prostitution and disease. The war permanently changed the crusade for public morals. Before 1917, reformers targeted commercial vice as a source of political and social corruption, but afterward they directed their efforts at women as carriers of disease.

The Army acted against liquor and prostitution, but it shrank from challenging racial injustice. At training camps in the South, clashes between uniformed African-American soldiers and white local officials easily turned violent. A riot in Houston in August 1917 began when soldiers from nearby Camp Logan rushed to the aid of an African-American woman being beaten by police. Twenty policemen and soldiers died and 54 soldiers received life sentences.

After the Houston riot, African-American units were dispersed to camps across the country. Training was continually interrupted by menial assignments like road building or freight handling. The Army remained segregated, and southern communities used military discipline to strengthen Jim Crow laws. Encouraged by the Army's "work or fight" order, which required draft-age men to either enlist or get a job, states and localities passed compulsory work laws that were intended to keep laborers in the fields and servants in the kitchens at prewar wages.

OVER THERE

When the U.S. Senate took up the enormous war budget the president submitted in April 1917, the finance committee questioned Major Palmer E. Pierce about what would be done with all of that money. "Clothing, cots, camps, food, pay," he replied, "and we may have to have an army in France." "Good Lord!" exclaimed Senator Thomas Martin of Virginia, "You're not going to send soldiers over there, are you?" After the horrors of the Somme and Verdun, where men died by the tens of thousands, it seemed mad to send Americans to such a place. "One would think that, after almost four years of war, . . . it would have been all but impossible to get anyone to serve," one veteran later recalled. "But . . . we and many thousands of others volunteered."

Americans went to France believing they could change the war and the peace. Trench warfare was not for them. They planned to sweep in formations across open fields, as Americans had at Antietam and Gettysburg. To a remarkable degree, they got the war they wanted. Europeans watched their civilization destroy itself in the Great War, but Americans saw theirs rising.

Citizens Into Soldiers

The job of enlisting, training, and transporting soldiers began with a rush of excitement. Camps housing 400,000 recruits went up in 30 days. A Wisconsin man found that Fort Sheridan had "an atmosphere somewhat like that of a college campus on the eve of a big game." Conscription went smoothly, and soon 32 camps were in operation, housing 1.3 million men. Commander John J. Pershing arrived in France in June with 40,000 men and the first of 16,000 women who would serve in the American Expeditionary Force (AEF).

Once Wilson was firmly committed to war, the British government revealed how financially desperate it was. London had barely enough dollar reserves to last another two weeks. Wilson advanced $200 million immediately, and loans to the Allies eventually amounted to $10 billion.

The Allies agreed that funds, food, and ammunition were needed more urgently than men, but that changed in October 1917, when German and Austrian forces smashed through the Italian lines at Caporetto, finishing the war on that front. When the Bolshevik Revolution curtailed Russian resistance in the east in November, Britain and France saw that by the next spring Germany would be able to break through to Paris. The war became a race between the United States and Germany to see who could place the most men on the western front in 1918.

To get troops to the war the United States needed ships, but for a time the United States had to cut back draft calls because it had scarcely a dozen ships for carrying men. The War Department confiscated 16 German passenger ships docked in U.S. ports, and the British converted freighters to use as transports. The Navy, meanwhile, cured the U-boat problem. The addition of the American destroyer fleet allowed the Allies to convoy effectively for the first time, cutting losses dramatically. When a torpedo was sighted, destroyers would sprint to the far end of its wake and deploy depth charges in a circle around the U-boat. By July 18, some 10,000 troops a day boarded the "Atlantic Ferry" for the ride to France.

The Fourteen Points

Meanwhile the Inquiry completed its work, sending the president a memorandum titled "The War Aims and the Peace Terms It Suggests" on Christmas Day, 1917. Consulting with Colonel Edward House, Wilson redrafted the report and presented it in an address to Congress on January 8, 1918. The Fourteen Points outlined U.S. objectives and suggested a new basis for peace. Unlike nineteenth-century wars waged for limited territorial or political objectives, the Great War was a total war, fought for unlimited aims. The principal belligerents—Britain, France, Russia, Germany, and Austria-Hungary—were global empires whose trade and law spanned continents and oceans. Each side wanted to destroy the other's future as a great power, economically and militarily. Wilson replaced these imperial visions of total victory with a peace based on limited gains and struck among nations, instead of empires.

The Fourteen Points were grouped around four themes: national self-determination; freedom of the seas; enforcement of peace by a league of nations; and open, instead of secret, diplomacy. The Inquiry's memorandum included maps marked with new European boundaries based on national, ethnic identities. The new state of Poland, for instance, should govern only territories with "indisputably Polish populations." Point III restated the Open Door, urging free trade. Wilson thus hoped to eliminate what he saw as the two leading causes of war, imperial and commercial rivalry. By calling for open diplomacy and national rights, he appealed directly to the people of Europe, over the heads of their governments. Creel printed 60 million copies of the Fourteen Points and had them distributed around the world. Planes dropped copies over Germany and Austria.

Wilson hoped the Fourteen Points would dispel not only the old dream of empire but also the new one of world socialist revolution. On November 7, Russian workers overthrew the Provisional Government of Alexander Kerensky. The one-party regime of the Bolsheviks, led by Vladimir Lenin, took its place and summoned workers everywhere to rise against their governments and to make peace. "The crimes of the ruling, exploiting classes in this war have been countless. These crimes cry out for revolutionary revenge." In December, Lenin sued for peace based on the principle of self-determination. The Council of People's Commissars allocated 2 million rubles to encourage revolutions around the world.

Two world leaders—Lenin and Wilson—now offered radically different visions of the new world order, and Lenin was putting his into effect. Wilson continued to hope that the revolution would move in a more liberal direction and that Russia would stay in the war. Those hopes ended with the Treaty of Brest-Litovsk, signed by Russia and Germany in March 1918. The treaty showed the fearful price of defeat in modern war. Russia lost the Ukraine, Poland, and Finland, three-quarters of its iron and steel, one-quarter of its population, and most of its best farmland. With its eastern front secure, Germany began transferring ten divisions a month to the west.

Wilson was the first, but not the last, American president to be haunted by the specter of a German–Russian alliance, uniting the immense war-making resources of Europe and Asia. He refused to recognize the Bolshevik government, and he sent 7,000 American troops to Russia to support anti-Bolshevik forces and to restart the war on the eastern front. U.S. troops joined Japanese forces invading Siberia from the east. Meanwhile, the battle for the control of Europe was about to begin.

The Final Offensive

The German high command knew the spring offensive would be the last. Risking everything, the German commander Erich Ludendorff launched his offensive on March 21, 1918. Specially trained shock troops hurled the British Fifth Army back to Amiens (see Map 22–1). In May they penetrated French lines as far as Soissons, 37 miles from Paris. As gaps opened in the lines, French General Ferdinand Foch and British General Douglas Haig appealed to Pershing to allow American troops to reinforce trenches under British and French command. Pershing opposed the idea. He wanted the American Army to play "a distinct and definite part" in the war to strengthen the United States' negotiating position and use his own strategy for defeating the Germans.

Pershing criticized European commanders for remaining on the defensive when the war could be won only by "driving the enemy out into the open and engaging him in a war of movement." He saw trenches not as protection against the murderous efficiency of modern weaponry but as symbols of inertia. Pershing favored overwhelming the main German force with massed assaults. Infantry commanders, he decided, "must oppose machine guns by fire from rifles." Pershing saw Europe's war as a replay of the American Civil War, revealing a habit of mind that would typify American geopolitical thinking for the next century: the belief that as the most advanced industrial nation, the United States was historically "ahead" of other countries, an advantage that allowed Americans to understand the world through the prism of their own experience.

The German onslaught interfered with Pershing's plans. On May 27, German divisions pierced French lines at Château-Thierry and advanced on Paris at a rate of 10 miles a day. Bowing to urgent requests, Pershing threw the AEF into the breach. Column after column of fresh American troops filled the roads from Paris to the front. Photographs show doughboys marching to meet the enemy across fields of wildflowers. Ahead of them lay five German divisions, poison gas, minefields, rolling artillery barrages, and machine guns. The Americans stopped the Germans, but at a fearful cost. The Marine brigade that took Belleau Wood lost half its men. Without artillery or tanks, they assaulted machine gun nests head on with rifles. The Americans, with help from a global influenza epidemic, stopped the German drive.

By mid-July, the initiative passed to the Allies. On September 12, Pershing tried his tactics against the Saint Mihiel salient, a bulge in the French lines. The doughboys

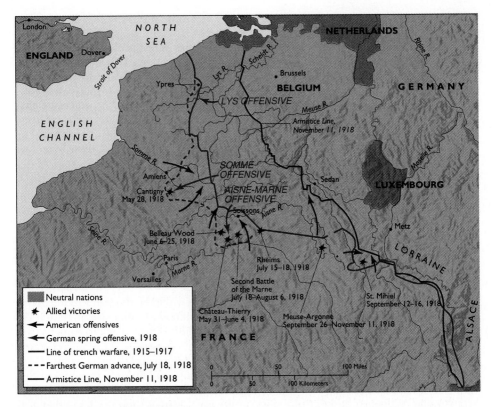

Map 22–1 Western Front, 1918
On the western front, the opposing armies fought from trenches fortified with earthworks and barbed wire. The parallel trench lines stretched thousands of miles from the North Sea to Switzerland.

raced behind the retreating enemy past their planned objectives, even outdistancing their own supply wagons. Saint Mihiel vindicated Pershing's strategy, and he yearned for another chance. It came two weeks later, at the battle of the Meuse-Argonne.

The Argonne Forest contained some of the most formidable natural and man-made defenses on the western front. Atop parallel ridges lay three fortified trench lines, or *stellung*, consisting of concrete pillboxes, barbed wire, artillery, and observation posts. Half a million German troops had defended these fortifications for four years. Against this force, Pershing arrayed the American First Army, 1,031,000 men. Pershing's battle plan called for overwhelming the German defenses with speed and numbers, breaching the first trench line and reaching the second, 10 miles inside the German front, the first day.

Breaking through the first line of German trenches after a day and a half, the battle turned into a deadly crawl up the Romagne heights into the teeth of the second *stellung*. In two weeks of fighting, 26,277 Americans died. French soldiers reported seeing the American dead lying in rows, cut down by machine guns as they marched in formation. Finally, on November 10, American troops reached their objective and dynamited the rail line connecting the cities of Metz and Sedan. Meanwhile, Germany announced that it would accept the Fourteen Points as the basis for an armistice and negotiations. At 11:00 a.m. on November 11, 1918, the guns fell silent.

African-American troops advance toward the sound of gunfire in northern France, 1918. "Our boys went on the battlefield last night singing," one wrote home.

American intervention had been decisive. The American economy lent its immense industrial and agricultural productivity to the Allies at a crucial moment. Pershing failed to transform strategy, but by striking the final blow, Americans had the illusion that their way of war had been triumphant.

Although they fought on the same battlefields, Americans and Europeans fought two vastly different wars. The Americans' war was swift and victorious; the Europeans' was a prolonged catastrophe that consumed an entire generation. For Europeans, the mental world of the prewar era, with its faith in modernity, science, and democracy, vanished forever. War validated Americans' confidence in the virtues of their own civilization, while reinforcing their suspicions of foreign systems and ideas. Confidence in the inevitability of progress became a distinctive feature of U.S. culture. In much of the world "American" became almost synonymous with "modern," but not everywhere. In the East another political and economic system shouted its claim to the future.

THE BLACK CLOUD IN THE EAST

Americans celebrated the armistice with bonfires, automobile horns, church bells, and uplifted voices. Outside the White House a choir from Howard University sang "The Spirit of Victory," a cantata written for the occasion, as army biplanes flew overhead. Wilson told Congress that "everything for which America fought has been accomplished," but he observed that the situation in Russia cast doubt on the durability of peace. Over the next months, revolutions broke out throughout Eastern Europe. Just as diplomats prepared to make peace in Europe, journalist Ray Stannard Baker wrote, there arose a "black cloud of the east, threatening to overwhelm and swallow up the world."

Wilson in Paris

For Wilson, the moment he had planned for in 1917 had arrived: The United States, he believed, would help set the terms of peace. Sure that the public would view the nation's victory as his victory, he made mistakes that undermined his support at home. First, he tried to turn the victory to political advantage. Republicans in the House and Senate had supported the president during the war, and the bipartisanship might have lasted had Wilson not dispelled it with an advertisement in the *New York Times*. "If you have approved my leadership," it read, "I earnestly beg that you will express yourself unmistakably to that effect by returning a Democratic majority to both the Senate and the House." Republicans attacked the ad as an insult to their patriotism. When the ballots were counted in the 1918 midterm elections, Republican majorities took power in both houses.

He next decided to go to Paris to negotiate himself, and passed up an opportunity to produce a bipartisan treaty by including a prominent Republican in the delegation. The chances for ratification would rest largely on Wilson's prestige and popularity.

In December 1918, Walter Lippmann, now an Army captain, stood on the balcony of the Crillon Hotel witnessing Wilson's triumphal entry into Paris. Huge crowds lined the streets, and as the procession entered the center of the city, a great cheer went up. For the next month, Wilson toured France, Italy, and Britain with cries of "Viva Veelson" ringing in his ears.

By the time he arrived for the treaty talks at the Palace of Versailles, two of the Fourteen Points had already been compromised, and Wilson's popularity provided little help at the negotiating table. Britain's David Lloyd George refused to accept the point on freedom of the seas, which would thwart the use of the Royal Navy in a future conflict. Wilson's own actions undercut his position on point six, respect for Russia's sovereignty, because American troops were occupying Russian territory in Siberia. Wilson was unable to prevent Britain, France, and Japan from dividing Germany's colonies among themselves and imposing harsh peace terms. Germany had to sign a humiliating "war guilt" clause and pay $33 billion in reparations, enough to cripple its economy for decades.

Wilson "growing grimmer and graver, day by day" concentrated his efforts on creating the League of Nations. He took the lead in drafting the League Covenant, which committed each member to submit disputes to arbitration and pledged them to take action against "any war or threat of war." Wilson presented the covenant to the peace delegations and declared, "A living thing is born."

The Senate Rejects the League

To many observers in the United States the Treaty of Versailles' imperial land grabs and severe treatment of the vanquished nations betrayed the goals Americans had fought to attain. Few in Congress and the press shared Wilson's confidence that the League of Nations would prevent future wars. They felt instead that it might only guarantee that the United States would be involved in the next conflict. To Republican leaders, like

Henry Cabot Lodge, the United States' best bet was to look to its own security and work out international relations independently rather than as part of a league.

In early March 1919, before the treaty was concluded, Lodge and 38 other senators—more than enough to defeat the treaty—signed a petition opposing the League of Nations. James A. Reed of Missouri said the covenant would turn American foreign policy over to foreigners. Senator William Borah called it "the greatest triumph for English diplomacy in three centuries of English diplomatic life." Wilson knew he would have to fight, but he believed that in the end the Senate would not reject the treaty.

In September, Wilson went "over the heads" of Congress and stumped for the treaty on a nationwide tour. Traveling more than 8,000 miles and speaking before large audiences without loudspeakers took a toll on the president's health. After a speech in Pueblo, Colorado, he became so ill that he was rushed back to Washington, where he suffered a stroke that left him paralyzed on his left side and unable to concentrate for more than a few minutes a day. Mrs. Wilson and the president's physician kept his condition secret and refused to allow anyone to see him.

With the League of Nations' champion secluded in the White House, the Senate defeated the treaty. Down to the end, Wilson refused to allow Senate Democrats to accept any modifications. Lodge and the Republicans were not ready to retreat into isolation, but they preferred diplomatic strategies that employed the United States' overwhelming economic power rather than its relatively weak military forces. They also saw Latin America as more critical than Europe to U.S. security.

Meanwhile, European governments organized the League of Nations without the United States or the Soviet Union. Over the next decade, U.S. influence abroad grew enormously. American automobiles, radios, and movies could be seen in far corners of the globe. However, the United States was cautious in its diplomatic dealings in Europe and Asia, to avoid being drawn into what the *New York Tribune* called the "vast seething mass of anarchy extending from the Rhine to the Siberian wastes."

Red Scare

On May 1, 1919, a dozen or more mail bombs were sent to prominent Americans, including J. P. Morgan, John D. Rockefeller, and Supreme Court Justice Oliver Wendell Holmes. None of the packages reached its intended target, but one blew up in the hands of a maid in the home of Senator Thomas Hardwick. A month later a bomb exploded outside the residence of Attorney General A. Mitchell Palmer in Washington. Investigations showed that the bombings were the work of lone lunatics, but many people concluded that communists were trying to overthrow the government. Since the Russian Revolution, newspapers, evangelists, and government officials had fed fears of Bolshevism.

The Communist risings in Europe terrified conservatives in the United States and led them to look for Soviet accomplices, particularly among immigrants and unionized workers. They drew no distinctions among Socialists, anarchists, Communists, and labor unionists; they were all "red." When steelworkers in Gary, Indiana, struck for higher wages and shorter hours in September 1919, Judge Elbert Gary, president of U.S. Steel, denounced them as Bolsheviks. Enlisting the help of local loyalty leagues, Judge Gary broke the strike.

Using the patriotic rhetoric of the war, industry leaders labeled strikers as dangerous aliens. They persuaded the courts to take action, and a series of Supreme Court decisions made union activity virtually illegal. In 1919 the court allowed antitrust suits under the Sherman Act to be filed against unions, and it later declared boycotts illegal and limited strikers' freedom to picket. In January 1920 a series of

CHRONOLOGY

1911	Mexican Revolution begins
1914	U.S. troops occupy Veracruz, Mexico World War I begins
1915	U.S. troops occupy Haiti (until 1934) *Lusitania* sunk
1916	U.S. forces invade Mexico in search of Pancho Villa U.S. forces enter the Dominican Repubic Woodrow Wilson re-elected
1917	Russian czar abdicates; parliamentary regime takes power U.S. declares war on Germany East St. Louis riot Houston riot October Revolution overthrows Russian government; Lenin takes power
1918	Wilson announces U.S. war aims: the Fourteen Points Wilson nationalizes railroads Sedition Act outlaws criticism of the U.S. government Armistice ends fighting on the western front
1919	Eighteenth Amendment outlaws manufacture, sale, and transport of alcoholic beverages Versailles Treaty signed in Paris Mail bombs target prominent government and business figures Gary, Indiana, steel strike U.S. Senate rejects Versailles Treaty
1920	Nineteenth Amendment secures the vote for women Palmer raids arrest thousands of suspected Communists Sacco and Vanzetti arrested on charges of robbery and murder

crackdowns known as the Palmer raids began. Some 250 members of the Union of Russian Workers were arrested and deported to Russia on an Army transport. In one night, 4,000 suspected Communists were arrested in raids across the country.

The most notorious case associated with the "Red Scare" began in May 1920 when Nicola Sacco and Bartolomeo Vanzetti, a shoemaker and a fish peddler, were arrested for robbing a shoe company in South Braintree, Massachusetts. Two men were killed during the robbery, and ballistics experts claimed that the bullets came from Sacco's gun. The trial, however, focused on the fact that the defendants were Italian and anarchists. The state doctored evidence and witnesses changed testimony, but the judge favored the prosecution. Despite Sacco's corroborated testimony that he was in Boston at the time of the robbery and the sworn confession of another man, Judge Webster Thayer sentenced Sacco and Vanzetti to death.

The appeals lasted six years, and protests for their release mounted. As the day of the execution approached, Europeans and Latin Americans organized boycotts of American products. Riots in Paris took 20 lives. Governments called on the president to intervene, but on August 23, 1927, Sacco and Vanzetti died in the electric chair.

Americans who had talked in 1917 about making the world safe for democracy now seemed ready to throw their freedoms away out of fear of anarchy. By the end of 1920, the original terror subsided, but labor unions and radicals would have to fend off the charge of communism for decades to come.

CONCLUSION

Wilson tried to lead America toward what he called a new world order, a world where nations and international law would count more than empires and where the United States could light the way toward progress, stability, and peace. He failed to recognize that for many Americans this future was filled with terrors as well as promise. The strains of war introduced new divisions in American society. Progressivism, which had given coherence and direction to social change, was a spent force. The growth of federal administration, the new powers of big business, internal migrations, and new social movements and values added up to what Lippmann called a "revolutionary world." Americans entered the 1920s with a sense of uneasiness. They knew that their nation was the world's strongest, but they were unsure about what that might mean for their lives.

FURTHER READINGS

Nancy K. Bristow, *Making Men Moral: Social Engineering During the Great War* (1996). How government and women's groups attempted to use military training to mold men into model citizens.

John Eisenhower, *Intervention! The United States and the Mexican Revolution, 1913–1917* (1993). The story of the U.S. occupation of Veracruz and Pershing's search for Pancho Villa.

Meirion Harries, *The Last Days of Innocence: America at War, 1917–1918* (1997). A lively anecdotal history of the war years.

David M. Kennedy, *Over Here: The First World War and American Society* (1980). The best study of the home front during World War I.

N. Gordon Levin, Jr., *Woodrow Wilson and World Politics* (1968). The progressive president's response to the disorder of world politics. Levin analyzes the idealism and realism of Wilsonian foreign policy.

H. C. Peterson and Gilbert C. Fite, *Opponents of War, 1917–1918* (1957). Still the best study on wartime peace movements and the Wilson administration's attempts to suppress dissent.

Ronald Steel, *Walter Lippmann and the American Century* (1980). More than any other journalist, Lippmann shaped American foreign policy in the twentieth century.

 Please refer to the document CD-ROM for primary sources related to this chapter.

23

The 1920s

"The Queen of Swimmers" • A Dynamic Economy • A Modern
Culture • The Limits of the Modern Culture • A "New Era" in
Politics and Government • Conclusion

"THE QUEEN OF SWIMMERS"

On August 6, 1926, Gertrude Ederle walked across the beach at Cape Gris-Nez on the French coastline. Her body and her bright red swimsuit were heavily greased. At 7:00 a.m., the 19-year-old from New York City plunged into the water and began to swim toward the coast of England.

"Trudy," the daughter of a German immigrant butcher, was a champion distance swimmer who had won medals at the 1924 Olympics, but no woman had ever completed the long, hazardous swim across the English Channel. In fact, only five men had accomplished the feat. Ederle herself had tried and failed the year before.

This time was different. Despite the tides, the chill water, and the threat of sharks, Ederle persevered, spurred on by her competitive instincts, her eagerness to please her mother, and her father's promise to buy her a new car, a roadster, if she succeeded.

Inspired by thoughts of that roadster, Ederle fought the choppy waves and hunted for a favorable tide. Finally, after 14 hours and 31 minutes in the water, she came ashore at Kingsdown, England, at 9:40 p.m. Ederle had become the first woman to swim the channel and had made the crossing faster than any of the men before her. Back in the United States, newspapers trumpeted Ederle's stunning achievement in page-one headlines and analyzed it in editorials. Ederle came home to a tumultuous ticker-tape parade in New York. "No President or king, soldier or statesman," reported the *New York Times*, "has ever enjoyed such an enthusiastic and affectionate outburst of acclaim by the metropolis as was offered to . . . the 'Queen of

Swimmers.'" She was overwhelmed with offers to endorse products and to appear on stage and in the movies.

Gertrude Ederle's enormous reception said a great deal about the United States in the 1920s. Once again at peace, America could afford to indulge an interest in the exploits of a long-distance swimmer. The nation's dynamic industrial economy seemed effortlessly to produce plenty of roadsters, movies, and prosperity.

Ederle herself exemplified a new national culture, rooted in the booming economy. Emphasizing the importance of pleasure, this modern culture celebrated leisure activities. The new culture glorified the purchase and consumption of material goods such as the roadster Ederle wanted and the merchandise she advertised. The teenage swimmer embodied still other aspects of the new culture—its fascination with youth, its endorsement of a child-centered family life, and its infatuation with pleasure-seeking, independent women.

In the euphoria of the ticker-tape parade, it was easy to conclude that Americans welcomed the emerging cultural and political order as much as they welcomed Trudy Ederle. In fact, many people were troubled by the changes of the 1920s. The new order did not speak to the social and economic inequalities that plagued national life. As a result, the new cultural and political order faced a powerful backlash, just as Ederle faced a hostile tide in the English Channel. Nevertheless, like the swimmer, the new culture and politics seemed to overcome all opposition as the decade moved to a close.

A DYNAMIC ECONOMY

By and large, the 1920s were a prosperous time for America. After a recession during 1920 and 1921, the economy stabilized and then grew. Consumer prices remained steady throughout the decade, and jobs were plentiful; the unemployment rate went as low as 1.8 percent in 1926. Wages jumped: The nation's net income—the value of its earnings from labor and property—leapt from $64.0 billion in 1921 to $86.8 billion in 1929. This prosperity was driven by the dynamism of the evolving industrial economy. New technologies, increased efficiency, a maturing automobile industry, and new businesses all contributed to the economic gains.

Despite the general prosperity, the transformation of the economy involved defeats for organized labor and decline for many farmers. The relative weakness of agriculture and the strength of industry helped to turn the United States into a predominantly urban nation. In the prosperous 1920s, as always, industrial capitalism was a transforming force.

The Development of Industry

Several long-term factors shaped the development of American industry in the 1920s. In their continuing quest for more efficient production, businessmen made use of new technologies and other innovations during the decade.

The switch from coal to electricity, underway since the 1910s, was an important innovation in factories. By the end of the 1920s, electricity powered more than two-thirds of American manufacturing plants.

Henry Ford's car company pioneered another critical innovation, the system that became known as mass production. By the 1910s, Ford, like other American manufacturers, used interchangeable parts, simple and accurate machine tools, and electric power to speed output at its Highland Park factory complex in Detroit, Michigan. However, auto production was slowed by a traditional manufacturing practice. Frames, transmissions, and other key subassemblies remained in place on stands while teams of workers moved from one stand to another to work.

Eager to meet the rising demand for the popular Model T car, Ford's managers reversed the process by "moving the work to the men." Beginning in 1913, the Ford plant used conveyor belts and chains to send subassemblies past groups of stationary workers. Instead of making an entire engine or subassembly, a worker might tighten a few bolts or install a single part. This led to an astonishing increase in output. In 1914, Ford produced 300,000 Model Ts. In 1923, the company produced more than 2 million. By that time, other manufacturers were racing to copy Ford's techniques.

Mass production, electrification, and other innovations spurred an extraordinary increase in productivity for American industry. Output per worker skyrocketed 72 percent from 1919 to 1929.

Along with increased productivity, the rise of several industries drove the economy. Auto production now dominated as textiles, railroads, iron, and steel had earlier. In 1921, there were 9.3 million cars on American roads. By 1929, the figure had reached 23 million. By producing all those cars, auto manufacturers stimulated demand for plate glass, oil, gasoline, and rubber.

Other sectors of the industrial economy also grew rapidly. The demand for processed foods, household appliances, office machinery, and chemicals increased dramatically. Emerging industries such as aircraft demonstrated their potential economic importance.

Arguably the first powered, fixed-wing flight had occurred in December 1903, when Wilbur and Orville Wright brought their "Flyer" to the beach at Kitty Hawk, North Carolina. With Orville lying at the controls, the fragile plane flew 120 feet in 12 seconds. But, the civilian airplane industry did not take off until the 1920s. Aircraft production rose from less than 300 in 1922 to more than 6,000 in 1929. By then, fledgling airlines were flying passengers on scheduled flights.

The Trend Toward Large-Scale Organization

The development of industry reinforced the trend toward large-scale organization that was basic to U.S. capitalism. Only big businesses had the financial resources to pay for mass production. By 1929, corporations produced 92 percent of the nation's manufactured goods.

The largest firms also benefited from more efficient organizational structures. When the recession of 1920 and 1921 left big corporations with too many unsold goods, companies reorganized. Now top managers, aided by financial, legal, and other experts, oversaw the work of semiautonomous divisions that supplied different markets. At General Motors, for example, the Chevrolet division produced huge numbers of relatively inexpensive cars, while the Cadillac division turned out a smaller number of expensive cars. The new organizational system made corporations more flexible, efficient, and responsive to changes in consumer demand.

Corporate growth was not confined to industry. Chains such as A & P grocers and F. W. Woolworth's variety stores increased their share of the nation's retail sales from 4 percent to 20 percent. One percent of the nation's banks managed nearly half of the country's financial assets.

Giant firms and their leaders had often been the targets of suspicion, hostility, and reform during the Progressive era, but many Americans softened their attitude toward business in the prosperous 1920s. Basking in the glow of public approval, big business confidently forecast a central role for itself in the nation's destiny.

The Transformation of Work and the Work Force

The modern corporation changed the nature of work and the work force in the 1920s. Industrial efficiency was not just a matter of electricity and machines. To speed up production, the managers at Ford and other factories had to speed up the labor process.

Accordingly, the spirit of scientific management continued to sweep through American industry. Laboring under ever tighter supervision, workers were pushed to work faster and harder. Ford's system of mass production shared Frederick Winslow Taylor's determination to simplify and regiment labor. The result was less satisfying work. Instead of making a whole engine, a Ford assembly-line worker might spend his day turning a few nuts on one engine after another.

The development of industry contributed to the transformation of occupational structure. As the economy became increasingly efficient, the nation experienced a net loss of about a million jobs in manufacturing, coal mining, and railroading. The growth of other kinds of employment more than compensated for this decrease, however. The ranks of white-collar workers increased 80 percent from 1910 to 1930, when nearly one worker in three did white-collar work rather than manual labor. The nation had already begun a long-term evolution from an industrial economy based on manual labor to a postindustrial economy based on white-collar work.

The development of the economy also encouraged the continuing, gradual movement of women into the paid work force. By the end of the 1920s, women made up a majority of clerical workers. Married women were more likely than ever to work outside the home.

Despite these changes, women still faced discrimination in the workplace. They were paid less than men who did comparable work. Hardly any women held high-level managerial jobs. Moreover, there was still resistance to the idea that women should work outside the home. Most people continued to believe that a woman's place was in the home, especially if she had children. Only economic necessities—families' need for income and employers' need for workers—reconciled American society to women's employment in the 1920s.

The Defeat of Organized Labor

The American labor movement did not respond effectively to the transformation of work and the work force. In an age of increasing economic organization, workers became less organized. In 1920 nearly one nonagricultural worker in five belonged to a union. By 1929, little more than one in 10 was a union member. The labor movement was especially weak in the developing mass-production industries such as automobiles and steel and barely addressed the growing ranks of clerks and other white-collar workers.

The weak state of organized labor partly resulted from prosperity. Earning relatively good wages, many workers were less interested in joining unions. To convince them that unions were unnecessary, corporations promoted *welfare capitalism*, a set of highly publicized programs ranging from lunch-hour movies to sports teams to profit-sharing plans.

While some firms tried to win over their workers with baseball teams and company unions, many employers used tougher tactics to battle the labor movement. Management crusaded for the "open shop"—a workplace free of labor organization—and found an ally in the judicial system. During the 1920s, rulings by the U.S. Supreme Court made it easier for lower courts to grant injunctions against union activities. State and federal courts issued injunctions to stop unions from striking and exercising their rights and allowed businesses to sue unions for damages.

The labor movement also hurt its own cause. The leadership of the major national organization, the AFL, was increasingly conservative and timid. The heads of the AFL, white males with Western European roots who represented skilled crafts, had little interest in organizing women workers and wanted nothing to do with socialists, radical unionists, or African-American workers. The AFL was slow to admit or even pay attention to the Brotherhood of Sleeping Car Porters, the assertive union of African-American workers organized in 1925 under socialist A. Philip Randolph. Despite pleas from Randolph and others, the AFL failed to organize unskilled workers, many of whom were African Americans or white immigrants from Eastern and Southern Europe.

Weakened by internal divisions, welfare capitalism, the open-shop crusade, and the courts, the labor movement did not challenge the ongoing transformation of industrial labor. Nationwide, the number of strikes and lockouts dropped from 3,411 in 1920 to 604 in 1928. All too often, these labor actions ended in defeat for workers.

The Decline of Agriculture

Against the backdrop of national prosperity, American agriculture continued its long decline. Prices for basic crops such as cotton and wheat fell, and the number of farms dropped.

The larger story of decline obscured important signs of growth and health. Some agricultural sectors were as dynamic as industry, and for the same reasons—increased efficiency promoted by new technologies and large-scale organization. Mechanization made farm labor more efficient, as did the increasing development of irrigation systems since the turn of the century. By the 1920s, the irrigated farms of the Southwest were producing bumper crops of cotton, fruits, and vegetables. The Southwest also witnessed the rise of huge farms with owners who could afford mechanization and irrigation. These innovative "factories in the fields" depended on the old-fashioned exploitation of farm labor, as well as on size and technology. In California's Imperial Valley and elsewhere, migrant workers labored in harsh conditions for low pay.

Ironically, the dynamism of the agricultural economy created a problem for many American farmers. Midsize farms could not compete with the "factories in the fields." Increased efficiency, meanwhile, led to bumper crops that did not always find a market at a good price. Farmers were hurt by changes in Americans' diet, such as declining consumption of bread and potatoes, as well as by the rise of competitors overseas. The resulting glut reduced the price of farm products. As their incomes lagged behind those of urban workers, farmers yearned for *parity*—the return of high pre-World War I agricultural prices.

Farmers' purchasing power did improve as nonagricultural prices dropped and farm prices rose toward the end of the decade, but the basic reality did not change. As a Georgia farmer observed, "The hand that is feeding the world is being spit upon."

The Urban Nation

The woes of agriculture contributed to a long-term shift in the geographical distribution of the American population. For the first time, according to the federal census of 1920, a majority of Americans—54 million out of 105 million—lived in urban territory. This did not mean the United States had become a nation of big cities. The census defined "urban territory" as places with as few as 2,500 people. Nevertheless, the United States was no longer predominantly rural.

The decline of farming spurred this transformation. As agricultural prices fell, millions of Americans fled the nation's farms, and the growth of the industrial economy swelled the population of towns and cities. In the 1920s, factory production was still centered in urban areas. Manufacturing gave many cities their identity. Detroit was becoming the "motor city." Pittsburgh, Pennsylvania, and Birmingham, Alabama, symbolized the steel industry. Most of the new white-collar jobs were located in cities.

The rise of the automobile also contributed to the emergence of the urban nation. The car made it practical for Americans to live in suburbs. In the 1920s, the suburban lifestyle was still mostly for the well-to-do. Elite suburbs, such as Grosse Pointe outside Detroit, and Glendale and Inglewood outside Los Angeles, grew explosively. The transformation of the countryside into suburbs was a powerful symbol of the new urban nation.

A MODERN CULTURE

The 1920s saw the full emergence of a modern culture. So perfectly symbolized by Gertrude Ederle, the new culture extolled the virtues of modernity, pleasure, leisure, and consumption. It reflected the needs of an industrial economy that had to sell the goods rolling off the assembly lines. Supported by advertising and installment buying, the culture of leisure and consumption offered spectator sports, movies, popular music, radio, and sex. The new culture entailed new views of gender, family life, and youth and placed renewed emphasis on the old values of individualism in an increasingly organized society.

The Spread of Consumerism

By the 1920s, many Americans, encouraged by big business, increasingly defined life as the pursuit of pleasure. People were invited to seek gratification through the consumption of goods and services. This philosophy of consumerism saturated American society by the end of the decade.

In addition to higher wages, many workers had more free time. For salaried, middle-class workers, the annual vacation had become a tradition by the 1910s. Although blue-collar workers seldom enjoyed a vacation, they spent less time on the job. Some employers, including Henry Ford, instituted a five-day work week during the 1920s. More commonly, businesses shortened their workday.

A change in attitude accompanied these changes in wages and workdays. The work ethic seemed less necessary in a prospering economy. Thanks to Fordism and Taylorism, work was less satisfying, too. In these circumstances, people justified pleasure as an essential antidote to labor.

The advertising industry encouraged the new attitude toward pleasure. During the 1920s, ads appeared everywhere—in newspapers and magazines, on billboards and big electric signs, and, by the end of the decade, on radio. Impressed by successful ad campaigns for such products as Listerine antiseptic and mouthwash and Fleischmann's yeast, big businesses increasingly turned to advertising agencies to sell goods and services. Expenditures for advertising leaped from $682 million in 1914 to nearly $3 billion by 1929.

Advertising, like the new culture, optimistically embraced change and innovation. According to advertisements, purchasing the right products would solve people's problems and thereby bring them fulfillment.

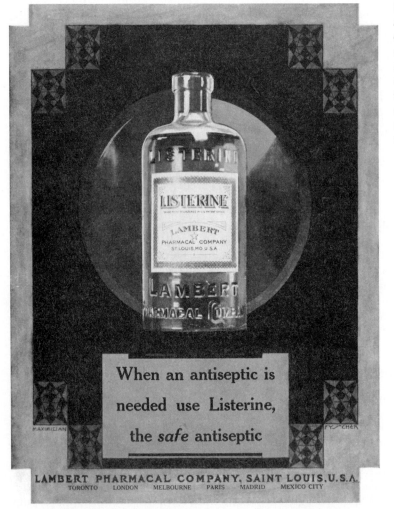

Selling mouthwash and consumerism. An elegant and rather restrained ad was part of the successful campaign to market Listerine to Americans.

Along with advertising, business used installment plans to encourage Americans to buy goods and services. The booming sales of such consumer goods as automobiles, radios, pianos, and washing machines depended on allowing customers to buy "on time." Credit buying spread so rapidly that the nation's total consumer debt more than doubled from 1922 to 1929.

New Pleasures

The culture of the 1920s offered many pleasures, especially spectator sports, movies, popular music, and radio. Gertrude Ederle was part of a golden age for spectator sports. Tennis, boxing, and auto racing flourished during the decade. The American Professional Football Association, which became the National Football League, played its first season in 1920. Baseball remained the most popular American sport, thanks in part to the exploits of the New York Yankees' home-run-hitting outfielder, Babe Ruth.

While spectator sports enthralled millions, another passive pleasure, the movies, was undeniably the most popular consumer attraction of the 1920s. Movies had matured into a big business commanding the loyalty of millions of Americans. Spreading through the cities and into the suburbs, theaters became larger and more elegant. By the 1920s, lavish movie "palaces," such as the Roxy in New York and the Tivoli in Chicago, were designed to evoke the Orient and other exotic far-away places.

Movie attendance doubled from 40 million a week in 1922 to 80 million a week in 1929. That attendance fueled the development of the handful of film companies that dominated the industry. By the 1920s, the center of movie production had shifted from New York to Hollywood, California. Technological innovation promised that this big business would grow still bigger. In 1927, Warner Brothers successfully released the first sound movie, *The Jazz Singer.*

It was fitting that the first sound movie was about the impact of jazz. Popular music in general and jazz in particular played an important role in the new consumer culture. Created by African Americans in the 1910s, jazz was a rhythmically and harmonically innovative music. The new music emerged in New Orleans, home to the first major jazz composer, Jelly Roll Morton, and to the first jazz superstar, trumpeter and singer Louis Armstrong. As jazz became nationally popular, its focus moved to Chicago and New York, as did so many African Americans.

For young white people, jazz was the music of outsiders, of African Americans. Soon white musicians were contributing to the evolution of the music. For many whites, jazz summed up a period seemingly dominated by the pursuit of liberating pleasures. The 1920s became known as the "Jazz Age."

The great popularity of jazz and other musical genres was made possible by the phonograph, originated by Thomas Edison in the 1870s and modified by other inventors. In the 1920s, the electrical recording microphone dramatically improved the sound quality of records and made the new music accessible to millions of Americans.

A newer technological innovation, the radio, also allowed Americans to hear popular music. After Italian inventor Guglielmo Marconi transmitted the first radio waves through the air in 1895, a series of innovations made possible the inauguration of commercial radio broadcasting in the United States by 1920. The federal government began licensing radio stations the next year.

Jazz pioneers: The Washingtonians, led by pianist, composer, and arranger Edward Kennedy "Duke" Ellington (seated at right). By the end of the 1920s jazz had swept across the nation, and Ellington had become one of the new music's great stars.

Like the movies, radio quickly became big business. By 1923, there were more than 500 stations. Americans tuned in to hear broadcasts of live music, news, sports, and soap operas. To meet the demand for radios, manufacturers turned out more than 2 million sets a year by 1925. Radio, like the movies, played a key role in disseminating the values of consumerism, as corporations rushed to advertise their products by sponsoring radio programs.

A Sexual Revolution

Along with such new pleasures as radio and movies, modern culture offered a new attitude toward an old pleasure, sex. By the 1920s, Americans' sexual attitudes and behavior were changing. During the progressive era, reformers forced the public discussion of such social issues as prostitution and venereal disease. The popular amusements of the 1910s and 1920s inundated Americans with sexual images.

The increased openness about sex reflected the growing belief that sexual pleasure was necessary and desirable, particularly within marriage. Married couples increasingly considered intercourse as an opportunity for pleasure as well as procreation.

The new view of marital sexuality helped to change attitudes toward contraception. By the 1910s, an emerging grassroots movement, led by socialists and other radicals, promoted sex education and contraceptives, which were largely illegal. The crusade's best known figure was the fiery former nurse and socialist organizer, Margaret Sanger. In 1915, Sanger coined the term "birth control." Birth control gradually became respectable—and widely practiced—in the 1920s.

Although most Americans still insisted publicly that sexual intercourse should be confined to marriage, and they still condemned homosexuality, a sexual revolution was underway. The emergent modern culture insisted that sexual pleasure was an integral aspect of life.

Changing Gender Ideals

The shifting attitude toward sex was closely tied to new gender ideals. By the 1920s, Americans' sense of what it meant to be female was changing. Since the late nineteenth century, Americans had been talking about the "New Woman," who claimed the right to attend school, vote, and have a career. The "New Woman" of the 1920s was now a sexual being, too. An object of male desire, she was also a fun-loving individual with desires of her own.

The most popular image of the American woman of the 1920s was the vivacious young "flapper," with her short skirt, bound breasts, and bobbed hair. The flapper was likely to wear cosmetics and to smoke cigarettes—practices once associated only with prostitutes.

Symbols of the fun-loving culture of the "Jazz Age": a flapper and two jazz musicians on the cover of McClure's Magazine.

Notions of masculinity were also changing. With the growing emphasis on female needs and desires, men were urged to be attentive and responsive and to focus on the home. As the world of work became less satisfying, experts told men to look for fulfillment in family life. The family man of the 1920s, unlike the stereotypical Victorian man, was not supposed to be a distant, stern patriarch. Instead, he was a companion to his wife and a doting friend to his children.

In practice, many men still defined themselves in terms of their work, rather than their domestic life. Moreover, American society still regarded women as the primary caretaker of children. Despite the clear change in domestic values, many men were still relative outsiders in the home.

The Family and Youth

Changing gender ideals were directly related to a reconsideration of family life and youth. In the 1920s, the American family no longer played a direct role in economic production. To most Americans, the family was no longer a group of productive workers. Child labor laws increasingly made sure that boys and girls spent their time in school rather than in the workplace. The family became primarily a unit of leisure and consumption. The home was the place where men, women, and children found pleasure and fulfillment, where they congregated around the radio and used their Fleischmann's yeast and Listerine mouthwash.

Reflecting the values of the modern culture, parents became more likely to indulge their children, who enjoyed more toys, possessions, spending money, and pleasures than had earlier generations. The automobile gave young people more mobility, too. With their new freedom, they could begin to create their own separate culture.

Most adults accepted this situation partly because they admired and envied youthfulness. The modern culture, unhappy with work and anxious for fun, glorified youth. "Flaming Youth" became a symbol of the culture of the 1920s.

The Celebration of the Individual

The emphasis on the individual, so evident in changing views of sex, gender, family, and youth, was a fundamental aspect of the modern culture. In addition to Gertrude Ederle and Babe Ruth, Americans admired a host of sports heroes and heroines, including tennis player Helen Wills Moody, boxer Jack Dempsey, golfer Bobby Jones, and football running back Red Grange. In the 1920s, the movie industry increasingly focused public attention on the distinctive personalities of stars. Individualism was basic to the "New Woman," too.

The resurgence of individualism was not surprising. The belief in the importance of the individual was deeply engrained in the American political economy. Paradoxically, the development of industrial capitalism intensified the importance of both individuals and organizations. As corporations grew larger and produced more, these giant firms needed to stimulate consumerism. Consumerism depended on a willingness to define life in terms of gratifying individual needs and desires.

There were serious obstacles to true individualism in the 1920s. Powerful organizations, including corporations, controlled individual life. Even the most famous individual exploit of the decade depended on organization. On May 20–21, 1927, Charles A. Lindbergh flew his monoplane, *The Spirit of St. Louis*, from New York City to Paris. This first nonstop solo crossing of the Atlantic made Lindbergh an international symbol of what an individual could accomplish, but Lindbergh's feat relied on a group of businessmen who put up the money and a corporation that built the plane. Organization and individualism, the new and the old, were interdependent in the 1920s.

THE LIMITS OF THE MODERN CULTURE

The modern culture had clear limits in the 1920s. For millions of Americans, much of the consumer lifestyle was out of reach. Despite general prosperity, low incomes and poverty persisted. As late as 1928, six out of ten American families made less than the $2,000 a year required for the "basic needs of life."

The spread of the new values was as limited as the spread of prosperity. Many Americans, among them artists and intellectuals, were unwilling to define their lives by the pursuit of pleasure, leisure, and consumption. For them the modern culture represented an unwelcome abandonment of old values. In different ways, fundamentalist Christians, immigration restrictionists, and the Ku Klux Klan demanded a return to an earlier United States. Others, such as Chicanos and African Americans, found that the new culture did not address their needs or had in reality changed very little.

The "Lost Generation" of Intellectuals

Many artists and intellectuals felt alienated from the United States of the 1920s. For white, mostly male writers and artists who came of age during World War I, the conflict represented a failure of Western civilization, a brutal and pointless exercise in destruction. Its aftermath left these Americans angry, alienated, and rootless. In a nation supposedly devoted to individualism, they did not feel free. They were, as the writer Gertrude Stein described them, a "Lost Generation."

However prosperous and peaceful, the postwar years did not reassure the Lost Generation about the course of American life. Artists and intellectuals argued that the nation had not changed much at all. In such works as *Winesburg, Ohio* (1919), novelist Sherwood Anderson portrayed a still-repressive society that denied people real freedom and individuality. The acid-tongued critic H. L. Mencken, editor of the magazine *The American Mercury*, excoriated a provincial and parochial culture.

At the same time, other American artists and intellectuals feared that their country had changed too much. Although excited by the potential of the machine, they noted the toll that industrialization exacted in increasingly routinized work and a culture devoted to the pursuit of superficial pleasures. In his 1922 novel, *Babbitt*, Sinclair Lewis satirized the life of a midwestern Republican businessman obsessed with consumerism. F. Scott Fitzgerald, in such fiction as *This Side of Paradise* (1920) and *The Great Gatsby* (1925), conveyed the sense of loss and emptiness in the lives of fashionable "Flaming Youth."

From a different angle, 12 southern intellectuals, including Allen Tate, Robert Penn Warren, Donald Davidson, and John Crowe Ransom, attacked the modern culture in *I'll Take My Stand: The South and the Agrarian Tradition* (1930). Their essays offered a spirited defense of the rural, traditional culture and lamented an industrial consumer society that demeaned work and exalted individualism.

The artists and intellectuals of the decade did not set off a mass rebellion against modern culture, but they did articulate the ambivalence and uneasiness many people felt. In different and contradictory ways, artists and intellectuals laid out an agenda for Americans as they came to terms with modern, consumer society in the decades to come.

Fundamentalist Christians and "Old-Time Religion"

For many Americans of faith, the rapid growth of the modern culture promoted a sense of profound and unsettling change. The new culture was troubling because it was so secular. American society seemed to define life in terms of material satisfaction rather than spiritual commitment. Many Protestants, feeling that their own churches had betrayed them, resented the influence of liberal Protestants who had tried to accommodate their faith to the methods and discoveries of science and scholarship.

Fundamentalists, or opponents of liberalism, took their name from *The Fundamentals*, a series of essays by conservative Protestant theologians that appeared in 1909. By the end of World War I, fundamentalists dominated the Southern Baptist Convention and were fighting liberals for control of the northern churches.

Fundamentalists rejected liberalism above all for its willingness to question the historical truth of the Bible. The fundamentalist movement urged people to return to biblical, patriarchal, and denominational authority, to what came to be called "old-time" religion.

The high point in the fundamentalist–liberal battle came in a courtroom in Tennessee in 1925. That year, a high school biology teacher, John Scopes, tested a new state law banning the teaching of "any theory that denies the story of the divine creation of man as taught in the Bible, and that teaches instead that man has descended from a lower order of animals." Scopes's trial became a national media event. The chief lawyer for the prosecution was William Jennings Bryan, the former Democratic presidential candidate and Secretary of State who had become a leading crusader for fundamentalism. While Bryan was a long-time champion of rural America, Scopes's attorneys—Clarence Darrow and Dudley Field Malone—represented the city and modern culture. (Malone had helped to finance Gertrude Ederle's swim across the English Channel.) In a dramatic confrontation, Darrow called Bryan to the stand and forced him to concede that the Bible might not be literally accurate. Although Scopes was convicted and fined, Bryan and the fundamentalists lost credibility.

Nativists and Immigration Restriction

While fundamentalist Christianity sought a return to old-time religion, a resurgent nativist movement wanted to go back to an earlier, supposedly more homogenous America. As mass migration from Europe to the United States resumed after World War I, nativist feeling revived among Americans from Western European backgrounds. Thanks to the Russian Revolution and the domestic Red Scare, they associated immigrants with anarchism and radicalism and called for a return to a simpler, less ethnically diverse nation.

This view decisively shaped public policy. In 1921, Congress overwhelmingly passed a law temporarily limiting the annual immigration from any European country to 3 percent of the number of its immigrants who had been living in the United States in 1910. This quota sharply reduced the number of new immigrants from Southern and Eastern Europe, but nativists wanted even tougher action. Congress responded with the National Origins Act of 1924. This limited the annual intake from a European country to 2 percent of the number of its immigrants living in the United States in 1890—a time when there were few Southern and Eastern Europeans in America. The Act also excluded Japanese immigrants altogether. The legislation had the desired effect: Immigration fell from 805,000 arrivals in 1921 to 280,000 in 1929 (see Table 23–1).

TABLE 23–1

The Impact of Nativism: Immigration, 1921–1929			
	(Arrivals in Thousands)		
Origin	**1921**	**1925**	**1929**
Eastern Europe & Poland	138	10	14
Southern Europe	299	8	22
Asia	25	4	4
Mexico	31	33	40
Total	805	294	280

Source: Historical Statistics of the United States, I, 401. (Note: Itemized groups do not add up to totals.)

The Rebirth of the Ku Klux Klan

Nativism and fundamentalism helped spur another challenge to the new cultural order of the 1920s. In 1915, the Ku Klux Klan, the vigilante group that had terrorized African Americans in the South during Reconstruction, was reborn and enjoyed explosive growth after World War I. The "Invisible Empire" borrowed the rituals of the nineteenth-century Klan, including its costume of white robes and hoods and its symbol of a burning cross. Like the old Klan, the twentieth-century version was driven by a racist hatred of African Americans, but the new Klan took on new targets, including Jews, Roman Catholics, immigrants, religious liberalism, and change in general.

The reborn Klan had extremist views but a mainstream, national membership, flourishing in every region, in cities as well as the countryside. The Klan was an extremist group with surprisingly strong roots in "respectable" America.

The Invisible Empire condemned modern culture, charging that the nation now valued "money above manhood." Klan rallies rang with denunciations of big business. Above all, the Klan condemned the new culture of leisure and pleasure. The Klan was hostile to the new gender ideals, to birth control and freer sexuality, and to the independence of youth. In essence, the Ku Klux Klan lamented the transformations of the twentieth century and yearned for an earlier America in which white Protestant males had power over women, youth, and other groups and had nothing to fear from big business.

For several years, the Klan proved extraordinarily successful. At its peak, the organization enrolled perhaps 3 to 5 million secret members. Because so many politicians sympathized with the Klan or feared its power, the organization had considerable political influence. Working with both major parties, the order helped to elect governors, senators, and other officials.

At the height of its power, however, the Invisible Empire collapsed under the weight of scandal. One former imperial wizard was revealed to have drunk alcohol, read pornography, and consorted with prostitutes. Assistants to the current imperial wizard were caught, drunk and nude, in an adulterous tryst. Incidents such as these, along with financial scandals, revealed the lawlessness and hypocrisy of the Klan's leadership. It had also become obvious that most Americans, however uneasy about the new culture, had no desire to support prejudice, lawbreaking, and violence. The Klan's membership dropped precipitously in the late 1920s.

White-robed men, women, and children of the Ku Klux Klan arriving in Cincinnati, Ohio, to celebrate the organization and its defense of "traditional" values.

Mexican Americans

Despite the activities of immigration restrictionists and the Klan, the United States remained a diverse nation at the end of the 1920s, in some ways, more diverse than ever. The struggle of Chicanos, ethnic Mexicans, to make a life in the United States revealed both the opportunities created by the dynamic economy and the limits of the new culture.

In the 1890s the migration of Mexicans began a dramatic, long-term increase. Perhaps a million to a million and a half Mexicans entered the United States legally or surreptitiously between 1890 and 1929. They left primarily to escape the transformation of Mexican agriculture that made it impossible for the rural poor to make a living off the land, and to avoid the upheaval of the Mexican Revolution of 1910 (see Chapter 22, "A Global Power"). Ironically, the restrictionist immigration legislation of the 1920s helped ensure that Mexicans would find work in the United States: Unable to get enough European or Asian workers, employers turned eagerly to Mexico as a source of cheap and often temporary seasonal labor. In particular the Southwest's rapidly developing economy needed workers for mines, railroads, construction gangs, and above all, farms. By the end of the 1920s, Chicanos dominated low-wage labor in the Southwest.

Like a large number of immigrants from Europe, many Mexican migrants did not plan to stay in the United States. They traveled back and forth to their homeland, or returned permanently. Gradually, however, many chose to stay as they developed economic and family ties in the United States. The National Origins Act, which made it costly, time-consuming, and often humiliating for Mexicans to cross the border, also encouraged migrants to remain in the United States. As a result, the Mexican population of the United States rose from 103,000 in 1900 to 478,000 by 1920. At the turn of the century, the majority of immigrants lived in Texas and Arizona, but California, with its booming agricultural economy, rapidly became the center of the Mexican population. The city of Los Angeles, growing phenomenally in the early twentieth century, particularly attracted Mexican migrants. The city's Mexican population, less than 5,000 in 1900, grew to perhaps 190,000 by 1930.

Chicanos, like so many other ethnic groups in the United States, wrestled with complex questions about their national identity. Were they still Mexicans or had they become Americans or some unique combination of the two nationalities? Those questions were more complicated because Mexican immigrants had left one rapidly changing country for another. The meaning of "Mexican" and the meaning of "American" were both fluid. In the United States, moreover, ethnic Mexicans received a mixed reception: While employers were eager for labor, they and many other native-born whites thought that Mexican workers should return to Mexico rather than live permanently in the United States. Many white Americans stereotyped Mexicans as a lazy and shiftless race who would take jobs from native-born workers and who could not be assimilated into American life and culture. Still other white Americans, drawing on the reform techniques of the progressive era, wanted to "Americanize" Chicanos by teaching them English and the middle-class values of thrift and time discipline.

The economy also presented Chicanos with a mixed message. Limited education and persistent discrimination prevented most from earning the larger incomes needed to enjoy American-style consumerism. In many towns and cities, they were effectively segregated in certain neighborhoods—*barrios*—in poor conditions.

Mexican immigrant workers, posed on the tracks of a railroad in Texas in the 1900s. It was the railroad that helped disrupt life in Mexico and offered the promise of jobs in the United States.

In the face of this ambivalent and often hostile reception, ethnic Mexicans forged their unique identities. In varying degrees, Chicanos clung to their old national identities and adapted to their new home. Mexican Americans, eager to hold onto the advantages they had won by birth and long-time residence in the United States, feared that the immigrants would compete for jobs and cause native-born whites to denigrate all Mexicans alike. The immigrants, in turn, often derided Mexican Americans as *pochos*—bleached or faded people—who had lost their true Mexican identity.

Nevertheless, ethnic Mexicans created a distinctive culture in the United States. For all their differences, Chicanos shared a sense of common cultural origins and common challenges. In a white-dominated society, they saw themselves as *La Raza*—the race—set apart by heritage and skin color.

Mexicans' response to the consumer culture helped create a common identity. Like other American workers, Mexicans went into debt to buy consumer goods. Largely ignored by corporations marketing goods nationwide, the Chicanos supported their own businesses, listened to their own Spanish-language radio programs, and bought records made by Mexican-American musicians. Among the most popular forms of Mexican-American music were *corridos*, the traditional folk ballads from rural Mexico adapted to life in the United States. Singing of things that Mexicans were often reluctant to say, *corridos* testified both to the distinctiveness of Chicanos' culture and to their uneasiness in American culture.

Nevertheless, hundreds of thousands of Mexicans came to the United States and struggled for equal rights and economic progress. In 1928, a farm workers' strike in the Imperial Valley led to the creation of the Federation of Mexican Workers Unions. A year later, Chicano businessmen and professionals in Texas formed the League of United Latin American Citizens (LULAC) in Texas.

African Americans and the "New Negro"

Like Chicanos, African Americans found the new cultural terrain of the United States appealing but unsatisfying. They enjoyed and helped to create the new culture, but modern culture did little to alter discrimination against blacks. Everywhere, African Americans lived with economic inequality.

While discrimination had not changed, many African Americans insisted that they had. The decade that saw the "New Woman" also witnessed the appearance of the "New Negro." This new ideal was partly the product of a fresh sense of freedom as African Americans left the southern countryside for the cities. It was also the product of frustration as African Americans encountered inequality along with opportunity in urban areas. The "New Negro" was militant and assertive in the face of mistreatment by whites.

The "New Negro" was also defined by a profound sense of racial difference. In the 1920s, African Americans applauded the distinctiveness of their life and culture. The Harlem Renaissance was a result of this effort. Harlem, the section of upper Manhattan in New York City where many African Americans had moved since the turn of the century, became a center of artistic and intellectual creativity. Novelists such as Zora Neale Hurston, Jessie Fauset, Claude McKay, Jean Toomer, and Dorothy West; poets such as Langston Hughes and Countee Cullen; and artists such as Aaron Douglas and Augusta Savage produced a new birth of African-American creativity.

The militance of the "New Negro" was reflected in the development of the NAACP, which turned increasingly to African-American leadership. The organization's key figure, W. E. B. Du Bois, became more critical of whites and more determined that white-dominated nations should return Africa to African control. The NAACP also pushed the cause of African-American civil rights more aggressively and attacked the white primary system that denied African Americans any say in the dominant Democratic Party organizations of the South. The NAACP continued a long-time antilynching campaign, which bore fruit in the 1920s, as southern whites were increasingly embarrassed by vigilante justice. In 1921, for example, white ministers in Athens, Georgia, condemned the burning of John Eberhardt, an African American accused of murder, as "barbarism."

For a time, the NAACP's efforts were overshadowed by the crusades of Marcus Garvey. A Jamaican immigrant to New York City, Garvey founded the Universal Negro Improvement Association (UNIA), which became the largest African-American political organization of the 1920s. Garvey focused on African-American self-help and on Africa. Garvey wanted African Americans to develop their own businesses and thus become economically self-sufficient. Like Du Bois, he insisted that the imperial powers give up their colonial control of the African continent. Sure that blacks could never find equality in a white-dominated nation, Garvey believed African Americans should return to Africa.

While the NAACP attracted mostly middle-class members, UNIA developed a vast following among the African-American working class. In 1919, Garvey launched an economic self-help project, the Black Star Line, which, he promised, would buy ships and transport passengers and cargo. Many of his followers invested in the Black Star Line, but it collapsed due to mismanagement. Garvey himself was indicted for mail fraud in connection with the project. By the end of the decade, federal authorities had deported him to Jamaica, and the UNIA had lost its mass following.

As the fate of the UNIA suggested, militance could be costly for African Americans. The NAACP also saw its membership drop dramatically during the decade. Nevertheless, African Americans' struggles during the 1920s laid the groundwork for more successful struggles in the future.

A "NEW ERA" IN POLITICS AND GOVERNMENT

Uneasiness with modern culture had only a limited impact on American politics and government. Other factors—the resurgence of individualism, the power of organizations, and the spread of consumerism—shaped public life more decisively in the 1920s. The decade witnessed the emergence of the modern political system characterized by advertising, weak parties, and low voter turnout. A succession of Republican presidents monopolized the White House during the decade. The Republican ascendancy brought the return of a political economic vision centered on minimalist government and a less internationalist foreign policy.

The Modern Political System

The 1920s marked the emergence of a political system that had been taking shape since the late nineteenth century. The major political parties grew weaker as their control over political culture loosened with the emergence of new media. Unlike newspapers, radio stations and movie theaters had no political affiliations. As a result, partisanship no longer engulfed Americans, and the number of independent voters probably increased.

As the parties weakened, a new, educational political style flourished, emphasizing the objective, nonpartisan presentation of facts. Pressure groups and other organizations used the educational style to lobby voters and legislators about public policies. In Washington, Congress was besieged by lobbyists from corporations, business groups, professional organizations, and single-issue pressure groups such as the Anti-Saloon League.

The other dominant political style of the 1920s drew its inspiration from consumerism. Copying big business, politicians used ads to appeal to voters. Because of the decline of intense partisanship, political advertising campaigns reflected the individualist focus of modern culture, selling the personality of individual candidates.

Nationwide, voter turnout fell from 79 percent for the presidential election of 1896 to just 49 percent in 1920 and 1924. A number of factors accounted for this drop-off: African Americans in the South had been effectively disfranchised, and newly enfranchised women were less likely to vote than men, but white male turnout dropped dramatically, too. The new political styles simply did not engage and motivate voters the way the old-style partisanship had.

The Republican Ascendancy

The chief beneficiaries of the new politics were the Republicans. Determined to win back the White House in 1920, the Republican Party chose an uncontroversial, conservative ticket. Handsome and charismatic, presidential nominee Warren G. Harding of Ohio had accomplished little during a term in the Senate. His running mate, Governor Calvin Coolidge of Massachusetts, was best known for his firm stance against a strike by the Boston police the year before.

The Republican ticket was not imposing, but neither was the opposition. The Democratic presidential nominee, Governor James M. Cox of Ohio, was saddled with the unpopularity of the Woodrow Wilson administration. His running mate, Franklin Roosevelt of New York, was a little-known cousin of former President Theodore Roosevelt who had served as Assistant Secretary of the Navy.

While the Democrats ran an ineffective campaign, the Republicans made excellent use of advertising. And Harding neatly appealed to the reaction against Wilson's activist government, offering a return to normal after the progressive innovations that had disrupted American society during and after the war.

Harding won a huge victory with 60.3 percent of the popular vote, a new record; he won 37 states for a total of 404 electoral votes. Cox carried only 11 southern and border states. The Republican Party substantially increased its majorities in the House and the Senate.

The Harding administration was plagued by revelations of fraud and corruption, some involving the so-called "Ohio Gang," political cronies from Harding's home state. The director of the Veterans' Bureau, caught making fraudulent deals with federal property, went to prison. One of the Ohio Gang, fearing exposure of the group's influence-peddling schemes, committed suicide in 1923.

Harding died suddenly of a misdiagnosed heart attack in August 1923, but the scandals continued. Congressional hearings revealed that former Secretary of the Interior Albert B. Fall had apparently accepted bribes in return for leasing U.S. Navy oil reserves at Teapot Dome, Wyoming, and Elk Hills, California. Teapot Dome, as the scandal came to be called, eventually earned Fall a fine and a jail term. In 1924, another member of Harding's cabinet, Attorney General Harry Daugherty, resigned because of his role in the Ohio Gang.

The parade of scandals damaged the reputation of the dead president, but they did not seriously harm his party or his successor, Calvin Coolidge. The former vice president proved well-suited to the political moment. The picture of rectitude, Coolidge restored public confidence in the presidency after the Harding scandals.

In 1924, Coolidge easily won the presidency in his own right against the Democrat John W. Davis, a colorless, conservative corporate lawyer from West Virginia, and the standard-bearer of the new Progressive Party, Senator Robert M. La Follette of Wisconsin. The choice, insisted Republicans, was either "Coolidge or Chaos." Holding onto the White House and to their majorities in Congress, the Republicans continued their ascendancy.

The Politics of Individualism

The Republicans practiced the politics of individualism. Eager to serve big business, they wanted a political economy driven by individualist values and minimalist government. They denounced the activist, progressive state and called instead for less government and more individual freedom. Coolidge declared that "the chief business of the American people is business."

Despite such slogans, Republicans sometimes used government power to spur economic development. The Federal Highway Act of 1921 provided federal matching grants to improve the nation's roads, and the Fordney–McCumber Tariff of 1922 restored high taxes on imports to shelter American producers from foreign competition.

These measures were exceptions, however. Above all, the Harding and Coolidge administrations called for reduced spending and lower taxes. The Republicans also condemned budget deficits and pledged to reduce the national debt; they succeeded on all counts. Federal expenditures dropped from $6.4 billion in 1920 to $3.1 billion in 1929 (see Figure 23–1). Congress repeatedly cut income and other taxes, but the federal government produced annual budget surpluses and reduced its debt.

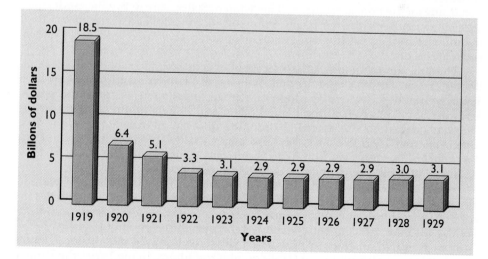

Figure 23–1   Shrinking Federal Spending, 1919–1929
Source: Historical Statistics of the United States, II, 1104.

Republicans' commitment to minimal government was obvious in their lax enforcement of progressive-era legislation. During the Harding and Coolidge administrations, the federal government made only weak attempts to enforce prohibition. Congress failed to commit enough money and manpower to stop the production and sale of illegal "bootleg" liquor.

Harding and Coolidge allowed the regulatory commissions of the Gilded Age and the progressive era to atrophy. The Interstate Commerce Commission (ICC) and the Federal Trade Commission (FTC) were effectively controlled by the businesses they were supposed to regulate.

Herbert Hoover, the Secretary of Commerce in both the Harding and Coolidge administrations, had a more activist view of the government's role in the economy than either of his bosses. Trained as an engineer, Hoover had become a national hero by supervising the government's effort to relieve famine in Europe during and after World War I. He aggressively sought ways to enlarge the size and power of the Commerce Department. Sensitive to business interests, Hoover promoted "associationalism"—organized cooperation among business trade groups. However, businessmen did not trust one another enough to make voluntary cooperation effective, and Hoover did not advocate federal action to force them to cooperate. Hoover believed above all in what he called "American individualism."

Republican Foreign Policy

After America's intense involvement in international affairs during World War I, the 1920s were a period of relative withdrawal. No crisis thrust foreign policy to the center of American life. Nevertheless, the United States, the world's greatest power, played an active role around the globe. In the aftermath of World War I, a surging international peace movement developed, supported in the United States by a broad range of women's groups and religious organizations. Their push for disarmament influenced the Harding administration to organize the Washington Naval Conference in 1921. The world's leading naval powers produced the first international arms-reduction agreement. The United States, Great Britain, and Japan agreed to scrap some of their largest ships and, along with France and Italy, to limit the tonnage of their existing large ships, abandon gas warfare, and restrict submarine warfare.

The peace movement was less successful in achieving its second goal, the outlawing of war. In 1928, the United States and 14 other countries signed the Kellogg–Briand Pact foreswearing war as an instrument of national policy. Enthusiastically received in the United States and elsewhere, the measure nevertheless contained no effective mechanism to stop a nation from going to war. U.S. membership in a World Court, the third major goal of the peace movement, was not achieved in the 1920s. Too many Americans believed that the court, like the League of Nations, would undermine U.S. sovereignty.

While Americans debated membership in the court, the U.S. economy became increasingly bound up in the world economy. American investment grew substantially overseas during the 1920s, American bankers made major loans around the world, and American companies exported their products around the world.

The growth of American economic activity abroad complicated the foreign policy priorities of the Harding and Coolidge administrations. In the 1920s, the United States had more interests than ever to protect overseas, but the American people were wary of government action that might lead to war. Many Americans were also uneasy about the nation's continuing military role in its own possessions and in supposedly sovereign nations.

In these circumstances, the Harding and Coolidge administrations tried to pull back from some imperial commitments. Marines withdrew from the Dominican Republic in 1924. American Marines also left Nicaragua in 1925 but returned the next year when the country became politically unstable.

The Harding and Coolidge administrations also attempted to promote a stable world in which American business would thrive. During the 1920s, the United States was involved in negotiations to increase Chinese sovereignty and thereby reduce the chances of conflict in Asia. The United States also tried to stabilize Europe in the years after World War I. With the quiet approval of Republican presidents, American businessmen intervened twice to help resolve the controversial issue of how much Germany should be expected to pay in reparation to the Allies.

Extending the "New Era"

The Republicans' cautious foreign and domestic policies proved popular. There was no serious challenge to the Republican ascendancy as the decade came to a close.

The backlash against modern culture hurt the Democrats more than the Republicans. The Democratic Party depended on support not only from nativists, fundamentalists, and Klansmen, but also from their frequent targets—urban Catholics and Jews. By the mid-1920s, these constituencies had split the party. The antagonism helped doom the Democrats' chances in the 1924 and 1928 elections.

In 1928, the Democrats nominated Al Smith, the governor of New York, for president. The first Irish Catholic presidential nominee of a major party, Smith displeased fundamentalists and nativists. Smith represented a new generation of urban, ethnic Democrats who were ready to use activist government to deal with social and economic problems. Their brand of urban liberalism would be influential in later years, but in 1928, Smith's politics and background could not galvanize a majority of voters.

Meanwhile, Herbert Hoover, the Republican nominee, polled 58.2 percent of the popular vote and carried 40 states for a total of 444 electoral votes—the Republicans' largest electoral triumph of the decade. Moreover, the Republicans increased their majorities in both the House and the Senate. The "New Era" would continue.

CONCLUSION

The Republicans' victory in 1928 underscored the limits of the resistance to modern culture. Like the tides that confronted Gertrude Ederle in the English Channel, nativists, fundamentalists, and Klansmen could not beat back the many changes of the "New Era." As Hoover prepared to take over the White House, the triumph of the new culture and politics seemed assured. The modern culture offered a renewed sense of individual worth and possibility, promised new freedom to women and youth, and held out an alluring vision of material pleasures.

Nevertheless, the modern culture and its Republican defenders were vulnerable. Perhaps more than ever before, the nation's dominant value system equated human happiness with the capacity to pay for pleasures. What would happen if Americans lost their jobs and their purchasing power? The new culture and the "New Era" had survived the dissent of alienated and excluded Americans, but it would not survive the sudden end of prosperity.

CHRONOLOGY

1913	Introduction of assembly line at Ford Motor Company
1919	Black Star Line founded by Marcus Garvey
1920	Beginning of recession Beginning of commercial radio broadcasting First season of the American Professional Football Association Warren G. Harding elected president
1921	Sheppard–Towner Maternity Act
1922	Fordney–McCumber Tariff Sinclair Lewis, *Babbitt*
1923	Death of Harding Calvin Coolidge succeeds as president
1924	Teapot Dome scandal Dawes Plan for German war reparations National Origins Act Calvin Coolidge elected president
1925	Founding of the Brotherhood of Sleeping Car Porters Scopes trial
1926	Gertrude Ederle's swim across the English Channel
1927	Charles Lindbergh's flight across the Atlantic Ocean First "talking picture," *The Jazz Singer*
1928	Kellogg–Briand Pact Herbert Hoover elected president

FURTHER READINGS

Nancy F. Cott, *The Grounding of Modern Feminism* (1987). Cott's book is a perceptive exploration of feminist ideas and activism.

Lynn Dumenil, *The Modern Temper: American Culture and Society in the 1920s* (1995). Dumenil surveys key elements of the modern culture, including consumerism and changing gender roles, and emphasizes the importance of large-scale organization in American life.

Paula S. Fass, *The Damned and the Beautiful: American Youth in the 1920s* (1977). This monograph details the emergence of a distinctive youth culture during the decade.

Robert H. Ferrell, *The Presidency of Calvin Coolidge* (1998). Ferrell's book offers a balanced examination of the Republicans' use of power in the 1920s.

Robert S. Lynd and Helen Merrell Lynd, *Middletown: A Study in Contemporary American Culture* (1929). This pioneering sociological study of Muncie, Indiana, charts the spread of modern culture in an American community.

Nancy MacLean, *Ku Klux Klan: The Making of the Second Ku Klux Klan* (1994). This study of Klan activity in a Georgia county stresses the importance of the Klansmen's hostility to the modern culture.

Roland Marchand, *Advertising the American Dream: Making Way for Modernity, 1920–1940* (1985). This study shows how the pioneering advertising men defined their profession and tried to shape popular tastes after World War I.

Michael E. McGerr, *The Decline of Popular Politics: The American North, 1865–1928* (1986). This monograph traces the cause of declining voter turnout to changes in political styles.

David Nasaw, *Going Out: The Rise and Fall of Public Amusements* (1993). Nasaw's book engagingly describes the evolution of movies, sports, and other amusements that helped to constitute the consumer culture of the 1920s.

George Sánchez, *Becoming Mexican American: Ethnicity, Culture, and Identity in Chicano Los Angeles, 1900–1945* (1993). A sensitive exploration of the Mexican encounter with life in the United States as the new consumer culture flourished.

 Please refer to the document CD-ROM for primary sources related to this chapter.

CHAPTER

A Great Depression and a New Deal

1929–1939

Sidney Hillman and the Search for Security • The Great Depression
• The First New Deal • The Second New Deal
Crisis of the New Deal • Conclusion

SIDNEY HILLMAN AND THE SEARCH FOR SECURITY

"The ideals of the labor movement" Sidney Hillman told his union in 1935, "must be security for every man and woman in the country." Hillman, leader of the Amalgamated Clothing Workers of America (ACWA), argued that the goal must be a fairer, government-moderated capitalism. Throughout the 1930s he worked tirelessly with President Franklin Delano Roosevelt's New Deal to create this new political economy that would, he hoped, provide a greater measure of security to working people.

Born in 1887 in Lithuania, Hillman grew up in a small Jewish village. He was supposed to become a rabbi, but instead embraced socialism and became involved in the revolutionary movements challenging the Russian czar. In 1907 he emigrated to the United States and found work in the clothing industry, where he recognized the insecurity faced by most working people and resolved to fight it.

In 1910 a massive strike in Chicago shaped Hillman's destiny. Begun by a few seamstresses angry at a wage cut, it quickly expanded to more than 40,000 workers and shut down clothing manufacture in the city for months. Hillman emerged as a practical leader who convinced his employer to recognize the union and to arbitrate the dispute.

In 1914 Hillman was offered the presidency of the ACWA, and the union grew rapidly. During World War I Hillman enlisted the help of the government to compel manufacturers of military clothing to accept the union. This move, and the overheated economy of wartime, expanded the ACWA's membership to nearly 140,000, making it the fourth largest union in the nation.

With the advent of the Great Depression in 1929, as the American economy tumbled, Hillman struggled to keep his union together. After the election of Franklin Roosevelt in 1932, Hillman took a prominent role in the National Recovery Administration and used its provisions for business, government, and labor cooperation to stabilize the clothing industry. This endeavor failed for a variety of reasons, including the fact that workers in most industries remained unorganized.

Hillman and others formed the Committee (later "Congress") on Industrial Organizations (CIO), which quickly organized hundreds of thousands of workers in the steel, auto, electric, and rubber industries. At the same time, Hillman formed Labor's Non-Partisan League to support the re-election of FDR. Roosevelt's triumph in 1936 cemented a decades-long marriage of organized labor and the Democratic Party.

The New Deal pushed America's political economy in the direction Hillman had struggled for all of his life. Government regulation of the financial system prevented the kind of collapse that took place after 1929. Federal officials no longer fought organized labor. The elderly and disabled were protected by Social Security. Unemployment insurance was available to millions of workers, and there was a minimum wage in many jobs. In line with Hillman's dreams, this was capitalism made more stable and more socially responsible.

THE GREAT DEPRESSION

In mid-October 1929 confidence in the continued growth of the stock market suddenly failed, sending tremors throughout the economy. On October 29, "Black Tuesday," stock values lost more than $14 billion, and within the month the market stood at only half its precrash worth. Although the stock market crash did not cause the ensuing depression, it did expose the underlying weakness of the economy.

Causes of the Great Depression

No single factor explains the onset and persistence of the Great Depression. Among the politicians, bureaucrats, and business leaders responsible for addressing the problem, nobody had a clear idea of why things had gone wrong. Today most scholars believe that numerous flaws in the national and international economic structure,

TABLE 24–1

Labor Force and Unemployment, 1929–1941 (Numbers in Millions)

Year	Labor Force	Unemployment Number	Unemployment % of Labor Force
1929	49.2	1.6	3.2
1930	49.8	4.3	8.7
1931	50.4	8.0	15.9
1932	51.0	12.1	23.6
1933	51.6	12.8	24.9
1934	52.2	11.3	21.7
1935	52.9	10.6	20.1
1936	53.4	9.0	16.9
1937	54.0	7.7	14.3
1938	54.6	10.4	19.0
1939	55.2	9.5	17.2
1940	55.6	8.1	14.6
1941	55.9	5.6	9.9

Source: United States Department of Commerce, Historical Statistics of the United States (1960), p. 70.

along with ill-conceived government policies, bear a large degree of responsibility for the catastrophe (see Table 24–1).

In the 1920s the base of the economy had begun to shift. New industries that sold complex consumer goods like automobiles, radios, clothing, and processed foods became the driving force. This shift toward a consumer-oriented economy was fueled by favorable business conditions, high rates of employment, and a new willingness to buy on credit. The limits of this market had, however, been reached even before the Great Crash. When the stock market fell, the sudden collapse of purchasing power slowed the transition to the new economy.

A rickety credit and financial system added to the problems of the late 1920s. Even in the boom times banks failed by the hundreds. For rural banks these failures could be traced directly to the crisis in the farm economy. But all over America, financial institutions suffered from inept and criminal management. Banks were free from regulation, and in the boom of the 1920s many invested their depositors' money in the shaky stock market or made risky loans. These practices magnified the impact of the crash by causing banks to fail.

Like the banks, the investment industry was free from regulation and given to misrepresentation, manipulation of stock prices, and corrupt inside deals. The corruption became apparent after the crash and inhibited the ability of legitimate companies to raise money.

Misguided government policies also played a role. The Republican administrations of the 1920s were committed to reducing the interference of government in the economy, lowering taxes on the wealthy, and reducing government spending. As a result, little was done to counter the chaotic state of banks, address the problems of farmers, or redistribute wealth. The Federal Reserve might have dampened speculation in stocks and forced banks to adopt sounder policies or, after the Depression had begun, expanded the currency to promote growth. Instead, the

Harding and Coolidge administrations and the Federal Reserve Board only made matters worse. Moreover, government lacked the data needed to understand and resolve the economic crisis.

The Great Depression was magnified by an international economic system still reeling from World War I. Unable to repay their war debts, Britain, France, and other allies had demanded large reparations from Germany and Austria. The United States had helped to reduce these reparations payments in the mid-1920s but refused to forgive the debts. While the American economy boomed, capital from the U.S. poured into Germany and Austria, flowed back through the Allied nations, and on to American vaults. This cycle was broken with the onset of depression in the United States. The European nations attempted to protect themselves by devaluing their currencies and raising trade barriers. The result was steady economic decline that made reparations and loan repayments impossible. In 1931, the international financial system crashed, bringing with it more American banks and deepening the economic crisis.

The United States Descends into Depression

The Great Depression was a year old when an unemployed worker in Pottstown, Pennsylvania, wrote a harsh letter to President Hoover. "I am one of the men out of work," he explained, "but the rich don't care so long as they have full and plenty." He pleaded with Hoover to speed up aid to "the struggling starving working class [of] under nourished men, women, and children."

Between 1929 and 1933 every index of economic activity showed a slide into depression. Gross national product shrank from $104.4 billion in 1929 to $74.2 billion in 1933. The combined incomes of American workers fell by more than 40 percent. Bank failures increased from 640 in 1928 to 2,294 in 1931. Both exports and imports fell by more than two-thirds.

As business activity collapsed, joblessness skyrocketed. Periodic bouts of unemployment had always been a feature of capitalist economies; what distinguished the Great Depression was the extent and duration of unemployment. At the lowest point of the slump in the early 1930s, between 20 and 30 percent of wage earners were out of work. In 1933 more than 12,600,000 Americans were unemployed.

Behind the grim statistics lay terrible human costs. In the spring of 1930, bread lines appeared in major cities. In the fall apple peddlers crowded street corners hoping to earn a few nickels. Unemployed men and women stood in lines at factory gates desperately seeking work, at soup kitchens hoping for a meal, and at overflowing homeless shelters.

The basic necessities were suddenly hard to get. Schoolteachers reported growing numbers of students listless from hunger. Big city hospitals began receiving children suffering from rickets, a disease caused by a deficiency of vitamin D and niacin. Inadequate protein caused another disease, pellagra, to reappear in many parts of the South. More and more tenants were evicted; more and more banks foreclosed on mortgages. Apartments stood vacant and homes went unsold, yet by 1932 more than 1 million homeless people occupied shanty towns on the outskirts of cities or slept in doorways and alleys. Hoboes traveled railroads and highways in search of something to eat, somewhere to live, and someplace to work.

Farmers faced both economic and environmental disaster. Grain and cattle farmers in the plains states and the West aggressively increased production in the 1920s and then watched the markets for corn, wheat, beef, and pork collapse after the Great Crash. Between 1929 and 1932, farmers' income dropped by two-thirds.

As the Depression deepened, bread lines appeared on the streets of cities all across America.

Then the drought struck. Between 1930 and 1936, the rains stopped in large parts of the South, Southwest, and Great Plains. Exposed by decades of wasteful farming practices, the earth dried up and blew away. Dust storms carried topsoil hundreds of miles, giving a new name—the Dust Bowl—to a large swath of the southern plains. Dust and depression ripped thousands of farm families from the land, sending them to California in search of work.

The Great Depression affected nearly everyone in America, but it was most severe for those already disadvantaged. While the environmental shock of the Dust Bowl affected many poor white farmers, the agricultural depression was more devastating for black and white sharecroppers, workers in the wheat fields of the Midwest, and the migrant labor pools that traveled the East and West Coasts picking fruits and vegetables. In cities, African Americans, who held the least secure jobs, found themselves pushed from unskilled work by desperate white workers.

By 1932 private charities, the major social safety net, failed to meet the needs of desperate citizens. Economic losses reduced the resources of charities and the ability of the better-off to give. Summing up the state of charities, Arthur T. Burns, the president of the Association of Community Chests and Councils, said, "The funds we have are altogether inadequate to meet the situation."

Public moneys were just as scarce. Only eight states provided unemployment insurance, most of it meager. State welfare agencies were poorly funded and stretched beyond their limits. Frustrated politicians and citizens looked to the federal government, but beyond pensions for veterans, little existed in the way of social welfare: no Social Security, no federal unemployment insurance, no food stamps.

The federal government thus found itself under unprecedented pressure to do something to relieve the Depression. Labor leaders and farmers' spokesmen, even bankers and businessmen, abandoned their traditional resistance to a strong cen-

A dust storm threatens to swallow up this prairie home.

tral government. The president of Columbia University suggested that a European-style dictatorship might provide more effective leadership. Others warned of social revolution if the government did not act swiftly.

Hoover Responds to the Depression

In 1928 Herbert Hoover was widely considered the most qualified man in the country to be president. Trained as an engineer at Stanford University, Hoover had roamed the world to build and manage mining operations and had become a millionaire by his mid-20s. Like many other young progressives, Hoover sought to apply business skills to social problems. He won fame as the brilliant administrator who saved Europe from starvation after World War I and then as the powerful Secretary of Commerce during the booming 1920s.

Hoover believed that a complex, modern political economy required accurate economic information, careful planning, and large-scale coordination. At the same time, he rejected the idea that only a large and overbearing government could provide these services. His political philosophy, termed associationalism, envisioned a federal government empowered to collect and disseminate information and structured to encourage voluntary cooperation among businesses but forbidden to intervene further.

Hoover easily won the presidency in 1928. Once in office, he quickly implemented his ideas. One of the first achievements of his administration was the Agricultural Marketing Act of 1929, enacted before the crash. The bill established a Federal Farm Board, which brought together representatives of various farming interests to establish agricultural cooperatives designed to purchase surplus crops and to make the distribution and sale of farm products more efficient.

When the market crashed, Hoover's initial goal was to get business to cooperate to maintain wages and investment. In 1931, as banks were failing at a rate of 25 a week, he encouraged the formation of the National Credit Corporation, in which banks could pool resources to stave off a general collapse.

Hoover approached relief for the unemployed in much the same way. He opposed government unemployment insurance or poor relief. Instead he first organized the President's Emergency Committee on Employment, which sought to convince companies not to lay off workers and cut wages. Next Hoover created the President's Organization on Unemployment Relief, designed to encourage individuals and corporations to contribute to charities to help the unemployed. But the breadth and depth of the Depression overwhelmed these schemes. Crop prices fell so low that the Farm Board could not afford to buy staple crops above the market price. Instead the cooperatives began to dump their surpluses onto the market, further depressing prices and aggravating the plight of farmers.

In September 1931, U.S. Steel cut wages across the board, and countless other companies followed suit. Moreover, parts of Hoover's own administration refused to cooperate with his programs. In November, Treasury Secretary Andrew Mellon, a former banker, refused to support the National Credit Corporation's effort to save the Bank of Pittsburgh from going under. By the beginning of 1932, Hoover's approach to the Depression had come to nothing, and he conceded the need for more aggressive government programs. Recognizing that the National Credit Corporation could not save the banks, he proposed that Congress create the Reconstruction Finance Corporation (RFC). The RFC was authorized to loan $2 billion to corporations and financial institutions to stimulate investment. Other measures to increase government revenues, cut expenditures, and allow the Federal Farm Board to distribute surpluses to the needy were also enacted, but it was too little too late.

Republican policies not only failed to relieve the Depression; they increased its severity. Unable to control his own party, Hoover watched helplessly as Congress passed the Hawley–Smoot Tariff in 1930, raising import duties to their highest level in history, stifling hope that international trade might help the economy, and causing damage to the weak nations of Europe. Despite the president's misgivings about the tariff, he signed the bill into law. At the same time Hoover vetoed massive public works bills sponsored by Congressional Democrats. Finally, Hoover's commitment to the gold standard, like his belief in a balanced budget, stifled economic growth and aggravated the effects of the Depression.

Hoover reinforced his reputation as a cold and aloof protector of the privileged classes by his response to the Bonus Marchers in 1932. In 1924 Congress had promised the veterans of World War I a "bonus" to be paid in 1945. But as the Depression threw millions out of work, veterans asked for their bonuses early. When the government declined, some veterans refused to take no for an answer.

In the summer of 1932 the veterans formed a "Bonus Expeditionary Force" to march on Washington. Riding freight cars and buses, more than 20,000 Bonus Marchers encamped on the Capitol grounds and the swamplands across the Anacostia River. "Families were there galore, just couples and families with strings of kids," one marcher remembered. Hoover ordered the Army to remove the marchers from downtown Washington; General Douglas MacArthur exceeded his orders and attacked the marchers' encampment with tanks and mounted cavalry.

The Bonus Expeditionary Force, or Bonus Marchers, arrived in Washington, DC, in the summer of 1932, the height of the Depression, asking that the government pay veteran's bonuses earlier than scheduled.

Major George S. Patton, with sabre drawn, galloped through the encampment, setting fire to the tents and shacks. Hoover's silent support of MacArthur solidified the president's reputation for callousness.

As Congress struggled to relieve unemployment and suffering, Hoover flatly dismissed the "futile attempt to cure poverty by the enactment of law." By the end of his presidency the "Great Humanitarian" had become sullen and withdrawn. It was a dispirited Republican convention that nominated Hoover for re-election in 1932.

THE FIRST NEW DEAL

When the Democratic convention chose its candidate for president in 1932, Franklin Delano Roosevelt flew to Chicago to accept the nomination in person, a dramatic gesture in an age new to air travel and personal politics. "I pledge myself," he told the enthusiastic crowd, "to a new deal for the American people." Ever since, the reforms enacted between 1933 and 1938 have been known as the New Deal. The programs came in two great waves commonly referred to as the "first" and "second" New Deals. The first commenced with the Hundred Days, a burst of executive and legislative activity following FDR's inauguration.

The Election of 1932

The Depression reached its lowest depths as the 1932 election approached, and the Republicans seemed headed for disaster. Hoover was a symbol of the government's failure. The Democrats had to overcome serious internal divisions if they were to take advantage of the situation.

Throughout the 1920s the Democratic Party had been split along cultural lines between the ethnically diverse, wet (i.e., anti-Prohibition), urban wing concentrated in the North and the East and the Anglo-Saxon Protestant rural southern and western wings. Many ideological divisions separated different constituencies within the party.

The leading candidate for the Democratic nomination, New York's governor Franklin D. Roosevelt, had the background to overcome these divisions. Because FDR came from an upstate rural district he was not associated with the machine politics of New York City. His interest in conservation endeared him to westerners. He had built strong ties to the southern Democrats while serving as Woodrow Wilson's Assistant Secretary of the Navy. As governor of New York Roosevelt had built a strong record of support for progressive social reforms that appealed to urban liberals.

FDR also had immense personal charm. Despite having been crippled by polio since 1921 he proved a tireless campaigner. He was a patrician, raised in wealth and educated at Groton and Harvard. Yet he spoke in clear, direct language that ordinary Americans found persuasive and reassuring.

During the campaign, Roosevelt simultaneously embraced old orthodoxies and enticed reformers with hints of change. He campaigned on a promise to cut government spending, balance the federal budget, and support the gold standard. Yet he also promised government relief for the poor. How he would finance such relief while also balancing the budget, FDR declined to say, but it hardly mattered. In November 1932, the Republicans were swept out of office, and FDR and the Democrats promised "a new deal" for the American people.

Behind the scenes during the campaign, Roosevelt worked to develop a program to fight the Depression. While governor of New York, FDR had surrounded himself with a group of intellectuals, the "Brains Trust," who attempted to convince him that the Depression was caused by the maldistribution of wealth within the United States. Because the rich held onto too large a share of the profits of American industry, the economy was producing much more than Americans could consume. Despite the influence of the Brains Trust, however, Roosevelt never fully bought their ideas and never allowed any one group to dominate his thinking.

It was FDR's comfort with experimentation and chaos that would allow his administration to confront the Depression. Where Hoover had retreated into dogmatism, FDR endorsed "bold, persistent experimentation." Above all, he ordered his officials, "try something." And rather than trying to unite his followers behind a single idea or policy, Roosevelt seemed to enjoy watching his advisers feud while he arranged the final bargains and compromises. FDR's goal, as one adviser put it, was "to put at the head of the nation someone whose interests are not special but general, someone who can understand and treat with the country as a whole."

Roosevelt Takes Command

In the weeks before the inauguration the ailing American banking system took a sharp turn for the worse. In mid-February the governor of Michigan declared an eight-day bank holiday. Stock prices dropped, and banks saw funds fly out of the tellers' windows at an alarming rate. On the morning of the inauguration, New York and Illinois, the two great centers of American finance, joined most of the other states in calling a bank holiday. The New York Stock Exchange and Illinois Board of Trade also closed. To many it seemed like the end of the American economy that had so recently been the envy of the world.

The nation turned expectantly to the new president: Roosevelt did not disappoint. "First of all," he declared, "let me assert my firm belief that the only thing we have to fear is—fear itself, nameless, unreasoning, unjustified terror." In the midst of a frightening financial collapse, FDR's speech, delivered with verve and determination, transformed the mood of the nation almost overnight.

Roosevelt knew that reassuring words alone would not end the banking crisis. He also declared a national bank holiday to last through the end of the week, instructed his Secretary of the Treasury to draft emergency legislation, and called Congress into special session. When Congress convened on March 9 the drafting team had barely finished a bill, but Congress was ready to act. Breaking all precedent, the House unanimously shouted its approval of the bill after less than one-half hour of debate; that evening the Senate did the same with only seven dissents. That night the president signed into law the Emergency Banking Act, a conservative bill aimed at shoring up the existing banking system. It gave the Treasury Secretary the power to determine which banks could safely reopen and which had to be reorganized. It also enabled the RFC to shore up sound banks by buying their stocks. The act legitimized Roosevelt's national bank holiday and extended it through the weekend to give the Treasury time to decide which banks could open the following Monday.

On Sunday night, one week after taking office, FDR went on national radio to deliver the first of his many "fireside chats." Sixty million people tuned their radios to hear Roosevelt explain, in his resonant, fatherly voice, his measures to address the banking crisis. He assured Americans that their money would be "safer in a reopened bank than under the mattress." This was a tremendous gamble because the government was not completely sure how solid most banks truly were, but it worked. The next day, 12,756 banks reopened. The run stopped and deposits began flowing back into the system. The immediate crisis was over.

To ensure that the financial system would remain sound in the long run, the administration next sponsored bills to implement more enduring reforms. The Glass–Steagall Banking Act of 1933 imposed conservative banking practices nationwide. Speculative loans, investments in the stock market, and shady business practices were outlawed. In addition, the newly created Federal Deposit Insurance Corporation protected the savings of individual depositors. Two years later, the Banking Act of 1935 reorganized the Federal Reserve, bringing the entire system under centralized and democratic control.

One reason the banking system had become so vulnerable was its ties to the unregulated securities markets. The banking reforms prohibited such ties, but they left the stock market unregulated. So the administration sponsored a Truth in Securities Act that required all companies issuing stock to file detailed financial reports with the FTC and to disclose accurate information to prospective buyers. The following year Congress passed the Securities and Exchange Act to regulate the markets that sold stocks. It prohibited inside trading and other forms of stock manipulation, gave the Federal Reserve Board the power to control how much credit was available for stock purchases, and established the Securities and Exchange Commission (SEC).

Federal Relief

Roosevelt's unemployment relief programs more sharply distinguished him from Hoover than had the banking measures passed in his first days in office. In May, Congress passed a bill providing a half-billion dollars for relief and creating the Federal Emergency Relief Administration (FERA) to oversee it. Headed by Harry Hopkins, a shrewd social worker and Roosevelt confidant, FERA distributed money at a terrific rate. As winter came on, however, Hopkins convinced Roosevelt that only a massive new federal program could avert disaster. At FDR's request Congress created the Civil Works Administration (CWA), which employed more than 4 million men and women. During the winter, the CWA built roads, schools, and other public buildings and paid teachers' salaries. When spring came the CWA was eliminated—Roosevelt did not want the nation to get used to a federal welfare program—but FERA continued to run programs on a smaller scale.

Roosevelt generally used relief only out of necessity, but he was enthusiastic about one program, the Civilian Conservation Corps (CCC). FDR believed that life in the countryside and service to the nation would have a positive moral impact on the young men of the cities. The CCC employed these young men building roads and trails in the national parks. By 1942 the program had transformed America's public lands and employed more than 3 million teenagers and young adults.

This poster advertises the Civilian Conservation Corps, which put thousands of unemployed Americans to work on conservation projects across the country in the 1930s.

The New Deal Confronts the Farm Crisis

By the spring of 1933, prices of basic commodities like corn, cotton, wheat, and to-bacco had fallen so low that it was not even worth the cost of harvesting them. The banking crisis left farmers without access to the necessary credit to continue, and millions faced foreclosure and homelessness. On the southern plains the Dust Bowl was destroying millions of acres of land. In the Midwest the Farmers' Holiday Association was calling for a nationwide strike if Washington did not take immediate action. New Deal efforts to reform the agricultural economy fell into three broad categories: land-use planning and soil conservation, modernization of rural life, and the effort to eradicate rural poverty. The program that came closest to fulfilling each of these goals was Tennessee Valley Authority (TVA). The TVA was a "corporation clothed with the power of government but possessed of the flexibility and initiative of a private enterprise." According to its administrator, it aimed to change the environment, the economy, the way of life, and the "habits, social, economic, and personal" of a region that spanned nine states.

One of the most ambitious projects of the entire New Deal, the TVA was also astonishingly successful. The dams it built served many purposes. They controlled flooding in the Tennessee Valley, created reservoirs for irrigation, and provided cheap hydroelectric power to new factory complexes. The TVA took responsibility for soil conservation, reforestation, improved navigation, and even the manufacture of fertilizer. The poor, mountainous region along the Tennessee–North Carolina border went from growing cotton to manufacturing. The average income of the area's residents increased tenfold. As a comprehensive, centrally planned development scheme, the TVA came closest to the brains trusters' vision. But it was an exception among New Deal programs, which tended to be more fragmented and improvisational.

Inspired by the success of the TVA, the Roosevelt administration established the Rural Electrification Administration (REA) in 1935; by 1945, 40 percent of America's farms had electricity, up from only 10 percent when the REA was founded. Electricity made life more comfortable for millions of farm families and allowed industry to move into new areas, bringing jobs to some of the poorest parts of the country.

In many other respects, however, the New Deal did little for the rural poor. Price supports, production controls, soil conservation, irrigation, rural electrification, and various long-term reforms tended to benefit independent commercial farmers. The landless poor—Mexican migrant workers in the Far West, and tenants and sharecroppers, black and white, in the cotton South—did not benefit from New Deal programs.

Native Americans suffered especially severe rural poverty. Shunted onto reservations in the late nineteenth century, by 1930 the majority of American Indians were landless, miserably poor, and subject to the corrupt paternalism of the Bureau of Indian Affairs. Alcoholism, crime, and infant mortality were all more common on reservations than among the poorest whites. John Collier, FDR's Commissioner of Indian Affairs, was determined to correct the situation, and the Indian Reorganization Act of 1934 gave him the power to try. Under the New Deal, forced land sales were ended and the reservations were enlarged. Tribal democracy replaced bureaucratic authority. In an effort to preserve Indian cultures, Collier used the agencies of the New Deal to build progressive schools on the reservations. The same agencies built hospitals and implemented soil conservation programs.

But the problems of Native Americans were too great even for someone as sympathetic and powerful as Collier. Congressional opponents remained committed to

Homeless share-croppers shortly after being evicted from their farms by the landowners.

the principle of forced assimilation. Even on its own terms Collier's plan could be only partially successful. What worked for the Pueblo Indians might not work for the Navajos, for example. And Indians themselves were divided over policies and goals. As a result, while the New Deal relieved some poverty among Native Americans, it did not solve the long-term problem.

The Flight of the Blue Eagle

Reviving manufacturing was the key to ending the Depression. However, FDR had no fixed plan for industrial recovery and preferred to wait until business interests could agree on one before acting. Congress, however, moved independently to pass a bill aimed at spreading employment by limiting the work week to 30 hours. Heading off what he thought an ill-conceived plan, Roosevelt put forward the National Industrial Recovery Act. It created a National Recovery Administration (NRA) and mandated that business, labor, and government officials negotiate a code of business conduct for each industry that would regulate trade practices, wages, hours, and production quotas. The hope was to raise prices by limiting production, simultaneously protecting the purchasing power of workers. Big businesses were granted exemptions from the antitrust laws if they signed onto the codes. Organized labor was guaranteed the right of collective bargaining. Finally, $3.3 billion was earmarked for job creation.

The NRA suffered from many of the same problems as Hoover's earlier schemes. It brought together representatives from hundreds of industries to draw up their respective codes, but the process tended to be dominated by business. Few strong unions existed, and the government lacked personnel trained in industrial management. Smaller businesses were shut out, leaving America's largest corporations to write the codes in their interest. For a time in 1933 and 1934 the NRA's

Blue Eagle, the symbol of compliance with the codes, flew proudly over the American economy. Soon, however, dissatisfaction dampened enthusiasm, and by 1935 the eagle had come to roost atop a shaky and unpopular agency.

THE SECOND NEW DEAL

The first Hundred Days had been extraordinary by any standard. Congress had given the president unprecedented power to regulate the economy. The financial system had been saved from collapse. Federal relief had been extended to the unemployed. The agricultural economy was given direct federal support. Almost everyone was dazzled by what had happened, but not everyone was pleased. If Hoover had been too rigid, FDR struck even his admirers as hopelessly flexible. By 1935 the New Deal was besieged by critics from all directions. But rather than becoming demoralized, Roosevelt responded to criticism by keeping Congress in session throughout the hot summer of 1935. The result was another dramatic wave of reforms, the second New Deal.

Critics Attack from All Sides

In May 1935 one of William Randolph Hearst's emissaries traveled to Washington to warn Roosevelt that the New Deal was becoming too radical. Hearst had long been one of the most powerful newspaper publishers in America, and like many businessmen he had "no confidence" in many of Roosevelt's advisers. Saving capitalism had always been one of Roosevelt's goals, but shortsighted businessmen and financiers never appreciated his efforts. The rising hostility of the business and financial communities was of concern to FDR's re-election campaign in 1936. These wealthy Americans rejected virtually all of the president's overtures. And after some initial gestures of cooperation, most industrialists became critics of the NIRA. In the long run they proved more potent critics than all of Roosevelt's radical opponents combined.

The fate of the Communist Party illustrates the difficulties radicals faced during the New Deal. On the one hand, the 1930s were "the heyday of American Communism." Jolted by the apparent collapse of the capitalist system, perhaps a quarter of a million Americans joined the Communist Party. The Communists had proved themselves skillful grassroots organizers at a critical moment in the history of American labor unions. The Communist Party also took the lead in defending the Scottsboro Boys, a group of nine young African-American men falsely accused of raping two white women in Alabama. Yet the party's appeal was greatest after 1935 when it adopted a "popular front" strategy of support for the New Deal. Thus the Communists were most popular when they were pragmatic rather than revolutionary. While Americans joined the Communist Party by the tens of thousands, they also left it by the tens of thousands.

The Socialists fared even worse. Notwithstanding the appeal of its lively and intelligent standard-bearer, Norman Thomas, the Socialist Party lost ground during the 1930s, polling 900,000 votes in the presidential election of 1932 but only 200,000 in 1936. The reason was simple: Roosevelt had stolen the socialists' thunder. Although FDR was committed to saving the capitalist system, he also believed that it was deeply flawed and needed fundamental reforms. Socialists were skeptical as to just how much reform Roosevelt wanted.

More troublesome to Roosevelt were Coughlinism, Townsendism, and Huey Longism. Father Charles Coughlin was a Catholic priest in Detroit who attracted listeners to his weekly radio show by blaming the Depression on international bankers and Wall Street as well as Communist and Jewish influence in Washington. His solution was to nationalize the banking system and inflate the currency. FDR was careful not to anger Coughlin, and at first the radio priest attacked the New Deal while defending Roosevelt personally. But by 1935 Coughlin was openly critical of the president. He formed the National Union for Social Justice to pressure Congress to enact further reforms.

In California, Dr. Francis Townsend offered a reform program that was especially popular among older Americans. Through a transaction tax of 2 percent, the government would fund generous retirement pensions. By requiring the elderly retirees to spend all of their pensions each month, the program would pump money into the economy and stimulate a recovery. Townsend's figures did not add up, but his following multiplied dramatically. Townsend clubs appeared across the country, and several dozen congressmen pledged their support.

Huey Long's "Share Our Wealth" program was more comprehensive than Townsend's and more popular than Father Coughlin's. As governor of Louisiana, Long had amassed nearly dictatorial powers, which he used to build roads, hospitals, and schools; his programs reduced adult illiteracy, enhanced the quality of Louisiana State University, improved conditions in prisons and mental asylums, and established more rigorous training for doctors and nurses. After moving from the governorship to the Senate, Long broke with the president and by 1934 was proposing his own alternative to the New Deal.

Because Long believed that the Depression was caused by the maldistribution of income, his program called for the redistribution of wealth through confiscatory taxes on the rich and a guaranteed minimum income of $2,500 per year. Like Townsend's and Coughlin's proposals, Long's "Share Our Wealth" program rested on a kernel of truth about the American economy. Elderly Americans were indeed desperate, the currency did need to be inflated, and wealth was unequally distributed in the United States. Hence the reforms proposed by Townsend, Coughlin, and especially Long seemed plausible to millions of Americans.

As criticism of the New Deal grew, the conservative-dominated U.S. Supreme Court struck down many of the key laws of the first Hundred Days. On May 27, 1935, the Court handed down a decision in *Schechter Poultry Corporation* v. *United States* that invalidated the NIRA. The justices ruled that the NIRA was unconstitutional and did so in a way that made it difficult for Congress to regulate the economy to any significant degree. Then, in January 1936, the Supreme Court overturned the Agricultural Adjustment Act. By the spring it seemed that the federal government was powerless to address the economic emergency.

Roosevelt Launches the Second Hundred Days

FDR loved a good fight. After 1935 the rhetoric flowing from the New Dealers became noticeably more radical. When the Supreme Court invalidated the NIRA, Roosevelt kept Congress in session through the sweltering Washington summer and forced through a raft of legislation in a "second Hundred Days," which marked the beginning of the second New Deal.

A few of the new proposals were designed to salvage important pieces of the NIRA. The Works Progress Administration (WPA), for example, revived the popular jobs program. Similarly, the Wagner Act recovered and strengthened Section 7(a) of the NIRA, which had guaranteed workers the right to bargain collectively.

Other reforms of the second Hundred Days were designed to silence radical critics. Hoping to undermine Huey Long, Roosevelt proposed a Revenue Act that would encourage a "wider distribution of the wealth" by raising estate and corporate taxes and raising personal income taxes in the top bracket to 79 percent.

Despite the political motives behind the bill, it made certain economic sense. Before the 1935 Revenue Act most New Deal programs had been financed by regressive sales and excise taxes. Thereafter programs were funded with progressive income taxes that fell most heavily on the rich.

The Wheeler–Rayburn Act was another major achievement of the second New Deal. The law grew out of Roosevelt's concern about the concentrated power of holding companies in the nation's utility industry. It gave the SEC the power to break up utilities that made no geographic sense. It took many years for the SEC to rationalize the nation's power industry, but forcing power companies to focus on specific regions actually made them more profitable.

The first New Deal had been preoccupied with the dire emergency of 1933. The second New Deal left a more enduring legacy. The administration put in place a Social Security system that became the centerpiece of the American welfare state for the remainder of the century, and it allied itself with organized labor, thereby creating a new and powerful Democratic Party coalition. By late August 1935, the most important achievements of the New Deal were in place.

Social Security for Some

Bolstered by big Democratic gains in the 1934 elections, FDR pursued a massive effort to fund work relief by sponsoring the Emergency Relief Appropriations Bill. Providing nearly $5 billion, more than the entire 1932 federal budget, it breathed new life into the relief programs of the first New Deal and created a new WPA, headed by Harry Hopkins. The WPA lasted for eight years, employing as many as 3.3 million Americans at one time. Two-thirds of WPA workers were unskilled, but the WPA also commissioned artists to decorate post offices and write plays, and WPA historians collected the stories of mill workers and former slaves. The program was hugely popular.

Critics complained with some justice that the WPA put people to work on meaningless "make-work" jobs or that the workers were incompetent. Political corruption was a more serious problem. WPA officials, especially at the local level, often used the agency as a patronage machine. Corruption was not rampant, but there was enough to provide ammunition to the WPA's opponents. Because the WPA paid its workers the "prevailing" local wage, its effectiveness differed from one locale to another. In many states, particularly in the South, local officials openly discriminated against poor African Americans. Finally, the WPA was never funded adequately, and its funds were doled out unpredictably, making it difficult to plan public-works projects rationally.

In the face of these obstacles, however, the WPA did a remarkable job. New York City used WPA employees to transform its public parks into a model for recreational facilities nationwide. In Georgia the WPA built 145 libraries, especially in isolated rural counties. The WPA Women's and Professional Division hired hundreds of thousands of women, and youth programs put hundreds of thousands of young men and women through high school and college. The WPA was never able to employ all those who needed work, but for millions of Americans it provided immediate relief from hunger and misery.

In addition to short-term relief, the New Deal created a permanent system of long-term economic security. In 1932 there were no national programs of unemployment insurance, workers' compensation, old-age pensions, or aid to needy children. As a result, most Americans had little or no protection from economic calamity.

The Social Security Act of 1935 took a critical first step toward providing such protection. It established matching grants to states that set up their own systems of workers' compensation, unemployment insurance, and aid to families with dependent children. Even more important, the federal government created a huge new Social Security system that guaranteed pensions to millions of elderly Americans. FDR insisted that it be funded as an insurance plan with payroll taxes paid by employees and employers to protect the system from the political attacks that welfare programs commonly encountered.

Most New Dealers had hoped to go further. Secretary of Labor Frances Perkins wanted to include agricultural laborers and domestic servants, mostly women and blacks, in the new Social Security system, but that would have provoked enough opposition from southern conservatives to kill the program.

Powerful conservative opposition thus limited the extent of the New Deal's plans for social welfare and economic security. As a result, welfare and insurance programs were weaker in the South than in the North and weaker for women and blacks than for white men. Despite such strong opposition, the New Deal actually accomplished a great deal. By 1939 every state had established a program of unemployment insurance and assistance to the elderly. More Americans than ever before were thereby protected from the ravages of unemployment, disability, poverty, and old age.

Labor and the New Deal

The 1930s saw unions take a new role in America's political economy. The number of Americans organized in unions leaped by the millions, and by 1940 nearly one in four nonfarm workers was unionized. Unions also became key players in the Democratic Party.

During the 1930s FDR moved from grudging acceptance to open support for organized labor. Section 7(a) of the NIRA, which had guaranteed workers the right to bargain collectively, was the first indication of this shift. Across the country workers sensed the change and responded with a spontaneous wave of strikes. At the same time, a talented group of national leaders, including John L. Lewis of the United Mine Workers, Sidney Hillman of the Amalgamated Clothing Workers, and David Dubinsky of the International Ladies' Garment Workers, all took advantage of Section 7(a) to launch huge organizing drives.

Employers fought back, using methods to intimidate workers—espionage, blacklisting, and armed assault—that had worked in earlier decades. But when it became clear that the federal government would now protect workers seeking to organize and bargain collectively, employers formed company unions to thwart independent action by workers. By 1935 the employers seemed to be winning, particularly when the Supreme Court declared the NIRA, including Section 7(a), unconstitutional. But the hopes of organized labor were kept alive by an influential and imaginative liberal senator from New York, Robert Wagner.

Wagner took the lead in expanding the limited protections of Section 7(a) into the National Labor Relations Act, also known as the Wagner Act. Wagner believed that workers had a basic right to join unions and hoped that effective unions would stimulate the economy by raising workers' wages. Like Section 7(a), the Wagner Act guaranteed workers the right to bargain collectively, but it also outlawed company unions, prohibited employers from firing workers after a strike, and restricted many traditional tactics companies used to inhibit the formation of unions. Most important, the Wagner Act created the National Labor Relations Board (NLRB) to enforce these provisions.

While Wagner and his colleagues moved in Congress, John L. Lewis and Sidney Hillman pressed the conservative leadership of the AFL to accept the principle of industrial unions, which would organize workers in an entire sector of the economy, such as steel manufacturing. The traditionalists of the AFL held fast to the notion that workers should instead be organized by crafts. Thwarted by the AFL leadership, Lewis, Hillman, and their allies formed a rival organization that eventually became the CIO.

The CIO organized some of the most powerful and prosperous industries in the country. The government's new attitude toward organized labor played an important role. For example, when the United Automobile Workers initiated a series of "sitdown strikes" against General Motors, neither FDR nor the Democratic governor of Michigan sent in troops to remove workers from the factories they were occupying. In addition, the NLRB protected the new unions from an employer counterattack during the recession of 1937.

Thus by the late 1930s a crucial political alliance had been formed. A newly vigorous labor movement had become closely associated with a reinvigorated Democratic Party. Having won the ability to organize, industrial workers used their power to increase their wages, enhance their job security, improve their working conditions, and secure their retirements. Organized labor now had a new stake in preserving the system from economic collapse. The successful unionization of industrial workers helped stabilize American capitalism.

The New Deal Coalition and the Triumph of 1936

Franklin Roosevelt believed that to overcome his varied opposition and win re-election he had to create a Democratic coalition far broader than that of 1932. Roosevelt was not interested in building a cult of personality but in rebuilding the party system. By 1936, under Roosevelt's charismatic leadership, the Democratic Party was transformed. For the first time since the Civil War, a majority of voters identified themselves as Democrats, and the Democrats retained majority status for decades. FDR achieved this feat by forging a coalition between the competing wings of the party. In the end, however, the coalition that made the New Deal possible also limited its progressivism.

The rural South had been overwhelmingly Democratic for a century, and it remained a crucial part of the party's coalition. But Democrats became the majority because the New Deal increased the party's appeal to urban voters in the North. This shift was well underway during the 1920s, but hard times and the New Deal confirmed the loyalty of ethnic blue-collar voters to the Democratic Party.

Both symbolism and substance attracted the urban working class to the New Deal. Jews and Catholics (Italian as well as Irish) served Roosevelt as advisers and cabinet officers. Many more accepted appointments to the federal judiciary. More important, thousands of working-class city dwellers found relief from the Depression through New Deal jobs programs. Those same programs generated patronage appointments that endeared Roosevelt to local Democratic machines. Finally, FDR's backing of the Wagner Act and his growing support for organized labor were reciprocated by the unions. The CIO poured $600,000 into Roosevelt's 1936 campaign, and its members helped get out the vote.

The New Deal's programs for the poor and unemployed help to explain the dramatic shift of allegiance among African-American voters. As they migrated to the urban North, blacks became a significant voting bloc, bringing with them their traditional allegiance to the Republicans, the party of Abraham Lincoln. But the Depression and the New Deal broke this pattern, and by 1936 northern blacks voted overwhelmingly for FDR and the Democrats. This was not because the

Democrats had suddenly become the party of civil rights: The New Deal sponsored no legislation against discrimination, and FDR sat silently as Congress rejected anti-lynching laws.

Nevertheless, New Deal agencies offered more assistance to poor, unemployed blacks than any previous federal programs, and some New Dealers were determined to run their agencies without discrimination. Mary McLeod Bethune, a prominent black educator and close friend of Eleanor Roosevelt, served as director of the National Youth Administration's Office of Negro Affairs, which gave jobs and training to 300,000 young African Americans. Bethune successfully pressured other New Deal administrators to open their programs to blacks. With perhaps a million black families depending on the WPA by 1939, black voters had solid economic reasons for joining the New Deal coalition.

A similar logic explains why prominent women reformers threw their support to the Democrats. FDR had no feminist civil rights agenda, and New Deal programs discriminated against women by offering them lower pay, restricting them to stereotypical "female" jobs, and terminating women's programs before all others. But as with blacks, women benefited in unprecedented numbers from New Deal programs. Through the first lady, Eleanor Roosevelt, a small but influential group of women suddenly assumed a prominent place in national politics. For the first time in American history a woman, Frances Perkins, was appointed to the cabinet.

The most prominent female reformer associated with the New Deal was Eleanor Roosevelt. She was the last representative of a woman's reform tradition of the late nineteenth and early twentieth centuries. She had worked in a settlement house and campaigned for suffrage and progressive causes. She became for many Americans the conscience of the New Deal, the person closest to the president who

New York Governor Herbert Lehman, Eleanor Roosevelt, and FDR after a speech in which the president rejected charges that his administration promoted communism. In fact, FDR was committed to saving capitalism by reforming it.

spoke most forcefully for the downtrodden. Her reputation for compassion protected her husband in at least two ways. Liberals who might have been more critical of the New Deal relied on Eleanor Roosevelt to push the president toward more progressive reform. At the same time, conservatives who were charmed by FDR's personality blamed all the faults of the New Deal on his wife.

Although four years of the New Deal had not lifted the Depression, the economy was steadily improving. Jobs programs had put millions of Americans to work. The banking crisis was over. The rural economy had stabilized. Based on this record and the backing of his powerful coalition of southern whites, northern urban voters, the labor movement, and blacks, FDR won re-election by a landslide in 1936. He captured over 60 percent of the popular vote and, in the electoral college, defeated his Republican opponent Alf Landon in every state but Maine and Vermont. The new Democratic coalition also won sweeping command of the Congress. Seventy-six Democratic senators faced a mere 16 Republicans; in the House, the Democratic majority was 333 to 89. Roosevelt now stood at the peak of his power.

CRISIS OF THE NEW DEAL

When the members of the new Congress took their seats in 1937 it seemed as if Roosevelt was unbeatable, but within a year the New Deal was all but paralyzed. A politically costly fight to "pack" the Supreme Court and a sharp recession encouraged the New Deal's enemies and provoked an intellectual crisis within the administration. In 1938, when the Republicans regained much of their Congressional strength, the reform energies of the New Deal were largely spent.

Conservatives Launch a Counterattack

With conservative opponents seemingly vanquished, progressives like Frances Perkins hoped that the legislation hastily passed in the rush of the first Hundred Days, or in compromises with Congressional conservatives, could now be strengthened.

FDR himself appeared to be poised to launch the next great wave of New Deal reforms, but one barrier stood in the way: the Supreme Court. The court had already struck down the NIRA and the AAA, and recent rulings made it seem that not much of the second Hundred Days would survive. Before he went on, Roosevelt wanted to change the court. Having had no opportunity to appoint any new justices, FDR instead launched a reckless and unpopular effort to "reform" the Court. He proposed legislation that would allow the president to appoint a new justice for every sitting member of the court over 70 years of age. This "court packing" plan, as Roosevelt's opponents labeled it, would have given the president as many as six new appointments.

Conservatives smelled their chance. Ever since the first Hundred Days they had complained that Congress had given the president "dictatorial" powers to meet the economic crisis. The court reform seemed to confirm their warnings. Conservatives formed the National Committee to Uphold Constitutional Government. They skillfully cultivated Congressional allies, allowing Democrats to take the lead in opposing court reform. Even the New Deal's allies refused to campaign for the president's bill. By the end of the summer of 1937, it was all over and the bill defeated.

Ironically, Roosevelt eventually won his point: The Supreme Court backed away from its narrow conception of the role of the federal government, and several of the justices soon retired, giving FDR the critical appointments he needed. As a result, New Deal legislation was protected from judicial assault.Nevertheless, FDR's court reform plan proved a costly political mistake. Its defeat emboldened the president's opponents. Critics who had remained silent for fear of presidential retribution now joined the opposition.

In November 1937 the administration's opponents gathered their forces and produced a Conservative Manifesto. In its call for balanced budgets, states' rights, lower taxes, and the defense of private property and the capitalist system, the manifesto heralded the themes around which conservatives would rally for the remainder of the century. Behind the Manifesto lay some hard political realities that drove the conservatives into opposition.

Southern congressmen were motivated by special regional concerns. Federal programs that offered an alternative to the bare subsistence wages of black and white agricultural workers compromised the ruling political economy of the South. Southern conservatives began to complain and to blame the New Deal.

In the South and West there were growing fears that the New Deal was too closely tied to the urban working class in the Northeast. To counteract this trend, conservatives appealed to the deeply rooted American suspicions of the central government. Still, the conservatives were not strong enough to block all New Deal legislation, because farm-state representatives needed Roosevelt's support. In late 1937 the administration succeeded in passing a Housing Act and a new Farm Tenancy bill. In 1938 Congress passed the Fair Labor Standards Act, the last of the major laws of the New Deal. It required the payment of overtime after 40 hours of work in a week, established a minimum wage, and eliminated child labor.

However, the 1938 Congressional elections gave the conservatives the strength they needed to bring New Deal reform to an end. Republicans gained 75 seats in the House and were now strong enough in the Senate to organize an effective anti-New Deal coalition with southern Democrats. By then, a jolting recession had created a crisis of confidence within the New Deal itself.

The "Roosevelt Recession" and the Liberal Crisis of Confidence

During the 1936 campaign Roosevelt was stung by conservative criticism of his failure to balance the budget. He had leveled the same charge against Hoover four years earlier, but the demands of the Depression made it dangerous to reduce spending. Furthermore, deficit spending seemed to be reviving the economy.

Hoping to silence his conservative critics after his re-election, Roosevelt ordered a sharp cutback in relief expenditures in 1937. On top of a contraction of the money supply ordered by the Federal Reserve and the removal of $2 billion from the economy by the new Social Security taxes, Roosevelt's economy measure was disastrous. Once again, the stock market crashed and industrial production plummeted. Even the relatively healthy automobile, rubber, and electrical industries were hurt. Opponents now carped about the "Roosevelt recession" and accused the administration of destroying business confidence.

This was an important turning point in the intellectual history of the New Deal, as well as twentieth-century American politics. Until 1938 the association between economic health and balanced budgets was firmly entrenched in government and the business community. Experience with the recession of 1937–1938 converted most young New Dealers to the newer economic theories of English economist John Maynard Keynes. During periods of economic stagnation, Keynes argued, the government needs to stimulate recovery through deficit spending. The goal of fiscal policy was no longer to encourage production, but to increase purchasing

CHRONOLOGY

1928	Herbert Hoover elected president
1929	Stock market crash
1931	National Credit Corporation authorized
1932	Franklin Roosevelt elected president
1933	FDR declares a bank holiday
	First Hundred Days
	Emergency Banking Act passed
	Economy Act passed
	Civilian Conservation Corps (CCC)
	U.S. goes off the gold standard
	Agricultural Adjustment Act (AAA)
	Emergency Farm Mortgage Act
	Tennessee Valley Authority (TVA)
	Truth in Securities Act
	Home Owners' Loan Act
	National Industrial Recovery Act (NIRA)
	Glass–Steagall Banking Act
	Farm Credit Act
1935	Second Hundred Days
	NIRA declared unconstitutional
	National Labor Relations Act
	Social Security Act
1936	AAA overturned
	Gone With the Wind published
	FDR re-elected
1937	FDR announces "court packing" plan
	Economy goes into recession
1938	Second Agricultural Adjustment Act
	Fair Labor Standards Act
	New Deal opponents win big in Congress
1939	Administrative Reorganization Act

power among ordinary consumers. Roosevelt himself never fully embraced these theories, but members of his administration found them attractive. Moreover, the massive inflow of government funds during World War II brought breathtaking economic revival and seemed to confirm the wisdom of Keynesian economics. Until the 1980s, presidents of both parties subscribed to Keynesian theory.

CONCLUSION

The New Deal did not bring an end to the Great Depression. Nevertheless, Franklin Roosevelt achieved other important goals. "I want to save our system," he told a White House visitor in 1935, "the capitalistic system." By this standard, the New Deal was a smashing success. Still more impressive, the New Deal allowed Americans to survive the worst collapse in the history of capitalism while preserving the democratic political system. Perhaps most important, the New Deal created a system of security for the majority of Americans. National systems of unemployment compensation, old-age pensions, and welfare programs grew from the stout sapling planted during the 1930s. Farm owners received new protections, as did the very soil of the nation. Workers won the right to organize, work hours were limited, child labor was ended, and a minimum wage was enacted. Moreover, the financial system was made more secure to the benefit of investors, depositors, and the economy as a whole.

America was a safer place at the end of the 1930s, but the world had become more dangerous. After 1938 the Roosevelt administration was increasingly preoccupied with the threatening behavior of nations that had responded poorly to the challenge of the Great Depression.

FURTHER READINGS

Alan Brinkley, *The End of Reform* (1995). An intellectual history of the "internal crisis" of the New Deal.

Lizabeth Cohen, *Making a New Deal: Industrial Workers in Chicago, 1919–1939* (1990). This work successfully combines labor history with the history of popular culture.

James Goodman, *Stories of Scottsboro* (1994). A highly readable retelling of the Scottsboro incident through the eyes of various participants.

Ellis W. Hawley, *The New Deal and the Problem of Monopoly: A Study in Economic Ambivalence* (1966). One of the first scholarly critiques of the New Deal.

Eric Hobsbawm, *The Age of Extremes: A History of the World, 1914–1991* (1994). This text puts the Depression into a global context.

Richard Hofstadter, *The American Political Tradition* (1948). The highly critical chapter on FDR is a classic that anticipated most later critiques.

David M. Kennedy, *Freedom From Fear: The American People in Depression and War* (1999). A strong recent synthesis of the period from 1933 to 1945.

William E. Leuchtenberg, *Franklin D. Roosevelt and the New Deal* (1963). Still the best short survey of the New Deal and the president who made it.

Arthur Schlesinger, Jr., *The Age of Roosevelt*, 3 vols. (1957–1960). A literary and scholarly masterpiece of heroic history.

 Please refer to the document CD-ROM for primary sources related to this chapter.

CHAPTER

25

The Second World War

1941–1945

A. Philip Randolph • Island in a Totalitarian Sea • Turning the Tide
Organizing for Production • Between Idealism and Fear
Closing with the Enemy • Conclusion

A. PHILIP RANDOLPH

"**W**ho is this guy Randolph?" Joseph Rauh asked. "What the hell has he got on the President of the U.S.?" It was June 1941 and Rauh, a government attorney, had just been instructed to draft a presidential order prohibiting discrimination on grounds of "race, color, creed, or national origin" in defense industries. Reversing decades of official support for legalized racism, it would use the economic muscle of the federal government to overturn job segregation nationwide. The president was bending to pressure, Rauh learned, from African Americans led by a labor organizer named A. Philip Randolph.

Randolph had founded the largest African-American labor union, the Brotherhood of Sleeping Car Porters, in 1925. Porters traveled the railroads as baggage handlers and valets, and during the Depression years Randolph's influence extended into every big-city station and small-town depot. According to the Federal Bureau of Investigation, which kept a secret file on Randolph's activities, he was a socialist. "Randolph believes race discrimination stems from the economic abuses of capitalism," a Bureau informant reported, "he joined the Socialist Party because it advocates unconditional social, political, and economic equality for Negroes."

In 1941, it looked to Randolph like only a matter of months before the United States would enter the war in Europe and Asia. President Franklin Roosevelt was sustaining Britain's struggle against Nazi Germany with weapons, food, and fuel, and Japan's drive into Southeast Asia threatened the U.S. colony in the Philippines. Randolph believed "that Negroes make most fundamental gains in periods of great social upheaval." War would create an opportunity to achieve equality, but only if African Americans demanded it.

In January 1941, Randolph called for African Americans to march to Washington to demand an end to job discrimination. The March on Washington Movement (MOWM) was largely a bluff. No buses were chartered, and there were no plans for where the thousands would sleep and eat, but Roosevelt and the FBI worried.

Roosevelt also had the power to accede to Randolph's demands. Using his leverage over thousands of manufacturers who had federal contracts in preparation for war, the president could single-handedly desegregate a large portion of the economy. The organizers agreed to cancel the march in return for a presidential directive—Executive Order 8802—establishing a Fair Employment Practices Committee to ensure fairness in hiring.

It was a victory for civil rights and for Randolph personally. Within a year, thousands of African Americans would be working at high-tech jobs in aircraft factories and arms plants. Randolph had recognized that war created an opening for changing the economic and political rules of the game. The social upheaval of war touched all Americans. The armed forces sent millions to serve and fight. Millions of others worked in plants producing war materiel. Government stepped in to run the economy, and corporations and labor fashioned new relationships to the federal government. War stimulated revolutionary advances in science, industry, and agriculture. The United States became the foremost military and economic power in the world.

These changes enlarged the discretionary powers of the federal government, particularly the presidency. As the MOWM proved, the president's enhanced powers could enlarge the freedoms and opportunities enjoyed by Americans, but they could also restrict individual liberties. FDR also ordered thousands of Japanese Americans to be "relocated" to internment camps and the FBI placed Randolph's name on a list of persons to be placed in "custodial detention" in the event of a national emergency. The war unsettled the economy and society, enlisting all Americans in a global crusade, and arousing both idealism and fear.

❧

ISLAND IN A TOTALITARIAN SEA

Randolph's movement capitalized on a world crisis that reached back to the end of World War I. Global depression heightened international tensions, turning regional conflicts in Africa, Europe, and Asia into tests of ideology and power. In 1937 Japan attacked China. Two years later when Germany invaded Poland, France and Britain declared war, beginning World War II in Europe.

Americans were divided on how their country should respond to the growing threat. Isolationists believed the United States should stay out of war, marshaling its defenses to secure the Western Hemisphere against attack. In contrast, Roosevelt and other internationalists believed the United States should support the nations fighting Germany and Japan while the war was still far from America's frontiers.

In 1940, most Americans opposed aid to the enemies of fascism, fearing that such aid would involve the United States in the fighting. When France's defeat left Britain to fight alone, more Americans saw aid to Britain as an alternative to U.S. involvement. Japan's attack on Pearl Harbor in December 1941 ended a debate that divided the nation.

A World of Hostile Blocs

In most of the world, economic growth in the 1920s had been less vigorous than in the United States. Europe stagnated under the burdens imposed by the Versailles Treaty. Germany had to pay $33 billion in war reparations to France and Britain, who in turn owed billions to the United States. The United States then loaned money back to Germany. Funds that could have created jobs, homes, and new industries went instead into this financial merry-go-round. One of the worst hit economies was in Italy, where unemployment contributed to the rise of Benito Mussolini's fascist government in 1922.

Like Italy, Japan was on the winning side of World War I, but its economy gained little from victory. Chinese consumers boycotted Japan to protest land grabs during the war. In 1923, an earthquake, fires, and a tidal wave leveled Tokyo and Yokohama, killing 150,000 people. Financial panics toppled companies and prime ministers. The one bright spot was in the foreign market for silk. Ninety percent of Japan's silk went into stockings worn by American women, and until 1930, that market seemed safe.

When the Depression hit, countries tied to a single commodity or to the American market suffered the most. After the crash, Americans stopped buying stockings, and the price of silk dropped by three-quarters. By the end of 1932, Japanese silk farmers were starving. International prices for Australian wool, Cuban sugar, Canadian wheat, Egyptian cotton, and Brazilian coffee plummeted. Everywhere the environment and the economy joined forces to destroy farmers. Those who survived bankruptcy succumbed to drought, floods, or famine.

In the industrial countries, jobless people stood in bread lines. More than 2 million workers were unemployed in Britain. American loans to Germany dried up in 1930, and by the end of the year more than 6 million Germans, 44 percent of the labor force, were out of work. This catastrophe, together with a hyperinflation that wiped out the savings of most of central Europe's middle class, silenced political moderates. In the worst economic crisis in memory, voters demanded extreme action.

The Depression destroyed the liberal international order based on free trade. For a century, governments around the world had favored policies that increased the movement of goods, people, and investment across borders. Movement toward an open-door world slowed during World War I and the 1920s and stopped completely with the Depression. World trade shrank from almost $3 billion a year in 1929 to less than $1 billion in 1933. Empires and nations restricted immigration, rationed the flow of capital, and imposed tariffs. The gold standard, the symbol of free trade, had once allowed dollars, pesos, and francs to be exchanged freely, but by 1936 Britain, the United States, and France had all abandoned it. Free trade had been replaced by autarky, the pursuit of national self-sufficiency.

Each country now looked out for itself, hoarding its scarce resources. Japan merged its colonies in Taiwan, Korea, and Manchuria into the Greater East Asia Co-Prosperity Sphere. The 1932 Ottawa Accords organized Britain, its empire, Canada, and Australia into a self-contained Sterling Bloc. To succeed, each bloc needed to have within its borders the ingredients of industrial growth—fuel, metals, skilled manpower, food—or it needed to take them from someone else.

In Germany, this policy was called *Grossraumwirtschaft*, the economics of large areas. It was the program of the National Socialist (Nazi) Party led by Adolf Hitler, who became chancellor in 1933. Hitler rose to power by playing on fears of economic chaos and resentment toward the Versailles Treaty. The harsh peace terms had been inflicted on Germany, he said, by a conspiracy of socialists and Jews. He promised to restore German greatness and carve out a German economic sphere in Eastern Europe and the Ukraine.

Autarky exacted heavy demands on citizens, requiring them to sacrifice prosperity, liberty, and lives for the nation. Efficiency was more important than democracy, and regimes around the world became more ruthless and less free. In Japan, secret groups within the army stalked and assassinated dissenting politicians. In Italy, Mussolini regimented the economy and outlawed opposition parties. Nazi ideology, in Hitler's words, placed "the good of the State before the good of the individual." Americans began to use a new word, *totalitarian*, to describe fascist and Communist regimes that demanded complete loyalty and obedience.

Even to Americans, dictatorships had a high-tech, modern sheen. Sleekly streamlined Italian trains and warships were the most beautiful in the world. Japan built a glistening new capital atop Tokyo's ruins and rationalized its economy with Frederick Taylor's time and motion techniques. Fascist economies pulled quickly out of the Depression, cutting unemployment and earning admirers in the United States.

Dictators enticed their followers with visions of imperial conquests and racial supremacy. Japanese schoolchildren learned that they belonged to a "Yamato race," purer and more virtuous than the inferior peoples they would rule. In Germany, Hitler built a state based on racism and brutality. Urging Germans to defend themselves against the *Untermenschen*, subhumans, in their midst—Jews, Gypsies, homosexuals—he suspended civil rights, purged non-Aryans from government and the professions, and compelled art, literature, and science to reflect the Nazi party's racial conception of the world.

Jews were the main target of Nazi terror. In 1935, the Nuremberg Laws stripped Jews of citizenship and outlawed intermarriage with Germans. On the night of November 9, 1938, Nazi stormtroopers and ordinary citizens rampaged throughout Germany, burning synagogues, destroying Jewish shops, homes, and hospitals, killing 100 Jews and arresting 30,000 more. Until *Kristallnacht*, the "night of the broken glass," Franklin Roosevelt had believed international opinion would restrain Hitler. Now he was no longer sure.

Germany, Italy, and Japan, known as the Axis powers, sought to solve their economic problems through military conquest. Italy invaded Ethiopia in 1935. In July 1937, Japan attacked China. The following year, Hitler's troops marched into Austria. American leaders feared that in a world of rival economic blocs, totalitarianism would outcompete democracy. Free markets and free labor might be no match for the ruthless, modern efficiency of the fascist states. "If Hitler destroys freedom everywhere else, it will perish here," *Fortune* magazine predicted. The United States would be "forced to become a great military power," to enlist industry, labor, and agriculture into a "state system, which, in its own defense, would have to take on the character of Hitler's system."

The Good Neighbor

Some Americans believed the United States ought to retreat into its own self-contained "dollar bloc," and in the early 1930s policy had briefly taken that direction. Industries and agriculture clamored for tariff protection. Free trade had been a hallmark of American foreign policy since John Hay proclaimed the open door policy in 1899, but Congress set the Smoot–Hawley Tariff of 1930 high enough to block most imports. Then, in April 1933, Roosevelt devalued the dollar. The move might have saved the banking system from collapse, but Roosevelt's own budget director called it "the end of Western civilization." One month after Roosevelt took office, the United States appeared to be moving toward autarky.

Within a year, Roosevelt reversed course and began pushing foreign trade as the answer to America's economic problems. He reacted partly to the failure of early New Deal programs but mainly to the vision of his single-minded Secretary of State, Cordell Hull, who believed the open door was the answer to the problems of dictatorship and depression. The best way to ensure peace, he argued, was to give all countries equal access to the world's markets.

Using loans and the lure of the vast American market, Roosevelt and Hull began to reopen markets in Latin America. The "Good Neighbor" policy meant encouraging trade ties and renouncing the use of force. Hull surprised the Pan American Conference at Montevideo, Uruguay, in 1933 by voting in favor of a declaration that no nation had the right to intervene in the affairs of another. Roosevelt tried to extend good neighborly policies to the rest of the world, urging peace-loving nations to "quarantine" aggressors, but the democracies were reluctant to join forces against the Axis powers.

In 1938, after absorbing Austria, Hitler demanded that Czechoslovakia cede part of its territory to Germany. Czechoslovakia's allies, Britain and France, agreed to negotiations, and in a meeting at Munich they yielded to Hitler's demands. The victors of World War I feared that a small war over Czechoslovakia would escalate into a larger one. After World War II, the term "Munich" came to symbolize the failure of attempts to appease aggressors, but in 1938 Americans were unsure how best to guard their freedoms in a hostile world.

America First?

Disillusioned by the results of the last war and anxious to concentrate on problems at home, Americans earnestly wanted to stay out of the conflicts in Europe and Asia. In 1935 and 1936, Congress passed temporary Neutrality Acts that prohibited loans and credits to nations engaged in war. In 1937 the act became permanent. A constitutional amendment requiring a national referendum to declare war narrowly missed getting a two-thirds majority in the House. Congress deliberated against the backdrop of the Spanish Civil War in which fascist forces, aided by Germany and Italy, fought against democratic, loyalist forces aided by the Soviet Union. Congress decided to stay out of the conflict, and the Neutrality Acts restricted the president's ability to aid the enemies of fascism just as Munich made the danger clear.

Between August 1939 and May 1940, Roosevelt watched as the United States became an island in a world dominated by force. The Soviet Union signed a nonaggression treaty with Germany. In September 1939, German armies struck Poland, using tanks and dive-bombers to slice deep into the interior. Hitler and Soviet leader Josef Stalin split Poland between them. Britain and France declared war on Germany.

The following April, Nazi armies invaded Denmark and Norway. On May 10, German tank columns pierced French lines in the Ardennes Forest and turned right toward the English Channel. France folded along with Belgium and the Netherlands. Britain stood alone against the German onslaught.

Roosevelt now had to face the possibility that Britain might collapse or surrender, placing the British fleet, control of the Atlantic, and possibly even Canada in Hitler's hands. Already the German air force, the *Luftwaffe*, was dueling for control of the skies over southern England. Determined to shore up this last line of defense, Roosevelt used his powers as commander in chief to bypass the Neutrality Acts. In June 1940, he submitted a bill to create the first peacetime draft in American history. He declared army weapons and supplies "surplus" so they could be sold to Britain. In September 1940, he traded Britain 50 old destroyers for leases to eight naval bases in Newfoundland, Bermuda, and the Caribbean.

Congress grumbled, but the isolationists now found themselves isolated. Sympathy for Britain grew as radio audiences heard the sounds of air attacks on London. Two-thirds of the public favored the draft, but isolationists were not ready to give up. In September 1940, the America First Committee launched a new campaign that urged Americans to distance themselves from Europe and prepare for their own defense.

Roosevelt worried that the 1940 election would become a referendum on intervention. Isolationist Senator Robert Taft was a leading contender for the Republican nomination. But the party's convention chose Wendell L. Willkie, a Wall Street lawyer with internationalist views. In his acceptance speech, Willkie endorsed the draft and expressed sympathy for Britain's struggle. Willkie stood by his principles, but it was a tactical error. With defense and foreign policy issues off the table, the only thing Willkie had to offer was a younger, fresher face. Roosevelt won an unprecedented third term by a 5-million-vote margin.

Means Short of War

British Prime Minister Winston Churchill waited until after election day to broach the urgent issue of war finances. Britain had been buying American arms on a "cash and carry" basis, but the Exchequer had run out of funds. Britain had defaulted on its World War I loans, and the Neutrality Act prohibited new loans. Churchill knew the chances of securing credits from Congress were slim, but without funds the war would stop. FDR produced a solution: Instead of loaning money, the United States would lend arms and equipment. Lend-Lease, as the program came to be called, put the U.S. "arsenal of democracy" on Britain's side and granted FDR unprecedented powers to extend aid in the nation's defense and to accept repayment "as the president deems satisfactory." The Lend-Lease bill passed the Senate by a two to one margin in 1941.

Repayment took the form of economic concessions. Hull insisted that in return for Lend-Lease aid, Britain discard the Sterling Bloc and open its markets to American trade. Churchill's economic adviser, John Maynard Keynes, reluctantly agreed. Britain was now, at least formally, committed to the open door. Later that year Churchill and Roosevelt met aboard cruisers off Newfoundland to issue a declaration of war aims, the Atlantic Charter. It assured all nations, "victor and vanquished," equal access to trade and raw materials.

In June 1941, Hitler stunned the world by launching a lightning invasion of the Soviet Union. Three million men backed by 3,000 tanks slashed through the Soviet defenses and rolled toward Moscow and Leningrad. Soviet involvement took pressure off Britain and gave the Allies a real chance to defeat Hitler. Roosevelt extended Lend-Lease aid to Moscow. The Germans advanced without interruption, but to the dismay of Hitler's officers, the Soviets did not collapse under the *Blitzkrieg* as France and Poland had.

The German Navy concentrated on severing Britain's trans-Atlantic lifelines, sinking half a million tons of shipping a month. To ease the burden on the British Navy, Roosevelt fought an undeclared naval war against Germany in the western Atlantic. The U.S. Navy convoyed merchant ships as far as Iceland, where British destroyers took over. Sparring between the American and German navies became common, and in September a German U-boat fired two torpedoes at the USS *Greer,* and the destroyer threw back depth charges. Roosevelt ordered aggressive patrols to expel German and Italian vessels from the western Atlantic. He had moved from neutrality to belligerency, and he appeared to be seeking an incident that would make it official.

Japan, meanwhile, probed into Southeast Asia in an effort to encircle China. In 1939, Japanese militarists had adopted a "go south" strategy, planning to capture oilfields in the Netherlands East Indies and cut China's lifelines through French Indochina and Burma. Because the Philippines, a U.S. territory, lay across the invasion route, the question for the Japanese was not whether to declare war on the United States, but when. In July 1941, Japanese troops established bases in French Indochina. Roosevelt saw this as a clear threat and opened talks with Japan while Marshall, the Army Chief of Staff, mobilized the Philippine Army. When Japanese

Japan's attack on the U.S. Navy's principal Pacific base at Pearl Harbor brought the United States into World War II. For Japan, it was the opening phase of a campaign to capture European and American colonies in Southeast Asia.

troop convoys moved into the South China Sea, Hull broke off negotiations and cut off Japan's only source of oil. On November 27, Marshall warned Army and Navy commands in Hawaii and the Philippines to expect "an aggressive move by Japan" in the next few days.

On Sunday afternoon, December 7, Americans listening to the radio heard that aircraft "believed to be from Japan" had attacked U.S. naval and air bases at Pearl Harbor in Hawaii. At 7:40 a.m. Hawaii time, 181 planes had bombed and strafed the airfields on Oahu, destroying or damaging more than 200 planes on the ground. Bombers then attacked the 96 ships of the U.S. Pacific Fleet anchored next to each other. The battleships *Oklahoma, Maryland,* and *Arizona* were lost, along with more than 2,000 men. Hours later, Japanese bombers caught American planes on the ground in the Philippines. The following day, President Roosevelt asked Congress for a declaration of war against Japan. On December 11, Germany honored its alliance with Japan and declared war on the United States.

Some historians have argued that Roosevelt knew of the approaching attack but withheld warnings to draw the United States into war. In fact, naval authorities at Pearl Harbor anticipated an attack, but they expected it to come in the form of sabotage or harassing raids. They doubted that Japan had the ability or audacity to project air and sea power across the Pacific in secrecy. Such preconceptions blinded commanders to the warning signs and reinforced their assumption that the Japanese would strike elsewhere.

Turning the Tide

For the Allies there was only bad news in the first half of 1942. In January, a German U-boat sank the tanker *Coimbra* off Long Island. Japan's Combined Fleet commanded the waters between Hawaii and India, striking at will. General Douglas MacArthur declared Manila an open city and braced for an Alamo-style defense of the Bataan peninsula and the fortress island of Corregidor. Bataan held out until April 9; Corregidor until May 6 (see Map 25–1).

Few could see it, but the tide was beginning to turn. The Soviets stopped the German advance in front of Moscow and held the line through the summer of 1942. On April 18, U.S. Colonel James Doolittle's B-25 bombers raided Tokyo, inflicting little damage but lifting American spirits. In Washington, leaders were trying to figure out how to build an overwhelming force and then how to use it. Roosevelt wanted to hold the line in the Pacific while coming to the aid of Britain and the Soviet Union as soon as possible. This meant stopping Japan's Combined Fleet, creating an American army, arming it, and putting it into action on the other side of the Atlantic. None of those jobs would prove to be easy.

Midway and Coral Sea

After Pearl Harbor, panic-stricken Americans imagined enemy landings on the California coast, but Japan's strategy was never so ambitious. It called for expelling the United States and Britain from the western Pacific and fortifying a defensive screen of islands to hold the Allies at bay until they sued for peace. After Pearl Harbor, the fleet turned west and south, raiding the coast of Australia and British bases in Ceylon, sinking thousands of tons of commercial shipping. "The fact that the Japanese did not return to Pearl Harbor and complete the job was the greatest help for us," Chester Nimitz, the U.S. Pacific commander, later

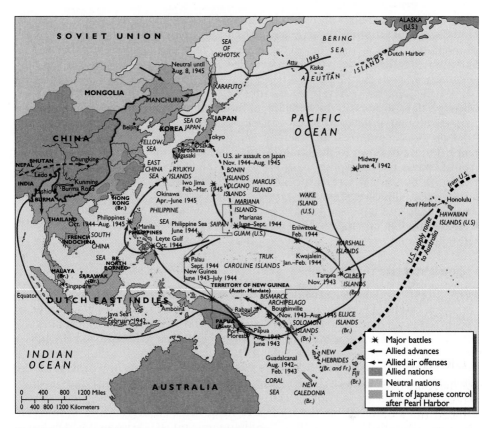

Map 25–1   World War II in the Pacific, 1942–1945
Japan established a barrier of fortified islands across the western Pacific. U.S. forces penetrated it west-ward from Hawaii and from Australia northward through the Solomon Islands to the Philippines.

remembered, "for they left their principal enemy with time to . . . rebuild his forces."

After the Doolittle raid, the Japanese realized their error and laid plans to lure the U.S. Pacific Fleet into battle. The increase in Japanese radio traffic helped Commander Joseph Rochefort, who had already partly succeeded in breaking the Japanese naval codes. In late April, he was confident enough to tell Nimitz that Japan was planning an attack on Port Moresby on the island of New Guinea. Nimitz dispatched two carriers, *Lexington* and *Yorktown*, to intercept the convoy. The Japanese expected American interference, but not from two flattops. The Battle of Coral Sea was the first engagement between carrier task forces in naval history. Sailors in the two fleets never saw the other's ships. Aircraft carried the battle to the enemy with devastating speed. The two sides withdrew after fighting to a draw. Port Moresby was saved.

Yamamoto next chose to attack the American fleet directly. Sending a small force north to mount a diversionary attack on the Aleutian Islands, he assembled a massive armada led by four carriers to assault Midway Island. Both targets were vital to the Americans, and Yamamoto gambled that Nimitz would divide his forces, allowing the Combined Fleet to crush the remnant guarding Hawaii. Trusting Rochefort's codebreakers, Nimitz knew the real target was Midway. He also learned from Coral Sea that aircraft, not battleships, were the winning weapons. He assembled task forces around the carriers *Hornet* and *Enterprise* and reinforced airfields on Midway and Oahu. Crews worked night and day to repair the *Yorktown*, damaged at Coral Sea, for the battle. The American fleet was still outnumbered, but this time surprise was on its side.

When Japanese aircraft encountered unexpectedly stiff resistance from Midway's flak gunners on the morning of June 4, they returned to their carriers and prepared for an unplanned second attack. With bombers, bombs, and aviation fuel littering their decks, the Japanese carriers were vulnerable. Japanese Zero fighters had been drawn down to the water by a U.S. attack. At that moment dive bombers from *Yorktown* and *Enterprise* burst out of the clouds, destroying three carriers in a matter of minutes. Before being sunk by American bombs, the remaining carrier launched an attack against the *Yorktown*. The mighty Combined Fleet ceased to exist. Midway put Japan on the defensive and allowed the United States to concentrate on building an army and winning the war in Europe.

Gone with the Draft

Long after the tank became the dominant land weapon, the U.S. Army continued to use horse cavalry. The German Army that overran France in May 1940 consisted of 136 divisions at a time when the United States could field only five. "Against Europe's total war," *Time* observed, "the U.S. Army looked like a few nice boys with BB guns."

Recognizing their weakness, U.S. officials drew up plans for the creation of a 10-million-man force that would invade Europe in July 1943. As in World War I, the United States had to house, equip, and transport the Army, but this time it would be five times larger. After the Selective Service Act passed in September 1940, 16 million men registered for the draft and those selected moved into hastily constructed camps. By December 1941, 2 million men and 80,000 women had enlisted. A year later the total exceeded 5 million. The draft revealed what a decade of Depression had done to the health and education of the country. Half of the recruits were rejected in 1941, mostly for bad teeth and eyes, signs of malnutrition. One-fifth were illiterate.

Buses rolled into the new camps and unloaded recruits in front of drill instructors who barked incomprehensible orders. Boot camp aimed to erase the civilian personality and replace it with an instinct for obedience and action. Selectees, as they were called, learned that there were three ways of doing things: the right way, the wrong way, and the Army way.

The new camps disrupted life in the towns and cities where they were located. Distinctions of apparel and race acted as stimuli for violence between recruits and locals. Southerners lynched African-American soldiers for wearing their uniforms. In 1943, sailors idled in Los Angeles attacked Mexican-American youths who wore fashionable "zoot suits." Aided by the Los Angeles police, the riot lasted for over a week, whereupon the city council passed an ordinance outlawing zoot suits. The problem for the council and for white southerners was what the clothes signified: the disintegration of the established social order, a process accelerated by the war.

The Army leadership struggled to preserve its racial traditions against the pressures of wartime expansion. Like the multiethnic imperial armies of Britain and France, the U.S. Army consisted of racially segregated units. African Americans served in the Army in segregated units, and until 1942 they were excluded from the Navy altogether. Roosevelt ordered the services to admit African Americans and appointed an African-American brigadier general, Benjamin O. Davis, but injustices remained. Even blood plasma was segregated in military hospitals.

Two issues aroused the most anger: treatment of African-American soldiers on and around southern bases and exclusion from combat. In a letter to *Yank* magazine in 1944, Corporal Rapiered Trimmingham described how he and five other GIs in uniform had been refused service in a Texas lunchroom where German prisoners of war were being served. Mutinies and race riots erupted at bases in Florida, Alabama, and Louisiana. The Army responded by moving African-American GIs to the war theaters.

Although desperately short of infantrymen, the Army kept African Americans out of front-line units, assigning them to menial chores. Combat symbolized full citizenship to both blacks and whites, and the NAACP pressed Roosevelt to create African-American fighting units. An African-American infantry division, the 92nd, went into battle in Italy; three air units—among them the 99th Pursuit Squadron, known as the Tuskegee Airmen—flew against the Luftwaffe; and one mechanized battalion, the 761st Tanks, received a commendation for action in the Ardennes. However, most African Americans went into the line as replacements when manpower was critically low. NAACP head Walter White observed that racially mixed units aroused few complaints in the field; resistance to desegregation came mainly from Washington.

With manpower in short supply, the armed forces hesitantly enlisted women to perform service roles. Eventually more than 100,000 women served as mechanics, typists, pilots, cooks, and nurses, but the unusual feature of women's service in the U.S. forces was not how many served, but how few. In nearly every other warring country women were fully mobilized for industry and combat, and the state stepped in to perform traditional female jobs, particularly caring for children, the sick, and the elderly, functions it continued to perform after the war. This "welfare state" came to be accepted and appreciated by the public in Europe, Canada, and Australia but not in the United States.

The 99th Pursuit Squadron, known as the Black Eagles, trained at Tuskegee Institute and engaged the Luftwaffe in the skies over North Africa.

The Winning Weapons

During World War II weapons technology advanced with blinding speed. Entering the war late, the United States gained a technological edge. American factories tooled up to produce models using the latest innovations, but many of these would not reach the fighting fronts until 1943 or later.

Until then, troops had to make do with weapons that were outclassed by their Axis counterparts. Marines went into action on Guadalcanal wearing World War I-era helmets and carrying the 1903 Springfield rifle. Japan's Zero was substantially faster and lighter than American fighter planes.

After 1943, the advantage began to pass to the Americans. Artillery was precise and lethal, and American crews became skilled at the devastating "time-on-target" technique, which delivered shells onto a target from several directions simultaneously. In the air, the elegant P-51 Mustang, a high-speed ultra-long-range fighter, dominated the French skies after D-Day. American four-engine bombers—the B-17 Flying Fortress and the B-24 Liberator—were superior in range and capacity to German or Japanese air weapons. In 1944, the B-29 Superfortress, with its 10-ton bomb load and awesome 4,200-mile range, took to the skies over the Pacific. Superforts incinerated Japanese cities one after another. American tanks, however, remained inferior to their German counterparts throughout the war, owing to the U.S. Army's failure to recognize the importance of this weapon.

American designers sometimes cut corners to make a product that could be mass produced. The results were impressive. When Allied troops landed in France in 1944, they enjoyed a superiority of 20 to 1 in tanks and 25 to 1 in aircraft. When Roosevelt set a production target of 50,000 aircraft in 1940, the Germans considered it a bluff, but American factories turned out almost 300,000 planes during the war. Often, abundance resulted in "attrition" tactics that pitted American numbers against Axis skill.

The War Department funded defense laboratories at Johns Hopkins, MIT, Harvard, and other universities, forging a permanent link between science and military research. American and British scientists invented one of the first "smart" bombs, the proximity fuse, which set its own range by bouncing a radio signal off its target. Collaboration between American and British scientists produced improvements in sonar and radar, penicillin, and the atomic bomb.

The Manhattan Project that produced the atomic bomb was the war's largest military-scientific-industrial enterprise. In 1939, three scientists who had fled Nazi Europe—Leo Szilard, Eugene Wigner, and Edward Teller—urged the famous physicist Albert Einstein to warn Roosevelt that the Germans might invent a nuclear weapon. General Leslie R. Groves was put in charge of the project, which eventually employed 600,000 people, cost $2 billion, and transformed the way science was done. Afterward, scientists would work in teams at government-funded laboratories on problems assigned by Washington.

The Second Front

To reassure Britain and the Soviet Union, FDR adopted a "Europe First" strategy, holding the line against Japan while directing the main effort at defeating Nazi Germany. The Allies had little in common except that Hitler had chosen them as enemies. Roosevelt needed to keep this shaky coalition together long enough to defeat Hitler. His greatest fear was that one or both of the Allies would make a separate peace or be defeated before the American economy could be fully mobilized.

As the Nazis closed in on the Soviet oilfields during the 1942 summer offensive, Stalin pleaded with Britain and the United States to launch a cross-channel invasion of France. Roosevelt and Marshall also wanted a second front to relieve pressure on the Soviets. To the British, however, the idea of a western front evoked the horrors of the trench warfare of World War I. Instead, Churchill wanted to encircle the Nazi empire, encourage insurrections, and finally invade when the enemy was weakened. He proposed attacking the Axis from the Mediterranean (see Map 25–2).

Concerned about the safety of the North Atlantic sea lanes—still prowled by U-boats—and about the inexperience of American troops, FDR reluctantly accepted Churchill's plan. A month after Pearl Harbor he promised Stalin a second front "this year." Finally, in June 1943, he told Stalin it would not take place until 1944.

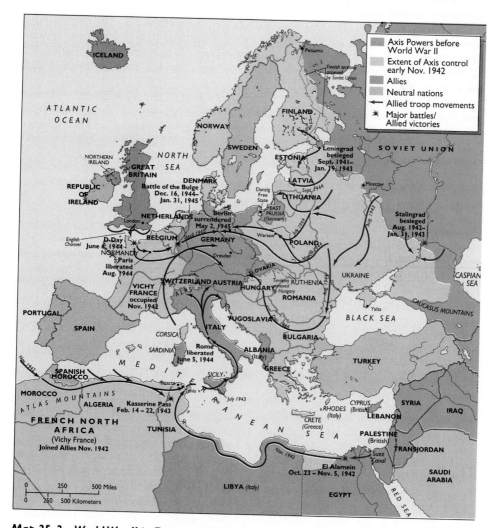

Map 25–2   World War II in Europe and North Africa, 1942–1945
While the Soviets reduced the main German force along the eastern front, the British and American allies advanced through Italy and France.

The delays reinforced Stalin's suspicions that the capitalist powers were waiting for the USSR's defeat.

Instead of invading Europe, the British and Americans chose a softer target, North Africa, and American troops commanded by Lt. General Dwight Eisenhower landed in Algeria and Morocco on November 8, 1942, moving east to link up with British forces. As Americans advanced on the mountainous Tunisian border in February 1943, General Erwin Rommel burst through the Kasserine Pass, trapping American columns in the high, rocky terrain. Panicky troops surrendered or fled, blowing up their ammunition stores. Rommel briefly had the chance to encircle and defeat the Allied forces, but his commanders ordered him to advance in another direction. Kasserine revealed fatal flaws in American organization and training.

Eisenhower sacked the corps commander responsible for defending the Kasserine and replaced him with Major General George S. Patton. The Army increased basic training from 13 to 17 weeks and reviewed its doctrine and weapons, discovering that American tanks were too small and artillery too weak. For Patton, Kasserine showed that firepower, delivered by air, tanks, and artillery, was more reliable than infantry. His preference for technology over bravery became ingrained in American strategy after the war.

Allied forces captured Tunis and Bizerte on May 7, bagging 238,000 German and Italian prisoners. Rommel fought the Americans again in France a year later. At that time he would encounter a larger, more experienced, and better equipped American Army. As it mobilized to fight, the United States was changing, too. Government took on new functions, and industry shifted into high gear.

ORGANIZING FOR PRODUCTION

To defeat regimented, totalitarian enemies, Americans had to gear their political economy for war. They willingly, even gladly, concentrated power in business, government, and labor. Big was beautiful because it made possible the "miracle of production" that both won the war and raised living standards on the home front. War contracts created 17 million new jobs and doubled industrial production. The employment dial reached "full" in 1942 and stayed there until Japan surrendered. People had money to save or spend. "People are crazy with money," a Philadelphia jeweler explained. "They purchase things . . . just for the fun of spending."

A Mixed Economy

Government planners were so enthusiastic about the potential for war production that military leaders felt a need to warn them against trying to beat Germany "by out-producing her." The Roosevelt administration created war mobilization agencies to control prices, assign labor, and gear up industry. It dusted off the tried-and-true methods from World War I—dollar-a-year-men and "cost plus" contracts—and added new incentives, such as tax breaks for retooling and federal loans and subsidies.

Output soared. At Willow Run, near Detroit, Ford turned out a fleet of B-24s larger than the Luftwaffe. Cargo ships, which took longer than a year to build in 1941, came out of the Kaiser Shipyards in an average of 56 days. Entirely new industries such as synthetic rubber (to replace natural rubber, grown in Japanese-controlled Southeast Asia) appeared overnight. Industrial techniques applied to agriculture—mechanization and chemical herbicides and pesticides—raised output by one-third while the number of farmers fell by 17 percent.

Business leaders regained the prestige they had lost during the Depression. Big business was now government's partner in the war effort. Major corporations were even running parts of the supersecret Manhattan Project. "The Government supplies most, if not all, of the capital, buys the goods produced, and generally controls operations, but with management in private hands," Edwin Witte, a member of the National War Labor Board explained. This produced "a mixed economy, which is not accurately described as either capitalism or socialism, as these terms have been used by the theorists."

Industry Moves South and West

Although Detroit got its share, the bulk of war contracts went to states in the South and Southwest and on the Pacific Coast, shifting industry's center of gravity. The B-29 Superfortress was manufactured in Seattle, Omaha, Wichita, and Marietta, Georgia. Three of the Manhattan Project's largest facilities—the gaseous diffusion plant in Oak Ridge, Tennessee, DuPont's plutonium factory in Hanford, Washington, and the bomb design laboratory at Los Alamos, New Mexico—likewise broke the historic pattern that had concentrated high-tech industry in the Northeast and Midwest.

There were several reasons for this shift. Industries that needed power gravitated to the huge hydroelectric grids created by the New Deal. The federal government also encouraged construction in the middle of the country to lessen the danger from enemy bombers. Corporations moved south and west to find low-wage nonunion workers. Southern and western senators, who controlled military appropriations, steered new factory development into their states.

The results were visible. The population of the West increased by 40 percent. Towns became cities overnight. Los Angeles, Houston, Denver, Portland, Seattle, and Washington, DC became wartime boomtowns. While "old" industries such as automobiles and steel remained the mainstay of the economy above the Mason-Dixon line, the South and West became the home of the gleaming industries of the future: plastics, aluminum, aircraft, and nuclear power.

Few people objected to government direction of the economy when it meant new jobs and industry in regions that had been poor. The war effort was so popular that the administration did not worry much about propaganda. Americans recognized that running a war was a complex business that required supervision from a large bureaucracy. Roosevelt and other war managers—many of them former progressives—had learned a lesson from World War I: In gaining public support, inducements worked better than coercion.

New Jobs in New Places

The following advertisement appeared in a Chattanooga, Tennessee, newspaper in September 1942: "Wanted: Registered druggist; young or old, deaf or dumb. Must have license and walk without crutches. Apply Cloverleaf Drug Store." Labor was in such short supply that prisoners were considered model employees. The need for workers pushed up wages, brought new employees into the work force, and set people on the move in search of better opportunities. It also swelled the ranks of organized labor from 10 million to almost 15 million between 1941 and 1945.

As it had with business, the federal government enlisted labor as a partner in the war effort. Wartime inflation and resistance from management created tremendous pressure to strike, even in plants producing vital war supplies. Through the National Defense Mediation Board (NDMB), the Roosevelt administration encouraged cooperative bargaining between unions and Washington. When United Auto Workers struck North American Aviation (NAA) plants in Los Angeles in 1941, the NDMB first called on union leadership to mediate. When that failed, the government sent the Army to break the strike, but the NDMB then forced NAA's management to accept the union's wage demands. Through a combination of carrots and sticks, federal administrators encouraged a more collaborative, managerial style of union leadership. Unions did not have to struggle as much for membership or recognition; in return, they curbed militant locals and accepted federal oversight.

Some 4 million workers, taking with them another 5 million family members, migrated as war mobilization redrew the map of economic opportunity. Some 200,000 Mexican farm workers, known as *braceros*, crossed the border to harvest crops. As they had during World War I, African Americans from the South proved especially willing to move. By leaving Mississippi to take a factory job in Los Angeles, a sharecropper could multiply his salary six- or sevenfold. In war plants, workers were protected by antidiscrimination clauses, and wages were federally set. Salaries of African Americans rose twice as fast during the war as those of whites.

Workers were generally happy with higher wages, but many would have been glad to have a decent place to live. War Manpower Commissioner Paul V. McNutt complained that all the new factories were going to places with no housing to spare. Frustrations over the housing shortage sometimes boiled over into racial conflict. In 1943, when the federal government constructed a housing project with 1,000 units in Detroit along the border between Polish and African-American neighborhoods, mob violence erupted over who would take possession of the dwellings.

Women in Industry

"Rosie the Riveter," the image of the glamorous industrial worker laboring to bring her man home sooner, was largely a creation of the Office of War Information. Some 36 percent of the wartime labor force was female, slightly more than in peacetime. Few women left housework for war work solely for patriotic reasons. Instead, the war economy shifted women workers into new roles, allowing women with factory jobs to take better paid and more highly skilled positions.

The number of manufacturing jobs for women grew from 12 million to 16.5 million, with many women moving into heavy industry as metalworkers, shipwrights, and assemblers of tanks and aircraft, jobs that had been off limits before. Women worked coke ovens in the hottest parts of steel plants; they operated blast furnaces and rolling mills. For many women, the war offered the first real chance for occupational mobility.

Even so, employers did not offer women pay equal to that of men. Unions either refused women membership or expelled them when the war ended. Despite government encouragement, neither employers nor federal agencies offered much help for women trying to juggle job and family. Under the Lanham Act, which provided the first federal support for day care, the government constructed 2,800 centers, but it was not nearly enough. Government experts and social scientists saw female labor as necessary for the war effort but dangerous in the long run. After the war, women were expected to yield their jobs to returning servicemen. They were blamed for neglecting their duties and encouraging juvenile delinquency, a backlash that began to build even before the war ended.

BETWEEN IDEALISM AND FEAR

In the movies Americans marched to war (and war plants) singing patriotic tunes, but in real life this war was noticeably free of high-minded idealism. A sentimental nationalism filled soldiers' letters in the Civil War and World War I, but GIs seldom wrote home to praise their leaders or their cause. Americans had already fought once to end all wars and keep the world safe for democracy. They were not ready to buy that bill of goods again quite yet. On the home front, to writer Dwight Macdonald the war seemed to represent "the maximum of physical devastation accompanied by the minimum of human meaning."

To fill this moral vacuum, wartime leaders took idealistic hyperbole to new heights. Churchill spoke of the triumph of the "English-speaking peoples." Roosevelt said Americans were fighting for the Four Freedoms: freedom of speech, freedom of worship, freedom from want, and freedom from fear.

Americans did know what they were fighting against: totalitarianism, Gestapos, and master races. Totalitarianism provided a powerful symbol of what America and Americans ought to oppose. "You don't wanna be like Hitler, do ya?" Frank Sinatra asked in a wartime ad. Nobody did, but while some groups found they could shame the government into living up to its own rhetoric, others found that in the face of wartime fears, the ideals voiced by leaders offered little protection.

Double V

African Americans improved their economic status in an atmosphere of seething racial hostility. In Maryland, Michigan, New York, and Ohio white workers engaged in "hate strikes" to prevent the hiring of African Americans. White employees of a naval shipyard burned black neighborhoods in Beaumont, Texas, in June 1943 when rumors circulated that their jobs would be given to African Americans. Curfews, rumors of riots, and white citizen's committees kept many other cities on edge.

African Americans responded by linking their struggle for equal rights in the United States to the global war against fascism. Thurgood Marshall, chief counsel for the NAACP, compared the Detroit rioters to "the Nazi Gestapo."

The nationwide African-American press and the blocs of black voters in northern cities made African Americans a more potent political force than they had been during World War I. In 1942, the *Pittsburgh Courier* launched the "Double V" campaign to join the struggles against racism and fascism. "Defeat Hitler, Mussolini, and Hirohito" it urged, "by Enforcing the Constitution and Abolishing Jim Crow." Membership in the NAACP grew tenfold during the war, and new groups that became household names during the civil rights movement of the 1960s began their work. In Chicago, activists inspired by the nonviolent tactics of Indian nationalist Mohandas Gandhi organized the Congress of Racial Equality (CORE), which desegregated restaurants and public facilities in the North. The NAACP won a legal victory in the Supreme Court case of *Smith* v. *Allwright* (1944), which invalidated all-white primary elections.

Along with other veterans, African-American soldiers received the benefits of the GI Bill. Many returned from the war determined not to accept discrimination any longer. The war prepared a generation of African Americans for the struggle ahead.

Japanese Internment

Idealism was no match for fear, and in the days after Pearl Harbor, journalists, politicians, and military authorities perpetrated an injustice on American citizens of Japanese descent. Ominous signs reading "Civilian Exclusion Order" went up in California and the Pacific Northwest in February 1942. They instructed "Japanese aliens and non-aliens" to report to relocation centers for removal from the Pacific coast "war zone." FBI investigators found no suspicious plots and told the president so, but the press continued to print rumors of Japanese saboteurs. Responding to the press, the military, and the California Congressional delegation, FDR ordered the relocation.

At assembly centers, armed soldiers met the families, inspected the few belongings they were allowed to bring, and herded them onto trains. Some 112,000 Japanese Americans were moved to 10 barbed-wire enclosures in remote regions of the West and Arkansas. Rows of wooden barracks were surrounded by guard towers, high fences, and sentry posts with machine guns facing inward. The internees reacted differently to their imprisonment. Some wanted to show loyalty by cooperating, while others were unwilling to repudiate Japanese culture or refrain from protest.

Internees and civil liberties lawyers challenged the legality of confining American citizens without charge or trial. Fred Korematsu, a welder from San Leandro, California, took a new name and had his face surgically altered in a futile attempt to stay out of the camps. When he was arrested, the American Civil Liberties Union used his case to challenge the exclusion order. Supreme Court Justice Hugo Black upheld the evacuation policy as justified by "military necessity."

No Shelter From the Holocaust

The United States might have saved more victims of Hitler's "final solution" had it chosen to do so. A combination of fear and anti-Semitism led American leaders to dismiss the Holocaust as someone else's problem. Between 1938 and 1941 the United States could have provided a haven for the millions of Jews trying to flee Europe. Instead, the State Department erected a paper wall of bureaucratic restrictions that kept the flow of immigrants to a trickle.

Nazi Germany's systematic extermination of the Jews made news in the United States. Stories in the *New York Times* as early as 1942 described the deportations and concluded that "the greatest mass slaughter in history" was underway. At Auschwitz, Poland, in the most efficient, high-tech death camp, 2,000 people an hour could be killed with Zyklon-B gas. Jewish leaders begged War Department officials to bomb the camp or the rail lines leading to it. The factory areas of Auschwitz were bombed twice in 1944, but John J. McCloy, the Assistant Secretary of War, refused to target the camp, dismissing it as a humanitarian matter of no concern to the Army. Roosevelt, who also knew of the Holocaust, might have rallied public support for Hitler's victims and made rescue a military priority. His inaction, according to historian David Wyman, was "the worst failure of his presidency."

When American soldiers penetrated Germany in 1945, they gained a new understanding of what they were fighting for and against. On April 15, Patton's Third Army liberated the Buchenwald death camp. Eisenhower ordered photographs and films to be taken, and he brought German civilians to witness the mass burial, by bulldozer, of the corpses. Many GIs doubted that the things they had witnessed would be believed.

Americans went into the First World War flushed with idealism and became disillusioned in victory's aftermath. The Second World War followed the reverse trajectory. Americans slowly came to see that their shopworn ideals offered what little protection there was against the hatred and bigotry that afflicted all nations, including their own.

CLOSING WITH THE ENEMY

The American Army was small—only 5 million compared to Germany's 9 million—but it was amply supplied and agile. Tactics emphasized speed and firepower. In 1944 and 1945 the United States carried the war to Japan and into the heart of Europe with a destructiveness never before witnessed.

Taking the War to Europe

Using North Africa as a base, the Anglo-American Allies attacked northward into Italy, knocking one of the Axis powers out of the war. In Sicily, where the Allies landed in July 1943, Patton applied the mobile, aggressive tactics he had advocated since 1940. Slicing the island in half and trapping a large part of the Italian Army, he swung east to Messina but arrived too late to block the Germans' escape. The defeat shook Italy. Strikes paralyzed the major cities, and Parliament deposed Mussolini and ordered his arrest. German troops took control and fiercely resisted the Allied landings at Salerno in September. Winter rains stopped the Anglo-American offensive south of Rome.

To break the deadlock, Churchill ordered an amphibious assault behind German lines at Anzio in January. Catching the Germans by surprise, three Anglo-American divisions came ashore unopposed, but the Germans quickly surrounded the small beachhead, pinning down the Allies in a siege that lasted until May. The Germans sent glider bombs and remote-controlled tanks filled with explosives into the Allied lines. American troops finally broke through to Rome on June 5, 1944.

The assault on France's Normandy coast the next day, D-Day, finally created the second front the Soviets had asked for in 1942. Early on the morning of June 6, 1944, the Allied invasion armada, thousands of supply and troop ships and hundreds of warships, assembled off England's channel coast and began the run into beaches designated Juno, Gold, Sword, Utah, and Omaha. Hitler had fortified the beaches with an "Atlantic Wall" of mines, underwater obstacles, heavy guns, and cement forts. On Omaha Beach the small boats headed straight into concentrated fire from shore batteries. The boats unloaded too soon, and men with full packs plunged into deep water. Floating tanks overturned and sank with crews inside. Commanders briefly considered calling off the attack, but soldiers in small groups began moving inland to outflank German firing positions. By the end of the day, they held the beach.

Eisenhower's greatest fear was another Anzio. The hedgerow country behind the beaches contained the most defensible terrain between the Channel and Germany. Each field and pasture was protected by earthen mounds topped with shrubs, natural walls that isolated troops. However, just as had happened on Omaha Beach, the defects of the generals' strategy were compensated by the initiative of GIs. On their own, tankers experimented with metal tusks to gouge holes through the hedgerows. By the end of the month the U.S. advance, led by "rhino tanks," broke through the German defenses and captured the critical port city of Cherbourg.

Once in the open country, highly mobile American infantry chased the retreating enemy across France to the fortifications along the German border. There, in the Ardennes Forest, Hitler's armies rallied for a final desperate counterattack.

Thirty divisions, supported by 1,000 aircraft, hit a lightly held sector of the American lines, broke through, and opened a "bulge" 40 miles wide and 60 miles deep in the Allied front. Two whole regiments were surrounded and forced to surrender, but the 101st Airborne held onto a critical road junction, slowing the German advance and allowing the Allies to bring in reinforcements. The Battle of the Bulge lasted a month and resulted in more than 10,000 American dead and 47,000 wounded, but the German Army had lost the ability to resist.

Island Hopping in the Pacific

To get close enough to aim a knockout blow at Japan, the United States had to pierce the barrier of fortified islands stretching from Alaska to Australia using only a fraction of the resources going to fight the war in Europe. The Army and the Navy bickered over supplies and the shortest route to Tokyo. MacArthur favored a thrust northward from Australia through the Solomon Islands and New Guinea to retake the Philippines. Nimitz preferred a thrust across the central Pacific to seize islands as staging areas for an air and land assault on Japan.

By November 1943, MacArthur's forces had advanced to Bougainville, the largest of the Solomon Islands and the nearest to the Japanese air and naval complex at Rabaul. Jungle fighting on these islands was especially vicious. Atrocity stories became self-fulfilling, as each side treated the other without mercy, killing prisoners and mutilating the dead. Air attacks pulverized Rabaul's airfields and harbor in early 1944, opening the way for an advance into the southern Philippines.

Meanwhile, Nimitz launched a naval attack on Japan's island bases. With 11 new aircraft carriers, each holding 50 to 100 planes, the Fifth Fleet attacked Tarawa, a tiny atoll that contained 4,500 Japanese troops protected by log bunkers and hidden naval guns. Tarawa, captured at a cost of more than 3,000 casualties, provided a base for an invasion of the Marshall Islands, which in turn, allowed an advance into the Marianas. Following a strategy called "island hopping," American forces bypassed strongly held enemy islands and moved the battle lines closer to Japan.

The Allied capture of Saipan, Tinian, and Guam in July 1944 brought Japan within range of B-29 bombers. General Curtis LeMay brought his 21st Bomber Command to Saipan in January 1945 and launched a new kind of air offensive against Japanese cities. LeMay experimented with low-level attacks using a mix of high explosives (to shatter houses and buildings) and incendiary bombs (to set fire to the debris). On the night of March 9, 1945, LeMay sent 334 bombers to Tokyo to light a fire that destroyed 267,000 buildings. The heat was so intense that the canals boiled, oxygen was burned from the air, and 83,000 people died from flames and suffocation. In the following months LeMay burned more than 60 percent of Japan's urban area.

Building a New World

As the war progressed across Europe and the Pacific, officials in Washington planned for the postwar future, and Allied leaders met to discuss their visions of the world after victory. Meeting in Casablanca in 1943, Roosevelt and Churchill agreed to demand the unconditional surrender of the Axis powers, to give the Allies a free hand to set the terms of peace. The U.S. State, War, and Navy departments undertook a comprehensive survey of the world, examining each country and territory to determine its importance to the United States. The planners believed that American security would depend on having a functioning international organization, a global system of free trade, and a worldwide network of American military bases.

Roosevelt envisioned a strong international organization led by the world's principal powers, who would act as "policemen" within designated spheres of influence. The new organization would work to disband empires, placing "trusteeships" over colonial territories preparing for self-government. The world after victory would be a world of nations, not empires or blocs. In September 1944, delegates from 39 nations met at Dumbarton Oaks and sketched out a plan for a United Nations comprised of a general assembly, in which all nations would be represented, and an executive council made up of the United States, China, the Soviet Union, Britain, and France.

To American leaders, the lesson of the 1930s had been that without prosperity there could be no peace. They wanted to create an open-door world, in which goods and money could move freely, eliminating the need for conquest. In July 1944, 44 nations attended a conference at Bretton Woods, New Hampshire, to create a system to manage and stabilize the international movement of money. The U.S. dollar would become an international currency, fixed against gold at the rate of $32 an ounce. Other countries would fix or "peg" the value of their currencies against the dollar, making it easy to set prices on the world market. To rescue unstable currencies, the delegates created an International Monetary Fund along with an International Bank for Reconstruction and Development (generally known as the World Bank). The "Bretton Woods system" gave rise to the network of regional development banks and international aid agencies that govern international finance today.

Military planners were not ready to stake America's future security on trade or international organizations. Pearl Harbor had shown that the Atlantic and Pacific Oceans offered no protection against aggression. Beginning in 1943, military leaders laid plans for a global system of military bases encircling the vast Eurasian land mass. Planners could not say who the next enemy would be, but with such an extensive base network, the United States could act preemptively against any challenger. Britain and the Soviet Union looked on this base system warily, suspecting they might be its targets, but American leaders were willing to take diplomatic risks to attain security.

The Fruits of Victory

Despite rumors of the president's failing health, Americans elected Franklin Roosevelt to a fourth term in 1944 by a margin of 53.5 percent to 46 percent for the challenger Thomas E. Dewey. On April 12, 1945, less than three months after his inauguration, Roosevelt died suddenly of a cerebral hemorrhage at Warm Springs, Georgia, days before Allied troops in Europe achieved the great victory for which Roosevelt had struggled and planned. On April 25, American and Soviet troops shook hands at Torgau in eastern Germany. On May 8, all German forces surrendered unconditionally.

Harry S Truman, the new vice president, was now commander in chief. Shortly after he took office, aides informed him that the Manhattan Project would soon test a weapon that might end the war in Asia. The first atomic explosion took place in the desert near Alamogordo, New Mexico, on July 16, 1945. Truman, meeting with Churchill and Stalin at Potsdam, Germany, was elated by the news. He informed Stalin while Churchill looked on, watching the expression of the Soviet leader. The bomb had been developed to be used against the Axis enemy, but by the time

Residents walk amid the ruins of Nagasaki, August 1945.

Truman learned about it, American leaders already saw it as a powerful instrument of postwar diplomacy. Stalin urged Truman to put the weapon to good use. Through intermediaries, Japanese diplomats had suggested an armistice on the condition that the emperor's life be spared, but Truman held out for unconditional surrender.

As American forces neared the Japanese home islands, defenders fought with suicidal ferocity. On Okinawa, soldiers and civilians retreated into caves and battled to the death. GIs feared the invasion of Japan's home islands, where resistance could only be worse. Then on August 6, a B-29 dropped an atomic bomb on Hiroshima. Two days later the Soviet Union declared war on Japan, and Soviet armies attacked deep into Japanese-controlled Manchuria. On August 9, the United States dropped a second atomic bomb, this time on Nagasaki. A few days later a French Red Cross worker saw the ruins of Hiroshima. "On what remained of the station facade the hands of the clock had been stopped by the fire at 8:15. It was perhaps the first time in the history of humanity that the birth of a new era was recorded on the face of a clock."

CONCLUSION

Emperor Hirohito announced Japan's unconditional surrender on August 14. In New York, crowds celebrated, but in most of the world there was silence and reflection. Thirty million people had been killed; great cities lay in ruins. At the end of the war, the United States' economic, scientific, and military mastery reached a pinnacle never attained by any of the great empires of history. America's air armada dominated the skies; its naval fleet had more ships than the navies of all its enemies and allies combined. Senator Claude Pepper asked Navy Secretary James Forrestal where he intended to put all of the 1,200 warships at his disposal. "Wherever there's a sea," Forrestal replied. Then there was the atomic bomb. The rest of the world looked for signs of how the United States would use its formidable wealth and power.

CHRONOLOGY

1930	Smoot–Hawley Tariff passed
1933	Hitler becomes chancellor of Germany President Roosevelt devalues the dollar The United States recognizes the Soviet Union
1934	Reciprocal Trade Act passed Export-Import Bank created
1935	Congress passes first Neutrality Act
1937	War begins in Asia
1938	Mexico nationalizes oil fields Munich agreement gives Hitler Sudetenland
1939	War begins in Europe
1940	Germany defeats France, Netherlands, Belgium Destroyers-for-bases deal between the U.S. and Britain
1941	Lend-Lease passed Executive Order 8802 ends discrimination in defense industries Roosevelt and Churchill sign Atlantic Charter Germany invades the Soviet Union Japan attacks the United States at Pearl Harbor U.S. declares war on Axis powers
1942	Philippines fall to Japan Internment of Japanese Americans begins Battles of Coral Sea and Midway turn the tide in the Pacific Allies land in North Africa
1943	Allies land in Sicily Churchill and Roosevelt meet at Casablanca U.S. troops advance to Bougainville Marines capture Tarawa
1944	U.S. troops capture Rome Allied landings in Normandy U.S. troops capture Saipan Bretton Woods Conference Roosevelt re-elected for fourth term
1945	Roosevelt dies Harry S Truman becomes president Germany surrenders Truman meets Churchill and Stalin at Potsdam Atomic bombs dropped on Hiroshima and Nagasaki Japan surrenders

FURTHER READINGS

Thomas Childers, *Wings of Morning* (1995). A historian reconstructs the lives and war experiences of the last B-24 crew shot down over Germany.

I. C. B. Dear, *The Oxford Companion to World War II* (1995). Easily the best single-volume reference work on the war. Contains full descriptions of battles and campaigns, biographies of leading figures, chronologies, maps, and as many statistics as you could want.

Michael D. Doubler, *Closing With the Enemy: How GIs Fought the War in Europe, 1944–1945* (1994). World War II has been seen as a "general's war," but Doubler explains how the tactics that beat the Nazis came from the bottom up. The U.S. Army's ability to listen to the lowliest GIs was its best asset.

Doris Kearns Goodwin, *No Ordinary Time: Franklin and Eleanor Roosevelt: The Home Front in World War II* (1994). The story of the nation at war through the eyes of the family that led it.

E. B. Sledge, *With the Old Breed at Peleliu and Okinawa* (1990). A classic memoir, the story of a Marine infantryman's war in the Pacific told with candor and feeling.

Ronald H. Spector, *Eagle Against the Sun: The American War With Japan* (1985). A comprehensive history of the Pacific War from a leading military historian.

 Please refer to the document CD-ROM for primary sources related to this chapter.

CHAPTER

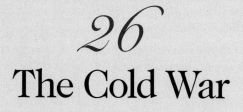

The Cold War

1945–1952

The Fall of Esther and Stephen Brunauer • The Origins of the Cold
War • Fighting the Cold War Abroad • The Reconversion of
American Society • The Frustrations of Liberalism • Fighting the
Cold War at Home • Conclusion

THE FALL OF ESTHER
AND STEPHEN BRUNAUER

*E*sther Caukin and Stephen Brunauer were an American success story. Born
in California in 1901, Esther graduated from Mills College, earned a
doctorate from Stanford University, and became an administrator for the
American Association of University Women. In 1931, she married Stephen
Brunauer, a successful chemist who had come to the United States from Hungary.

The Brunauers hated fascism. In the 1930s, Esther tried to educate Americans
about the threat from Adolf Hitler's Germany. When World War II came, she went
to work in the State Department. Stephen also worked for the government as a Navy
explosives expert. After the war, he traveled to Hungary to gather intelligence for the
government and help Hungarian scientists emigrate.

With fascism defeated and their careers well launched, the Brunauers should
have looked forward to a happy, prosperous future. But in 1947 a U.S. congressman
accused Esther of being one of the "pro-Communist fellow travelers and muddle
heads" in the State Department, and a federal agency refused to let Stephen attend a
meeting about atomic energy because in the 1920s he had belonged to a group with
Communist ties.

Then things got worse. On March 13, 1950, Senator Joseph R. McCarthy of Wisconsin suggested that Esther and Stephen were supporting Communism. Esther, McCarthy testified, had engaged in "Communist-front activities"; Stephen, purportedly a member of the Communist Party, had access "to some of the topmost secrets" of the U.S. military. McCarthy demanded that the Senate subcommittee subpoena federal records to find out whether the Brunauers had betrayed their country.

Two weeks later Esther took the witness stand to defend herself and her husband before the subcommittee. She accused McCarthy of betraying American values. Esther revealed how much McCarthy's accusations had already hurt her family. They had received "anonymous telephone calls at all hours of the day and night, accompanied by threats and profanity. All of you who have families . . . how would you feel if it were happening in your home?"

The subcommittee's report concluded that McCarthy's charges against the Brunauers were "contemptible," and "a fraud and a hoax." But the damage had been done. The Brunauers' employers, the State Department and the Navy, were unwilling to keep such controversial people on the job. In 1951 both were suspended. Stephen quit his job; Esther tried to fight her suspension but found herself charged with "close and habitual association" with her husband. In 1952, the State Department fired her as a "security risk."

How had it happened? At the end of World War II, things had seemed so promising. Americans lived in a country and a world that had been saved from ruin. At home, the economic boom of World War II had swept away the Great Depression. Abroad, the United States had helped to destroy the threat of fascism. Understandably, Americans expected the postwar world to be stable and safe.

Before two years had passed, however, the cold war disrupted American life. Convinced that the Soviets intended to expand their power and spread Communism across Europe, U.S. leaders challenged their former allies. The confrontation with Communism was deeply rooted in the long-standing values and the new conditions of the American political economy at the close of World War II. Partly the product of the political economy, the cold war in turn deeply affected it. To contain Soviet expansion, the U.S. government took unprecedented peacetime actions—massive foreign aid, new alliances, and a military buildup—that helped to transform the political economy.

The new American policies did not prevent the cold war from widening and intensifying. By 1950, the nation was fighting a hot war in Korea, and the Soviet Union had nuclear weapons that could conceivably devastate the United States. In response, the Truman administration stepped up military spending and developed more powerful nuclear weapons. As the cold war seemed to spiral out of control, fear gripped American society. In one way or another, the cold war unsettled the lives of all Americans for years to come.

THE ORIGINS OF THE COLD WAR

In just two years, the United States and the Soviet Union went from a wartime alliance to the strained relations known as the cold war. From the outset, the United States and the Soviet Union tried to blame the cold war on each other. For a long time, Americans wanted to believe that the Soviet Union, authoritarian and expansionist, was solely responsible. However, historians generally agree that both countries helped to start the cold war.

Ideological, political, military, and economic factors all played a role in the conflict. Ever since the founding of the Soviet Union toward the end of World War I, Soviets and Americans were ideological adversaries. Despite their differences, the two countries were allies in World War II, but in peacetime, the Soviet Union and the United States were the only countries strong enough to threaten each other. Moreover, they had quite different political, military, and economic interests which, by 1947, produced open antagonism.

Ideological Adversaries

The Russian Revolution of 1917 created the Soviet Union and committed the new nation to Communism. The Bolshevik revolutionaries installed a government dominated by the Communist Party. They also installed a socialist economy in which the state—the government—owned all property. At home, the Soviet Union limited individual rights, including freedom of speech and religion. Abroad, the new nation endorsed the revolutionary overthrow of capitalism.

The Soviets' Communist ideology set them at odds with the political economy of the United States. The vast majority of Americans favored a capitalist economy, individualism, freedom of speech, freedom of religion, and democratic government based on free elections. Although the United States did not always live up to these values, most Americans were sure that the "Red" Soviet Union never would.

Nevertheless, open conflict between the two countries was not inevitable. The Soviet Union posed no military threat to the United States in the 1920s and 1930s. President Franklin Roosevelt, eager to promote U.S. trade and restrain Japanese expansion, officially recognized the Soviet Union in 1933.

Uneasy Allies

World War II demonstrated that the United States and the Soviet Union could become allies. Still, the wartime alliance also laid the groundwork for trouble. For many Americans, the lesson of the war was that no new dictator should ever take over other European countries unopposed, as Adolf Hitler had in the 1930s. It was easy to view authoritarian Soviet Communism as another kind of fascism and the brutal Soviet leader Josef Stalin as another Hitler.

Wartime decisions also promoted tensions between the United States and the Soviet Union. The delay of the Allied invasion of France until 1944 embittered the Soviets, who were desperately resisting the Germans at the cost of millions of lives. The American government further strained relations by sharing news of its atomic bomb project with the British but not with the Soviets.

Decisions about the postwar world led to trouble as well. At a conference in Yalta in the Soviet Union during February 1945, Franklin Roosevelt, Josef Stalin, and British Prime Minister Winston Churchill promoted conflicting visions of the postwar world.

On the one hand, the "Big Three" supported the self-determination of nations, and in a Declaration of Liberated Europe, stated that nations would be free and democratic. The three leaders also laid plans for the United Nations, an organization that would encourage states to cooperate in keeping the world free, safe, and secure.

On the other hand, the Big Three believed that powerful nations such as theirs were entitled to spheres of influence in which they would exercise power independently and limit the self-determination of smaller states. Clearly, spheres of influence and unilateral action conflicted with democracy, self-determination, and collective action.

The conflict was made apparent when the three leaders dealt with the future of Poland, the Soviet Union's neighbor to the west. Stalin wanted to install a Polish government loyal to the Soviet Union. He could not risk an independent Poland that might become the staging area for another invasion of the USSR. Churchill and Roosevelt, however, favored a self-governing Poland. Stalin agreed to elections, but seemingly felt that Roosevelt promised him a free hand in postwar Poland. This lack of clarity set the stage for future misunderstandings.

So did differences over the future of Germany. The United States wanted Germany, safely controlled by the Allies, to become a healthy part of the world economy. Stalin, determined never to be attacked by Germany again, wanted the country formally divided and weakened. In the end, the Big Three agreed that Germany would be temporarily divided into four separate zones of occupation, administered by the United States, the USSR, Great Britain, and France. Although Berlin, the German capital, lay within the Soviet zone, the four conquering powers would each control a section of the city.

Coldwar leaders at Potsdam in July 1945. The determined expressions of British Prime Minister Winston Churchill, U.S. President Harry Truman, and Soviet Premier Josef Stalin reveal the tensions that would produce confrontation after World War II.

The uncertainties and contradictions of the Yalta meeting quickly led to Soviet–American disagreements. When Vice President Harry Truman succeeded Roosevelt in April 1945, he objected to the Soviets' attempt to control Poland. Promising to "stand up to the Russians," Truman held a tense meeting in Washington with the Soviet foreign minister.

When Truman met with Stalin and the British prime minister at the German city of Potsdam in July, relations were more cordial, and Truman reluctantly accepted the realities of power. Because Soviet troops occupied most of Eastern Europe and much of Germany, Truman had to go along with Stalin's demand that some German territory be given to Poland. There was no progress on planning the future reunification of Germany.

From Allies to Antagonists

After the war, the relationship between the United States and the Soviet Union eroded rapidly. With vastly different political economies and visions of the postwar world, the two nations defined their national security interests in conflicting ways (Map 26–1).

Stalin and the Soviet leadership took a cautious approach. Although they were committed to the overthrow of capitalism, their immediate concern was to protect

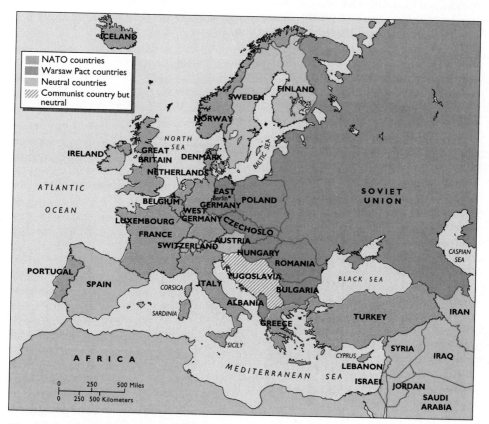

Map 26–1   Cold War in Europe, 1950
Five years after World War II, the cold war had divided Europe into hostile camps, with NATO members allied to the United States and Warsaw Pact signers tied to the Soviet Union.

the Soviet Union from invasion. In addition to establishing a pro-Soviet Eastern Europe, Stalin wanted to make sure he could not be attacked from the south, through Turkey and Iran, and that Germany and Japan never menaced his country again. Trying to rebuild the war-torn USSR, Stalin promoted national economic independence and had little interest in encouraging speedy rebuilding and easy trade relations for other nations.

The leaders of the United States looked at the postwar world differently. Truman did not have to worry about the immediate security of U.S. borders or fear any other military power. But American leaders feared that some other power might seize control of parts of Europe and Asia, making the United States isolated and susceptible to attack.

To avoid this dismaying scenario, American leaders took nearly the opposite of the Soviet approach to the postwar world. Truman favored the quick reconstruction of nations, including Germany and Japan, that would participate in a world economy based on free trade. The United States needed healthy trading partners to maintain prosperity at home. America also needed contented allies who would accept U.S. military bases on their soil.

The different needs and interests of the Soviet and U.S. political economies soon translated into combative rhetoric. In February 1946 Stalin declared that capitalism and Communism were incompatible. A month later, Winston Churchill, no longer prime minister of Great Britain, ominously declared that "an Iron Curtain has descended across the Continent" of Europe.

American leaders thought that Stalin wanted more than just safety from invasion. The Soviet Union, they concluded, aimed to expand abroad. George Kennan, an American diplomat in Moscow, sent to the State Department a long telegram that shaped the thinking of American policymakers. The Soviet leadership, explained Kennan, believed "there can be no permanent peaceful coexistence" between capitalism and socialism. Stalin and his regime were sure that capitalist nations would attack socialist nations and one another. Acting on this unfounded fear, the USSR would try to destabilize capitalist nations, especially the United States. The Soviet "problem," Kennan concluded, could be resolved without war, but the solution was "undoubtedly the greatest task our diplomacy has ever faced and probably . . . will ever have to face."

Truman's words and actions reflected Kennan's analysis. In 1946 the president tried to counter the apparent expansionism of the USSR, warning the Soviets against trying to increase their influence over Iran and Turkey. When the Soviets kept troops in Iran past the agreed-on deadline for their withdrawal, Truman sent a battleship to the eastern Mediterranean and successfully pressed Moscow to withdraw.

Relations between the United States and the Soviet Union deteriorated further in 1947, as Truman took aggressive steps to counter apparent Soviet expansionism in Turkey and Greece. The USSR had been pressing for a role in Turkey for some time. In Greece, the monarchist regime was under attack from Communist guerrillas, seemingly aided by pro-Soviet Eastern European nations. Great Britain had played the key role in supporting the Greek and Turkish governments, but by 1947 the British could no longer afford this aid. For Truman and his advisors, British withdrawal was disastrous. Control of Turkey would have given the Soviets access to the Indian Ocean and to the oil fields of the Middle East. Worse, successes in Greece and Turkey could have helped Communism everywhere in Europe and the Middle East.

To prevent this disaster, the Truman administration wanted to provide $400 million in aid to the Greek and Turkish governments. To persuade Congress to appropriate the money, Truman told a joint session of Congress on March 12, 1947, that the world once again faced a choice between freedom and totalitarianism. The president announced what became known as the Truman Doctrine. "I believe," he said, "that it must be the policy of the United States to support free peoples who are resisting attempted subjugation by armed minorities or by outside pressures." Congress voted overwhelmingly to provide the aid to Greece and Turkey.

The crisis marked the turning point in the U.S.–Soviet relationship. By 1947 the term *cold war* was being used to describe the American–Soviet confrontation. Dividing the world into good and evil, the United States was ready to support "free peoples" and oppose Communism. Former allies were now bitter antagonists.

Was the confrontation inevitable? It is difficult to see how the United States and the Soviet Union could have avoided antagonism. They had a history of tension and hostility, and they both possessed great military power. Most important, the two nations' political economies had produced clashing ideologies and needs.

It is much harder to say that the precise form of that confrontation was inevitable. The cold war was the product of human choices, such as Truman's decision to "scare hell out of the American people," and of human mistakes, such as Kennan's erroneous conclusion that the Soviets were bent on territorial expansion. Those choices and mistakes were certainly not inevitable. With good reason, Americans would wonder for decades whether the cold war could have been different.

FIGHTING THE COLD WAR ABROAD

The cold war intensified almost as soon as it started. In the late 1940s the United States implemented a strategy of containment to combat Soviet expansion. Moreover, the cold war quickly widened beyond Europe to include the entire world and, at the same time, became more dangerous. When the Soviets exploded their own atomic bomb, the United States dramatically stepped up military spending and built the hydrogen bomb. As the arms race spiraled, the cold war seemed frighteningly out of control.

The Strategy of Containment

Committed to opposing Soviet and Communist expansion, the Truman administration had to figure out how to fight the cold war. Once again, diplomat George Kennan helped give expression to American thinking. In 1947 Kennan argued "that the main element of any United States policy toward the Soviet Union must be that of a long-term, patient but firm and vigilant containment of Russian expansive tendencies."

The term containment aptly described American policy for the next 40 years, but it was a broad, rather vague concept. Truman and his successors had to decide just where and when to contain the Soviet Union as well as what combination of diplomatic, economic, and military programs to use.

To implement containment, Truman and his advisors revolutionized American policies on foreign aid, overseas alliances, and national defense. Soon after the decision to help Greece and Turkey, the United States had to confront the slow recovery of war-ravaged Europe. Given their fears that an impoverished Europe would hurt the U.S. economy and embrace Communism, Truman and his advisors were determined to help the continent rebuild. In a speech at Harvard University in June 1947, Truman's new Secretary of State, General George C. Marshall, proposed a European Recovery Plan to promote "political and social conditions in which free institutions can exist." Sixteen nations eagerly supported what became known as the Marshall Plan, and in 1948 Congress approved the plan with bipartisan support.

The Marshall Plan, the largest aid program ever initiated by any nation, served its purposes remarkably well. From 1948 to 1952, $13 billion went to restore agricultural production, boost industrial output, increase exports, and promote economic cooperation. Politically, the return of prosperity helped stabilize Western European governments and weaken the region's Communist parties. In the process, Western European nations were bound more tightly to the United States. Because of the Marshall Plan, Communism seemed much less likely to spread into Western Europe.

In addition to aid programs, containment demanded the kind of peacetime alliances that the United States had historically avoided because of fears that such agreements might drag the nation into war. Facing the unique challenge of the cold war, American leaders saw alliances as a way of preventing armed conflict. By promising to defend other countries if they were attacked, the United States could make the Soviet Union think twice about pushing further into Europe.

This thinking led the Truman administration to forge the first peacetime military alliance with Europe. In 1949, the United States joined ten Western European nations and Canada to form the North Atlantic Treaty Organization (NATO). Under the NATO agreement, an attack on any member nation would be treated as an attack on every member nation. Congress appropriated $1.3 billion in military aid for NATO countries, and Truman ordered American troops to Europe under the command of General Dwight D. Eisenhower.

As these actions suggested, containment also depended on a strong military establishment. The Truman administration pushed for the reorganization of the military. In 1947 Congress passed the National Security Act, which put the Army, Navy, and Air Force under a single cabinet secretary, the Secretary of Defense. This act also created both the Central Intelligence Agency (CIA) to gather information on national security and the National Security Council (NSC) to advise the president on security matters.

To build up the military, Congress passed a new Selective Service Act in 1948, allowing the government to draft men between ages 19 and 25 in peacetime. Finally, in 1949, Congress adopted another National Security Act, which brought together the Joint Chiefs of Staff, the heads of each of the armed services, to advise the president on military matters.

The Dangers of Containment

Containment exposed the United States to dangers. Confrontation with the Soviets had the potential to get out of hand and become a war. The dangers became clear in 1948 during a showdown over access to Berlin. That spring, the Americans, British, and French began to unify their zones of occupation in Germany into a single administrative unit. Faced with the prospect of a wealthy, unified, anti-Communist Western Germany, Stalin threw a blockade around Berlin, the German capital, located within the Soviet zone but jointly occupied by all four former allies. The 2.5 million people in the American, British, and French sections of Berlin were at risk of running out of food and coal. If the U.S. military tried to bring in supplies over land across the Soviet zone of Germany, there might have been war.

Instead, the Truman administration sent relief to Berlin by air. American transport planes carried 2,500 tons of food and fuel a day to the people of Berlin. In May

1949 the Soviets ended the blockade. Put to the test, the strategy of containment had worked, but the risks were obvious.

The dangers of containment became even greater for the United States later that year, when American reconnaissance planes over the Pacific collected evidence that the Soviet Union had exploded an atomic bomb. The U.S. monopoly on nuclear weapons was over, and confrontation with the Soviets now had potentially lethal consequences for the American people.

The Globalization of the Cold War

While the dangers of the cold war became frighteningly clear, the scope of the conflict widened. Events in China played a key role in this globalization of the cold war.

At the end of World War II, the Chinese nationalist government of Jiang Jieshi, America's ally, faced a revolution led by the Communist Party of Mao Zedong. The Truman administration, concluding that the nationalist regime could not be saved, agreed to $2 billion in aid for the nationalists but refused to send American troops. In December 1949 the defeated nationalists fled the Chinese mainland for the island of Formosa, also known as Taiwan.

The Chinese Revolution widened the cold war. Although Stalin did not direct the Chinese Communists, Americans saw Jiang's defeat as a victory for the Soviet Union. The Truman administration refused to recognize the new mainland Chinese regime, the People's Republic of China.

By this time American policymakers believed that Communism was a potential threat in almost every part of the world. The United States moved to make sure that Communism did not spread to Latin America. At a conference in the Brazilian city of Rio de Janeiro in August 1947, the United States and 20 Latin American republics agreed to the Inter-American Treaty of Reciprocal Assistance. Under the terms of the Rio Pact, the United States promised to train Latin American military leaders, regulate the flow of military supplies, and coordinate the defense of the region. In 1948 the United States joined with Latin American nations to create the Organization of American States (OAS). This body promoted hemispheric solidarity and economic development and enforced the Rio Pact.

Even Africa, which was not critical to the defense of the United States, became a battlefield of the cold war. In 1948 Truman improved diplomatic relations with the white supremacist government of South Africa, partly because of its opposition to Communism and Soviet expansionism.

The Cold War Turns Hot in Korea

With the United States working to hold off Communism around the world, it was not surprising that the nation was drawn into war. Americans were startled when their soldiers went into battle in South Korea in 1950 (see Map 26–2), but the Korean War was firmly rooted in the logic of the cold war.

Korea had been liberated from the Japanese in 1945. American troops occupied the territory south of the 38th Parallel while Soviet troops occupied the territory to the north. Despite American policymakers' professed support for self-determination, they opposed a left-wing movement of Koreans who wanted their nation to become an independent "people's republic." The Truman administration aided the anti-Communist government of Syngman Rhee in the South, while the Soviet Union promoted the regime of the Communist Kim Il Sung in the North. In 1948 the United States went along with the permanent division of Korea at the 38th

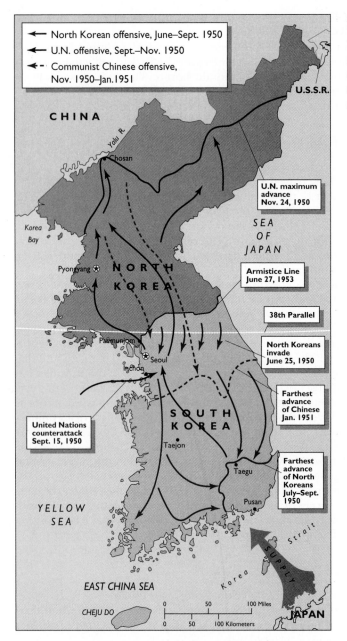

Map 26–2 The Korean War, 1950–1953
The shifting lines of advance mark the back-and-forth struggle that would end with stalemate and the permanent division of Korea.

Parallel. Then, in June 1950, after a series of incidents along the border, North Korea invaded South Korea.

The Korean invasion was the greatest crisis of Truman's presidency. The president and his advisors clearly believed that the Soviet Union was responsible for the North Korean attack. After the "loss" of China, the Truman administration could not afford to allow Communism to advance further in Asia and secured approval from the United Nations for international action in Korea. Although troops from 15 countries eventually fought for the United Nations, nine out of ten soldiers came from the United States. America was at war then, or was it? Claiming that the conflict was only a "police action," Truman never asked Congress for a declaration of war.

At first, the fighting did not go well. U.S. troops had to fall back before the North Korean army. But in the summer, U.N. forces under the leadership of American general Douglas MacArthur halted the North Koreans' advance. In September, American troops stormed ashore at Inchon on the west coast of South Korea. Within weeks, the South was reclaimed.

Then Truman and his advisers made a fateful decision. Truman gave the order to invade North Korea and push for the reunification of the Korean peninsula. MacArthur, who privately thirsted for war with the Chinese Communists, pushed quickly northward, ever closer to China. Fearing an American invasion, the Chinese unleashed a broad attack on U.N. troops. As MacArthur's army fled back south to the 38th Parallel, the general admitted it was an "entirely new war."

The Korean "police action" settled into a troubling stalemate. MacArthur wanted to expand the war effort and fight back aggressively, but the Truman administration, giving up on Korean reunification, was prepared to accept the division at the 38th Parallel. When MacArthur broke the U.S. military's unwritten rule against public criticism of its civilian leadership, Truman fired his popular general. Meanwhile, the war dragged on.

The Korean stalemate underscored some difficult realities of the cold war. The confrontation with Communism had the potential to sacrifice American lives in seemingly insignificant countries far away from the United States. American soldiers had to go into battle without a declaration of war and accept a less-than-total victory. Moreover, the American people had to acknowledge that the fighting could easily spread into a wider war, perhaps even a nuclear war with the Soviet Union.

Escalating the U.S. Effort

The "loss" of China, the Soviet atomic bomb, and the Korean War had important consequences for American policy. The Truman administration increased its support for anti-Communist causes, such as the French war in Southeast Asia.

Vietnam, along with Laos and Cambodia, made up Indochina, a southeast Asian colony of France. After losing Indochina to Japan during World War II, the French were ready to take over again in 1945. By then, however, many Vietnamese wanted their land to be independent. Led by the Communist and nationalist Ho Chi Minh, the Viet Minh freedom fighters declared Vietnamese independence and appealed to the Truman administration for support in 1945 and 1946. However, the United States refused to oppose the interests of a valued European ally. Truman did not even answer Ho's letters.

With help from the Soviets and the Chinese Communists, the Viet Minh frustrated the French Army. By 1950, France needed help from the United States, and the Truman administration gave military equipment and direct financial aid to the French war effort in Vietnam.

Another consequence of the events of 1949 and 1950 was the escalation of the arms race. To deploy troops around the world and counter Soviet nuclear weapons, the United States had to strengthen its forces. In April 1950 the NSC approved a secret guideline for American policy, NSC 68, which warned that America, vulnerable to Soviet attack, must develop "clearly superior overall power." Increased defense spending was an absolute necessity.

In September 1950, at the president's urging, Congress passed the Defense Production Act, which nearly doubled defense spending in a single year. By 1952, defense expenditures had nearly doubled again, to $44 billion, and the armed forces grew from 1.5 million before the Korean War to 3.6 million in 1952 (see Figure 26–1).

The president had already made perhaps the most momentous decision of all. Early in 1950, Truman ordered the building of "the so-called hydrogen or super-bomb." Successfully tested in November 1952, the hydrogen bomb had far more explosive power than the earlier atomic bomb. Less than a year later, the USSR had its own H-bomb.

The confrontation with Communism was transforming the American political economy. To fight the cold war, Americans accepted things they had long feared in peacetime: alliances, foreign aid, and a massive standing army. These innovations magnified the role of the federal government in the economy and society. The president held more power than ever before. The federal government, its budget swollen by military expenditures, had new power to shape the economy.

THE RECONVERSION OF AMERICAN SOCIETY

While the cold war escalated, the United States confronted domestic challenges that tested the political economic arrangements of the Depression and World War II. With the end of the war, Americans focused on reconversion, the restoration of the economy and society to a peacetime footing. Reconversion was a welcome process, but also a cause for worry. Americans feared a return to the bleak economic conditions of the 1930s; labor, women, and African Americans feared losing their wartime gains.

The Postwar Economy

As World War II ended, economists and policymakers worried that the end of the federal government's massive spending for the war effort would force businesses to lay off workers and cut investment. Americans questioned whether the economy could provide enough jobs for the returning servicemen.

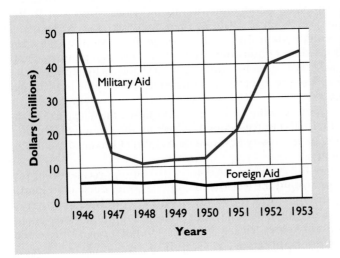

Figure 26–1   The Cost of the Cold War: U.S. Military and Foreign Aid Expenditures

Source: Statistical Abstract of the United States, 1952, p. 199; 1953, pp. 225, 886; 1957, p. 879; Historical Statistics of the United States, II, p. 1124.

The economic disaster never came. Unemployment rose to almost 4 percent in the first few years after the war, but never approached the double-digit rates of the 1930s. Despite brief downturns, the economy remained healthy.

This strong performance reflected several factors. Returning servicemen and women did not put excessive strain on the economy, partly because so many of them went back to school rather than look for work. Thanks to the generous provisions of the GI Bill of 1944, half of the nation's 15.4 million returning veterans went to school or received technical training.

Spending by the federal government also helped to prevent a return to the economic conditions of the 1930s. The GI Bill illustrated how that spending stimulated the economy. Pumping nearly $14.5 billion into the educational system, the bill encouraged colleges and universities to expand and to hire new faculty. Entire new educational systems, such as the State University of New York, were created.

Reconversion also went well because of the gradual transformation of the economy. In the late 1940s, the United States was still an industrial nation, with production centered in the Northeast and Midwest, but during and after the war, economic activity shifted toward the South and West, and the nature of the economy changed. In 1945, coal provided more than half the nation's energy. Five years later oil and natural gas provided the majority of energy. New technologies and industries, such as plastics and aviation, grew rapidly. This economic dynamism eased the process of reconversion.

Finally, the dominant role of the United States in the world economy facilitated reconversion. At the end of World War II, America was the only major industrial nation whose economy was undamaged. As late as 1950, America, with only 6 percent of the world's population, accounted for 40 percent of the value of all the goods and services produced around the globe. Demand for American exports helped to provide jobs for returning veterans and to sustain the economy.

Although the economy did not suffer from unemployment, it did confront inflation. The strong job market contributed to a rise in prices. With steady paychecks, Americans were eager to buy the appliances, cars, and houses that had been unavailable during the war. Driven by shortages of houses and other goods, the consumer price index rose 14.4 percent in 1946. By the late 1940s production caught up with demand, inflation decreased, and an economic boom continued.

The Challenge of Organized Labor

Reconversion posed special challenges for workers and the labor movement. After pledging not to strike during World War II, organized labor was eager to test and expand its power in peacetime. The unions wanted wage increases; some also wanted more control over the way corporations did business. Not surprisingly, corporate executives were reluctant to give up their power or profits.

The result was a huge wave of strikes as soon as the war ended in August 1945. At the start of 1946, 2 million workers were on strike. Machinists in San Francisco, longshoremen in New York City, and other workers across the country called a record 4,985 strikes that year.

Late in 1945, the United Auto Workers (UAW) struck General Motors (GM) for a 30 percent raise in hourly wages, access to the company's account books, and more of a say in the company's decisions. UAW vice president Walter Reuther insisted that higher wages would stimulate consumption without forcing the prosperous car company to raise prices; however, GM refused access to its books and rejected union interference in management decisions. When the strike finally ended after

113 days, the UAW won only some of its wage demands. The GM strike marked a turning point. Unions never again made such bold demands to participate in management, focusing instead on questions of pay and benefits.

The coal and railroad strikes were even more contentious than the GM work stoppage. The United Mine Workers (UMW) and the railway unions refused to accept federal arbitration. As the coal supply dwindled, power systems suffered and railroad passengers were stranded. The situation tested the strong relationship between the liberal Democratic Party and organized labor as an angry President Truman ordered federal takeovers of both the mines and the railroads. The strikes came to an end in May. When the UMW struck again in November, Truman took the union to court for violating a federal injunction. Forced to pay heavy fines, the union ended its walkout. Although angry unionists condemned Truman, much of the public applauded the president's action, believing that union leaders had become too powerful for the good of the country.

Counting on the public's unhappiness with unions, Congress soon moved to limit the power of organized labor. In 1947, Republicans and conservative Democrats passed the Taft–Hartley Act, which made it easier for employers to hire nonunion workers and to oppose the formation of unions. The bill also limited unions' right to organize supervisors, boycott employers, and engage in political activity. Most humiliating of all, it compelled union leaders to swear that they did not belong to the Communist Party. To angry unionists and their Democratic allies, the measure was the "Tuff–Heartless Act." Truman vetoed it, but Congress overrode him in June 1947.

The passage of the Taft–Hartley Act was not the end of organized labor's problems. A drive to unionize the low-wage industries of the South went poorly, in part because of divisions between white and African-American workers. Labor's attempts to force the repeal of Taft–Hartley failed.

Despite these setbacks, workers and unions prospered. In 1948 the UAW won guaranteed cost-of-living adjustments (COLAs) and an annual wage increase tied to rises in worker productivity. In 1950 the UAW obtained other increases and a pension plan. In return for pensions and protection against inflation, the auto workers gave management stable, predictable labor relations over the long term.

Opportunities for Women

Reconversion also posed special challenges to the status of American women. During World War II, the shortage of male civilian labor had expanded women's employment opportunities. At the end of the war, most working women did not want to give up those opportunities. But there was a widespread belief that women should surrender jobs to returning servicemen. American culture still assumed that women's ideal place was in the home.

Employers gave away women's jobs—high-paying industrial positions, in particular—to male veterans. The number of women in the labor force dropped 13 percent from 1945 to 1946, but three-quarters of the women who wanted to stay at work managed to find jobs.

Women's role in the postwar workplace was the product of both their desire and financial necessity. By 1953 the number of women in the work force matched the level of 1945. A higher percentage of women was employed than before World War II. The number of women in nontraditional jobs increased, too. More women than ever before were skilled craftspersons, forepersons, physicians, and surgeons.

The number of married women in the postwar labor force was especially notable. Traditionally, married women were expected to devote themselves to husbands and children, not jobs and careers. However, in the late 1940s there was a shortage of single female workers, so employers needed married women workers. By 1947 there were already more married women than single women in the wage labor force.

Reconversion did not cause a return to the prewar days when women had almost no place in the military. In 1947 Congress passed the Army–Navy Nurse Act, which granted women permanent status in the armed forces. The next year Congress merged the separate women's military organizations, such as the Women's Army Corps, into the regular armed services.

Despite these gains, women continued to face discrimination in the workplace. The vast majority of female workers had to settle for traditionally female, low-paying jobs. Women's hourly pay rose only half as much as men's in the first years after the war. In the military, women were largely confined to traditionally female roles such as nursing.

Women faced discrimination in the larger society as well. There was little interest in women's rights. After a meeting with female activists, Truman dismissed a constitutional amendment guaranteeing equal rights for women as a "lot of hooey." Nevertheless, women's opportunities gradually expanded after World War II as the combination of women's desires and the economy's needs slowly promoted the feminization of the labor force.

Civil Rights for African Americans

Like women, African Americans made significant gains during World War II. They played new roles in the military, filled higher paying jobs in the civilian economy, and pushed their demand for civil rights. Like women, African Americans wanted to preserve and extend their rights and opportunities in the postwar period but faced substantial resistance.

Several factors, including economic change, legal rulings, and wartime experiences, stimulated African Americans' drive for equal rights and opportunities. By the end of the war, the transformation of the southern economy was undermining the old system of segregation and denial of voting rights. African Americans continued to leave farms for the region's growing cities and for the North and West. One of the fundamental rationales for segregation—the need for an inexpensive and submissive labor force to work the fields—was gradually disappearing. Meanwhile, the African-American migrants to northern and western cities increased black votes and political influence in the nation.

During the 1940s, a series of Supreme Court decisions struck at racial discrimination. In *Smith* v. *Allwright* in 1944, the court banned whites-only primary elections. In *Morgan* v. *Virginia* in 1946, the court ruled that interstate bus companies could not segregate passengers. In *Shelley* v. *Kraemer* in 1948, the court banned restrictive covenants, private agreements between property owners not to sell houses to African Americans and other minorities. These and other court decisions made long-established forms of discrimination seem vulnerable and showed that African Americans might have a judicial ally in their struggle for justice.

African Americans' own wartime experiences also encouraged them to demand more from the United States. African-American veterans, having fought for their country, now expected justice. "Our people are not coming back with the idea of just taking up where they left off," an African-American private wrote.

That kind of determination spurred civil rights activism. In the South, African Americans increasingly demanded the right to vote after *Smith* v. *Allwright*. The National Association for the Advancement of Colored People (NAACP) set up citizenship schools in southern communities to show African Americans how to register to vote. Across the South, local organizations challenged the disfranchisement of African Americans. The voting campaign was driven, too, by grassroots, often spontaneous action. In July 1946 Medgar Evers, a combat veteran, tried to vote in the Democratic Party primary in Decatur, Mississippi. Such activism met resistance from many southern whites. A white mob kept Medgar Evers from voting. In Georgia, whites killed an African-American voter. More often, whites manipulated registration laws to disqualify would-be black voters. An African-American voter might have to answer such questions as "How many bubbles are there in a bar of soap?" African-American voter registration in the South, only 2 percent in 1940, rose to 12 percent by 1947. With that increasing percentage came the election of a few black officials and better service from local government.

While the campaign for voting rights went forward in the South, civil rights activists fought segregation in all parts of the country. To test the Supreme Court's decision in *Morgan* v. *Virginia*, the Congress of Racial Equality (CORE) sent an integrated team of activists on a bus trip through the upper South in 1947. The activists' attempt to desegregate buses and bus terminals met with violence and arrests. That year, an interracial CORE group forced the integration of an amusement park in New Jersey. Civil rights activists had more success promoting antidiscrimination laws in the North than in ending legal segregation in the South. By 1953 fair-employment laws had been adopted in 30 cities and 12 states.

Activists also pressured President Truman to support civil rights. In the spring and summer of 1946, picketers marched outside the White House with signs that read, "SPEAK, SPEAK, MR. PRESIDENT." Racial discrimination was an embarrassment for a nation claiming to represent freedom and democracy around the world, but support for civil rights was a political risk. Nevertheless, Truman took significant steps to fight discrimination.

In the fall of 1946, the president set up a Committee on Civil Rights. The committee's report, *To Secure These Rights*, called for strong federal action, including suppression of lynching, protection of African-American voters, enforcement of civil rights laws, desegregation of the armed forces, and promotion of equal employment opportunities. Admitting that "there is a serious gap between our ideals and some of our practices," Truman insisted "this gap must be closed."

African Americans, meanwhile, kept the heat on. To protest continuing discrimination in the military, A. Philip Randolph, the head of the Brotherhood of Sleeping Car Porters, proposed an African-American boycott of the draft. In July 1948 Truman responded with Executive Order 9981, which created the Committee on Equality of Treatment and Opportunity in the Armed Services. The committee moved vigorously to end discrimination in the military. At the same time, Truman established the Fair Employment Board, which moved more slowly against discrimination in federal hiring.

During the Truman years, the most publicized blow to racial inequality landed not in the White House or the courts, but rather on the baseball diamond. When the Brooklyn Dodgers called up infielder Jackie Robinson from the minor leagues in 1947, he became the first black man in decades to play in the majors. Fast, powerful, and exciting, Robinson finished the season as the National League's Rookie of the Year, and his success paved the way for increasing numbers of African-American players in the major leagues over the next several years.

"President Truman, We Need Your Help." African Americans picket the White House to demand justice for the black victim of a lynching in Georgia. The placards condemning powerful white southern Democrats—Senator Eugene Talmadge, Senator Theodore Bilbo, and Representative John Rankin—are a reminder that Truman risked alienating white support if he responded to black demands for civil rights.

On the whole, African Americans preserved and sometimes expanded their wartime gains. Nevertheless, they still encountered injustice and inequality in most aspects of daily life. Legalized segregation and disfranchisement remained in the South. Although improving, the median income of African-American families was little more than half that of white families at the end of the 1940s. Moreover, most whites were not eager to redress these inequalities.

For African Americans, women, and organized labor, reconversion turned out to be better than feared and worse than hoped. All struggled to preserve and expand their rights and opportunities in the political economy of the late 1940s and confronted the limits of their power to change society.

Instead of falling back into economic depression, America generally prospered. The political economic arrangements that had emerged from the Depression and World War II seemed to work well enough, but the difficulties of African Americans, women, and organized labor were unfinished business that the United States grappled with for the next half-century.

THE FRUSTRATIONS OF LIBERALISM

During the Great Depression, liberalism, in the form of Franklin Roosevelt's New Deal, had reshaped the American political economy. The liberal Democratic agenda had stalled during World War II, and after the war liberalism met with frustration.

The Democrats' Troubles

An accidental president, Harry Truman faced skepticism from many Americans. They wondered whether this unassuming, plain-spoken man could take the place of Franklin Roosevelt. Liberals wondered, too, whether Truman really shared their ideas.

At the same time, the president was handicapped by skepticism about the Democrats' liberal approach to the political economy. During the Great Depression, Americans had been willing to endorse the liberals' faith in an activist government, but in a fairly prosperous peacetime, people felt less need for government and more need for individual freedom.

The president embraced more of liberalism than the liberals expected. Shortly after he took office in 1945, Truman presented a 21-point legislative program that included liberal proposals on education, employment, insurance, social security, and civil rights. Yet a Full Employment Bill met overwhelming conservative and moderate opposition. Watered down by Congress, the resulting Employment Act of 1946 did nothing to increase the role of the federal government in promoting employment.

Truman and the liberals suffered an even sharper defeat over the president's proposal for a compulsory health insurance system that would guarantee medical care to all Americans. Conservatives and the medical profession condemned Truman's proposal as "the kind of regimentation that led to totalitarianism in Germany." The bill failed to pass Congress, and so did the rest of Truman's proposals.

Nevertheless, the federal government's role in national life continued to grow. For example, even though national health insurance was defeated, federal intervention in the health-care system increased. The Veterans Administration established a vast network of federal hospitals. The Hill–Burton Act appropriated federal money for hospital construction, and Congress created the Communicable Disease Center (later called the Centers for Disease Control) to monitor infectious diseases, reorganized the National Institutes of Health, and established the National Institute of Mental Health.

While Truman struggled with domestic and foreign policy, he became increasingly unpopular. The president looked weak and ineffective to some Americans and tyrannical and overbearing to others. In the 1946 Congressional elections, voters gave the Republican Party a majority in both the House and the Senate for the first time in 16 years.

Truman's Comeback

The 1946 elections seemed to point toward Truman's certain defeat in the presidential contest two years later, but the president managed a stunning comeback. The turnaround began with the victorious Republican majority of the Eightieth Congress that convened in 1947. Led by Senator Robert Taft of Ohio, the Congressional Republicans hoped to beat back New Deal liberalism. Taft, the son of former president William Howard Taft, believed in limited government and wanted "free Americans freely working out their destiny."

The Republicans did win passage of the Taft–Hartley Act, which was a blow to labor, liberals, and the president, but Taft and the Republicans found themselves hamstrung by Americans' ambivalence about liberalism. People did not want bold new liberal programs such as national health insurance, but Americans clearly wanted to hold on to the government benefits they had won in the Depression and World War II. Besides the Taft–Hartley Act, the Eightieth Congress did not accomplish much of the Republican agenda.

Nevertheless, things looked bleak for Harry Truman. By March 1948 only 35 percent of the people approved of his performance in office. Moreover, his party was splitting apart. On the left, his former Secretary of Commerce Henry Wallace was running for president as a Progressive appealing to liberals. On the right, Democratic Governor Strom Thurmond of South Carolina was running as a "Dixiecrat," appealing to white supporters of segregation.

Truman's Republican opponent, Governor Thomas E. Dewey of New York, thought Truman was certain to lose. Dewey believed he could get away with a mild, uncontroversial campaign. But Truman worked hard to pull the Democratic New Deal majority back together. Climbing aboard his railway car, Truman visited more than half the states on an old-fashioned "whistle-stop" campaign, reaching out to African Americans, labor, farmers, senior citizens, and other beneficiaries of New Deal liberalism. "Give 'em hell, Harry," the crowds shouted, and he did, deriding the "do-nothing" Republican Congress. "The Democratic Party puts human rights and human welfare first," he declared. "These Republican gluttons of privilege . . . want a return of the Wall Street economic dictatorship."

On election day Dewey attracted fewer votes than he had four years before. Holding together the New Deal coalition, Truman won the presidency in his own right with only 49.5 percent of the vote. Moreover, the Democrats recaptured the House and the Senate.

Truman soon discovered that an election victory did not mean a mandate for his ideas. In his State of the Union address in January 1949, Truman declared that "every individual has a right to expect from our Government a fair deal." But the president's Fair Deal legislation made little headway in Congress. The liberal vision of the political economy could not command the politics of cold war America.

"Give 'em hell, Harry!" President Harry Truman speaks to a crowd from the back of his railroad car during the 1948 election campaign.

FIGHTING THE COLD WAR AT HOME

While conservatives and liberals battled over domestic policy, the cold war increasingly affected life in the United States. Billions of dollars in defense expenditures eventually stimulated economic growth, but in the short run, the main domestic by-product of the cold war was a largely irrational fear of Communist subversives. By the 1950s, this fear was a powerful force capable of destroying the lives of thousands of Americans, including Esther and Stephen Brunauer.

Doubts and Fears in the Atomic Age

Despite the U.S. triumph in World War II, American culture was surprisingly dark and pessimistic in the late 1940s. The rise of fascism, the Holocaust, and the bombings of Hiroshima and Nagasaki raised troubling questions. The cold war did nothing to calm those concerns. People felt small and powerless in an age of giant corporations, big unions, big government, and super bombs.

Nuclear weapons were perhaps the greatest source of fear. The unprecedented power of the atomic bomb dominated the popular imagination. For many Americans, this was the Atomic Age. They dealt with their anxiety in a variety of ways. Some people tried humor. Americans drank "atomic cocktails" and danced to the "Atomic Polka." But the Soviets' development of the atomic bomb and the hydrogen bomb was impossible to laugh away.

Americans' fear was also reflected in the hardening of attitudes toward foreigners who wanted to live in the United States. The Immigration and Nationality Act of 1952 continued tight restrictions on immigration, particularly from Asia. It also kept out Communists and homosexuals and allowed the deportation of American citizens suspected of disloyalty.

The Anti-Communist Crusade Begins

Americans might have feared disloyalty most of all. The search for traitors quickly became a panicky "Red Scare," much like the one that followed World War I.

Historians debate the origins of the second Red Scare. Anti-Communism was already deeply rooted in American culture, but the powerful politicians of both major parties gave domestic anti-Communism its particularly dangerous form.

The crusaders had to search hard for Communism at home. The Communist Party of the United States of America (CPUSA), a legal political party, never received more than 0.3 percent of the popular vote in any presidential election. Nevertheless, the party became the target of persecution. In June 1948 the Truman administration charged 12 American Communist leaders with violations of the 1940 Smith Act, which had criminalized membership in "a group advocating . . . the overthrow of the government by force." Eleven were convicted and jailed.

With so little open Communism, some Americans searched for secret Communists. The hunt was led by the House of Representatives' Committee on Un-American Activities, known as the House Un-American Activities Committee (HUAC). In 1947 the HUAC held hearings to lay bare a supposed Communist plot in Hollywood. Much of the film industry cooperated with the HUAC, but eight screenwriters, a producer, and a director, who were Communists, cited their First Amendment rights and declined to testify about their political beliefs and activities.

The "Hollywood Ten" were convicted of contempt of Congress and sent to jail for up to a year, with the eventual concurrence of the Supreme Court.

Hollywood got the message. Film studios refused to hire writers, directors, and actors even remotely suspected of Communist ties. The studios put out over-wrought anti-Communist movies such as *The Red Menace.*

Afraid of looking "soft" on Communism, the Truman administration helped promote the Red Scare by encouraging the idea that there was a real problem with domestic Communism. "Communists," declared Truman's Attorney General, Tom Clark, "are everywhere . . . and each carries with him the germs of death for society."

In 1947 the president created a permanent Federal Employee Loyalty Program. Any civil servant could lose his or her job by belonging to any of the "totalitarian, Fascist, Communist or subversive" groups listed by the attorney general. People accused of disloyalty were denied due process and had to prove their own inno-cence. Although only about 300 employees were actually discharged for disloyalty, the program helped create the impression that there was a serious problem with Communism in Washington.

The Hunt for Soviet Spies

There was, in fact, spying going on inside the federal government. The Soviet Union, like the United States, carried out espionage abroad. In 1945 an illegal raid by the Office of Strategic Services, the predecessor of the CIA, turned up secret U.S. government documents in the offices of *Amerasia,* a magazine that favored the Chi-nese Communists. The Canadian government found evidence of a spy ring that had passed American atomic secrets to the Soviets during World War II.

Thanks to information from the Canadian case, the FBI began to suspect that Alger Hiss, an aide to the secretary of state, was a Soviet agent. Hiss was quietly eased out of his job. Then, in 1948, the HUAC took testimony from Whittaker Chambers, an editor of *Time* magazine, who accused Hiss of being a Communist. Hiss denied the charge against him, said he had never even met Chambers, and sued the magazine editor for libel.

The suave Hiss appeared far more credible than the rumpled Chambers, who was an admitted perjurer, but Republican Congressman Richard Nixon of California forced Hiss to admit that he had known Chambers under an alias. Chambers charged that Hiss had given him secret information in the 1930s. In front of reporters at his farm in Maryland, Chambers pulled rolls of microfilm out of a hollowed-out pumpkin. The film contained photographs of secret documents, some of which had apparently been typed on a typewriter belonging to Hiss's fam-ily. Under the statute of limitations, it was too late to try Hiss for spying, but it was not too late to indict him for lying to Congress. Hiss was convicted in January 1950. While Hiss sat in prison for almost four years, Chambers wrote a bestseller and Nixon became a senator. The case was a triumph for Republicans and conservatives and a blow to Democrats and liberals.

As the Hiss case ended, another scandal stimulated Americans' fears. In early 1950, British authorities arrested Klaus Fuchs, a physicist who had worked at the nuclear research facility in Los Alamos, New Mexico. The investigation led to David Greenglass, who had worked on the atomic bomb project during World War II. Greenglass admitted that he had passed information about the bomb to his brother-in-law, Julius Rosenberg. Rosenberg, a former member of the Communist Party, and his wife Ethel were convicted in a controversial trial on charges of conspiracy to commit espionage and sentenced to death in April 1951. The Supreme Court refused to review the case. Ignoring appeals for clemency from around the world, the federal government finally electrocuted the Rosenbergs in June 1953. The controversy over their guilt has continued to the present day.

There now seems little disagreement over the reality of Soviet spying in the early years of the cold war. The USSR obtained some American nuclear secrets, but the impact was not as great as conservatives feared or as minimal as liberals insisted. Most likely, espionage sped up the Soviets' work on an atomic bomb that they would have developed anyway.

The Rise of McCarthyism

Two weeks after Hiss's conviction, one week after Truman's announcement of the decision to build the hydrogen bomb, and days after the arrest of Klaus Fuchs, Senator Joseph McCarthy of Wisconsin took command of the anti-Communist crusade.The previously obscure senator claimed to have the names of 205 Communists working for the State Department. In fact, McCarthy had no names of State Department Communists at all. Instead, he named other people as subversives, including Esther and Stephen Brunauer. A Democratic-controlled Senate subcommittee dismissed McCarthy's charges.

Nevertheless, frightened by the developments of the last five years, many people believed McCarthy. Some Americans shared McCarthy's resentment of New Dealers and other privileged elites—the powerful figures he derided as "egg-sucking phony liberals."

Many Democrats hated McCarthyism, but they were afraid to challenge such a powerful political force. Frightened Democratic legislators even helped Congress pass the Internal Security Act of 1950, which forced the registration of Communist and Communist-front groups, allowed the internment of suspicious persons in national emergencies, provided for the deportation of allegedly subversive aliens, and barred Communists from defense jobs. Truman vetoed the bill, but Congress overrode his veto.

Eventually, McCarthy went too far. Angry that one of his aides, David Schine, had not received a draft deferment, the senator launched an investigation of the Army. The Secretary of the Army, Robert T. Stevens, claimed that McCarthy had pressured the service to take care of Schine. In April 1954, before a television audience of 20 million people, McCarthy failed to come up with evidence of treason in the Army. When he tried unjustifiably to smear one of the Army's young lawyers as a Communist, McCarthy was suddenly exposed. "Have you no sense of decency, sir, at long last?" asked the Army's Chief Counsel, Joseph Welch. It was an electric moment. McCarthy's popularity ratings dropped sharply, and the Senate condemned him for "unbecoming conduct." Three years later he was dead.

The fall of McCarthy did not end McCarthyism, however. Americans were looking everywhere for Communists in the 1950s. At several universities, faculty members lost their jobs. Communism had become a useful charge to hurl at labor unions, civil rights, and even modern art. Politicians and communities attacked nonrepresentational, abstract expressionist artists as "tools of the Kremlin" and "our enemies." The Cincinnati Reds renamed their team the "Redlegs." Across the country, Americans became more careful about what they said out loud. Containment abroad seemed to have produced an uncontainable fear at home.

CHRONOLOGY

1945	Yalta conference Harry S Truman's succession to the presidency Potsdam conference Beginning of postwar strike wave
1946	Winston Churchill's "Iron Curtain" speech George Kennan's "long telegram" on Soviet expansionism Employment Act of 1946 *Morgan* v. *Virginia* Election of Republican majorities in the House and Senate
1947	Announcement of Truman Doctrine Beginning of Federal Employee Loyalty Program CORE's Journey of Reconciliation Integration of Major League baseball by Jackie Robinson HUAC Hollywood hearings Rio Pact Taft–Hartley Act National Security Act of 1947 Report by Presidential Committee on Civil Rights, *To Secure These Rights*
1948	*Shelley* v. *Kraemer* Congressional approval of Marshall Plan Truman's Executive Order 9981 Beginning of Berlin crisis Selective Service Act Truman elected president
1949	Formation of North Atlantic Treaty Organization Communist takeover of mainland China
1950	NSC 68 Alger Hiss's conviction for perjury Joe McCarthy's speech in Wheeling, West Virginia Treaty of Detroit Beginning of Korean War Internal Security Act of 1950
1951	Truman fires General Douglas MacArthur
1952	Immigration and Nationality Act Test of hydrogen bomb
1953	Execution of Ethel and Julius Rosenberg
1954	Army–McCarthy Hearings

Conclusion

By the time Esther Brunauer lost her job in 1952, the cold war had deeply disrupted American life. To contain Communism, the United States had made unprecedented peacetime commitments that transformed the nation's political economy. Despite these changes, the cold war had widened and intensified. Just seven years after dropping the first atomic bomb on the Japanese, Americans lived with the threat of nuclear annihilation. They lived, too, with the frenzied search for domestic Communists.

As Esther and Stephen Brunauer moved back to Illinois to find peace and rebuild their lives, other Americans needed peace as well. They wanted the fighting in Korea to end. Anxious to avoid a nuclear holocaust, they wanted the cold war confrontation with the Soviets to stabilize. Meanwhile, American society needed to focus on the unfinished business of reconversion, including the rights of labor, women, and African Americans. However, it would be impossible to avoid the consequences of the cold war.

Further Readings

Richard M. Fried, *Nightmare in Red: The McCarthy Era in Perspective* (1990). Provides a concise overview of the anti-Communist crusade.

William Graebner, *The Age of Doubt: American Thought and Culture in the 1940s* (1991). Probes the fears and insecurities that shaped American society during the cold war.

Alonzo L. Hamby, *Man of the People: A Life of Harry S. Truman* (1995). A full biography of the first cold war president.

Melvyn P. Leffler, *A Preponderance of Power: National Security, the Truman Administration, and the Cold War* (1992). One of several important conflicting accounts of the origins of the cold war.

Nelson Lichtenstein, *The Most Dangerous Man in Detroit: Walter Reuther and the Fate of American Labor* (1995). Examines the hopes and frustrations of the labor movement after World War II.

David M. Oshinsky, *A Conspiracy So Immense: The World of Joe McCarthy* (1983). An engaging, even-handed biography of the most famous anti-Communist crusader.

Arnold Rampersad, *Jackie Robinson: A Biography* (1997). Explores the complicated man who integrated Major League Baseball.

Richard Rhodes, *Dark Sun: The Making of the Hydrogen Bomb* (1995). An engaging narrative account of a key development in the nuclear arms race.

Allen Weinstein, *Perjury: The Hiss–Chambers Case* (1978). Provides a thorough, controversial study of one of the most controversial episodes of the cold war.

 Please refer to the document CD-ROM for primary sources related to this chapter.

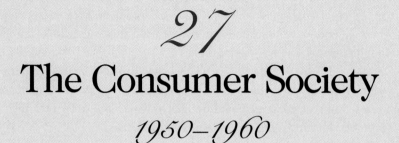

CHAPTER

27

The Consumer Society

1950–1960

E. J. Korvettes • Living the Good Life • A Homogeneous Society?
The Eisenhower Era at Home and Abroad • Challenges to the
Consumer Society • Conclusion

E. J. KORVETTES

At the end of World War II, Harry Ferkauf owned two luggage stores in midtown Manhattan in New York City. An immigrant Jewish man from Eastern Europe, he haggled with customers over prices in the old way and made a decent living. He did not want or expect much more.

Harry's son, Eugene, was unwilling to accept the old limits. After the war, Gene began offering discounts on luggage, watches, and other goods. Other neighborhood storeowners resented this low-priced competition. Father and son argued frequently. In 1948, Gene quit the business and put all his savings into his own discount store that would compete with the full-priced stores of the other merchants.

Gene envisioned a new kind of store, where customers could buy appliances and other goods without haggling, at low, fixed prices. Discounting his merchandise by a quarter and even a third, Gene could not make much money from a single sale. But if he sold enough televisions and refrigerators, he would earn more than his father ever had. Gene and his wife distributed thousands of cards announcing the new store on East 46th Street. On opening day, crowds filled the small shop and spent $3,000. Harry, who usually took in about $50 a day, was impressed.

In a few years, Gene had five successful discount stores in and around New York City. The business was called "E. J. Korvettes"—E for Eugene, J for his partner Joe

Zwillenberg, and Korvettes after the small, quick Canadian warships of World War II. Korvettes appealed to a new generation, young men and women eager to buy televisions and other appliances and unafraid to go into debt. Prosperous, they were leaving their parents' neighborhoods in the city for new suburbs. Gene Ferkauf understood these people; he was one of them.

In December 1953 Gene opened a vast new department store in Westbury, Long Island, where farmland was giving way to new suburban housing developments. The crowds were so big that salesmen could not get back into the store after their lunch hours. The suburban store pulled in $28 million in a year.

Riding the suburban wave, Gene Ferkauf had made it big. Gene closed the stores in New York City and kept expanding into the suburbs. He had left his father's world behind.

Gene Ferkauf's success reflected one of the central developments that shaped American society after World War II. Along with the cold war, economic prosperity transformed the nation in a host of ways. Just as Gene left his father's world behind, American society left behind the sense of economic limits and constraints that marked the Great Depression and the war. The 1950s marked the culmination of the nation's long transformation into a full-fledged consumer society. Gene Ferkauf profited because mainstream culture celebrated consumption and pleasure instead of work and self-restraint and because televisions and suburbs defined the consumer lifestyle.

The emergence of the consumer society strongly affected the American political economy, producing a more homogeneous, seemingly more harmonious society, characterized by decreasing class differences, changing gender relations, and a baby boom. In later years, American culture would look back nostalgically at the 1950s, but the consumer society had its conflicts, failures, and limits. In different ways, teenagers and some other Americans rebelled against the conformity and constraints of the 1950s. The benefits of the consumer society did not reach every group; consumerism did not solve the problem of racial inequality or end the cold war. By the close of the decade, many Americans worried about the inadequacies of the consumer society, even as they enjoyed its benefits.

LIVING THE GOOD LIFE

Consumerism was not a new development, but it was only in the 1950s that consumer values and habits finally dominated the American economy and culture. Never before had so many Americans had the chance to live the good life.

They tended to define that "good life" in economic terms. A dynamic, evolving economy provided more leisure and income. Sure of prosperity, Americans had the confidence to spend more of their time and money in the pursuit of pleasure. Millions of people lived the dream of homeownership in new suburbs, bought flashy automobiles, purchased their first televisions, and enjoyed a new openness about sex.

Economic Prosperity

Consumerism could not have flourished without prosperity. Despite three short recessions, the 1950s were a period of economic boom. The economy grew solidly, and the gross national product—the value of all the country's output of goods and services—grew at an average of 3.2 percent a year.

Several major factors spurred this economic growth. The shortage of consumer goods during and just after World War II had left Americans with money to spend. Because of the cold war, the federal government was also ready to spend money. Washington's expenditures for the defense buildup and foreign aid helped to stimulate the demand for American goods and services. At the same time, the industrial economy was evolving. Traditional heavy manufacturing—the production of steel and automobiles—was still crucial to national prosperity, but newer industries—electronics, chemicals, plastics, aviation, and computers—became increasingly important.

The emergence of the computer business was especially significant for the long-term transformation of the economy. In 1946, two engineers at the University of Pennsylvania, J. Presper Eckert, Jr., and John William Mauchly, completed the first fully electronic digital computer, loaded with hot bulky vacuum tubes. The Electronic Numerical Integrator and Computer (ENIAC) weighed more than 30 tons and filled a large room. Then Eckert and Mauchly produced the UNIVAC 1 (Universal Automatic Computer), a more advanced machine that was used to count census data in 1951 and presidential election returns in 1952.

As tiny solid-state transistors replaced vacuum tubes, computers became smaller, more powerful, and more common. By 1958, American companies were producing $1 billion worth of computers a year. Because computers were still so large and expensive, they were used mostly by universities, corporations, the Department of Defense, and other federal agencies. By 1961, there were about 10,000 computers in use, and the nation was on the brink of the computer age.

As American industry continued to evolve, the nation's distribution and service sectors played a larger economic role than ever before. While the number of manufacturing jobs barely changed, employment in retail stores like E. J. Korvettes increased 19 percent. Jobs in the service sector, such as restaurants, hotels, repair shops, hospitals, and universities, jumped 32 percent. The United States had begun to develop a post-industrial economy, less dependent on production and more dependent on service and consumption.

The prosperity of the 1950s also rested on relative labor peace. After the instability of the late 1940s, relations between workers and employers settled down. Unionized workers, their wages and benefits rising, seldom challenged employers.

Economic prosperity greatly benefited big business. In the 1950s, corporations loomed larger than ever before. New firms such as E. J. Korvettes emerged and grew. Established corporations became still larger. By 1960, corporations earned 18 times as much income as the rest of the nation's businesses combined.

Corporations enjoyed public approval as well as economic prosperity. Business executives now seemed to be leading the nation into an economic golden age. As a result, the popular suspicion of big business, so strong during the Depression, evaporated. Even liberals, once critical of corporate power, now celebrated the benefits of large-scale business enterprise.

American workers also benefited from the prosperity of the 1950s, enjoying high employment, low inflation, and rising incomes. Typically, less than 5 percent of the work force was out of a job at one time. Wages rose dramatically. Factory workers' average hourly pay more than doubled between 1945 and 1960. Moreover, consumer prices rose less than 2 percent per year. The percentage of people living in poverty declined.

The economy also gave Americans more leisure time. By the 1950s, the 40-hour work week was commonplace in American factories. Many workers now looked forward to two- or three-week paid annual vacations. As life expectancy increased and the economy boomed, more and more Americans could expect to retire at age 65 and then live comfortably off their pensions and Social Security.

The impact of World War II and the cold war, the development of the industrial and service sectors, and stable labor relations fostered a comfortable sense of economic well-being. Corporations and consumers alike had the means to live the good life.

The Suburban Dream

For growing numbers of people, the good life lay outside the city. In the 1950s, many urban and rural Americans dreamed of living in a house in the suburbs. American culture had long idealized homeownership, and suburbs, developing since the nineteenth century, were nothing new. Yet the suburbs had been mainly for the well-to-do. Most Americans had never owned their own homes. But entrepreneurship, efficient construction methods, inexpensive land, and generous federal aid made possible a host of affordable housing developments outside the nation's cities. Along with Gene Ferkauf and his family, much of America moved to the suburbs in the 1950s.

William J. Levitt's pioneering development, Levittown, illustrated how entrepreneurship, low-priced land, and new construction techniques fueled a suburban housing boom. Levitt came back from military service in World War II with an optimistic vision of the future. He wanted to make houses affordable for middle-class and working-class people. Drawing on the assembly-line techniques of automaker Henry Ford, he intended to build houses so efficiently that they could be sold at remarkably low prices. Levitt bought 1,000 acres of cheap farmland on New York's Long Island. He put up simple houses, with prefabricated parts, no basements, and low price tags. The original Cape Cod-style house cost $7,990, an appealing price for young couples buying their first homes.

Like Korvettes, Levittown quickly became a huge success. Buyers signed 1,400 contracts for houses on a single day in 1949. The development grew to 17,500 dwellings housing 82,000 people. Levitt soon built more Levittowns, as did imitators all around the country.

The Pursuit of Pleasure

The consumer society depended on Americans' eagerness to pursue pleasure. Businesses made sure that nothing would prevent Americans from buying goods and services. If their wages and salaries were not enough, consumers could borrow. Along with federally guaranteed mortgage loans, people could now get credit cards. In 1950, the Diner's Club introduced the credit card for well-to-do New Yorkers. By the end of the decade, Sears Roebuck credit cards allowed more than 10 million Americans to spend borrowed money. In 1945, Americans owed only $5.7 billion for consumer goods other than houses. By 1960, they owed $56.1 billion.

In the 1950s, discount stores such as Korvettes made shopping seem simpler and more attractive, and so did another new creation, the shopping mall. In 1956, Southdale, the nation's first enclosed suburban shopping mall, opened outside

Symbol of the consumer society: The first McDonald's fast food restaurant, opened by the McDonald brothers in San Bernadino, California, in 1948.

Minneapolis, Minnesota. Consumers bought meals more easily, too. The first McDonald's fast-food restaurant opened in San Bernardino, California, in 1948. Taken over by businessman Ray Kroc, McDonald's began to grow into a national chain in the mid-1950s.

To get to McDonald's, the Southdale Mall, Korvettes, and Levittown, Americans needed cars. In the 1950s, cars reflected Americans' new sense of affluence and self-indulgence. Big, high-compression engines burning high-octane gasoline powered ever bigger cars. Unlike the drab autos of the Great Depression, the new models had "Passion Pink" and "Horizon Blue" interiors and two-tone and even three-tone exteriors studded with shiny chrome.

Automakers used that chrome to solve one of the main problems of a consumer society—getting people who already had plenty to want to buy even more. How could Detroit persuade Americans to trade in old cars that were running just fine and purchase new ones? The answer was to make the new models look different from the old ones. The result was what General Motors's chief designer called "dynamic obsolescence," the feeling that the old model with last year's styling was somehow inadequate (see Table 27–1).

More than ever, automakers offered cars as a reflection of a driver's identity. The car of the 1950s clearly announced its owner's affluence. General Motors's line of cars rose up the socioeconomic ladder, from the ordinary Chevrolet, to the more prosperous Pontiac, Oldsmobile, and Buick, all the way up to the sumptuous Cadillac.

Automobiles also spoke to sexual identity. Detroit designed the interior of cars to appeal to women. Inside, the autos of the 1950s had to seem like comfortable or

TABLE 27–1

Automobiles and Highways, 1945–1960			
Year	Factory Sales (in 1,000s)	Registrations (in 1,000s)	Miles of Highway (in 1,000s)
1945	69.5	25,796.9	3,035
1946	2,148.6	28,217.0	5,057
1947	3,558.1	30,849.3	15,473
1948	3,909.2	33,355.2	21,725
1949	5,119.4	36,457.9	19,876
1950	6,665.8	40,339.0	19,876
1951	5,338.4	42,688.3	17,060
1952	4,320.7	43,823.0	22,147
1953	6,116.9	46,429.2	21,136
1954	5,558.8	48,468.4	20,548
1955	7,920.1	52,144.7	22,571
1956	5,816.1	54,210.9	23,609
1957	6,113.3	55,917.8	22,424
1958	4,257.8	56,890.5	28,137
1959*	5,591.2	59,453.9	32,633
1960	6,674.7	61,682.3	20,969

*Denotes first year for which figures include Alaska and Hawaii.

Source: Historical Statistics of the United States, 1976, Vol. 2, pp. 711, 716.

luxurious living rooms. The exterior offered men a combination of power and sexuality. Automakers tried to make men feel like they were flying supersonic jets. While the back of a 1950s car looked like the winking afterburners of a jet, the front spoke to something else. The chrome protrusions on 1950s Cadillacs were known as "Dagmars" after the name of a large-breasted female television star. A car, as a Buick ad promised, "makes you feel like the man you are."

It was not remarkable that the chrome on a Cadillac would make Americans think of a television star. In the 1950s, television became a central part of American life. Technological advances made TV sets less expensive. As sales boomed, there were new opportunities for broadcasters. By 1950, the Federal Communications Commission (FCC) had licensed 104 TV stations, mostly in cities. By 1960, 90 percent of the nation's households had a television (see Table 27–2). In 15 years, TV had become a part of everyday life.

From its early days, television reinforced the values of consumer society. Advertisements for consumer products paid for programming that focused mainly on pleasure and diversion. Nightly national news broadcasts lasted only 15 minutes. There were operas, documentaries, and live, original dramas in what some critics consider television's "golden age," but most of the broadcast schedule was filled with variety shows, sports, westerns, and situation comedies.

One of the hallmarks of American culture in the 1950s was a new openness about sexuality. To his surprise, Dr. Alfred C. Kinsey of Indiana University commanded enormous public attention with two pioneering academic studies—*Sexual*

TABLE 27–2

Year	Television Stations	Households With Television Sets (in 1,000s)
1941	2	—
1945	9	—
1950	104	3,875
1955	458	30,700
1960	579	45,750

Source: George Thomas Kurian, Datapedia (Lanham, MD: Bernan Press, 1994), pp. 299–300.

Behavior in the Human Male (1948) and *Sexual Behavior in the Human Female* (1953). To his readers' surprise, Kinsey reported that Americans were more sexually active outside of marriage than had been thought.

The new candor about sexuality was probably best represented by *Playboy* magazine, first published by Hugh Hefner in December 1953. Hefner presented sex as one part of a hedonistic, consumer lifestyle complete with flashy cars, expensive stereos, and fine liquor.

The different tall tail fins of two late-1950s Cadillacs epitomized the gaudy "dynamic obsolescence" of the consumer society.

The success of *Playboy*, along with the popularity of TV and tail fins, underscored how much American attitudes had changed since the Great Depression. Armed with money, leisure, and confidence, many Americans devoted more of life to enjoyment. Business encouraged them with credit cards, shopping malls, fast-food restaurants, and dynamic obsolescence. Before long, it became clear that many Americans could not afford consumerism, but for a while at least, the nation seemed to be living the good life.

A HOMOGENEOUS SOCIETY?

The spread of consumerism reinforced a sense of sameness in America during the 1950s. Declining class differences strengthened the feeling that people were becoming more alike, as did a rush to attend church and have children. Along with the renewed emphasis on religion and family, Americans faced pressure to conform to gender roles.

Nevertheless, the United States remained a heterogeneous society. While ethnic differences among whites decreased, race remained a powerful divider. Despite fears of conformity, the nation still encouraged difference and individuality.

The Discovery of Conformity

In the years after World War II, sociologists and other writers noticed a disturbing uniformity across American society. People were becoming increasingly alike, partly because they shared more and more experiences, such as consumerism and suburban lifestyles. Some commentators and social critics feared the loss of the personal freedom and individuality that seemed so basic to American life.

A variety of factors promoted homogeneity. During the frenzied search for domestic Communists, people did not want to risk accusations by appearing different or unusual. Moreover, as corporations merged and small businesses disappeared, Americans worked for the same giant companies. The new suburbs intensified the sense of homogeneity.

To some observers, this similarity was more than a matter of shared experience. Americans, they believed, wanted to be like one another. In *The Lonely Crowd* (1950), sociologist David Riesman suggested that instead of following their own internalized set of values, Americans adjusted their behavior to meet the expectations of the people around them. In *The Organization Man* (1956), William H. Whyte, Jr., described the conformist style of white-collar workers in big corporations. In the office or at home in the suburbs, the "organization man" was all too willing to go along with others.

The Decline of Class Differences

The homogeneity of American society was reinforced by the apparent decline of class differences. By the 1950s, the old upper class—the families of the Gilded Age industrialists and financiers—had lost much wealth and power thanks to the Great Depression, income and inheritance taxes, and sheer waste and mismanagement. In his book *The Power Elite* (1956), sociologist C. Wright Mills argued that an interlocking military, political, and economic elite ran the country. However, this rather drab group did not have the bold, public swagger of the old, opulent upper class.

American farmers had also been disappearing for a long time. Since the late nineteenth century, the increasing efficiency of American agriculture, along with overseas competition, had meant the nation needed fewer farmers. The number of American farms fell from more than 6 million in 1944 to just 3.7 million 15 years later.

In contrast, the working class remained large and apparently healthy. Manual and service workers, some 33 million strong, were still the nation's largest occupational group in 1960. About one-third of workers belonged to unions. The labor movement's size and power were underscored in 1955 when the AFL and the CIO merged to become the gigantic AFL-CIO.

Well-paid blue-collar workers appeared content with American society and their role within it. Labor leaders endorsed consumerism and anti-Communism. Some observers argued that American workers had become essentially middle class in their buying habits and social values.

This apparent transformation, along with the decline of farmers and the upper class, made it easier to think of the United States as a classless society. Different social groups were evidently becoming more middle class in their values and outlook. The middle class itself was burgeoning. By 1960, the white-collar sector made up 40 percent of the work force.

Even the ethnic differences no longer seemed significant. Whites from different ethnic backgrounds mixed together in the new suburbs. The rate of intermarriage between ethnic groups increased. Anxious to prove their loyalty during the cold war, newer Americans were reluctant to emphasize their origins. Ethnicity had apparently disappeared in the national melting pot of the consumer society.

Many Americans, especially powerful ones, had long wanted to believe that the United States was a unified society devoted to middle-class values. In the 1950s, there was probably more basis for this belief than ever before. Nevertheless, prosperous Americans were ignoring some troublesome realities. The very poor remained concentrated in inner cities and remote rural areas. Social classes still differed significantly. The completely unified, classless society was an illusion, but many people preferred this illusion to reality.

The Resurgence of Religion and Family

Americans went back to church in the 1950s. Church membership doubled to 114 million between 1945 and 1960. The surge in attendance mostly benefited Christian denominations. By 1960, there were 64 million Protestants, 42 million Roman Catholics, and fewer than 6 million Jews (see Table 27–3).

Denominations encouraged the attendance boom by adapting religion to the consumer society. Naturally, they made use of television. Charismatic preachers such as Roman Catholic Bishop Fulton J. Sheen and evangelist Billy Graham became TV stars. The nation's political leaders encouraged the religious revival, too. Freedom of religion, they insisted, differentiated the United States from allegedly godless Communist nations. To underscore the national commitment to religion, the federal government put the words "In God We Trust" on all its currency.

American culture celebrated the family along with religion in the 1950s. Detroit presented its big automobiles as "family" cars. Manufacturers promoted television as a way of holding families together. American society venerated what McCall's magazine christened family "togetherness."

This "togetherness" meant the nuclear family, with a mother, a father, and plenty of children. After decades of decline, the birth rate rose during and after World War II. Beginning in 1954, Americans had more than 4 million babies a year. Thanks to new drugs, more of these babies survived. Antibiotics reduced the risk of diphtheria, typhoid fever, influenza, and other infections. The Salk and Sabin vaccines virtually wiped out polio. The average number of children per family went from 2.4 in 1945 up to 3.2 in 1957, and the population grew by a record 29 million people to reach 179 million.

TABLE 27–3

Religious Revival and Baby Boom, 1945–1960

Year	Membership of Religious Bodies (in 1,000s)	Live Births (in 1,000s)
1945[1]	71,700	2,858
1946[1]	73,673	3,411
1947	77,386	3,817
1948	79,436	3,637
1949	81,862	3,649
1950	86,830	3,632
1951	88,673	3,823
1952	92,277	3,913
1953	94,843	3,965
1954	97,483	4,078
1955	100,163	4,104
1956	103,225	4,218
1957	104,190	4,308
1958[2]	109,558	4,255
1959*	112,227	4,245
1960	114,449	4,258

*Denotes first year for which figures include Alaska and Hawaii.
[1]Based on 50 percent sample for 1951–1954, 1956–1960.
[2]Includes Alaska

Source: George Thomas Kurian, Datapedia (Lanham, MD: Bernan Press, 1994), pp. 37, 146.

Like the religious revival, the "baby boom" of the 1940s and 1950s is somewhat difficult to explain. For more than 100 years, Americans had reduced the size of their families. The economic prosperity of the cold war era may have persuaded couples that they could afford to have more children. But prosperity alone did not explain why American culture became so much more child-centered during these years.

Maintaining Gender Roles

In the 1950s, American culture strongly emphasized differences between the sexes: Women were expected to be homemakers and men, providers. The reality was more complicated. Women's roles, in particular, changed. Both sexes, meanwhile, were warned against deviating from gender stereotypes.

American culture underscored the differences between genders in a variety of ways. Standards of beauty highlighted the physiological differences between women and men. Popular movie actresses such as Marilyn Monroe and Jayne Mansfield were large-hipped, large-breasted women. During the baby boom, women were expected to be helpful wives and devoted mothers. Men were encouraged to define themselves primarily as family providers.

However, traditional gender roles evolved during the 1950s. Society stressed a man's domestic role more than before. Experts urged husbands to do some of the housework and to spend more time nurturing their children, although few men lived up to the new ideal.

Female roles evolved more dramatically. Women were not simply confined to the domestic sphere. To help pay for the consumer lifestyle, many wives went to work outside the home. Gene Ferkauf's wife, while taking care of their child, helped publicize the first Korvettes store. By 1960, almost one married woman in three held a job, and women made up more than one-third of the labor force.

To a degree, American culture supported the expanding role of women outside the home. In the cold war competition with the Soviets, Americans celebrated the supposedly greater freedom and opportunity for women in the United States. Television featured situation comedies with feisty women who stood up to their men.

Nevertheless, women faced a difficult situation with relatively little help. Congress voted an income tax deduction for child-care costs in 1954, but little first-class child care was available. At work, women were expected to watch men get ahead of them. Women's income was only 60 percent of men's in 1960.

American culture strongly condemned women and men who strayed outside conventional gender norms. *Modern Woman: The Lost Sex*, a 1947 bestseller by Marynia Farnham and Ferdinand Lundberg, censured feminism as the "deep illness" of "neurotically disturbed women" with "penis envy." Psychologists and other experts demonized lesbians, who had become a more visible subculture during the 1940s.

Like women, men faced condemnation if they failed to play conventional social roles. In the 1950s, unmarried men risked accusations of homosexuality. Along with lesbian women, gay men became targets of abuse during the cold war. Police cracked down on gay bars. The message was clear: Men were supposed to be heterosexual; they were supposed to be husbands and fathers. Those roles, in turn, forced men to conform to social expectations.

Persisting Racial Differences

In spite of the many pressures toward conformity, American society was still heterogeneous. Society continued to segregate and discriminate against African Americans and Native Americans. The rapid growth of the Hispanic population helped to ensure that the United States would remain a multiracial nation.

Although suburbanization broke down ethnic differences among whites, it intensified the racial divide between those whites and African Americans. The nation's suburbs were 95 percent white in 1950. As whites moved into Levittown and other suburbs, African Americans took their place in cities. By 1960, more than half of the black population lived in cities. By custom in the North and law in the South, African Americans were clearly set apart from white Americans.

Native Americans, living on their reservations, were also set apart. In 1953, Congress did try to "Americanize" the Indians by approving the termination of Indians' special legal status. Termination meant the end of federal aid to tribes and the end of many reservations. The new policy was intended to turn Indians into full members of the consumer society.

It did not turn out that way. As reservations became counties, Indians had to sell valuable mineral rights and lands to pay taxes. Despite short-term profits, tribes faced poverty, unemployment, and social problems. Encouraged by the federal government's new Voluntary Relocation Program, about one in five Native Americans moved to cities. But whether they lived on reservations or crowded city blocks, the nation's quarter of a million Indians remained largely separate and ignored.

The increasing migration of Puerto Ricans also reinforced the multiracial character of American society. Beginning in the 1940s, a large number of Puerto Ricans, who were U.S. citizens, left their island hoping for more economic opportunity on the mainland. By 1960, the Puerto Rican population in the mainland United States had reached 887,000, two-thirds of it concentrated in the East Harlem section of New York City. These new migrants found opportunities in the United States, but they also found separation and discrimination.

Mexican immigration further contributed to racial diversity. After 1945, increasing numbers of Mexicans left their impoverished homeland for the United States, particularly the booming Southwest. Congress, bowing to the needs of southwestern employers, continued the Bracero Program, the supposedly temporary wartime agreement that had brought hundreds of thousands of laborers, or *braceros,* to the United States. Meanwhile, illegal Mexican migration increased dramatically.

Like other Mexican migrants before them, the newly arrived Chicanos met with ambivalence. As in the years before World War II, Mexicans already living in the United States worried that the new arrivals would compete for jobs, drive down wages, and feed American prejudice. Mexican Americans feared that the federal government would use the provisions of the Internal Security Act of 1950 and the Immigration and Nationality Act of 1952 to deport Mexicans and thereby break up families. The government's intention became clear in 1954 with the launching of Operation Wetback, which sent more than 1 million immigrants back to Mexico in that year alone.

About 3.5 million Chicanos were living in the United States by 1960. The great majority worked for low wages in the cities and on the farms of the Southwest. Many Chicanos continued to live in *barrios* apart from whites. Because of Operation Wetback and other instances of prejudice, some Mexican Americans became more vocal about their circumstances and their rights. The League of United Latin American Citizens denounced the impact of the Immigration and Nationality Act. More outspoken was the American GI Forum, an organization of Mexican-American veterans. Ernesto Galarza, an official of the National Agricultural Workers' Union, also spoke out about the plight of Mexicans.

The experiences of Hispanics, Native Americans, and African Americans underscored the continuing importance of race in the United States. Mostly living apart, whites and nonwhites faced different conditions and different futures. Prosperity and consumerism did not change that reality. As long as race was such a potent factor in national life, the United States would never be a homogeneous society.

The Survival of Diversity

Along with race, a variety of forces ensured the survival of diversity. Despite the appearance of suburbs all over the country, the states continued to differ from each other. As in the past, internal migration and the expansion of national boundaries promoted diversity. During the 1950s, more than 1.6 million people, many of them retired, moved to Florida. As a result, the state increasingly played a distinctive national role as a center for retirement and entertainment.

Meanwhile, Americans moved westward. During the 1950s, California gained more than 3 million new residents. California earned a reputation as the pioneer state of the consumer society, the home of the first Disneyland amusement park and the first McDonald's.

The admission of two new states highlighted the continuing diversity of the United States. In 1959, Alaska and Hawaii became, respectively, the 49th and 50th states in the union. Racially and culturally diverse, climatically and topographically distinctive, they helped make certain that America was not simply a land of corporations and Levittowns.

Popular music also exemplified the continuing diversity of the United States. Swing bands gave way rapidly to such popular singers as Frank Sinatra and Patti Page. Jazz split into different camps—traditional, mainstream, and modern. Country music, rooted in white rural culture, included cowboy songs, Western swing, honky-tonk, and bluegrass. A range of African-American musical forms, including blues, jazz, and vocal groups, became known as "rhythm and blues" (R & B).Gospel music thrilled white and African-American audiences. Mexican Americans made Tejano music in Texas, and Cajuns played Cajun music in Louisiana.

R & B collided with country music to create rock and roll. By 1952, white disc jockey Alan Freed was playing R & B on his radio show, "Moondog's Rock 'n' Roll Party," out of Cleveland. By 1954, a white country group, Bill Haley and the Comets, had recorded the first rock-and-roll hit, "Rock Around the Clock." Rock and roll produced both African-American and white heroes in its first years.

The biggest rock-and-roll sensation of all was a young white singer and guitar player, Elvis Presley. Born in Mississippi and raised in near poverty in Memphis, Tennessee, Presley grew up hearing a wide range of music. Beginning with his first commercial record, "That's All Right, Mama," in 1954, Presley sang in a distinctive style that listeners could never quite pigeonhole.

Because of Presley and other musicians, the sound of American popular music was anything but homogeneous. Because of the distinctiveness of Florida, California, Alaska, Hawaii, and other states, the United States was hardly monolithic. In these ways, at least, American society remained diverse after World War II.

THE EISENHOWER ERA AT HOME AND ABROAD

Prosperity encouraged Americans to demand less from government in the 1950s. In a period of rapid social change and continuing international tensions, most people wanted reassurance rather than boldness from Washington. The politics of the decade were dominated by President Dwight D. Eisenhower, a moderate leader well-suited to the times. His middle-of-the-road domestic program, "Modern Republicanism," appealed to a prosperous electorate wary of government innovation. But Eisenhower's anti-Communist foreign policy did little to diminish popular anxieties about the cold war.

"Ike" and 1950s America

Dwight Eisenhower, a charismatic military hero with a bright, infectious grin, would have been an ideal public figure in almost any era of American history, but the man known affectionately as "Ike" was especially suited to the 1950s. Throughout his life, Eisenhower managed to reconcile the old and the new. Raised on the individualistic values of the Midwest, Eisenhower adopted the bureaucratic style of modern organizations. He succeeded in the military after World War I, not because he was a great fighter or strategist, but because he was a great manager. A believer in teamwork, Eisenhower was the quintessential "organization man." As a commander in World War II, Eisenhower worked to keep sometimes fractious allies together. After the war, he deepened his organizational experience as president of Columbia University and then as the first commander of the armed forces of NATO.

Just as he accommodated the rise of big organizations, Eisenhower accommodated the extension of the nation's commitment abroad. Ike had grown up in the isolationist Midwest, among people who feared American involvement in the world's problems. But his military career rested on his acceptance of an activist role for the United States around the world.

Eisenhower easily fit the dominant culture of the 1950s. He was an involved, loving husband and father. In a society zealously pursuing pleasures, he was famous for his many hours on the golf course. His wife, Mamie, eagerly wore the "New Look" fashions inspired by designer Christian Dior and avidly watched television soap operas.

Nominated for president by the Republicans in 1952, Eisenhower ran against Adlai Stevenson, the liberal Democratic governor of Illinois. Stevenson, witty and eloquent, was no match for Eisenhower. Running a moderate, conciliatory campaign, the former general avoided attacks on the New Deal and promised to work for an end to the Korean War. Meanwhile, his running mate, Senator Richard Nixon of California, accused Stevenson of being soft on Communism. The Republican ticket won 55 percent of the popular vote and 442 electoral votes. The Republican Party took control of the White House and both houses of Congress for the first time in 20 years.

Modern Republicanism

Eisenhower advocated Modern Republicanism for the American political economy. This philosophy attempted to steer a middle course between traditional Republican conservatism and Democratic liberalism. With a conservative's faith in individual freedom, the president favored limited government and balanced budgets, but Eisenhower the organization man believed that Washington had an important role to play in protecting individuals. Eisenhower also recognized that most Americans did not want to give up such liberal programs as Social Security and farm subsidies.

Accordingly, the president took some steps to limit governmental control over the economy, such as tax cuts for the wealthy and decreased federal regulation of business. With the Submerged Lands Act of 1953, the federal government turned over offshore oil resources to the states for private exploitation. With the Atomic Energy Act of 1954, Washington allowed private firms to sell power produced by nuclear reactors.

Nevertheless, the Eisenhower administration did little to undermine the legacy of the New Deal and the Fair Deal. Eisenhower went along with increases in Social Security benefits and farm subsidies. Despite his belief in balanced budgets, his administration produced several budget deficits. Federal spending, including the highway program, helped fuel the consumer economy.

Modern Republicanism frustrated liberals as well as conservative "old-guard" Republicans, but many Americans appreciated the president's moderation. "The public loves Ike," a journalist observed. "The less he does the more they love him."

Eisenhower's popularity was confirmed at the polls in 1956. The president once again headed the Republican ticket with Richard Nixon, and the Democrats nominated Adlai Stevenson. This time Eisenhower won an even bigger victory, with 58 percent of the popular vote and 457 electoral votes.

An Aggressive Approach to the Cold War

Like President Harry Truman before him, Eisenhower was committed to opposing Communism at home and around the world. The president helped the crusade against alleged Communist subversives and tolerated its excesses. He refused to criticize the tactics of Senator Joseph R. McCarthy in public and declined to stop the execution of the convicted atomic spies, Julius and Ethel Rosenberg, in 1953. Eisenhower denied the security clearance that J. Robert Oppenheimer, the former director of the Manhattan Project, needed to continue work on the government's nuclear projects. Thousands of other alleged security risks also lost their federal jobs during the Eisenhower era.

Campaigning in 1952, Eisenhower and his advisers talked of rolling back Soviet power in Europe. Moving beyond containment, Eisenhower spoke of the need to free already "captive peoples" from Communism. Presumably, that would mean contesting Soviet control of Eastern Europe. This assertive approach seemed more likely to lead to armed confrontation with the Soviets.

In office, Eisenhower and Secretary of State John Foster Dulles coupled their rhetoric with a new national security policy. Dulles threatened "instant, massive retaliation" with nuclear weapons in response to Soviet aggression. To support this threat, the U.S. military adopted the "New Look," a strategy that de-emphasized costly conventional armies and increased the nuclear arsenal with long-range bombers, missiles, and the first nuclear-powered submarines. Not surprisingly, massive retaliation and the New Look stirred fears of nuclear war.

The president also used the CIA to counter Communism by stealthier means. At the president's direction, the CIA carried out secret activities: As a presidential commission observed, the cold war was "a game" with "no rules." At home, the agency explored the possible uses of lysergic acid diethylamide—the dangerous hallucinogenic drug known as LSD—by using it on hundreds of unwitting Americans. Abroad, the agency gave secret aid to pro-American regimes and ran secret programs against hostile governments.

In August 1953 a covert CIA operation, code-named Ajax, orchestrated a coup that removed Mohammed Mossadeq, the nationalist prime minister of oil-rich Iran. Eisenhower and Dulles feared that this "madman," who had nationalized oil fields, would open the way for Communism and the Soviet Union. He was replaced by the young Shah Mohammed Reza Pahlavi, who gratefully accepted $45 million in U.S. aid, turned his back on the Soviets, and made low-priced oil available to American companies.

The next year, Pbsuccess, a secret CIA operation modeled on Ajax, overthrew another foreign leader. Eisenhower and Dulles worried that a "Communist infection" in the Central American nation of Guatemala could spread to the United States-controlled Panama Canal and further north to Mexico. In fact, the Soviet Union had made no effort to help Guatemala's new president, Jacob Arbenz Gúzman, who supported the redistribution of land and threatened the interests of a powerful American corporation, United Fruit. In June, Pbsuccess used misleading "disinformation," a small force of Guatemalan exiles, and CIA-piloted bombing raids to persuade Arbenz Gúzman to resign.

Avoiding War with the Communist Powers

Despite the tough talk, the Eisenhower administration tried to avoid direct confrontation with the two major Communist powers, the People's Republic of China and the Soviet Union. Eisenhower knew he had to end the Korean conflict. As he promised in his 1952 campaign, Eisenhower traveled to Korea to observe conditions firsthand before his inauguration. Once in office, he pushed to end the military stalemate that ultimately killed 33,629 Americans. A cease-fire agreement in July 1953 left the United States without a victory. Although North and South Korea remained divided, the agreement ended a costly, difficult war. It was, Eisenhower declared, "an acceptable solution."

Ending an old war with one Communist power, the Eisenhower administration avoided a new conflict with the other. In October 1956, Hungarians rose up against their pro-Soviet government. The Soviet Union sent troops to break the rebellion. Despite all its tough talk, the Eisenhower administration did not intervene to help the Hungarian rebels. The United States would not contest Soviet control of Eastern Europe after all.

More broadly, Eisenhower was cautious about military confrontation with the Soviets and the Chinese. Eisenhower declined to unleash nuclear weapons that would "destroy civilization." Although he sent out CIA agents to conduct covert operations, the president was more reluctant than Truman to send American soldiers into open battle.

At the same time Eisenhower, like Truman, knew the cold war was an economic and political fight. The Eisenhower administration maintained foreign-aid programs and fought a propaganda war with the Soviets. In front of a model American kitchen in Moscow in 1959, Vice President Richard Nixon and Soviet leader Nikita Khrushchev argued the merits of the their two systems. Not surprisingly, Nixon turned this "Kitchen Debate" into a celebration of the prosperity and freedom of the consumer society.

The Eisenhower administration took some modest steps to improve relations with the Soviets. After the death of Soviet leader Josef Stalin in 1953, his successors signaled their desire for "peaceful coexistence" with the United States and the West. Responding cautiously, Eisenhower told the United Nations that he wanted to pursue disarmament and the peaceful use of atomic power with the Soviets. The president proposed an "Atoms for Peace" plan in which an international agency would experiment with nonmilitary uses for nuclear materials. The Soviets, however, dragged their feet. Although the International Atomic Energy Agency was formed in 1957, the United States and the Soviet Union did not cooperate significantly to control the nuclear arms race during the Eisenhower years.

The president made another attempt at improving relations with the Soviets. In July 1955, Eisenhower joined Soviet leader Nikita Khrushchev in Geneva, Switzerland, for the first meeting between an American president and Soviet rulers since World War II. The relatively amicable Geneva talks sparked some optimism about American–Soviet relations. That optimism ended by May 1960, when the Soviets shot down an American U-2 spy plane flying high over the USSR.

The U-2 incident underscored the continuing rivalry between the United States and the major Communist powers. The Eisenhower administration refused even to recognize the Communist Chinese regime officially.

Crises in the Third World

Although Eisenhower worried most about the fate of Western Europe, his administration increasingly focused on the threat of Communist expansion in Africa, Asia, Latin America, and the Middle East. These regions, which made up the industrializing third world, were enmeshed in the confrontation between the first world of industrial, non-Communist nations and the second world of industrial, Communist countries. Often plagued by poverty, violence, and civil war, many third-world societies struggled to break free from imperial domination.

Under Khrushchev, the Soviet Union tried to exploit third-world discontent and conflict. Anxious to preserve America's influence and access to natural resources, the Eisenhower administration stood ready to counter Soviet moves with the techniques of containment—aid, trade, and alliances. Eisenhower offered increased foreign aid to third-world countries and tried to stimulate trade with them. He also encouraged closer military ties: The United States signed individual defense pacts with the Philippines, South Korea, and Taiwan.

Eisenhower's approach to the third world was sorely tested in Southeast Asia. When he took office in 1953, the United States continued to support France's war to hold onto Vietnam and its other Southeast Asian colonies. The president feared that a Communist victory in Vietnam would deprive the West of raw materials and encourage the triumph of Communism elsewhere. Comparing the nations of Asia and the Pacific to "a row of dominoes," Eisenhower explained that the fall of the first domino—Vietnam—would lead to the fall of the rest.

Despite vast American aid, the French could not defeat the nationalist forces of the Viet Minh, led by the Communist Ho Chi Minh and helped by the mainland Chinese. By 1954, the Viet Minh had surrounded French troops at Dienbienphu in northern Vietnam. Unwilling to fight another land war in Asia, Eisenhower refused to send American troops. The president also rejected the use of atomic bombs. Without further help from the United States, France surrendered Dienbienphu in May.

In 1954, peace talks at Geneva produced an agreement to cut Vietnam, like Korea, in half. Ho Chi Minh's forces would stay north of the 17th Parallel; his pro-French Vietnamese enemies would stay to the south of that line. The peace agreement stipulated that a popular election would unite the two halves of Vietnam in 1956. Certain that Ho Chi Minh and the Communists would win the election, the United States refused to sign the agreement.

Instead, the Eisenhower administration worked to create an anti-Communist nation south of the 17th Parallel. To protect South Vietnam, the United States created the South East Asian Treaty Organization (SEATO) in 1954 (see Map 27–1). To ensure South Vietnam's loyalty, the Eisenhower administration backed Ngo Dinh Diem, an anti-Communist who established a corrupt, repressive government. The United States sent military advisers and hundreds of millions of dollars to Diem.

By thwarting the Geneva Accords and establishing an unpopular regime in the South, Eisenhower ensured that Vietnam would be torn by civil war in the years to come. In the short run, however, Eisenhower had avoided war and seemingly stopped the Asian dominoes from falling.

Eisenhower soon confronted another crisis in the Middle East. Gamal Abdel Nasser, who had seized power in Egypt in 1954, emerged as a forceful spokesman for Arab nationalism and Middle Eastern unity. Fearing that Nasser would open the way for Soviet power in the Middle East, John Foster Dulles withdrew an offer to aid the Egyptians. Nasser struck back by taking over the British- and French-owned Suez Canal in 1956. In retaliation, Britain and France, with Israel's cooperation, moved against Nasser. As Israeli troops fought their way into Egypt in October, Britain and France stood ready to take back the Suez Canal. Eisenhower feared the invasion could give the Soviets an excuse to move into the Middle East and threatened economic sanctions. Khrushchev threatened to launch Soviet rockets in defense of the Egyptians. The British, French, and Israelis soon withdrew.

After the Suez crisis, in January 1957, the president announced what became known as the Eisenhower Doctrine. The United States, he promised, would intervene to help any Middle Eastern nation threatened by Communist armed aggression. The next year, in an illustration of his doctrine, Eisenhower sent troops to Lebanon. The soldiers were not really needed, but they did send a message about American power and resolve. The president underscored that message in 1959, when the United States encouraged the formation of another regional defense organization patterned after NATO. The new group, which included Turkey and

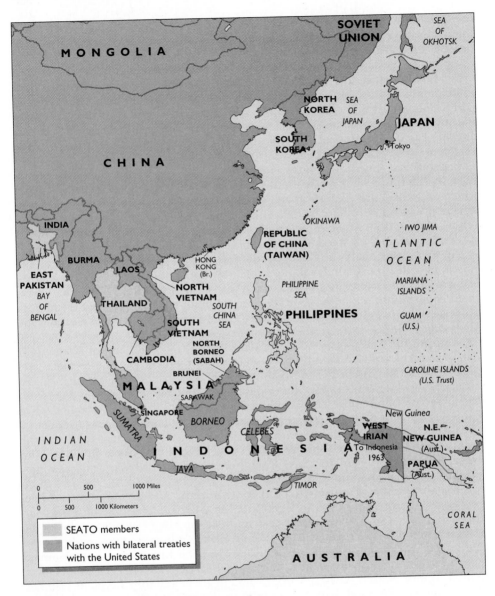

Map 27–1 America's Cold War Alliances in Asia
Members of SEATO (the South East Asian Treaty Organization) and signers of other treaties with the United States. Through these pacts, the Eisenhower administration hoped to hold back the threat posed by Communist mainland China.

Iran, was known as the Central Treaty Organization (CENTO) for its geographical position between NATO and SEATO.

Eisenhower had helped to stabilize the Middle East for a time, but as in Vietnam, his policy had intensified local divisions. The two third-world crises had been resolved temporarily, but Eisenhower's actions had increased the odds of future trouble. During the 1960s and 1970s, the United States would have to deal with Eisenhower's legacy in the third world.

CHALLENGES TO THE CONSUMER SOCIETY

While the Eisenhower administration managed crises abroad, American society confronted challenges at home. In different ways, a rebellious youth culture, the alienated beat movement, and the divisive civil rights struggle upset the stability of the Eisenhower era. They demonstrated that consumerism had not solved all the nation's problems or won over all of its citizens.

Rebellious Youth

In the 1950s, the emergence of a distinct youth culture, built around rock and roll, customized cars, comic books, and premarital sexual exploration, troubled many adults. The youth culture was the culmination of a trend apparent since the 1920s and 1930s. As more and more teenagers attended high school, they were segregated in their own world. Within that world, they developed their own values and practices. In the 1950s, young people claimed rock and roll as their own music. They wore blue jeans; they read comic books and teen magazines. Expressing their individuality, boys modified standard Detroit cars into customized "hot rods." Teens were attracted to alienated and rebellious movie characters such as the troubled son played by James Dean in *Rebel Without a Cause* (1955). A wave of juvenile delinquency appeared to be sweeping the country.

Many young people were rebellious, but not nearly as much as adults feared. Despite all the publicity, juvenile delinquency did not actually increase after World War II and neither did rates of sexual intercourse among teenagers. Most young people never questioned the political system. On the whole, youth culture exaggerated rather than rejected the values of adult, consumer society.

The early career of Elvis Presley illustrated the boundaries of youthful rebellion. Presley's appeal rested on an unsettling combination of rock-and-roll music and open sexuality. Presley's style—his sensual mouth, disheveled "duck's ass" haircut, and gyrating hips—powerfully amplified the music's sexuality.

Despite his appeal to teenagers, Presley remained relentlessly polite and softspoken, devoted to his parents and deferential to interviewers. Buying a pink Cadillac and other luxury cars, he was caught up in the consumer culture. Like Gene Ferkauf and millions of other Americans, Presley joined the suburban migration when he bought his house, Graceland, on the outskirts of Memphis, Tennessee. Presley was a new version of the old American dream of upward mobility.

Still, many adults blamed Presley, rock and roll, and mass media for the spread of dishonesty, violence, lust, and degeneration among young Americans. One popular television program showed Presley only from the waist up. To get rid of blue jeans and other teenage fashions, high schools imposed dress codes on their students. There was a crusade against comic books, teen magazines, and movies that were supposedly "brainwashing" teenagers. In well-publicized hearings, the Senate's Subcommittee to Investigate Juvenile Delinquency focused attention on the corrupting power of the mass media. However, the campaign against youth culture had little impact in a society devoted to free speech and consumerism.

The Beat Movement

A second group of rebels was smaller in numbers but a bit older and much more critical of American society. The beat movement, which emerged in New York City in the 1940s, expressed a sense of both alienation and hope. Worn down by contemporary culture, the beats searched hopefully for a way to get beyond it.

Elvis Presley delights a crowd—particularly its female members—in Long Beach, California, in June 1956.

Uptown at Columbia University and downtown in Greenwich Village, Allen Ginsberg, Jack Kerouac, John Clellon Holmes, William Burroughs, and others wanted, as one of them put it, "to emote, to soak up the world." Beats explored their sexuality, sampled mind-altering drugs, and investigated the spirituality of Eastern religions.

The beats had a dark vision of American society and were fascinated by outsiders and outcasts. Like the teen culture, the beats were drawn to the culture of African Americans. But while teenagers danced to the relatively simple and upbeat sounds of African-American R & B, the beats embraced the rhythmically and harmonically challenging bop music of black jazz musicians. Moreover, the beats were not nearly as positive about the consumer culture. In a society captivated by bright colors, "beatniks" declared their alienation from consumerism by wearing black.

Few in number, the beats sometimes seemed absurd, but the media's attention suggested just how important they were. The beat movement was a clear sign of budding dissatisfaction with consumer society, conventional sexual mores, and politics as usual.

The Struggle for Civil Rights

The African-American struggle for civil rights also challenged the political moderation of the Eisenhower era. By the 1950s, segregation was under increasingly effective attack in the courts and on the streets.

As in the 1940s, the NAACP fought segregation in the courts. Focusing on public schools, the organization directly assaulted the discriminatory legacy of the

Supreme Court's *Plessy* v. *Ferguson* ruling of 1896. In 1951 the NAACP's special counsel, Thurgood Marshall, combined five different lawsuits aimed at segregation in the public schools. In one of these lawsuits, an African-American welder, Oliver Brown, challenged the constitutionality of a Kansas state law that allowed cities to segregate their schools. When the Brown case reached the Supreme Court in December 1952, Thurgood Marshall attacked the *Plessy* argument that justified "separate but equal" facilities for whites and African Americans. As a result of segregation, Marshall maintained, African Americans received both an inferior education and a sense of their own inferiority. He concluded that segregation violated the citizenship rights guaranteed by the Fourteenth Amendment.

In May 1954, the court, led by new Chief Justice Earl Warren, handed down its ruling in *Brown* v. *Board of Education, Topeka, Kansas.* Overturning the *Plessy* decision, the justices ruled unanimously that public school segregation was unconstitutional under the Fourteenth Amendment. Warren's tenure as chief justice was one of the most important in the history of the court; no ruling of the Warren Court would prove more significant than the decision in the Brown case. African Americans and white liberals were jubilant. Marshall foresaw the dismantling of school segregation before the end of the decade.

It did not work out that way. When the Supreme Court ruled on the enforcement of school desegregation in May 1955, the justices turned to local school boards, dominated by whites, to carry out the integration of the schools. Federal district courts were to oversee the process of desegregation, which should occur with "all deliberate speed." In other words, school segregation had to end, but not right away.

Taking heart from this ruling, many whites refused to give up Jim Crow. For some white southerners, as one put it, a "reasonable time" for the end of segregation would be "one or two hundred years." Amid calls for massive resistance to desegregation, White Citizens' Councils formed to prevent schools from integrating. Some states passed laws intended to stop school integration. There was violence, too. In 1955, white Mississippians killed Emmett Till, a 14-year-old black boy from Chicago.

African Americans, encouraged by the court's action, were ready to fight even harder against segregation. On December 1, 1955, Rosa Parks, a 42-year-old African-American tailor's assistant in Montgomery, Alabama, boarded a bus to go home from work. State law dictated segregation on city buses. Local custom required an African American to give up her seat to a white passenger and then move to the back of the bus, but when the bus driver told her to move, Parks would not get up. The angry driver had Parks arrested.

Local African-American leaders, who had encouraged her to test the law, seized on the arrest of this respectable woman to challenge segregation. African-American men and women began to boycott the city's bus system. Twenty-six-year-old Martin Luther King, Jr., pastor of the Dexter Avenue Baptist Church, agreed to lead the boycott. The son of a noted Atlanta preacher, King was already developing a brilliant oratorical style and a philosophy of nonviolent protest against segregation.

The boycott met immediate resistance. The city outlawed carpools and indicted the leaders; African-American homes and churches were bombed. In November 1956, however, the U.S. Supreme Court ruled Alabama's bus segregation law unconstitutional. By then, the boycott had cost the bus company and downtown storeowners dearly, and the white community had lost the will to resist. The city settled with the boycotters and agreed to integrate the buses.

Montgomery showed that a combination of local activism and federal intervention could overcome Jim Crow in southern communities. It established a charismatic new leader with a powerful message, and it soon brought forward a new civil rights

A white student heckles an African-American student trying to integrate Central High School in Little Rock, Arkansas, in September 1957.

organization, the Southern Christian Leadership Conference. For one journalist, Montgomery "was the beginning of a flame that would go across America."

The flame did not travel easily. In 1957, the school board of Little Rock, Arkansas, accepted a federal court order to integrate the city's Central High School, but in September the state's segregationist governor, Orval Faubus, called out National Guard troops to stop black students from enrolling. Even after meeting with President Eisenhower, Faubus would not order the troops away from the school. When he finally did remove the soldiers, an angry mob of whites made it impossible for the African-American students to stay.

Little Rock created a dilemma for the president. Not a believer in racial equality, Eisenhower wanted to avoid the divisive issue of civil rights. The president knew, however, that his government was being defied in Little Rock and humiliated around the world. So Eisenhower sent in troops of the crack 101st Airborne of the U.S. Army. With that protection, nine African-American students went to Central High.

Like the Montgomery bus boycott, Little Rock demonstrated that a combination of federal action, however reluctant, and African-American courage could triumph. The Central High crisis showed, too, how the cold war helped tip the balance against segregation. Competing with the Soviets for support from the multiracial third world, no president could afford the embarrassment of racial inequality at home. Segregation and discrimination would continue to upset the stability of Eisenhower's America. It was, the president concluded, "troublesome beyond imagination."

An Uneasy Mood

Youth culture, the beat movement, and the civil rights struggle contributed to an uneasy mood in America by the end of the 1950s. Even people who did not share the beats' values worried that the consumer society was flawed. Consumerism itself could seem like a trap. In his bestseller *The Hidden Persuaders* (1957), Vance Packard played on the fears that advertisers were manipulating American consumers.

Americans were troubled, too, by signs of corruption in the consumer society. In 1958, they learned that record companies had paid Alan Freed and other disc jockeys to play particular records on the radio. The same year, Americans were shocked by revelations that contestants on popular TV quiz shows had secretly been given the answers to questions in advance.

While Americans worried about whether the consumer society was corrupt, they wondered whether it could meet the challenge of the cold war. In October 1957, the Soviet Union sent Sputnik, the world's first satellite, into orbit, setting off a wave of fear in the United States. If the Soviets could send up a satellite, they could be ahead in nuclear weapons and economic growth too.

Sputnik intensified concerns about the quality of American education. A diverse and growing student population, along with rising parental demands, had strained the nation's schools. Now Americans worried that the schools were not preparing children to compete with the Soviets in science and technology. In 1958, Congress, previously reluctant to provide aid to schools, passed the National Defense Education Act. This wide-ranging measure promoted instruction in science, math, and foreign languages, supported construction of new schools, and offered loans and fellowships to students.

Sputnik forced Washington to accelerate the space program. The first U.S. satellite launch collapsed in flames. In January 1958 the government successfully launched its first satellite, Explorer I. Later that year, Congress created the National Aeronautics and Space Administration (NASA) to coordinate space exploration. These initiatives did not wipe away fears about the fate of a society caught up in consumerism and the cold war, however.

Eisenhower did little to change the national mood. Slowed by poor health, the president now seemed old and out of ideas. A few days before the end of his presidency in January 1961, Eisenhower fed the uncertain mood with a warning about the political economy in his farewell address. Noting that cold war spending had built up the military and the defense industry, he warned against allowing this "military-industrial complex" to gain too much power. It was a stunning admission that the cold war's transformation of the political economy might destroy rather than save democracy in America.

Eisenhower's difficulties were a sign of new stresses on American society. The great majority of Americans were not about to give up the benefits of the prosperous consumer economy, but many people worried whether consumerism and Modern Republicanism were enough to meet the challenges of the cold war world.

CONCLUSION

Along with the cold war, the triumph of consumerism dramatically affected the United States in the 1950s. The booming consumer economy gave Gene Ferkauf and other Americans a new sense of security and affluence during the unsettling confrontation with Communism. Breaking with the past, they moved to the suburbs, had record numbers of children, bought televisions at E. J. Korvettes, and defined life as the pursuit of material pleasures. Consumerism helped promote homogeneity and conformity in American society and spurred the victory of Dwight Eisenhower and his moderate approach to the political economy.

CHRONOLOGY

1947	Opening of Levittown suburban development
1948	Opening of first McDonald's fast-food restaurant
	Alfred Kinsey, *Sexual Behavior in the Human Male*
1950	Introduction of Diner's Club credit card
1951	UNIVAC 1 computer
1952	Dwight D. Eisenhower elected president
1953	Opening of first suburban E. J. Korvettes store
	First issue of *Playboy* magazine
	Beginning of Federal Termination policy for Native American reservations
	CIA Operation Ajax in Iran
	Cease-fire in Korea
	Eisenhower Atoms for Peace proposal
1954	Atomic Energy Act
	"Baby boom" birth rate over 4 million per year
	Bill Haley and the Comets, "Rock Around the Clock"
	Supreme Court school desegregation decision, *Brown* v. *Board of Education, Topeka, Kansas*
	Federal Operation Wetback
	Army–McCarthy Senate hearings
	CIA Operation Pbsuccess in Guatemala
	Creation of divided Vietnam in Geneva peace talks
	Beginning of Senate hearings on juvenile delinquency

For a moment, perhaps, it seemed as if America had achieved stability and harmony in a dangerous cold war world, but that feeling did not last. At the end of the 1950s, many Americans questioned whether the consumer society could provide prosperity, equality, and security for all its citizens. The next decade, a tumultuous time, would give them an unsettling answer.

FURTHER READINGS

Stephen E. Ambrose, *Eisenhower*, 2 vols. (1983–1984). Evenhandedly chronicles the life of the general and president.

David L. Anderson, *Trapped by Success: The Eisenhower Administration and Vietnam, 1953–1961* (1993). Examines the American decision to support South Vietnam after the French withdrawal.

Taylor Branch, *Parting the Waters: America in the King Years, 1954–1963* (1988). A lively narrative focusing on the role of Martin Luther King, Jr., in the civil rights struggle.

1955	Formation of AFL-CIO
	Eisenhower Open Skies proposal
	Beginning of bus boycott in Montgomery, Alabama
1956	National System of Defense Highways Act
	William H. Whyte, Jr., *The Organization Man*
	Opening of Southdale suburban shopping mall
	Suez crisis
	C. Wright Mills, *The Power Elite*
	Re-election of President Eisenhower
1957	Announcement of Eisenhower Doctrine
	Confrontation over school desegregation in Little Rock, Arkansas
	Jack Kerouac, *On the Road*
	Soviet Sputnik satellite launch
1958	National Defense Education Act
	Rock-and-roll "payola" scandals
	TV quiz show scandals
1959	Alaska and Hawaii statehood
	Nixon–Khrushchev "Kitchen Debate" in Moscow
1960	President Eisenhower's Commission on National Goals
	Soviet downing of U.S. U-2 spy plane
1961	Eisenhower's farewell address on "military-industrial complex"

John P. Diggins, *The Proud Decades: America in War and in Peace, 1941–1960* (1988). Gives a broad overview of the postwar period.

Barbara M. Kelly, *Expanding the American Dream: Building and Rebuilding Levittown* (1993). Details the evolution of the quintessential suburban development.

Karal Ann Marling, *As Seen on TV: The Visual Culture of Everyday Life in the 1950s* (1994). Engagingly explores the emerging consumer culture.

Joanne Meyerowitz, ed., *Not June Cleaver: Women and Gender in Postwar America, 1945–1960* (1994). An important set of essays that collectively change our understanding of women in the postwar period.

Grace Palladino, *Teenagers: An American History* (1996). Persuasively describes the development of youth culture in the 1950s.

 Please refer to the document CD-ROM for primary sources related to this chapter.

CHAPTER

28

The Rise and Fall of the New Liberalism

1960–1968

"We Would Never Be Beaten": Vietnam, 1968 • The Liberal Opportunity • Implementing the Liberal Agenda • Winning Civil Rights • Fighting the Cold War • The American War in Vietnam The Great Society Comes Apart • Conclusion

"WE WOULD NEVER BE BEATEN": VIETNAM, 1968

On the night of January 10, 1968, Second Lieutenant Fred Downs of the U.S. Army looked up at the stars over the coast of South Vietnam. Only 23, he was thousands of miles from the Indiana farm where he had grown up. Why was he so far from home?

Downs's presence in South Vietnam reflected two factors that shaped American life after 1945: the cold war and prosperity. Downs was in South Vietnam because of the ongoing U.S. opposition to the spread of Communism. His job was to protect South Vietnam's government from forces loyal to the North Vietnamese Communists. Downs was there, too, because of his country's wealth. Only a prosperous society could afford to send several hundred thousand military personnel to fight halfway around the world.

Downs's presence in South Vietnam also emphasized a critical change in the United States from the 1950s to the 1960s. During the 1950s, the U.S. government had a cautious sense of the limits of American power, but leaders in the 1960s, buoyed by the prosperous economy, were more daring. Faced with the likely collapse of South Vietnam, the U.S. government had sent its troops to battle in 1965.

Fred Downs shared his leaders' confidence. "I knew we would never be beaten," he declared. Still, the months in Vietnam had tested his confidence. He worried about stepping on land mines and booby traps. He worried whether he could trust the South Vietnamese. He worried whether his country was fighting the war the right way.

Downs was wounded four times, but the Army rewarded him with medals for bravery and he put aside his worries. "My men thought I was invulnerable," he reported. "I did too." On the night of January 10 he saw "no clouds on my horizon." "Nothing would happen to me," he believed.

The next morning, his platoon moved out. At 7:45, he went through a gate at the top of a hill and stepped on a mine. The explosion threw Downs into the air, ripped through his ear drums, tore away pieces of his legs and hips, mutilated his right hand, laid bare the bones of his right arm, and blew off his left arm at the elbow. Horrified, Downs looked at his wounds. "I felt," he recalled, "the total defeat of my life."

Fred Downs's story mirrored the experience of his country in the 1960s. With growing confidence in its wealth, power, and wisdom, the United States tried bold projects. Americans turned to a vigorous liberalism that took an activist approach to the political economy. The nation's leaders pledged to fight Communism abroad and to reform life at home. By the mid-1960s, the federal government had gone to war in Vietnam and had begun to create a "Great Society" in the United States. The country tried to wipe out poverty, heal race relations, protect consumers and the environment, and improve education and health care. Fred Downs's fate reflected the fate of his nation. By 1968 the United States had to confront the limits of its power, just as Fred Downs had to confront the new limits of his life without an arm.

THE LIBERAL OPPORTUNITY

Americans' uneasiness about their society, rather unfocused in the 1950s, became increasingly focused in the 1960s. During the new decade, people realized that the prosperous consumer economy had left millions in poverty and damaged the environment. Meanwhile, the grassroots protests of African Americans dramatized the persistence of racial inequality.

These popular discontents created an opportunity for new ideas and new leaders in the 1960s. A fresh brand of liberalism promised a new approach to the political economy. Confident that the federal government could keep the economy growing, liberals wanted to use more of the nation's wealth to improve life at home and to confront the Communist challenge abroad.

Discontent in the Consumer Society

Despite the economic boom after World War II, the percentage of Americans living in poverty had hardly budged by 1960. Millions of people lived the consumerist good life, but millions of others did not. By the standards of the day, about one in five people were poor, and the majority of the poor were white.

By the 1960s the rest of country found it harder and harder to ignore the poor or to blame poverty on the failings of poor people. In his influential book *The Other America* (1962), Michael Harrington stressed that the poor remained poor because of racism and a lack of opportunity, not because of personal shortcomings. Thanks in part to Harrington, more Americans began to ask why their affluent consumer society failed to provide decent housing, education, and jobs for all citizens.

At the same time, people were asking why the economy had to do so much ecological damage. Americans could no longer ignore the fact that their large, flashy automobiles, the symbol of the consumer society, were polluting the air. They began to criticize society's cavalier attitude toward the natural world. In the mid-1950s, environmentalists had blocked the construction of the Echo Park Dam in the upper basin of the Colorado River that would have inundated the Dinosaur National Monument. A new environmental movement, determined to protect wilderness lands from development, emerged from that battle. Americans became further sensitized to the threat that the consumer economy posed to the countryside because of the bestselling book *Silent Spring* (1962), which emphasized the dangerous power that human beings held over the natural world. The author, marine biologist Rachel Carson, warned that environmental contamination, like nuclear weapons, threatened human survival.

In the 1960s, some Americans recognized that pollution was not the only threat to consumers. The uncritical approval of corporations in the 1950s gave way to a more skeptical view of big business. In 1965, Ralph Nader, an intense young lawyer, published a disturbing book, *Unsafe at Any Speed*, charging that car manufacturers cared more about style and sales than about safety. American cars lacked safety features, such as seat belts, that could save lives. Moreover, Nader reported, executives at General Motors had ignored safety defects in the Chevrolet Corvair. Faced with these revelations, General Motors seemed to confirm its arrogance by trying to discredit Nader rather than promising immediately to improve the Corvair.

The End of Deliberate Speed

In the early 1960s, Americans expressed their growing discontent with consumer culture largely through bestsellers and polite speeches. In contrast, the civil rights movement increasingly protested racial inequality with bold grassroots action. A new generation of African Americans was impatient with the slow "deliberate speed" of integration that the Supreme Court had mandated in *Brown* v. *Board of Education* and was prepared to confront segregation in the South. In 1960, the spirit of grassroots activism inspired a wave of sit-ins and the formation of a new civil rights organization.

The sit-ins began in Greensboro, North Carolina. On February 1, 1960, four black male students from North Carolina Agricultural and Technical College politely insisted on being served at a whites-only lunch counter. When the white waitress refused their order, the students, who would become known as the Greensboro Four, stayed all afternoon. Returning the next day with 30 colleagues, the Greensboro Four were again denied service. Soon hundreds of African-American students from North Carolina A & T and other campuses, along with some white students, were besieging lunch counters.

The sit-in resembled the protests of the 1940s, but it had a far greater impact. Sit-ins spread across Greensboro and North Carolina, and then to other states. The demonstrations forced reluctant whites to open up lunch counters and other facilities to black patrons. The demonstrations also helped produce a new civil rights organization, the Student Nonviolent Coordinating Committee (SNCC). The SNCC (pronounced "Snick") brought together white and African-American young people, influenced by "Judaic-Christian traditions" and eager to create "a social order permeated by love."

The Emergence of the New Liberalism

By the 1960s, liberals were offering a fresh agenda that responded to the discontents of the consumer society, to the civil rights movement, and to the continuing cold war confrontation with Communism. The key to this new liberalism was faith in American economic growth. To meet its domestic and international challenges, the United States needed to expand its economy. As one liberal economist observed, growth would provide "the resources needed to achieve great societies at home and grand designs abroad." The liberals charged that the Eisenhower administration had failed to expand the economy enough in the prosperous 1950s, and they were confident that greater growth could be achieved in the 1960s. By manipulating its budget, they reasoned, the federal government could keep the economy growing. The right amount of taxes and expenditures would ensure full employment, strong consumer demand, and a rising gross national product.

Growth alone would not make America great, the liberals cautioned. Economic growth had to be used to create a better, more satisfying life for all Americans. Because the private sector could not solve pressing national problems, the federal government had to step in to deal actively with poverty, racial inequality, pollution, housing, education, world Communism, and other problems.

Like the liberals of the 1930s and 1940s, liberals at the start of the 1960s believed in using government to correct problems created or ignored by the private sector. They also remained staunchly anti-Communist. Nevertheless, the new liberalism differed from the old in important ways. New Dealers had worried most of all about restoring and maintaining prosperity; the new liberals almost took prosperity for granted. They were sure that the economy could pay for a host of reforms. The old liberals had feared that big business and class conflict posed dangers for the United States. Their successors generally saw racial divisions as the country's greatest domestic problem. Most of all, the new liberalism rested on a powerful feeling of confidence in America's prosperity and power.

The Presidential Election of 1960

The presidential election of 1960 seemed to offer a clear choice between a vaguely liberal future and the status quo. The Democratic nominee, Senator John F. Kennedy of Massachusetts, was open to the liberals' agenda and shared their optimism. Kennedy was youthful, energetic, and charismatic. Although he had compiled an undistinguished record in Congress, he promoted a sense of expectation. The candidate exuded, said one of his speechwriters, "the promise, almost limitless in dimensions, of enormous possibilities yet to come."

Kennedy gave voice to that promise during the campaign. Americans, he explained, stood "on the edge of a New Frontier—the frontier of the 1960s—a frontier of unknown opportunities and paths, a frontier of unfulfilled hopes and threats." The

United States needed to foster economic growth, rebuild slums, end poverty, improve education for the young, and enhance retirement for the old.

In contrast, Kennedy's Republican opponent, Vice President Richard Nixon of California, represented the cautious Eisenhower administration that favored balanced budgets and limited government. As a result, the campaign presented an apparent choice between maintaining the stability of the 1950s and exploring an exciting but unclear liberal future.

Kennedy's stirring rhetoric did not produce a great victory; in fact the election was the closest in history. Kennedy polled 49.7 percent of the vote to Nixon's 49.5 percent (see Map 28–1). Kennedy managed to keep much of the Democratic New Deal coalition of liberals, workers, and African Americans together, but he won by less than 120,000 votes. However narrowly, the voters had turned to a Democrat, influenced by liberal ideas, who was eager to explore the New Frontier.

Kennedy's Unfulfilled Promise

From the first moments of his presidency, Kennedy voiced the confident liberal faith in America's unlimited power and responsibility. "Let every nation know," he declared in his inaugural address in January 1961, "that we shall pay any price, bear any burden, meet any hardship, support any friend, oppose any foe to assure the survival and the success of liberty." Kennedy's extravagant promise perfectly captured the optimistic spirit of the early 1960s. So did the dramatic escalation of the space race.

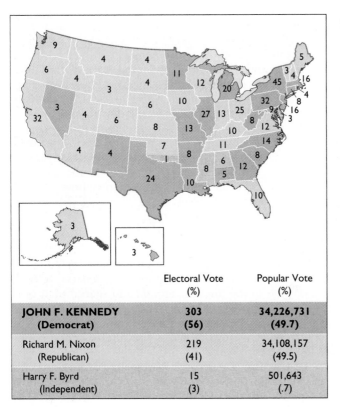

Map 28–1   The Presidential Election, 1960

Democrat John F. Kennedy's clear margin in the electoral vote belies just how narrowly he outpolled Republican Richard M. Nixon in the popular vote.

	Electoral Vote (%)	Popular Vote (%)
JOHN F. KENNEDY (Democrat)	**303 (56)**	**34,226,731 (49.7)**
Richard M. Nixon (Republican)	219 (41)	34,108,157 (49.5)
Harry F. Byrd (Independent)	15 (3)	501,643 (.7)

The exploration of space seemed like an ideal occupation for confident Americans in the 1960s. Moreover, the space race allowed Kennedy to reject the cautious Eisenhower policies of the 1950s and to confront the Soviet challenge. In April 1961 the Soviet Union sent up the first astronaut to orbit Earth. The next month, NASA managed only to launch astronaut Alan Shepard for a brief, suborbital flight. Once again Americans feared "that the wave of the future is Russian."

The Kennedy administration responded with dramatic rhetoric and the abundant resources of the growth economy. The president boldly pledged to land "a man on the moon . . . before the decade is out." With 60,000 workers and billions of dollars, the Apollo program began. In February 1962 astronaut John Glenn became the first American to orbit Earth. That year the United States launched Telstar, a sophisticated communications satellite. In all, the space program mixed practical achievements such as Telstar with less practical, more symbolic gestures such as manned space flights.

That mixture of style and substance reflected the Kennedy administration as a whole. The president maintained a dynamic, energetic image, but his administration, hampered by a weak electoral mandate, did not venture too far out onto the liberal New Frontier.

How much Kennedy might have accomplished would never be known. On a trip to Dallas, Texas, on November 22, 1963, the president was shot while riding in an open limousine at 12:33 P.M. Two bullets tore through Kennedy's throat and skull, and doctors pronounced him dead half an hour later. That afternoon, police arrested Lee Harvey Oswald for the shooting. A quiet former Marine, Oswald had spent

The Kennedy assassination, November 22, 1963. Jacqueline Kennedy tries to help her mortally wounded husband, John F. Kennedy, as his motorcade drives through Dallas.

time in the Soviet Union. Two days later, as police transferred him from one jail to another, he was shot and killed by Jack Ruby, the troubled owner of a local nightclub.

Americans were shocked and numbed by the assassination and its aftermath. Some could only believe the assassination was the product of a dark conspiracy, but there was never any proof of such a plot. The presidency of John Kennedy, little more than 1,000 days long, left a sad sense of unfulfilled promise. Kennedy gave voice to the new liberalism, but he seldom translated liberal ideas into action.

Lyndon Johnson's Mandate

In background and personality, the new president, Lyndon Johnson, seemed far different from his slain predecessor. Johnson was never an eloquent public speaker or a charismatic figure. He lacked Kennedy's polish and glamour. He himself was often blunt and crude, rather than cool and suave, but he was an especially effective legislator who knew better than Kennedy how to bully and cajole Senate colleagues into making a deal.

Despite the obvious differences in style and background, there were more fundamental similarities between Johnson and Kennedy. Both were members of the Democratic Party that engineered the New Deal, won World War II, and fought the cold war. Both shared the liberals' sense of limitless possibility for the United States. "We're the richest country in the world, the most powerful," Johnson declared. "We can do it all."

Johnson seemed to feel he could do it all after his landslide victory in the presidential election of 1964. The contest gave voters an unusually clear choice between competing visions of the political economy. Johnson stood for activist government, growth economics, and the new liberalism. His Republican opponent, Senator Barry Goldwater of Arizona, just as plainly stood for an emerging brand of conservatism. Goldwater flatly opposed liberal domestic policy, including civil rights and activist government.

It was not much of a contest. Goldwater was too outspoken for many voters. The Johnson campaign portrayed him as a dangerous radical who would gut liberal programs and perhaps start a war. Johnson, in contrast, was supposed to be a statesman and a man of peace. He won 61.1 percent of the popular vote, 44 states, and 486 electoral votes. Moreover, the Democrats increased their majorities in the House and Senate. Goldwater represented the wave of the future; by 1980 his views would not seem extreme. But in 1964 Johnson spoke for the mass of Americans.

IMPLEMENTING THE LIBERAL AGENDA

In the 1960s the federal government attempted to create what Lyndon Johnson called the Great Society, "a society of success without squalor, beauty without barrenness, works of genius without the wretchedness of poverty." The Democratic-controlled Congress passed a wave of new laws, the most important body of legislation since the New Deal, that aimed to wipe out poverty and enhance the quality of life for all Americans. At the same time, the Supreme Court afforded new protections for individual rights. By 1967 the principles of the new liberalism, turned into law, were transforming American government and society.

Declaring War on Poverty

For liberals, the persistence of poverty amid prosperity stood as a chief failure of the consumer society and an embarrassment for the United States around the world. Liberals argued that the poor needed help from the federal government to become productive workers and contribute to economic growth. Increasing the productivity of the poor was not a simple matter, however. Liberals contended that the battle against poverty should include improved housing, education, health, and job opportunities, as well as job training.

Kennedy supported some modest antipoverty measures. In 1961 he signed into law the Area Redevelopment Act to help revive depressed areas. He also signed the Omnibus Housing Act to clear slum housing and bring urban renewal to inner cities. But these measures were not enough to wipe out poverty.

Declaring its "unconditional war on poverty," the Johnson administration embraced a much broader range of liberal programs. In 1964 Congress created an independent federal agency, the Office of Economic Opportunity (OEO), to spend nearly $1 billion on antipoverty programs. The OEO managed Volunteers in Service to America (VISTA), whose workers taught literacy and other skills in impoverished areas. It ran the Job Corps, which taught necessary job skills to poor youth, and implemented Community Action Programs (CAPs), which encouraged the poor to organize themselves in American cities.

In 1965 and 1966 Congress continued the war on several fronts. It established an expanded food stamp program and created Head Start, which provided early schooling, meals, and medical exams for impoverished preschool-aged children. To protect the rights of the poor, the Legal Services Program brought lawyers into slums. To improve urban life, the Model Cities Program targeted 63 cities for slum clearance and redevelopment. The War on Poverty was at least a partial success. Mainly because of the ongoing economic boom, the percentage of people living in poverty decreased to 13 percent by 1970. But that meant that 25 million Americans were still poor. Moreover, poverty was unevenly distributed. About a third of African Americans and a quarter of Americans of Spanish origin were impoverished as the 1970s began. Still, the liberal War on Poverty made a significant, enduring difference in American life.

Improving the Quality of Life

Johnson wanted the Great Society to improve the quality of life for all Americans. Beginning in 1964, Congress enacted measures affecting health care, consumer protection, education, and culture, using the fruits of economic growth to furnish security, opportunity, and cultural enrichment.

One of the fundamental commitments of New Deal liberalism was to provide greater economic security for Americans. Federally subsidized health insurance was part of that goal. The Great Society took a major step toward national health insurance when Congress created Medicare in 1965. This program provided the elderly with insurance coverage for doctors' bills, surgery, and hospitalization. At the same time Congress created Medicaid, a program that helped the states provide medical care to the nonworking poor. The Johnson administration also dealt with the issue of consumer protection. Congress passed the National Traffic and Motor Vehicle Safety Act of 1966, which set the first federal safety standards for automobiles, and the Highway Safety Act, which required states to establish highway safety programs.

The president and Congress adopted the new liberals' belief in using the federal government to support education at all levels. The Elementary and Secondary School Act of 1965 channeled $1.3 billion into school districts around the country. The Higher Education Act of 1965 encouraged youth to attend college by offering federally insured educational loans.

TABLE 28–1

						Education &
Year	**Civilian Employees (thous.)**	**Total Spending (millions)**	**Defense (millions)**	**Space (millions)**	**Health (millions)**	**Manpower (millions)**
1955	2,397	$ 68,509	$40,245	$ 74	$ 271	$ 573
1960	2,399	$ 92,223	$45,908	$ 401	$ 756	$1,060
1965	2,528	$118,430	$49,578	$5,091	$ 1,704	$2,284
1970	2,982	$196,588	$80,295	$3,749	$12,907	$7,289

Expanding the Federal Government, 1955–1970

Source: Historical Statistics of the United States (1976), II, pp. 1102, 1116.

The Great Society included programs for cultural enrichment. In 1965 Congress established the National Endowment for the Arts to fund the visual and performing arts and the National Endowment for the Humanities to support scholarly research. The Public Broadcasting Act of 1967 established a nonprofit corporation to support educational and cultural programming. Before long, the Corporation for Public Broadcasting would be giving money for such commercial-free television shows as *Sesame Street*.

The Great Society's programs added up to a major change in the American political economy. Government claimed more authority than ever to manage many Americans' daily lives. The Great Society brought a massive expansion of the size, cost, and power of the federal government (see Table 28–1).

That expansion would be controversial for years to come. Some Great Society measures—Medicare in particular—proved to be enormously expensive. Conservatives did not welcome an enlarged federal government, and some corporations resented the government's regulation of business in the name of consumer protection. Despite these concerns, the various attempts to improve the quality of life represented some of the greatest successes of the new liberalism.

Protecting the Environment

Protection of the environment was a natural issue for liberals to address. Here was a problem, created by the booming consumer economy, that government could solve. During Johnson's presidency, more than 300 pieces of legislation led to the expenditure of more than $12 billion on environmental programs. In 1963 the Clean Air Act encouraged state and local governments to set up pollution control programs. Two years later, amendments established the first pollution emission standards for automobiles. The Air Quality Act of 1967 further strengthened federal authority to deal with air pollution. Meanwhile, the Water Quality Act of 1965 and the Clean Waters Restoration Act of 1966 enabled states and the federal government to fight water pollution. The Wilderness Act of 1964 responded to environmentalists' calls for a system of wilderness lands protected from development.

Preserving Personal Freedom

The new liberalism contained a paradox: Liberals wanted to enhance the power of the federal government and to expand individual rights. Their concern for individual rights was apparent in their support for civil rights for African Americans and in a series of decisions by the Supreme Court, led by Chief Justice Earl Warren.

In *New York Times* v. *Sullivan* in 1964, the justices encouraged free speech by making it more difficult for public figures to sue news media for libel. In addition, two important decisions protected the rights of people accused of crimes. In 1963 the court ruled in *Gideon* v. *Wainwright* that governments had to provide lawyers to poor felony defendants. Three years later, *Miranda* v. *Arizona* required police to inform individuals of their rights when they were arrested, including the right to remain silent and the right to an attorney.

The Warren Court also protected sexual and religious freedom. In 1965 in *Griswold* v. *Connecticut* the court threw out a state law that banned the use of contraceptives. In 1963 the court acted to prohibit mandatory prayer in the nation's public schools. *School District of Abington Township* v. *Schempp* prohibited state and local governments from requiring public school students to say the Lord's Prayer or read the Bible.

The Supreme Court's rulings were controversial. Some people charged that the court was "driving God out" of the classroom. Others believed that the court had gone too far to protect the rights of alleged criminals. Through its rulings, the liberal majority on the court substantially increased individual freedom, but few people had yet thought much about the tension between expanding both individual rights and government power.

Much of the liberal agenda had been accomplished by 1967. The Great Society dealt with the key issues of the political economy, such as poverty, health care, and consumer protection. The most significant body of legislation since the New Deal, Johnson's program vastly expanded the reach of the federal government and changed the lives of Americans for decades to come.

WINNING CIVIL RIGHTS

Of all the domestic challenges confronting the Great Society, none was more difficult than civil rights. The fervor of the grassroots civil rights movement helped spur the new liberalism in the 1960s, yet many whites were still determined to preserve the old racial order. Civil rights activists needed allies in the federal government, and the Great Society produced major legislation outlawing segregation and restoring black voting rights in the South—at least on paper.

White Resistance and Federal Reluctance

The civil rights movement did not win any easy victories in the South during the early 1960s. In one location after another, attempts to break down segregation and promote African-American voting met with resistance. The character of white resistance became evident in the spring of 1961. After the Supreme Court outlawed the segregation of interstate bus terminals, a small group of African-American and white "Freedom Riders" traveled south on buses to test the decision. The Freedom Riders met with beatings from white citizens and harassment from local authorities. Only then did the Kennedy administration send federal marshals to protect them.

White resistance could prove effective, especially if there were no federal marshals around. In 1961, when SNCC started a voter-registration drive in Mississippi, white people struck back. SNCC workers were beaten and shot. When SNCC tried to register black voters in the small city of Albany, Georgia, members of the Albany Movement, as it was called, were beaten and arrested. Martin Luther King, Jr.,

The price of civil rights: Freedom Riders outside their burning bus, which was set on fire by a white mob determined to stop the desegregation of southern bus terminals in May 1961.

leader of the Southern Christian Leadership Conference (SCLC) and veteran of the Montgomery bus boycott of 1955–1956, came to Albany and got arrested, too, but segregation still ruled in the city.

SNCC activists resented the lack of presidential support for their work, and the defiance of southern whites gradually pushed Kennedy toward action. In 1962 the governor of Mississippi, Ross Barnett, disregarded a federal court order by preventing a black student from enrolling at the University of Mississippi. When federal marshals escorted the student, James Meredith, to school, white students pelted them with rocks and Molotov cocktails. After the rioting killed two people and wounded more than 100 marshals, Kennedy called in federal troops to stop the violence and allow Meredith to enroll.

Two confrontations in Alabama forced the president's hand in 1963. In April, Martin Luther King, Jr., and the SCLC tried to end segregation in the Southern steel-making center, Birmingham, perhaps the most segregated city in America. The city's Public Safety Commissioner, Eugene "Bull" Connor, was a stereotypical racist white southern law enforcement officer. To win a badly needed victory, King and local allies planned to boycott department stores and overwhelm the jails with arrested protesters. Calling for the end of segregation, King laid down the gauntlet to Connor and the white community. In the next days, Connor's officers arrested demonstrators by the hundreds. King ignored a judge's injunction against further protests and ended up in solitary confinement. In a powerful statement, *Letter From Birmingham Jail*, King responded to critics of the demonstrations. "We know through painful experience," he wrote, "that freedom is never voluntarily given by the oppressor; it must be demanded by the oppressed." King rejected further patience: "We must come to see . . . that 'justice too long delayed is justice denied.'" Out on bail, King and the SCLC pushed harder for justice with demonstrations by thousands of young African-American students.

Goaded by the new protests, "Bull" Connor turned fire hoses on young demonstrators, set dogs on them, and hit them with clubs. Shocking pictures of the scenes, shown around the world, increased the pressure on the white leadership of Birmingham and on President Kennedy. Mediators from Kennedy's Justice Department arranged for a deal in which the SCLC gave up the demonstrations and local businesses gave up segregation and promised to hire African Americans. However, soon thereafter the Ku Klux Klan marched outside the city and bombs went off at the home of King's brother and at SCLC headquarters. In response, African Americans rioted in the streets of Birmingham. Kennedy was forced to send federal troops to keep the peace.

A second confrontation in Alabama drew the president still deeper into the civil rights struggle. The state's segregationist governor, George Wallace, defied federal officials and tried to stop two black students from enrolling at the University of Alabama. Only then did President Kennedy take an open stand on civil rights in an eloquent televised address and propose sweeping civil rights legislation.

Two months later, on August 28, a march on Washington brought together a crowd of nearly 200,000 people, including 50,000 whites, at the Lincoln Memorial to commemorate the 100th anniversary of the Emancipation Proclamation and to

Martin Luther King, Jr., and his wife, Coretta Scott King, at the front of the civil rights march from Selma, Alabama, on March 30, 1965. Male and female, old and young, black and white, the marchers illustrate the diversity of the coalition that walked with linked arms and determined faces to demand the right to vote for African Americans.

demand "jobs and freedom." Whites and African Americans, workers and students, singers and preachers joined hands to sing the stirring civil rights anthem, "We Shall Overcome." Martin Luther King, Jr., moved the nation with his vision of racial harmony. "I have a dream," he said, "that one day . . . little black boys and black girls will be able to join with little white boys and white girls as sisters and brothers." King looked forward to "that day when . . . black men and white men, Jews and Gentiles, Protestants and Catholics, will be able to join hands and sing . . . 'Free at last! Free at last! Thank God Almighty, we are free at last!'"

Kennedy's address and the March on Washington marked a turning point. The surging grassroots movement for racial equality had created broad-based support for civil rights and finally forced the federal government to act.

The Death of Jim Crow

In the 10 weeks after the Birmingham confrontation, 758 demonstrations led to 14,733 arrests across the United States. When a bomb killed four African-American girls in a Baptist church in Birmingham in September, African-American rioters burned stores and destroyed cars, and the police killed two more children.

The violence continued the following year: CORE, SNCC, SCLC, and the NAACP had created the Council of Federated Organizations (COFO) to press for African-American voting rights in Mississippi. Robert Moses, an African-American schoolteacher, led the COFO crusade that united young African-American and white activists to register black voters and start "Freedom Schools" for African-American children. The effort, known as Freedom Summer, met hostility from whites. In June 1964 two white activists, Michael Schwerner and Andrew Goodman, and one African-American activist, James Chaney, disappeared near Philadelphia, Mississippi. They were found a month later, shot to death. Eventually a white deputy sheriff, a local Klan leader, and five other whites were convicted of "violating the rights" of Chaney, Goodman, and Schwerner.

The violence continued in Mississippi throughout the Freedom Summer of 1964. Homes and churches were burned, and three more COFO workers were killed.

Lyndon Johnson could not escape the events in Mississippi. In the summer of 1964, the Mississippi Freedom Democratic Party (MFDP) sent a full delegation to the Democratic National Convention in Atlantic City, New Jersey. The MFDP delegates, including the eloquent Fannie Lou Hamer, hoped at least to share Mississippi's convention seats with the whites-only Democratic Party delegation. Hamer, the daughter of sharecroppers, told the national Democratic Party's Credentials Committee how she had been jailed and beaten for trying to register African-American voters. Afraid of alienating white southern voters, Johnson tried to stop the publicity and offered the delegates two seats in the convention. "We didn't come all this way for no two seats," Hamer retorted. The MFDP delegation went away empty-handed.

Johnson and the Democratic Party were clearly not ready to share power with African-American activists, but they were ready to end legalized segregation. In July, with Johnson's prodding, Congress adopted the Civil Rights Act, which outlawed racial discrimination in public places. The measure also set up an Equal Employment Opportunity Commission (EEOC) to stop discrimination in hiring and promotion. Even the schools gradually became integrated. In 1964 hardly any African-American students attended integrated schools; by 1972 nearly half of African-American children attended integrated schools.

However, across the South, most African Americans still could not vote. In January 1965 the SCLC and SNCC tried to force the voting rights issue with protests in Selma, Alabama. Predictably, the demonstrations produced violent opposition and helpful publicity. The sight of state troopers using tear gas, cattle prods, and clubs on peaceful marchers built support for voting rights.

Seizing the moment, Johnson called for the end of disfranchisement, and Congress passed the Voting Rights Act of 1965. This powerful measure forced southern states to give up literacy tests used to disfranchise black voters and empowered federal officials to make sure that African Americans could register to vote. In three years, Mississippi saw African-American registration increase from 6 percent to 44 percent of eligible voters.

Together with the Civil Rights Act of 1964, the Voting Rights Act transformed the South. These twin achievements of the civil rights movement effectively doomed Jim Crow and laid a foundation for African-American political power. However, the struggle for racial equality was far from over.

FIGHTING THE COLD WAR

The new liberalism was staunchly anti-Communist, but the New Frontier and the Great Society modified the defense and foreign policies of the 1950s. More confident about American power and wisdom, the Kennedy administration increased the nation's defense spending and international commitments and confronted Communism throughout the third world. Meanwhile, Kennedy and Johnson maintained the core American commitment to containing the Soviet Union that helped to produce dangerous crises in the early 1960s.

Flexible Response and the Third World

Although Kennedy shared President Eisenhower's commitment to containing Communism, Kennedy believed the nation could afford to spend more money on the military. He also abandoned the doctrine of massive retaliation, Eisenhower's threat to use nuclear weapons against any Soviet aggression. Kennedy and his advisers preferred flexible response, a strategy that allowed the president to choose different military options, not just nuclear weapons, in dealing with the Soviets. While spending generously on nuclear weapons, the Kennedy administration built up the country's conventional ground forces and special forces—the highly trained troops, known as Green Berets, who could fight in guerilla wars. Flexible response better prepared the United States for challenges around the world.

Kennedy was more willing than Eisenhower to intervene in the affairs of the third world. This was partly a reflection of Kennedy's characteristic confidence about American power and partly a response to Soviet actions. In January 1961 Nikita Khrushchev announced Soviet support for "wars of national liberation" against established governments in Asia, Africa, and Latin America. In reply, Kennedy used different, even contradictory strategies to keep Communism out of the third world in the 1960s. His administration encouraged democracy and prosperity in developing countries. However, the United States also helped to thwart third-world independence and democracy in the name of anti-Communism.

To stop the spread of Communism, Kennedy supported modernization in Africa, Asia, and Latin America; that is, policymakers wanted these continents to develop capitalist, democratic, independent, and anti-Communist regimes along the lines of the American political economy. To encourage modernization, the

Kennedy administration created the Peace Corps in 1961, sending thousands of young volunteers around the world to promote literacy, public health, and agriculture. The Peace Corps reflected both the idealism and anti-Communism of the Kennedy years as well as many Americans' arrogant sense of superiority.

To promote the modernization of Latin America, Kennedy announced the formation of the Alliance for Progress in 1961. Over the next eight years, this venture provided $20 billion for housing, health, education, and economic development for poorer countries in the Western Hemisphere. The Kennedy administration did not always support independence and democracy. In some cases, the United States intervened in the domestic affairs of supposedly independent countries. In the Belgian Congo (now the Democratic Republic of Congo), which later became known as Zaire, the CIA engineered the election of an anti-Communist leader. The United States also backed antidemocratic, but anti-Communist, regimes and went along with the military overthrow of legitimate governments.

In Cuba, Kennedy inherited a plan from the Eisenhower administration for a CIA-directed invasion by anti-Communist Cuban exiles. The president wanted to bring down Fidel Castro, whose successful revolution was an example for the rest of Latin America. To conceal U.S. responsibility for the invasion, Kennedy canceled U.S. flights that would have protected the invaders. As a result, nearly all 1,500 exiles who landed at the Bay of Pigs in April 1961 were killed or captured by Castro's troops. Embarrassed, Kennedy turned to the CIA, which launched an unsuccessful secret campaign to kill or depose Castro. The Cuban leader, aware of the American plot, declared himself a Communist and turned to the Soviets for help.

Kennedy's assassination made little difference for American defense and foreign policies. Johnson too was a committed cold warrior with an optimistic view of American power. He kept flexible response in place and was equally willing to undermine the independence of third-world countries. In 1965, Johnson sent 22,000 American troops to the Dominican Republic to stop an increasingly violent struggle for political power. The president acted without obtaining evidence of a Communist threat and without consulting Latin American countries as required by treaty.

The U.S. intervention in the Dominican Republic and Cuba underscored the increased importance of the third world for American policymakers. Anxious to stop the Soviets, Kennedy and Johnson were willing to ignore the sovereignty of Latin American, African, and Asian countries as well as the idealistic commitment to democracy reflected in the Peace Corps and the Alliance for Progress. As would become clear in Vietnam, the costs of the U.S. preoccupation with the third world could be enormous.

Two Confrontations With the Soviets

Kennedy faced two direct confrontations with the Soviet Union. In 1961, Khrushchev threatened to stop Western traffic into West Berlin, which was surrounded by Soviet-dominated East Germany. In response, Kennedy called up reserve troops, asked Congress to increase defense spending, and hinted at a pre-emptive nuclear strike against the Soviets. Khrushchev backed down, but the East German government built a barbed-wire and concrete fence between East Berlin and West Berlin. By halting the embarrassing flight of East Germans to freedom in West Berlin, the so-called Berlin Wall defused the crisis and became a symbol of cold war Europe, a visible "iron curtain" that separated Communists and non-Communists.

In 1962 Kennedy entered a more dangerous confrontation with the Soviet Union. On October 15 photos from an American spy plane showed that the Soviets were building launch sites in Cuba for nuclear missiles that could strike the United States. To force the Soviet Union to withdraw the missiles, the president put ships in place on October 22 to intercept Soviet vessels bound for Cuba. That night, a somber Kennedy told a television audience about the Russian missiles and demanded their removal. Khrushchev backed down and withdrew the missiles in exchange for the removal of obsolete American missiles from Turkey.

The Cuban Missile Crisis both eased and intensified the cold war. The close call with nuclear war gave both sides a chance to think carefully about a nuclear conflict; neither found the prospect appealing, and both sought to ease tensions. A teletype "hotline" was installed between the White House and the Kremlin so that Soviet and American leaders could communicate quickly during a crisis. In 1963 the two powers also approved a Limited Test Ban Treaty halting aboveground tests of nuclear weapons. On the other hand, the crisis made both the Soviets and the Americans more determined to stand firm against each other.

The Berlin and Cuban crises were reminders that the heart of the cold war was the confrontation between the United States and the Soviet Union. The Test Ban Treaty might have marked the beginning of the end of the cold war, but that confrontation was still far from over.

THE AMERICAN WAR IN VIETNAM

The war in Vietnam was a decisive episode for the new liberalism and the nation in the 1960s. American participation in the conflict reflected the liberals' determined anti-Communism and their boundless sense of power and responsibility. Driven by these beliefs, Kennedy deepened the U.S. commitment to protect South Vietnam in the early 1960s, and Johnson made the fateful decision to send American troops into battle in 1965. As the fighting stretched on, Americans divided passionately over the conflict, and the economy faltered. By the end of 1967 the war was beginning to destroy the Great Society.

Kennedy's Deepening Commitment

Kennedy inherited a deteriorating situation in South Vietnam in 1961. Ngo Dinh Diem's non-Communist government faced increasing attacks from the Viet Cong, guerrillas determined to overthrow his regime. Diem also faced a new political organization, the National Liberation Front, that was trying to mobilize his Communist and non-Communist opponents. In addition, he faced the continuing hostility of Ho Chi Minh's Communist government in North Vietnam, which was secretly sending soldiers and supplies into South Vietnam.

Like Eisenhower, Kennedy tried to shore up the Diem government, providing advice and financial aid. Further, Kennedy sent American advisers, including the Special Forces, to teach the South Vietnamese Army how to stop the Viet Cong insurgency. Before Kennedy took office, there were 900 American troops filling noncombat roles in South Vietnam. At his death, there were more than 16,000.

Despite all this support, Diem's regime spiraled downward. His army could not stop the Viet Cong. A cold, unpopular ruler, he alienated his own people. Losing confidence in Diem, the Kennedy administration did nothing to stop a military coup that resulted in the murder of the South Vietnamese leader at the beginning of November.

Kennedy's interventions made South Vietnam weaker, not stronger. After the assassination, some Americans wanted to believe that the president would have kept the United States out of the Vietnam War if he had lived. Yet there was no compelling evidence that Kennedy intended to withdraw American troops. Instead, Kennedy's commitment had only made it more difficult for his successor to pull the United States out of Vietnam.

Johnson's Decision for War

At first, Johnson followed Kennedy's policy. The new president believed in the domino theory, the idea that the fall of one country to Communism would lead to the fall of others. Like many Americans who witnessed the rise of Adolf Hitler in the 1930s, Johnson thought it was a mistake to tolerate any aggression. Finally, the president felt he could not turn his back on commitments made by Kennedy, Eisenhower, and Truman. Johnson sent more aid and advisers to South Vietnam and stepped up covert action against the North.

This covert action helped Johnson get Congressional approval to act more aggressively. On August 2, 1964, a U.S. destroyer, the *Maddox*, was cruising a few miles off the coast of North Vietnam in the Gulf of Tonkin. When three North Vietnamese patrol boats unsuccessfully attacked the *Maddox*, the American ship sank two of the boats and damaged a third. Two days later the *Maddox*, along with a second U.S. destroyer, fired mistakenly at a nonexistent North Vietnamese attack. Johnson ordered retaliatory strikes from U.S. aircraft carriers and asked Congress for the power to protect American military personnel. Congress approved what became known as the Tonkin Gulf Resolution, which gave the president the authority, without a declaration of war, to use military force to safeguard South Vietnam. After American soldiers were killed in a Viet Cong attack on a U.S. base in February 1965, Johnson authorized air strikes against North Vietnam itself. In March the U.S. began Operation Rolling Thunder, a series of bombing raids on military targets in North Vietnam.

When the raids failed to deter the North Vietnamese and Viet Cong, Johnson had a disagreeable but clear choice. If he wanted to save both South Vietnam and his reputation, he had to commit American ground troops to battle; otherwise, he would be blamed for the loss of South Vietnam to Communism. In July 1965, Johnson gave the order to send 180,000 soldiers to fight in South Vietnam.

Johnson's decision was the ultimate expression of the new liberalism. The president went to war not only because he opposed Communism, but also because he had faith in American wealth and wisdom. Johnson believed that the United States could transform a weak, divided South Vietnam into a strong, united, modern nation. Even though he was cautious about going to war, Johnson could not accept that the United States might lose. Moreover, he believed that the United States could afford to fight a war abroad and build a Great Society at home.

Fighting a Limited War

Johnson and his advisers believed the United States did not need all its power to save South Vietnam (see Map 28–2). Vietnam was to be a limited war in which American forces, led by General William Westmoreland, would use conventional weapons against military targets. The goal was to kill enough enemy soldiers to persuade the North Vietnamese and the Viet Cong to give up. The measure of American success would be the number of dead North Vietnamese and Viet Cong. Relying on America's superior technology, Westmoreland expected the United States to prevail by the end of 1967.

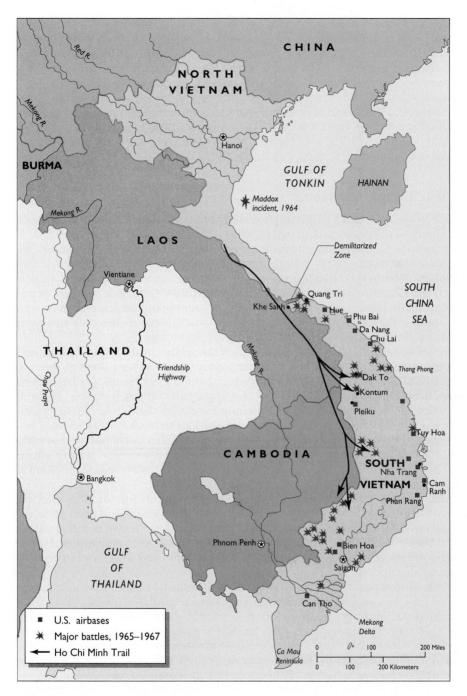

Map 28–2   America's War in Vietnam, 1965–1968
The many military bases suggest how much power the United States had to commit to South Vietnam; the many major battles show how hard American troops had to fight to protect the South Vietnamese regime from the Viet Cong and from the North Vietnamese soldiers who traveled the Ho Chi Minh Trail.

Westmoreland's strategy turned out to be poorly suited to the realities of Vietnam. As Fred Downs discovered, the North Vietnamese and the Viet Cong usually escaped by hiding in tunnels, fleeing through the jungle, fighting mainly at night, or retreating into Cambodia, Laos, and North Vietnam. Their strategy was to live long enough for a frustrated U.S. military to leave South Vietnam.

At the close of 1967, when the war should have been ending, too many North Vietnamese and Viet Cong were still alive and committed to the overthrow of South Vietnam. Even though there were now half a million troops in Westmoreland's command, he had not won the war. He had not lost the war, either; the United States had just run out of time to fight (see Table 28–2).

The War's Impact at Home

The war in Vietnam had a major impact back home. An impassioned antiwar movement emerged to condemn American policy.

To antiwar protesters, mostly students on college and university campuses, the Vietnam War epitomized the failings of the Great Society. The war revealed how undemocratic America had become. Johnson, the radicals pointed out, had ignored the Constitution by sending troops into battle without a declaration of war. In addition, the selective service law was forcing a repugnant choice on young men: They could either fight this illegal war or obtain student deferments to stay in school and prepare for empty lives in the consumer society.

Forced to rethink their basic assumptions about the United States and the cold war, a growing number of liberals and Democrats shared at least some of the radicals' analysis. These "doves" acknowledged that the United States was backing an antidemocratic government in a brutal and apparently unnecessary war. The conflict appeared to be a civil war among Vietnamese rather than some plot to expand Soviet or Chinese influence. Meanwhile, the war had shattered many liberals' and Democrats' overconfident view of the Great Society. The United States, confessed Senator J. William Fulbright of Arkansas in 1966, was a "sick society" suffering from an "arrogance of power." The nation apparently could not solve major problems as readily as the liberals had believed a few years earlier.

Some African Americans viewed the conflict as a painful illustration of American racism. A disproportionate number of poor African Americans, unable to go to college and avoid the draft, were being sent to kill nonwhites abroad on behalf of a racist United States. First SNCC and then Martin Luther King, Jr., condemned the war. Refusing to be drafted, boxer Muhammad Ali was sentenced to jail and stripped of his championship in 1967. The growing opposition to the war produced large and angry demonstrations. In 1965 students and faculty staged "teach-ins" at college campuses to explore and question American policy in Vietnam. In April, 20,000 people gathered at the Washington Monument to protest the war. Some young men risked jail by returning or burning their draft cards. On campuses, students protested the presence of recruiters trying to hire workers for defense contractors. Radicals in Oakland, California, tried to shut down an Army draft induction center. Meanwhile, nearly 100,000 people rallied in Washington, DC, to protest the war.

Yet most Americans supported the war. To many people, the demonstrators were unpatriotic. "America—Love It or Leave It," read a popular bumper sticker. "Hawks," mostly conservative Republicans and Democrats, wanted Johnson to fight harder. Nevertheless, by October 1967 support for the war in one public opinion poll had fallen to 58 percent, and only 28 percent of the people approved of Johnson's conduct of the war.

TABLE 28–2

The Escalating War in Vietnam, 1960–1968

Year	U.S. Troops	U.S. Battle Deaths	S. Vietnamese Battle Deaths	N. Vietnamese & Viet Cong Battle Deaths (estimated)
1961	3,164	11	(three-year	12,000
1962	11,326	31	total =	21,000
1963	16,263	78	13,985)	21,000
1964	23,310	147	7,457	17,000
1965	184,000	1,369	11,403	35,382
1966	385,000	5,008	11,953	55,524
1967	486,000	9,378	12,716	88,104
1968	536,000	14,589	27,915	181,149

Sources: Michael Clodfelter, Vietnam in Military Statistics, pp. 46, 57, 209, 258; Fox Butterfield, ed., Vietnam War Almanac, pp. 50, 54, 57, 64, 102, 132, 158, 192; Shelby Stanton, ed., Vietnam Order of Battle, p. 333.

Bad economic news contributed to the public mood. Massive government spending for the war and the Great Society had overstimulated the economy. With jobs plentiful, strong consumer demand drove up prices, which in turn put upward pressure on wages. Anxious about inflation, the Federal Reserve contracted the money supply, making it harder for businesses to get loans. When interest rates reached their highest levels since the 1920s, there were fears of a financial panic. Despite liberal economic policies, the United States had not created perpetual prosperity after all.

By the end of 1967 the war had put enormous stress on the Great Society. It undermined liberals' commitment to anti-Communism and their confidence in American power and wisdom. By dividing the nation, the conflict also undermined support for the Great Society. By weakening the economy, furthermore, the Vietnam War made it harder to pay for the Great Society. The United States could not, as Johnson believed, "do it all." The new liberalism had reached its crisis.

THE GREAT SOCIETY COMES APART

Liberals attained power in the early 1960s because their agenda responded to popular discontent with the consumer society, but even as Congress enacted that agenda, many Americans were expressing new dissatisfactions that liberalism could not accommodate. The Black Power movement, the youth rebellion, and a reborn women's movement exposed the limits of the liberal vision. In 1968 the strain of new demands, the Vietnam War, and economic realities tore apart the Great Society, destroyed the fortunes of Lyndon Johnson, and badly wounded the Democratic Party and the new liberalism.

The Emergence of Black Power

For many African Americans, the Great Society's response to racial inequality was too slow and too weak. As the controversy over the MFDP delegation suggested, Johnson and many white Democrats were unwilling to share power with African

Americans. Meanwhile, other events dramatized the gap between the promise of the Great Society and the reality of life in black America. Even as the civil rights movement reached its climax in the mid-1960s, a wave of race riots spread across the United States. When a white policeman shot a 15-year-old African American in New York in July 1964, angry African Americans burned and looted buildings. In August 1965 friction between white police and African-American citizens touched off a riot in Los Angeles. In five days more than 1,000 fires burned, and 34 people died. The wave of riots peaked in Detroit in July 1967 when 43 people died. There were more than 300 race riots from 1964 to 1969 in all parts of the country, not just the South.

The disturbances flowed from the real frustrations of African Americans. Despite the civil rights movement's successful challenge to legalized segregation in the South, African Americans still lived with poverty and discrimination all across the country. The riots signaled that the civil rights movement and the new liberalism had not addressed some of the most difficult problems of racial inequality.

For years King and other activists had relied on nonviolent demonstrations and ties to white liberals to achieve integration, but that approach proved ineffective in the North. In 1965, King went north to confront "the Negro's repellent slum life" in Chicago and join marches protesting the de facto segregation of the city's educational system. King faced the determined opposition of the city's Democratic political boss, Mayor Richard Daley. Reluctant to challenge the powerful mayor, the Johnson administration would not give King real support. In 1966, King returned to lead the "Chicago Movement" to wipe out slums and win access to better housing in white neighborhoods. Daley accepted a compromise on fair housing but repudiated it as soon as King left town. Under the leadership of 24-year-old Jesse Jackson, Operation Breadbasket threatened demonstrations and boycotts against businesses that refused to hire African Americans. The project produced few results; King's nonviolent tactics had failed.

African Americans already had the example of a different approach to the problem of black/white relations. The Nation of Islam believed that whites were devils and African Americans were God's chosen people. The Black Muslims, as they were known, preached separation of the races and the self-reliance of African Americans. One of the Muslims' most powerful preachers was Malcolm X, who angrily rejected integration and nonviolence. He moderated his view of whites before being gunned down, apparently by Muslims, in 1965, but Malcolm X was best known for his militant call "for the freedom of the 22 million Afro-Americans by any means necessary."

By the mid-1960s, many African Americans were willing to follow at least some of Malcolm X's example. Rejecting the longtime goal of integration, they now emphasized maintaining and celebrating a separate African-American identity, declaring that "black is beautiful." In asserting their distinctive identity, some African Americans accentuated their African heritage. They wore African robes and dashikis, explored African language and art, and observed the seven-day holiday Kwanzaa, based on an African harvest festival.

In rejecting nonviolence and integration, a number of African-American activists adopted a more militant stance that was encapsulated in the new slogan "Black Power." The new slogan had different meanings for different people. The most radical interpretation came from the Black Panthers, who were first organized in Oakland, California, by Huey P. Newton and Bobby Seale. Dressed in black clothes and black berets, the Panthers armed themselves to protect their neighborhoods from white police. The Panthers also founded schools and promoted peaceful community activism, but they were best known in the media for their aura of violent militance.

Particularly because of the violent image of the Black Panthers, many Americans, African American and white, were hostile to the new slogan. For King and his allies, Black Power all too obviously meant repudiation of nonviolent integration. For white leaders like Richard Daley, Black Power meant giving up political authority to African Americans. For Lyndon Johnson, Black Power obviously meant a rejection of his Great Society.

The Youth Rebellion

By the early 1960s many students felt confined and oppressed in overcrowded and impersonal colleges and universities. Moreover, these schools ordered students' lives through rules that governed eating in dining halls, drinking alcohol, keeping cars on campus, and socializing in dorm rooms. Female students were subject to particularly strict rules, including curfews.

Campuses across the country witnessed rebellions against these rules in the 1960s. Demanding greater sexual freedom, students sharply criticized regulations that restricted the mixing of male and female students in dorms. By the end of the decade, students were living together before marriage, to the consternation of college authorities and other adults.

Meanwhile, a much smaller number of students was beginning to see the shortcomings of colleges and universities as symptoms of broader social problems. These youth created the New Left, a radical movement that attempted to confront liberalism and create a more democratic nation. The key organization of the New Left was Students for a Democratic Society (SDS).

During its national convention at Port Huron, Michigan, in 1962, SDS approved an "Agenda for a New Generation" that laid out their developing vision. The Port Huron Statement, as it became known, argued that American society denied people real choice and real power in their lives. The answer, SDS claimed, was "participatory democracy." The members of SDS did not believe that liberalism would promote real democracy in America. Instead, the Port Huron Statement looked to students to lead the way by fighting for control of their schools.

The battle began at the University of California at Berkeley in 1964. That fall, the university's administration banned political speaking and organizing at the one street corner where it had been allowed. When a civil rights activist was arrested for defying the ban in October, hundreds of students sat down around the police cars, trapping the officers for 32 hours. After the stand-off, students created the Free Speech Movement (FSM) to demand greater student involvement in the educational process. When the university refused to accept that demand, students took over the main administration building. The administration eventually succumbed to faculty protests and a student boycott of classes and agreed to new rules on free speech.

Americans had never seen anything quite like the Berkeley protests. Here were privileged students, on their way to comfortable middle-class lives, condemning society, storming a building, and being dragged off by the police. Many people were infuriated; running for governor of California in 1966, the conservative former movie actor Ronald Reagan vowed to "clean up the mess at Berkeley." Many younger Americans were inspired by the FSM; SDS membership rose from 2,500 in December 1964 to 10,000 in October 1965. By then, the New Left had found a perfect issue to dramatize the failings of liberalism—the Vietnam War. Student radicals became the backbone of the antiwar movement.

While the New Left flourished, young people were also creating the rebellious lifestyle that became known as the counterculture. Less politically oriented than the

New Left, the counterculture challenged conventional social values. By the mid-1960s, many younger Americans were condemning conformity, careerism, materialism, and sexual repression as they groped toward an alternative lifestyle.

The counterculture rested on the enjoyment of rock music, drugs, and sexual freedom. Beginning in 1964, the sudden popularity of the Beatles, the Rolling Stones, and other British rock groups brought back a rebellious note to rock and roll. Young Americans loved the Beatles' first movie, *A Hard Day's Night* in 1964, because, a student wrote, "all the dreary old adults are mocked and brushed aside."

Rock also became more socially and politically conscious in the 1960s. Bob Dylan, Simon and Garfunkel, and other musicians rooted in folk music sang about racism, nuclear weapons, and other issues.

Rock music often sang of the virtues of drugs and sex, two more elements of the counterculture. Many young people hoped that the counterculture would weave sex, drugs, and rock into a new lifestyle. Novelist Ken Kesey joined with his followers, the Merry Pranksters, to set up a commune outside San Francisco. The Merry Pranksters used drugs to synchronize with the cosmos and attain a state of ecstasy. By 1965 Kesey had created the "acid test," which fused drugs, rock, and light shows into a multimedia experience. The acid test helped establish the popularity of "acid rock," the "San Francisco sound" of the Jefferson Airplane and the Grateful Dead.

The purest form of the countercultural lifestyle was created by the hippies, who appeared in the mid-1960s. Hippie culture centered in San Francisco. Rejecting materialism and consumerism, hippies celebrated free expression and free love. They wanted to replace competition and aggression with cooperation and community. One group of hippies, the Diggers, tried to transcend the consumer economy by giving away used clothes at their "free store" in Haight-Ashbury, handing out free food, and staging free concerts.

The counterculture had obvious roots in the beat movement and the rebellious style of Elvis Presley and James Dean in the 1950s. The counterculture also had roots in the orthodox culture it attacked. By the close of the 1950s, adults themselves had become ambivalent about consumerism and conventional morality. Sexual freedom for youth was encouraged partly by the greater sexual openness of mainstream culture, the Supreme Court's *Griswold* decision, and the introduction of the oral contraceptive (the "pill") in 1960. Moreover, the countercultural lifestyle itself became a form of consumerism, as young Americans flocked to buy the right clothes and record albums. Nevertheless, the counterculture was a disruptive force in 1960s America. Like the Black Panthers, hippies were a small minority, but they and the counterculture deeply influenced young people and adults. The counterculture encouraged Americans to question conventional values and authority and to seek a freer way of life.

By 1967, the New Left, the counterculture, and the other forms of youth rebellion were upsetting the Great Society. Adults feared that young people were out of control, and a society already divided by race was increasingly divided by generation.

The Rebirth of the Women's Movement

By the 1960s American women were reacting against the difficult social roles enforced on them after World War II. More women than ever went to college, but they were not expected to pursue long-term careers. More women than ever worked outside the home, but they were still expected to devote themselves to home and family. Women also had to put up with the continuing double standard of sexual behavior, which granted men more freedom to seek sexual gratification outside of marriage. As the new decade began, educated middle-class women be-

The counterculture comes together. The three dancers epitomize the joyful quest for freedom at the heart of the youth rebellion of the 1960s; the rest of the crowd is a reminder of how many young people sat and watched.

gan to question their second-class status. In part, they were inspired by the example of the civil rights movement.

Two best-selling books reflected these women's complaints. In *The Feminine Mystique* (1963), journalist Betty Friedan described "the problem that has no name," the growing frustration of educated, middle-class wives and mothers who had subordinated their own aspirations to the needs of men. Meanwhile, journalist Helen Gurley Brown rejected unequal sexual opportunities in her book, *Sex and the Single Girl* (1962). Brown did not challenge male sexual ethics, just as Friedan did not challenge male careerism. Instead, like Friedan, Brown wanted equal opportunity for women, both in and out of marriage. She explained, coyly, that "nice, single girls do."

In 1963 Congress passed the Equal Pay Act, which mandated the same pay for men and women who did the same work, but the measure, full of loopholes, had little impact on women's comparatively low wages and salaries. A year later, Title VII, a provision of the Civil Rights Act of 1964, prohibited employers from discriminating on the basis of sex in hiring and compensating workers. Yet the Equal Employment Opportunity Commission (EEOC) did little to enforce the law.

Male insensitivity and inaction soon pushed women to organize. In 1966 Betty Friedan and a handful of other women, angry at the EEOC, formed the National Organization for Women (NOW). Although frustrated with the Great Society, Friedan and the founders of NOW expressed essentially liberal values. They saw NOW as "a civil rights organization," and wrote a "Bill of Rights" for women that focused on government action to provide rights and opportunities. NOW also demanded access to contraception and abortion.

NOW's platform was too radical for many women and not radical enough for others. Some younger women, particularly activists in the civil rights movement and the New Left, wanted more than liberal solutions to their problems. By the fall of 1967, activists were forming new groups dedicated to "women's liberation." Influenced by the New Left, radical feminists blamed the capitalist system for the oppression of women, but a growing number of radicals saw men as the problem. Like African Americans in the Black Power movement, radical women talked less about rights and more about power and had little interest in collaboration with male liberal politicians.

Few in number, radical feminists nevertheless commanded public attention. In September 1968 New York Radical Women organized a protest against the annual Miss America pageant in Atlantic City, New Jersey. The pageant, they said, was an act of "thought control" intended "to further make women oppressed and men oppressors; to enslave us all the more in high-heeled, low-status roles." The protesters threw bras, girdles, make-up, and other "women-garbage" into a "Freedom Trash Can." Then they crowned a sheep "Miss America."

Not surprisingly, men were generally uncomfortable with radical feminism. Second-wave feminism, like Black Power and the New Left, did not fit comfortably within the political economy of white, male-dominated new liberalism.

1968: A Tumultuous Year

In 1968 the stresses and strains of the Great Society came together to produce the most tumultuous year in the United States since World War II. While Fred Downs lay wounded in an Army hospital, the Viet Cong and North Vietnamese launched bold, sometimes suicidal attacks all over South Vietnam on the first day of Tet, the Vietnamese new year. Although U.S. and South Vietnamese forces inflicted punishing losses on the attackers, the Tet Offensive shocked Americans. If the United States was winning the war, how could the North Vietnamese and the Viet Cong have struck so daringly? Many Americans who had supported the decision to send troops into South Vietnam now began to believe the war was unwinnable.

The Tet Offensive doomed Johnson's increasingly troubled administration. The president needed to send reinforcements to Vietnam, but he knew public opinion would oppose the move. As it was, he could not even pay for more troops. The economy would not support both the war and the Great Society any longer. The political situation was bad, too. On March 12 Senator Eugene McCarthy, an antiwar candidate, nearly beat Johnson in New Hampshire's Democratic primary. Four days later, Senator Robert Kennedy, the younger brother of John Kennedy, announced his own candidacy for the Democratic nomination. Besieged by the war, the economy, and the presidential campaign, Johnson went on television the night of March 31. He announced that he had halted the bombing of much of North Vietnam and indicated his willingness to talk peace with the North Vietnamese. Then Johnson, drained by events, announced that he would not run again for president.

Johnson had painfully accepted new limits on the war, the economy, the Great Society, and his own career. During 1968, Congressional leaders forced him to agree to spending cuts for Great Society programs. Johnson did not have the money or the clout for new welfare programs, new initiatives to improve race relations, or even the space program, that symbol of great liberal dreams. The president continued the Apollo program but abandoned other space projects. The Great Society was coming back down to earth.

Meanwhile, the United States was torn by upheaval and violence. In the first six months of 1968, students carried out demonstrations at 101 colleges and universities. On April 4, Martin Luther King, Jr., was assassinated in Memphis, Tennessee, where he had gone to support striking African-American and white sanitation workers. King's assassination set off riots in more than 100 cities. Forty-one African

Americans and five whites died. African Americans "have had all they can stand," two black psychologists wrote.

The violence soon spread to the presidential campaign. After winning the California Democratic primary on the evening of June 5, Robert Kennedy was shot. Kennedy's death the next morning left Eugene McCarthy to contest the Democratic presidential nomination with Vice President Hubert Humphrey of Minnesota, who still supported the American war effort in Vietnam. Humphrey won the nomination at the Democratic convention in Chicago in August, but the party was deeply divided. Outside the convention hall, Mayor Daley's police battled in the streets with antiwar demonstrators.

The Republican Party nominated Richard Nixon, the man who lost to John Kennedy in 1960. A critic of the Great Society, Nixon promised to end the Vietnam War and unify the country. Nixon tried to exploit the nation's social divisions with promises to speak for "the forgotten Americans, the nonshouters, the nondemonstrators." Running as a third-party candidate, the segregationist former governor of Alabama, George Wallace, reached out even more bluntly to middle- and working-class whites who increasingly resented African Americans and their liberal benefactors.

Like 1960, the 1968 election produced a narrow outcome with large consequences, but this time, Nixon was the winner. Although Humphrey gained in the polls by distancing himself from Johnson's Vietnam policy, the vice president could not overcome the troubles of the Democratic Party and the Great Society. Nixon attracted 43.4 percent of the popular vote to Humphrey's 42.7 percent and Wallace's 13.5 percent. Although the Democrats retained control of the House and Senate, the liberals' eight-year hold on the White House had been broken.

Over the course of 1968, the new liberalism had finally lost its hold on the nation. The Johnson administration could not handle the demands of African Americans, youth, and women, win the war in Vietnam, or stabilize the economy. The violence of 1968 testified to the frustration of many Americans with the Great Society, as did the outcome of the presidential election.

CONCLUSION

In 1960 Nixon's defeat signaled the rise of the new liberalism. In 1968 his victory marked liberalism's fall. The end of liberal dominance marked the end of illusions about limitless American power. John Kennedy's confident America—able to "pay any price, bear any burden, meet any hardship, support any friend, oppose any foe"—had vanished. By 1968 the American economy could no longer "pay any price." The United States could not successfully support its friends in South Vietnam or defeat the North Vietnamese and the Viet Cong. The government could not fulfill the ambitious plans of the New Frontier and the Great Society. Instead, the nation was deeply divided by generation, race, and gender. The assassinations of Robert Kennedy and Martin Luther King, Jr., dramatized the breakdown of the political system. The liberal approach to political economy depended on the state to reform and regulate society, but now the American state no longer seemed to work.

Back in the United States in the spring of 1968, Fred Downs had to deal with his own losses. His left arm, his confidence, and his plans were gone. He had to learn how to use a prosthetic arm and to accept the break-up of his marriage. He had to learn how to deal with a divided, angry America. On the street one day, a man pointed to the hook sticking out of Downs's left sleeve. "Get that in Vietnam?" the man asked. Downs said he had. "Serves you right," the man snapped, and walked away. The United States, like that man, would have a difficult time coming to terms with the events of the 1960s.

CHRONOLOGY

1960	Lunch counter sit-ins at Greensboro, N.C. Founding of Student Nonviolent Coordinating Committee (SNCC) Formation of Students for a Democratic Society (SDS) John Kennedy elected president
1961	Bay of Pigs invasion of Cuba First U.S. suborbital space flight, by Alan Shepard Freedom Rides Beginning of SNCC voter-registration drive in Mississippi Beginning of Albany Movement in Albany, Georgia Erection of Berlin Wall Creation of Peace Corps
1962	Michael Harrington, *The Other America* Rachel Carson, *Silent Spring* First U.S. orbital space flight, by John Glenn Integration of University of Mississippi Cuban Missile Crisis
1963	Betty Friedan, *The Feminine Mystique* Clean Air Act Limited Test Ban Treaty Civil rights protests in Birmingham, Alabama Civil rights march on Washington, DC Assassination of Ngo Dinh Diem Assassination of John F. Kennedy in Dallas Lyndon B. Johnson succeeds to the presidency
1964	Beatlemania Wilderness Act Civil Rights Act of 1964

FURTHER READINGS

Terry H. Anderson, *The Movement and the Sixties: Protest in America From Greensboro to Wounded Knee* (1995). A sweeping chronicle of the varieties of protest in the 1960s.

David Farber, *The Age of Great Dreams: America in the 1960s* (1994). Offers a readable account of the decade.

Betty Friedan, *The Feminine Mystique* (1963). Explores the plight of middle-class women that helped produce liberal feminism.

Samuel P. Hays, *Beauty, Health, and Permanence: Environmental Politics in the United States* (1987). A broad study of the emergence of the modern environmental movement.

Announcement of Lyndon Johnson's "War on Poverty"
Economic OpportunityAct
Free Speech Movement
Harlem race riot
Tonkin Gulf incidents
Lyndon Johnson's landslide election as president

1965 Decision to send U.S. troops into battle in South Vietnam
Voting Rights Act of 1965
Creation of Medicare and Medicaid
Elementary and Secondary School Act
Water Quality Act
Watts race riot
Creation of National Endowment for the Arts and National
Endowment for the Humanities
Griswold v. *Connecticut*
Ralph Nader, *Unsafe at Any Speed*

1966 Founding of National Organization for Women (NOW)
Clean Waters Restoration Act
Miranda v. *Arizona*

1967 Air Quality Act
Public Broadcasting Act
Stop the Draft Week

1968 Tet Offensive in Vietnam
Assassination of Martin Luther King, Jr.
Assassination of Robert Kennedy
New York Radical Women's Miss America Protest
Richard Nixon elected president

George C. Herring, *America's Longest War: The United States and Vietnam, 1950–1975* (1996). A balanced overview of the war.

Jim Miller, *"Democracy Is in the Streets": From Port Huron to the Siege of Chicago* (1987). Explores the SDS's efforts to define and promote "participatory democracy."

Howell Raines, *My Soul Is Rested: Movement Days in the Deep South Remembered* (1977). A moving collection of interviews that vividly recreate the struggle against segregation.

 Please refer to the document CD-ROM for primary sources related to this chapter.

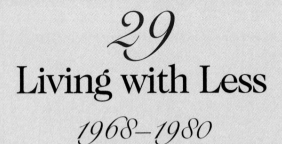

29
Living with Less
1968–1980

"*Panic at the Pump*," 1973–1974 • A New Crisis: Economic Decline
Confronting Decline: Nixon's Strategy • Refusing to Settle for
Less: Struggles for Rights • Backlash: From Radical Action to
Conservative Reaction • Political Crisis: Three Troubled
Presidencies • Conclusion

"PANIC AT THE PUMP," 1973–1974

*A*cross the country in the fall and winter of 1973–1974, frustrated drivers waited in long lines to buy gasoline. Like most Americans, these men and women took for granted cheap, abundant energy. Suddenly, the price of gas skyrocketed. Many service stations had little or no gas to sell. One news magazine reported about the "Panic at the Pump." Service-station attendants faced curses, threats, guns, and even a hand grenade in one case.

The energy shortage and its effects spread well beyond gas stations. In Pennsylvania, Ohio, and other states, truck drivers blockaded highways to protest the high cost of fuel and low speed limits. Lack of fuel grounded some commercial flights. Heating oil for homes and businesses was also in short supply. Communities opened shelters for people who could not afford to heat their homes.

The crisis dramatized a turning point in American life. Beginning in the early 1960s, the United States had been unable to produce all the oil it needed. By 1974, the nation had to import over a third of its oil, particularly from the Middle East. The energy needs of the United States and other Western countries empowered the Organization of Petroleum Exporting Countries (OPEC), third-world nations that had joined together to get higher prices for their oil. In October 1973 Arab members of OPEC refused to send petroleum to the United States and other nations that supported Israel and raised oil prices nearly 400 percent. The result was the panic at the pump.

Although the Arabs ended the oil embargo in March 1974, the underlying conditions that encouraged it remained. After the soaring liberal hopes of the early 1960s, Americans confronted sobering new realities in the 1970s. The nation did not have enough oil and other natural resources. Its economy, long prosperous, was vulnerable to foreign nations. The federal government was not strong enough to challenge those nations. Americans' consumer lifestyle now seemed as impractical as the big cars built by Detroit. As a magazine concluded, Americans were "Learning to Live With Less."

The 1970s were a difficult period of adjustment for the American political economy. Workers, employers, politicians, and families struggled with the consequences of limited resources and power. This task was made more difficult because of new demands for economic opportunity and political rights from many disadvantaged Americans, who had already lived with less for too long. By the end of the decade, the United States had not solved the problem of equality and the other challenges of living with less.

✄

A New Crisis: Economic Decline

The crises of the 1960s had focused attention on the apparent weaknesses of American politics and government. The Great Society had not established racial harmony and equality; the government had not won the Vietnam War. After the assassinations of John F. Kennedy, Robert F. Kennedy, and Martin Luther King, Jr., Americans even wondered if their society was capable of democratic politics and peaceful change.

The events of the 1970s intensified concerns about the capacity of government to achieve national goals and serve the people. They also focused Americans' attention on a new crisis—the economy. By the end of the 1970s, Americans wondered whether the economy, like the political system, would ever work smoothly again.

The Sources of Economic Decline

There were signs of economic decline almost everywhere. Although the economy continued to grow, the productivity of American workers peaked in 1966 and then began to fall. Corporate profits dropped off after the mid-1960s; the growth rate of the gross national product slowed; poverty remained; unemployment increased; and inflation, which usually dropped when unemployment rose, also increased. The unprecedented combination of high unemployment and high inflation led to the coining of a new word—stagflation.

There were several major reasons for American economic decline. Along with the energy crisis, the United States suffered from increasing competition from Japan, West Germany, and other nations, which, thanks to American aid after World

War II, now had efficient, up-to-date industries. As a result, these nations rivaled the United States not only abroad, but even in the American market.

The rise of Japan was the most dramatic of these developments. By the 1970s, Japan's factories turned out high-quality products. Japanese televisions and other electronic goods filled American homes. Japanese cars—small, well made, and fuel efficient—attracted American buyers worried about the high price of gas.

Because of such competition, the United States fell back in the international economic race. In 1950, the nation had accounted for 40 percent of the value of all the goods and services produced around the globe. By 1970 that figure was down to 23 percent. During these years, the American share of world trade dropped nearly 50 percent. By the end of the 1970s, the United States imported more manufactured goods than it exported.

Long an emblem of security and stability, American corporations suddenly appeared vulnerable. In 1970, the Penn Central Railroad went bankrupt, and only massive aid from the federal government saved the giant Lockheed Aircraft company. Other corporations thrived by becoming multinationals, building factories and other facilities overseas and thus directing jobs and dollars away from the American economy.

The federal government also played a part in the economic predicament. Massive government spending, particularly for defense, had stimulated the economy from the 1940s to the 1960s, but by the 1970s defense spending did not have the same effect. In addition, the government's huge expenditures for the Vietnam War promoted inflation.

In the 1960s, the liberal followers of John Maynard Keynes had been confident that they understood the secret of maintaining prosperity. They believed the federal government could manipulate its budget to stabilize the economy. The economists were unprepared for the novel problem of stagflation. "The rules of economics," admitted the chairman of the Federal Reserve, "are not working quite the way they used to."

The Impact of Decline

Shaped by a broad range of factors, economic decline began to reshape life in the United States. By the 1970s, it seemed as if the industrial revolution was being reversed. As factories closed, Americans witnessed the deindustrialization of their country. Huge steel plants, the symbol of American industrial might, stood empty. Manufacturers switched the production of televisions to Canada, Japan, Taiwan, and Hong Kong. Food-processing companies moved their operations to Mexico. These developments intensified the trend, first evident in the 1950s, toward a service-centered economy. In the 1970s, most new jobs were in the sales and retail sectors.

For American workers, the consequences of deindustrialization were devastating. Heavy industry had been the stronghold of the labor movement. Organized labor lost members, power, and influence. By the late 1970s, less than one in four workers belonged to a union.

The shift away from unionized industrial jobs eroded Americans' incomes. After rising from the 1950s into the 1960s, workers' spendable income began to drop by the mid-1970s. To keep up, more and more women took full-time jobs outside the home, but not all Americans could find work. As the huge baby-boom generation came of age, the economy did not produce enough jobs.

Economic decline accelerated the transformation of America's regions. People and power had been moving from north to south and east to west for a long time.

Population Change

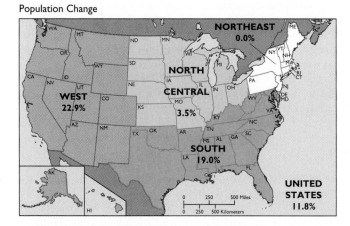

Map 29–1   Movement from Rustbelt to Sunbelt
The percentages track the shift of population (top) and manufacturing jobs (bottom) from the Northeast and the Midwest to the South and West between 1970 and 1980.

Source: D.K. Adams et al., An Atlas of North American Affairs, 2nd ed. (London and New York: Methuen).

Manufacturing Output

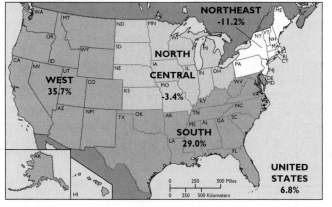

The energy crisis and deindustrialization sped up that movement (see Map 29–1). The Northeast and the Midwest, home to so many aging steel mills and auto plants, suffered especially.

Fleeing deindustrialization, many northerners migrated south to the band of states ranging from Florida to California. As the Sunbelt boomed, farms turned into suburbs and cities such as Orlando, Houston, Dallas, Phoenix, San Diego, and Anaheim exploded in size.

With mild winters, the Sunbelt did not suffer so much from high oil prices. If anything, Texas and the southwestern states, rich in oil and natural gas reserves, profited from the energy crisis. The Sunbelt was also home to new high-technology businesses: aerospace firms, electronics companies, and defense contractors. The Sunbelt was also at the cutting edge of the service economy, with its emphasis on leisure and consumption.

CONFRONTING DECLINE: NIXON'S STRATEGY

Richard Nixon was the first president to confront the decline of America's post-World War II prosperity and power. Nixon and his administration understood that the American political economy would have to live with less. The president also recognized that the failure of the war effort in Vietnam marked the end of America's cold-war pretensions. Nixon would not claim that the nation had unlimited power.

Nixon also recognized that the upheavals of the 1960s had weakened liberalism and its supporters. According to the president, the troubles of Lyndon Johnson's Great Society demonstrated the failings of the activist, liberal approach to the political economy. He believed, too, that the crises of the 1960s created opportunities for new people and new political economic approaches. Abroad and at home, the new president tried to take advantage of those opportunities.

A New Foreign Policy

The president and his national security advisor, Henry Kissinger, still regarded Communism as a menace and saw the cold-war rivalry between the United States and the Soviet Union as the defining reality of the modern world. However, Nixon and Kissinger understood that the relative decline of American power dictated a new approach to the cold war. During Nixon's presidency, the United States pulled back from its promise to intervene around the world to stop the spread of Communism. Nixon moved to ease tensions with the Soviet Union and the People's Republic of China and to end American participation in the Vietnam War. By the end of Nixon's presidency, the role of the United States in the world had changed considerably.

The twin pillars of the new foreign policy were the Nixon Doctrine and détente. In a speech in July 1969, the president announced that the United States "cannot—and will not—conceive all the plans, design all the programs, execute all the decisions and undertake all the defense of the free nations of the world." America would continue to provide a nuclear umbrella, but its allies would have to defend themselves. This Nixon Doctrine amounted to a repudiation of the Truman Doctrine, the 1947 promise "to support free peoples who are resisting attempted subjugation by armed minorities or by outside pressures."

The United States also pursued a new relationship with the Soviet Union and the People's Republic of China. Nixon and Kissinger wanted to lessen the cost of America's rivalry with these two Communist nuclear powers. Separate agreements with the Soviet Union and China would, the American leaders hoped, keep those two nations from combining forces against the United States. Nixon and Kissinger therefore worked to establish détente, the relaxation of tensions.

At the start of Nixon's presidency, the United States had not recognized the legitimacy of the People's Republic of China. Instead, America supported the Communists' bitter foes, the Nationalist Chinese regime on Taiwan. In February 1972, Nixon became the first American president to go to mainland China. He gave the Chinese leaders what they most wanted—a promise that the United States would eventually withdraw its troops from Taiwan. The two sides also made clear that they opposed any Soviet attempt to dominate Asia.

Nixon's trip brought American policy in line with the reality of the 1970s and underscored the gradual ending of anti-Communist hysteria back home in America. As Nixon intended, the trip also left the Soviets with the frightening possibility of a Chinese–American alliance.

Nixon did not want a confrontation with the Soviets. The United States no longer had clear military superiority. Instead, the president sought détente. Above all, he wanted the Soviets to agree to limit their long-range or strategic nuclear arsenals. The Soviets also wished to reduce the expense and danger of the cold war and to counter Nixon's overture to the Chinese. Moreover, they badly needed American grain to help feed their own people.

Under these circumstances, the two sides began talks on the Strategic Arms Limitations Treaty (SALT I) in 1969. In May 1972, three months after his trip to China, Nixon became the first American president to travel to Moscow, where he signed the SALT treaty, limiting for five years the number of each nation's nuclear missiles. An Anti-Ballistic Missile (ABM) treaty sharply limited the number of defensive missiles that the two sides could deploy. Although they did not stop the arms race, the ABM and SALT treaties symbolized the American and Soviet agreement that "there is no alternative to . . . peaceful coexistence."

Ending the Vietnam War

Along with other motivations, the Nixon administration sought better relations with the Soviet Union and the People's Republic of China to help end the Vietnam War. Nixon and Kissinger hoped the Soviets and the Chinese would pressure the North Vietnamese to accept a peace agreement. The president needed such an agreement. Nixon knew the United States could not win the Vietnam War. Meanwhile, the ongoing conflict divided the American people and undermined American prestige and power around the world.

To appease public opinion, Nixon began to bring American soldiers home in 1969. Without those soldiers, he had a hard time persuading North Vietnam to accept the continued existence of South Vietnam. The president attempted to resolve this dilemma with a policy known as "Vietnamization," or encouraging the South Vietnamese to take over their own defense. However, the South Vietnamese military alone could not beat back the Communists.

Accordingly, Nixon turned to U.S. airpower to support South Vietnamese troops. In March 1969, he authorized B-52 raids on North Vietnamese sanctuaries in Cambodia. Because bombing this neutral country might outrage American and world opinion, the president kept the raids secret. However, the Cambodian operation did not force North Vietnam to make peace. Secret negotiations between Henry Kissinger and North Vietnamese diplomats also went nowhere.

Meanwhile, Nixon's actions angered many Americans. News of the secret bombings leaked out. In October, millions of Americans participated in Moratorium Day, a dramatic break from business as usual, to protest the war. In November, more than 250,000 people staged a "March Against Death" in Washington. That month, Americans learned about one of the most troubling episodes of the war. On March 16, 1968, United States soldiers had shot and killed between 200 and 500 unarmed South Vietnamese women, children, and old men in the hamlet of My Lai. This atrocity led to the 1970 court martial and eventual conviction of Lieutenant William Calley, Jr., for mass murder.

Demonstrations and public opinion did not stop the president from using violence to force a peace agreement. When General Lon Nol, the new pro-American leader of Cambodia, appealed for United States aid to stop a Communist insurgency, a joint United States–South Vietnamese force invaded Cambodia in April 1970. The Cambodian invasion produced turmoil in the United States. Students demonstrated on campuses across the country. On May 4, National Guard troops fired at an unarmed crowd of protesters at Kent State University in Ohio. Four students died. Ten days later, state police killed two African-American students at

Death at Kent State University: The body of one of four students shot by the Ohio National Guard during protests over the U.S. invasion of Cambodia in 1970.

Jackson State College in Mississippi. These deaths intensified the outrage over the invasion of Cambodia. Students went out on strike at about 450 campuses.

As American troop withdrawals continued, the war and the peace negotiations dragged on. Vietnamization continued to founder. Meanwhile, the *New York Times* began publishing the so-called Pentagon Papers, a secret history of the American involvement in Vietnam. The documents, which made clear that the Johnson administration had misled the American people, further undermined support for the war. The Nixon administration tried unsuccessfully to persuade the Supreme Court to block publication of the papers.

Unable to stop the publication of the Pentagon Papers or secure a peace agreement, Nixon stepped up efforts to pressure North Vietnam into a settlement. When the North Vietnamese Army swept across the border into South Vietnam in March 1972, the president struck back with Operation Linebacker, an aerial attack against North Vietnam. When negotiations stalled again, the president intensified the air raids in December. On January 27, 1973, negotiators signed a peace agreement in Paris. For the United States, at least, the Vietnam War was over.

The United States had gone to war to preserve an anti-Communist South Vietnam, but the peace agreement did not guarantee South Vietnam's survival or require the North Vietnamese to pull their troops out of South Vietnam. The cease-fire came at a heavy cost. Twenty thousand Americans and more than 600,000 North and South Vietnamese soldiers had died since Nixon took office in 1969. The number of civilian casualties will never be known. Nixon had ended U.S. participation in the Vietnam War, but the president's critics asked whether four more years of fighting had really been necessary when the result was such a flawed peace agreement.

Chile and the Middle East

Détente did not end U.S. opposition to Communist initiatives around the world. It also did not restore American power abroad. Nixon, like the presidents before him, refused to accept the establishment of a Communist regime in the Western Hemisphere. In 1970, he ordered the CIA to block the election of Salvador Allende, a Marxist, as president of Chile. Allende was elected anyway. The CIA then destabilized Allende's regime by helping right-wing parties, driving up the price of bread, and encouraging demonstrations. When a military coup murdered Allende and thousands of his followers, the United States denied responsibility and offered financial assistance to the new leader, Augusto Pinochet.

In the Middle East, the Nixon administration also displayed its hostility to Communism and its inability to shape events decisively. During the Six Day War in 1967, Israel defeated Egyptian and Syrian forces and occupied territory belonging to Egypt, Syria, and Jordan. Seeking revenge, Egypt and Syria attacked Israel in October 1973, on Yom Kippur, the holiest day of the Jewish calendar. When the United States sent critical supplies to Israel, Arab countries responded with an oil embargo. Meanwhile, the Soviets supplied the Arabs and pressed for a role in the region. Determined to keep out the Soviet Union, Nixon put American nuclear forces on alert. Kissinger mediated between the combatants, who agreed to pull back their troops in January 1974. Although the embargo ended, American weakness was obvious. Supporting Israel, the United States still needed the Arabs' oil. Nixon and Kissinger held back the Soviet Union, but they could not bring peace to the Middle East.

A Mixed Domestic Record

Nixon had a mixed domestic record. In some areas, his administration shrank the federal government and the Great Society. In others, it accepted new liberal initiatives. Meanwhile, the president had little success in dealing with an ailing economy. The problem of decline, imaginatively addressed in Nixon's foreign policy, proved more difficult to handle at home.

Nixon took office with conventional Republican goals. He wanted the federal government to balance its budget and shed some of its power. In 1969, the president called for a New Federalism, in which Washington would return "a greater share of control to state and local governments and to the people."

During the Nixon years, there were spending cuts for some programs, including defense. The fate of the space program epitomized the new budgetary realities. On July 20, 1969, a lunar landing module touched down on the moon. As astronaut Neil Armstrong set foot on the surface, he proclaimed, "That's one small step for man, one giant leap for mankind." The United States had beaten the Soviets to the moon. This triumph suggested that there was still no limit to what Americans could do. There were, however, firm limits to what the space program could do. The administration slashed NASA's budget.

The New Federalism also put limits on Washington. In 1972 the administration persuaded Congress to pass a revenue-sharing plan that allowed state and local governments to spend funds collected by the federal government. But the president left largely intact the massive New Deal and Great Society programs. By 1971, the unsettled economy and the cost of big government had produced a huge budget deficit.

The president did try to reform the federal welfare system put in place by the New Deal. His administration tried to replace the largest federal welfare program,

Aid to Families with Dependent Children, with a controversial system inspired by presidential aide Daniel Patrick Moynihan, a Harvard sociologist. Moynihan's Family Assistance Plan would have provided poor families with a guaranteed minimum annual income, but it also would have required the heads of poor households to accept any available jobs. Opposed by both liberals and conservatives, the program failed to pass Congress.

Meanwhile, the Nixon administration went along with several liberal initiatives that expanded the government's regulatory powers. By the end of the 1960s, the middle class worried that corporations did not protect workers, consumers, or the environment. A grassroots environmental movement grew rapidly, and in April 1970 tens of millions of Americans celebrated the first Earth Day.

Liberals in Congress responded to popular opinion by establishing three new federal regulatory agencies: the Environmental Protection Agency (EPA), the Occupational Safety and Health Administration (OSHA), and the Consumer Product Safety Commission. These agencies considerably enhanced the government's power over corporations, as did a series of measures to safeguard coastlines and endangered species and to limit the use of pesticides, the strip-mining of coal, and the pollution of air and water.

An Uncertain Economic Policy

Nixon reluctantly accepted liberal policies as he struggled with the economy. The Nixon administration faced inflation, rising unemployment, and falling corporate profits. Beginning in 1970, the president tried unsuccessfully to persuade business to control price increases and organized labor to limit wage demands.

The situation was complicated by the U.S. dollar's role in the international monetary system. Since the Bretton Woods conference during World War II, many other nations had tied the value of their own currencies to the dollar. The value of the dollar, in turn, had been supported by the U.S. commitment to the gold standard. The federal government had promised to give an ounce of gold in return for 35 dollars. By the 1970s, however, strong European economies held too many dollars and the United States held too little gold. If other countries had demanded gold for their dollars, panic could have followed.

In response, Nixon announced his New Economic Policy in August 1971. To prevent a gold crisis, the president took the United States off the gold standard. To strengthen the United States against foreign competition, Nixon lowered the value of the dollar and slapped new tariffs on imports. To slow inflation, he authorized a freeze on wages and prices.

Wage and price controls did not solve the underlying economic problems that caused inflation. The ongoing cost of the Vietnam War, along with the Arab oil embargo, continued to drive up prices. Nixon and his advisers had no domestic counterpart to détente.

REFUSING TO SETTLE FOR LESS: STRUGGLES FOR RIGHTS

In the late 1960s and 1970s, African Americans and women continued their struggles for rights that they had long been denied. Their example and the optimistic promises of liberalism spurred other disadvantaged groups to demand recognition. By the end of the 1970s, American society—however tentatively and reluctantly— was more committed to equality for women and minorities.

African Americans' Struggle for Racial Justice

After the assassination of Martin Luther King, Jr., in 1968, the NAACP, the SCLC, and other civil rights organizations continued to press for integration. By the 1970s, national attention focused on two relatively new and controversial means of promoting racial equality—affirmative action and mandatory school busing.

First ordered by the Johnson administration, affirmative action required businesses, universities, and other institutions receiving federal money to provide opportunities for women and nonwhites. Supporters viewed the policy as a way to make up for past and present discrimination. Opponents argued that affirmative action was itself a form of discrimination that reduced opportunities for whites, particularly white men.

Nixon generally supported the principle of affirmative action. His administration developed the Philadelphia Plan, which encouraged the construction industry to meet targets for hiring minority workers. In 1978, the Supreme Court offered qualified support for affirmative action with its decision in *Regents of the University of California v. Allan Bakke.* While the court barred schools from using fixed admissions quotas for different racial groups, it did allow educational institutions to use race as an admissions criteria. By the end of the 1970s, affirmative action had become an important means of increasing diversity in schools and other institutions.

School busing was more controversial than affirmative action. By the late 1960s, the Supreme Court had become impatient with delays in integrating the nation's schools. Even in the North, where there had been no de jure or legal segregation, there was still extensive de facto segregation. In *Swann v. Charlotte-Mecklenburg Board of Education,* the court upheld the mandatory busing of thousands of children to desegregate schools. To its advocates, busing seemed to be the best way to ensure equal education for African-American pupils. But many Americans opposed the policy because they did not want integration or because they did not want children taken out of neighborhood schools.

Nixon sided with the opponents of busing. Privately ordering his aides to enforce busing less vigorously, the president publicly called for a "moratorium" on new busing plans. Some communities implemented busing peacefully. Others faced protest and turmoil. In 1974, a federal court ordered busing in Boston. When the white-dominated local school committee refused to comply, a federal judge imposed a busing plan on the community. Working-class and lower middle-class whites protested plans to bus students between the predominantly African-American neighborhood of Roxbury and the largely Irish-American neighborhood of South Boston. In "Southie," whites taunted and injured black students. The violence spread to Roxbury and continued through the fall. With busing and affirmative action, the civil rights movement seemed to have reached its limits.

Women's Liberation

By the 1970s, the movement for women's liberation was flourishing. To commemorate the 50th anniversary of the ratification of the women's suffrage amendment to the Constitution, the Women's Strike for Equality took place on August 26, 1970.

The women's liberation movement, like the struggle for African-American equality, was diverse. Liberal feminist groups, such as the National Organization for Women (NOW), concentrated on equal public opportunities for women. Radical feminists focused on a broader range of private and public issues. Oppression, they insisted, took place in the bedroom and the kitchen as well as the school and the

Police break up a crowd of demonstrators opposed to court-ordered busing to integrate public schools in Boston in 1974.

workplace. Some radical feminists blamed women's plight on the inequalities of capitalism; others traced the oppression of women to men. Cultural feminists insisted that women's culture was different from and superior to male culture. They felt that women should create their own separate institutions rather than seek formal equality with men. Some lesbian feminists took this separatist logic one step further to argue that women should avoid heterosexual relationships.

Women's liberation made its mark on the media. In 1972, Gloria Steinem began to publish the feminist magazine *Ms.* On television, popular sitcoms portrayed independent women. Some feminists condemned the availability of pornography, which, they argued, incited violence against women.

In the 1970s, female activists focused on three public issues—access to abortion, equal treatment in schools and workplaces, and passage of the Equal Rights Amendment (ERA) to the Constitution. Abortions were generally illegal and unsafe; in the 1970s, women went to court to challenge the law. In *Roe* v. *Wade* in 1973, the Supreme Court ruled a Texas antiabortion law unconstitutional on the grounds that it violated the "right to privacy" guaranteed by the Ninth and Fourteenth Amendments. With this decision, abortion began to become legal and widely available.

Like the civil rights movement, the women's movement demanded equal treatment in schools and workplaces. Women filed many complaints against discrimination by employers. At first reluctant, the Nixon administration moved to open up government employment to women and to press colleges and businesses to end discriminatory practices. In 1972, Congress approved Title IX of the Higher Education Act, which required schools and universities receiving federal funds to give equal opportunities to women and men in admissions, athletics, and other programs.

The women's movement also continued the long-time struggle to enact the ERA. "Equality of rights under the law," the amendment read, "shall not be denied or abridged by the United States or by any State on account of sex." In 1972 Congress passed the ERA. If 38 states had ratified the amendment within 7 years, it would have become law. Within a year, 28 states had ratified.

Despite this progress, the ERA and women's liberation encountered considerable opposition. To male critics, feminists were a "small band of braless bubbleheads" who suffered from "defeminization." Conservative women activists led a backlash against feminism and equal rights. Phyllis Schlafly organized an effective campaign against the ERA. Although more states ratified the amendment, some rescinded their votes, and the ERA never became law.

The ERA's defeat underscored the challenges that the women's movement faced. Women still did not have full equality in American society. Nevertheless, women had more control over their bodies, more access to education, and more opportunity in the workplace, and women's issues were at the center of American public life.

Mexican Americans and "Brown Power"

In the 1960s and 1970s, Mexican Americans, the second-largest racial minority in the United States, developed a new self-consciousness. Proudly identifying themselves as Chicanos, Mexican Americans organized to protest poverty and discrimination.

Despite the federal efforts to keep out Mexican immigrants, the Mexican-American population grew rapidly. By 1980, at least 7 million Americans claimed Mexican heritage. The great majority lived in Arizona, California, Colorado, New Mexico, and Texas. By the 1970s, most Chicanos lived in urban areas. More than 1 million lived in Los Angeles. Chicanos as a group earned substantially less than did Anglos (white Americans of non-Hispanic descent). One in four Mexican-American families lived in poverty in the mid-1970s.

Chicanos faced racism and discrimination. The media stereotyped them as lazy and shifty. Schools in Chicano neighborhoods were underfunded. In some California schools, Mexican-American children could not eat with Anglo children. California and Texas law prohibited teaching in Spanish.

Although Chicanos were not legally prevented from voting, gerrymandering diluted their political power. Despite its large Mexican-American population, Los Angeles had no Hispanic representative on the city council at the end of the 1960s. The justice system often treated Chicanos unfairly.

The combination of poverty and discrimination marked Chicano life. Many Mexican Americans were crowded into *barrios*, rundown neighborhoods. In the countryside, many lived without hot water or toilets. Infant mortality was high, and life expectancy was low. Nationwide, almost half of the Mexican-American population was functionally illiterate.

Encouraged by the civil rights movement, Mexican Americans protested against poverty and injustice for migrant farm workers. In the fertile San Joaquin Valley of California, the Mexican Americans who labored for powerful fruit growers earned as little as 10 cents an hour and lived in miserable conditions. César Chávez, a former migrant worker influenced by Martin Luther King, Jr.'s nonviolent creed, helped them organize the National Farm Worker Association. In 1965 this union went on strike. The growers, accusing Chávez of Communist ties, called on police, strikebreakers, intimidation, and violence. Chávez's nonviolent tactics, which included a 25-day hunger strike in 1968, gradually appealed to liberals and other

Americans. Chávez also initiated a successful nationwide consumer boycott against grapes. Under this pressure, the grape growers began to settle with the union.

While Chávez turned for inspiration to Martin Luther King, Jr., other Chicanos responded to the nationalism of the Black Power movement. In New Mexico, Reies López "Tiger" Tijerina, a former preacher, favored separatism over integration and nationalism over assimilation. He created the Alianza Federal de Mercedes (Federal Alliance of Land Grants) to take back land that the United States had supposedly stolen from Mexicans. In 1967, Tijerina's raid on a courthouse and other militant acts earned him a jail sentence and a reputation as the Robin Hood of New Mexico.

Chicano activism flourished in the late 1960s. In California in 1969, college students began the Movimiento Estudiantil Chicano de Aztlán (Chicano Student Movement of Aztlán). The organization was known by its initials, MEChA, which spelled the word for "match" in the Spanish dialect of Mexican Americans. MEChA was meant to be the match that would kindle social change for Chicanos. In Crystal City, Texas, a boycott of Anglo businesses led to the formation of La Raza Unida, a political party that won control of the local school board in 1970. Thousands of students marked September 16, 1969, Mexican Independence Day, with the First National Chicano Boycott of high schools.

All these protests and organizations reflected a strong sense of Chicano pride and a desire to preserve Chicano heritage. Protesters wanted bilingual education and Mexican-American studies in the schools and equal opportunity and affirmative action in schools and workplaces. Most fundamentally, Mexican-American activism reflected the desire for empowerment, for what some called "Brown Power."

Asian-American Activism

Asian Americans also pressed for rights and recognition as the 1960s ended. Like Chicanos, Asian Americans confronted a history of discrimination in the United States. They, too, had to contend with denigrating stereotypes and hurtful epithets.

The small size of the Asian-American population limited organization and protest, but the Immigration Act of 1965 had made possible increased Asian migration to the United States. From the 1960s through the 1970s, the war in Southeast Asia, political conditions in the Philippines, and economic opportunity spurred waves of Asian immigration. By 1980 America was home to more than 3 million Asian immigrants, including 812,000 Chinese, 781,000 Filipinos, and 716,000 Japanese. Overall, there were 3.7 million Americans of Asian descent. The majority lived in the Pacific states and in cities.

Asian-American activism followed the pattern of other minority movements. By the late 1960s, Asian Americans were demonstrating a new ethnic self-consciousness and pride. Many Asian Americans saw themselves not only as Chinese or Japanese, inheritors of a particular national and ethnic heritage, but as members of a broader, pan-Asian group.

In 1968, the Asian American Political Alliance (AAPA) emerged on the campus of the University of California at Berkeley to unite Chinese, Japanese, and Filipino students. Asian Americans pushed for Asian studies programs on college campuses. By the end of the 1970s, a number of colleges and universities had responded to Asian-American students' demands for courses and programs.

Asian-American activism spread beyond campuses. In 1974 protests forced the hiring of Chinese-American workers to help build the Confucius Plaza complex in New York City's Chinatown. In San Francisco, activists brought suit against the public school system on behalf of 1,800 Chinese pupils. In *Lau* v. *Nichols* in 1974, the

Supreme Court declared that school systems had to provide bilingual instruction for non-English-speaking students.

Japanese groups demanded compensation for the U.S. government's internment of Japanese Americans during World War II. In 1976 Washington did rescind Executive Order 9066, the 1942 presidential directive that allowed internment to occur. But the federal government did not make a more comprehensive settlement until 1988.

Asian Americans, like Chicanos, made only limited gains by 1980. However, Asian Americans had developed a new consciousness and new organizations; they had also forced real change at the local and national levels.

The Struggle for Native-American Rights

African-American activism also inspired Native Americans. Native Americans' struggle also reflected their distinctive relationship with the federal government.

After many years of decline and stagnation, the Indian population had grown rapidly since World War II (see Map 29–2). By 1970, there were nearly 800,000 Native Americans, half of whom lived on reservations. Native Americans were divided into about 175 tribes and other groups, but, like Mexican Americans and African Americans, they were united by poor living conditions and persistent discrimination. Native Americans had the lowest average family income of any ethnic group. Reservations had especially high unemployment rates. Many Indian children attended substandard schools.

Native-American life was shaped by the Indians' unique relationship with the federal government. Many resented the Bureau of Indian Affairs (BIA), which had long patronized and exploited tribes. Like African-American and Mexican-American separatists, some Native Americans began to see themselves as a nation apart. Calling themselves "prisoners of war," these Native Americans struck an aggressive stance, expressed in such slogans as "Custer Had It Coming" and "Red Power."

Beginning in the 1960s, a Native-American movement emerged to protest federal policy, combat stereotypes, unite tribes, and perpetuate their cultures. Native Americans called for an end to employment discrimination and to the sale of Indian lands and resources to corporations. Native Americans also condemned the use of Indian symbols by schools and sports teams and demanded Indian-centered school curricula.

Some Indians favored more radical action. Copying the Black Panthers, a group of Native Americans in Minneapolis, Minnesota, formed an "Indian Patrol," clad in red berets, to defend against the police. The patrol evolved into the American Indian Movement (AIM), which spread to other cities. In 1969, AIM activists occupied the abandoned federal prison on Alcatraz Island in San Francisco Bay and told the authorities to leave. The occupiers unsuccessfully offered the government "$24 in glass beads and cloth" for the prison, which they planned to convert into a Native-American museum and center. In 1972 and 1973, AIM took over BIA headquarters in Washington and the BIA office in Wounded Knee, South Dakota.

The Native-American rights movement made few gains in a society worried about limited resources and an uncertain future. Through the Indian Self-Determination Act of 1975, the federal government did allow Native Americans more independence on the reservations. Still, Native Americans themselves were divided about their relationship to the government. Many tribal leaders wanted to continue selling off their lands through the BIA, but AIM assailed Native Americans

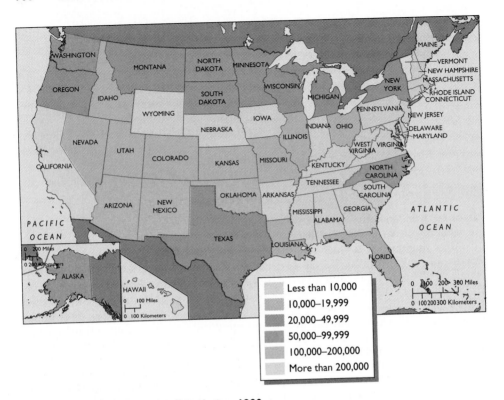

Map 29–2   Native-American Population, 1980
After rapid growth in the years following World War II, the Native-American population remained largest west of the Mississippi River, and above all, across the Southwest. But there were substantial numbers of Native Americans in every region.
Source: Data from Statistical Abstract of the United States, 1973, p. 348; and 1984, pp. 375–376, 463, 760.

who accepted the BIA's authority. Despite such divisions, the movement had forced American society to confront the inequitable treatment of Indians more directly than at any time since the Great Depression.

Homosexuals and Gay Power

Singled out for persecution in the McCarthy era, most homosexual men and women had learned to conceal their sexual identity in public. Mainstream American culture mercilessly ridiculed homosexuals as "faggots," "queers," and "dykes." The medical profession treated homosexuality as an illness. In the late 1960s, that began to change.

A catalyst for change was the struggle of women, racial minorities, and students. Another was a police raid on the Stonewall Inn, a gay bar in New York City's Greenwich Village, in June 1969. Such raids were commonplace, but this time, to the surprise of the police, gay men resisted.

Stonewall became a rallying cry for gay activism. The Gay Liberation Front, the Student Homophile League, and other organizations appeared. Activists picketed companies that discriminated against gays, and homosexuals socialized more openly. On the first anniversary of Stonewall, 10,000 gay men and lesbians paraded down New York's Sixth Avenue. "Two, four, six, eight!" marchers chanted. "Gay is just as good as straight!" Their movement began to have an effect on mainstream culture. In 1974, the American Psychiatric Association decided that homosexuality was not a "mental disorder" and that homosexuals deserved equal rights.

The emerging movements for gay, Native-American, and Chicano rights, along with the ongoing crusades of women and African Americans, made a deep impact on the 1970s. American society could not escape demands for equal rights and opportunities for all people. Women, gays, African Americans, Native Americans, and Chicanos did not win full equality, of course, but these groups made important gains in the 1970s.

BACKLASH: FROM RADICAL ACTION TO CONSERVATIVE REACTION

By the close of the 1960s, American society reverberated with demands to end the war in Vietnam and allow equal rights at home. Surrounded by protests, some hopeful activists believed the United States would be torn apart and remade, but the revolution never came. Radical movements squabbled and fell apart. Many Americans abandoned activism for their own private concerns; others angrily rejected protest movements. Encouraging this backlash, President Nixon won re-election in 1972.

"The Movement" and the "Me-Decade"

Many activists believed that the struggles of women and minorities, along with student protests and the antiwar movement, were creating a single coalition, known simply as "the Movement." At the start of the 1970s, it seemed as if the Movement might take shape, but the different protest groups never merged, and they were often hostile to each other.

In addition, key groups within the Movement fell apart. Plagued by internal divisions, SDS held its last convention in 1969. The violent Weathermen called for "Days of Rage" in the "pig city" of Chicago in October 1969, but only a few hundred protesters showed up. Transient radical groups bombed or burned corporate headquarters and other "establishment" targets but succeeded only in giving the New Left and the Movement a bad name. The FBI secretly penetrated Black Panther chapters and worked to discredit the organization. Panther leaders fled the country, went to jail, or died at the hands of police. Radical feminist groups also declined as women's liberation increasingly focused on liberal demands, such as the ERA.

Some protest movements lost their targets. After the widespread demonstrations of 1970, the antiwar movement declined as the U.S. pulled out of Vietnam. The student movement declined as young people lost some of their grievances. Around the country, colleges and universities eased parietal rules and other regulations. In 1971, the states completed ratification of the Twenty-Sixth Amendment to the Constitution, which lowered the voting age to 18.

The revolution also failed to materialize because many people turned away from activism and political engagement. Some were disillusioned by the failure of the Great Society and the duplicity of the Johnson and Nixon administrations. Others were disappointed by the limited accomplishments of radical movements. Still others found themselves caught up in therapeutic and religious movements, as Americans focused on their inner needs rather than on political change.

The 1970s, announced the writer Tom Wolfe, were the "Me-Decade." Wolfe and other observers believed Americans had become self-absorbed and narcissistic. The cause, explained the historian and social critic Christopher Lasch, was the crisis of capitalism in "an age of diminishing expectations." The fears about the self-absorbed Me-Decade were as exaggerated as the hopes for the revolutionary Movement. People did not stop hoping and working for change, but in a time of economic uncertainty and political disappointment, many Americans felt they could not afford the expansive liberal dreams of the 1960s. They had to look out for themselves.

The Plight of the White Ethnics

The "new American revolution" was a victim of anger as well as apathy. Many lower middle-class and working-class whites rejected the Movement. They felt abandoned by liberal politicians, they believed the Great Society did too little for them and too much for minorities, and they felt threatened by urban renewal projects and court-ordered busing. They resented the students and protesters who had avoided fighting in Vietnam, and many resented the women's movement. Most of all, they feared the consequences of economic decline. In a decade of deindustrialization, they faced the loss of their jobs and their standard of living.

The media painted an unflattering portrait of these Americans. The popular television comedy *All in the Family* derided its main character, the conservative Archie Bunker, who was upset with his feminist daughter, his liberal son-in-law, and all the social change around him. Underneath Archie's outbursts was frustration: "He'll never be more than what he is now," his wife Edith said, "even though he had dreams once."

In reality, the white working and lower-middle classes were not so racist and forlorn. They took renewed pride in the ethnic heritage that set them apart from other Americans. "White ethnics" used their heritage to affirm an alternative set of values—their own counterculture. For them, ethnicity meant a commitment to family, neighborhood, and religion in place of the individualistic American dream and the centralizing federal government. Most important, the white ethnics formed a large potential voting bloc, attractive to politicians.

The Conservative Counterattack

During the 1970s, the white ethnics became an important part of a conservative counterattack against radicalism, liberalism, and the Democratic Party. Assailing the Movement, Richard Nixon and the Republicans put together a coalition of white ethnics in the North and white voters in the Sunbelt. That coalition rewarded Nixon with a landslide re-election in 1972.

The Nixon administration condemned radicalism and demonstrations. "Anarchy," the president fumed, "this is the way civilizations begin to die." The Nixon administration used more than words against protesters. The president ordered IRS investigations to harass liberal and antiwar figures. He used the FBI to infiltrate and disrupt the Black Power movement, the Brown Berets, and the New Left. He made illegal domestic use of the CIA to obstruct the antiwar movement.

To oppose all the forces of disruption, Nixon also called for support from "the great silent majority of my fellow Americans." With his "southern strategy," Nixon reached out to Sunbelt voters by opposing busing, rapid integration, crime, and radicalism. He also tried to create a more conservative, less activist Supreme Court. In 1969, he named the cautious Warren Burger to succeed Earl Warren as chief justice. To fill another vacancy on the court, he nominated first a conservative South Carolina judge, Clement Haynsworth, who had angered civil rights and union leaders, and then Judge G. Harrold Carswell of Florida, a former avowed white supremacist. Both nominations failed, but the president had sent an unmistakable message to the "silent majority" and to white southerners.

The 1972 Election

The conservative counterattack paid off in the 1972 presidential election. The Republican ticket of Nixon and Vice President Spiro Agnew benefited from some unforeseen occurrences in 1972. More than any other politician, George Wallace, the segregationist governor of Alabama, rivaled Nixon's appeal to the "silent majority." But Wallace's campaign for the Democratic nomination came to an end when a would-be assassin's bullet paralyzed him from the waist down. In addition, the Democratic vice presidential nominee, Senator Thomas Eagleton of Missouri, had to withdraw over revelations about his treatment for depression.

Nixon did not really need good luck in 1972. The Democrats chose a strongly liberal senator, George McGovern of South Dakota, as the party nominee for president. McGovern's eventual running mate was another unabashed liberal, Sargent Shriver, a brother-in-law of the Kennedys. The Democratic ticket, which endorsed busing and affirmative action and opposed the Vietnam War, alienated white ethnics, white southerners, and organized labor.

Carrying 49 out of 50 states, Nixon easily won re-election in November 1972. With nearly 61 percent of the popular vote, the president scored almost as big a triumph as Lyndon Johnson in 1964, but Nixon's victory was deceptive. The election had not produced a partisan political realignment. The Democrats still controlled both houses of Congress.

Nevertheless, the 1972 election was a sign that the traditional Democratic coalition was breaking up. More broadly, Nixon's triumph, along with the failure of the Movement, the rise of the white ethnics, and the self-absorption of the Me-Decade, showed that the glory days of liberalism and radicalism were over.

POLITICAL CRISIS: THREE TROUBLED PRESIDENCIES

Nixon's triumph, the 1972 election, soon turned out to be his undoing. The discovery of illegal activities in the president's campaign led to the revelation of other improprieties and, finally, to his resignation. Nixon's successors, Gerald Ford and Jimmy Carter, could not master the problems of a divided nation discovering the limits of its power. The 1970s ended like the 1960s had, with Americans wondering whether their political system still worked.

Watergate: The Fall of Richard Nixon

Nixon's fall began when five men were caught breaking into the offices of the Democratic National Committee in the Watergate complex in Washington, DC, just before 2:00 a.m. on June 17, 1972. The five burglars had ties to Nixon's campaign organization, the Committee to Re-Elect the President (CREEP). They were attempting to repair an electronic eavesdropping device that had been previously planted in the Democrats' headquarters.

At first, Watergate had no impact on the president. He won re-election easily, but gradually, a disturbing story emerged. Two reporters for the *Washington Post*,

Bob Woodward and Carl Bernstein, revealed payments linking the five burglars to CREEP and to Nixon's White House staff. The burglars went on trial with two other former CIA agents, G. Gordon Liddy and E. Howard Hunt, who had directed the break-in for CREEP. Faced with heavy sentences in March 1973, the burglars admitted that "higher-ups" had planned the break-in and orchestrated a cover-up. One of those higher-ups, Nixon's presidential counsel John Dean, revealed his role in the Watergate affair to a grand jury. To emphasize his commitment to justice, Nixon named a special federal prosecutor, Archibald Cox, to investigate Watergate.

A Senate committee, chaired by Sam Ervin of North Carolina, began hearings on Watergate in May 1973. Testifying before the committee, a White House aide revealed that a secret taping system routinely recorded conversations in the president's Oval Office. Claiming "executive privilege," Nixon refused to turn over tapes of his conversations after the break-in. When Archibald Cox continued to press for the tapes, Nixon ordered him fired on Saturday, October 20, 1973. Attorney General Elliott Richardson and a top aide refused to carry out the order and resigned. A third official finally discharged Cox. Nixon's "Saturday Night Massacre" set off a storm of public anger. Nixon had to name a new special prosecutor, Leon Jaworski. The Democratic-controlled House of Representatives began to explore articles of impeachment against the president. "I am not a crook," Nixon insisted.

By 1974, it became clear that the Nixon administration had engaged in a shocking range of improper and illegal behavior. Infuriated by news leaks in 1969, Henry Kissinger had ordered wiretaps on the phones of newspaper reporters and his own staff. Two years later, the White House had created the "Plumbers," a bumbling group of operatives led by Liddy and Hunt, to combat leaks, including the release of the Pentagon Papers. Anxious to win in 1972, Nixon's men had also engaged in dirty tricks to sabotage Democratic presidential aspirants. Nixon's personal lawyer had collected illegal political contributions, "laundered" the money to hide its source, and then transferred it to CREEP.

Nixon himself had ordered the secret and illegal bombing of Cambodia. He had impounded (i.e., refused to spend) money appropriated by Congress for programs he disliked. He had secretly approved the use of federal agencies to hurt "our political enemies."

As a result of the Watergate break-in and other scandals, many of Nixon's associates had to leave office. No fewer than 26, including former Attorney General John Mitchell, went to jail. Vice President Spiro Agnew was found to have accepted bribes as the governor of Maryland in the 1960s. In October 1973 Agnew accepted a plea bargain deal and resigned as vice president. He was replaced by Republican Congressman Gerald R. Ford of Michigan.

Finally, the president himself had to leave office. Under growing pressure to release his tapes, Nixon tried to get away with publishing selected edited transcripts. Revealing a vulgar, rambling, and inarticulate president, the transcripts only fed public disillusionment. In July 1974 the House Judiciary Committee voted to recommend to the full House of Representatives three articles of impeachment—obstruction of justice, abuse of power, and defiance of subpoenas.

Nixon still wanted to fight the charges, but the Supreme Court ruled unanimously that the president had to turn over his tapes to the special prosecutor. The tapes showed that Nixon himself had participated in the cover-up of Watergate as early as June 23, 1972. The president had conspired to obstruct justice and had lied repeatedly to the American people. Almost certain to be impeached, the president agreed to resign rather than face a trial in the Senate. On August 9, 1974, Nixon left office in disgrace. "My fellow Americans, our long national nightmare is over," the new president, Gerald Ford, declared. "Our constitution works."

Gerald Ford and a Skeptical Nation

At first, Gerald Ford was a welcome relief for a nation stunned by the misdeeds of Richard Nixon. Modest and good-humored, the new president seemed unlikely to abuse the authority of the White House. But Ford also seemed stumbling and unimaginative in the face of the nation's declining prosperity and power. Moreover, his administration had no popular mandate. Ford was the first unelected vice president to succeed to the presidency. His vice president, former New York governor Nelson Rockefeller, had not been elected either.

Ford had to govern a nation that had grown skeptical about politicians. Johnson's deceitful conduct of the Vietnam War and Nixon's scandals raised fears that the presidency had grown too powerful. To re-establish its authority, Congress passed the War Powers Act of 1973, which allowed the president to send troops to hostile situations overseas for no more than 60 days without obtaining Congressional consent. In 1975 Congress conducted hearings on the secret operations of the CIA. Amid revelations about the agency's improper roles in domestic spying and the assassination of foreign leaders, the House and Senate created permanent committees to oversee the agency. Ford had to ban the use of assassination in American foreign policy.

Soon after taking office, Ford himself fed public skepticism about the presidency by offering Nixon a full pardon for all crimes committed as president. Ford's popularity dropped immediately and his presidency never fully recovered.

A moderate Republican, Ford did not want the federal government to take an active role in managing the economy. But like Nixon, he could not stop some liberal initiatives. Congress strengthened the regulatory power of the FTC and extended the 1970 Clean Air Act.

Ford had no solutions for deindustrialization and stagflation. Believing inflation was the most serious problem, Ford did little to stop rising unemployment. His anti-inflation program, known as WIN for "Whip Inflation Now," mainly encouraged Americans to control price increases voluntarily. Ford wore a WIN button on his lapel, but inflation continued.

In foreign affairs, the president had to accept limits on American power. Despite the 1973 cease-fire agreement, the fighting continued in Vietnam. Ford promised to protect South Vietnam, but Congress cut the administration's requests for monetary aid to the Saigon government. Sending American armed forces to South Vietnam was out of the question. When North Vietnamese troops invaded early in 1975, panicked civilians fled southward and Congress refused to provide any more aid. As Saigon was overrun, the last Americans evacuated in helicopters. For more than 20 years, the United States had worked to preserve an independent, anti-Communist South Vietnam. Yet, on April 30, 1975, South Vietnam surrendered, and Ford could not prevent the final, ignominious failure of America's Vietnam policy.

The policy of détente with the Soviet Union was supposed to help America cope with its limited power, but détente was clearly in trouble during the Ford administration. The United States and the Soviets failed to agree to a second Strategic Arms Limitation Treaty (SALT II). American critics of détente, including Democratic Senator Henry Jackson of Washington, claimed that the policy sapped

American defenses and overlooked human rights violations by the Soviets. In 1974, Jackson added an amendment to a trade bill linking increased commerce to increased freedom for Soviet Jews to emigrate. The Jackson–Vanik Amendment helped sour the Soviets on détente. In turn, Ford further alienated American conservatives when he traveled to Helsinki, Finland, in 1975 to sign an agreement accepting the post-World War II boundaries of European nations.

Ford's troubles were reflected at the polls. The Democrats made large gains in the Congressional elections in 1974. In 1976, Ford won the Republican nomination for president, replacing Rockefeller with a more conservative vice presidential nominee, Senator Robert Dole of Kansas. The Democrats' presidential choice was former Georgia governor Jimmy Carter, a far cry from the liberal George McGovern. Carter chose a liberal running mate, Senator Walter Mondale of Minnesota, but the Georgian ran as a moderate who could appeal to businessmen and white southerners.

With low turnout at the polls, Carter won 50.1 percent of the vote to Ford's 48 percent. The outcome was less an endorsement of Carter than a rejection of Ford, who became the first sitting president to lose an election since Herbert Hoover.

Jimmy Carter: Why Not the Best?

As he took office in 1977, Jimmy Carter seemed capable and efficient. A graduate of the Naval Academy, he had served as an engineer in the Navy's nuclear submarine program and successfully managed his family's peanut farm before entering politics as a state legislator. Carter's commitment to perfectionism was captured in the title of his autobiography, *Why Not the Best?*

Carter responded more energetically and imaginatively than Ford to the nation's problems, and he had the advantage of working with a Congress controlled by his own party. But Carter came to be seen as a weak, uncertain leader. More important, he faced the same intractable problems that had bedeviled Ford. In the 1970s, it seemed that no president could resolve the nation's economic, political, and diplomatic crises.

Like Ford, Carter had trouble putting to rest the recent past. Carter met angry criticism when he pardoned most American men who had resisted the draft during the Vietnam War, offending many veterans and conservatives.

Carter also had to contend with increasing popular resentment of government. Many Americans believed that government regulation and taxation had gotten out of hand. When the Endangered Species Act of 1973 forced a halt to the construction of a Tennessee dam because it threatened the survival of the snail darter, a small local fish, it seemed as if the federal government worried more about fish than about people's need for electricity and recreation.

The West was the stronghold of antigovernment sentiment in the 1970s. Assailing the bureaucrats in Washington, DC, the Sage Brush Rebellion demanded state control over federal lands in the West. Businessmen in the West also wanted the government to allow more exploitation of oil, forests, and other resources on federal lands. Meanwhile, California became the center of an antitax movement in 1978. Angered by high taxes and government spending, California voters passed Proposition 13, which sharply reduced property taxes.

As always, antigovernment sentiment was inconsistent. Many of the same people who attacked taxes and regulation expected aid and benefits from Washington. When the giant automaker Chrysler faced bankruptcy in 1979, the government had to save the company with a $1.5 billion loan guarantee. When Carter moved to cancel supposedly wasteful federal water projects in the West in 1977, he encountered a storm of protest from the Sage Brush Rebellion.

Carter was most successful when he moved to limit government. By the 1970s, some economists were advocating deregulation of businesses as a way to lower costs, increase competition, and improve services. In 1978, the government removed price controls on the airline industry. In the short run the move lowered fares, but in the long run it drove some airlines out of business.

Deregulation was a sign of a changing balance of political power. Big business, under attack since the 1960s, now lobbied effectively against regulation, organized labor, and taxes. Liberals, meanwhile, had lost influence. As a result, Congress never created the Consumer Protection Agency advocated by consumer activists. Legislation to make labor organization easier also failed. Congress watered down the Humphrey–Hawkins bill, which reasserted the government's responsibility to ensure full employment. When Carter tried to raise taxes on business, Congress instead cut taxes on capital gains and added more loopholes to the tax law.

Carter attempted, with mixed results, to adjust the economy to the realities of living with less. His program of voluntary wage and price controls did not stop soaring inflation. After fuel shortages forced some schools and businesses to close in the harsh winter of 1976–1977, Carter addressed the energy crisis. He proposed the establishment of the Department of Energy, taxes on gas-guzzling automobiles and large consumers of oil, tax incentives to stimulate production of oil and gas, and development of nuclear power. Conservatives thought the program expanded government authority. Liberals and environmentalists objected to its support for nuclear power and oil-company profits. The final plan, passed in 1978, was considerably weakened, but it did encourage conservation.

Nuclear power, a key part of Carter's energy plan, soon lost much of its appeal. In March 1979 a nuclear reactor at Three Mile Island, near Harrisburg, Pennsylvania, nearly suffered a catastrophic meltdown. As 100,000 frightened residents fled their homes, the reactor had to be permanently closed. Around the country, utilities scrapped plans for new nuclear power plants.

Three Mile Island also fed broader anxieties about the environmental damage caused by industrial capitalism. Americans wondered whether their neighborhoods would suffer the fate of Love Canal, located near Niagara Falls, New York. There, hazardous waste buried by a chemical company caused so many health problems that residents had to move away. Despite business concerns about regulation, Washington created a "superfund" of $1.6 billion to clean up hazardous waste sites. The Carter administration also took control of 100 million acres of Alaska to prevent damage from economic development.

At first, Carter had more success with foreign policy than with domestic affairs. Continuing Nixon's de-escalation of the cold war, Carter announced that "we are now free of the inordinate fear of Communism." The president did not abandon Nixon's emphasis on détente with the Soviet Union, but he focused on supporting human rights and building harmony around the world. In 1978, Carter won Senate approval of a treaty yielding ownership of the Panama Canal to Panama at the end of the century. The treaty signaled a new and more respectful approach to Central and Latin America.

In 1978, Carter also mediated the first peace agreement between Israel and an Arab nation. Bringing together Israeli and Egyptian leaders at the Camp David presidential retreat, Carter helped forge a framework for peace that led to Israel's withdrawal from the Sinai Peninsula and the signing of an Israeli–Egyptian treaty. The agreement did not settle the fate of the Israeli-occupied Golan Heights and

A poster of President Jimmy Carter, carried in a demonstration near the American embassy in Tehran, mocks U.S. weakness during the Iranian hostage crisis in 1979.

Gaza Strip or the future of the Palestinian people, but it did establish a basis for future negotiations in a region torn by conflict for centuries.

Carter's foreign policy suffered from the eventual collapse of détente. The president did reach agreement with the Soviets on the SALT II treaty, but the Senate was reluctant to ratify the agreement. Then, in December 1979, the Soviet Union invaded its southern neighbor, Afghanistan. In response, Carter withdrew the SALT II treaty, stopped grain shipments to the Soviet Union, forbade American athletes to compete in the 1980 Olympics in Moscow, and increased American military spending. These moves had no effect on the Soviet invasion, but détente was obviously over, and the direction of American foreign policy had become unclear.

By 1979, Carter was a deeply unpopular president. He had not stabilized the economy or set out a coherent foreign policy. After pondering the situation at the Camp David retreat for 11 days in July, the president came back to tell a television audience that the nation was suffering a "crisis of spirit." The president offered a number of proposals to deal with the energy crisis, but he spoke most strongly to the state of the nation: "What is lacking is confidence and a sense of community." The speech only seemed to alienate more Americans.

Carter became still more embattled when the Shah of Iran was overthrown by the followers of an Islamic leader, the Ayatollah Ruholla Khomeini, early in 1979. The Shah had long received lavish aid from the United States. Now, the Iranian revolutionaries, eager to restore traditional Islamic values, condemned America for imposing the Shah and modern culture on their nation. In the wake of the revolution, oil prices rose. Once again, Americans had to contend with gas lines and inflation spread through the economy.

The situation worsened when Khomeini condemned the United States for allowing the Shah to receive medical treatment in New York. On November 4, students loyal to Khomeini overran the United States embassy in Tehran, the Iranian capital, and took 60 Americans hostage. Carter froze Iranian assets in the United States, but he could not compel the release of the hostages. As days passed, the United States seemed helpless. In the spring of 1980, the frustrated president ordered a secret military mission to rescue the hostages. On April 24, eight American helicopters headed for a desert rendezvous with six transport planes carrying troops and supplies. However, when two helicopters broke down and another became lost, the mission had to be aborted, and the hostages remained in captivity.

CONCLUSION

The failure of that rescue mission summed up the problems of the United States at the start of the 1980s. The nation was no longer strong enough to protect its own citizens abroad. The presidency seemed weak and ineffectual. The military seemed unable to project its power overseas. The nation had not yet adjusted to the challenges of living with less.

FURTHER READINGS

Stephen E. Ambrose, *Nixon*, 3 vols (1987–1991). A readable narrative of Nixon's many triumphs and ultimate failure.

Terry H. Anderson, *The Movement and the Sixties: Protest in America From Greensboro to Wounded Knee* (1995). A sweeping chronicle of the many protests in both the 1960s and 1970s that created the Movement.

Peter N. Carroll, *It Seemed Like Nothing Happened: The Tragedy and Promise of America in the 1970s* (1983). A fresh, journalistic account that is still the best general social history of the 1970s.

Ronald P. Formisano, *Boston Against Busing: Race, Class, and Ethnicity in the 1960s and 1970s* (1991). Nicely analyzes the white resistance to school desegregation.

Ignacio Garcia, *Chicanismo: The Forging of a Militant Ethos Among Mexican Americans* (2000). Offers a balanced account of the emerging Chicano rights movement.

Seymour Hersh, *The Price of Power: Kissinger in the Nixon White House* (1983). A harsh, fascinating study of the architect of détente.

CHRONOLOGY

1968	My Lai Massacre in South Vietnam Founding of American Indian Movement (AIM)
1969	Secret bombing of Cambodia ordered by President Richard Nixon Stonewall Riot in New York's Greenwich Village *Apollo 11* moon landing Announcement of Nixon Doctrine Founding of Chicano student organization MEChA "Days of Rage" protests by Weathermen in Chicago
1970	First Earth Day Creation of Environmental Protection Agency (EPA) United States–South Vietnam invasion of Cambodia Killing of students at Kent State University and Jackson State College Women's Strike for Equality
1971	Conviction of Lieutenant William Calley, Jr., for role in My Lai Massacre Publication of Pentagon Papers by *New York Times* Nixon takes U.S. off gold standard Ratification of Twenty-Sixth Amendment, lowering voting age to 18 Supreme Court busing decision, *Swann* v. *Charlotte-Mecklenburg Board of Education*
1972	President Nixon's trips to the People's Republic of China and the Soviet Union Strategic Arms Limitation Treaty (SALT I) and Anti-Ballistic Missile (ABM) Treaty signed

Burton I. Kaufman, *The Presidency of James Earl Carter, Jr.* (1993). A fair-minded treatment of a troubled presidency.

Stanley I. Kutler, *The Wars of Watergate: The Last Crisis of Richard Nixon* (1990). A balanced, clear account of the scandal that brought down Richard Nixon.

Eric Marcus, *Making History: The Struggle for Gay and Lesbian Equal Rights, 1945–1980* (1992). Moving, candid oral histories that personalize the gay and lesbian liberation movement.

Winifred D. Wandersee, *On the Move: American Women in the 1970s* (1988). A detailed study of the different social and political phases of women's liberation in the 1970s, including the fight for the Equal Rights Amendment.

	Congressional passage of Equal Rights Amendment Operation Linebacker bombing raids on North Vietnam Watergate burglary Re-election of President Nixon
1973	Peace agreement to end Vietnam War signed Beginning of Arab oil embargo Supreme Court ruling to legalize abortion, *Roe* v. *Wade* Resignation of Vice President Spiro Agnew
1974	Beginning of struggle over busing in Boston Resignation of President Nixon Succession to presidency by Gerald Ford
1975	Surrender of South Vietnam to North Vietnam Helsinki Agreement
1976	Announcement of the "Me-Decade" by Tom Wolfe Jimmy Carter elected president
1977	President Carter proposes energy plan
1978	Camp David peace accords Supreme Court affirmative action decision, *Regents of the University of California* v. *Allan Bakke*
1979	Accident at Three Mile Island nuclear power plant Iranian revolution
1980	Failed mission to rescue U.S. hostages in Iran

 Please refer to the document CD-ROM for primary sources related to this chapter.

CHAPTER

30
The Triumph of a New Conservatism
1980–1988

The Trumps' American Dream • A New Conservative Majority
The Reagan Revolution at Home • The Reagan Revolution
Abroad • The Battle Over Conservative Social Values
The Limits of the New Conservatism • Conclusion

THE TRUMPS' AMERICAN DREAM

In the 1980s Donald and Ivana Trump were one of the most famous couples in the United States. Rich, glamorous, and powerful, they appeared to prove that the American dream could still come true.

Donald, the son of a prosperous real estate developer, seemed unaffected by recent history. Going into business in New York in the 1970s, Trump refused to be pessimistic about the city's depressed real estate market and uncertain finances. While the nation learned to live with less, Trump aggressively acquired land and buildings at low prices.

Trump's strategy paid off in the 1980s. By 1986, Trump had accumulated one of the largest fortunes in America. He owned apartment houses and hotels. He built the posh Trump Tower on Fifth Avenue, with condominiums priced as high as $10 million. He had a glitzy gambling casino, Trump's Castle, in Atlantic City, New Jersey. He owned an airline, the Trump Shuttle. He owned a football team, the New Jersey Generals. He even had his own bestselling book, naturally titled *Trump*.

Trump's wife, Ivana, lived both an old dream for immigrants and a new dream for women. Born in Austria and raised in Czechoslovakia, she found riches and happiness in the United States. A modestly successful skier and model, Ivana married the man she called "The Donald" in New York in 1977 and became "a stunning prototype of the truly fashionable world-class billionairess."

Ivana's life with "The Donald" seemed to prove that a modern American woman could have it all. After bearing three children she remained, an admiring biographer exclaimed, a "celebration of the body perfect." Ivana gracefully combined family and career, helping to supervise interior decoration for Donald's projects and managing Trump's casino.

To some observers, the Trumps' self-promoting lifestyle was flashy, excessive, and insubstantial. Donald's brash business methods seemed to trample ordinary people. Over the years, tenants accused him of cruel treatment. The U.S. Justice Department charged the Trump Organization with racial discrimination.

Donald and Ivana survived the criticism, but the couple did not avoid personal and financial troubles. Donald removed Ivana as manager of his casino in May 1988 because of lagging profits. Then she discovered his apparent affair with a model. After their much-publicized breakup, she confessed to "a tremendous sense of failure." She wondered, too, about the free-wheeling capitalism that had put the Trumps on top. Meanwhile, that system nearly destroyed Donald's empire. By 1990, he was deep in debt trying to fund his glitziest casino, the Trump Taj Mahal. To stave off bankruptcy, he had to sell the Trump Shuttle and other properties.

The Trumps' story reflected a central theme of the 1980s. Still coming to terms with economic and political decline, the United States turned toward an older, business-centered, conservative vision of the political economy. Rejecting the pessimism of the 1970s, many Americans wanted to believe that success like the Trumps' was still possible. Downplaying the idealism of the 1960s, Americans exalted the material satis-factions of consumerism and favored a more conservative state that promised to restore prosperity and left businesspeople like Donald Trump free to make a fortune.

The trend toward conservatism had wide-ranging consequences. A broad-based coalition elected a conservative Republican, Ronald Reagan, to the presidency. Eager to restore old social, economic, and political values, Reagan set out to recast the American political economy by cutting taxes, reducing government regulation, and diminishing union power to restore economic growth. Abroad, he carried out a foreign policy dedicated to confronting Communism. With Reagan's re-election in 1984, the new conservatism seemed triumphant.

Before the 1980s ended, however, many Americans wondered whether the conservative triumph, like the Trumps' fortune, was real after all. The conservatives' social agenda had met strong opposition. The nation's renewed prosperity seemed fragile and uneven. Like Donald's empire, the wealth of the 1980s depended on borrowed money and shaky deals. And, like Donald's tenants, some Americans found themselves ignored or exploited. By the close of the decade, ordinary people were learning Ivana's lesson: They could not have it all.

A New Conservative Majority

By 1980, a new conservatism had emerged in the United States. This New Right drew strength from ongoing changes in the economy and Americans' economic values. The rapid growth of a conservative coalition became clear in the 1980 presidential election, when voters sent Ronald Reagan to the White House.

The End of Economic Decline?

The decline of the American economy appeared to halt in the 1980s. The continuing growth of the Sunbelt fueled optimism. Rustbelt industrial cities such as Pittsburgh, Detroit, and Gary, Indiana, lost population, while some counties in Georgia, Florida, and Texas more than doubled in population. The movement of population had political consequences, too. Reapportionment in 1980 gave more Congressional seats and electoral votes to the relatively conservative states of the Sunbelt.

Across the country, technological innovations encouraged hopes for economic revival. Microwave ovens, pocket calculators, compact disc players, cordless telephones, and fax machines were just a few features of a consumer electronics revolution. Videocassette recorders, remote controls, satellites, and cable television transformed Americans' television viewing habits.

The most important new product was the microcomputer. In 1977 a new company, Apple, offered its first microcomputer for sale. Four years later, the computing giant IBM introduced its first personal computer, or PC. By the end of the 1980s, Americans were buying 7 million PCs a year.

These explosive sales produced optimistic visions of the U.S. economy. Computers seemed to promise a way out of national economic decline. Whereas Asian manufacturers built most consumer electronics products, American companies dominated the computer industry. The microcomputer bolstered older companies such as IBM, created new companies such as Apple and Compaq, and fed the growth of the Sunbelt. Compaq's headquarters were in Houston. Apple was one of many computer firms clustered in Silicon Valley just outside San Francisco. The microcomputer also seemed to be reviving parts of the Rustbelt. In Massachusetts, a string of computer companies sprang up around Boston along Route 128 to replace the textile mills and shoe factories that had long since left the state.

The growth of the computer industry rested on the seemingly limitless possibilities of the microcomputer, which inspired utopian dreams of a high-technology society built on the production of knowledge rather than things. Promoting literacy and education, the computer would then lift up the poor and disadvantaged. Unlike the old industrial economy, the computerized economy could cut down on pollution and the consumption of raw materials. By enabling people to work at home, the microcomputer could eliminate commuting and relieve urban congestion.

While the 1980s pointed to a utopian future, the decade also recalled the cutthroat capitalism of the turn of the twentieth century. A wave of corporate takeovers and mergers swept across the economy. Aggressive investment bankers and entrepreneurs such as Michael Milken and Ivan Boesky used a variety of techniques, such as junk bonds, high-risk, high-paying securities, to finance takeovers. Executives agreed to sell their own companies in return for golden parachutes, huge payments these executives received when they lost their jobs. Enormous deals merged some of the largest American corporations. In 1985 General Electric bought RCA for $6 billion. In 1986 alone there were more than 4,000 mergers worth a total of $190 billion. The biggest deal of all came in 1988 when

RJR Nabisco was sold for $25 billion and the company's executives received a $100-million golden parachute.

The takeovers sparked criticism from Americans worried about expensive deals and the concentration of so much economic power. But other observers saw the takeovers as a sign of economic vitality. They argued that the mergers created larger, more efficient companies that could compete more successfully. These observers praised Milken, Boesky, and other wealthy takeover artists as models of entrepreneurial energy and creativity.

The Rehabilitation of Business

The takeover wave, along with the growth of the Sunbelt and the computer industry, encouraged hopes for an economic revival. In turn, those hopes helped rehabilitate business and its values, which had been assailed in the 1960s and 1970s. The media enthusiastically reported the achievements and opinions of Donald Trump, Michael Milken, Ivan Boesky, Bill Gates, and Steve Jobs. Business was more respectable than at any time since the 1950s.

So was materialism. The Trumps and other business figures helped legitimize the pursuit and enjoyment of wealth. There was renewed interest in luxurious living. "Thank goodness it's back," gushed *The New York Times*, "that lovely whipped cream of a word—luxury."

The baby-boom generation reflected the new appeal of business values. Abandoning social action, former 1960s radicals such as the Yippie leader Jerry Rubin took up business careers. By 1983 the media were talking about the emergence of yuppies, young urban professionals. Uninterested in reform, these self-centered baby boomers were supposedly eager to make lots of money and then spend it on BMW cars, Perrier water, and other consumer playthings. The yuppies made up perhaps only five percent of the baby-boom generation. Nevertheless, the yuppie stereotype underscored the resurgence of business values, as many Americans aspired to a more conservative, money-centered way of life.

The Rise of the Religious Right

At the same time American culture celebrated materialism, many Americans still turned to religion to find meaning in their lives. But the ongoing transformation of religious life also reinforced conservative values. Conservative denominations, especially evangelical Christian churches, grew rapidly, and evangelical leaders took conservative stands on social and economic issues. By 1980 they had become a powerful political movement, the religious right.

The rise of the religious right reflected a long-term trend. Such mainline Protestant denominations as the United Methodist Church, the Episcopal Church and the Presbyterian Church, USA, had been dropping sharply in membership since at least 1940. Meanwhile, evangelical churches boomed (see Map 30–1).

The changing balance between mainline and evangelical churches had social and political consequences. The mainline denominations often took moderate or liberal positions on such social issues as civil rights and abortion, but the evangelical churches were much more likely to support conservative positions. Troubled by social change and emboldened by their own growth, evangelicals wanted to spread a conservative message across American culture and politics.

The emergence of so-called "televangelists" was the most obvious result of these efforts. From 1978 to 1989 the number of Christian television ministries grew from

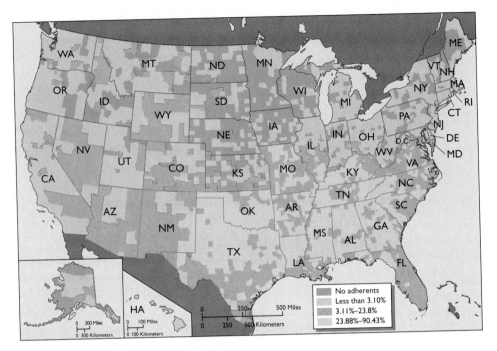

Map 30–1   The Growth of Evangelical Christianity
The Southern Baptist Convention's share of the population, by county, reveals its gradual spread beyond its traditional base in the South by 1990.

Source: Peter L. Halvorson & William M. Newman, Atlas of Religious Change in America, 1952–1990 (Cincinnati, Ohio; Glenmary Research Center, 1994), p. 120.

25 to 336. Pat Robertson, a born-again Baptist from Virginia, hosted *The 700 Club* and ran the Christian Broadcast Network. Jerry Falwell, a fundamentalist who believed in the literal interpretation of the Bible, hosted *The Old Time Gospel Hour* and founded Liberty Baptist College in Virginia. He also organized the Moral Majority, a political pressure group. A televangelist couple, Jim and Tammy Faye Bakker, started Heritage Park, USA, complete with a hotel and water park, in South Carolina.

Deeply conservative, the televangelists condemned many of the social changes of the 1960s and 1970s, such as women's liberation, abortion, gay rights, and liberal Great Society programs. They wanted prayer in public schools. Earning millions of dollars, they praised low taxes, limited government, and financial success. As materialistic as the Trumps, Jim and Tammy Faye Bakker proudly showed off their six homes and their air-conditioned doghouse. By 1980, the televangelists were moving into politics. Through their broadcasts, organizations, and fundraising, they were creating a conservative political force, a religious right.

The Conservative Counterestablishment

Conservatives and Republicans had long despised the liberal establishment, the northeastern, Ivy League educated men who supposedly ran Wall Street and Washington. The establishment was never the powerful, tightly knit organization that its critics imagined, but conservatives endeavored to stop the establishment by creating their own counterestablishment.

Money helped build the conservative counterestablishment. Wealthy donors, such as brewer Joseph Coors, contributed to conservative organizations and campaigns. Televangelists and such conservative fundraisers as Richard Viguerie collected small contributions from millions of less wealthy Americans.

All this money helped to create and sustain a range of conservative institutions and activities. The John M. Olin Foundation and other philanthropic organizations supported conservative causes and initiatives. The National Conservative Political Action Committee (NCPAC) and other pressure groups lobbied for conservative legislation and supported conservative political candidates. Think tanks such as the Heritage Foundation and the American Enterprise Institute publicized conservative ideas and policies. Conservative publications such as *The Public Interest, Human Events, The National Review,* and *The Wall Street Journal* offered a conservative alternative to establishment news outlets.

Like conservative businessmen and Republicans a century earlier, the New Right praised unrestricted free enterprise and minimal regulation of economic life and blended hostility to activist liberal government with a hatred of Communism. Evangelical Christians wanted to use government power to enforce their views on such social issues as abortion, school prayer, and gay rights, but libertarians believed government should leave people as free as possible. Despite these differences, the conservative counterestablishment offered a powerful cluster of ideas, influenced by economic, social, religious, and political change since the 1960s.

The 1980 Presidential Election

The power of the new conservatism became evident in the presidential election of 1980. The Republican Party nominated a charismatic conservative, Ronald Reagan. Confronting a divided Democratic Party and an unpopular president, Reagan won a stunning victory.

Reagan's life story reflected the rise of the Sunbelt and the new conservatism. Born into a lower middle-class family in Illinois in 1911, Reagan left the Midwest during the Great Depression for California. From the 1930s through the early 1960s, he starred in movies and television shows in Hollywood. A staunch Democrat, he supported Franklin Roosevelt and Harry Truman. Reagan then moved to the right: Angry over high income taxes, he attacked big government while serving as a corporate spokesman for General Electric. In the 1960s, Reagan became a Republican, and his conservative views won him election as governor of California in 1966 and 1970.

The conservative tide carried Reagan along in 1980. Although he chose a moderate running mate, George Bush of Texas, his campaign offered a conservative vision of less government, lower taxes, and renewed military power.

Meanwhile, the Democratic nominee, incumbent President Jimmy Carter, could not overcome the double burdens of a weak economy and the ongoing hostage crisis in Iran. His moderate and sometimes conservative policies alienated liberal Democrats. His poor economic record alienated the party's white ethnics. Moderate Republican Congressman John Anderson of Illinois, who ran as an independent, drew votes away from Carter.

Reagan pulled off the rare feat of defeating an incumbent president (see Map 30–2). The Democrats held on to the House of Representatives, but the Republicans took control of the Senate for the first time since 1952. The nation had turned sharply to the right. Reagan's victory marked the emergence of a conservative majority.

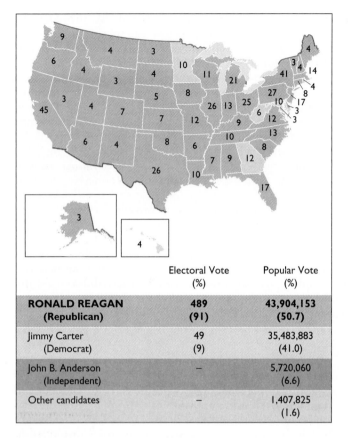

Map 30–2 The Presidential Election, 1980

	Electoral Vote (%)	Popular Vote (%)
RONALD REAGAN (Republican)	**489** **(91)**	**43,904,153** **(50.7)**
Jimmy Carter (Democrat)	49 (9)	35,483,883 (41.0)
John B. Anderson (Independent)	–	5,720,060 (6.6)
Other candidates	–	1,407,825 (1.6)

THE REAGAN REVOLUTION AT HOME

Ronald Reagan probably shaped American life more decisively than any president since Franklin Roosevelt. Reagan's style—folksy and optimistic—made him popular, but the Reagan years were more than a triumph of style. With some justice, his supporters believed that the president spurred a sweeping conservative transformation of the American political economy.

The Reagan Style

The Reagan Revolution was partly a matter of style. Despite the frustrations of the 1960s and 1970s, Reagan exuded optimism. Rather than teach Americans how to live with less, he embraced luxury. Nevertheless, he retained a common touch. After the troubled presidencies of the 1970s, Reagan made the job seem manageable again.

Reagan's presidency signaled a confident, even opulent, new era. On Inauguration Day, as if to mark the belated end of the frustrating 1970s, the Iranian government finally released its American hostages. In his inaugural address, Reagan firmly rejected pessimism about the nation's future. "We are not," the new president declared, "doomed to an inevitable decline." That night, he and his wife Nancy danced at a series of lavish balls. The Reagan inaugural cost five times more than Jimmy Carter's had four years earlier.

Even while the Reagans continued their lavish lifestyle in the White House, the president remained popular. He knew how to speak simply and effectively to the American people. Although the president did not always master the details of issues, he became known as the "Great Communicator."

Reagan also appeared to enjoy and master his job. Although all his recent predecessors had faded under the pressures of the job, Reagan appeared to delight in the presidency; even though he took office as America's oldest president at the age of 69, he projected an image of vigor and energy.

The president even managed to survive an assassination attempt. On March 30, 1981, John W. Hinckley, a troubled young loner, shot and wounded Reagan, his press secretary, and a policeman. Reagan's chest wound was more serious than his spokesmen admitted, but the president met the situation with good humor. "Honey," he told his wife, "I forgot to duck." The president's popularity soared in opinion polls.

Shrinking Government

Reagan's administration offered a clear conservative alternative to the liberal policies of the New Deal and the Great Society. Above all, Reagan denied that a large, activist federal government could deal with the challenges of American life in the 1980s. Accordingly, he wanted to shrink the government's size and reduce its power.

Reagan's efforts to shrink the federal government met with mixed success. In his 1982 State of the Union address, the president endorsed the New Federalism, a plan to transfer federal programs and tax revenues to the states. Reagan insisted the New Federalism would promote efficiency and economic growth, but governors worried that their states would be saddled with expensive responsibilities. In the end, the federal government passed on only a few programs.

Reagan also created a commission, headed by business executive J. Peter Grace, to explore ways the federal government could save money. The Grace Commission claimed that Washington could save more than $400 billion over three years, partly by making it more difficult for Americans to qualify for welfare, pension, and other benefits. Congress was unwilling to make such reforms. The commission also called for the line-item veto, which would allow a president to reject particular spending programs in Congress's annual budget without having to veto the entire budget bill. Congress was not ready to give Reagan so much new power.

The president had more success when he attacked social welfare programs. Like many other conservatives, Reagan condemned antipoverty programs as a waste of federal resources that sapped the work ethic and the morals of the poor. Reagan and his followers believed that the political economy worked best when workers had to succeed or fail on their own. He wanted reductions in food stamps, school meal programs, and aid to cities. In response, Congress cut appropriations for urban public housing and eliminated job training for the unemployed.

Reagan found it nearly impossible to touch Medicare and Social Security, two expensive and popular programs that benefited most Americans. The Social Security system proved especially difficult to cut. By the 1980s there was growing concern that workers' Social Security payments would eventually not be enough to cover the cost of benefits to retirees. After a long struggle, Congress produced the Social Security Reform Act of 1983, which raised the minimum age for full benefits from 65 to 67 and made retirees pay taxes on some benefits. The measure did little to reduce the total cost of the program, and by 1984 Reagan was promising not to cut Social Security.

Despite his eagerness to reduce the size of government, Reagan did not tear down the federal system of welfare and other benefits. Expenditures for these programs continued to rise, but the Reagan administration managed to slow the growth of welfare. Benefits did not expand dramatically; there were no costly new programs. As expenditures for national defense grew, welfare outlays fell from 28 percent of the federal budget in 1980 to 22 percent by 1987.

Reaganomics

For Reagan and his followers, shrinking the government meant decreasing Washington's role in the economy. They argued that the nation prospered most when government left Americans free to manage their own businesses and keep their own earnings. The Reagan administration worked to lower taxes, deregulate business, and cut federal support for unions. Reaganomics changed the American political economy by reducing the role of the federal government.

Reagan's economic policy drew on a new theory known as supply-side economics. Beginning in the 1970s, economist Arthur Laffer had offered an alternative to the liberal, Keynesian economics that had guided federal policy since the New Deal. While Keynesians believed that increased consumer demand would spur economic growth, Laffer contended that an increased supply of goods and services was the key to growth. He rejected the Keynesian prescription for raising government spending to put more money in the hands of consumers. To promote prosperity, he believed government should cut taxes. By leaving more money in the hands of businesses, government would allow them to invest in more production of goods and services. The increase in supply would stimulate prosperity and increase tax revenues. The tax cut, Laffer concluded, would not even produce a federal budget deficit.

Supply-side economics was controversial. To liberal critics it seemed to be an excuse to let the rich keep more of their money. Even some Republicans doubted that a tax cut would produce more tax revenues. Nevertheless, Reagan asked a joint session of Congress in 1981 to cut taxes dramatically. Impressed by Reagan's popularity and the electorate's increasing conservatism, the Democratic-controlled House joined the Republican-dominated Senate to pass the Economic Recovery Act of 1981 (also known as the Kemp–Roth Bill). This measure cut federal income taxes five percent the first year and then 10 percent in each of the next two years. It especially benefited the wealthy by making the tax structure less progressive and by reducing the tax rate on the highest individual incomes and on large gifts and estates.

Like other conservatives, Reagan believed that federal rules and requirements hamstrung American business and prevented economic growth. Accordingly, his administration stepped up the campaign for deregulation begun by Jimmy Carter. The government cut the budgets of regulatory agencies and made sure that government officials did not strictly enforce regulatory rules and laws. Further, the administration deregulated the telephone industry. In 1982 the government broke up the giant American Telephone and Telegraph Company, allowing new firms such as Sprint and MCI to compete for AT&T's long-distance business.

Reagan moved particularly to lift environmental restrictions on American businesses. His administration made it easier for timber and mining companies to exploit wilderness areas and allowed oil companies to drill off the Pacific coast. The administration also opposed environmentalists' demands for laws to protect against acid rain—air pollution, caused by industrial emissions, that harmed lakes, forests, and crops in the Northeast and Canada.

Reaganomics also meant weakening organized labor. Like most conservatives, Reagan believed that unions obstructed business and limited the freedom of individual workers. Unions were already weakening when Reagan took office. Thanks mainly to deindustrialization, the number of unionized workers dropped from 21 million in 1970 to 17 million in 1986.

Reagan took steps to weaken the labor movement even further. He made probusiness appointments to the National Labor Relations Board. Most important, he took a strong antiunion stance during a strike by the Professional Air Traffic Controllers Organization (PATCO) in 1981. Despite a law forbidding strikes by federal workers, PATCO walked out to protest unsafe conditions in the air traffic control system. Reagan fired the striking controllers, refused to hire them back, and replaced them with nonunion workers.

Reaganomics did not quite have the effect that its supporters anticipated. In the short run, Reagan's measures could not prevent a sharp recession, which began in the fall of 1981. As the Federal Reserve Bank fought inflation by raising interest rates, the economy slowed, and unemployment increased. Reaganomics also increased the federal budget deficit. The supply-side theory that tax cuts would boost tax revenues and balance the budget proved incorrect.

By the spring of 1984, the recession had ended. Thanks largely to the Federal Reserve's monetary policy, the high inflation of the 1970s was over. The economy began a long period of growth and higher employment, and Reagan's supporters gave the president credit. His critics charged that the deficit rather than Reaganomics had produced the boom and that the deficit would ultimately hurt the economy. In the mid-1980s, however, Reaganomics appeared to be a success.

The 1984 Presidential Election

The unclear results of Reaganomics helped to shape national politics. In the depths of the recession, the Republicans lost 26 House seats in the midterm Congressional elections of 1982. With the return of prosperity, and his popularity on the rise, the president was easily renominated in 1984. Reagan ran against a liberal Democratic nominee, former Vice President Walter Mondale of Minnesota. The Democrat, confronting a popular incumbent, made bold moves. Mondale chose the first female vice-presidential nominee of a major party, Representative Geraldine Ferraro of New York. To prove his honesty and openness, Mondale announced that he would raise taxes as president.

Election day revealed both the strength and the weakness of the Reagan Revolution. The contest was a personal triumph for the president. With his conservative message, Reagan polled 58.8 percent of the popular vote and lost only the District of Columbia and Mondale's home state of Minnesota. Reagan's big vote did not translate into a sweeping victory for his party. Holding on to the Senate, the Republicans failed to win a majority in the House of Representatives.

THE REAGAN REVOLUTION ABROAD

Reagan's foreign policy, like his domestic policy, rested on old values. The president rejected the main diplomatic approaches of the 1970s—Richard Nixon's détente with the Soviet Union and Jimmy Carter's support for international human rights. Instead, the Reagan Revolution revived the strident anti-Communism of the 1940s and 1950s. Communism, however, had little to do with such difficult international issues as conflict in the Middle East, terrorism, and economic relations with Japan and developing nations.

Restoring American Power

After losing the Vietnam War, the United States had cut back its armed forces and become reluctant to risk military confrontations abroad. Reagan set out to restore American power in the 1980s.

Like most conservatives, the president did not believe that cutting government spending should include cutting the armed forces. Under Reagan, the nation's defense spending more than doubled, from $134 billion in 1980 to more than $300 billion by 1989. Construction of the B-1 strategic jet bomber, stopped by Jimmy Carter, resumed. Reagan began development of the B-2 Stealth bomber, an innovative plane that could evade detection by enemy radar. He won Congressional approval for the MX Peacekeeper, a nuclear missile with multiple warheads. He also persuaded Congress to authorize work on the neutron bomb, a nuclear weapon that could spread lethal radiation over a half-mile radius.

As he pursued his military buildup, Reagan faced a growing mass movement against nuclear weapons. In both Europe and the United States, millions of people called for a halt to the introduction of new nuclear arms. In June 1982, a crowd of 700,000 gathered in New York to demand a nuclear freeze. The National Conference of Catholic Bishops supported the freeze and declared nuclear war immoral. Reagan rejected the freeze movement as naïve and Communist-infiltrated. The best way to ensure peace, he believed, was to keep developing weapons.

The military buildup was a matter of attitudes as well as weapons and budgets. In the wake of the Vietnam War, many Americans seemed reluctant to endorse U.S. intervention abroad. This Vietnam syndrome threatened the Reagan administration's foreign policy. The president could not afford to let other countries think the United States would not back up its words with action. Accordingly, Reagan used his speeches to stir up patriotic emotion.

By the mid-1980s, Reagan had succeeded in restoring much of America's military power. It remained to be seen, however, whether Americans were willing to use that power abroad.

Confronting the "Evil Empire"

The main purpose of the military buildup was to contain the Soviet Union. Suspicion of the Soviets and their Communist ideology was the heart of Reagan's diplomacy. In the early 1980s, Reagan called the USSR the "evil empire" and insisted that the Soviet Union and its Communist allies were doomed by failing economies and unpopular regimes.

Reagan avoided cooperation with the Soviet Union and held no summit meetings during his first term. The Reagan administration openly supported the *mujahedeen*, the Afghan rebels who were resisting the Soviets.

More important, the president avoided arms-control agreements with the Soviets during his first term. Reagan refused to submit the second Strategic Arms Limitation Treaty, signed by Jimmy Carter, to the Senate for ratification. In response to the United States's deployment of new intermediate-range nuclear missiles in Western Europe, the Soviets walked out of arms-control talks in 1983.

That year, Reagan put even more pressure on the USSR when he announced plans for the Strategic Defense Initiative (SDI), a space-based missile-defense sys-

A nuclear freeze rally in New York City in 1982. For a time, the movement to halt the introduction of new nuclear weapons challenged President Reagan's plans for an arms buildup.

tem that would use lasers and other advanced technology to shoot down nuclear missiles launched at the United States. Although funded by Congress, SDI was a long way from reality in 1983. Critics, convinced SDI was science fiction, called the plan Star Wars.

The U.S. initiative pressed the Soviets to expend scarce resources to develop their own SDI. It also seemingly made the USSR more vulnerable to nuclear attack. Since the 1950s, the Americans and the Soviets had relied on the concept of *mutual assured destruction* as a deterrent to nuclear war, but SDI might enable the United States to survive a nuclear attack. The Soviets faced the possibility that the United States, no longer facing assured destruction, might start a nuclear war.

While the United States challenged the Soviets aggressively, the Reagan administration did not confront the other major Communist power, the People's Republic of China. The Chinese, less active in promoting third-world Communism, seemed less of a threat than the Soviets. Instead, Reagan traded visits with China's premier in 1984 and encouraged cultural exchanges, economic cooperation, and a nuclear weapons agreement.

The Reagan Doctrine in the Third World

The Reagan administration also changed American foreign policy toward the third world. Jimmy Carter had wanted the United States to support human rights around the globe, but his successor preferred to support America's national security interests, including anti-Communism.

Reagan, along with other conservatives, had been impatient with the Carter administration's attempts to promote human rights abroad. The United States, conservatives believed, needed to back anti-Communist, pro-American governments, whether or not they respected human rights. Jeane J. Kirkpatrick, who became Reagan's ambassador to the United Nations, called for a distinction between totalitarian regimes hostile to the U.S. and authoritarian governments friendly to American interests. Kirkpatrick's view became known as the Reagan Doctrine.

During the president's first term, his administration applied the Reagan Doctrine aggressively in Central America and the Caribbean (see Map 30–3). Determined to keep Communism out of the Western Hemisphere, the United States opposed the Marxist Sandinista government of Nicaragua and supported the repressive anti-Communist government of neighboring El Salvador.

The Sandinistas had come to power in the late 1970s by overthrowing the dictatorship of Anastasio Somoza with the encouragement of the Carter administration. The Reagan administration believed the Sandinistas were too friendly to the Soviet Union and to leftist rebels in El Salvador. Reagan halted aid to Nicaragua in

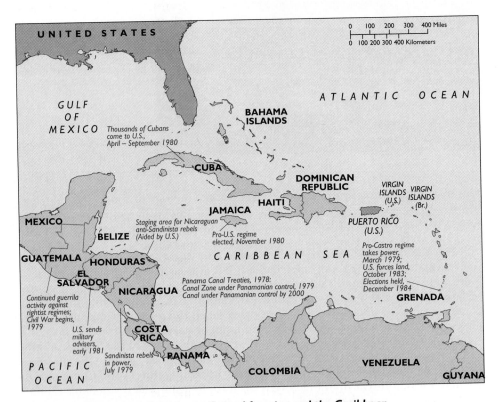

Map 30–3   The Reagan Doctrine in Central America and the Caribbean
Events that shaped Reagan's anti-Communist initiative in the Western Hemisphere.

April 1981 and directed the CIA to train, arm, and supply the Contra rebels who opposed the Sandinistas. Many of the Contras had ties to the oppressive Somoza government, but Reagan praised them as "freedom fighters."

Meanwhile, the president strongly backed the brutal right-wing government of El Salvador. Although the regime engaged in kidnapping and terror, Reagan did not want it to fall to pro-Sandinista and pro-Cuban rebels. El Salvador, the president explained, was "a textbook case of indirect armed aggression by Communist powers."

Despite such anti-Communist rhetoric, the Reagan administration could not persuade Congress to support its Central American policy. Congressional Democrats, like many Americans, did not want to risk another Vietnam War in Central America. They were skeptical about the Communist threat to El Salvador and Nicaragua and troubled by the antidemocratic character of the Salvadoran government and the Contra rebels. In 1983 Congress approved Reagan's Caribbean Basin Initiative, an economic development package, but Reagan did not get the military aid he wanted for the Salvadoran government. Instead, in September 1982 Congress passed the Boland Amendment, which restricted aid to the Contras and banned efforts to topple the Sandinista regime.

The president applied the Reagan Doctrine more successfully in the Caribbean. On October 25, 1983, U.S. troops invaded the small West Indian island of Grenada, supposedly to protect about 1,000 Americans, mostly medical students, from a Marxist regime. The invading force quickly secured the island and replaced the government with a pro-American regime.

The president also implemented the Reagan Doctrine in Africa. The Carter administration had condemned the long-standing policy of *apartheid*—racial separation—pursued by the white government of South Africa. Reagan would not take a similarly strong stance. Rather than impose economic sanctions on the South African regime, the president endorsed a mild policy of diplomatic discussions known as "constructive engagement."

The Middle East and Terrorism

The Reagan Doctrine was not much help in dealing with the Middle East and the growing problem of terrorism. As before, the United States wanted to ensure its supply of oil and to support its longtime ally, Israel. There was no new Arab oil embargo during the Reagan years, but the administration could not bring peace to the Middle East or end the threat of terrorism.

Reagan found it difficult to build on the Camp David Accords between Israel and Egypt, which were supposed to lead to self-government for the Palestinian Arabs who lived in the Israeli-occupied West Bank and Gaza Strip. However, Israel and the Palestine Liberation Organization (PLO) remained at odds. The PLO continued to threaten Israel from bases in neighboring Lebanon. In the spring of 1982, the Israelis invaded Lebanon, which was already convulsed by a civil war between Muslims and Christians.

To end the Israeli invasion and stabilize Lebanon, the United States sent Marines to join an international peacekeeping force. On October 23, 1983, a terrorist killed 241 Americans by driving a truck bomb into Marine headquarters at Beirut. The attack shocked Americans and marked a low point of Reagan's administration. The president pulled out the soldiers in 1984, but there was still no peace in Lebanon and no agreement between the Israelis and the PLO.

The attack on the Marine headquarters illustrated the growing threat of terrorism against the United States and its allies. Reagan vowed to make terrorists "pay for their actions," but terrorism proved hard to stop. Acts of terrorism by Palestinians and Libyans drew quick American reprisals in the 1980s, but the threat of terrorism did not go away.

Reagan also acted to safeguard America's oil supply. During a war between Iran and Iraq, the United States sent Navy ships to protect oil tankers in the Persian Gulf. In May 1987 Iraqi missiles struck the U.S. destroyer *Stark*, killing 37 of its crew. The Reagan administration, unwilling to help Iran, accepted Iraq's apology. In July 1988, the U.S. missile cruiser *Vincennes* accidentally shot down an Iranian airliner, killing 290 passengers. An American apology did little to quell Iranian anger, but the Iran–Iraq war soon ended, and with it the threat to America's oil supply.

The United States and the World Economy

Middle Eastern oil was only one of the economic factors shaping Reagan's foreign policy. The president had to deal with strains on the world economy.

By the end of the 1980s, the developing nations of the third world owed foreign banks more than $1.2 trillion in loan payments. Mexico was more than $100 billion in debt. American banks stood to lose heavily if Mexico and other nations defaulted on loans. American producers stood to lose, too, if these countries could not afford to buy U.S. goods. The Reagan administration nevertheless refused to protect American banks from loan defaults, instead forcing debtor countries to adopt austerity programs in return for new loans.

The Reagan administration had much less power to dictate trade policy with Japan. As Japanese exports flowed into the United States, Americans increasingly resented Japan's domination of the Japanese home market. Congress, believing the Japanese discriminated against American goods, pushed for retaliation. Japan placed voluntary quotas on its export of steel and automobiles to the United States. Although the Reagan administration devalued the dollar to make American goods cheaper, the trade imbalance continued. In 1988 the president signed the Omnibus Trade and Competitiveness Act, which allowed the government to place high tariffs on Japanese goods if Japan continued to discriminate against American goods. However, as long as Americans wanted to buy Japanese products, retaliation was unlikely.

THE BATTLE OVER CONSERVATIVE SOCIAL VALUES

For all of Ronald Reagan's success in the early 1980s, the new conservatism met with considerable opposition. Eager to combat the legacies of the 1960s, many conservatives wanted to restore supposedly traditional values and practices. The conservative agenda collided head-on with one of the chief legacies of the 1960s—disadvantaged groups' demands for equal rights and opportunities. Moreover, many Americans were unwilling to abandon the social changes of the last generation. Faced with such opposition, conservatives failed to achieve much of their vision for American society.

Attacking the Legacy of the 1960s

The new conservatism was driven by a desire to undo the liberal and radical legacies of the 1960s. Conservatives blamed federal courts for much of the social change in the United States over the last generation. In the 1960s and 1970s liberal justices with an activist conception of the courts' role had supported defendants' rights, civil rights, affirmative action, busing, and abortion and rejected such conservative causes as school prayer.

Determined to take control of the courts, Reagan appointed many staunch, relatively young conservatives to the federal bench and the Supreme Court. In 1981 Sandra Day O'Connor, a fairly conservative judge from Arizona, became the court's first woman justice. When Chief Justice Warren Burger retired, Reagan replaced him with conservative William Rehnquist. With the appointments of two more conservatives, Antonin Scalia and Anthony Kennedy, the Supreme Court seemed ready to turn away from liberalism.

It did not quite work out that way. In the 1980s the court followed conservative views in limiting the rights of defendants: Ruling in *United States* v. *Leon* and *Nix* v. *Williams* in 1984, the justices made it easier for prosecutors to use evidence improperly obtained by police. However, on a variety of other issues, the court took a moderate stance. In *Wallace* v. *Jaffree* in 1985, the court invalidated an Alabama law that allowed schools to devote a minute each day to voluntary prayer or meditation.

Conservatives believed that the federal government had played too large a role in the schools since the 1960s. Conservative educational reformers wanted to dismantle the federal Department of Education. In addition, they wanted the government to enable parents to choose the best schools—public or private—for their children, by means of a system of federally funded vouchers or tax credits.

Because many Americans were worried about the quality of the schools, conservatives had a golden opportunity. In 1983 a federal study, *A Nation at Risk*, documented American students' shortcomings, especially in math and science. Despite such revelations, Congress refused to adopt the voucher system or to abolish the Department of Education.

In the early 1980s, the sale and use of crack, especially in the cities, led to crime and violence. In 1986 the president and his wife, Nancy, announced a "national crusade" for a "drug-free" America, encouraging young people to "Just Say No" to drugs. Reagan also instituted drug testing for federal employees. The "war on drugs" was controversial. Critics ridiculed the "Just Say No" slogan as naïve and ineffective. Despite the new penalties and expenditures, drug use did not decrease appreciably.

Women's Rights and Abortion

One of the chief legacies of the 1960s was the women's rights movement. Many conservatives, especially evangelical leaders, believed that women were undermining family life by leaving home for jobs and blamed feminists and liberal government for encouraging women to abandon their traditional role. The conservative movement was especially determined to halt federal initiatives, such as affirmative-action programs and the ERA, that used government power to protect women's rights.

The conservative agenda on women's rights met with mixed results. The campaign for the ERA ended unsuccessfully, but affirmative-action programs, designed to promote the hiring of women, continued. So did women's push into the workplace and public life as more and more American families needed two incomes. By 1983 women made up half of the paid work force. As their economic role expanded, American women received more recognition from the political system. Ironically, Reagan himself gave women new public prominence by choosing Jeane J. Kirkpatrick and Sandra Day O'Connor for important offices.

Women still did not enjoy equality in America. They were generally paid less than men doing the same sort of work, and they had less opportunity to break through the glass ceiling and win managerial jobs. Moreover, commentators had begun to note the feminization of poverty. Unmarried or divorced women, many with children, made up an increasing percentage of the poor.

For many conservatives, abortion was the most troubling sign of the changed status of women. A growing Right to Life movement passionately denounced abortion as the murder of the unborn, practiced by selfish women who rejected motherhood and family.

Conservatives failed to narrow abortion rights significantly in the 1980s. Reagan successfully urged Congress to stop the use of federal funds to pay for abortions, but a constitutional amendment outlawing abortion stalled in the Senate. In 1983 and 1986, the Supreme Court made rulings that upheld *Roe* v. *Wade*.

Gays and the AIDS Crisis

The gay rights movement was another legacy of the 1960s that troubled many conservatives. Evangelical leaders such as Jerry Falwell condemned homosexuality on religious grounds. Some people believed that the public acceptance of equal rights for gay men and women would promote immorality and corrupt children.

Despite such opposition, the gay rights movement made progress in the 1980s. By the end of the decade, most states had repealed sodomy laws that criminalized

Anti-abortion protestors, part of the Right to Life movement that challenged the legitimacy of the Supreme Court's Roe v. Wade *decision in the 1980s.*

gay sex. In 1982 Wisconsin became the first state to pass a law protecting the rights of gay men and women.

The battle over gay rights took place against a tragic backdrop. In 1981 the Centers for Disease Control began reporting cases of acquired immune deficiency syndrome (AIDS), a disease that destroyed the body's immune system and left it unable to fight off infections and rare cancers. By the mid-1980s, researchers had traced AIDS to different forms of the human immunodeficiency virus (HIV) that were transmitted in semen and blood. By 1990 there were nearly 100,000 recorded deaths from AIDS in the United States.

Because 75 percent of the first victims were gay men, Americans initially considered AIDS a homosexual disease. Some people, including evangelical leaders, believed this "gay cancer" was God's punishment for the alleged sin of homosexuality. As soon became clear, however, AIDS could also be transmitted by heterosexual intercourse, by intravenous drug use that involved sharing needles, and by tainted blood transfusions.

Public understanding of AIDS and HIV gradually increased. Nevertheless, the specter of "gay cancer" promoted homophobia and slowed the public response to the disease. Gay activists pushed for government action. The AIDS Coalition to Unleash Power, known as ACT UP, and other organizations staged demonstrations and acts of civil disobedience to focus attention on the crisis. Nevertheless, the Reagan administration did not fund research on AIDS for several years.

African Americans and Racial Inequality

Conservatives were uneasy with still another legacy of the 1960s, the expansion of African-American civil rights and benefits guaranteed by the federal government. Conservatives believed that the liberal policies of the Great Society hurt, rather than helped, black people. They maintained that individual initiative, and not government action, would promote racial equality. In keeping with these ideas, President Reagan opposed renewal of the Voting Rights Act and condemned busing and affirmative action.

Compared with the 1950s and 1960s, African Americans' crusade for justice and opportunity generally slowed in the 1970s and 1980s. Despite legal equality, African Americans faced persisting racism and discrimination. After years of improvement, African Americans' economic status relative to whites stagnated or declined during the Reagan era. African Americans still made less money than whites did for comparable work and had much less chance to attain managerial positions.

Economic hardship and persistent discrimination did not affect all African Americans equally. Among college-educated Americans, the incomes of black men rose faster than those of whites into the mid-1980s. Meanwhile, working-class African Americans found their wages stagnating or falling compared with those of white workers. In the 1970s and 1980s, poverty rates rose faster among African Americans than among whites. The feminization of poverty hit black families particularly hard. In 1985, 75 percent of poor African-American children lived in families headed by a single female. Observers feared that there was now a permanent African-American underclass living segregated in inner-city neighborhoods with poor schools and widespread crime.

African Americans mobilized to fight for equality and opportunity in the 1980s. Across the country, the number of African-American elected officials increased markedly. The Reverend Jesse Jackson, a protégé of Martin Luther King, Jr., won wide attention. Preaching self-esteem and economic self-help for African Americans, Jackson was the leader of Operation PUSH—People United to Save Humanity. In 1984 Jackson challenged Walter Mondale for the Democratic presidential nomination. His campaign suggested how far American society had come in accepting African-American political participation.

African-American activism made it difficult for Reagan and other conservatives to undo the civil rights revolution, as did the persistence of discrimination and inequality. Most Americans seemed to accept that some federal action was essential to redress the imbalance between races in America. Despite Reagan's opposition, in 1982 Congress voted to extend the Voting Rights Act for 25 years. In 1983 the Supreme Court ruled overwhelmingly against Bob Jones University, an evangelical institution that attempted to retain its tax-exempt status despite discriminatory policies. The court also rejected the Reagan administration's bid to set aside local affirmative-action programs. In other decisions, the justices limited affirmative action somewhat, but this important liberal program survived the Reagan administration.

The battles over the rights of African Americans, gays, and women demonstrated that conservative social values were controversial. Many Americans were not ready to undo the legacy of the 1960s. The result was a stalemate. Disadvantaged groups made relatively little progress in the 1980s, but conservatives also made little progress in their social agenda.

THE LIMITS OF THE NEW CONSERVATISM

The Reagan administration was hurt by policy setbacks, economic woes, and its own scandals. For a time, the conservatives' triumph, like the Trumps' fortune, was seriously in doubt.

Business and Religious Scandals

In the late 1980s the new conservatism suffered from a series of scandals. Even before Donald Trump's fortunes declined in the late 1980s, other famous entrepreneurs were in trouble. In 1986 Ivan Boesky, the swaggering Wall Street dealmaker, was indicted for insider trading, the illegal use of secret financial information. Rather than go to trial, he agreed to give up stock trading, inform on other law breakers, spend two years in jail, and pay a $100-million fine. In 1987 Michael Milken, the junk-bond king, was indicted on fraud and racketeering charges. His eventual plea bargain agreement included a ten-year jail sentence and a stunning $600-million fine.

These scandals provoked second thoughts about the celebration of business and materialism. Critics pointed out that Boesky's and Milken's business methods had hurt the economy by saddling corporations with a great deal of debt and little cash to pay for it. Lavish lifestyles no longer seemed quite so attractive.

Scandal touched religion as well as commerce. Leading televangelists were caught in embarrassing predicaments. In 1987 Americans learned that Jim Bakker had defrauded investors in Heritage Park, USA, and paid hush money to hide an adulterous liaison. The scandal hurt the reputation of Jerry Falwell, who had taken over Bakker's organization. In 1988 Falwell resigned from his own Moral Majority. That same year, televangelist Jimmy Swaggart admitted that he "had sinned" with prostitutes.

Political Scandals

The Reagan administration had its own scandals. Almost from the start, some observers decried its lax ethical standards. Before the end of the president's first term, more than 20 officials of the EPA resigned or were fired over charges of favoritism toward lobbyists and polluters. In 1985 Secretary of Labor Raymond Donovan resigned after becoming the first cabinet officer ever indicted. In 1988 Reagan's friend and attorney general, Edwin Meese III, resigned amid questions about his role in the corrupt awarding of government contracts to a defense firm. To critics of the administration, the president and his followers encouraged fraud and corruption with their contemptuous attitude toward government and their eagerness to please business.

In his second term, Reagan faced much more damaging accusations. In October 1986, Sandinista soldiers in Nicaragua shot down a transport plane attempting to supply the Contra rebels. It soon became clear that the plane had been part of a secret effort by the Reagan administration to violate the Boland Amendment's ban on aid to the Contras. Then, in November, a Lebanese magazine reported that the United States had traded arms to Iran. Despite denials from the president, the government had sold arms to win the release of American hostages held by terrorists in Lebanon. The Reagan administration had broken the president's pledge not to negotiate with terrorists and had violated a ban on arms sales to Iran. Americans soon learned that the arms deal and the Nicaraguan plane crash were connected. Government officials had illegally used proceeds from the arms sale to pay for supplying the Contras.

The scandal that became known as the Iran-Contra affair had the potential to drive Reagan from office. If the president had ordered or known about the arms deal and the supply effort, he might have faced impeachment. The Reagan administration underwent three separate investigations: one by a special commission appointed by the president and headed by former Senator John Tower; one by a special prosecutor appointed by the attorney general; and one by a special Congressional committee. These inquiries made clear that Reagan was probably deeply involved in the Iran-Contra affair, but none turned up enough evidence to impeach him.

Nevertheless, the Iran-Contra affair badly damaged Reagan's reputation. Several of his associates left office and faced jail sentences. Former National Security Adviser Robert "Bud" McFarlane pleaded guilty to withholding information from Congress. His successor, Rear Admiral John Poindexter, was allowed to resign. Poindexter's charismatic aide, Marine Lieutenant Colonel Oliver North, had to be fired. Tried and sentenced for their actions, Poindexter and North had their convictions overturned on technical grounds. Meanwhile, the director of the CIA, William Casey, died in 1987, the day after testimony implicated him in the effort to aid the Contras.

Setbacks for the Conservative Agenda

Against this backdrop of scandal, conservatives faced a series of policy setbacks during Reagan's second term. Even though Democrats controlled the House of Representatives, during his first term Reagan had usually persuaded Congress to back his conservative agenda. The Democrats were less cooperative during his second term. The Democrats became even more combative after winning majorities in both the House and Senate in the Congressional elections of 1986.

Accordingly, Reagan sometimes had to compromise with Congress. In 1985 the president called for a Second American Revolution, a comprehensive overhaul of the income tax system. But the Tax Reform Act that Congress passed in 1986 did not lower and simplify income taxes nearly as much as the president had wanted.

Reagan also met outright defeat in Congress. In 1988, a coalition of Democrats and Republicans passed a bill compelling large companies to give workers 60 days' advance notice of plant closings and layoffs. Reagan opposed this liberal, prolabor measure, but he allowed the bill to become law without his signature.

The president faced repeated defeat on environmental policy. During the 1980s there was growing concern about environmental hazards. In December 1984 the subsidiary of a U.S. corporation accidentally allowed toxic gas to escape from a pesticide plant in Bhopal, India. The emission killed more than 2,500 people and injured 200,000. In April 1986 an explosion and fire allowed radioactive material to escape a nuclear power plant at Chernobyl in the Soviet Union. The accident killed more than 30 people, injured more than 200, exposed countless others to radioactivity, and caused extensive environmental damage.

In this alarming context, Reagan had to accept the extension of the federal Superfund program to clean up hazardous waste in the United States in 1986. The next year, Congress overrode his veto of a bill renewing the Water Quality Control Act. In 1988 the Reagan administration signed an international agreement placing limits on emissions linked to acid rain.

A Vulnerable Economy

Even the economy, the centerpiece of the Reagan Revolution, became a problem during the president's second term. During the 1980s the gap between rich and poor widened sharply. While the average family income, after taxes, of the highest paid tenth of Americans rose 27 percent from 1977 to 1988, the average family income of the poorest tenth fell 11 percent (see Figure 30–1). In the 1980s only the rich earned more and kept more. Other Americans faced economic stagnation or decline.

The falling incomes of the poorest Americans ensured the persistence of poverty. Twenty-nine million Americans lived below the poverty line in 1980. Ten years later, that figure had grown to almost 37 million. Despite Reaganomics, the United States had one of the highest poverty rates among industrialized nations.

One of the most visible consequences of poverty was homelessness. In the 1980s the number of homeless Americans increased markedly. The sight of men and women, their belongings in shopping carts, sleeping on sidewalks, was common during the Reagan years.

Homelessness, poverty, and inequality produced a spirited debate in the 1980s. Democrats and liberals blamed these problems on Reaganomics. The president, they charged, had done nothing to stop the erosion of high-paying factory jobs. His welfare, housing, and job-training cuts hurt the poor, while his tax cuts and deregulation helped the rich.

In response, conservatives and Republicans maintained that activist, liberal government had hurt manufacturing and weakened the economy. Moreover, welfare programs caused poverty by destroying poor people's work ethic and making them dependent on handouts.

Not surprisingly, neither side persuaded the other. In reality, both liberal and conservative policies had produced flawed economic results. Lyndon Johnson's spending for the Great Society, along with the cost of the Vietnam War, had begun

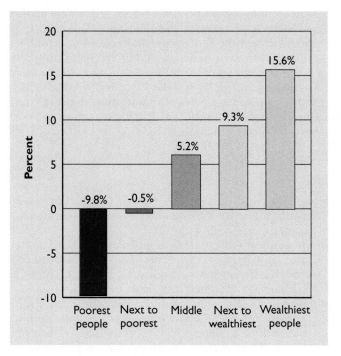

Figure 30–1   Changes in Families' Real Income, 1980–1990

Source: Copyright © 1989 by the New York Times Co. Reprinted by permission.

to undermine the economy in the 1960s. His antipoverty programs had been less effective than liberals wanted to admit, but the Reagan Revolution had offered no solution to poverty, either. Reaganomics did not reinvigorate manufacturing or boost middle-class incomes.

There were other signs of economic vulnerability by the mid-1980s. The federal budget deficit did not disappear. Instead, between 1981 and 1986, as the government cut taxes and increased defense spending, the deficit soared from $79 billion to $221 billion—a staggering new record.

Like poverty and inequality, the deficit was controversial: Some economists believed the deficit was a sign of great economic weakness; others believed it did not matter. Democrats and liberals blamed Reagan for the budgetary red ink. Reagan's supporters blamed Congress for failing to cut the budget.

In fact both the president and Congress were to blame. Neither Republicans nor Democrats wanted to reduce such popular benefits as Medicare and Social Security. Congress enacted the Balanced Budget and Emergency Deficit Control Act of 1985, known as the Gramm–Rudman Act, which promised automatic cuts to balance the budget by 1990. The next year a Supreme Court ruling critically weakened the measure. The deficit remained high during Reagan's last years in office, and the national debt—the total amount owed by the federal government to its creditors—reached $2.6 trillion.

Along with this burgeoning debt, the Reagan years produced a growing international trade deficit. In 1980 the annual value of imports was $25.4 billion greater than the value of the nation's exports. By 1986 that gap had grown to $145.1 billion. Consumers at home and abroad found foreign goods more attractive than ever. Reaganomics had not solved the problem of America's relative decline in the world economy.

Doubts about Reagan's economic policy increased when the stock market plummeted unexpectedly on Monday, October 19, 1987, losing 508 points, or 23 percent of its value. The market drop reflected underlying economic problems including the federal budget deficit, the trade deficit, and deindustrialization, plus lax regulation of Wall Street by the Reagan administration. "What crashed was more than just the market," a journalist concluded. "It was the Reagan Illusion: the idea that there could be a defense buildup and tax cuts without a price, that the country could live beyond its means indefinitely." In the late 1980s, the American economy, like Ivana Trump, apparently could not have it all.

Reagan's Comeback

By 1987 the Reagan presidency, beset by scandals and economic troubles, appeared to be in jeopardy. Reagan's accomplishments, like the Trumps' success, seemed uncertain. Then the president began a comeback.

Reagan benefited from his political skills and his popularity. Continuing economic growth overshadowed the stock market crash and other woes. Most important, perhaps, changes in the Soviet Union led to a dramatic easing of cold-war tensions. By the end of his presidency, Reagan had won back his popularity.

During his second term, Reagan showed a remarkable ability to withstand scandal and defeat. Opponents dubbed him the "Teflon president" because nothing seemed to stick to him. That was a tribute to Reagan's political skills as well as many Americans' real affection for him. After a series of disappointing presidencies, Americans seemed unwilling to let Reagan fail.

The economy also helped the president. Notwithstanding Americans' fears, the stock market crash did not lead to depression or recession. The market soon recovered. The economy continued to grow. The nation was arguably more prosperous than during the 1970s.

Reagan's comeback was probably helped most of all by the transformation of the Soviet Union. By the mid-1980s the USSR suffered from a weakening economy, an unpopular war in Afghanistan, and a costly arms race. At this critical juncture, Mikhail Gorbachev became General Secretary of the Communist Party. The dynamic and charismatic Gorbachev signaled a new era with a series of stunning reforms. At home, he called for restructuring the economy (*perestroika*) and tolerating more open discussion (*glasnost*). Abroad, he sought an easing of tensions with the United States and the West.

Gorbachev's reforms gave the U.S. government a politically popular opportunity to thaw cold-war tensions. Reagan met with the Soviet leader in a series of positive summits beginning in Geneva, Switzerland, in November 1985. Meanwhile, it became apparent that the Soviets were, in fact, changing their foreign policy, as they withdrew their troops from Afghanistan and began to ease control over the Communist regimes of Eastern Europe.

Simultaneously, the United States and the Soviets made striking progress on arms control. In December 1987 Reagan and Gorbachev signed the Intermediate-Range Nuclear Forces Treaty (INF), promising to destroy more than 2,500 intermediate-range nuclear missiles. For the first time, the two powers had agreed to give up a weapon altogether.

The INF treaty signaled a permanent easing of tensions. The cold war, so intense just a few years earlier, suddenly seemed to be ending. Conservatives and Republicans insisted that the president's defense buildup had forced the Soviets to

CHRONOLOGY

1980	Ronald Reagan elected president
1981	Introduction of the IBM personal computer Air traffic controllers' strike Economic Recovery Act passes Appointment of Sandra Day O'Connor to the Supreme Court AIDS cases first publicly reported
1982	Breakup of AT&T Nuclear freeze rally in New York City Passage of the Boland Amendment Extension of the Voting Rights Act
1983	Announcement of Strategic Defense Initiative Congress approves Caribbean Basin Initiative Social Security Reform Act of 1983 U.S. invasion of Grenada Terrorist attack on U.S. Marines in Lebanon Publication of *A Nation at Risk*
1984	Report of the Grace Commission Re-election of Ronald Reagan
1985	General Electric purchases RCA Gramm–Rudman Act
1986	US bombing of Libya Nuclear power plant accident in Chernobyl, USSR Tax Reform Act Indictment of Ivan Boesky Revelation of Iran-Contra affair
1987	Iraqi missile attack on U.S. destroyer *Stark* Indictment of Michael Milken Jim Bakker scandal Stock market crash Intermediate-Range Nuclear Forces Treaty
1988	Omnibus Trade and Competitiveness Act U.S. accidentally shoots down Iranian airliner

capitulate. Democrats and liberals maintained that the buildup and the president's harsh rhetoric had actually slowed the thaw in U.S.–Soviet relations.

As Reagan left office in January 1989, his comeback seemed complete. The economy was growing; the cold war was ending. He had the highest popularity rating of any president since the beginning of modern polling in the 1930s.

CONCLUSION

Reagan's comeback emphasized the triumph of the new conservatism. Americans would debate the nature of that triumph for years to come. Certainly the conservative victory, like the Trumps' success, was never as great as it seemed in the early 1980s. Americans did not embrace much of the conservative social agenda. The Reagan Revolution did not solve such basic economic problems as poverty. It even worsened some problems, such as inequality and the budget deficit.

Nevertheless, the conservative triumph, like the Trumps' fortune, was real. In the 1980s American culture celebrated the wealth and values of Trump and other business figures. A new conservative coalition elected Reagan. Moreover, Reagan combatted the sense of national decline that pervaded America in the 1970s.

The accomplishments of the new conservatism, as Reagan's troubled second term indicated, were fragile. The nation's economic revival was shaky, as was the revival of its spirit. Americans were still worried about the future. "I think," Donald Trump concluded, "the '90s are going to be much trickier than the 1980s."

FURTHER READINGS

Connie Bruck, *The Predators' Ball: The Inside Story of Drexel Burnham and the Rise of the Junk Bond Raiders* (1989). This work vividly describes some of the new, controversial business practices of the 1980s.

Theodore Draper, *A Very Thin Line: The Iran-Contra Affairs* (1991). A careful reconstruction of the major scandal of the Reagan presidency.

Susan Faludi, *Backlash: The Undeclared War Against American Women* (1991). Faludi's book captures the contentiousness surrounding gender issues in the 1980s.

Marshall Frady, *Jesse: The Life and Pilgrimage of Jesse Jackson* (1996). Frady presents a full biography of the most prominent African-American leader of the 1980s.

Paul Freiberger and Michael Swaine, *Fire in the Valley: The Making of the Personal Computer* (1974). An interesting anecdotal account of a critical development in the computer revolution.

Paul Gottfried, *The Conservative Movement* (1993). A balanced analysis, particularly strong on conservative ideas.

Haynes Johnson, *Sleepwalking Through History: America in the Reagan Years* (1991). A journalist's vivid chronicle of major developments in the 1980s.

William E. Pemberton, *Exit With Honor: The Life and Presidency of Ronald Reagan* (1997). One of the first full assessments of Reagan's career by a professional historian.

James M. Scott, *Deciding to Intervene: The Reagan Doctrine and American Foreign Policy* (1996). Scott's book focuses on the anti-Soviet aims of the Reagan administration.

Randy Shilts, *And the Band Played On: Politics, People, and the AIDS Epidemic* (1987). A moving account of the response to AIDS.

 Please refer to the document CD-ROM for primary sources related to this chapter.

CHAPTER

31

A New America?

1989–

Felix Andreev and "The Blessing of America" • A New Economy
Political Deadlock • Struggles Over Diversity and Rights
From the Cold War to the War on Terrorism • Conclusion

FELIX ANDREEV AND "THE BLESSING OF AMERICA"

elix Iosifovich Andreev felt trapped in the Soviet Union. He chafed under the restraints of the Communist political and economic system. A Jew, he resented discrimination against his religion. For years, he had loved American movies, American books, and American jazz. The United States, Andreev believed, was a place of "liberty and generous people." However, for years Soviet immigration law made it impossible for him to leave. Then, in the late 1980s, the Soviet leader Mikhail Gorbachev loosened immigration restrictions, and in 1989, Andreev moved with his family to the Brighton Beach section of Brooklyn in New York City.

From the long perspective of American history, Andreev's story was not unusual. Immigrants, escaping oppression and seeking opportunity, had been migrating to America for centuries. From another perspective, Andreev's arrival in Brooklyn was remarkable. For more than 40 years, the cold war had blocked migration between the Soviet Union and the United States. The emerging crisis of deindustrialization in the 1970s had made the United States a less obvious symbol of economic opportunity. Immigrants had played a lessened role in national life since World War II.

As Felix Andreev's arrival suggested, things were changing. At the end of the 1980s, the cold war was ending. Instead, such forces as immigration were reshaping the nation. Andreev was one of millions of immigrants from Russia, Asia, and Latin America who arrived in the United States in the 1980s and 1990s. These new Americans both changed their adopted country and were changed by it.

Andreev's Brighton Beach showed the process at work. Russian immigrants were transforming this one-and-a-half-mile strip of Brooklyn. Restaurants and stores had signs written in Russia's distinctive Cyrillic alphabet. People spoke Russian in the streets. But the immigrants did not want to re-create the Soviet Union they had left behind. They wanted to share what Andreev called "the blessing of America." But in the early 1990s, the new Russian residents of Brighton Beach struggled to find jobs and make their way. As Andreev's wife admitted, the Russians "do not yet fit into" American society.

Brighton Beach symbolized the promise and the uncertainty of the nation as it ended one century and began another. Despite all the upheavals since the 1960s, the United States still represented freedom and prosperity. The United States, however, was plainly changing. An older nation, defined by the cold war, New Deal liberalism, and heavy industry, was disappearing. A new America had not yet taken its place. Despite the declaration of a new war on terrorism, the nation's role in the world was unclear. As the industrial revolution ran its course, the outlines of a postindustrial economy were still incomplete. In the 2000s, the United States was much like Felix Andreev: The nation had left behind much of its recent past but had not yet defined its future.

A NEW ECONOMY

Felix Andreev and other immigrants were drawn to the United States partly by the promise of its changing economy. As manufacturing played a smaller economic role, the service sector, led by computer companies and other high-technology firms, drove the economy. Like the industrial revolution before it, the computer revolution seemed to have the power to transform American life, but the nature of the new, postindustrial economy remained uncertain at the start of the twenty-first century.

Toward a Postindustrial Economy

Underway since the 1950s, the transition from an industrial to a postindustrial economy picked up momentum in the 1990s. Manufacturing played a smaller role in the economy. American corporations continued to move their manufacturing operations abroad to take advantage of lower wages and production costs. Consequently, workers had less chance to hold relatively high-wage factory jobs.

Those workers were increasingly likely to find employment in the service sector, the fastest growing part of the economy. More and more Americans worked in restaurants, retail stores, and offices instead of factories. By 1994 the service sector accounted for about 70 percent of the nation's economic activity.

Many Americans believed that high technology would dominate the postindustrial economy. In the 1990s the electronics revolution continued to transform communications. More and more Americans carried cellular telephones. High-speed fiber-optic cables and satellite dishes expanded the power and reach of telephone and television systems.

The most powerful symbol of the new economy was still the computer, however. Computers became smaller, faster, more powerful, and more common. By 1999 more than half of the nation's households had at least one computer.

The most dramatic computing development in the 1990s was the explosive growth of the Internet, the communications network linking computer users around the nation and the world. Begun by the Department of Defense in the late 1960s, the Internet had spread through universities and across American society by the end of the century. Originally, people used the Internet to send and receive e-mail, but by the middle of the 1990s millions of Americans began to explore the World Wide Web, the segment of the Internet that blended text, graphics, audio, and video. Americans used the Web to communicate, to do research, to create and exhibit art, to listen to music, and to buy and sell online.

These developments spurred the old utopian dream that the computer would define the postindustrial society. Thanks to the computer and other electronic innovations, the dream held, Americans would process information instead of raw materials. Postindustrial America would be a prosperous information society, sustained by the computerized e-commerce of an "Internet economy."

At the start of the twenty-first century, there were many reasons to believe this utopian dream was coming true. The computer revolution seemed to be repeating the industrial revolution. As in the late 1800s and early 1900s, corporations that best took advantage of new technologies were pushing to the forefront of American capitalism: Microsoft and Oracle, Dell Computer and Intel, Amazon.com and eBay, and America Online. Established companies, meanwhile, rushed to do business online.

Like the industrial revolution, the computer revolution spurred a wave of corporate mergers and acquisitions. The ABC television network, already merged with Capital Cities Communications in the 1980s, was taken over by Walt Disney in 1995. That year, media giant Time-Warner, the product of a merger in 1989, bought out Turner Broadcasting. Then, in a sign of the growing importance of the Internet, America Online arranged to purchase Time-Warner in 2000.

The computer revolution also paralleled the industrial revolution by producing a new, hugely wealthy elite. The most famous of this new corporate elite was Bill Gates, the cofounder of Microsoft, who became the wealthiest American since John D. Rockefeller, the cofounder of Standard Oil, nearly a century before. Like Standard Oil, Microsoft became the target of a federal antitrust suit that ended in a judge's order to break up the company into smaller units.

Like the industrial revolution, the computer revolution also produced uncertainty and fear. At the end of the twentieth century, as at the beginning, many Americans worried about the economic and political power of giant new companies and new fortunes. Microsoft, like Standard Oil, became a symbol of monopoly power, and like Standard Oil, Microsoft became the target of state and federal prosecutors. In 2000, a federal judge ordered that Microsoft, like Standard Oil, be broken up into smaller companies to restore competition. The many parallels between the computer revolution and the industrial revolution seemed to prove that the postindustrial economy had indeed arrived, but in some ways the computerized,

Internet economy remained a dream. Few companies made substantial profits from e-commerce. Many online companies quickly failed. General Motors and Ford—old-fashioned manufacturing companies—remained the largest corporations in America. At the start of the twenty-first century, it was not clear that computers, like machine tools and railroads before them, had boosted the productivity of workers.

Moreover, most new service positions were low paying, involved limited technology, and required little education. As a result, the growth of the service sector inspired fears of a low-tech future as well as dreams of a high-tech utopia.

At the start of the twenty-first century, no one could predict the outcome of America's ongoing economic transformation with much confidence. The postindustrial age had begun, but Americans could not be sure what it would bring.

Toward a Global Economy

There was at least one economic certainty at the start of the new century. The American economy was becoming ever more tightly bound up in a single global economy. Americans owned more stock in foreign companies than ever before, and foreigners had more financial investments in the United States than ever before. U.S. exports and imports both jumped about 50 percent in the five years from 1990 to 1995.

International trade remained intensely competitive in the 1990s. Even though the United States still imported more than it exported, the nation seemed to fare better in its rivalry with other industrial nations. American corporations continued their efforts to become more efficient. By 1993 one study rated the United States, rather than Japan, the most competitive national economy in the world.

International competition involved governments as well as corporations. Since World War II, Western European nations had moved gradually toward economic and political cooperation. That trend culminated with the formation of the European Union in 1993. Through the Union, such nations as France, Germany, and Great Britain planned to coordinate their economic and political policies and create a single vast economic unit. The member countries would then, it was believed, find it easier to trade with one another, and other countries, including the United States, might find it harder to compete in Europe.

The United States responded by creating an economic bloc in North America. In 1992 Canada, Mexico, and the United States announced the North American Free Trade Agreement (NAFTA), which established the world's largest and richest low-tariff trading zone. NAFTA won considerable support from U.S. corporations, but organized labor feared that NAFTA would encourage those corporations to transfer even more jobs from the United States to Mexico. Environmentalists worried that the agreement would weaken the battle against industrial pollution. Despite this opposition, the Senate ratified the agreement in 1993.

Downsizing America

Global competition helped spur a wave of downsizing in the 1990s. Some of America's largest and most advanced corporations announced stunning cutbacks in their operations. For instance, AT&T decided in 1996 to trim 40,000 positions. This and other corporate cutbacks were remarkable for a number of reasons: They came during a period of relative prosperity, they involved some of the largest and seemingly most stable American companies, and they affected many white-collar workers. Large corporations had traditionally been slow to cut loose white-collar workers, but now managers and professionals were vulnerable as well.

Several factors helped produce this situation. Fundamentally, American businesses wanted to cut costs and increase profits. They worried about remaining efficient and competitive in the world economy. Also, the end of the cold war affected American corporations. As the federal government downsized the military, defense contractors had to downsize as well.

Downsizing dramatically affected American workers, particularly members of the middle class, who had to abandon some of their cherished assumptions. In the 1990s the middle class realized what blue-collar workers had known since the 1970s: Even the largest corporations were not as stable and secure as they seemed. Accordingly, middle-class status itself was not as stable and secure as in the past.

An Uneasy Prosperity

In spite of the pangs of downsizing, the productivity of American workers and the vitality of the service sector helped keep the economy expanding throughout most of the 1990s. Inflation was negligible, interest rates were low; unemployment rose during a recession early in the decade, then dropped off to record lows, only to inch up in 2000. Driven by excitement about computer-related companies, the stock market reached one record high after another, until it peaked in early 2000 (see Figure 31–1).

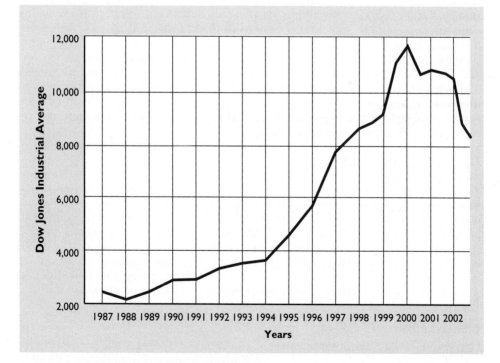

Figure 31–1   The Stock Market, 1987–2002
The Dow Jones Industrial Average had a long, steady rise during the 1990s and a precipitous decline in the early 2000s.

Source: Phyllis S. Pierce, ed., The Dow Jones Averages, 1885–1995 (1996); World Almanac, 1998, p. 510; Standard and Poor's Daily Stock Price Record, NYSE, 1996, vol. 2, and 1997, vol. 2; http://www.forecasts.org/data/data/djiaM.htm.

Despite the good economic news of the 1990s, Americans remained uneasy. Downsizing was one reason; falling wages were another. Allowing for inflation, the average weekly earnings of American workers in 1998 were less than they were in 1970. After 2000, the falling stock market eliminated gains many middle-class people were relying on for retirement.

Americans also worried about whether they could afford the rapidly increasing costs of health care. The United States, almost alone among developed nations, had no national health insurance plan for its citizens. By the 1990s America was spending a greater proportion of its gross domestic product on health care than were the other developed nations. Amid calls for more federal control over health care, many Americans feared the government could not control medical costs without denying people the right to choose their own doctors. As a result, Congress failed to pass a proposal for sweeping health care reform in 1993, and insurance companies were left to attempt to control rising costs. After leveling off in the mid-1990s, by the early 2000s health care costs, including insurance premiums, were again rising rapidly, and the number of uninsured Americans was over 44 million. Congress debated various ways to provide prescription drug coverage to the elderly as part of Medicare, but the larger problem of costs and access was not addressed.

Americans feared, too, that they could not afford retirement. Since the 1980s experts and politicians had debated whether the Social Security system was headed for bankruptcy. With the aging of the baby-boom generation, many people believed there would not be enough money to pay their pensions. Social Security needed reform, but the federal government was reluctant to act. As a result, with a booming stock market, politicians, including George W. Bush, advocated allowing Americans to invest part of their Social Security contributions in stock. A falling stock market silenced that debate, but few other possible reforms were brought forward.

The Social Security and health care issues, along with the corporate downsizing and falling wages, fostered an undertone of anxiety in the midst of prosperity. As the stock market faltered in the early 2000s, Americans were unsure that the future would be prosperous. Leaving the industrial era behind, Americans were not yet sure what the postindustrial era would bring.

POLITICAL DEADLOCK

The economic uncertainty at the start of the twenty-first century was accompanied by a pervasive political deadlock. At the end of the 1980s, conservatives and Republicans believed that Ronald Reagan's presidency had revolutionized the American political economy. The Reagan Revolution had, they expected, realigned politics, government, and the economy for years to come. Despite these hopes, the 1990s brought, instead of a decisive shift to the right, political moderation and uncertainty. No party or philosophy seemed able to mold politics and government—a situation dramatized by a virtual dead heat in the presidential election of 2000.

George Bush and the End of the Reagan Revolution

Conservatives were disappointed even before Reagan left office. The natural choice for his successor, Vice President George Bush of Texas, was a moderate willing to make political compromises. Nevertheless, Bush had loyally served Reagan through two terms, and he had a broad background of government service.

Bush easily won the general election in 1988. Committing himself to Reagan's economic policy, Bush made a popular pledge never to raise taxes. "Read my lips," he vowed. "No new taxes." At the same time, Bush softened the image of the new conservatism by supporting education and the environment. He easily defeated the Democratic nominee, former Governor Michael Dukakis of Massachusetts. Bush polled 53 percent of the popular vote and carried 40 states for a total of 426 electoral votes.

Despite Bush's triumph, the election revealed the weak electoral impact of the Reagan Revolution. Once again, the Republicans had failed to break the Democrats' hold on the House and Senate.

The Republicans' limited victory in 1988 reinforced Bush's instinct for political moderation. Bush disappointed conservatives by signing the Clean Air Act of 1990, which cut emissions from power plants and automobiles, and by signing measures to increase federal funding for education. Above all, he alienated conservatives by agreeing to a tax increase in 1990 to help decrease the federal budget deficit.

Bush's moderation did not ensure his popularity. The abandonment of his no-tax pledge reinforced the sense that he was a weak leader. Then an economic recession in 1991 and 1992 intensified Americans' dissatisfaction with the president.

The Rebellion Against Politics as Usual

Americans' unhappiness with George Bush was part of their broader dissatisfaction with politicians and government. By the 1990s there were signs of a brewing popular rebellion against politics as usual. In 1964, 76 percent of Americans had believed they could trust the government to do what was right always or most of the time. By 1994 only 19 percent of the people felt they could trust government. Americans were troubled by the feeling that politicians were ineffective as well as unethical. During Bush's term, the president and Congress seemed unable to cooperate on critical issues; Bush vetoed legislation more than 40 times. Unable to agree on a budget with Congress, the president shut down "nonessential" government services over Columbus Day weekend in 1990. That episode epitomized many Americans' sense that the government no longer served their needs.

People were still more frustrated because politicians seemed unwilling to reform. By the 1990s there was widespread agreement that money played too large a role in elections. Americans feared that huge donations from special-interest groups and wealthy individuals were corrupting politics. Although Congress and the president talked about the need for campaign finance reform, attempts to reform election spending failed repeatedly.

Americans tried other ways to reform Washington. There was considerable interest in limiting the number of terms that officials could serve in Congress, but Americans settled instead for a more modest reform. For many years the states had not ratified the Twenty-Seventh Amendment to the Constitution, which would keep a Congressional pay increase from taking effect until after the next election. The measure ensured that members of a Congress had to face the voters before getting a raise. Amid the popular anger at Congress, the amendment was finally ratified in 1992.

For a moment that year, it seemed as if popular disaffection was about to revolutionize American politics. Running a tired campaign for re-election in 1992, George Bush faced a sudden challenge from the strongest independent candidate in years, H. Ross Perot of Texas. Perot played to Americans' unhappiness with the political system by promising to end political gridlock, balance the budget, and reform campaign finances.

When voters began to wonder whether the quirky Perot could be an effective president, it was the Democratic nominee, Governor Bill Clinton of Arkansas, who seemed to embody hopes for change. Calling himself a "New Democrat," the charismatic Clinton polled 43 percent of the popular vote to Bush's 37 percent and Perot's surprisingly strong 19 percent. Holding on to African-American support, the Arkansas governor won back many white southerners and workers, the so-called Reagan Democrats. With the Democrats in control of the White House and both houses of Congress, it seemed as if "gridlock" would come to an end.

Bill Clinton and the Disappointment of Reform

In some ways, Clinton's election marked a change in American political life. Clinton was the first of the baby-boom generation to enter the White House. Clinton's rise from modest origins to become a Rhodes Scholar and then the nation's youngest governor reassured an unsettled America that upward mobility was still possible.

Clinton did act like a New Democrat by balancing traditional liberal activism with more conservative efforts to shrink government. Convinced that the federal government could not play an effective social role or maintain prosperity without balancing the budget, the president moved to cut the size of the federal work force. Through budget cuts and tax increases, Clinton and Congress reduced the size of the federal deficit. By 1998 the government posted a budget surplus.

Nevertheless, the promise of the Clinton presidency was limited by the resurgent power of the Republican Party. Clinton's most sweeping liberal proposal, his plan for dramatically increasing the federal role in medical care, went down to defeat. In 1994 voters awarded control of the House of Representatives to Republicans for the first time in 40 years. The new Republican majority chose an outspoken conservative, Newt Gingrich of Georgia, as Speaker of the House. The Republicans vowed to enact a conservative "Contract With America" that featured a balanced budget amendment to the Constitution, term limits, increased defense spending, welfare reform, and tax cuts. The Republicans never won enough popular support to enact key provisions of their "contract." Still, the Republican Party controlled both houses of Congress for the remainder of the decade.

The Republicans' strength forced Clinton to slight key liberal principles and make sometimes controversial compromises with conservatism. Clinton signed a welfare bill in 1996 that significantly reduced federal support for the poor, especially children. Reflecting the conservative vision of political economy, the measure replaced Aid to Families with Dependent Children (AFDC), which had long guaranteed federal payments to the poor, with grants to the states for use as they saw fit. The bill limited welfare recipients to five years of assistance over their lifetime and required heads of households on welfare to find work within two years. To discourage extramarital pregnancies, the bill imposed restrictions on unwed teenage mothers who were receiving benefits and offered bonuses for states with declining rates of illegitimate childbirth. Many Democrats and liberals angrily claimed that the president had betrayed the poor.

Running for re-election in 1996, Clinton benefited from the strength of the economy and the weakness of his opponents. Ross Perot had created a new Reform Party, but his candidacy could not rekindle the enthusiasm of 1992. The Republicans turned to moderate Bob Dole of Kansas, the Senate Majority Leader, who seemed to epitomize the compromising career politician so many Americans distrusted. Clinton won a clear victory with 49 percent of the popular vote. Dole attracted 41 percent of the popular vote and Perot only 8 percent.

Despite his re-election, Clinton no longer seemed like an agent of political change. Damaged by his compromises with conservatism, his reformist image was destroyed by a series of scandals. Soon after taking office, the president, along with the first lady, faced allegations that they had engaged in corrupt deals involving a real estate project, the Whitewater Development Corporation, in Arkansas in the 1970s and 1980s. Meanwhile, there were charges that the Clinton administration had improperly fired White House staff and obtained confidential FBI files on more than 600 people. In 1994, Paula Corbin Jones filed a lawsuit charging Bill Clinton with unwanted sexual advances while he was governor of Arkansas.

Scandal engulfed Clinton's second term. There were charges of illegal fundraising for the president's campaign. Expanding the Whitewater investigation, special prosecutor Kenneth Starr and a grand jury explored whether Clinton had obstructed justice in the Jones lawsuit by covering up an alleged sexual relationship with a young White House page, Monica Lewinsky. After months of denial, Clinton finally admitted to a grand jury in August 1998 that he had had "inappropriate intimate contact" with Lewinsky.

For a time, Clinton's presidency hung in the balance. In November 1998 the president settled Jones's suit by agreeing to pay her $500,000. In December the Republican-dominated House of Representatives voted two articles of impeachment charging Clinton with perjury and obstruction of justice. The following month, he became only the second president to go on trial in the Senate. The Constitution required a two-thirds majority to convict a president, but Republican and Democratic senators alike were well aware that Clinton remained surprisingly popular. In February 1999, the Senate acquitted Clinton on both articles of impeachment.

Like Andrew Johnson in 1868, Clinton held on to the presidency, but he lost the opportunity to make a major impact on public policy in his second term. Clinton's legacy would rest on his shrewd management of the economy and on his attempts to chart a course between liberalism and conservatism. His compromises and personal scandals ensured that his presidency would end with a sense of unfulfilled promise.

Emphasizing the unpopular impeachment issue in the fall elections in 1998, the Republicans barely managed to hold on to their majority in the House of Representatives. In the aftermath of the elections, Speaker of the House Newt Gingrich, plagued by questions about his own ethics, resigned from Congress. His designated successor suddenly admitted extramarital affairs and left as well.

Against this backdrop of frustration, the Republicans nominated George W. Bush, the governor of Texas, for president in 2000. The son of former president George Bush, the candidate benefited from the unity and enthusiasm of Republicans eager to reclaim the White House. He benefited, too, from the decision of the Democratic nominee, Vice President Al Gore of Tennessee, to distance himself from the record of the Clinton administration.

The cautious campaign suddenly became riveting on election night when the contest turned out to be too close to call. As the vote counts stretched into days and then weeks without a clear result, there were fears of a constitutional crisis. The battle turned on the vote in Florida, where Bush held a fluctuating lead of a few hundred votes. Determined to overcome that lead, the Gore campaign called for recounts in key counties, where the votes of his supporters had supposedly been rejected or undercounted. Inevitably, the contest spilled into local courts, the Florida Supreme Court, and the United States Supreme Court. Risking their credibility, the justices of the nation's highest court settled the partisan battle with a close 5-to-4 ruling that effectively halted the recounts. Certified the victor in Florida, George W. Bush became the president-elect.

With no clear winner in the presidential election of 2000, attention focused on the closely contested state of Florida. Here, a judge and an observer try to decide how a voter's ballot should be counted in Broward County.

It was nearly the closest presidential election in American history. Gore actually won the popular ballot by 550,000 votes, but Bush won the electoral college, and therefore the election, with 271 votes to Gore's 266. The narrow margin of victory and the narrow differences between the two candidates emphasized the persistence of political deadlock and uncertainty. No party and no philosophy dominated American public life as the new century began.

STRUGGLES OVER DIVERSITY AND RIGHTS

In the 1990s Americans continued to struggle with the diversity of their society. The wave of immigration made the nation even more heterogeneous than it was during the 1970s and 1980s. Since the 1940s, individuals and groups had been asserting their rights vigorously. In the 1990s the quest for rights took new and sometimes disturbing forms, as some Americans demanded the right to live without government interference.

The Impact of Immigration

Felix Andreev was part of a wave of immigration that took shape in the 1980s and crested in the 1990s. By 1999 the immigrant population had reached 26.3 million, nearly 10 percent of the population, the largest percentage of immigrants since before World War II.

The new immigrants were significant because of their origins as well as their numbers. Only 15 percent were European. In the 1990s more than a quarter of the immigrant population came from Mexico alone. Large numbers also came from the Philippines, China, Cuba, Jamaica, El Salvador, Poland, and the former East Germany.

The shift in immigrant origins should not have been surprising. The people of Eastern Europe and the third world, living with economic and political upheaval, had strong reason to come to the United States. Drawn by a strong job market throughout the United States, the new immigrants settled in all sorts of communities. Mexican immigrants, for instance, settled in small Midwestern towns and cities where semiskilled and unskilled jobs paid 10 and 15 times more than jobs in Mexico.

The majority of immigrants settled in only six states—California, Florida, New York, Texas, Illinois, and New Jersey—and were likely to live in large cities. As a result, the impact of the new immigration was highly concentrated and highly visible.

The effects of large, concentrated, non-western European immigration were especially evident in Miami, Florida. Since the 1960s, migration, particularly from nearby Cuba, had remade this formerly white-majority city. By the 1990s one-third of Miami's 2 million residents had Cuban origins. With substantial numbers of Colombians, Dominicans, Mexicans, Nicaraguans, and Peruvians as well, Miami had become the first major city with a Hispanic majority. The new immigration put considerable strain on Miami. Its schools and hospitals were overcrowded, and many longtime residents resented the new arrivals.

That was what some Americans believed would happen to the United States as a whole. By 2000, non-whites made up one-quarter of the population. Americans of Hispanic origin, both white and non-white, numbered some 35 million—almost 13 percent of the nation's population.

This was a disturbing prospect for some native-born Americans. They worried that immigration would hurt the country. In the short run, the critics of immigration charged, legal and illegal aliens would compete with the native-born population for jobs and drive down wages with their willingness to work cheaply. Native-born Americans complained that they had to pay high taxes to provide health care, education, and welfare for poor immigrants. In the long run, some native-born Americans feared, Spanish would rival English, immigrant cultures would dilute the dominant culture, and whites would lose political power.

Other native-born Americans were not so fearful. Immigration, they believed, had made the United States great in the first place. Instead of undermining the economy, they felt, immigrants would improve it; as in the past, immigrants would invigorate rather than overwhelm the dominant culture. Because of immigrants, the United States would remain a diverse, dynamic nation.

Inevitably, the disagreement over immigration spilled into politics. A new effort to restrict immigration began with the passage of the Immigration Reform and Control Act in 1986, which imposed penalties on Americans who knowingly brought illegal aliens into the country and hired them. The measure also offered amnesty to illegal aliens who had arrived since 1981.

The critics of immigration did not have much success when they tried to go further. In 1990 a revision of the federal immigration law raised the annual quota of immigrants who would be admitted. Illegal aliens were another matter. In 1994 California passed a state referendum denying illegal aliens access to public education and other benefits. In 1996 Congress appropriated more resources to stop the flow of illegal immigrants from Mexico.

Debating Diversity

Disagreements about diversity were at the heart of the immigration controversy. They also drove debates over two other charged issues: the status of the family and American culture. By the 1990s the ongoing transformation of the American family had become unmistakable. Married couples with children, 40 percent of all households as late as 1970, made up only 24 percent by 2000 (see Table 31–1). More Americans were living alone: The percentage of single-person households rose from 17 percent in 1970 to 26 percent in 2000. Families themselves were less likely to fit the traditional model. By 2000, 31 percent of families with children contained one parent rather than two.

A number of factors led to these changes. Americans were marrying later, having fewer children, and having them later in life. The divorce rate doubled from 1960 to 1990. In the 1990s about half of all marriages ended in divorce. As women's wages gradually rose, more women could afford to live alone or to head families by themselves.

Many conservatives and Republicans blamed these developments on the nation's moral decline. Allegedly, the counterculture of the 1960s, liberals, the media, feminists, gays, and others had undermined the nation's "family values." Some defenders of the family suggested that single mothers should receive fewer welfare benefits and that divorce should be made more difficult. Liberals fought back by denying that the family was dying. Instead, they argued, it was simply adapting to change as it always had. The different forms of the family, like diversity in general, were supposedly a good thing.

Liberals and conservatives also fought over the state of culture in America. Since the 1960s, the authority of the Western literary, artistic, and philosophical heritage had been under attack from several directions. Literary critics and other advocates of "deconstruction" had argued that Western culture was revered not because of intrinsic merit but because it reflected the interests of powerful Europeans and Americans. Other people, these critics felt, should be free to place a lesser value on Western culture.

Beginning in the 1960s, several groups did just that. Feminists, African Americans, gays, and other groups maintained that society in general and schools in particular needed to recognize the cultural contributions of the disadvantaged and the oppressed. Instead of worshiping one culture, America needed to practice multiculturalism. That demand horrified conservatives. Western cultural values were, they insisted, vitally important for the well-being of American society. The conservatives charged that the multiculturalists were destroying Western heritage and threatening free speech by making it impossible for anyone to question their positions.

TABLE 31–1

The Changing American Family, 1960–2000*

Year	Households	Families	Married-Couple Families	Single-Parent Families	One-Person Households
1960	52,799	44,905	23,358	3,332	6,917
1970	63,401	51,456	25,541	3,271	10,851
1980	80,776	58,426	24,961	6,061	18,296
1990	93,347	66,090	24,537	7,752	22,999
2000	104,705	72,025	25,248	9,357	26,724

Source: U.S. Census Bureau Web Site:
http://www.census.gov/population/socdemo/hh-fam/tabHH-1.xls and http://www.census.gov/population/socdemo/hh-fam/tabHH-4.xls
*Numbers given in thousands.

The conservatives also attacked the National Endowment for the Humanities (NEH) and the National Endowment for the Arts (NEA) for funding academic and artistic projects that flouted Western values. Liberals, academics, artists, and others defended the NEH, the NEA, and multiculturalism. It was the conservatives, they asserted, who were trying to censor curricula and wipe out diversity.

In the end, the controversies over culture and the family did little to undermine the new diversity of American life. Although Congress cut the budgets of the NEH and the NEA, these agencies survived the conservative attack. States did virtually nothing to make divorce more difficult. The trends toward diverse households and multiculturalism continued, but the controversies revealed just how deeply Americans were divided over diversity.

The Status of African Americans

While Americans debated diversity, individual groups continued to confront their unequal status. From the 1980s into the 1990s, African Americans made economic and political gains. The black middle class continued to grow. African Americans also made progress in electoral politics: In 1992 more than 10,000 African Americans held public office nationwide.

These achievements hardly marked the end to racial injustice and conflict. During the 1990s three episodes, each involving the nation's legal system, dramatized the continuing unequal status of African Americans. In 1991 George Bush nominated an African-American judge, Clarence Thomas, to succeed Thurgood Marshall on the Supreme Court. Thomas's selection proved controversial because of his conservative views, his lack of distinguished credentials, and allegations of sexual harassment made against him by a former subordinate, Anita Hill, an African-American lawyer. Angrily denying her story, Thomas denounced the hearings as "a high-tech lynching for uppity blacks." The Senate confirmed his nomination to the court, but Americans were left to wonder whether Thomas had been singled out for public embarrassment because of his race.

Soon after the Thomas hearings, a second episode exposed the legal system's unequal treatment of African Americans, provoked a race riot, and left lingering questions about the status of African Americans. In Los Angeles in 1991, white police stopped a black motorist, Rodney King, for drunk driving and then savagely beat him. Unknown to the officers, an onlooker had videotaped the beating. Despite the tape, an all-white jury acquitted four of the policemen of all charges on April 29, 1992. The stunning verdict set off rioting in the predominantly African-American community of South Central Los Angeles. Three days of violence left 51 people dead, 1,800 injured, and nearly 3,700 buildings burned.

In the aftermath, Americans debated whether the legal system offered justice to African Americans. They also argued over the cause of poverty and despair in South Central Los Angeles and other black communities. The Bush administration seemed to blame the welfare policy and other liberal programs of the Great Society. Democrats pointed to the welfare cuts and other policies of the Reagan administration. Neither side had concrete solutions for South Central Los Angeles. Subsequent rulings, which convicted two of the police for depriving King of his civil rights and awarded King $3.8 million in damages, failed to wash away the basic messages of the King beating and its violent aftermath. African Americans were less likely than whites to receive fair treatment from the police and the courts. More broadly, society seemed to have no answer for the problems of African-American poverty and inequality.

"We will not rest." In the spring of 1992, rioters in South Central Los Angeles protest the acquittal of white police officers charged with beating an African-American driver, Rodney King.

Less than three months after the damage award to King, another criminal case in Los Angeles raised some of the same questions about race and justice. In June 1994 Los Angeles police charged O.J. Simpson, a charismatic African-American actor, sports announcer, and former football star, with the stabbing murders of his white ex-wife and her male friend. During Simpson's criminal trial for the killings, his lawyers suggested that racist white police had lied and planted evidence. The mostly African-American jury acquitted Simpson in October 1995, but in a civil trial in February 1997, a mostly white jury ordered Simpson to pay millions of dollars in damages to the families of the victims. The Simpson case laid bare deep differences in outlook between whites and African Americans. Most whites believed him guilty; most African Americans believed him innocent.

The Simpson case, the King beating, and the Thomas hearings provoked passionate debate but relatively little action. The federal government did not take sweeping action to deal with African-American inequality. The administrations of both George Bush and Bill Clinton reflected Americans' apparent pessimism about race relations and government activism. Bush disliked affirmative action, but affirmative action programs largely remained in place. The president did sign the Civil Rights Act of 1991, which helped workers sue their employers for discrimination on the basis of race or sex. Although Clinton was supportive of affirmative action and civil rights, his administration did little to deal with the problems dramatized by the Thomas, King, and Simpson episodes.

Contesting Women's Rights

The economic gap between women and men continued to narrow during the decade. The percentage of adult women in the work force rose, as did the percentage of women in high-paying white-collar jobs. Women also played a larger role in government. After the 1992 elections, a record 53 women held seats in Congress.

Clinton selected the first female attorney general, Janet Reno, in 1993; the second female justice of the Supreme Court, Ruth Bader Ginsburg, in 1993; and the first female secretary of state, Madeleine Albright, in 1997.

Nevertheless, women faced continuing discrimination. A woman was likely to make less money than a man. She was also much more likely to live in poverty. Like African Americans, women were still underrepresented in government.

Controversies over sexual harassment also underscored the persistence of gender inequality. Several highly publicized incidents provoked widespread public discussion about the nature of relationships between men and women. The Clarence Thomas confirmation hearings were not only about race; they were also about gender. For many Americans, Thomas's alleged treatment of Anita Hill dramatized the widespread harassment of women in the workplace. President Clinton's affair with Monica Lewinsky further raised the issue of how men exploited their power over women.

As more women entered the military, the armed services also had to deal with the issue of harassment. In 1996 and 1997, the Army was rocked by numerous allegations that drill sergeants had sexually harassed female recruits. Then, in 2000, the Army supported a claim by its highest ranking female general that she had been sexually harassed by a male general.

Despite such revelations, the organized feminist movement did not grow dramatically. Many Americans seemed to accept the expansion of women's rights but to reject feminism. Feminists often found themselves defending earlier accomplishments rather than pushing for new objectives.

Abortion provided a case in point. From the 1980s into the 1990s the conservative Right to Life movement continued its passionate campaign against abortion. Protesters picketed abortion clinics and tried to discourage women from having abortions. Some radicals resorted to violence, including the murder of clinic workers. Meanwhile, George Bush condemned abortion as "murder" and, like Reagan before him, named anti-abortion judges to the federal courts.

In spite of this assault, the right and practice of abortion continued in the 1990s. In *Planned Parenthood* v. *Casey* in 1992, the Supreme Court voted narrowly to uphold much of a Pennsylvania law limiting access to abortions. But the court also declared that a woman's right to choose an abortion was "a component of liberty we cannot renounce." Later that year, Bush's defeat by Clinton, a strongly prochoice Democrat, made abortion rights seem secure. Nevertheless, the struggle to shut down clinics and overturn *Roe* v. *Wade* continued.

Contesting Gay and Lesbian Rights

In a society struggling over diversity, homosexuality remained perhaps the most controversial difference of all. Like women and African Americans, gay men and lesbian women had made real gains since the 1960s. During the Bush administration, the federal government committed more resources to AIDS research. Meanwhile, gays became more accepted in society. Two openly gay men served in Congress. Many businesses, including Disneyland, welcomed gay customers. Leading corporations, including General Motors and Ford, began providing benefits to the partners of gay employees.

Nevertheless, homosexuals' calls for equal rights met with opposition. Although most Americans believed businesses should not discriminate on the basis of sexual preference, a majority still believed that homosexuality was morally wrong. Every year, there were hundreds of documented instances of violence against gays and lesbians. In 1998, Matthew Shepherd, a gay student at the University of Wyoming in

Laramie, was beaten, robbed, tied to a fence, pistol whipped, and left to die by two homophobic men who were later convicted of murder.

The resistance to gay rights was especially strong in the armed services. Officially barred from serving, homosexuals had long concealed their sexual orientation to remain in the military. By the 1990s, however, many gays called on the armed forces to allow openly homosexual officers and enlisted personnel. Then, in 1992 for the first time, a federal court ordered the Navy to reinstate an openly gay petty officer who had been discharged. Campaigning for president that year, Bill Clinton promised to lift the ban on gays in the armed services. Once in office, he met stiff resistance from military leaders and compromised by instituting a "don't ask, don't tell" policy. The military would no longer ask recruits whether they were gay, and gays and lesbians would continue to conceal their sexual orientation. It was unclear how long this uneasy compromise would survive.

There was no compromise in the struggle over legal protection for gay and lesbian rights in civilian life. In communities and states, homosexuals demanded laws that would prevent businesses from discriminating on the basis of sexual orientation. Conservatives moved to block these measures. In 1992 Colorado voters passed a state referendum forbidding communities to pass laws protecting gay rights, but the state's supreme court declared the referendum unconstitutional. In 1996 Congress passed the Defense of Marriage Act, which denied federal benefits to same-sex couples and allowed states to refuse to recognize same-sex marriages from other states. In 2000, the Supreme Court upheld the right of the Boy Scouts of America to dismiss a homosexual troop leader in New Jersey, despite the existence of a state gay rights law.

New Demands for Rights

While old battles for rights continued, the 1990s also saw new and unsettling demands for rights. A small number of Americans claimed the right for religious or political reasons to live free from governmental authority. That claim inevitably brought them into conflict with the federal government. The result was a series of deadly episodes that raised difficult questions about the way Washington used its power.

In 1992 Randy Weaver, a white separatist, failed to appear for a trial on weapons charges. Federal agents then converged on his remote cabin in Ruby Ridge, Idaho, to arrest him, but Weaver resisted. An 11-day siege, punctuated by two gun battles, ended with the deaths of Weaver's wife, one of his sons, and a federal marshal. For some Americans, Ruby Ridge demonstrated the arrogance and deceitfulness of the federal government. They felt vindicated in 1995 when Weaver was acquitted of assault and the U.S. Justice Department agreed to pay him a $3.1 million settlement. Five federal agents were suspended for misconduct, and one was convicted of obstruction of justice.

In 1993 another tragic siege provoked more charges about the arrogance of federal power. David Koresh, the leader of the tiny Branch Davidian religious sect, had gathered about 100 heavily armed followers in a compound outside Waco, Texas, to wait for the end of the world. When the federal Bureau of Alcohol, Tobacco, and Firearms (ATF) moved to arrest Koresh on weapons charges, a fierce gun battle killed four ATF agents and at least five Branch Davidians. Hundreds of law enforcement officers surrounded the compound. The stand-off continued for 51 days, until April 19, when federal agents pumped tear gas into the compound and it burned down. At least 72 Branch Davidians, including Koresh and 17 children, died—some from bullets fired by members of the sect. Many Americans blamed the horrifying fire on the insanity of Koresh, who considered himself the messiah. Others blamed the federal government, which had refused to delay its assault even though there were children in the compound. For critics of the government, Waco stood as a symbol of Washington's intolerance of personal and religious freedom.

The Waco and Ruby Ridge incidents inspired thousands of people to join right-wing paramilitary groups, known as "Patriots" and "civil militias," which trained with weapons to protect themselves from a supposedly hostile government. Some believed that the federal government, secretly controlled by foreign countries, was planning to take away Americans' guns and freedom. Others denied that local, state, or national government had the right to tax American citizens.

A handful of antigovernment extremists apparently did more than train with guns and denounce Washington. On April 19, 1995—the second anniversary of the Waco tragedy—a car bomb exploded in front of a federal building in Oklahoma City, Oklahoma. The blast killed 169 people, including small children in a day-care center. Americans were stunned over what was then the worst terrorist attack in the

The impact of domestic terrorism: Rescue workers and residents mourn the victims killed in the bombing of the Alfred P. Murrah Federal Building in Oklahoma City in 1995.

nation's history and were shocked when they learned the likely terrorists were not foreigners but Americans. In 1997 Timothy McVeigh, an Army veteran with ties to a right-wing militia group, was convicted of murdering victims of the bombing. A friend of McVeigh's confessed to a role in planning the bombing and another friend was convicted of conspiracy and manslaughter.

The Oklahoma City attack was followed by other incidents that raised fears of domestic terrorism, culminating at the 1996 Olympic games in Atlanta, Georgia, where a bomb went off in a crowded park, killing one person. The leading suspect in the bombing had vague ties to white supremacist, antigovernment groups.

The sudden spread of domestic terrorism emphasized that Americans' sense of rights was unsettling and divisive. The struggles over rights in a diverse society would continue, but Americans would soon be forced to focus on even greater threats from abroad.

FROM THE COLD WAR TO THE WAR ON TERRORISM

America's role in the world, so plainly fixed for nearly half a century, suddenly became uncertain when the cold war ended with the collapse of Communist regimes in Eastern Europe and the Soviet Union. No longer preoccupied with the Soviet threat, Americans had to reconsider their needs and obligations as the only superpower in a changed world. For a moment in 1991, victory in the Persian Gulf War suggested that the United States might serve as an active international policeman in a "New World Order," but the moment passed. Americans were ambivalent about involvement in crises abroad. Then, in 2001, the worst terrorist attack in the nation's history led to a war on terrorism. As this unprecedented conflict began, it remained to be seen whether a new principle had emerged to guide American foreign policy in the post-cold-war world.

Victory in the Cold War

As President Ronald Reagan left office in 1989, the cold war continued to wind down. Fear and hatred no longer dominated relations between the United States and the Soviet Union. After more than 40 years of cold-war confrontations and crises, most Americans realized that neither the United States nor the Soviet Union was likely to attack the other without provocation. Both sides recognized that the cold war was enormously expensive and potentially tragic.

Reflecting this understanding, George Bush, built cautiously on the initiatives of the second Reagan administration. In 1990 Bush and Soviet leader Mikhail Gorbachev signed an agreement to end production of chemical weapons and reduce existing stockpiles. The next year, Bush and Gorbachev signed the START (Strategic Arms Reduction Talks) Treaty, which called for the United States and the USSR to cut back their arsenals of nuclear weapons by as much as 30 percent. Nuclear war seemed increasingly unlikely.

Gorbachev was willing to cooperate with the United States in part because his regime had grown so weak. In 1989 the Soviet Union could do nothing to stop the collapse of its repressive Communist allies in Eastern Europe. That year, the unpopular Communist regimes in Hungary and Poland had to agree to free elections. Hardline Communist regimes collapsed in Bulgaria, Czechoslovakia, and Romania as well. Most dramatically, a new East German government agreed to allow travel through the Berlin Wall. Intended to keep East Berliners from escaping into non-Communist West Berlin, the wall had long symbolized the cold-war division of Europe. As jubilant Berliners dismantled the wall, it symbolized the collapse of Communism in 1989.

The cold war ends: A man attacks the Berlin Wall, dividing East and West Germany, as onlookers cheer in 1989.

Powerless to stop its allies from abandoning Communism, the Soviet leadership soon found that it could not save itself. Despite Gorbachev's attempts to improve life in the Soviet Union, many people, like Felix Andreev, were still unhappy with the low standard of living, an unpopular war in Afghanistan, and the repressiveness of Communism. In 1990 Russia chose a charismatic president, Boris Yeltsin, who quit the Communist Party, supported independence for the republics, and challenged Gorbachev. The next year, Gorbachev resigned as party leader and president of the Soviet Union. The Soviet parliament suspended the Communist Party. As one republic after another declared its independence, the USSR ceased to exist.

The cold war was over, and the United States and its allies had clearly won. Around the world, capitalism and democracy seemed to be pushing back Communism. The United States now stood as the sole military superpower.

America's Role in a Changed World

With the cold war over, Americans had to reconsider their role in a changed world. Some Republicans called for a new, less internationalist foreign policy, insisting that the United States should no longer provide so much aid and military protection to other countries, especially in Europe.

In contrast, internationalists in both the Democratic and Republican parties believed the United States could protect itself and advance its political and economic interests only by participating actively in world affairs. Even though the cold war was over, America still faced a variety of challenges abroad. The best way to face those challenges was through international cooperation with NATO and the United Nations.

The most powerful internationalist was President Bush, who believed that American commitment to international freedom had won World War II, preserved the peace, and sustained the nation's economy for so many years. With the help of other powerful countries, Bush felt, America should use foreign aid, military strength, NATO, and the United Nations to maintain a stable international system, a New World Order. Like Woodrow Wilson and Harry Truman before him, Bush mixed together idealism and self-interest in his vision of the international political economy: A free world would be good both for other nations and for the United States. However, the president concluded, only American leadership could preserve that world.

The New World Order was a broad, vague concept. Bush and other internationalists had a hard time explaining just what overseas commitments America needed to make. It was also unclear whether the American people would endorse armed intervention abroad. Critics noted a tension between Bush's call for order and his support for democracy. Should the United States protect antidemocratic countries in the name of international stability and national prosperity?

There was also a tension between Bush's commitment to international cooperation and the long-standing tendency for the United States to act alone in its own hemisphere. While the president spoke of the New World Order, he intervened unilaterally in Panama in 1989. Frustrated with General Manuel Noriega, the Panamanian leader who engaged in drug sales to the United States and thwarted democratic elections, Bush dispatched American troops, who captured Noriega and sent him to the United States for prosecution on drug charges. Bush's unilateral action contradicted his rhetoric about international collaboration in the post-cold-war world.

The Persian Gulf War

The test of the New World Order came soon enough. On August 2, 1990, Iraq, led by President Saddam Hussein, overran Kuwait, its oil-rich but defenseless neighbor to the south. Entrenched in Kuwait, Iraq now threatened its much larger western neighbor, oil-producing Saudi Arabia. Hussein's actions clearly jeopardized America's oil supply and its Saudi Arabian ally and challenged George Bush's calls for a stable New World Order of free nations.

The president reacted firmly. Comparing Hussein to Hitler, Bush created an international coalition opposing Iraq. By the end of 1990 more than half a million U.S. troops had joined with forces from more than 30 nations in Operation Desert Shield to protect Saudi Arabia. Meanwhile, the United Nations imposed economic sanctions on Iraq and authorized the use of force if the Iraqis did not withdraw by January 15, 1991. Bush also obtained Congressional approval for the use of force.

When Hussein refused to pull back, Operation Desert Shield became Operation Desert Storm. As television audiences watched around the world on the night of January 17, coalition forces began an intensive air attack against Iraq. Hussein struck back by launching Scud missile attacks against America's ally, Israel, hundreds of miles away. The missiles did little damage and failed to provoke Israeli retaliation that might have split the coalition. Instead, coalition forces, led by U.S. General Norman Schwarzkopf, began a ground attack against the Iraqi army. In just

Saddam Hussein, the Iraqi president, speaks into a bank of microphones at a press conference.

100 hours, Schwarzkopf's solders swept into Kuwait, devastated the Iraqis, and pushed on into Iraq. Bush called a halt before the invasion reached the Iraqi capital of Baghdad and toppled Hussein.

At first, the Persian Gulf War seemed like a great victory. The United States lost only 148 troops while killing thousands of Iraqis. American technology appeared to work perfectly. Bush's popularity soared. The New World Order, at least for a moment, seemed like a practical reality.

Americans' euphoria over the Gulf War did not last, however. Studies showed that U.S. weapons had not worked quite so well, after all. Gulf War veterans began to suffer health problems possibly caused by exposure to Iraqi chemical weapons. Saddam Hussein held on to power and hindered implementation of the agreement ending the war. His aircraft soon encroached on so-called "no-fly" zones over northern and southern Iraq. Hussein also obstructed United Nations inspectors charged with searching for Iraqi chemical and nuclear weapons. In February 2001, the newly inaugurated George W. Bush ordered missile attacks against Iraqi forces in retaliation for violations of the no-fly zones. Despite his father's massive war effort, the goals of the New World Order had not been achieved. Hussein remained a threat to his neighbors and to American interests in the new century. In 2002 George W. Bush again considered the use of American force to topple Saddam Hussein, countered by opposition from within the United States and abroad.

Retreating from the New World Order

After the Persian Gulf War, the United States retreated from George Bush's vision of a New World Order. The American people were reluctant to accept the dangers of involvement abroad. That reluctance was apparent when violence followed the collapse of Communist rule in Yugoslavia in 1990. As this Eastern European country broke apart, three major ethnic groups—Muslim Slavs, Serbs, and Croatians— fought a bitter civil war in the newly independent province of Bosnia-Herzegovina. The remnants of the old Yugoslavia, under the harsh leadership of Slobodan Milosevic, aided the Serbs as they carried out "ethnic cleansing," the forcible expulsion of Muslims and Croats. Faced with the worst mass brutality in Europe since World War II, first George Bush and then Bill Clinton were unwilling to risk military involvement. In 1994 American and NATO planes and missiles attacked Bosnian Serb forces from the air. The following year, the warring parties accepted a peace agreement brokered by the United States. The Clinton administration committed 20,000 troops to join a peacekeeping force.

Yugoslavia posed a challenge again when the Milosevic regime mistreated and attacked ethnic Albanians in the region of Kosovo. The Clinton administration supported a NATO air offensive against the Yugoslavian government in March 1999. The 78-day war killed between 2,000 and 5,000 people, badly damaged Yugoslavia's infrastructure, and forced Milosevic to accept a multinational peacekeeping force. Ultimately, the United States had helped restore some peace to the regions of the former Yugoslavia. Yet, critics charged, millions had suffered and thousands had died before a cautious America had been willing to employ even a minimum of force.

The New World Order depended on maintaining the American power built up during the cold war, but reluctance to spend money and make international commitments diminished that power. As their budget declined, military leaders cut troops, closed bases, and reduced orders for new weapons. In 1993 the government officially abandoned the Strategic Defense Initiative or "Star Wars" project to create a space-based missile defense system. Meanwhile, intelligence operations struggled with tight budgets, low morale, and public criticism. The federal government's foreign aid budget stagnated in the 1990s. Washington also failed to keep up its promised payments to support the work of the United Nations.

The War on Terrorism

As the New World Order faded away, no single overarching principle emerged to direct the nation's diplomacy. After the cold war, anti-Communist passion no longer animated American foreign policy, and economic interests often swayed policy. For years, the United States had withheld diplomatic recognition of the Communist regime in Vietnam, mainly because of the possibility that MIAs—Americans missing in action during the war—might still be held captive. By the 1990s, there was no evidence that MIAs remained alive. Eager for trade with Vietnam, President Clinton announced full diplomatic recognition of this Communist nation in 1995.

Economic interests helped shape policy toward another Asian Communist regime, the People's Republic of China. Although the Chinese leadership clearly violated the human rights of its people, first George Bush and then Bill Clinton proved unwilling to disrupt developing economic ties with the world's most populous country. The Clinton administration pressed Congress to ease trade relations with the Asian nation.

As Clinton's policy toward China suggested, the American commitment to human rights was fairly weak. During Clinton's first term, he offended human rights advocates by sending boatloads of refugees back to Haiti to avoid angering voters who objected to the cost of caring for the new immigrants.

While Americans failed to show much enthusiasm for the New World Order, terrorism gradually forced them to reconsider the nation's foreign policy. In 1993, Middle Eastern terrorism reached into the United States. A car bomb exploded in the underground garage of one of the twin towers of New York City's giant office building complex, the World Trade Center. Six people were killed and more than 1,000 were injured. Investigators traced the attack to followers of a radical Islamic spiritual leader from Egypt, Sheikh Omar Abdel-Rahman. Rahman and more than a dozen associates were convicted for the World Trade Center bombing and other plots. In 1995 and 1996, terrorist bombings killed American soldiers and civilians in Saudi Arabia. In August 1998 bombs killed at least 190 people and wounded 5,000 at U.S. embassies in Kenya and Tanzania. Blaming the embassy attacks on Islamic fundamentalist terrorists funded by Saudi businessman Osama bin Laden, the United States launched missile attacks on targets in Afghanistan and the Sudan linked to bin Laden's organization.

Fire fighters work in the smoking rubble of one of the towers of the World Trade Center in New York City on September 11, 2001.

CHRONOLOGY

1988	George Bush elected president
1989	Collapse of Communist regimes in Eastern Europe Invasion of Panama
1990	Clean Air Act of 1990 signed First assisted suicide involving Jack Kevorkian Partial shutdown of federal government
1991	START (Strategic Arms Reduction Talks) Treaty with Soviet Union Persian Gulf War Civil Rights Act of 1991 Clarence Thomas named to U.S. Supreme Court Collapse of the Soviet Union
1992	Riot in Los Angeles after first Rodney King verdict Ruling in *Planned Parenthood* v. *Casey* Federal confrontation with Randy Weaver in Ruby Ridge, Idaho Bill Clinton elected president Ratification of Twenty-Seventh Amendment
1993	Car bombing of World Trade Center, New York City Burning of Branch Davidian complex at Waco, Texas Family and Medical Leave Act of 1993 signed Cancellation of Strategic Defense Initiative ("Star Wars") Ratification of North American Free Trade Agreement (NAFTA)

Despite these episodes, Americans remained fairly unconcerned about the threat of international terrorism. But on September 11, 2001, small groups of men linked to bin Laden hijacked four U.S. passenger jets soon after takeoff and aimed them at targets in New York City and Washington, DC. As onlookers watched in horror, two of the jets crashed into the upper floors of the World Trade Center's twin towers. Within two hours, both towers collapsed in clouds of smoke and debris, killing and wounding thousands of people. A third jet crashed into the Pentagon, killing and wounding hundreds. The fourth jet, apparently intended for a target in or near Washington, DC, crashed in western Pennsylvania. To stunned Americans, the attacks were a shocking revelation of their nation's vulnerability.

In the aftermath of the attacks, President George W. Bush committed the United States to a war on terrorism around the world. The President sent U.S. military forces to Afghanistan, whose ruling power, the Taliban, had sheltered bin Laden and his organization, Al-Qaeda. With the aid of British forces, the United States quickly drove the Taliban from power and paved the way for a new regime. Using sophisticated weaponry improved by experience in the Gulf War, American forces suffered hardly any casualties. But, as the fighting wound down in 2002, it

1994	Appointment of independent counsel Kenneth Starr in Whitewater affair
	Accusation of sexual harassment against Bill Clinton by Paula Jones
	Murder of Nicole Brown Simpson and Ronald Goldman
	Election of Republican majority to House of Representatives
	Adoption of Proposition 187 in California
1995	Bombing of federal building in Oklahoma City, Oklahoma
	Peace treaty in Bosnia-Herzegovina civil war
	U.S. diplomatic recognition of Socialist Republic of Vietnam
	Repeal of federal 55-mile-an-hour speed limit
	Million Man March
1996	Enactment of welfare reform
	Re-election of Bill Clinton as president
1998	Investigation of Bill Clinton's relationship with White House intern Monica Lewinsky
1999	Acquittal of Bill Clinton in Senate impeachment trial
	NATO air war against Yugoslavia
	Dow Jones Industrial Average over 10,000 for first time
2000	America Online acquisition of Time-Warner
	Breakup of Microsoft ordered by federal court
	Dow Jones Industrial Average begins historic decline
2001	George W. Bush elected president

was unclear whether bin Laden and much of Al-Qaeda had managed to escape to attack the United States again.

The uncertainty about bin Laden's fate was the not the only reason Americans remained fearful about terrorism. The attacks of September 11—known as 9/11—led to changes in American life. Air travelers had to undergo long, careful screening. A new federal agency, charged with protecting homeland security, issued regular alerts about the likelihood of terrorist attacks. Americans discovered, too, that those attacks could take a variety of deadly forms. Not long after 9/11, a series of letters apparently spread anthrax, a deadly bacteria, in postal facilities, federal offices, and newspaper and television news headquarters, killing two people and leaving several others ill.

Although the threat of terrorism changed American life, its impact was not as sweeping or as novel as many people expected. In some ways, the war on terrorism echoed the cold war. Like earlier presidents who confronted communism, George W. Bush did not seek a declaration of war, dramatically alter economic policy, or call on Americans to make major economic sacrifices to fight the new foreign threat. Despite 9/11, the daily routine of most Americans changed very little.

Nevertheless, the war on terrorism was unpredictable. Much as Americans feared terrorist attacks, they also worried about the challenge of combating terrorism. As the campaign in Afghanistan ended, George W. Bush increasingly focused on the threat posed by the regime of Saddam Hussein in Iraq. The president accused Hussein of supporting terrorism and attempting to build weapons of mass destruction. The prospect of war with Iraq underscored how difficult it was to reorient American foreign policy around the confrontation with terrorism. Abroad, American allies warned that an invasion of Iraq would cost the United States political support. At home, even Republican supporters of the Bush administration worried that such an invasion was too costly. It was by no means clear that Americans were ready to accept a war on terrorism as the guiding principle of their nation's foreign policy.

Conclusion

At the start of the twenty-first century, Americans lived with uncertainty. An older nation, defined by the cold war, New Deal liberalism, and the industrial economy, was fading away, but the outlines of a new America remained indistinct. For Felix Andreev and other Americans, the United States still meant prosperity and freedom, but how would prosperity and freedom be maintained? There was no sure answer. The postindustrial economy was still evolving, as was the nation's role in the post-cold-war world. American politics, caught between liberalism and conservatism, reflected all these uncertainties. Like so many people before them, Felix Andreev and the rest of the nation would define the meaning of America in a new century.

Further Readings

Stephanie Coontz, *The Way We Really Are: Coming to Terms With America's Changing Families* (1997). Coontz's book details family life in the 1990s.

Lawrence Freedman and Efraim Karsh, *The Gulf Conflict, 1990–1991: Diplomacy and War in the New World Order* (1993). This work carefully analyzes the international context of the Gulf War.

Raymond L. Garthoff, *The Great Transition: American–Soviet Relations and the End of the Cold War* (1994). A thorough narrative of the end of the US–USSR confrontation.

Jane Mayer and Jill Abramson, *Strange Justice: The Selling of Clarence Thomas* (1994). A journalistic account of the Hill–Thomas confrontation.

New York Times, ed., *The Downsizing of America* (1996). A detailed investigation of the social impact of corporate cutbacks.

Herbert S. Parmet, *George Bush: The Life of a Lone Star Yankee* (1997). The first scholarly biography of George H. Bush by a historian.

Sanford J. Ungar, *Fresh Blood: The New American Immigrants* (1995). A readable account, based on interviews, of the social and political aspects of the new immigration.

 Please refer to the document CD-ROM for primary sources related to this chapter.

APPENDIX

— ✄ —

The Declaration of Independence

When in the course of human events it becomes necessary for one people to dissolve the political bands which have connected them with another and to assume, among the powers of the earth, the separate and equal station to which the laws of nature and of nature's God entitle them, a decent respect to the opinions of mankind requires that they should declare the causes which impel them to the separation.

We hold these truths to be self-evident, that all men are created equal; that they are endowed by their Creator with certain unalienable rights; that among these are life, liberty, and the pursuit of happiness. That, to secure these rights, governments are instituted among men, deriving their just powers from the consent of the governed; that, whenever any form of government becomes destructive of these ends, it is the right of the people to alter or to abolish it, and to institute a new government, laying its foundation on such principles, and organizing its powers in such form, as to them shall seem most likely to effect their safety and happiness. Prudence, indeed, will dictate that governments long established should not be changed for light and transient causes; and, accordingly, all experience hath shown that mankind are more disposed to suffer, while evils are sufferable, than to right themselves by abolishing the forms to which they are accustomed. But when a long train of abuses and usurpations, pursuing invariably the same object, evinces a design to reduce them under absolute despotism, it is their right, it is their duty, to throw off such government and to provide new guards for their future security. Such has been the patient sufferance of these colonies, and

such is now the necessity which constrains them to alter their former systems of government. The history of the present King of Great Britain is a history of repeated injuries and usurpations, all having, in direct object, the establishment of an absolute tyranny over these States. To prove this, let facts be submitted to a candid world:

He has refused his assent to laws the most wholesome and necessary for the public good.

He has forbidden his governors to pass laws of immediate and pressing importance, unless suspended in their operation till his assent should be obtained; and, when so suspended, he has utterly neglected to attend to them.

He has refused to pass other laws for the accommodation of large districts of people, unless those people would relinquish the right of representation in the legislature, a right inestimable to them and formidable to tyrants only.

He has called together legislative bodies at places unusual, uncomfortable, and distant from the depository of their public records, for the sole purpose of fatiguing them into compliance with his measures.

He has dissolved representative houses, repeatedly for opposing, with manly firmness, his invasions on the rights of the people.

He has refused, for a long time after such dissolutions, to cause others to be elected; whereby the legislative powers, incapable of annihilation, have returned to the people at large for their exercise; the state remaining, in the meantime, exposed to all the danger of invasion from without and convulsions within.

He has endeavored to prevent the population of these States; for that purpose, obstructing the laws for naturalization of foreigners, refusing to pass others to encourage their migration hither, and raising the conditions of new appropriations of lands.

He has obstructed the administration of justice by refusing his assent to laws for establishing judiciary powers.

He has made judges dependent on his will alone for the tenure of their offices and the amount and payment of their salaries.

He has erected a multitude of new offices and sent hither swarms of officers to harass our people and eat out their substance.

He has kept among us, in time of peace, standing armies, without the consent of our legislatures.

He has affected to render the military independent of, and superior to, the civil power.

He has combined with others to subject us to a jurisdiction foreign to our Constitution and unacknowledged by our laws, giving his assent to their acts of pretended legislation—

For quartering large bodies of armed troops among us;

For protecting them, by mock trial, from punishment for any murders which they should commit on the inhabitants of these States;

For cutting off our trade with all parts of the world;

For imposing taxes on us without our consent;

For depriving us, in many cases, of the benefit of trial by jury;

For transporting us beyond seas to be tried for pretended offences;

For abolishing the free system of English laws in a neighboring province, establishing therein an arbitrary government, and enlarging its boundaries, so as to render it at once an example and fit instrument for introducing the same absolute rule into these colonies;

For taking away our charters, abolishing our most valuable laws, and altering, fundamentally, the powers of our governments.

For suspending our own legislatures and declaring themselves invested with power to legislate for us in all cases whatsoever.

He has abdicated government here by declaring us out of his protection and waging war against us.

He has plundered our seas, ravaged our coasts, burnt our towns, and destroyed the lives of our people.

He is, at this time, transporting large armies of foreign mercenaries to complete the works of death, desolation, and tyranny already begun with circumstances of cruelty and perfidy scarcely paralleled in the most barbarous ages, and totally unworthy the head of a civilized nation.

He has constrained our fellow citizens, taken captive on the high seas, to bear arms against their country, to become the executioners of their friends and brethren, or to fall themselves by their hands.

He has excited domestic insurrections amongst us and has endeavored to bring on the inhabitants of our frontiers, the merciless Indian savages, whose known rule of warfare is an undistinguished destruction of all ages, sexes, and conditions.

In every stage of these oppressions, we have petitioned for redress in the most humble terms; our repeated petitions have been answered only by repeated injury. A prince whose character is thus marked by every act which may define a tyrant is unfit to be the ruler of a free people.

Nor have we been wanting in attention to our British brethren. We have warned them, from time to time, of attempts made by their legislature to extend an unwarrantable jurisdiction over us. We have reminded them of the circumstances of our emigration and settlement here. We have appealed to their native justice and magnanimity, and we have conjured them, by the ties of our common kindred, to disavow these usurpations, which would inevitably interrupt our connections and correspondence. They, too, have been deaf to the voice of justice and consanguinity. We must, therefore, acquiesce in the necessity which denounces our separation, and hold them, as we hold the rest of mankind, enemies in war, in peace, friends.

We, therefore, the representatives of the United States of America, in general

Congress assembled, appealing to the Supreme Judge of the world for the rectitude of our intentions, do, in the name and by the authority of the good people of these colonies, solemnly publish and declare, that these united colonies are, and of right ought to be, free and independent states: that they are absolved from all allegiance to the British Crown, and that all political connection between them and the state of Great Britain is, and ought to be, totally dissolved; and that, as free and independent states, they have full power to levy war, conclude peace, contract alliances, establish commerce, and to do all other acts and things which independent states may of right do. And, for the support of this declaration, with a firm reliance on the protection of Divine Providence, we mutually pledge to each other our lives, our fortunes, and our sacred honor.

THE CONSTITUTION OF THE UNITED STATES OF AMERICA

We the people of the United States, in order to form a more perfect union, establish justice, insure domestic tranquillity, provide for the common defense, promote the general welfare, and secure the blessings of liberty to ourselves and our posterity, do ordain and establish this Constitution for the United States of America.

Article I

SECTION 1. All legislative powers herein granted shall be vested in a Congress of the United States, which shall consist of a Senate and House of Representatives.

SECTION 2. 1. The House of Representatives shall be composed of members chosen every second year by the people of the several States, and the electors in each State shall have the qualifications requisite for electors of the most numerous branch of the State legislature.

2. No person shall be a representative who shall not have attained to the age of twenty-five years, and been seven years a cit-

izen of the United States, and who shall not, when elected, be an inhabitant of that State in which he shall be chosen.

3. Representatives and direct taxes[1] shall be apportioned among the several States which may be included within this Union, according to their respective numbers, which shall be determined by adding to the whole number of free persons, including those bound to service for a term of years, and excluding Indians not taxed, three fifths of all other persons.[2] The actual enumeration shall be made within three years after the first meeting of the Congress of the United States, and within every subsequent term of ten years, in such manner as they shall be law direct. The number of representatives shall not exceed one for every thirty thousand, but each State shall have at least one representative; and until such enumeration shall be made, the State of New Hampshire shall be entitled to choose three, Massachusetts eight, Rhode Island and Providence Plantations one, Connecticut five, New York six, New Jersey four, Pennsylvania eight, Delaware one, Maryland six, Virginia ten, North Carolina five, South Carolina five, and Georgia three.

4. When vacancies happen in the representation from any State, the executive authority thereof shall issue writs of election to fill such vacancies.

5. The House of Representatives shall choose their speaker and other officers; and shall have the sole power of impeachment.

SECTION 3. 1. The Senate of the United States shall be composed of two senators from each State, chosen by the legislature thereof,[3] for six years; and each senator shall have one vote.

2. Immediately after they shall be assembled in consequence of the first election, they shall be divided as equally as may be into three classes. The seats of the senators of the first class shall be vacated at the expiration of the second year, of the second class at the expiration of the fourth year, and of

[1]See the Sixteenth Amendment.
[2]See the Fourteenth Amendment.
[3]See the Seventeenth Amendment.

the third class at the expiration of the sixth year, so that one third may be chosen every second year; and if vacancies happen by resignation, or otherwise, during the recess of the legislature of any State, the executive thereof may make temporary appointments until the next meeting of the legislature, which shall then fill such vacancies.[4]

3. No person shall be a senator who shall not have attained to the age of thirty years, and been nine years a citizen of the United States, and who shall not, when elected, be an inhabitant of that State for which he shall be chosen.

4. The Vice President of the United States shall be President of the Senate, but shall have no vote, unless they be equally divided.

5. The Senate shall choose their other officers, and also a president pro tempore, in the absence of the Vice President, or when he shall exercise the office of the President of the United States.

6. The Senate shall have the sole power to try all impeachments. When sitting for that purpose, they shall be on oath or affirmation. When the president of the United States is tried, the chief justice shall preside: and no person shall be convicted without the concurrence of two thirds of the members present.

7. Judgment in cases of impeachment shall not extend further than to removal from office, and disqualification to hold and enjoy any office of honor, trust or profit under the United States: but the party convicted shall nevertheless be liable and subject to indictment, trial, judgment and punishment, according to law.

SECTION 4. 1. The times, places, and manner of holding elections for senators and representatives, shall be prescribed in each State by the legislature thereof; but the Congress may at any time by law make or alter such regulations, except as to the places of choosing senators.

2. The Congress shall assemble at least once in every year, and such meeting shall be on the first Monday in December, unless they shall by law appoint a different day.

[4]See the Seventeenth Amendment.

SECTION 5. 1. Each House shall be the judge of the elections, returns and qualifications of its own members, and a majority of each shall constitute a quorum to do business; but a smaller number may adjourn from day to day, and may be authorized to compel the attendance of absent members, in such manner, and under such penalties as each House may provide.

2. Each House may determine the rules of its proceedings, punish its members for disorderly behavior, and, with the concurrence of two thirds, expel a member.

3. Each House shall keep a journal of its proceedings, and from time to time publish the same, excepting such parts as may in their judgment require secrecy; and the yeas and nays of the members of either house on any question shall, at the desire of one fifth of those present, be entered on the journal.

4. Neither House, during the session of Congress, shall, without the consent of the other, adjourn for more than three days, nor to any other place than that in which the two Houses shall be sitting.

SECTION 6. 1. The senators and representatives shall receive a compensation for their services, to be ascertained by law, and paid out of the Treasury of the United States. They shall in all cases, except treason, felony, and breach of the peace, be privileged from arrest during their attendance at the session of their respective Houses, and in going to and returning from the same; and for any speech or debate in either House, they shall not be questioned in any other place.

2. No senator or representative shall, during the time for which he was elected, be appointed to any civil office under the authority of the United States, which shall have been created, or the emoluments whereof shall have been increased, during such time; and no person holding any office under the United States shall be a member of either House during his continuance in office.

SECTION 7. 1. All bills for raising revenue shall originate in the House of Representatives; but the Senate may purpose or concur with amendments as on other bills.

2. Every bill which shall have passed the House of Representatives and the Senate, shall, before it become a law, be presented to the President of the United States; if he approves he shall sign it, but if not he shall return it, with his objections, to that House in which it shall have originated, who shall enter the objections at large on their journal, and proceed to reconsider it. If after such reconsideration two thirds of that House shall agree to pass the bill, it shall be sent, together with the objections, to the other House, by which it shall likewise be reconsidered, and if approved by two thirds of that House, it shall become a law. But in all such cases the votes of both Houses shall be determined by yeas and nays, and the names of the persons voting for and against the bill shall be entered on the journal of each House respectively. If any bill shall not be returned by the President within ten days (Sundays excepted) after it shall have been presented to him, the same shall be a law, in like manner as if he had signed it, unless the Congress by their adjournment prevent its return, in which case it shall not be a law.

3. Every order, resolution, or vote to which the concurrence of the Senate and the House of Representatives may be necessary (except on a question of adjournment) shall be presented to the President of the United States; and before the same shall take effect, shall be approved by him, or being disapproved by him, shall be repassed by two thirds of the Senate and House of Representatives, according to the rules and limitations prescribed in the case of a bill.

SECTION 8. The Congress shall have the power

1. To lay and collect taxes, duties, imposts, and excises, to pay the debts and provide for the common defense and general welfare of the United States; but all duties, imposts, and excises shall be uniform throughout the United States.

2. To borrow money on the credit of the United States;

3. To regulate commerce with foreign nations, and among the several States, and with the Indian tribes;

4. To establish a uniform rule of naturalization, and uniform laws on the subject of bankruptcies throughout the United States;

5. To coin money, regulate the value thereof, and of foreign coin, and fix the standard of weights and measures;

6. To provide for the punishment of counterfeiting the securities and current coin of the United States;

7. To establish post offices and post roads;

8. To promote the progress of science and useful arts, by securing for limited times to authors and inventors the exclusive right to their respective writings and discoveries;

9. To constitute tribunals inferior to the Supreme Court;

10. To define and punish piracies and felonies committed on the high seas, and offenses against the law of nations;

11. To declare war, grant letters of marque and reprisal, and make rules concerning captures on land and water;

12. To raise and support armies, but no appropriation of money to that use shall be for a longer term than two years;

13. To provide and maintain a navy;

14. To make rules for the government and regulation of the land and naval forces;

15. To provide for calling forth the militia to execute the laws of the Union, suppress insurrections and repel invasions;

16. To provide for organizing, arming, and disciplining the militia, and for governing such part of them as may be employed in the service of the United States, reserving to the States respectively, the appointment of the officers, and the authority of training the militia according to the discipline prescribed by Congress;

17. To exercise exclusive legislation in all cases whatsoever, over such district (not exceeding ten miles square) as may, by cession of particular States, and the acceptance of Congress, become the seat of the government of the United States, and to exercise like authority over all places purchased by the consent of the legislature of the State in which the same shall be, for the

erection of forts, magazines, arsenals, dock-yards, and other needful buildings; and

18. To make all laws which shall be necessary and proper for carrying into execution the foregoing powers, and all other powers vested by this Constitution in the government of the United States, or any department or officer thereof.

SECTION 9. 1. The migration or importation of such persons as any of the States now existing shall think proper to admit, shall not be prohibited by the Congress prior to the year one thousand eight hundred and eight, but a tax or duty may be imposed on such importation, not exceeding ten dollars for each person.

2. The privilege of the writ of habeas corpus shall not be suspended, unless when in cases of rebellion or invasion the public safety may require it.

3. No bill of attainder or ex post facto law shall be passed.

4. No capitation, or other direct, tax shall be laid, unless in proportion to the census or enumeration herein-before directed to be taken.[5]

5. No tax or duty shall be laid on articles exported from any State.

6. No preference shall be given by any regulation of commerce or revenue to the ports of one State over those of another: nor shall vessels bound to, or from, one State be obliged to enter, clear, or pay duties in another.

7. No money shall be drawn from the treasury, but in consequence of appropriations made by law; and a regular statement and account of the receipts and expenditures of all public money shall be published from time to time.

8. No title of nobility shall be granted by the United States: and no person holding any office of profit or trust under them, shall, without the consent of the Congress, accept of any present, emolument, office, or title, of any kind whatever, from any king, prince, or foreign State.

SECTION 10. 1. No State shall enter into any treaty, alliance, or confederation; grant letters of marque and reprisal; coin money;

emit bills of credit; make any thing but gold and silver coin a tender in payment of debts; pass any bill of attainder, ex post facto law, or law impairing the obligation of contracts, or grant, any title of nobility.

2. No State shall, without the consent of the Congress, lay any imposts or duties on imports or exports, except what may be absolutely necessary for executing its inspection laws: and the net produce of all duties and imposts laid by any State on imports or exports, shall be for the use of the treasury of the United States; and all such laws shall be subject to the revision and control of the Congress.

3. No State shall, without the consent of the Congress, lay any duty of tonnage, keep troops, or ships of war in time of peace, enter into any agreement or compact with another State, or with a foreign power, or engage in war, unless actually invaded, or in such imminent danger as will not admit of delay.

Article II

SECTION I. 1. The executive power shall be vested in a President of the United States of America. He shall hold his office during the term of four years, and, together with the Vice President, chosen for the same term, be elected, as follows:

2. Each State shall appoint, in such manner as the legislature thereof may direct, a number of electors, equal to the whole number of senators and representatives to which the State may be entitled in the Congress: but no senator or representative, or person holding any office of trust or profit under the United States, shall be appointed an elector.

The electors shall meet in their respective States, and vote by ballot for two persons, of whom one at least shall not be an inhabitant of the same State with themselves. And they shall make a list of all the persons voted for, and of the number of votes for each; which list they shall sign and certify, and transmit sealed to the seat of the government of the United States, directed to the president of the Senate. The president of the Senate shall, in the presence of the Senate and House

[5]See the Sixteenth Amendment.

of Representatives, open all the certificates, and the votes shall then be counted. The person having the greatest number of votes shall be the President, if such number be a majority of the whole number of electors appointed; and if there be more than one who have such majority, and have an equal number of votes, then the House of Representatives shall immediately choose by ballot one of them for President; and if no person have a majority, then from the five highest on the list the said House shall in like manner choose the President. But in choosing the President, the votes shall be taken by States, the representation from each State having one vote; a quorum for this purpose shall consist of a member or members from two thirds of the States, and a majority of all the States shall be necessary to a choice. In every case after the choice of the President, the person having the greatest number of votes of the electors shall be the Vice President. But if there should remain two or more who have equal votes, the Senate shall choose from them by ballot the Vice President.[6]

3. The Congress may determine the time of choosing the electors, and the day on which they shall give their votes; which day shall be the same throughout the United States.

4. No person except a natural born citizen, or a citizen of the United States, at the time of the adoption of this Constitution, shall be eligible to the office of President; neither shall any person be eligible to the office who shall not have attained to the age of thirty-five years, and been fourteen years a resident within the United States.

5. In case of the removal of the President from office, or of his death, resignation, or inability to discharge the powers and duties of the said office, the same shall devolve on the Vice President, and the Congress may by law provide for the case of removal, death, resignation or inability, both of the President and Vice President, declaring what officer shall then act as President, and such officer shall act accordingly until the disability be removed, or a President shall be elected.

[6]Superseded by the Twelfth Amendment.

6. The President shall, at stated times, receive for his services a compensation which shall neither be increased nor diminished during the period for which he shall have been elected, and he shall not receive within that period any other emolument from the United States, or any of them.

7. Before he enter on the execution of his office, he shall take the following oath or affirmation:—"I do solemnly swear (or affirm) that I will faithfully execute the office of president of the United States, and will to the best of my ability, preserve, protect and defend the Constitution of the United States."

SECTION 2. 1. The President shall be commander in chief of the army and navy of the United States, and of the militia of the several States, when called into the actual service of the United States; he may require the opinion in writing, of the principal officer in each of the executive departments, upon any subject relating to the duties of their respective offices, and he shall have power to grant reprieves and pardons for offenses against the United States, except in cases of impeachment.

2. He shall have power, by and with the advice and consent of the Senate, to make treaties, provided two thirds of the senators present concur; and he shall nominate, and by and with the advice and consent of the Senate, shall appoint ambassadors, other public ministers and consuls, judges of the Supreme Court, and all other officers of the United States, whose appointments are not herein otherwise provided for, and which shall be established by law; but the Congress may by law vest the appointment of such inferior officers, as they think proper, in the President alone, in the courts of laws, or in the heads of departments.

3. The President shall have power to fill up all vacancies that may happen during the recess of the Senate, by granting commissions which shall expire at the end of their next session.

SECTION 3. He shall from time to time give to the Congress information of the state of the Union, and recommend to their consideration such measures as he shall judge necessary and expedient; he may, on extraordinary occasions, convene both houses, or either of them, and in case of disagreement between them with respect to the time of adjournment, he may adjourn them to such time as he shall think proper; he shall receive ambassadors and other public ministers; he shall take care that the laws be faithfully executed, and shall commission all the officers of the United States.

SECTION 4. The President, Vice President, and all civil officers of the United States, shall be removed from office on impeachment for, and conviction of, treason, bribery, or other high crimes and misdemeanors.

Article III

SECTION I. The judicial power of the United States shall be vested in one Supreme Court, and in such inferior courts as the Congress may from time to time ordain and establish. The judges, both of the Supreme and inferior courts, shall hold their offices during good behavior, and shall, at stated times, receive for their services, a compensation, which shall not be diminished during their continuance in office.

SECTION 2. 1. The judicial power shall extend to all cases, in law and equity, arising under this Constitution, the laws of the United States, and treaties made, or which shall be made, under their authority;—to all cases of admiralty and maritime jurisdiction;—to controversies to which the United States shall be a party;[7]—to controversies between two or more States;—between a State and citizens of another State;—between citizens of different States;—between citizens of the same State claiming lands under grants of different States, and between a State, or the citizens thereof, and foreign States, citizens or subjects.

2. In all cases affecting ambassadors, other public ministers and consuls, and those in which a State shall be party, the Supreme Court shall have original jurisdiction. In all the other cases before mentioned, the Supreme Court shall have appellate juris-

diction, both as to law and fact, with such exceptions, and under such regulations as the Congress shall make.

3. The trial of all crimes, except in cases of impeachment, shall be by jury; and such trial shall be held in the State where the said crimes shall have been committed; but when not committed within any State, the trial shall be such place or places as the Congress may by law have directed.

SECTION 3. 1. Treason against the United States shall consist only in levying war against them, or in adhering to their enemies, giving them aid and comfort. No person shall be convicted of treason unless on the testimony of two witnesses to the same overt act, or on confession in open court.

2. The Congress shall have power to declare the punishment of treason, but no attainder of treason shall work corruption of blood, or forfeiture except during the life of the person attained.

Article IV

SECTION I. Full faith and credit shall be given in each State to the public acts, records, and judicial proceedings of every other State. And the Congress may by general laws prescribe the manner in which such acts, records and proceedings shall be proved, and the effect thereof.

SECTION 2. 1. The citizens of each State shall be entitled to all privileges and immunities of citizens in the several States.[8]

2. A person charged in any State with treason, felony, or other crime, who shall flee from justice, and be found in another State, shall on demand of the executive authority of the State from which he fled, be delivered up to be removed to the State having jurisdiction of the crime.

3. No person held to service or labor in one State under the laws thereof, escaping into another, shall, in consequence of any law or regulation therein, be discharged from such service or labor, but shall be delivered up on claim of the party to whom such service or labor may be due.[9]

[7]See the Eleventh Amendment.

[8]See the Fourteenth Amendment, Sec. 1.
[9]See the Thirteenth Amendment.

SECTION 3. 1. New States may be admitted by the Congress into this Union; but no new State shall be formed or erected within the jurisdiction of any other State, nor any State be formed by the junction of two or more States, or parts of States, without the consent of the legislatures of the States concerned as well as of the Congress.

2. The Congress shall have power to dispose of and make all needful rules and regulations respecting the territory or other property belonging to the United States; and nothing in this Constitution shall be so construed as to prejudice any claims of the United States, / particular State.

SECTION 4. The United States shall guarantee to every State in this Union a republican form of government, and shall protect each of them against invasion; and on application of the legislature, or of the executive (when the legislature cannot be convened) against domestic violence.

Article V

The Congress, whenever two thirds of both Houses shall deem it necessary, shall propose amendments to this Constitution, or, on the application of the legislatures of two thirds of the several States, shall call a convention for proposing amendments, which in either case shall be valid to all intents and purposes, as part of this Constitution, when ratified by the legislatures of three fourths of the several States, or by conventions in three fourths thereof, as the one or the other mode of ratification may be proposed by the Congress; Provided that no amendment which may be made prior to the year one thousand eight hundred and eight shall in any manner affect the first and fourth clauses in the ninth section of the first article; and that no State, without its consent, shall be deprived of its equal suffrage in the Senate.

Article VI

1. All debts contracted and engagements entered into, before the adoption of this Constitution, shall be as valid against the United States under this Constitution, as under the Confederation.[10]

2. This Constitution, and the laws of the United States which shall be made in pursuance thereof; and all treaties made, or which shall be made, under the authority of the United States, shall be the supreme law of the land; and the judges in every State shall be bound thereby, any thing in the Constitution or laws of any State to the contrary notwithstanding.

3. The senators and representatives before mentioned, and the members of the several State legislatures, and all executive and judicial officers, both of the United States and of the several States, shall be bound by oath or affirmation to support this Constitution; but no religious test shall ever be required as a qualification to any office or public trust under the United States.

Article VII

The ratification of the conventions of nine States shall be sufficient for the establishment of this Constitution between the States so ratifying the same.

Done in Convention by the unanimous consent of the States present the seventeenth day of September in the year of our Lord one thousand seven hundred and eighty-seven, and of the independence of the United States of America the twelfth. In witness whereof we have hereunto subscribed our names.

Articles in addition to, and amendment of, the Constitution of the United States of America, proposed by Congress, and ratified by the legislatures of the several States, pursuant to the fifth article of the original Constitution.

Amendment I

[First ten amendments ratified December 15, 1791]

Congress shall make no law respecting an establishment of religion, or prohibiting the free exercise thereof; or abridging the freedom of speech, or of the press; or the right of the people peaceably to assemble, and to petition the government for a redress of grievances.

Amendment II

A well regulated militia, being necessary to the security of a free State, the right of the people to keep and bear arms, shall not be infringed.

---

[10]See the Fourteenth Amendment, Sec. 4.

Amendment III

No soldier shall, in time of peace be quartered in any house, without the consent of the owner, nor in time of war, but in a manner to be prescribed by law.

Amendment IV

The right of the people to be secure in their persons, houses, papers, and effects, against unreasonable searches and seizures, shall not be violated, and no warrants shall issue, but upon probable cause, supported by oath or affirmation, and particularly describing the place to be searched, and the persons or things to be seized.

Amendment V

No person shall be held to answer for a capital or otherwise infamous crime, unless on a presentment or indictment of a grand jury, except in cases arising in the land or naval forces, or in the militia, when in actual service in time of war or public danger; nor shall any person be subject for the same offense to be twice put in jeopardy of life or limb; nor shall be compelled in any criminal case to be a witness against himself, nor be deprived of life, liberty, or property, without due process of law; nor shall private property be taken for public use, without just compensation.

Amendment VI

In all criminal prosecutions, the accused shall enjoy the right to a speedy and public trial, by an impartial jury of the State and district wherein the crime shall have been committed, which district shall have been previously ascertained by law, and to be informed of the nature and cause of the accusation; to be confronted with the witnesses against him; to have compulsory process for obtaining witnesses in his favor, and to have the assistance of counsel for his defense.

Amendment VII

In suits at common law, where the value in controversy shall exceed twenty dollars, the right of trial by jury shall be preserved, and no fact tried by a jury shall be otherwise reexamined in any court of the United States, than according to the rules of the common law.

Amendment VIII

Excessive bail shall not be required, nor excessive fines imposed, nor cruel and unusual punishments inflicted.

Amendment IX

The enumeration in the Constitution of certain rights shall not be construed to deny or disparage others retained by the people.

Amendment X

The powers not delegated to the United States by the Constitution, nor prohibited by it to the States, are reserved to the States respectively, or to the people.

Amendment XI [January 8, 1798]

The judicial power of the United States shall not be construed to extend to any suit in law or equity, commended or prosecuted against one of the United States by citizens of another State, or by citizens or subjects of any foreign State.

Amendment XII [September 25, 1804]

The electors shall meet in their respective States, and vote by ballot for President and Vice President, one of whom, at least, shall not be an inhabitant of the same State with themselves; they shall name in their ballots the person voted for as President, and in distinct ballots, the person voted for as Vice President, and they shall make distinct lists of all persons voted for as President and of all persons voted for as Vice President, and of the number of votes for each, which lists they shall sign and certify, and transmit sealed to the seat of the government of the United States, directed to the President of the Senate;—The President of the Senate shall, in the presence of the Senate and House of Representatives, open all the certificates and the votes shall then be counted;—The person having the greatest number of votes for President, shall be the President, if such number be a majority of the whole number of electors appointed; and if no person have such majority, then from the persons having the highest numbers not exceeding three on the list of those voted for as President, the House of Representatives shall choose immediately, by ballot, the President. But in choosing the President, the votes shall be taken by

States, the representation from each State having one vote; a quorum for this purpose shall consist of a member or members from two thirds of the States, and a majority of all the States shall be necessary to a choice. And if the House of Representatives shall not choose a President whenever the right of choice shall devolve upon them, before the fourth day of March next following, then the Vice President shall act as President, as in the case of the death or other constitutional disability of the President. The person having the greatest number of votes as Vice President shall be the Vice President, if such number be a majority of the whole number of electors appointed, and if no person have a majority, then from the two highest numbers on the list, the Senate shall choose the Vice President; a quorum for the purpose shall consist of two thirds of the whole number of Senators, and a majority of the whole number shall be necessary to a choice. But no person constitutionally ineligible to the office of president shall be eligible to that of Vice President of the United States.

Amendment XIII [December 18, 1865]

SECTION 1. Neither slavery nor involuntary servitude, except as punishment for crime whereof the party shall have been duly convicted, shall exist within the United States, or any place subject to their jurisdiction.

SECTION 2. Congress shall have power to enforce this article by appropriate legislation.

Amendment XIV [July 28, 1868]

SECTION 1. All persons born or naturalized in the United States, and subject to the jurisdiction thereof, are citizens of the United States and of the State wherein they reside. No State shall make or enforce any law which shall abridge the privileges or immunities of citizens of the United States; nor shall any State deprive any person of life, liberty, or property, without due process of law; nor deny to any person within its jurisdiction the equal protection of the laws.

SECTION 2. Representatives shall be apportioned among the several States according to their respective numbers, counting the whole number of persons in each State, excluding Indians not taxed. But when the right to vote at any election for the choice of electors for President and Vice President of the United States, representatives in Congress, the executive and judicial officers of a State, or the members of the legislature thereof, is denied to any of the male inhabitants of such State, being twenty-one years of age, and citizens of the United States, or in any way abridged, except for participating in rebellion, or other crime, the basis of representation there shall be reduced in the proportion which the number of such male citizens shall bear to the whole number of male citizens twenty-one years of age in such State.

SECTION 3. No person shall be a senator or representative in Congress, or elector of President and Vice President, or hold any office, civil or military, under the United States, or under any State, who having previously taken an oath, as a member of Congress, or as an officer of the United States, or as a member of any State legislature, or as an executive or judicial officer of any State, to support the Constitution of the United States, shall have engaged in insurrection or rebellion against the same, or given aid or comfort to the enemies thereof. But Congress may by a vote of two thirds of each House, remove such disability.

SECTION 4. The validity of the public debt of the United States, authorized by law, including debts incurred for payment of pensions and bounties for services in suppressing insurrection or rebellion; shall not be questioned. But neither the United States nor any State shall assume or pay any debt or obligation incurred in aid of insurrection or rebellion against the United States, or any claim for the loss or emancipation of any slave; but all such debts, obligations, and claims shall be held illegal and void.

SECTION 5. The Congress shall have the power to enforce, by appropriate legislation, the provisions of this article.

Amendment XV [March 30, 1870]

SECTION 1. The right of citizens of the United States to vote shall not be denied or abridged by the United States or by any State on account of race, color, or previous condition of servitude.

SECTION 2. The Congress shall have power to enforce this article by appropriate legislation.

Amendment XVI [February 25, 1913]
The Congress shall have power to lay and collect taxes on incomes, from whatever source derived, without apportionment among the several States, and without regard to any census or enumeration.

Amendment XVII [May 31, 1913]
The Senate of the United States shall be composed of two senators from each State, elected by the people thereof, for six years; and each senator shall have one vote. The electors in each State shall have the qualifications requisite for electors of the most numerous branch of the State legislature.

When vacancies happen in the representation of any State in the Senate, the executive authority of such State shall issue writs of election to fill such vacancies: Provided, That the legislature of any State may empower the executive thereof to make temporary appointments until the people fill the vacancies by election as the legislature may direct.

This amendment shall not be so construed as to affect the election or term of any senator chosen before it becomes valid as part of the Constitution.

Amendment XVIII[11] [January 29, 1919]
After one year from the ratification of this article, the manufacture, sale, or transportation of intoxicating liquors within, the importation thereof into, or the exportation thereof from the United States and all territory subject to the jurisdiction thereof for beverage purposes is thereby prohibited.

The Congress and the several States shall have concurrent power to enforce this article by appropriate legislation.

This article shall be inoperative unless it shall have been ratified as an amendment to the Constitution by the legislatures of the several States, as provided in the Constitution, within seven years from the date of the submission hereof to the States by Congress.

Amendment XIX [August 26, 1920]
The right of citizens of the United States to vote shall not be denied or abridged by the United States or by any State on account of sex.

Congress shall have the power to enforce this article by appropriate legislation.

Amendment XX [January 23, 1933]

SECTION 1. The terms of the President and Vice President shall end at noon on the 20th day of January and the terms of Senators and Representatives at noon on the 3d day of January, of the years in which such terms would have ended if this article had not been ratified; and the terms of their successors shall then begin.

SECTION 2. The Congress shall assemble at least once in every year, and such meeting shall begin at noon on the 3d day of January, unless they shall by law appoint a different day.

SECTION 3. If, at the time fixed for the beginning of the term of president, the President-elect shall have died, the Vice President-elect shall become President. If a President shall not have been chosen before the time fixed for the beginning of his term, or if the President-elect shall have failed to qualify, then the Vice President-elect shall act as president until a President shall have qualified; and the Congress may by law provide for the case wherein neither a President-elect nor a Vice President-elect shall have qualified, declaring who shall then act as President, or the manner in which one who is to act shall be selected, and such person shall act accordingly until a President or Vice President shall have qualified.

SECTION 4. The Congress may by law provide for the case of the death of any of the persons from whom, the House of Representatives may choose a President whenever the right of choice shall have devolved upon them, and for the case of the death of any of the persons from whom the Senate may choose a Vice President whenever the right of choice shall have devolved upon them.

[11]Repealed by the Twenty-first Amendment.

SECTION 5. Sections 1 and 2 shall take effect on the 15th day of October following the ratification of this article.

SECTION 6. This article shall be inoperative unless it shall have been ratified as an amendment to the Constitution by the legislatures of three-fourths of the several States within seven years from the date of its submission.

Amendment XXI [December 5, 1933]

SECTION 1. The Eighteenth Article of amendment to the Constitution of the United States is hereby repealed.

SECTION 2. The transportation or importation into any State, Territory, or possession of the United States for delivery or use therein of intoxicating liquors in violation of the laws thereof, is hereby prohibited.

SECTION 3. This article shall be inoperative unless it shall have been ratified as an amendment to the Constitution by conventions in the several States, as provided in the Consitution, within seven years from the date of the submission thereof to the States by the Congress.

Amendment XXII [March 1, 1951]

No person shall be elected to the office of the President more than twice, and no person who has held the office of President, or acted as President, for more than two years of a term to which some other person was elected President shall be elected to the office of the President more than once.

But this article shall not apply to any person holding the office of President when this article was proposed by the Congress, and shall not prevent any person who may be holding the office of President, or acting as President, during the term within which this article becomes operative from holding the office of President or acting as President during the remainder of such term.

This article shall be inoperative unless it shall have been ratified as an amendment to the Constitution by the legislatures of three-fourths of the several States within seven years from the date of its submission to the States by the Congress.

Amendment XXIII [March 29, 1961]

SECTION 1. The District constituting the seat of Government of the United States shall appoint in such manner as the Congress may direct.

A number of electors of President and Vice President equal to the whole number of Senators and Representatives in Congress to which the District would be entitled if it were a State, but in no event more than the least populous State; they shall be in addition to those appointed by the States, but they shall be considered, for the purposes of the election of President and Vice Presient, to be electors appointed by a State; and they shall meet in the District and perform such duties as provided by the twelfth article of amendment.

SECTION 2. The Congress shall have power to enforce this article by appropriate legislation.

Amendment XXIV [January 23, 1964]

SECTION 1. The right of citizens of the United States to vote in any primary or other election for President or Vice President, for electors for President or Vice President, or for Senator or Representative in Congress, shall not be denied or abridged by the United States or any State by reason of failure to pay any poll tax or other tax.

SECTION 2. The Congress shall have power to enforce this article by appropriate legislation.

Amendment XXV [February 10, 1967]

SECTION 1. In case of the removal of the President from office or of his death or resignation, the Vice President shall become President.

SECTION 2. Whenever there is a vacancy in the office of the Vice President, the President shall nominate a Vice President who shall take office upon confirmation by a majority of both Houses of Congress.

SECTION 3. Whenever the President transmits to the President pro tempore of the Senate and the Speaker of the House of Representatives his written declaration that he is unable to discharge the powers and duties of his office, and until he transmits to them a written declaration to the contrary, such powers and duties shall be discharged by the Vice President as Acting President.

SECTION 4. Whenever the Vice President and a majority of either the principal officers of the executive departments or of such other body as Congress may by law provide, transmit to the President pro tempore of the Senate and the Speaker of the House of Representatives their written declaration that the President is unable to discharge the powers and duties of his office, the Vice President shall immediately assume the powers and duties of the office as Acting President.

Thereafter, when the President transmits to the President pro tempore of the Senate and the Speaker of the House of Representatives his written declaration that no inability exists, he shall resume the powers and duties of his office unless the Vice President and a majority of either the principal officers of the executive departments or of such other body as Congress may by law provide, transmit within four days to the President pro tempore of the Senate and the Speaker of the House of Representatives their written declaration that the President is unable to discharge the powers and duties of his office. Thereupon

Congress shall decide the issue, assembling within forty-eight hours for that purpose if not in session. If the Congress, within twenty-one days after receipt of the latter written declaration, or, if Congress is not in session, within twenty-one days after Congress is required to assemble, determines by two-thirds vote of both houses that the President is unable to discharge the powers and duties of his office, the Vice President shall continue to discharge the same as Acting President; otherwise, the President shall resume the powers and duties of his office.

Amendment XXVI [June 30, 1971]

SECTION 1. The right of citizens of the United States who are eighteen years of age or older to vote shall not be denied or abridged by the United States or by any State on account of age.

SECTION 2. The Congress shall have power to enforce this article by appropriate legislation.

Amendment XXVII [May 8, 1992]

No law, varying the compensation for the services of the Senators and Representatives, shall take effect, until an election of Representatives shall have intervened.

Demographics of the United States

Population Growth		
Year	Population	Percent Increase
1630	4,600	—
1640	26,600	478.3
1650	50,400	90.8
1660	75,100	49.0
1670	111,900	49.0
1680	151,500	35.4
1690	210,400	38.9
1700	250,900	19.2
1710	331,700	32.2
1720	466,200	40.5
1730	629,400	35.0
1740	905,600	43.9
1750	1,170,800	29.3
1760	1,593,600	36.1
1770	2,148,100	34.8
1780	2,780,400	29.4
1790	3,929,214	41.3
1800	5,308,483	35.1
1810	7,239,881	36.4
1820	9,638,453	33.1
1830	12,866,020	33.5
1840	17,069,453	32.7
1850	23,191,876	35.9
1860	31,443,321	35.6
1870	39,818,449	26.6
1880	50,155,783	26.0
1890	62,947,714	25.5
1900	75,994,575	20.7
1910	91,972,266	21.0
1920	105,710,620	14.9
1930	122,775,046	16.1
1940	131,669,275	7.2
1950	150,697,361	14.5
1960	179,323,175	19.0
1970	203,235,298	13.3
1980	226,545,805	11.5
1990	248,709,873	9.8
2000	281,421,906	13.1

Source: Historical Statistics of the United States (1975); Statistical Abstract of the United States (1991 and 2001).
Note: Figures for 1630–1780 include British colonies within limits of present United States only; Native-American population included only in 1930 and thereafter.

Immigration, by origin

(in thousands)

Period	Europe	Americas	Asia
1820–30	106	12	—
1831–40	496	33	—
1841–50	1,597	62	—
1851-60	2,453	75	42
1851-60	2,453	75	42
1861–70	2,065	167	65
1871–80	2,272	404	70
1881–90	4,735	427	70
1891–1900	3,555	39	75
1901–10	8,065	362	324
1911–20	4,322	1,144	247
1921–30	2,463	1,517	112
1931–40	348	160	16
1941–50	621	355	32
1951–60	1,326	997	150
1961–70	1,123	1,716	590
1971–80	800	1,983	1,588
1981–90	706	3,581	2,817
1991–1998	1,086	3,744	2,427

Source: Historical Statistics of the United States (1975); Statistical Abstract of the United States (1991 and 2001)

Racial Composition of the Population

(in thousands)

Year	White	Black	Indian	Hispanic	Asian
1790	3,172	757	(NA)	(NA)	(NA)
1800	4,306	1,002	(NA)	(NA)	(NA)
1820	7,867	1,772	(NA)	(NA)	(NA)
1840	14,196	2,874	(NA)	(NA)	(NA)
1860	26,923	4,442	(NA)	(NA)	(NA)
1880	43,403	6,581	(NA)	(NA)	(NA)
1900	66,809	8,834	(NA)	(NA)	(NA)
1910	81,732	9,828	(NA)	(NA)	(NA)
1920	94,821	10,463	(NA)	(NA)	(NA)
1930	110,287	11,891	(NA)	(NA)	(NA)
1940	118,215	12,866	(NA)	(NA)	(NA)
1950	134,942	15,042	(NA)	(NA)	(NA)
1960	158,832	18,872	(NA)	(NA)	(NA)
1970	178,098	22,581	(NA)	(NA)	(NA)
1980	194,713	26,683	1,420	14,609	3,729
1990	208,741	30,517	2,067	22,479	7,467
2000	226,232	35,307	2,434	32,440	11,159

Source: U.S. Bureau of the Census, U.S. Census of Population: 1940, vol. II, part 1, and vol. IV, part 1; 1950, vol. II, part 1; 1960, vol. I, part 1; 1970, vol. I, part B; and Current Population Reports, P25-1095 and P25-1104; and unpublished data; Statistical Abstract of the United States, 2001.

Work Force

Year	Total Number Workers (1000s)	Farmers as % of Total	Women as % of Total	% Workers in Unions
1810	2,330	84	(NA)	(NA)
1840	5,660	75	(NA)	(NA)
1840	5,660	75	(NA)	(NA)
1860	11,110	53	(NA)	(NA)
1870	12,506	53	15	(NA)
1880	17,392	52	15	(NA)
1890	23,318	43	17	(NA)
1900	29,073	40	18	3
1910	38,167	31	21	6
1920	41,614	26	21	12
1930	48,830	22	22	7
1940	53,011	17	24	27
1950	59,643	12	28	25
1960	69,877	8	32	26
1970	82,049	4	37	25
1980	108,544	3	42	23
1990	117,914	3	45	16
2000	140,863	3	47	13.5

Source: Historical Statistics of the United States (1975); Statistical Abstract of the United States (1991, 1996, and 2001).

BIBLIOGRAPHY

⸎

This Bibliography contains a selected listing of the extensive body of literature available on American History. It is compiled chapter-by-chapter, enabling the reader to easily find additional references in a given area, and offers an expanded compilation of literature for students who wish to explore topics in fuller detail.

CHAPTER 16

Belz, Herman, *Emancipation and Equal Rights: Politics and Constitutionalism in the Civil War Era* (1978). _____, *Reconstructing the Union: Theory and Policy during the Civil War* (1969). Benedict, Michael Les, *A Compromise of Principle: Congressional Republicans and Reconstruction* (1974). Brock, W. R., *An American Crisis: Congress and Reconstruction, 1865–1867* (1963). Cox, LaWanda, *Lincoln and Black Freedom: A Study in Presidential Leadership* (1981). Current, Richard, *Those Terrible Carpetbaggers* (1988). Donald, David, *The Politics of Reconstruction, 1864–1867* (1967). DuBois, Ellen Carol, *Feminism and Suffrage: The Emergence of an Independent Women's Movement in America, 1848–1869* (1978). Edwards, Laura, *Gendered Strife and Confusion: The Political Culture of Reconstruction* (1977). Fields, Barbara Jeanne, *Slavery and Freedom on the Middle Ground: Maryland during the Nineteenth Century* (1985). Foner, Eric, *Freedom's Lawmakers: A Directory of Black Officeholders during Reconstruction* (1993). _____, *Nothing But Freedom: Emancipation and Its Legacy* (1983).

Gillette, William, *Retreat from Reconstruction, 1869–1879* (1979). Hermann, Janet Sharp, *The Pursuit of a Dream* (1981). Holt, Thomas G., *Black over White: Negro Political Leadership in South Carolina during Reconstruction* (1977). Hyman, Harold, *A More Perfect Union: The Impact of the Civil War and Reconstruction on the Constitution* (1973). Jaynes, Gerald David, *Branches without Roots: Genesis of the Black Working Class in the American South, 1862–1882* (1986).

McCrary, Peyton, *Abraham Lincoln and Reconstruction: The Louisiana Experiment* (1978). McFeely, William S., *Grant: A Biography* (1981). _____, *Yankee Stepfather: General O. O. Howard and the Freedmen* (1968). McGerr, Michael, *The Decline of Popular Politics: The American North, 1865–1928* (1986). McKitrick, Eric L., *Andrew Johnson and Reconstruction* (1960). Montgomery, David, *Beyond Equality: Labor and the Radical Republicans, 1861–1872* (1967). Morgan, Lynda J., *Emancipation in Virginia's Tobacco Belt, 1850–1870* (1992). Nieman, Donald L., *To Set the Law in Motion: The Freedmen's Bureau and Legal Rights for Blacks, 1865–1869* (1979). Perman, Michael, *Reunion without Compromise: The South and Reconstruction, 1865–1879* (1973). _____, *The Road to Redemption: Southern Politics, 1868–1879* (1984). Powell, Lawrence N., *New Masters: Northern Planters during the Civil War and Reconstruction* (1980). Rabinowitz, Howard N., *Race Relations in the Urban South, 1865–1890* (1978). Rose, Willie Lee, *Rehearsal for Reconstruction: The Port Royal Experiment* (1964). Royce, Edward, *The Origins of Southern Sharecropping* (1993).

Saville, Julie, *The Work of Reconstruction: From Slave to Wage Laborer in South Carolina, 1860–1870* (1994). Sproat, John G., *"The Best Men": Liberal Reformers in a Gilded Age* (1968). Summers, Mark, *Railroads, Reconstruction and the Gospel of Prosperity: Aid Under the Radical Republicans, 1865–1877* (1984). Trelease, Allen W., *White*

Terror: The Ku Klux Klan Conspiracy and Southern Reconstruction (1971). Wayne, Michael, The Reshaping of Plantation Society: The Natchez District, 1860–1880 (1983). Wiener, Jonathan, Social Origins of the New South: Alabama, 1860–1885 (1978). Williamson, Joel, After Slavery: The Negro in South Carolina during Reconstruction, 1861–1877 (1965). Wright, Gavin, Old South, New South: Revolutions in the Southern Economy Since the Civil War (1986).

CHAPTER 17

Ayers, Edward L., The Promise of the New South: Life after Reconstruction (1992). Bledstein, Burton J., The Culture of Professionalism: The Middle Class and the Development of Higher Education in America (1976). Bodnar, John E., The Transplanted: A History of Immigrants in Urban America (1985). Brody, David, Steelworkers in America: The Nonunion Era (1960). Cochran, Thomas, and William Miller, The Age of Enterprise: A Social History of Industrial America (1942). Dubofsky, Melvin, Industrialism and the American Worker (1975). Dykstra, Robert R., The Cattle Towns (1968). Fite, Gilbert C., The Farmer's Frontier (1963).

Goldfield, David, and Blaine Brownell, Urban America: A History, 2nd. ed. (1990). Gutman, Herbert G., Work, Culture and Society in Industrialising America (1976). Handlin, Oscar, The Uprooted: The Epic Story of the Great Migrations that Made the American People (1951, 1973). Hearnden, Patrick H., Independence and Empire: The New South's Cotton Mill Campaign, 1865–1901 (1982). Jackson, Kenneth T., Crabgrass Frontier: The Suburbanization of the United States (1985). Jeffrey, Julie Roy, Frontier Women (1979). Johnson, Susan Lee, Roaring Camp: The Social World of the California Gold Rush (2000). Josephson, Matthew, The Robber Barons: The Great American Capitalists, 1861–1901 (1934). Limerick, Patricia Nelson, Legacy of Conquest: The Unbroken Past of the American West (1987). Lingenfelter, Richard, The Hardrock Miners: A History of the Mining Labor Movement in the American West, 1863–1893 (1974).

Montgomery, David, Workers' Control in America: Studies in the History of Work, Technology, and Labor Struggles (1979). Rabinowitz, Howard, Race Relations in the Urban South, 1865–1890 (1978).

Slotkin, Richard, The Fatal Environment: The Myth of the Frontier in the Age of Industrialization (1985). Taylor, Philip A. M., The Distant Magnet: European Emigration to the U.S.A. (1971). Teaford, Jon C., City and Suburb: The Political Fragmentation of Metropolitan America, 1850–1970 (1979). Thernstrom, Stephen, The Other Bostonians: Poverty and Progress in the American Metropolis, 1880–1970 (1973). Utley, Robert M., The Indian Frontier of the American West, 1846–1890 (1984). Wiebe, Robert, The Search for Order, 1877–1920 (1967). Wyman, Mark, Hard Rock Epic: Western Miners and the Industrial Revolution, 1860–1910 (1979).

CHAPTER 18

Addams, Jane, Twenty Years at Hull House (1910). Archdeacon, Thomas, Becoming American: An Ethnic History (1981). Banner, Lois, American Beauty (1981). Barth, Gunther, City People: The Rise of Modern City Culture in Nineteenth-Century America (1980). Beisel, Nicola Kay, Imperiled Innocents: Anthony Comstock and Family Reproduction in Victorian America (1997). Bodnar, John, The Transplanted: A History of Immigrants in Urban America (1985). Boorstin, Daniel J., The Americans: The Democratic Experience (1973). Boyer, Paul S., Purity in Print: The Vice-Society Movement and Book Censorship in America (1968). Danly, Susan, and Cheryl Leibold, et al., Eakins and the Photograph (1994). Fabian, Ann, Card Sharps and Bucket Shops: Gambling in Nineteenth-Century America (1999). Fredrickson, George, The Black Image in the White Mind: The Debate on Afro-American Character and Destiny, 1817–1914 (1971).

Gilfoyle, Timothy, City of Eros: New York City, Prostitution, and the Commercialization of Sex, 1820–1920 (1992). Gorn, Elliot J., The Manly Art: Bare-Knuckle Prize Fighting in America (1986). Graff, Gerald, Professing Literature: An Institutional History (1987).

Green, Harvey, *Fit for America: Health, Fitness, Sport, and American Society* (1986). Harris, Neil, *Cultural Excursions: Marketing Appetites and Cultural Tastes in Modern America* (1990). Hawkins, Mike, *Social Darwinism in European and American Thought, 1860–1945: Nature as Model and Nature as Threat* (1997). Higham, John, *Send These To Me: Jews and Other Immigrants in Urban America* (1984). Hofstadter, Richard, *Social Darwinism in American Thought* (1992). Lears, T. J. Jackson, *No Place of Grace: Antimodernism and the Transformation of American Culture, 1880–1920* (1981). Lott, Eric, *Love and Theft: Blackface Minstrelsy and the American Working Class* (1993). Lucie-Smith, Edward, *American Realism* (1994).

May, Henry, *Protestant Churches and Industrial America* (1949 and 1963). Mintz, Steven, *A Prison of Expectations: The Family in Victorian Culture* (1983). Nasaw, David, *Going Out: The Rise and Fall of Public Amusements* (1993). Novak, Barbara, *American Painting of the Nineteenth Century: Realism, Idealism, and the American Experience*, 2nd ed. (1979). Rodgers, Daniel, *The Work Ethic in Industrial America, 1850–1920* (1970). Rothman, Sheila M., *Woman's Proper Place: A History of Changing Ideals and Practices, 1870 to the Present* (1978). Rydell, Robert, *All the World's a Fair: Visions of Empire at American International Expositions, 1876–1916* (1984).

Sollors, Werner, *Beyond Ethnicity: Consent and Descent in American Culture* (1986). Toll, Robert, *On with the Show: The First Century of Show Business in America* (1976). Trachtenberg, Alan, *Reading American Photographs: Images as History, Mathew Brady to Walker Evans* (1989).

CHAPTER 19

Baker, Paula C., *The Moral Frameworks of Public Life: Gender, Politics, and the State in Rural New York, 1870–1930* (1991). Beatty, Bess, *A Revolution Gone Backward: The Black Response to National Politics, 1876–1896* (1987). Beisner, Robert L., *From the Old Diplomacy to the New, 1865–1900* (1975). Bordin, Ruth, *Frances Willard: A Biography* (1986). Brock, William R., *Investigation and Responsibility: Public Responsibility in the United States, 1865–1900* (1984). Buhle, Mary Jo, *Women and American Socialism, 1870–1920* (1981). Campbell, Ballard, *Representative Democracy: Public Policy and Midwestern Legislatures in the Late Nineteenth Century* (1980). Campbell, Charles S., *The Transformation of American Foreign Relations, 1865–1900* (1976).

Garraty, John A., *The New Commonwealth, 1877–1890* (1968). Gould, Lewis L., *The Presidency of William McKinley* (1980). Hays, Samuel P., *The Response to Industrialism, 1885–1914*, 2nd ed. (1995). Jensen, Richard J., *The Winning of the Midwest: Social and Political Conflict, 1888–1896* (1971). Keller, Morton, *Affairs of State: Public Life in Late-Nineteenth-Century America* (1977). Kleppner, Paul J., *The Cross of Culture: A Social Analysis of Midwestern Politics, 1850–1900* (1970).

McCormick, Richard L., *The Party Period and Public Policy: American Politics from the Age of Jackson to the Progressive Era* (1986). McMath, Robert C., Jr., *The Populist Vanguard: A History of the Southern Farmers' Alliance* (1975). Mink, Gwendolyn, *Old Labor and New Immigrants in American Political Development: Union, Party, and the State, 1875–1920* (1986). Morgan, H. Wayne, *From Hayes to McKinley: National Politics, 1877–1896* (1969). Nugent, Walter T. K., *Money and American Society, 1865–1880* (1968). Orren, Karen, *Belated Feudalism: Labor, the Law, and Liberal Development in the United States* (1991). Painter, Nell Irvin, *Standing at Armageddon: The United States, 1877–1919* (1987). Peskin, Allan, *Garfield: A Biography* (1978). Reeves, Thomas C., *Gentleman Boss: The Life of Chester Alan Arthur* (1975).

Skowronek, Stephen, *Building A New American State: The Expansion of National Administration Capacities, 1877–1920* (1982). Socolofsky, Homer Edward, and Allan B. Spetter, *The Presidency of Benjamin Harrison* (1987). Teaford, Jon C., *The Unheralded Triumph: City Government in America, 1870–1900* (1984). Terrill, Tom E., *The Tariff,*

Politics and American Foreign Policy, 1874–1900 (1973). Tomsich, John, *A Genteel Endeavor: American Culture and Politics in the Gilded Age* (1971). Unger, Irwin, *The Greenback Era: A Social and Political History of American Finance, 1865–1879* (1964).Weinstein, Allen, *Prelude to Populism: Origins of the Silver Issue, 1867–1878* (1970). Welch, Richard E., Jr., *The Presidencies of Grover Cleveland* (1988). Wiebe, Robert H., *The Search for Order, 1877–1920* (1967).

CHAPTER 20

Adams, Henry, *The Education of Henry Adams* (1918). Ayers, Edward L., *The Promise of the New South: Life After Reconstruction* (1992). Bailey, Thomas A., *A Diplomatic History of the American People* (1958). Brands, H. W., *The Reckless Decade: America in the 1890s* (1995). Chernow, Ron, *The House of Morgan: An American Banking Dynasty and the Rise of Modern Finance* (1990). Cochran, Thomas C., and William Miller, *The Age of Enterprise: A Social History of Industrial America* (1961). Dulles, Foster Rhea, *Labor in America: A History* (1960).

Gilbert, James B., *Perfect Cities: Chicago's Utopias of 1893* (1991). Ginger, Ray, *Age of Excess: The United States from 1877 to 1914* (1965). _____, *Altgeld's America: The Lincoln Ideal Versus Changing Realities* (1958). Kanigel, Robert, *The One Best Way: Frederick Winslow Taylor and the Enigma of Efficiency* (1997). Karnow, Stanley, *In Our Image: America's Empire in the Philippines* (1989). Lewis, David L., *W. E. B. Du Bois: Biography of a Race, 1868–1919* (1993).

McCloskey, Robert Green, *American Conservatism in the Age of Enterprise, 1865–1910* (1951). McCormick, Richard L., *The Party Period and Public Policy* (1986). McCormick, Thomas J., *China Market: America's Quest for Informal Empire, 1893–1901* (1967). McDougall, Walter A., *Let the Sea Make a Noise: A History of the North Pacific from Magellan to MacArthur* (1993). McGerr, Michael E., *The Decline of Popular Politics: The American North, 1865–1928* (1986). Montgomery, David, *The*

Fall of the House of Labor: The Workplace, the State, and American Labor Activism, 1865–1925 (1987). Musicant, Ivan, *Empire by Default: The Spanish American War and the Dawn of the American Century* (1998). Richardson, Dorothy, *The Long Day: The Story of a New York Working Girl* (1990). Rosenberg, Emily S., *Spreading the American Dream: American Economic and Cultural Expansion, 1890–1945* (1982).

Salvatore, Nick, *Eugene V. Debs: Citizen and Socialist* (1982). Schirmer, Daniel B., *Republic or Empire: American Resistance to the Philippine War* (1972). Slotkin, Richard, *Gunfighter Nation: The Myth of the Frontier in Twentieth-Century America* (1993). Strouse, Jean, *Morgan: American Financier* (1999). Trask, David F., *The War with Spain in 1898* (1981).

CHAPTER 21

Brands, H. W., *T. R.: The Last Romantic* (1997). Bringhurst, Bruce, *Antitrust and the Oil Monopoly: The Standard Oil Cases, 1890–1911* (1979). Clark, Norman H., *Deliver Us from Evil: An Interpretation of American Prohibition* (1976). Cooper, John Milton, Jr., *The Warrior and the Priest: Theodore Roosevelt and Woodrow Wilson in American Politics* (1983). Crichon, Judy, *America 1900: The Turning Point* (1998). Diner, Steven J., *A Very Different Age: Americans in the Progressive Era* (1998). Dulles, Foster Rhea, *Labor in America* (1955). Faulkner, Harold Underwood, *The Quest for Social Justice, 1898–1914* (1931). Filene, Peter G., "Narrating Progressivism: Unitarians v. Pluralists v. Students," *Journal of American History*, 79 (1993) 4, 1546–1561.

Gould, Lewis L., *The Presidency of Theodore Roosevelt* (1991). Harbaugh, William H., *Power and Responsibility: The Life and Times of Theodore Roosevelt* (1961). Kessler-Harris, Alice, *Out to Work: A History of Wage Earning Women* (1982). Lewis, David Levering, *W. E. B. Du Bois: Biography of a Race, 1868–1919* (1993). Lukas, J. Anthony, *Big Trouble: A Murder in a Small Western Town Sets Off a Struggle for the Soul of America* (1997).

McGerr, Michael E., *The Decline of Popular Politics* (1986). McMurry, Linda O., *To Keep the Waters Troubled: The Life of Ida B. Wells* (1998). Ninkovich, Frank, *Modernity and Power: A History of the Domino Theory in the Twentieth Century* (1994). Rodgers, Daniel T., "In Search of Progressivism," *Reviews in American History*, 10 (1982) 4, 113–132. Rosen, Ruth, *The Lost Sisterhood: Prostitution in America, 1900–1918* (1982).

Salvatore, Nick, *Eugene V. Debs: Citizen and Socialist* (1982). Schiesl, Martin J., *The Politics of Efficiency: Municipal Administration and Reform in America, 1800–1920* (1977). Scully, Eileen P., "Taking the Low Road to Sino-American Relations: 'Open Door' Expansionists and the Two China Markets," *Journal of American History*, 82 (1995) 1, 62–83. Shannon, David A., *The Socialist Party of America: A History* (1955). Sklar, Kathryn Kish, *Florence Kelley and the Nation's Work: The Rise of Women's Political Culture, 1830–1900* (1995). Starr, Kevin, *Inventing the Dream: California Through the Progressive Era* (1985). Thelen, David, *Robert M. La Follette and the Insurgent Spirit* (1976). Weibe, Robert H., "The Anthracite Strike of 1902: A Record of Confusion," *Mississippi Valley Historical Review*, 48 (1961) 2, 229–251. _____, *The Search for Order, 1877–1920* (1967).

CHAPTER 22

Bailey, Thomas A., "The Sinking of the Lusitania," *The American Historical Review*, 41 (1935) 1, 54–73. Bird, Kai, *The Chairman: John J. McCloy, The Making of the American Establishment* (1992). Butler, Gregory S., "Visions of a Nation Transformed: Modernity and Ideology in Wilson's Political Thought," *Journal of Church and State*, 39 (Winter 1997) 1, 37–51. Chatfield, Charles, "World War I and the Liberal Pacifist in the United States," *American Historical Review*, 75 (1970) 7, 1920–1937. Clark, Norman H., *Deliver Us from Evil: An Interpretation of American Prohibition* (1976). Clifford, John Garry, *The Citizen Soldiers: The Plattsburg Training Camp Movement, 1919–1920* (1972). Davis,

Richard Harding, "The Plattsburg Idea," *Collier's* (October 9, 1915) 7–9. Ferrell, Robert H., *Woodrow Wilson and World War I, 1917–1921* (1985).

Horne, Alistair, *The Price of Glory* (1964). Katz, Freidrich, "Pancho Villa and the Attack on Columbus, New Mexico," *American Historical Review*, 83 (1978) 1, 101–130. _____, *The Secret War in Mexico: Europe, the United States, and the Mexican Revolution* (1981). Levin, N. Gordon, Jr., *Woodrow Wilson and World Politics* (1968).

Miles, Lewis W., "Plattsburgh," *Sewanee Review*, 24 (January 1916) 1, 19–23. Miller, William D., *Pretty Bubbles in the Air: America in 1919* (1991). Page, Ralph W., "What I Learned at Plattsburg," *World's Work* (November 1915), 105–108. Perry, Ralph Barton, "Impressions of a Plattsburg Recruit," *New Republic* (October 2, 1915), 229–231. Rudwick, Elliott M., *Race Riot in East Saint Louis, July 2, 1917* (1964). Russell, Francis, *Tragedy in Dedham: The Story of the Sacco-Vanzetti Case* (1962).

Schaffer, Ronald, *America in the Great War: The Rise of the War Welfare State* (1991). Schoonover, Thomas D., "To End All Social Reform: A Progressive's Search for International Order," *Reviews in American History*, 21 (1993), 647–654. Tuchman, Barbara, *The Guns of August* (1976). Ward, Robert D., "The Origin and Activities of the National Security League, 1914–1919," *Mississippi Valley Historical Review*, 47 (January 1960) 1, 51–65. Wynn, Neil A., *From Progressivism to Prosperity: World War I and American Society* (1986).

CHAPTER 23

Barron, Hal S., *Mixed Harvest: The Second Great Transformation in the Rural North, 1870–1930* (1997). Blee, Kathleen M., *Women of the Klan: Racism and Gender in the 1920s* (1991). Burner, David, *Herbert Hoover: A Public Life* (1979). _____, *The Politics of Provincialism: The Democratic Party in Transition, 1918–1932* (1968). Chandler, Alfred D., Jr., *Strategy and Structure* (1962). Coben, Stanley, *Rebellion*

Against Victorianism: The Impetus for Change in 1920s America (1991). Cohen, Warren I., *Empire Without Tears: America's Foreign Relations, 1921–1933* (1987). De Benedetti, Charles, *Origins of the Modern American Peace Movement: 1915–1929* (1978). D'Emilio, John, and Estelle Freedman, *Intimate Matters: A History of Sexuality in America* (1988). Douglas, Ann, *Terrible Honesty: Mongrel Manhattan in the 1920s* (1995). Douglas, Susan J., *Inventing American Broadcasting, 1899–1922* (1987).

Gordon, Linda, *Woman's Body, Woman's Right: A Social History of Birth Control in America* (1977). Griswold, Robert, *Fatherhood in America: A History* (1993). Gutierrez, David, *Walls and Mirrors: Mexican Americans, Mexican Immigrants, and the Politics of Ethnicity* (1995). Hawley, Ellis W., *The Great War and the Search for a Modern Order: A History of the American People and Their Institutions, 1917–1933* (1992). _____, ed., *Herbert Hoover as Secretary of Commerce: Studies in New Era Thought and Practice* (1981). Hogan, Michael J., *Informal Entente: The Private Structure of Cooperation in Anglo-American Economy, 1918–1929* (1977). Hounshell, David A., *From the American System to Mass Production, 1800–1932: The Development of Manufacturing Technology in the United States* (1984). Huggins, Nathan I., *Harlem Renaissance* (1971). Jackson, Kenneth T., *The Ku Klux Klan in the City, 1915–1930* (1967). Kennedy, J. Gerald, *Imagining Paris: Exile, Writing and American Identity* (1993). Kern, Stephen, *The Culture of Time and Space, 1880–1918* (1983). Koszarski, Richard, *An Evening's Entertainment: The Age of the Silent Feature Picture, 1915–1928* (1990). Ladd-Taylor, Molly, *Mother-Work: Women, Child Welfare, and the State, 1890–1930* (1994). Lears, Jackson, *Fables of Abundance: A Cultural History of Advertising in America* (1994). Leffler, Melvyn P., *The Elusive Quest: America's Pursuit of European Stability and French Security, 1919–1933* (1979). Lemons, J. Stanley, *The Woman Citizen: Social Feminism in the*

1920s (1973). Lichtman, Alan J., *Prejudice and the Old Politics: The Presidential Election of 1928* (1979).

Marsden, George M., *Fundamentalism and American Culture: The Shaping of Twentieth-Century Evangelicalism, 1870–1925* (1980). Meyerowitz, Joanne J., *Women Adrift: Independent Wage Earners in Chicago, 1880–1930* (1988). Montgomery, David, *The Fall of the House of Labor: The Workplace, the State, and American Labor Activism, 1865–1925* (1987). Moore, Leonard J., *Citizen Klansmen: The Ku Klux Klan in Indiana, 1921–1928* (1991). Peretti, Burton W., *The Creation of Jazz: Music, Race, and Culture in Urban America* (1992).

Schlesinger, Arthur M., Jr., *The Crisis of the Old Order: 1919–1933* (1957). Seymour, Harold, *Baseball: The Golden Age* (1971). Singal, Daniel Joseph, *The War Within: From Victorian to Modernist Thought in the South, 1919–1945* (1982). Trani, Eugene P., and David L. Wilson, *The Presidency of Warren G. Harding* (1977). Zunz, Olivier, *Making America Corporate, 1870–1920* (1990).

CHAPTER 24

Badger, Anthony J., *The New Deal: The Depression Years, 1933–1940* (1989). Bernstein, Irving, *The Lean Years* (1960). _____, *The Turbulent Years* (1970). Bernstein, Michael A., *The Great Depression: Delayed Recovery and Economic Change in America, 1929–1939* (1987). Bird, Caroline, *The Invisible Scar* (1966). Brinkley, Alan, *Liberalism and Its Discontents* (1998). _____, *Voices of Protest* (1982). Burns, James MacGregor, *Roosevelt: The Lion and the Fox* (1956). Carnegie, Dale, "Grab Your Bootstraps," *Colliers*, March 5, 1938, 14–15. Carter, Dan T., *Scottsboro: A Tragedy of the American South*. Rev. ed. (1979). Cooke, Blanche Wiesen, *Eleanor Roosevelt*, 2 vols. (1992–1999). Daniels, Roger, *The Bonus March* (1971). Denning, Michael, *The Cultural Front: The Laboring of American Culture in the Twentieth Century* (1997). Edwards, Anne, *Road to Tara* (1983). Eichengreen, Barry, *Golden Fetters: The Gold Standard and the Great Depression, 1919–1939* (1995). Ellis, Edward Robb, *A Nation in Torment: The Great American Depression, 1929–1939* (1970). Fraser, Steve, *Labor Will Rule: Sidney Hillman and the Rise of American Labor* (1991). _____, and Gary Gerstle, *The Rise and Fall of the New Deal Order, 1930–1980* (1989).

Galbraith, John Kenneth, *The Great Crash: 1929* (1961). Gourevitch, Peter, *Politics in Hard Times: Comparative Responses to International Economic Crises* (1986). Granberry, Edward, "The Private Life of Margaret Mitchell," *Colliers*, March 13, 1937, 22–24. Greenberg, Cheryl Lynn, "*Or Does it Explode?": Black Harlem in the Great Depression* (1991). Gregory, James, *American Exodus: The Dust Bowl Migration and Okie Culture in California* (1989). Harriman, Margaret Case, "He Sells Hope," *Saturday Evening Post*, August 14, 1937, 12–34. Hofstadter, Richard, *The Age of Reform* (1956). Kelley, Robin D. G., *Hammer and Hoe: Alabama Communists during the Great Depression* (1990). Kennedy, David M., *Freedom from Fear: The American People in Depression and War* (1999). Kindelberger, Charles, *The World in Depression* (1973). Kirby, John B., *Black Americans in the Roosevelt Era* (1980). Klehr, Harvey, *The Heyday of American Communism: The Depression Decade* (1984). Leuchtenberg, William E., *Franklin D. Roosevelt and the New Deal* (1963).

Manchester, William, *The Glory and the Dream* (1973). McElvaine, Robert S., *The Great Depression: America, 1929–1941* (1984). Nelson, Bruce, *Workers on the Waterfront: Seamen, Longshoremen, and Unionism in the 1930s* (1988). Patterson, James, *Congressional Conservatism and the New Deal* (1967). _____, *The New Deal and the States* (1969). Pells, Richard, *Radical Visions and American Dreams: Culture and Social Thought in the Depression Years* (1973). Plotke, David, *Building a Democratic Political Order: Reshaping American Liberalism in the 1930s and 1940s* (1996). Pyron, Darden Asbury, *Southern Daughter* (1991).

Schulman, Bruce J., *From Cotton Belt to Sunbelt: Federal Policy, Economic Development, and the Transformation of the South, 1938–1980* (1991). Sitkoff, Harvard, *A New Deal for Blacks* (1978). Temin, Peter, *Lessons from the Great Depression* (1996). Watkins, T. H., *The Hungry Years* (1999). Williams, T. Harry, *Huey Long: A Biography* (1969). Wilson, Joan Hoff, *Herbert Hoover: Forgotten Progressive* (1975). Worster, Donald, *The Dust Bowl: The Southern Plains in the 1930s* (1979).

CHAPTER 25

Adams, Michael C. C., *The Best War Ever: America and World War II* (1994). Alperovitz, Gar, *The Decision to Use the Atomic Bomb and the Architecture of an American Myth* (1995). Ambrose, Stephen, *American Heritage New History of World War II* (1997). _____, *Citizen Soldiers* (1997). Bendiner, Elmer, *The Fall of Fortresses* (1980). Bergerud, Eric, *Touched with Fire: The Land War in the South Pacific* (1996). Blum, John Morton, *V Was for Victory* (1976). Blumenson, Martin, *Kasserine Pass* (1966). Deighton, Len, *Blood, Tears and Folly: An Objective Look at World War II* (1993). Dower, John W., *War without Mercy* (1986). Feingold, Henry L., *The Politics of Rescue: The Roosevelt Administration and the Holocaust, 1938–1945* (1970). Finkle, Lee, "The Conservative Aims of Militant Rhetoric: Black Protest During World War II," *Journal of American History*, 60 (December 1973) 3, 692–713. Flower, Desmond, and James Reeves, eds., *The War, 1939–1945: A Documentary History* (1997). Fussell, Paul, *Wartime* (1989).

Harris, William H., "A. Philip Randolph as a Charismatic Leader, 1925–1941," *Journal of Negro History*, 64 (Autumn 1979) 4, 301–315. Heinrichs, Waldo, *Threshold of War* (1988). Hobsbawm, Eric, *The Age of Extremes*

(1994). Houston, Jeanne Wakatsuki, and James D., *Farewell to Manzanar* (1973). Hynes, Samuel, *Flights of Passage* (1988). Kennedy, Paul, *The Rise and Fall of the Great Powers* (1987). Kimball, Warren F., *The Juggler: Franklin Roosevelt as Wartime Statesman* (1991). Leffler, Melvyn P., *The Specter of Communism* (1994).

Manchester, William, *The Glory and the Dream: A Narrative History of America, 1932–1972* (1973). Milward, Alan S., *War, Economy and Society 1939–1945* (1977). Morison, Samuel Eliot, *Coral Sea, Midway and Submarine Actions* (1949). _____, *The Two-Ocean War* (1963). O'Neill, William L., *A Democracy at War* (1993). Perrett, Geoffrey, *Days of Sadness, Years of Triumph* (1973). Pogue, Forrest C., *George C. Marshall: Ordeal and Hope, 1939–1942* (1965). Prange, Gordon W., *Miracle at Midway* (1982). Rosenberg, Emily S., *Spreading the American Dream: American Economic and Cultural Expansion, 1890–1945* (1982).

Sitkoff, Harvard, "Racial Militancy and Interracial Violence in the Second World War," *Journal of American History*, 58 (December 1971) 3, 661–681. Spickard, Paul R., *Japanese Americans: The Formation and Transformations of an Ethnic Group* (1996). United States, Federal Bureau of Investigation, "FBI File: A. Philip Randolph" (1990). Weighley, Russell F., *Eisenhower's Lieutenants* (1981). Wright, Gordon, *The Ordeal of Total War, 1939–1945* (1997).

CHAPTER 26

Blackwelder, Julia Kirk, *Now Hiring: The Feminization of Work in the United States, 1900–1995* (1997). Boyer, Paul, *By the Bomb's Early Light: American Thought and Culture at the Dawn of the Atomic Age* (1985). Cumings, Bruce, *The Origins of the Korean War*, 2 vols. (1981–1990). Dalfiume, Richard, *Desegregation of the U.S. Armed Forces: Fighting on Two Fronts, 1939–1953* (1969). Donovan, Robert J., *Conflict and Crisis: The Presidency of Harry S Truman, 1945–1948* (1977). _____, *Tumultuous Years: The Presidency of Harry S Truman,*

1948–1953 (1982). Egerton, John, *Speak Now Against the Day: The Generation Before the Civil Rights Movement in the South* (1994). Fried, Richard M., *The Russians Are Coming! the Russians Are Coming!: Pageantry and Patriotism in Cold-War America* (1999).

Gaddis, John Lewis, *The United States and the Origins of the Cold War, 1941–1947* (1972). _____, *We Now Know: Rethinking Cold War History* (1997). Hamby, Alonzo L., *Beyond the New Deal: Harry S. Truman and American Liberalism* (1973). Hartmann, Susan M., *The Home Front and Beyond: American Women in the 1940s* (1982). _____, *Truman and the 80th Congress* (1971). Heller, Francis H., ed., *Economics and the Truman Administration* (1981). Hogan, Michael J., *The Marshall Plan: America, Britain, and the Reconstruction of Western Europe, 1947–1952* (1987). Knox, Donald, *The Korean War: An Oral History*, 2 vols. (1985–1988). Lacey, Michael J., ed., *The Truman Presidency* (1989). LaFeber, Walter, *America, Russia, and the Cold War, 1945–1992* (1993). Lawson, Steven M., *Black Ballots: Voting Rights in the South, 1944–1969* (1976).

May, Lary, ed., *Recasting America: Culture and Politics in the Age of Cold War* (1989). McCoy, Donald, and Richard Ruetten, *Quest and Response: Minority Rights and the Truman Administration* (1973). Meier, August, and Elliott Rudwick, *CORE: A Study in the Civil Rights Movement, 1942–1968* (1973). Merrill, Dennis, ed., *Documentary History of the Truman Presidency*, 20 vols. (1995–1997). Nadel, Alan, *Containment Culture: American Narratives, Postmodernism, and the Atomic Age* (1995). Navasky, Victor S., *Naming Names* (1989). Patterson, James T., *Mr. Republican: A Biography of Robert A. Taft* (1972). Poen, Monte M., *Harry S. Truman Versus the Medical Lobby: The Genesis of Medicare* (1979). Polan, Dana, *Power and Paranoia: History, Narrative, and the American Cinema, 1940–1950* (1986). Radosh, Ronald, and Joyce Milton, *The Rosenberg File: A Search for the Truth* (1984). Renshaw, Patrick, *American Labor and Consensus Capitalism, 1935–1990* (1991).

Stueck, William, *The Korean War: An International History* (1995). Sugrue, Thomas J., *The Origins of the Urban Crisis: Race and Inequality in Postwar Detroit* (1996). Weiner, Lynn Y., *From Working Girl to Working Mother: The Female Labor Force in the United States, 1820–1980* (1985). Whitfield, Stephen J., *The Culture of the Cold War* (1991).

CHAPTER 27

Baughman, James L., *The Republic of Mass Culture: Journalism, Filmmaking and Broadcasting in America since 1941* (1991). Beschloss, Michael R., *Mayday: Eisenhower, Khrushchev and the U-2 Affair* (1991). Bowie, Robert R., and Richard H. Immerman, *Waging Peace: How Eisenhower Shaped an Enduring Cold War Strategy* (2000). Breines, Wini, *Young, White, and Miserable: Growing Up Female in the Fifties* (1992). Broadwater, Jeff, *Eisenhower and the Anti-Communist Crusade* (1992). Burk, Robert Fredrick, *The Eisenhower Administration and Black Civil Rights, 1953–1961* (1984). Cullather, Nick, *Illusions of Influence: The Political Economy of United States-Philippines Relations, 1942–1960* (1994). Divine, Robert, *The Sputnik Challenge* (1993). Dockrill, Saki, *Eisenhower's New-Look National Security Policy, 1953–1961* (1996). Dudziak, Mary, *Cold War Civil Rights: Race and the Image of American Democracy* (2000). Foreman, Joel, ed., *The Other Fifties: Interrogating Midcentury American Icons* (1997). Fried, Richard M., *Nightmare in Red: The McCarthy Era in Perspective* (1990).

Gardner, Lloyd C., *Approaching Vietnam: From World War II through Dienbienphu* (1988). Gartman, David, *Auto Opium: A Social History of American Automobile Design* (1994). Graebner, William, *Coming of Age in Buffalo: Youth and Authority in the Postwar Era* (1990). Guralnick, Peter, *Last Train to Memphis: The Rise of Elvis Presley* (1994). Gutierrez, David, *Walls and Mirrors: Mexican Americans, Mexican Immigrants, and the Politics of Ethnicity* (1995). Horowitz, Daniel, ed., *American Social Classes in the 1950s: Selections from Vance Packard's* The

Status Seekers (1995). Jackson, Kenneth, *Crabgrass Frontier: The Suburbanization of the United States* (1985). Jones, Gerard, *Honey, I'm Home! Sitcoms: Selling the American Dream* (1992). Karabell, Zachary, *Architects of Intervention: The United States, the Third World, and the Cold War, 1946–1962* (1999). Kluger, Richard, *Simple Justice: The History of* Brown *v.* Board of Education *and Black America's Struggle for Equality* (1977). Korrol, Virginia Sanchez, *From Colonia to Community: The History of Puerto Ricans in New York City* (1994). Kunz, Diane B., *The Economic Diplomacy of the Suez Crisis* (1991). Lhamon, Ward T., *Deliberate Speed: The Origins of a Cultural Style in the American 1950s* (1990).

May, Elaine Tyler, *Homeward Bound: American Families in the Cold War Era* (1988). Meier, Matt S., and Feliciano Ribera, *Mexican Americans, American Mexicans: from Conquistadors to Chicanos* (1993). O'Neill, William L., *American High: The Years of Confidence, 1945–1960* (1986). Pach, Chester J., and Elmo Richardson, *The Presidency of Dwight D. Eisenhower* (1991). Raines, Howell, *My Soul Is Rested: Movement Days in the Deep South Remembered* (1977). Ramos, Henry A. J., *The American G.I. Forum: In Pursuit of the Dream, 1948–1993* (1998). Rawls, James J., *Chief Red Fox Is Dead: A History of Native Americans Since 1945* (1996). Rupp, Leila J., *Survival in the Doldrums: The American Women's Rights Movement, 1945 to the 1960s* (1987).

Takeyh, Ray, *The Origins of the Eisenhower Doctrine: The U.S., Britain, and Nasser's Egypt, 1953–57* (2000). Watson, Steven, *The Birth of the Beat Generation: Visionaries, Rebels, and Hipsters, 1944–1960* (1995).

CHAPTER 28

Appy, Christian G., *Working-Class War: American Combat Soldiers and Vietnam* (1993). Beschloss, Michael, *The Crisis Years: Kennedy and Khrushchev, 1960–1963* (1991). Blum, John Morton, *Years of Discord: American Politics and Society, 1961–1974* (1991).

Brands, H. W., *The Wages of Globalism: Lyndon Johnson and the Limits of American Power* (1995). Brick, Howard, *Age of Contradiction: American Thought and Culture in the 1960s* (2000). Burner, David, *John F. Kennedy and a New Generation* (1988). Carson, Clayborne, *In Struggle: SNCC and the Black Awakening of the 1960s* (1981). Chafe, William H., *Civilities and Civil Rights: Greensboro, North Carolina, and the Black Struggle for Freedom* (1980). Dallek, Robert, *Flawed Giant: Lyndon Johnson and His Times, 1961–1973* (1991). Davies, Gareth, *From Opportunity to Entitlement: The Transformation and Decline of Great Society Liberalism* (1996). Dickstein, Morris, *Gates of Eden: American Culture in the Sixties* (1977). Dittmer, John, *Local People: The Struggle for Civil Rights in Mississippi* (1994). Douglas, Susan J., *Where the Girls Are: Growing Up Female with the Mass Media* (1994). Downs, Frederick, *The Killing Zone: My Life in the Vietnam War* (1978). Evans, Sara, *Personal Politics: The Roots of Women's Liberation in the Civil Rights Movement and the New Left* (1979). Farber, David, ed., *The Sixties: From Memory to History* (1994).

Garrow, David J., *Bearing the Cross: Martin Luther King, Jr., and the Southern Christian Leadership Conference* (1986). Giglio, James N., *The Presidency of John F. Kennedy* (1991). Halberstam, David, *The Best and the Brightest* (1972). Haley, Alex, *The Autobiography of Malcolm X* (1966). Harrison, Cynthia, *On Account of Sex: The Politics of Women's Issues, 1945–1968* (1988). Harvey, Mark W. T., *A Symbol of Wilderness: Echo Park and the American Conservation Movement* (1994). Hodgson, Godfrey, *America in Our Time: From World War II to Nixon* (1976). Hoffman, Elizabeth Cobbs, *All You Need Is Love: The Peace Corps and the Spirit of the 1960s* (1998). Horne, Gerald, *Fire This Time: The Watts Uprising and the 1960s* (1996). Horowitz, Daniel, *Betty Friedan and the Making of the Feminine Mystique: The American Left, the Cold War, and Modern Feminism* (1998). Jeffreys-Jones, Rhodri, *Peace Now!: American Society and the Ending of the Vietnam War* (1999). Kahin, George McT., *Intervention: How America Became Involved in Vietnam* (1986). Kaiser, David E., *American Tragedy: Kennedy, Johnson, and the Origins of the Vietnam War* (2000). Krepinevich, Andrew F., Jr., *The Army and Vietnam* (1986). Linden-Ward, Blanche, and Carol Hurd Green, *Changing the Future: American Women in the 1960s* (1993).

Macedo, Stephen, ed., *Reassessing the Sixties: Debating the Political and Cultural Legacy* (1997). McAdam, Doug, *Freedom Summer* (1988). McDougall, Walter A., . . . *the Heavens and the Earth: A Political History of the Space Age* (1985). Moïse, Edwin E., *Tonkin Gulf and the Escalation of the Vietnam War* (1996). Paterson, Thomas G., ed., *Kennedy's Quest for Victory: American Foreign Policy, 1961–1963* (1989). Payne, Charles M., *I've Got the Light of Freedom: The Organizing Tradition and the Mississippi Freedom Struggle* (1995). Pearson, Hugh, *The Shadow of the Panther: Huey Newton and the Price of Black Power in America* (1994). Ralph, James R., Jr., *Northern Protest: Martin Luther King, Jr., Chicago, and the Civil Rights Movement* (1993). Rorabaugh, W. J., *Berkeley at War: The 1960s* (1989). Rothman, Hal K., *The Greening of a Nation: Environmentalism in the United States since 1945* (1998).

Schlesinger, Arthur M., Jr., *Robert Kennedy and His Times* (1978). Schwartz, Bernard, *Super Chief: Earl Warren and His Supreme Court* (1983). Steigerwald, David, *The Sixties and the End of Modern America* (1995). Summer, Harry G., Jr., *On Strategy: A Critical Analysis of the Vietnam War* (1982). Szatmary, David P., *Rockin' in Time: A Social History of Rock-and-Roll* (1997). Van Deburg, William L., *New Day in Babylon: The Black Power Movement and American Culture, 1965–1975* (1992). Wells, Tom, *The War Within: America's Battle Over Vietnam* (1996).

CHAPTER 29

Adam, Barry D., *The Rise of a Gay and Lesbian Movement*, Rev. ed. (1995). Barnet, Richard J., and Ronald E. Müller, *Global Reach: The Power of the Multinational Corporations (1974). Bartley, Numan V., *The New South, 1945–1980: The Story of the South's Modernization* (1995). Bernstein, Carl, and Bob Woodward, *All the President's Men* (1974). Bernstein, Michael A., and David E. Adler, eds., *Understanding American Economic Decline* (1994). Bill, James A., *The Eagle and the Lion: The Tragedy of American-Iranian Relations* (1988). Brands, H. W., *Since Vietnam: The United States in World Affairs, 1973–1995* (1996). Campisi, Jack, *The Mashpee Indians: Tribe on Trial* (1991). Carter, Dan T., *The Politics of Rage: George Wallace, the Origins of the New Conservatism, and the Transformation of American Politics* (1995). Chan, Sucheng, *Asian Americans: An Interpretive History* (1990). D'Emilio, John, *Sexual Politics, Sexual Communities: The Making of a Homosexual Minority in the United States, 1940–1970* (1983). Duberman, Martin, *Stonewall* (1993). Engelhardt, Tom, *The End of Victory Culture: Cold War America and the Disillusioning of a Generation* (1995). Espiritu, Yen Le, *Asian American Panethnicity: Bridging Institutions and Identities* (1992). Ford, Daniel F., *Three Mile Island: Thirty Minutes to Meltdown* (1982). Frye, Gaillard, *The Dream Long Deferred* (1988).

Garrow, David J., *Liberty and Sexuality: The Right to Privacy and the Making of* Roe v. Wade (1994). Garthoff, Raymond L., *Détente and Confrontation: American-Soviet Relations from Nixon to Reagan* (1994). Gartman, David, *Auto Opium: A Social History of American Automobile Design* (1994). Greene, John Robert, *The Limits of Power: The Nixon and Ford Administrations* (1992). Isaacs, Arnold R., *Without Honor: Defeat in Vietnam and Cambodia* (1983). Isaacson, Walter, *Kissinger: A Biography* (1992). Jones, Charles O., *The Trusteeship Presidency: Jimmy Carter and the United States Congress* (1988). Kimball, Jeffrey P., *Nixon's Vietnam War* (1998). LaFeber, Walter, *The Panama Canal Crisis in Historical Perspective* (1989). Lasch, Christopher, *The Culture of Narcissism: American Life in an Age of Diminishing Expectations* (1979). Lawson, Steven F., *Running for Freedom: Civil Rights and Black Politics in America since 1941* (1997).

Marin, Marguerite V., *Social Protest in an Urban Barrio: A Study of the Chicano Movement, 1966–1974* (1991). Nagel, Joanne, *American Indian Ethnic Renewal: Red Power and the Resurgence of Identity and Culture* (1996). Rieder, Jonathan, *Canarsie: The Jews and Italians of Brooklyn Against Liberalism* (1985). Rosen, Ellen Israel, *Bitter Choices: Blue-Collar Women In and Out of Work* (1987). Ryan, Paul B., *The Iranian Rescue Mission and Why It Failed* (1986).

Sale, Kirkpatrick, *Power Shift: The Rise of the Southern Rim and Its Challenge to the Eastern Establishment* (1975). Schlesinger, Arthur M., Jr., *The Imperial Presidency* (1973). Schulman, Bruce J., *From Cotton Belt to Sun Belt: Federal Policy, Economic Development, and the Transformation of the South, 1938–1980* (1991). Schur, Edwin, *The Awareness Trap: Self-Absorption Instead of Social Change* (1976). Small, Melvin, *The Presidency of Richard Nixon* (1999). Smith, Gaddis, *Morality, Reason, and Power: American Diplomacy in the Carter Years* (1986). Stern, Kenneth S., *Loud Hawk: The United States versus the American Indian Movement* (1994). Szasz, Andrew, *EcoPopulism: Toxic Waste and the Movement for Environmental Justice* (1994). Takaki, Ronald, *Strangers from a Different Shore: A History of Asian Americans* (1989). Thurow, Lester, *The Zero-Sum Society: Distribution and the Possibilities for Economic Change* (1980). Vigil, Ernesto, *The Crusade for Justice: Chicano Militancy and the Government's War on Dissent* (1999). Wei, William, *The Asian American Movement* (1993). Wicker, Tom, *One of Us: Richard Nixon and the American Dream* (1991). Wilkinson, J. Harvie, III, *From Brown to Bakke: The Supreme Court and School Integration, 1954–1978* (1979). Wolfe, Alan, *America's Impasse: The Rise and Fall of the Politics of Growth* (1981).

CHAPTER 30

Adam, Barry D., *The Rise of a Gay and Lesbian Movement*, Rev. ed. (1995). Anderson, Martin, *Revolution: The Reagan Legacy* (1988). Berman, William C., *America's Right Turn: From Nixon to Bush* (1994). Blumenthal,

Sidney, *The Rise of the Counter-Establishment: From Conservative Ideology to Political Power* (1986). Campbell-Kelly, Martin, and William Aspray, *Computer: A History of the Information Machine* (1996). Cannon, Lou, *Ronald Reagan: The Role of a Lifetime* (1991). Davis, Flora, *Moving the Mountain: The Women's Movement in America since 1960* (1991). Ferree, Myra Marx, and Beth B. Hess, *Controversy and Coalition: The New Feminist Movement across Three Decades of Change* (1994). Friedman, Benjamin M., *Day of Reckoning: The Consequences of American Economic Policy under Reagan and After* (1988).

Gallagher, John, *Perfect Enemies: The Religious Right, the Gay Movement, and the Politics of the 1990s* (1996). Garthoff, Raymond L., *Détente and Confrontation: American-Soviet Relations from Nixon to Reagan* (1994). _____, *The Great Transition: American-Soviet Relations and the End of the Cold War* (1994). Gillon, Steven M., *The Democrats' Dilemma: Walter F. Mondale and the Liberal Legacy* (1992). Hill, Dilys M., et al., *The Reagan Presidency: An Incomplete Revolution?* (1990). Hodgson, Godfrey, *The World Turned Right Side Up: A History of the Conservative Ascendancy in America* (1996). Hoeveler, J. David, *Watch on the Right: Conservative Intellectuals in the Reagan Era* (1991). Hurt, Harry, *The Lost Tycoon: The Many Lives of Donald J. Trump* (1993). Jaynes, Gerald David, and Robin M. Williams, Jr., eds., *A Common Destiny: Blacks and American Society* (1989). Fitzgerald, Frances, *Way Out There in the Blue: Reagan and Star Wars and the End of the Cold War* (2000). Jeffords, Susan, *Hard Bodies: Hollywood Masculinity in the Reagan Era* (1994). Jorstad, Erling, *Holding Fast/Pressing On: Religion in America in the 1980s* (1990). Lewis, Michael, *Liar's Poker: Rising Through the Wreckage on Wall Street* (1989). Lofland, John, *Polite Protesters: The American Peace Movement of the 1980s* (1993).

Martin, William C., *With God on Our Side: The Rise of the Religious Right in America* (1996). McGirr, Lisa, *Suburban Warriors: The Origins of the New American Right* (2001). Meyer, Jane, and Doyle McManus, *Landslide: The Unmaking of the President, 1984–1988* (1988). Murray, Charles, *Losing Ground: American Social Policy, 1950–1980* (1984). Noonan, Peggy, *What I Saw at the Revolution: A Political Life in the Reagan Era* (1990). Phillips, Kevin P., *The Politics of Rich and Poor: Wealth and the American Electorate in the Reagan Aftermath* (1990). Rayack, Elton, *Not So Free to Choose: The Political Economy of Milton Friedman and Ronald Reagan* (1987). Reed, Adolph L., *The Jesse Jackson Phenomenon: The Crisis of Purpose in Afro-American Politics* (1986).

Schaller, Michael, *Reckoning with Reagan: America and Its President in the 1980s* (1992). Scheer, Robert, *With Enough Shovels: Reagan, Bush, and Nuclear War* (1982). Taylor, John, *Circus of Ambition: The Culture of Wealth and Power in the Eighties* (1989). Thelen, David P., *Becoming Citizens in the Age of Television: How Americans Challenged the Media and Seized Political Initiative during the Iran-Contra Debate* (1996). Thompson, Mark, ed., *Long Road to Freedom: The Advocate History of the Gay and Lesbian Movement* (1994). Wolters, Raymond, *Right Turn: William Bradford Reynolds, the Reagan Administration, and Black Civil Rights* (1996).

CHAPTER 31

Abramson, Jeffrey, ed., *Postmortem: The O. J. Simpson Case: Justice Confronts Race, Domestic Violence, Lawyers, Money, and the Media* (1996). Beschloss, Michael R., and Strobe Talbott, *At the Highest Levels: The Inside Story of the End of the Cold War* (1993). Bingham, Clara, *Women on the Hill: Challenging the Culture of Congress* (1997). Button, James W., et al., *Private Lives, Public Conflicts: Battles Over Gay Rights in American Communities* (1997). Campbell, Colin, and Bert A. Rockman, eds., *The Clinton Presidency: First Appraisals* (1996). Dertouzos, Michael L., *What Will Be: How the New World of Information Will Change Our Lives* (1998). Drew, Elizabeth, *Showdown: The Struggle Between the*

Gingrich Congress and the Clinton White House (1996). Duignan, Peter, and L. H. Gann, eds., *The Debate in the United States Over Immigration* (1998). Dunnigan, James F., and Austin Bay, *From Shield to Storm: High-Tech Weapons, Military Strategy, and Coalition Warfare in the Persian Gulf* (1992).

Gitlin, Todd, *The Twilight of Common Dreams: Why America Is Wracked by Culture Wars* (1995). Gordon, Avery, and Christopher Newfield, eds., *Mapping Multiculturalism* (1996). Green, John C., et al., eds., *Religion and the Culture Wars: Dispatches from the Front* (1996). Greenberg, Stanley B., *Middle Class Dreams: The Politics and Power of the New American Majority* (1995). Greene, John Robert, *The Presidency of George Bush* (2000). Haas, Richard N., *The Reluctant Sheriff: The United States After the Cold War* (1997). Hafner, Katie, and Matthew Lyon, *Where Wizards Stay Up Late: The Origins of the Internet* (1998). Hogan, Michael, ed., *The End of the Cold War: Its Meanings and Implications* (1992). Lind, Michael, *The Next American Nation: The New Nationalism and the Fourth American Revolution* (1995). Lowi, Theodore J., and Benjamin Ginsberg, *Embattled Democracy: Politics and Policy in the Clinton Era* (1995).

Maraniss, David, *First in His Class: A Biography of Bill Clinton* (1995). Matteo, Sherri, ed., *American Women in the Nineties: Today's Critical Issues* (1993). McGuckin, Frank, ed., *Terrorism in the United States* (1997). Morris, Roger, *Partners in Power: The Clintons and Their America* (1996). Newman, Katherine S., *Declining Fortunes: The Withering of the American Dream* (1993). Nolan, James L., Jr., ed., *The American Culture Wars: Current Contests and Future Prospects* (1996). Phillips, Kevin P., *The Politics of Rich and Poor: Wealth and the American Electorate in the Reagan Aftermath* (1990). Posner, Gerald L., *Citizen Perot: His Life and Times* (1996). Ripley, Randall B., and James M. Lindsay, eds., *U.S. Foreign Policy After the Cold War* (1997). Rivlin, Gary, *The Plot to Get Bill Gates* (1999). Rubin, Lillian B., *Families on the Fault Line: America's Working Class Speaks about the Family, the Economy, Race, and Ethnicity* (1994).

Skocpol, Theda, *Boomerang: Clinton's Health Security Effort and the Turn Against Government in U.S. Politics* (1996). Slessarev, Helene, *The Betrayal of the Urban Poor* (1991). Spain, Daphne, and Suzanne M. Bianchi, *Balancing Act: Motherhood, Marriage, and Employment Among American Women* (1996). Stern, Kenneth S., *A Force Upon the Plain: The American Militia Movement and the Politics of Hate* (1996). Stewart, James B., *Blood Sport: The President and His Adversaries* (1996). Thomas, Evan, et al., *Back from the Dead: How Clinton Survived the Republican Revolution* (1997). Toobin, Jeffrey, *A Vast Conspiracy: The Real Story of the Sex Scandal That Nearly Brought Down a President* (2000). Wray, Matt, and Annalee Newitz, eds., *White Trash: Race and Class in America* (1997).

PHOTO CREDITS

— ✂ —

INDEX

⚜

A

A & P supermarket, 547
Abolition of slavery. *See*
African Americans,
free slaves
Abortion
Roe v. Wade, 702,
734, 757
Victorian era, 433
Acid rain, 726
Acid rock, 686
Acquired immune
deficiency syndrome
(AIDS), 735
ACT UP, 735
Adams, Charles Francis,
454
Adams, Samuel
Hopkins, 504
Adams Express
Company stock, 409
Addams, Jane, 503, 523
Advertising
consumerism, 550
and women's
suffrage, 529
World War I, 529
Affirmative action,
701
Afghanistan, terrorist
presence in, 766–7
Africa
apartheid, 731
Reagan Doctrine,
731
World War II, 609
African Americans
affirmative action,
701
busing, 701
civil rights, 629–31
Double V campaign,
607
Great Migration,
531–2
Jim Crow laws,
482–3
lynchings, 483
March on
Washington
Movement
(MOWM), 592
music, 651
and New Deal,
585–6

Niagara Movement,
506
post World War II,
629–31
poverty, 735
renaissance of 1920s,
560–1
riots, 684
Rodney King
incident, 755
segregation, 483
Simpson trials, 756
soldiers, World War
II, 600–1
Thomas hearings,
755
Voting Rights Act,
736
World War I, 531–2
World War II,
600–1, 606–7
African Americans, free
slaves
Banks Plan, 372
contract labor, 375–7
land ownership,
desire for, 373–5
massacre of, 377–8
nationwide suffrage,
390
sharecropping,
384–6
sharecropping
becomes wage
labor, 415–16
Agnew, Spiro, 711
Agricultural
Adjustment Act, 582
Agricultural Marketing
Act, 573–4
Agriculture
decline of, 548–9
during Great
Depression, 571–2
Agriculture,
Department of, 463
Aguinaldo, Emilio,
491–2
AIDS, 735
Air Quality Act, 672
Air traffic controllers,
727
Airline industry
beginning of, 546
after 9/11 attacks,
767

Airplanes
Lindbergh flight,
554–5
Wright brothers'
flight, 546
Aitken, Annie, 407
Alabama, 389
Alamogordo, New
Mexico, 612
Alaska
purchase of, 461
statehood, 650–1
Albany Movement,
673–4
Alcohol consumption,
"Crusade" against,
450–2
Alcott, Louisa May, 444
Alexander II,
assassination of, 405
Alger, Horatio, 434
Ali, Muhammad, 682
All in the Family, 708
Allende, Salvador, 699
Allies
World War I, 524,
535–6
World War II,
609–10
Al-Qaeda, 766
Amalgamated Clothing
Workers of America
(ACWA), 568–9
America First
Committee, 596
America Online, 745
American
Expeditionary Force
(AEF), 535
American Federation of
Labor (AFL), 478,
548
and New Deal, 486
American Indian
Movement (AIM),
705
American Medical
Association (AMA),
433
American Missionary
Association, 373
American Plan, 534–5
American Protective
League (APL), 529
American Railway
Union, 478

American Telephone
and Telegraph
Company (AT & T),
726
American Union
Against Militarism,
523
The American Mercury,
555
Anderson, Mary, 534
Anderson, Sherwood,
555
Andreev, Felix
Iosifovich, 743–4
Annexation
Canada, 462
Cuba, 462
Hawaii, 462
Anthrax, 767
Anti-Ballistic Missile
(ABM) treaty, 697
Anti-Communist
crusade, 615–16,
634–6
Anti-Imperialist
League, 491
Anti-imperialists,
491–2
Anti-Saloon League,
534, 562
Apartheid, 731
Apple, 720
Arab-Israeli conflict
Camp David
accords, 713–14
Six Days War, 699
Yom Kippur War,
699
Ardennes Forest,
609–10
Argonne Forest, 538
Arms race
Defense Production
Act, 626
escalation of, 625–6
H-bomb, 626
Armstrong, Neil, 699
Army-Navy Nurse Act,
629
Arnold, Matthew, 438
Art, realism in, 443–6
Arthur, Chester A., 457
Artists
realists, 426
renaissance of 1920s,
560

Asian Americans
activism of, 704–5
organizations of, 704–5
Assassinations
Alexander II, 405
attempt on Ronald Reagan, 725
Garfield, James A., 457
Kennedy, John F., 669–70
King, Martin Luther, Jr., 688–9
McKinley, William, 510
"Atlanta Compromise," 483–4
Atlantic Charter, 596
Atlantic City, New Jersey, 688
Atlantic Monthly, 443
Atomic Age, 634
Atomic bomb
Manhattan Project, 602, 605, 612
World War II, 612
Atomic Energy Act, 652
Atoms for Peace, 654
Auschwitz, Poland, 608
Autarky, 593–5
Automobiles
consumerism, 643–6
mass production, 546
Model T car, 546
ownership in 1950s, 643–6
sexuality, 644
and suburban growth, 643–6
Axis powers, World War II, 594, 609–10

B

B-24 Liberator, 602
B-29 Superfortress, 602, 605
Babbit (Lewis), 555
Baby-boom, 648, 721
Baker, Ray Stannard, 475, 504
Bakker, Jim, 722, 736
Bakker, Tammy Faye, 722
Ballinger, Richard, 515
Banking
banking crisis, Great Depression, 576–7
devaluing dollar, 595
Emergency Banking Act, 577
Federal Reserve Act, 517
Federal Reserve Board, 517

Glass-Steagall Banking Act, 577
New Deal legislation, 576–7
Banks, Nathaniel, 372
Banks Plan, 372
Barrios, 559, 650, 703
Baruch, Bernard, 531
Baseball, 429–30
African Americans in, 630
Bay of Pigs, 678
Beat movement, 657–8
The Beatles, 686
Beatniks, 658
Bellamy, Edward, 466
Berkeley, California, 685
Berlin airlift, 622–3
Berlin Wall, 760–1
Berlin Wall Crisis, 678
Bernstein, Carl, 710
Bicycling, 430
Bin Laden, Osama, 765–6
Birmingham riots, 674–6
Birth control, 552
Bison, 419
Black, Hugo, 608
Black and Decker Company, 531
Black Codes, 376–7
Black Hills, gold found in, 418
Black Monday, 740
Black Muslims, 684
Black Panthers, 684–5
Black Power, 684–5
Black Star Line, 561
Black Tom, 528
Black Tuesday, 569
Blaine, James G., 453
Bland-Allison Act, 460
Blue Eagle, 580–1
Boesky, Ivan, 720–1, 736
Bolshevik Revolution, 536–7
Bonfield, James, 468
Bonus Marchers, 574–5
Bosnia-Herzegovinia civil war, 764
Boxer Rebellion, 492–3
Boxing, 429
Bozeman Trail, 418
Bracero Program, 650
Brady, Mathew, 446
Brains Trust, 576
Branch Davidians, 758–9
Bread lines, 572, 593
Brest-Litovsk, Treaty of, 537
Bretton Woods, New Hampshire, 611

Brighton Beach, 743–4
Brotherhood of Sleeping Car Porters, 548, 591
Brown, Helen Gurley, 687
Brown v. Board of Education, 659, 666
Brunauer, Esther, 615–16
Brunauer, Stephen, 615–16
Bryan, William Jennings
"Cross of Gold" speech, 480
election of 1896, 481
resignation as Secretary of State, 525
Scope's trial, 556
Bryant, William Cullen, 452
Buchenwald death camp, 608
Bulge, Battle of, 610
Bureau of Indian Affairs (BIA), 705
Burger, Warren, 708
Burroughs, William, 658
Bush, George
election of 1988, 748–9
New World Order, 762–3
presidency, 749
Bush, George W.
controversy of election, 751–2
election of 2000, 751–2
Busing, African Americans, 701

C

California
growth in 1950s, 650
Proposition 13, 712
California, University of, 442
Calley, William, Jr., 697
Cambodia, 697
Camp David, 713
Camp David accords, 713–14
Canada
annexation issue, 462
North American Free Trade Agreement (NAFTA), 746
Capitalism
communism compared, 617
ideology of, 617

industrialism of nineteenth century, 407–12
large-scale organization, 546–7
Caribbean
peacekeeping, Wilson administration, 523
Reagan Doctrine, 730–1
Carnegie, Andrew, 407, 478
biographical information, 407–8
as financier, 409
Pennsylvania Railroad, 408
in steel industry, 409–11
Carnegie, Margaret, 407
Carnegie, Will, 407
Carranza, Venustiano, 522–3
Carson, Rachel, 666
Carter, Jimmy
election of 1976, 712
foreign policy, 713–15
presidency, 712–15
Casey, William, 737
Cassettari, Rosa, 401–3
Castro, Fidel, Bay of Pigs, 678
Catholic Church
anti-Catholic sentiment, 455
and immigrants, 435, 437
Catt, Carrie Chapman
Woman's Peace Party, 523
World War I, 533
Cattle, 419–20
Cattlemen, 419–20
Centers for Disease Control (CDC), 632
Central America
Cold War, 653
Reagan Doctrine, 730–1
Central High crisis, 660
Central Intelligence Agency (CIA), 622
and Allende regime, 699
Bay of Pigs, 678
Cold War operations, 653
hearings on, 711
Central Powers, World War I, 524

Central Treaty Organization (CENT), 655–6
Chambers, Whittaker, 635
Charismatic preachers, 647
Chávez, César, 703–4
Cherbourg, France, 609
Chernobyl, 738
Cherokee Strip, 475
Cheyenne Indians, massacre of, 418
Chicago
    fire of 1871, 407
    ghettos, 532
    high culture, 441
    mob attack of African Americans, 532
    typhoid epidemic, 496–7
    World's Columbian Exposition, 431, 475
    world's fair, 431
Chicago Defender, 532
Chicago Inter Ocean, 452
Chicago Movement, 684
Chicago Record, 475
Chicanos, 558–60
Chile, Allende regime, 699
China
    Boxer Rebellion, 492–3
    Japan, war with, 487–8
    Open Door Note, 492–3
    Taiping Rebellion of 1848, 404
Chinese Exclusion Act, 404
Chopin, Kate, 444
Christian Advocate, 460
Christy Minstrels, 427
Churchill, Winston
    Potsdam Conference, 619
    World War II, 596, 603–4, 611–12
    Yalta Conference, 617–19
Ci Xi, 492–3
Cities and urban growth
    African Americans, 482
    crime and, 407
    deindustrialization and, 695
    disease and, 407
    insecurity of, 498–9

progressivism and local governments, 507–9
southern cities, 482
trend towards, 406–7
urban nation, emergence of, 549
vice and, 425–7
City governments and taxes, 463–4
City services, improvement of, 508
Civil militias, 758–60
Civil Rights Act, 378–9, 395, 676–7, 756
Civil Rights Cases of 1883, 399
Civil rights movement
    Albany Movement, 673–4
    Birmingham riots, 674–6
    Brown v. Board of Education, 659
    Central High crisis, 660
    Freedom Riders, 673
    Freedom Summer, 676
    Greensboro Four, 666
    King, Martin Luther, Jr., 673–4
    March on Washington, 675–6
    Montgomery bus boycott, 659–60
    NAACP, 658–9
    Rosa Parks and bus boycott, 659
    SCLC, 674–5
    sit-ins, 666–7
    Student Nonviolent Coordinating Committee (SNCC), 667
    white resistance, 673–6
Civil Service Commission, 455
Civil Works Administration (CWA), 578
Civilian Conservation Corps (CCC), 578
Class differences, decline of, 646–7
Classless society, illusion of, 647
Clayton Antitrust Act, 517
Clean Air Act, 672, 711, 749

Clean Water Restoration Act, 672
Cleveland, Grover
    presidency of, 457–8
    re-election of, 458
    tariff reform issue, 458
Climate of western territory, 421–3
Clinton, Bill
    biographical information, 750
    Bosnia-Herzegovinia civil war, 764
    election of 1992, 749–50
    election of 1996, 750
    federal deficit reduction, 750
    gays in military, 758
    impeachment trial, 751
    presidency, 750–1
    scandals, 751
Clothing industry and working class, 414
Cody, Buffalo Bill, 427
Cold War, 615–38
    Central America, 653
    CIA involvement, 653
    containment strategy, 621–3
    covert operations, 652–3
    Eastern Europe, 653–4
    end of, 760–1
    Europe (1950), map of, 619
    globalization of, 623
    Intermediate-Range Nuclear Forces Treaty (INF), 740
    Korean War, 653–4
    Massive Retaliation strategy, 653
    origins of, 617–21
    Third World countries, 654–6
Collier, John, 579–80
Combined Fleet, 597–8, 600
Commerce and Labor, Department of, 510
Commercial farmers, 420–1
Committee on Equality of Treatment and Opportunity in the Armed Services, 630
Committee on Industrial

Organizations (CIO), 569, 585
Committee on Public Information (CPI), 529
Committee to Re-Elect the President (CREEP), 710–11
Communications satellites, 669
Communism
    anti-Communist crusade, 615–16, 634–5
    Bay of Pigs, 678
    Berlin Wall Crisis, 678
    capitalism compared, 617
    China, 623
    Hollywood Ten, 634–5
    ideology of, 617
    McCarthyism, 615–16
    Red Scare, 634–5
Communist Party, New Deal and, 581
Communists in America
    anti-Communist crusade, 636
    Communist Party of the United States of America (CPUSA), 634
    McCarthyism, 636
    red scare, post-World War I, 541–3
Compaq, 720
Computer industry
    beginning of, 641–2
    growth in 1990s, 745
    growth of, 720
    microcomputer, 720
Computer revolution, 745–6
Comstock, Anthony, 425–6, 447
Comstock Law, 425
Congress, World War I, 527–8
Congress of Racial Equality, 607
Congressional Government, 516
Congressional reconstruction, 380–6
Conkling, Roscoe, 456
Conscription, 528
Conservationist, Theodore Roosevelt as, 512

Conservatives
  Conservative
    Manifesto, 588
  counter-
    establishment,
    708–9, 722–3
  National committee
    to Uphold
    Constitutional
    Government, 587
  social values,
    732–6
Consumer Product
  Safety Commission,
  700
Consumer Protection
  Agency, 713
Consumerism
  advertising industry
    and, 550
  automobiles, 643–6
  credit buying and,
    551
  credit cards, 643
  discontent with, 666
  economic prosperity
    and, 641–2
  in 1920s, 549–51
  retail discount
    stores, 639–40, 642
  shopping malls, 643
  spread of, 549–51
  suburban home
    ownership, 642–3
  technological
    innovations, 720
Containment strategy
  dangers of, 622–3
  overview, 621–2
Contract labor, 375–7
Cooke, Jay, 396
Coolidge, Calvin
  foreign policy, 564–5
  presidency of, 563–5
  re-election of, 563
Coral Sea, Battle of, 599
Corporate
  consolidation, 479
Corporations
  downsizing, 746–7
  large-scale
    organization,
    546–7
  mergers, 720–1, 745
  takeovers, 720–1
  work and work
    force,
    transformation of,
    547
Corruption. See
  Scandals
Cosmopolitan, 504
Cost-of-living
  adjustments
  (COLAs), 628
Coughlin, Charles,
  581–2

Counterculture, youth
  of 1960s, 685–6
Covert operations of
  Cold War, 652–3
Cowboys, 419–20
Cox, Archibald, 711
Coxey, Jacob, 475
Crack cocaine, 733
Crazy Horse, 418
Credit buying and
  consumerism, 551
Credit cards, 643
Credit Mobilier, 393
Creel, George, 529
Crime and cities, 407
"Cross of Gold" speech,
  480
"Crusade" against
  alcohol
  consumption, 450–2
Crystal Palace, 431
Cuba
  annexation issue,
    462
  Spanish-American
    War, 488–91
Cuban Missile Crisis,
  678–9
Culture
  and city life, 427–31
  counterculture of
    1960s, 685–6
  popular culture, 426
Culture and Anarchy
  (Arnold), 438
Currency, gold
  standard, 479–80
Custer, George
  Armstrong
    Cheyenne Indians,
      massacre of, 418
    Little Bighorn, 418
  Custer's Last Stand,
    418–19
Czolgosz, Leon, 510

D

Daguerre, Louis, 446
Daley, Richard, 684
Daniels, Josephus, 529
Darrow, Clarence,
  Scope's trial, 556
Darwin, Charles, 442–3
Darwinism, 442–3, 476
Daugherty, Harry, 562
Davidson, Donald, 555
Davis, Benjamin O., 600
Davis, Henry Winter,
  373
Dawes Severalty Act,
  419, 458
D-Day, 609
Dean, James, 657
Dean, John, 711
Debs, Eugene V., 478,
  486, 501

Deephaven (Jewett), 444
Defense of Marriage
  Act, 758
Defense Production
  Act, 626
Del Monte company,
  436
Democratic Party
  decline of, 565
  liberalism, 631–2
  and New Deal, 585
Denmark, World War
  II, 596
Dennett, John Richard,
  369–71
Denver, growth of, 423
Depressions
  Great Depression,
    569–89
  Panic of 1873, 403
  Panic of 1893, 403,
    473–9
Deregulation, 713, 726
Détente, 711
Devaluing dollar, 595
Diem, Ngo Dinh, 680
Disease
  AIDS, 735
  cities and urban
    growth and, 407
  human
    immunodeficiency
    virus (HIV), 735
  Interdepartmental
    Board of Social
    Hygiene, 534–5
  typhoid, 496–7
  venereal disease,
    534–5
Disenfranchisement,
  485
Dole, Bob, 750
Dole, William P., 419
Dollar diplomacy, 515
Domestic terrorism,
  759–60
Dominican Republic,
  389–90
Donovan, Raymond,
  737
Doolittle, James, 418,
  598
Double V campaign,
  607
Doughboys, 537–8
Downs, Fred, 664–5,
  689
Downsizing, 746–7
Downtown, creation of,
  406–7
Draft
  World War I, 527–8
  World War II, 600–1
Drugs
  crack cocaine, 733
  Just Say No slogan,
    733

Du Bois, William
  Edward Burghardt,
    505–7, 561
Dukakis, Michael, 749
Dulles, John Foster, 653
Dust Bowl, 572

E

E. J. Korvettes, 639–40,
  642
Eakins, Thomas, 444–6
Earth Day, 700
Eastern Europe, Cold
  War, 653–4
Eckert, J. Presper, Jr.,
  641
E-commerce, 746
Economic prosperity
  and consumerism,
    641–2
Economic Recovery
  Act, 726
Economic
  transformation of,
    419–23
Ederle, Gertrude, 544–5
Edison, Thomas, 551
Education
  freed African
    Americans and,
    373
  reform,
    progressivism, 505
  women, 500–1
Efficiency experts, 477
Eighteenth
  Amendment, 534
Eight-Hour Leagues,
  392
Einstein, Albert, 602
Eisenhower, Dwight
  biographical
    information,
    651–2
  Cold War, 652–3
  election of 1952, 652
  election of 1956, 652
  farewell address, 661
  Geneva talks,
    654–565
  Modern
    Republicanism,
    652
  World War II, 604,
    608–9
Eisenhower, Mamie,
  652
Eleanor Roosevelt,
  influence of, 586
Electoral fraud, 397
Electronic Numerical
  Integrator and
  Computer
  (ENIAC), 641

Elementary and
Secondary School
Act, 671
Elite
decline of, 646
nonpartisan politics,
advocates of,
454–5
sports, view of, 430
Elkins Act, 511
Embassy attacks, 765
Emergency Banking
Act, 577
Emergency Relief
Appropriations Bill,
583
Employment Act, 632
Endangered Species
Act, 712
Energy crisis, 713
Enforcement Acts, 389
Enterprise, 600
Environment,
transformation of,
421–3
Environmental
protection, 672
Environmental
Protection Agency
(EPA), 700
Equal Pay Act, 687
Equal Rights
Amendment (ERA),
702–3, 734
Espionage Act, 528
Ethnic identity
diversity in music
and, 651
immigrant
transformation to
ethnic Americans,
435–6
Mexican Americans,
559–60
middle class, 438
working class, 438
Eugenics, 504
Europe First strategy,
World War II, 602–3
European involvement
in World War II ,
map of, 603
Evangelical churches,
721–2
Everybody's, 504
Evinrude, World War I,
531
Exodusters, 416
Expansionism
commercial
expansion, 461–2
foreign policy and
commercial
expansion, 460–2
foreign policy and
commercialism,
475–7

Experts, rise of, 504–5
Exported goods
Japan's export
quotas, 732
World War I, 524

F

F. W. Woolworth
variety stores, 547
Fair Employment
Practices
Committee, 592
Fair Labor Standards
Act, 588
Fall, Albert B., 562
Falling wages, 748
Falwell, Jerry, 722, 736
Family structure
immigration and,
754–5
in 1920s, 554
in 1950s, 647–8
resurgence of family,
647–8
single parent
families, 754
transformation by
1990, 754
Farmers' Alliance,
469–70
Farming industry
agriculture, decline
of, 548–9
decline of, 646
Farmers' Alliance,
469–70
Federal Farm Board,
574
Grange, 469
National Farmers'
Alliance and
Industrial Union,
469–70
Ocala Platform,
469–70
Patrons of
Husbandry, 469
sharecropping,
384–6
sharecropping
becomes wage
labor, 415–16
Tennessee Valley
Authority (TVA),
579
Farnham, Marynia,
649
Faubus, Orval, 660
Federal budget deficit,
739
Federal
Communications
Commission (FCC),
644
Federal Emergency
Relief

Administration
(FERA), 577–8
Federal Employee
Loyalty Program,
635
Federal employees, 463
Federal Farm Board,
574
Federal Highway Act,
563
Federal Reserve Act,
517
Federal Reserve Bank,
727
Federal Reserve Board,
517
Federal Trade
Commission (FTC),
517, 563
The Feminine Mystique
(Friedan), 687
Ferkauf, Eugene,
639–40
Ferraro, Geraldine, 727
Fielden, Samuel, 468
Fifteenth Amendment,
380, 390, 392
Financial panic sets off
depression, 395–6
Fire departments,
creation of, 407
Fire of 1871, 407
Fireside chats,
Roosevelt, Franklin
D., 577
First Hundred Days,
576–81
First launches, 669
First Reconstruction
Act, 381–2
Fish, Hamilton, 462
Fitzgerald, F. Scott,
555
Five-day work week,
549
Flappers, 553
Florida
presidential election
controversy, 751
retirees in, 650
Fontana, Marco, 436
Ford, Gerald R.
presidency, 711–12
as vice-president,
711
Ford, Henry, 546, 549
Ford Motor Company,
531
Fordney-McCumber
Tariff, 563
Foreign policy and
commercial
expansion, 460–2
Foreign policy and
commercialism,
475–7
Fort Laramie, 417–18

Fort Laramie Treaty,
418
Forten, Charlotte, 374
Fourteen Points, 536–7
Fourteenth
Amendment, 379–80
France
World War I, 537–40
World War II, 595–6
Fraud and racketeering,
736
Free slaves. *See* African
Americans, free
slaves
Free Speech Movement
(FSM), 685
Freed, Alan, 651, 660
Freedmen's Bureau,
369–71, 374
Freedmen's Bureau Bill,
378–9
Freedom Riders, 673
Freedom Summer, 676
Frick, Henry Clay, 478
Friedan, Betty, 687
Fuchs, Klaus, 635
Full Employment Bill,
632
Fundamentalists, 556
The Fundamentals, 556

G

Galarza, Ernesto, 650
Garfield, James A.
assassination of, 457
election of, 456–7
Garvey, Marcus, 561
Gary, Elbert, 541
Gates, Bill, 745
Gay Liberation Front,
706
Gender ideals, changing,
553
Gender roles
in 1950s, 648–9
Victorian era, 432–3
General Federation of
Women's Clubs, 500
General Motors, 546
safety defects in
Chevrolet
Corvair, 666
strikes, 585
Geneva Accords,
654–565
George, Henry, 464–6,
508
German Americans and
Catholicism, 437
Germany
post World War I,
593–4
post World War II,
618
Russian alliance, 537

Germany (*cont'd*)
Soviet Union,
invasion of, 596–7
submarine warfare,
524–6
U.S., declaring war
on, 597
World War I, 524–43
World War II,
595–6, 609–12
Ghettos, 532
GI Bill, 627
Gilman, Daniel Coit,
442
Gingrich, Newt, 750–1
Ginsberg, Allen, 658
Glass-Steagall Banking
Act, 577
Glenn, John, 669
Global economy, move
towards, 746
Globalization, 623
Goethals, George W.,
513
Gold
in Black Hills, 418
resumptionists'
desire to return to
gold standard,
459–60
Gold Rush, 423
Gold standard, 479–80
end of, 700
Goldwater, Barry, 670
Gompers, Samuel, 486
Good Neighbor policy,
595
Gorbachev, Mikhail,
740
resignation of, 761
Strategic Arms
Reduction Talks
(START), 760
Gore, Al, 751–2
Gorgas, William C., 513
Gould, Jane, 416–17
Grace Commission, 725
Graceland, 657
Graham, Billy, 647
Gramm-Rudman Act,
739
Grange, 469
Grant, Ulysses S.
election of, 389
foreign policy,
389–90
re-election of, 394
Gray, Asa, 442
Great Depression,
569–89
agriculture during,
571–2
Black Tuesday, 569
causes of, 569–71
Hoover's actions,
573–5
New Deal, 575–89

unemployment,
570–1
unemployment
insurance, 572
Great Migration, 531–2
Great Pile Up, 530–1
Great Western Railroad,
403
The Great Gatsby
(Fitzgerald), 555
Greeley, Horace, 394,
452
Green Berets, 677
Greenback-Labor Party,
460
Greenbacks, 459–60
Greenglass, David, 635
Greensboro Four, 666
*Griswold v.
Connecticut*, 673
The Gross Clinic
(Eakins), 445
Groves, Leslie R., 602
Guam, annexation of,
491
Gúzman, Arbenz, 653

H

Haitian immigrants,
sending back, 764
Haley, Bill, 651
Hall v. DeCuir, 399
Hamilton, Alice, 496–7,
503
Hanford, Washington,
605
Hanna, Marcus, 481
A Hard Day's Night,
686
Harding, Rebecca, 443
Harding, Warren G.
death of, 562
election of, 562
presidency, 562
Harlem, Renaissance of
1920s, 560
Harper's Magazine, 438
Harper's Weekly, 478–9
Harrington, Michael,
666
Harrison, Benjamin
presidency of, 458
Harrison-McKinley
Tariff, 458, 477
Haverly, J. H., 428
Hawaii
annexation of, 462,
491
dethroning of
queen, 462, 491
Pearl Harbor, 597
statehood, 650–1
sugar plantations,
462, 491
World War II, 597
Hawley-Smoot Tariff,
574

Hay, John, 492–3
Hayes, Rutherford B.
election of, 397, 456
presidency of, 456
Haymarket Square,
468–9
H-bomb, 626
Health care
Medicaid, 671
Medicare, 671
rising costs of, 748
Hearst, William
Randolph, 488, 581
Hefner, Hugh, 645
The Hidden Persuaders
(Packard), 660
Higginson, Thomas
Wentworth, 439
High culture, 438–43
museums, 441
opera, 440–1
orchestral music,
440–1
Shakespeare, 440
theater, 440
universities, 441–2
Higher Education Act,
671
Highway Safety Act,
671
Hill, Anita, 757
Hill-Burton Act, 632
Hillman, Sidney,
568–9
Hillsboro, Ohio, 450–1
Hinckley, John W., 725
Hippies, 686
Hiroshima, 612
Hiss, Algier, 635
"History of the
Standard Oil
Company"
(Tarbell), 504
Hitler, Adolf
Jewish
extermination, 594
Nazi Party, 594
Poland, conquering,
595
Soviet Union,
invasion of, 596–7
World War II,
594–5, 609–10
Ho Chi Minh trail, 681
Hoffman, Frederick L.,
443
Hog Island, 530–1
Hollywood Ten, 634–5
Holmes, John Clellon,
658
Holocaust, 608–9
Homelessness, 738
Homer, Winslow, 444–6
Homestead,
Pennsylvania, 478
Homestead Act, 416
Homestead mill, 478

Homogeneous society,
646–51
Homosexuality
ACT UP, 735
activism of 1970s,
706–7
AIDS, 735
conservative
opposition to,
734–5
Defense of Marriage
Act, 758
gays in military, 758
legal protection, lack
of, 758
organizations of,
706–7
in 1950s, 649
Victorian era, 433–4
Hoover, Herbert, 564
election of, 565
Hopkins, Harry, 577–8,
583
Hornet, 600
House of Morgan, 409
House Un-American
Activities
Committee
(HUAC), 634–5
Housing for wealthy,
412
Houston riot, 535
*How the Other Half
Lives* (Riis), 407, 446
Howard, Oliver Otis,
374
Howells, William Dean,
443
Huckleberry Finn
(Twain), 434, 444
Huerta, Victoriano, 522
Hughes, Charles Evans,
508, 525–6
Hull, Cordell, 595
Hull House, 496–7,
503
World War I, 528
Human
immunodeficiency
virus (HIV), 735
Hunt, E. Howard, 711
Huntington, Collis P.,
410
Hussein, Saddam,
762–3, 767–8

I

IBM, 720
*I'll Take My Stand: The
South and the
Agrarian Tradition*,
555
Illegal aliens, 753
Immigrant Americans
and Catholic
Church, 435, 437
criticism of, 435

ethnic Americans, transformation to, 435–6
family size, 438
nativist attack, 455
political economy, 437–8
Immigration
attack on, Josiah Strong's, 435
Chinese Exclusion Act, 404
criticism of, 753–5
illegal aliens, 753
immigrants of 1990s, 752–5
Immigration Reform and Control Act, 753
Jewish immigration, 405–6
political economy of, 404–6
political upheaval and its effect on, 404–6
restrictions on, 556
Immigration laws
Chinese Exclusion Act, 404
Immigration and Nationality Act, 634
Immigration Reform and Control Act, 753
National Origins Act, 556
Imperialism, 487
In re Debs, 486
Independent voters, increase in, 561–2
Indian Reorganization Act, 579
Individualism, 554–5
politics of, 563–4
Industrial unions, 486
Industrial Workers of the World (IWW)
origin of, 502
World War I, 528–9
Industry
innovations of 1920s, 545–6
political economy, 545–9
white collar workers, increase in, 547
women, discrimination of, 547
work and work force, transformation of, 547

World War II, 604–7
Inflation
Carter era, 713
and stagflation, 693–4
Inquiry, 527
Insider trading, 736
Inter-American Treaty of Reciprocal Assistance, 623
Interdepartmental Board of Social Hygiene, 534–5
Internal Security Act, 636
International Cigar Makers Union, 486
International labor market, emergence of, 404
International Monetary Fund, 611
Internationalists, 761–2
Internet, 745
Internet economy, 745
Interstate Commerce Act, 458, 463
Interstate Commerce Commission (ICC), 463, 510–11, 563
Invisible Empire, 557
Iran
hostage crisis, 715, 724
Iraq, war with, 732
Iran-Contra affair, 737
Iran-Iraq war, 732
Iraq
Iran, war with, 732
Persian Gulf War, 762–3
Irish Americans and Catholicism, 437
Iron curtain, 678
Island hopping, 610
Italian Americans
and Catholic Church, 437
family size, 438
nativist attack, 455

J

Jackson, Henry, 711–12
Jackson, Jesse, 735–6
Operation Breadbasket, 684
presidential campaign, 735–6
Jackson State College, 697–8
Jackson-Vanik Amendment, 712
James, Henry, 434
Japan
China, war with, 487–8

Combined Fleet, 597–8, 600
export quotas, 732
industrial rise of 1970s, 694
post World War I, 593–4
World War II, 597–600, 610, 612
Japanese internment during World War II, 608
Jaworski, Leon, 711
Jazz Age, 551
Jazz music, 551, 651
The Jazz Singer, 551
Jehovah's Witnesses, pacifism of, 529
Jewett, Sarah Orne, 444
Jews
immigration of, 405–6
nativist attack, 455
Nazi extermination, 594
Jieshi, Jiang, 623
Jim Crow laws, 482–3, 659, 676–7
Jingoes, 486–93
John Hopkins University, 442
Johnson, Andrew
impeachment of, 386–8
presidency of, 375–89
and reconstruction, 375–80
trial of, 388
Johnson, Lyndon
biographical information, 670
election of, 670
presidency of, 670
Vietnam War, 680–2
Joint Committee on Reconstruction, 378
Jones, Paula Corbin, 751
Jones, Samuel "Golden Rule," 508
Just Say No slogan, 733
Justice, Department of, 463
World War I, 528–9
Juvenile delinquency in 1950s, 657

K

Kasserine Pass, 604
Kelley, Florence, 500, 503
Kellogg-Briand Pact, 564
Kemp-Roth Bill, 726
Kennan, George, 620–1

Kennedy, Anthony, 733
Kennedy, John F.
assassination of, 669–70
Berlin Wall Crisis, 678
Cuban Missile Crisis, 678–9
election of 1960, 667–8
inaugural address, 668
presidency, 677–80
Third World policy, 677–8
Vietnam War, 679–80
Kennedy, Robert, 688–9
Kent State University, 697
Kerouac, Jack, 658
Kersands, Billy, 428
Kesey, Ken, 686
Keynes, John Maynard, 588–9, 596
Keynesian economics, 588–9
Keystone Bridge Company, 409
Khomeini, Ayatollah Ruholla, 715
Khrushchev, Nikita
Geneva Accords, 654–565
Kitchen Debate, 654
King, Martin Luther, Jr., 659, 673–4
Albany Movement, 673–4
assassination of, 688–9
Birmingham riots, 674–6
Chicago Movement, 684
March on Washington, 675–6
King, Rodney, 755
Kinsey, Alfred C., 644–5
Kirkpatrick, Jeane J., 730
Kissinger, Henry
détente, 696–7
Vietnam War, 697–8
Kitchen Debate, 654
Kitchin, Claude, 528
Kittyhawk, North Carolina, 546
Kleeck, Mary Van, 534
Knights of Labor, 468–9
Knights of the White Camelia, 389
Knox, Philander, 510–11
Korean War, 625, 653–4
Korematsu, Fred, 608

Koresh, David, 758–9
Kroc, Ray, 643
Ku Klux Klan
  Reconstruction era, 389
  resurgence in 1920s, 557

L

La Follette, Robert M., 509, 523
Labor movement
  deindustrialization, 694–5, 727
  open shops, 548
  organized labor, decline in, 547–8
  welfare capitalism, 548
Labor unions
  American Federation of Labor (AFL), 486
  industrial unions, 486
  politics, split from, 486
  United Mine Workers (UMW), 511–12
Laffer, Arthur, 726
Lakota Sioux Indians, 418
Lanham Act, 606
Lasch, Christopher, 707–8
Lathrop, Julia, 503
Latin America
  dollar diplomacy, 515
  peacekeeping, Wilson administration, 523
  Roosevelt Corollary, 513
Lau v. Nichols, 704–5
League of Nations, 540–1
League of United Latin American Citizens (LULAC), 560
Lebanon, 731
LeConte, Joseph, 442–3
Leisure time, 427–31
LeMay, Curtis, 610
Lend-Lease program of World War II, 596–7
Lenin, Vladimir, 536–7
Levit, William J., 643
Levittown, 643
Lewinsky, Monica, 751, 757
Lewis, Diocletian, 450
Lewis, Sinclair, 555
Liberal Republicans revolt, 394–5

Liberalism
  Democratic Party and, 631–2
  Kennedy era, 667–70
  post World War II, 631–3
  War on Poverty, 670–1
Liddy, G. Gordon, 711
"Life in the Iron Mills" (Harding), 443
Lindbergh, Charles A., 554–5
Lindbergh flight, 554–5
Lippman, Walter, 520–1
Literary realism, 443–4
Little Bighorn, 418
Little Rock, Arkansas, 660
Lloyd, Henry Demarest, 403
Local government
  city services, improvement of, 508
  progressivism, 507–9
  reform mayors, 508
Loewe v. Lawlor, 486
The Lonely Crowd (Riesman), 646
Long, Huey, 582
Looking Backward (Bellamy), 466
Los Alamos, New Mexico
  Manhattan Project, 605
Lost Generation, 555
Love Canal, 713
Ludendorff, Erich, 537
Luftwaffe, 596
Lundberg, Ferdinand, 649
Lusitania, 524–5
Lynchings, 483
Lysergic acid diethylamide (LSD), CIA experimentation, 653

M

MacArthur, Douglas
  Bonus Marchers, 574–5
  World War II, 597–8, 610
Madero, Francisco, 522
Magazines
  feminist magazines, 702
  muckraker expose, 504
  public opinion and, 504

sexually-explicit, 645
Mahan, Alfred Thayer, 487
Mail bombs, 541
Maine, 489
Malcom X, 684
Malone, Dudley Field, 556
Manhattan Project, 602, 605, 611–12
Mansfield, Jayne, 648
March on Washington, 675–6
March on Washington Movement (MOWM), 592
Marconi, Guglielmo, 551
Marshall, George C., 621–2
Marshall, Thurgood, 607
Marshall Plan, 622
Mass media. *See also* Magazines; Television
  and political campaigns, 525
Mass production of automobiles, 546
Massive Retaliation strategy, Cold War, 653
Materialism, 721
Mauchly, John William, 641
May Laws, 406
McArthur, Douglas, 625
McCarthy, Joseph, 616, 636
McCarthyism, 615–16, 636
McCloy, John J., 608
McClure's, 504
McCumber, Porter J., 528
McDonald's, 643
McFarlane, Robert, 737
McGovern, George, 709
McKinley, William
  assassination of, 510
  campaign platform, 480–1
  re-election of, 481
McVeigh, Timothy, 760
Me-Decade, 707–8
Media. *See* mass media
Medicaid, 671
Medicare, 671
Medicine Lodge Treaty, 418
Meese, Edwin, 737
Mellon, Andrew, 574
Memphis, race riots, 379–80
Mencken, H. L., 555

Mennonites, pacifism of, 529
Mergers, 479, 720–1, 745
Merry Pranksters, 686
Mexican Americans, 558–60
  activism of, 703–4
  barrios, 559, 650, 703
  Bracero Program, 650
  discrimination, 650
  ethnic identity, 559–60
  League of United Latin American Citizens (LULAC), 5560
  music, 651
  organizations of, 650, 703–4
  racism/ discrimination, 703
  work/jobs of, 650, 703–4
  World War II, 606
Mexico
  Mexican Revolution, 522–3
  North American Free Trade Agreement (NAFTA), 746
  and U.S. commercial expansion, 462
Miami, Florida, 753
Microcomputer, 720
Microsoft, 745
Middle class
  consolidation of, 413
  downsizing, effect of, 747
  ethnicity, 438
  faith, loss of, 439
  lifestyles of, 413
  partisan politics, decline of, 499
  radicalism, 464–7
Middle East
  oil embargo, 692–3, 699
  Palestine Liberation Organization (PLO), 731
  Reagan era, 731–2
  Six Days War, 699
  Suez crisis, 655
Milken, Michael, 720–1, 736
Mills, C. Wright, 646
Milosevic, Slobodan, 764
Minh, Ho Chi, 625, 655
Minstrel shows, 427–8

Miss Amelia C. van Buren (Eakins), 446
Miss America Pageant, 688
Model T car, 546
Modern Republicanism, 652
Modern Woman: The Lost Sex (Franham and Lundberg), 649
Mondale, Walter, 727
Mongrel Tariff, 457
Monopoly power, 745
Monroe, Marilyn, 648
Montgomery, Alabama, 659
Montgomery bus boycott, 659–60
Moral Majority, 722
Morgan, J. P., 407–8, 410, 473–4, 479
Morgan v. Virginia, 629–30
Morrison, John, 413–14
The Movement, 707–8
Movies
  of 1920s, 551
  of 1950s, 657
Ms., 702
Muckrakers, 504
Muir, John, 512
Muller, Friedrich Max, 442
Museums, 441
Music
  and African Americans, 651
  and ethnic diversity, 651
  jazz, 551, 651
  and Mexican Americans, 651
  opera, 440–1
  orchestral music, 440–1
  rhythm and blues (R & B), 651
  rock and roll, 651, 686
Mussolini, Benito, 593
My Lai, 697

N

Nader, Ralph, 666
Nagasaki, 612
Nasser, Gamal Abdel, 655
The Nation, 369, 455
Nation of Islam, 684
National Aeronautics and Space Administration (NASA), 660–1, 699
National American Women's Suffrage Association (NAWSA), 501, 533
National Association for the Advancement of Colored People (NAACP), 499, 507, 560–1, 658–9
National Association of Manufacturers, 476–7
National Civil Service Reform League, 455
National Consumers' League, 500
National Credit Corporation, 574
National Defense Education Act, 660
National Defense Mediation Board (NDMB), 606
National Endowment for the Arts (NEA), 672, 755
National Endowment for the Humanities (NEH), 672, 755
National Farmers' Alliance and Industrial Union, 469–70
National Foreign Trade Council, 531
National Industrial Recovery Act (NIRA), 580, 584
National Institute of Mental Health, 632
National Institutes of Health, 632
National Labor Relations Board (NLRB), 584–5
National Labor Union (NLU), 392
National League (baseball), 429–30
National Organization for Women (NOW), 687, 701
National Origins Act, 556
National Recovery Administration (NRA), 580–1
National Refiner's Association, 411
National Security Act, 622
National Security Council (NSC), 622
National Traffic and Vehicle Safety Act, 671
National Union for Social Justice, 582
National War Labor Board, 534, 605
National Woman's Party, 501, 533
The National Review, 723
Nationalist Clubs, 466
Nationwide suffrage, 390
Native American reservations
  flaws in system, 418
  origin of system, 417–18
Native Americans
  American Indian Movement (AIM), 705
  Custer's Last Stand, 418–19
  Dawes Severalty Act, 419
  Fort Laramie Treaty, 418
  Great Depression, 579–80
  Indian Reorganization Act, 579
  Medicine Lodge Treaty, 418
  New Deal legislation, 579–80
  pro-Indian reformers, 419
  termination of legal status, 649
  Wounded Knee, 419
Nativism, 455, 556
Naval expansion, 487
Nazi Party, 594
Neutrality Acts, 595–6
Neutrality policy, 524
New Deal, 575–89
  African Americans, 585–6
  American Federation of Labor (AFL), 486
  Civil Works Administration (CWA), 578
  Civilian Conservation Corps (CCC), 578
  conservatives and, 587–8
  critics/opposition to, 581–2, 587–8
  Eleanor Roosevelt, influence of, 586
  Emergency Banking Act, 577
  Emergency Relief Appropriations Bill, 583
  Fair Labor Standards Act, 588
  Federal Emergency Relief Administration (FERA), 577–8
  First Hundred Days, 576–81
  Glass-Steagall Banking Act, 577
  Indian Reorganization Act, 579
  and labor unions, 584–5
  legislation, 576–7
  National Industrial Recovery Act (NIRA), 580, 584
  National Labor Relations Board (NLRB), 584–5
  National Recovery Administration (NRA), 580–1
  Revenue Act, 582–3
  Rural Electrification Administration (REA), 579
  Second Hundred Days, 582–3
  Social Security Act, 583–4
  Tennessee Valley Authority (TVA), 579
  Truth in Securities Act, 577
  Wheeler-Rayburn Act, 583
  Works Progress Administration (WPA), 582–3
New Freedom, 516–17
New Nationalism, 515–16
New Orleans, race riots, 379–80
New World Order, 762–3
New York Central Railroad, 403
New York City
  beat movement, 657–8
  Harlem, Renaissance of 1920s, 560
  World Trade Center destruction, 765–6
New York Customs House, 456
New York Evening Post, 452
New York Herald, 489

New York Journal, 488
New York Sun, 489
The New York Times,
608, 698
New York Times v.
Sullivan, 673
New York Tribune,
452
Newlands Reclamation
Act, 512
Newton, Huey P., 684
Nez Percé Indians, 419
Niagara Movement,
506
Night Riders, 389
Nimitz, Chester,
599–600, 610
9/11 attacks, 765–7
Nineteenth
Amendment, 533
Nix v. Williams, 733
Nixon, Richard, 635
détente, 696–7
domestic policies,
699–700
economic decline,
strategy for,
695–700
economic policy,
700
election of 1968, 689
election of 1972,
708–9
foreign policy, 696–7
Kennedy, loss of
presidency to,
667–8
Kitchen Debate, 654
Nixon Doctrine, 696
resignation of,
710–11
Watergate, 709–11
Nobel Peace Prize,
Theodore Roosevelt,
513
Noble and Holy Order
of Knights of Labor,
468–9
Nonpartisan politics,
advocates of, 454–6
Noriega, Manuel, 762
Norris, George W.,
523
North, Oliver, 737
North American Free
Trade Agreement
(NAFTA), 746
North Atlantic Treaty
Organization
(NATO), 622
Northern Plains
Indians, 418
Norway, World War II,
596
Nuclear freeze
movement, 728
Nuclear weapons

Anti-Ballistic
Missile (ABM)
treaty, 697
nuclear freeze
movement, 728
post World War II,
634
Strategic Arms
Limitations Treaty
(SALT I), 697
Nuremberg Laws, 594

O

Oak Ridge, Tennessee
Manhattan Project,
605
Ocala Platform, 469–70,
480
Occupational Safety and
Health
Administration
(OSHA), 700
O'Connor, Sandra Day,
733
Office of Economic
Opportunity
(OEO), 671
Ohio Gang, 562
Oil embargo, 692–3, 699
Oil supplies
energy crisis, 713
Iran-Iraq war, 732
oil embargo, 692–3,
699
Okinawa, 612
Oklahoma City, federal
building bombing,
759–60
Old Time Gospel Hour,
722
Old-time religion, 556
Olympic games
bombing at 1996
games, 760
U.S. boycott, 714
Omaha platform, 480
Omnibus Trade and
Competitiveness
Act, 732
On the Origin of Species
(Darwin), 442–3
Open Door Note,
492–3
Open shops, 548
Open-range herding,
420
Opera, 440–1
Operation Breadbasket,
684
Operation Desert
Shield, 762
Operation Desert
Storm, 762–3
Operation Rolling
Thunder, 680
Oppenheimer, J.
Robert, 653

Orchestral music, 440–1
Oregon, 489
Oregon, progressivism
and, 508–9
Organization of
American States
(OAS), 623
The Organization Man
(Whyte), 646
Organization of
Petroleum
Exporting Countries
(OPEC), 692–3
Organized labor
decline in, 547–8
National Defense
Mediation Board
(NDMB), 606
reconversion and,
627–8
World War II, 605–6
Oswald, Lee Harvey,
669
The Other America
(Harrington), 666
Ottawa Accords, 594
Our Country (Strong),
435
Overland Trail, 416–17

P

P-51 Mustang, 602
Pacific involvement in
World War II, map
of, 599
Packard, Vance, 660
Page, Patti, 651
Palace of Versailles, 540
Pale of Settlement, 406
Palestine Liberation
Organization
(PLO), 731
Panama Canal, 513, 713
Pan-American
Conference, 462
Panic of 1873, 403
Panic of 1893, 403,
473–9
Parks, Rosa, 659
Parochial education, 437
Partisan politics
critics of, 454–6
decline of, 499
political campaigns,
452–3
Patriotism, World
War I, 528–9
Patronage system, 457
Patrons of Husbandry,
469
Patton, George S.
Bonus Marchers,
575
World War II, 604,
608
Paul, Alice, 501, 533

Payne-Aldrich Tariff,
515
Peace Corps, 678
Pearl Harbor, 597
Pendleton Act, 457
Pennsylvania Railroad,
403, 408
Pentagon Papers, 698
People's Party, 470–2
People's Republic of
China
Nixon's visit, 696
origin of, 623
trade relations, 764
Pepperell Mills, 408
Perkins, Frances, 584,
586
Perot, H. Ross, 749–50
Pershing, John J., 537–8
Persian Gulf War, 760,
762–3
Personnel management,
477
Philadelphia Inquirer,
453
The Philadelphia Negro
(Du Bois), 505
Philippine-American
War, 492
Philippines
massacre by U. S.,
492
Philippine-
American War,
492
Spanish control of,
491
Spanish-American
War, 488–91
U.S. purchase of,
491
World War II, 597
Phillips, Wendell, 391
Phonograph, invention
of, 551
Photography, 445–7
Pinchot, Gifford, 512
Pinochet, Augusto, 699
Plains Indians, 418
Planned Parenthood v.
Casey, 757
Playboy magazine, 645
Plessy, Homer, 482
Plessy v. Ferguson,
482–3
Pogroms, 405–6
Poindexter, John, 737
Poland, conquering, 595
Police departments
brutality, incidents
of, 755
creation of, 407
Polish immigrants,
family size, 438
Political campaigns
female participation
in, 453

male participation
in, 453
partisan politics and,
452–3
partisan politics,
critics of, 454–6
Political economy
competition from
other nations,
693–4
contract labor, 375–7
downsizing, 746–7
economic decline of
1970s, 693–5
falling wages, 748
federal budget
deficit, 739
global economy,
move towards,
746
immigrants, 404–6,
437–8
industrialization,
545–9
Internet economy,
745
post World War I
economy, 593–4
post World War II
economy, 626–7
postindustrial
economy, 744–6
Reaganomics, 726–7,
738–40
service sector, 745
of sharecropping,
384–6
stagflation, 693–4
trade deficit, 739
World War I, 529–31
World War II,
604–7
Political parties. See also
Democratic party;
Republican party
People's Party,
470–2
Populists, 470–2
success of system,
452–3
Politics, labor unions
split from, 486
Pollution, 666
Popular culture, 426
Populism, 470–2
Populists, 470–2
Postindustrial economy,
744–6
Potsdam Conference,
619
Poverty, 670–1, 738
Powers, Johnny, 507
The Power Elite (Mills),
646
Presley, Elvis, 651, 657
Prisoners From the
Front (Homer), 445

Producers' ideology,
464–6
Professional Air Traffic
Controllers
Organization
(PATCO), 727
Progress and Poverty
(George), 464–6, 508
Progressive Party, 516
Progressivism, 502–15
education reform,
505
experts, rise of,
504–5
and local
governments,
507–9
muckrakers, 504
overview, 502–3
and racial
discrimination,
505–7
settlement houses,
503–4
social workers,
503–4
and state
governments,
508–9
Pro-Indian reformers,
419
Propaganda, World
War I, 529
Proposition 13, 712
Prostitution, World
War I, 534–5
Protestants, 437, 556
Puerto Ricans, 650
Puerto Rico, annexation
of, 491
Pullman, George, 409
Pullman Company, 478
Pullman strike, 478–9

Q

Quality of life, 671–2
Queen of Swimmers,
544–5
Quiz show scandals, 660

R

"The Race Problem in
the South"
(LeConte), 443
Race riots, 379–80
Race Traits and
Tendencies of the
American Negro
(Hoffman), 443
Radical feminism, 688
Radical reconstruction,
382–3
Radicalism, middle
class, 464–7
Radicals, 373
Radio, origin of, 551–2

Rahman, Omar Abdel,
765
Railroad industry
Jim Crow laws,
482–3
stocks, 409
strikes, 403
World War I, 530–1
Randolph, A. Philip,
548, 591–2, 630
Ransom, John Crowe,
555
Reagan, Ronald
African American
policy, 735–6
assassination
attempt, 725
biographical
information, 723
election of 1980,
723–4
election of 1984,
727
environmental
policy, neglect of,
726, 738
foreign policy,
727–32
inaugural address,
724
Iran-Contra affair,
737
Middle East actions,
731–2
military buildup,
728
popularity, return
of, 740–1
Reagan Doctrine,
730–1
Reaganomics, 726–7,
738–40
reduction of federal
government,
725–6
Soviet relations,
728–9
Strategic Defense
Initiative (SDI),
728–9
Third World, 730–1
women's rights,
733–4
Reagan Doctrine,
730–1
Reagan Revolution, 724,
727–32
Reaganomics, 726–7,
738–40
Realism in art, 443–6
Rebel without a Cause,
657
Recession and Franklin
D. Roosevelt,
588–9
Reconstruction
Banks Plan, 372

congressional
reconstruction,
380–6
corruption as
national problem,
392–4
depression, 395–9
end of, 392–6
financial panic sets
off depression,
395–6
First Reconstruction
Act, 381–2
and Johnson, 375–80
Joint Committee on
Reconstruction,
378
land ownership, free
slaves' desire for,
373–5
liberal Republicans
revolt, 394–5
in the North, 390–2
race riots, 379–80
radical
reconstruction,
382–3
radicals, 373
Second
Reconstruction
Act, 382
Ten-Percent Plan,
372–3
Wade-Davis Bill,
373
Reconstruction Finance
Corporation (RFC),
574
Reconversion of
American society,
626–31
Red Cloud, 418
The Red Menace, 635
Red scare. See
communists in
America
Red Shirts, 389
Redeemers, 396
Reform mayors, 508
Regents of the
University of
California v. Allan
Bakke, 701
Rehnquist, William, 733
Religion
evangelical churches,
721–2
freed African
Americans and,
373
and homosexuality,
734–5
and personal
freedom, 672–3
resurgence of, 647–8
rise of religious
right, 721–2

Religion (*cont'd*)
televangelists, 721–2
World War I, 529
Remington, Frederic, 478–9
Republican Party
modern Republicanism, 652
and politics of individualism, 562–5
Resumptionists' desire to return to gold standard, 459–60
Retail discount stores, 639–40, 642
Retirement, Social Security and, 748
Retrenchment policies, 463–4
Revenue Act, 582–3
Rhythm and blues (R & B), 651
Richardson, Elliott, 711
Riesman, David, 646
Right to Life movement, 757
Riis, Jacob, 407, 446
Rio Pact, 623
Riots, 755
Birmingham riots, 674–6
Houston riot, 535
Memphis riots, 379–80
New Orleans riots, 379–80
The Rise of Silas Lapham (Howells), 443
Robber barons, 410
Robertson, Pat, 722
Robinson, Jackie, 630
Rochefort, Joseph, 599
Rock and roll, 651, 657, 686
Rockefeller, John D., 410–12, 461
exposure of, 504
Rockefeller, Nelson, 711
Roe v. Wade, 702, 734, 757
Rommel, Erwin, 604
Roosevelt, Franklin D.
biographical information, 576
Brains Trust, 576
death of, 611
election of 1932, 575–6
election of 1936, 585–6
election of 1940, 596
election of 1944, 611
fireside chats, 577

Good Neighbor policy, 595
as governor of New York, 576
New Deal, 575–89
recession and, 588–9
Yalta Conference, 617–18
Roosevelt, Theodore
biographical information, 509–10
as conservationist, 512
foreign policy, 512–13
labor disputes, 511–12
New Nationalism, 515–16
and Nobel Peace Prize, 513
Panama Canal, 513
Progressive Party, 516
Rough Riders, 489–91
trust busting, 510–11
Roosevelt Corollary, 513
Rosa Cassettari's Autobiography, 402
Rosa Parks and bus boycott, 659
Rosenberg, Ethel, 635–6
Rosenberg, Julius, 635–6
Rosie the Riveter, 606
Rough Riders, 489–91
Ruby, Jack, 670
Ruby Ridge, 758
Ruef, Abraham, 498
Rural Electrification Administration (REA), 579
Russia
Bolshevik Revolution, 536–7
German alliance, 537
Rustbelt, 720

S

Sabin vaccine, 647
Sacco, Nicola, 542–3
Sage Brush Rebellion, 712–13
Salk vaccine, 647
Salvation Army, 499
San Francisco
Gold Rush, 423
growth of, 423
Sanger, Margaret, 500–1, 552

Santo Domingo (Dominican Republic), 389–90
Scalia, Antonin, 733
Scandals
Alan Freed, 660
Boesky insider trading, 736
Clinton era, 751
corruption as national problem, 392–4
Iran-Contra affair, 737
Milkin fraud and racketeering, 736
Monica Lewinsky, 751
Reagan era, 736–7
televangelists, 736
TV quiz shows, 660
Whitewater Development Corporation, 751
Schechter Poultry Corporation v. United States, 582
Schine, David, 636
School District of Abington Township v. Schempp, 673
Schools
Elementary and Secondary School Act, 671
government role in, 733
Vietnam war protests, 697
Schwab, Charles M., 530–1
Schwarzkopf, Norman, 762–3
SCLC, 674–5
Scopes, John, 556
Scope's trial, 556
Scott, Tom, 408–9
Seale, Bobby, 684
Second Hundred Days, 582–3
Second Reconstruction Act, 382
Second-wave feminism, 688
Securities and Exchange Act, 577
Securities and Exchange Commission (SEC), 577
Sedition Act, 528
Segregation, 483
Selective Service Act, 600, 622
Service sector, 745
Sesame Street, 672

Settlement houses, 503–4
700 Club, 722
17th parallel, 655
Seward, William
Alaska, purchase of, 389, 461
as secretary of state, 460–1
Sex and the Single Girl (Brown), 687
Sexual Behavior in the Human Female (Kinsey), 645
Sexual Behavior in the Human Male (Kinsey), 644–5
Sexual harassment, 757
Sexuality
and automobiles, 644
birth control and, 552
openness in 1950s, 644–5
and rock music, 651, 657
sexual revolution of 1920s, 552
Victorian view of, 432–4
Shakespeare, William, 440
"The Shame of the Cities" (Steffen), 504
Share Our Wealth program, 582
Sharecropping, 384–6
becomes wage labor, 415–16
Sheen, Fulton J., 647
Shelley v. Kraemer, 629
Shepard, Alan, 669
Shepherd, Matthew, 757–8
Sherman, William Tecumseh, 374, 418
Sherman Anti-Trust Act, 458, 463, 510–11
Shopping malls, 643
Sierra Club, 499
Silent Spring (Carson), 666
Simpson, O. J., 756
Sinatra, Frank, 607, 651
Sinclair, Upton, 498
Single parent families, 754
Single Tax, 465–6
Sit-ins, 666–7
Sitting Bull, 418–19
Six Days War, 699
Smith, Al, 565
Smith v. Allwright, 607, 629–30

Social housekeeping, 500–1
Social order. *See also* Middle Class; Wealthy; Working class
Social sciences, 442–3
Social Security Act, 583–4
Social Security Reform Act, 725
Social Security System, 725
Social work, 503–4
Socialism
Industrial Workers of the World (IWW), 502
labor movement and, 501–2
Socialist Party of America (SPA), 501
Socialist Party
New Deal and, 581
World War I, 528
Society for the Suppression of Vice (SSV), 426
Soldiers, training and transportation of, World War I, 535–6
The Souls of Black Folk (Du Bois), 506
South East Asian Treaty Organization (SEATO), 655
Southern Plains Indians, 418
Soviet Union, 669
communism, ideology of, 617
expansion of, 520
invasion of, 596–7
nuclear weapons, 729
Space program
communications satellites, 669
first launches, 669
first man on moon, 699
first satellite, 669
National Aeronautics and Space Administration (NASA), 660–1
Soviet Union, 669
Sputnik, 660–1
Spanish-American War, 488–91
The Spirit of Saint Louis, 554
"The Spirit of Victory," 539

Sports
baseball, 429–30
bicycling, 430
boxing, 429
elite view of, 430
in 1920s, 551
popularity of, 430
Sputnik, 660–1
Stalin, Josef
Poland, conquering, 595
Potsdam Conference, 619
World War II, 603–4, 611–12
Yalta Conference, 617–19
Standard Oil, 461
Standard Oil Trust, 411–12
Stanton, Edwin M., 387
Stanton, Elizabeth Cady, 391–2
State governments
progressivism, 508–9
retrenchment policies, 463–4
Steel industry
Carnegie's domination over, 409–11
Thompson Works, 410
Union Iron Company, 409
Steffens, Lincoln, 498, 504
Stein, Gertrude, 555
Steinem, Gloria, 702
Stellung, 538
Stock market
Adams Express Company stock, 409
Black Monday, 740
gains of 1990s, 747–8
railroad stocks, 409
Securities and Exchange Act, 577
Securities and Exchange Commission (SEC), 577
Truth in Securities Act, 577
Stonewall Inn, 706
Stowe, Harriet Beecher, 447
Strategic Arms Limitations Treaty (SALT I), 697
Strategic Arms Limitations Treaty (SALT II), 711, 714, 728

Strategic Arms Reduction Talks (START), 760
Strategic Defense Initiative (SDI), 728–9, 764
Strikes
air traffic controllers, 727
auto workers, 627–8
coal miners, 628
General Motors, 585, 627–8
government intervention, 541–2
Haymarket Square, 468–9
Homestead mill, 478
Knights of Labor, 468–9
Pullman strike, 478–9
railroad workers, 403, 628
UMW, 511–12
Strong, Josiah, 435
Student Homophile League, 706
Student Nonviolent Coordinating Committee (SNCC), 667
Students for a Democratic Society (SDS), 685
Submarine warfare, 524–6
Submerged Lands Act, 652
Suburban home ownership, 642–3
Suez crisis, 655
Suffrage
Voting Rights Act, 677, 736
women, 390–2, 501
Sugar plantations, 462, 491
Sullivan, John L., 429
Sunbelt, 695, 720–1
Supply-side economics, 726
Sussex Pledge, 525
Swaggart, Jimmy, 736
Swann v. Charlotte-Mecklenburg Board of Education, 701
Swift, Gustavus, 410
The Swimming Hole (Eakins), 445–6
Sylvis, William, 392
Szilard, Leo, 602

T

Taft, Robert, 596, 632
Taft, William H.
election of, 513
presidency of, 513–15
Taft-Hartley Act, 628, 632
Taiping Rebellion of 1848, 404
Taiwan, 623, 696
Takeovers, 720–1
Taliban, 766
Tarbell, Ida, 504
Tate, Allen, 555
Tax Reform Act, 738
Taxes, city governments, 463–4
Taylor, Frederick Winslow, 477
Technological innovations, 720
Telegraph, 404
Televangelists, 647, 721–2, 736
Television
charismatic preachers, 647
in 1950s, 644
quiz show scandals, 660
white ethnic stereotypes, 708
Teller, Edward, 602
Telstar, 669
Temperance movement, 450–2, 466–7, 534
Tennessee Valley Authority (TVA), 579
Ten-Percent Plan, 372–3
Tenure of Office Act, 388
Terrorism
domestic terrorism, 759–60
embassy attacks, 765
Lebanon incident, 731
Reagan era, 731–2
World Trade Center destruction, 765–6
Tet Offensive, 688
Texas Pacific Railroad, 403
Theater, 440
Third World, Cold War era, 654–6
Thirteenth Amendment, 380
38th Parallel, 623–5
This Side of Paradise (Fitzgerald), 555
Thomas, Clarence, 755, 757

Thomas, Norman, 581
Thompson Works, 410
Thomson, J. Edgar, 408, 410
Three Mile Island, 713
Thurmond, Strom, 633
Tijerina, Reies López "Tiger," 704
Tilden, Samuel J., 397
Time-Warner, 745
Title IX, 702
Tocqueville, Alexis de, 440
Tonkin Gulf Resolution, 680
Total war, 529–30
Totalitarian regimes, 594
Tourgée, Albion, 482
Townsend, Francis, 582
Trade deficit, 739
Traps for the Young (Comstock), 426
Triangle Shirtwaist Company, 498
Truman, Harry
    election of 1948, 632–3
    Korean War, 623–5
    Potsdam Conference, 619
    Truman Doctrine, 621
    whistle-stop campaign, 633
    World War II, 611–12
Truman Doctrine, 621
Trump, Donald, 718–19
Trump, Ivana, 718–19
Trusts
    Standard Oil Trust, 411–12
    trust busting, 510–11
Truth in Securities Act, 577
Turner, Frederick Jackson, 475–6
Tuskegee Airmen, 601
Twain, Mark, 434, 444
Tweed, William Marcy, 393
Twenty-sixth Amendment, 707
Twenty-seventh Amendment, 749
Typhoid epidemic, 496–7

U

U-2 spy plane, 654
Uncle Tom's Cabin (Stowe), 427–8
Underwood-Simmons Tariff, 516–17

Unemployment
    in Great Depression, 570–1
    insurance, 572
Union Iron Company, 409
Union Pacific Railroad, 393
United Auto Worker (UAW), 627–8
United Mine Workers (UMW), 486, 511–12, 628
United Nations, creation of, 611
United States v. Leon, 733
Universal Automatic Computer (UNIVAC 1), 641
Universal Negro Improvement Association (UNIA), 561
Universities and colleges, 441–2
    Vietnam war protests, 697
Unsafe at Any Speed (Nader), 666
Unterseeboot, 524
Urban culture, 427–31
    minstrel shows, 427–8
    spectator sports, 429–31
    vaudeville, 428–9
    world's fairs, 431
Urban nation, emergence of, 549
U'Ren, William S., 508–9
U.S. Steel, 479

V

Vanzetti, Bartolomeo, 542–3
Vaudeville, 428–9
Venereal disease, 534–5
Versailles, Treaty of, 540–1, 593
Veterans, 689
Vice
    cities and urban growth, 425–7
    World War I era reform, 534–5
Victorian era
    abortion, 433
    gender roles, 432–3
    homosexuality, 433–4
    sexuality, 432–4
    women, 432–3

Viet Cong actions, 679–82
Vietnam
    diplomatic recognition of, 764
    division into north and south, 655
    independence effort, 625
    Vietnamization, 697
Vietnam War
    economic effects, 683
    end of, 697–8
    hawk position, 682
    Ho Chi Minh trail, 681
    Johnson actions, 680–2
    Kennedy actions, 679–80
    Nixon era, 697–8
    Operation Rolling Thunder, 680
    Pentagon Papers, 698
    protest movement against, 682
    Tet Offensive, 688
    Tonkin Gulf Resolution, 680
    troop withdrawals, 697–8
    veterans, 689
    Viet Cong actions, 679–82
    Vietnamization, 697
Vietnamization, 697
Villa, Francisco "Pancho," 522–3
Volstead, Andrew J., 534
Volstead Act, 534
Volunteers in Service to America (VISTA), 671
Voter participation, decline in, 485, 499–500, 562
Voting Rights Act, 677, 736

W

Waco, Texas, 758
Wade, Benjamin F., 373
Wade-Davis Bill, 373
Wage labor, sharecropping as, 415–16
Wagner, Robert, 584
Wagon trains, 416–17
The Wall Street Journal, 723
Wallace, George, 709

Wallace, Henry, 632–3
Wallace v. Jaffree, 733
Walt Disney, 745
War Industries Board (WIB), 531
War measures, World War I, 532–3
War on Poverty, 670–1
War Powers Act, 711
War socialism, 531
Warehouse Act, 517
Warren, Earl, 659, 673, 708
Warren, Robert Penn, 555
Washington, Booker T., 483–4, 506
Washington Naval Conference, 564
Water Quality Act, 672
Watergate, 709–11
Wealthy
    housing, 412
    lifestyles of, 412–13
    partisan politics, decline of, 499
    scandals of 1980s, 736
Weapons. See also Nuclear weapons
    World War II, 602
Weaver, Randy, 758
Weir, John Ferguson, 444
Welch, Joseph, 636
Welfare capitalism, 548
Welfare state, 601
Wells-Barnett, Ida, 483, 505–7
Western states, population increase during World War II, 605
Western territory
    cattle, 419–20
    cattlemen, 419–20
    climate of, 421–3
    commercial farmers, 420–1
    cowboys, 419–20
    economic transformation of, 419–23
    environment, transformation of, 421–3
    Homestead Act, 416
    open-range herding, 420
    wagon trains, 416–17
Western Union, 409
Westmoreland, William, 680–2
Westward migration
    Exodusters, 416

Overland Trail, 416–17
Weyler, Valeriano, 488
Wheeler-Rayburn Act, 583
"Whiskey Ring," 393
Whistle-stop campaign, 633
White collar workers, increase in, 547
White ethnics, 708
Whitewater Development Corporation, 751
Whitman, Walt, 434, 444, 447
Whyte, William H., Jr., 646
Wigner, Eugene, 602
Wild West Show, 427
Wilderness Act, 672
Wilkie, Wendell L., 596
Willard, Frances, 451, 466–7
Wilson, Woodrow
  antitrust laws, 517
  banking system reform, 517
  Congressional Government, 516
  election of, 516
  neutrality policy, 524
  New Freedom, 516–17
  presidency of, 516–17
  re-election of, 525–6
  tariff policy, 516–17
  World War I, 525–43
Winesburg, Ohio (Anderson), 555
Witte, Edwin, 605
Wolfe, Tom, 707
Woman's Christian Temperance Union (WCTU), 451–2, 466–7, 534
Woman's Peace Party, 523
Women. *See also* Gender roles
  activism, increase in, 500–1
  American Plan, 534–5
  discrimination of, 547
  education, 500–1

flappers, 553
gender ideals, changing, 553
and New Deal, 586
in 1950s, 648–9
political activism, 496–7
political campaigns, 453
post World War II, 628–9
realism in art and, 444
reconversion, 628–9
social housekeeping, 500–1
social work, 503–4
suffrage movement, 390–2, 501
Victorian era, 432–3
Woman's National Loyal League, 390–1
working class, 414
World War I, 533–4
World War II, 606–7
Women's rights
  movement, 686–8
  abortion issue, 702, 734, 757
  Equal Rights Amendment (ERA), 702–3, 734
  National Organization for Women (NOW), 687
  radical feminism, 688
  Roe v. Wade, 702, 734, 757
  second-wave feminism, 688
  sexual harassment, 757
  Title IX, 702
Women's Trade Union League, 534
Woodruff Sleeping Car Company, 409
Woodward, Bob, 710
Work and work force, transformation of, 547
Working class, 413–15
  clothing industry and, 414
  ethnicity, 438
  families, 415
  hierarchy of wages, 414

in 1950s, 647
populism, 470–2
women, 414
Works Progress Administration (WPA), 582–3
World Bank (International Bank for Reconstruction and Development), 611
World Court, 564
World Trade Center
  bombing in 1993, 765
  destruction in 2001, 765–6
World War I, 520–43
  advertising/propaganda, 529
  African-American workers, 531–2
  conscription, 528
  draft, 527–8
  Fourteen Points, 536–7
  Lusitania, 524–5
  soldiers, training and transportation of, 535–6
  and suffrage movement, 532–3
  temperance movement, 534
  Versailles, Treaty of, 540–1
  vice reform, 534–5
  war goals of U.S., 526–7
  war measures, 532–3
  women and, 533–4
World War II, 592–5, 609–10
  African-American discrimination, 607
  African-American soldiers, 600–1
  American entry, 597
  Atlantic Charter, 596
  atomic bomb, 612
  D-Day, 609
  draft, 600–1
  Europe First strategy, 602–3
  Europe involvement, map of, 603

Germany, 611–12
Hitler and Nazi Germany, 593–4
Holocaust, 608–9
Japan, 597–600, 610, 612
Japanese internment, 608
Lend-Lease program, 596–7
Manhattan Project, 602, 605, 611–12
Pacific involvement, map of, 599
Pearl Harbor, 597
political economy, 604–7
prewar sentiment, 592–3
Selective Service Act, 600
weapons, 602
women's activities, 601, 606–7
World's Columbian Exposition, 431, 475
World's fairs, 431
Wounded Knee, 419
Wright, Orville, 546
Wright, Wilbur, 546
Wright brothers' flight, 546

Y

Yalta Conference, 617–19
Yeltsin, Boris, 761
Yom Kippur War, 699
Yorktown, 600
Young Men's Christian Association (YMCA), 430–1
Youth culture
  of 1920s, 554
  of 1950s, 657
  rebellion of 1960s, 685–6
Yuppies, 721

Z

Zapata, Emiliano, 522
Zedong, Mao, 623
Zimmerman Telegram, 526
Zoot suits, 600
Zyklon-B gas, 608